AGAINST THE CURRENT

Readings for Writers

AGAINST THE CURRENT

Readings for Writers

PAMELA J. ANNAS
University of Massachusetts / Boston

ROBERT C. ROSEN
William Paterson University

 Prentice Hall, Upper Saddle River, New Jersey 07458

Against the current : readings for writers / [compiled by] Pamela J.
  Annas, Robert C. Rosen.
        p.   cm.
  Includes index.
  ISBN 0-13-097924-4
    1. College readers.   2. English language—Rhetoric—Problems,
  exercises, etc.   3. Report writing—Problems, exercises, etc.
  I. Annas, Pamela J.   II. Rosen, Robert C.
  PE1417.A33   1998
  808'.0427—dc21   97-37429

Editor-in-Chief: *Charlyce Jones Owen*
Executive Editor: *Leah Jewell*
Editorial Assistant: *Patricia Castiglione*
Production Liason: *Fran Russello*
Editorial/Production Supervision: *Publications Development Company of Texas*
Prepress and Manufacturing Buyer: *Mary Ann Glorilande*
Cover Design: *Wendy Alling Judy*
Marketing Manager: *Rob Mejia*

This book was set in 10.5/12.5 point Goudy by Publications Development Company of Texas
and was printed and bound by Courier Companies, Inc.

The cover was printed by Phoenix Color Corp.

© 1998 by Prentice-Hall, Inc.
Simon & Schuster/A Viacom Company
Upper Saddle River, New Jersey 07458

Printed in the United States of America
10 9 8 7 6 5 4 3 2 1

ISBN 0-13-097924-4

Prentice-Hall International (UK) Limited, *London*
Prentice-Hall of Australia Pty. Limited, *Sydney*
Prentice-Hall Canada, Inc., *Toronto*
Prentice-Hall Hispanoamericana, S.A., *Mexico*
Prentice-Hall of India Private Limited, *New Delhi*
Prentice-Hall of Japan, Inc., *Tokyo*
Simon & Schuster Asia Pte. Ltd., *Singapore*
Editora Prentice-Hall do Brasil, Ltda., *Rio de Janeiro*

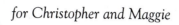

for Christopher and Maggie

CONTENTS

T W O
EDUCATION

T H R E E
MASS CULTURE

F O U R
GENDER

F I V E
RACE AND ETHNICITY

SIX
MONEY, WORK, AND SOCIAL CLASS

Introduction   354

S E V E N
SCIENCE AND TECHNOLOGY

E I G H T
NATURE/THE ENVIRONMENT

Introduction 473

NINE
WAR

TEN
PROTEST AND CHANGE

E L E V E N
ART AND THE ARTIST

PREFACE

The eighty-six works of nonfiction collected in *Against the Current: Readings for Writers* offer models of socially engaged and socially responsible writing. The writers included here—whether they are remembering, describing, explaining, analyzing, satirizing, arguing, philosophizing—are all cognizant of themselves in relation to their social context. They take positions, sometimes implicitly, more often explicitly, on social issues: from the cumulative neurological effects of television or toys on children's creativity (Mander, Barthes) to the "corrosive bitterness" of the legacy of racism (Baldwin); from serious topics such as the confining effects of ethnic stereotyping (Cofer, Parenti) to lighter topics, such as what the American obsession with lawns tells us about the national psyche (Pollan) and what mail order catalogs seek to tell us about ourselves (Jones).

Rather than floating downstream, trailing one hand in the water oblivious to water moccasins and snapping turtles, these writers have chosen to paddle against the current. Many write out of a lifetime commitment to critical perspectives on twentieth-century culture and society. From Barry Commoner in "At War with the Planet" to June Jordan in "Nobody Mean More to Me Than You and the Future of Willie Jordan," these writers, some already famous and some relatively unknown, perform necessary acts of responsible citizenship in a democratic society. They hold up a mirror to current trends, asking us to see the causes and effects of our actions, both when we intend these actions and when they reveal our unintentional complicity in systems larger than ourselves. Their critical perspectives are informed by choices alternative to the main stream. They explore eddies of possibility, branch streams that would change our direction of travel and offer us new vistas. They question authoritative, accepted, and conventional explanations; they reframe the issues and the very questions that inform everyday life. They are involved in education in its highest sense, education not merely to explain the way the world is, but to consider how we, as creative and intelligent beings endowed with more power than most of us think we have or know what to do with, can accept a responsible stewardship of ourselves, our children, and the earth on which we live. A sense of ethics, an appreciation of history, a respect for the individual, and a belief in community anchor the writings within each section.

Each of the eleven thematic sections includes seven to nine nonfiction writings that provide an array of perspectives on a given topic: Growing Up and Growing Older; Education; Mass Culture; Gender; Race and Ethnicity; Money, Work, and Social Class; Science and Technology; Nature/The Environment; War; Protest and Change; Art and the Artist. Unlike anthologies that offer a *debate* format, providing opposing viewpoints on topics such as abortion or affirmative action, *Against the Current* instead offers a *conversation* among writers who take various critical stances on specific aspects of a broad theme, such as gender or race/ethnicity. That is, we offer an array of socially critical perspectives on each theme. In some cases, we have included a more conservative if quirky viewpoint, such as Joyce Carol Oates's provocative and engagingly written "Against Nature," which offsets a group of pieces—essays, feature journalism, memoir, prose poem—that develop various facets of a pro-environmentalist stance. In its own way, each of the thematic sections constructs a collective analysis of the way things are and ponders alternatives. The section on Gender, for example, is composed of writing by four men and four women. All of them consider the ways their gender, the social construction of gender, and the social expectations around gender affect their own lives and the lives of people around them.

The selections are carefully chosen to represent a variety of critical perspectives on a wide range of important contemporary issues. They also represent the diversity of perspectives currently available in an increasingly heterogeneous United States. (The overwhelming majority of readings are by North American writers.) More than half the readings are by women and over a third are by people of color. Working-class, gay and lesbian, Native American, Italian American, Asian American, Indian, Latina and Latino, African American, Jewish American, female and male perspectives appear throughout the eleven thematic sections as well as in sections like Gender or Race and Ethnicity explicitly devoted to issues of diversity. In the section on Nature/The Environment, for example, Elizabeth Martinez writes about "When People of Color Are an Endangered Species." In Science and Technology, Joy Harjo's "Three Generations of Native American Women's Birth Experience" offers traditional alternatives, from her own and her culture's history, to the increasing technologization of the act of giving birth. Growing Up and Growing Older, the opening section of *Against the Current*, demonstrates our commitment to providing an array of diverse and particular perspectives on "universal" topics. Five memoirs of growing up in the United States—female, gay, Asian American, Jewish American, and African American—represent in vivid particularity the pain and possibility inherent in positioning oneself, or in finding oneself positioned, against the current of mainstream America. The three other essays also included in that section consider a lesbian perspective on birth and motherhood, the institutional treatment of the elderly, and the challenges of coping with physical disability, which by the end of Nancy Mairs's "Carnal Acts" becomes a challenge thrown back at the reader to accept his or her own embodied self in all its complexity.

These narratives and essays—autobiography, memoir, journal, prose poem, editorial, feature journalism, sociological study, exposition, description, speech, epistle, analysis, argument, persuasion—invite readers to participate from the inside in experiences and ways of thinking that might be different from their own. The study questions and writing exercises appended to each selection promote critical reading, taking readers through each piece toward a thorough understanding of both content and form. What are the issues? How does the writer develop her narrative or argument or exposition? How does he use figurative language and rhetorical devices? How might the reader, in response or in emulation, construct an essay, a memoir, a satire of his or her own? These selections are intended as invitations, as readings for writers. They demonstrate the vitality, range, and brilliance of an alternative tradition of nonfictional prose and they encourage beginning and more advanced writers to explore the particulars of their own experience, to discover and forge their own principled position on issues, and to practice and cultivate their own writing skills.

ACKNOWLEDGMENTS

We would like to thank a number of friends for their suggestions and help with this project: Linda Dittmar, Emily Filardo, Linda Hamalian, Jim Hauser, Reamy Jansen, Mary Jane Karp, Dan Perlstein, Donna Perry, Neill Rosenfelt, Stephen Rosskamm Shalom, Saul Slapikoff, and Zippie Bauman. Thanks also to the students in Introductory Composition at the University of Massachusetts/Boston.

Finally, we would like to thank a few people connected with Prentice Hall: Alison Reeves and Mary Jo Southern for their advice and encouragement, Harriet Prentiss for her invaluable work on the headnotes and footnotes, and Charlyce Jones Owen and Leah Jewell for helping us see the book to completion.

Pamela J. Annas
University of Massachusetts/Boston
Robert C. Rosen
William Paterson University

GROWING UP AND GROWING OLDER

No matter how old or how young we might be, we carry our past around with us. For some of us it may seem shut up in suitcases we lug in each hand; for others it may seem to trail out behind us like a long scarf. Even in a culture focused on the present tense or the current moment, the store of our experiences and thoughts connects us on a continuum to the past and goes a long way toward explaining who we are in the present. Even in a society in love with individualism, no one of us is in fact that lone hero riding into town on a dusty horse. We are from a range of ethnic backgrounds, races, regions, and religions. We are constructed not only by our individual experiences but by our families, our communities, and the cultural traditions that are passed down to us in overt and in subtle ways.

Childhood experiences can be accessed suddenly and unexpectedly by an old photograph, the smell of cinnamon or cilantro, a loud angry voice, the taste of hot cornbread with honey, a hand brushing the hair off one's face. All of us, but particularly professional writers, pull up images out of the reservoir of memory. We, like most of the writers in this section, construct stories out of those memories as well as use them to figure out some aspect of life that is puzzling. We use them to build and to renovate identity, to figure out where and how we fit into our social context. Five of the eight essays in this section—Charlotte Nekola's "Good Mothers, Bad Daughters," Tommi Avicolli's "He Defies You Still: The Memoirs of a Sissy," the excerpt from Lydia Minatoya's *Talking To High Monks in the Snow: An Asian American Odyssey*,

Alfred Kazin's "The Kitchen," and James Baldwin's "Notes of a Native Son"—are accounts of growing up in the United States. The perspectives represented are, respectively, female, gay, Japanese American, Jewish American, and African American.

In "Good Mothers, Bad Daughters," Charlotte Nekola vividly recreates for us what it was like to grow up female in the 1950s, that "*Ozzie and Harriet*" era when Moms presumably stayed home, wore pressed aprons over their shirtwaist dresses, and baked chocolate chip cookies for children who walked back to white picket-fenced homes after school, rather than, as is often now the case, staying in aftercare until a tired, stressed-out parent picks them up at 5:30, struggles home through rush hour traffic, and tries to throw together a nutritious dinner amid the clutter left by that morning's rush out the door. Nekola's portrait of her mother probes the actual complex woman underneath the conventional facade, a mother who played sad old tunes on the piano, who had a college education which she wasn't able to use, who had wanted to be a writer, who had a friend who lived by herself and wrote books, and who took her children to meet that friend. To frame this portrait of her mother and herself, Nekola uses three fairy tales: "Sleeping Beauty," "The Little Mermaid," and "The Red Shoes." Notice how Nekola employs these pieces of Anglo-European culture to add complexity to her exploration of how girls were socialized in mid-twentieth-century America. Also notice how mothers both acquiesed in and subtly subverted that socialization.

Using a formal combination of drama and commentary, Tommi Avicolli presents his own often painful childhood to the reader, immersing us in scene after remembered scene of cruel homophobic taunting from his years in a Catholic high school. He found himself harassed by classmates, priests, and his father; some harassed him out of a sincere desire to help him be "a man," others out of a meanspirited fear of anyone different from who they were supposed to be. Interspersed with the dramatic scenes and their direct visceral effect on the reader are reflections on the meanings of concepts like "sissy," "faggot," "queer," "homosexual," "effeminate," "gay," and "men." In this exploration of his identity as a gay man, Avicolli particularly pinpoints the (unsuccessful) attempts to erase who he is—to make him walk differently, to desire and love differently, to erase through silence the many important figures in history who were also gay. "It was all a secret. . . . No history—a faggot."

The importance of names is where Lydia Minatoya begins in the excerpt from her memoir, *Talking to High Monks in the Snow: An Asian American Odyssey.* As Japanese Americans raising children in the post-World War II period, her parents remembered well the "relocation camps" of a few years earlier in which they, like other Japanese Americans, had been interned behind barbed wire. Her parents wanted to pick out for her a nice American name that would camouflage their daughter, make her less conspicuous. But, as the writer points out, "I remained unalterably alien . . . in those days, everyone knew all real American families were white." Even so, at four years old, Lydia believes in the American Dream. "This is America. . . . I can grow up to be anything that I want." The elementary school scenes she recounts demonstrate the tension between these two beliefs which help to shape who she is.

In a more deliciously comforting memoir, Alfred Kazin in "The Kitchen" evokes for us his New York Jewish childhood. Kazin chooses to structure his childhood memories primarily through setting or place. The peacefulness of Friday evenings after his mother had cleaned the kitchen and filled the table with "company" food and his father had arrived home from his work as a painter evokes longings for a childhood characterized by security and anticipated pleasure. Unlike Nekola's mildly satiric and conflicted look at family life and particularly at her mother's role as homemaker, Kazin's memoir nostalgically enthrones his mother as the heart of her family. The setting in Kazin's essay, unlike Nekola's middle-class suburbia, is working class and urban; Kazin's mother, a seamstress, worked all the time, the kitchen her workshop. Kazin's mother, too, had her dark side—Kazin refers to her endless labor and loneliness—but, Kazin says, "one good look at the street would revive her." Along with differences in ethnicity and time period, differences in gender can be instructive. For example, how men and women variously remember a mother or a father. "The kitchen held our lives together," Kazin writes. That he chooses the kitchen as focal point of his memoir also gives him scope to include marvelously sensual descriptions of food that evoke our senses of sight, smell, and taste and pull us into the scene.

The last of the family of origin memoirs we include here is James Baldwin's classic essay about coming of age as an African American man in America, "Notes of a Native Son." A defining moment comes for the narrator when his father dies; at age nineteen, Baldwin realizes his father's legacy to his son as a black man in America is also the legacy of racism—a corrosive bitterness. This poison, which later in the essay he refers to as gangrene, has a toxic effect on individuals, families, communities, and the larger social body. From beginning to end, Baldwin's essay, in form and content, considers all these levels of society. Through memories of his father's life, recollections of incidents in his own life, a current narrative of his father's funeral, and a more general account of what simultaneously is happening in the surrounding community, Baldwin lays his father to rest. He realizes that "now it had been laid to my charge to keep my own heart free of hatred and despair."

We move from Baldwin's coming of age story to another life stage most of us will participate in: raising a family. Some of us will conceive and raise a child early in life, some later; some with ease, some with great difficulty and perhaps technological help; some within a marriage, some outside of marriage; some in relative luxury, some in material poverty. As the *Sesame Street* jingle suggests, we come in all kinds of family structures. Leslie Lawrence's mysteriously titled "The Death of Fred Astaire" is a very contemporary account of one woman's process of redefining herself as a mother, on her own terms. As a lesbian in her mid-thirties, the narrator faces more conscious choices about conception and motherhood than is usual for those taking more conventional routes than hers. Will she have a child? Will she do so in or out of a relationship? Will she try artificial insemination or ask a trusted male friend to have intercourse? Will her family accept her choices? Fortunately she had no financial, social class, or racial issues to concern her; these would, as Lawrence herself points out, have affected her choices and her experiences. Finally, what does ballroom dancing have to do with Lawrence's unconventional journey toward motherhood?

The sole essay in this section written from a third-person point of view is Jules Henry's sociological study of a hospital for the aged, Muni San (short for Municipal Sanitarium). As in Tommi Avicolli's essay about growing up gay, Henry's approach in "Human Obsolescence" involves combining genres. As Avicolli mixes dramatic scenes with commentary, Henry mixes commentary with sociological observation. At least half of Henry's essay consists of reports from the study's "observers," who logged many hours in the nursing home and wrote detailed and vivid descriptions of people and setting as well as reporting the patients' dialogue. Henry builds his own analysis from these reports and develops an argument about how old people in our society are silenced, isolated, discarded, dehumanized, made obsolete, and consigned to what he terms "a human junkyard."

We end this section with the title essay of Nancy Mairs's book, *Carnal Acts*, a complex and intellectually challenging essay whose particular focus is learning to live with, learning to live in spite of, and even continuing to thrive with a degenerative disease like multiple sclerosis. We all tend to take the healthy functioning of our bodies for granted—like we take the mechanical competence of our cars, refrigerators, and computers for granted—until something goes wrong and they don't work. And sometimes they can't be fixed. All of us, sooner or later, will have to cope with the body's dysfunctions and deteriorations, certainly as we age, often long before. What makes "Carnal Acts" so compelling is not simply Mairs's narrative power to present the particular. She also provides us with a philosophical exploration of attitudes toward the body. First, she explores the traditional Western attitude toward the body—our sense not that we *are* our bodies but that we have or possess a body. Second, through the experience of disability she shares with us her discovery of her own embodied voice as a writer.

The material most of the writers in this section work with is the same material all of us have access to in our memories and in our current observations: the richly sensual detail of our own lives. Notice the formal choices each of these writers makes as she or he selects moments, details, and stories and arranges them to provide the reader with a vivid experience, a shared perspective, and, often, an argument about how we shape and are shaped by our social context.

GOOD MOTHERS, BAD DAUGHTERS

Charlotte Nekola

Charlotte Nekola was born in St. Louis in 1952, studied at Drew and the University of Michigan, and now teaches English at William Paterson University. Her poetry has appeared in a number of publications and she is coeditor of Writing Red: An Anthology of Radical American Women Writers, 1930–1940 *(1988). The following is a chapter from* Dream House: A Memoir *(1993).*

Reading "Sleeping Beauty" one night to my own daughter, I was stunned to recognize my own mother's face in the picture of the thirteenth fairy—the scowly one, the one the other fairies forgot to invite to the party. Suddenly my mother's sighs and resignation and the occasional cross look, the thirteenth-fairy look, crossing over her face took on new meaning.

When I was a child, my mother appeared to me to be the same as the mother in the Dick and Jane readers.[1] This woman decorated pastel birthday cakes, produced new kittens from her apron pockets for surprises, and sat on lawn chairs with her ankles crossed. She set up lunches for her children on card tables under shady maple trees, she put pennies in their coin purses, she held her children's hands on little trips to the bakery or the pet store. She wore Orlon sweaters, skirts, and pumps and sat next to the father for family outings in the car.

My mother provided correct-looking activities and birthday cakes for her children. She seemed benign, at least, if not radiant or even happy or even content. It wasn't until twenty or more years later that I understood that this pastel mother had a darker side. I know now that she was trying very hard to appear benign, because she thought she should, or perhaps because nothing else seemed possible—not the stories she planned to write, not the teaching job she had trained for. Somehow, by the time she was my mother, the elements of her life were quarrels with the butcher, a mostly absent husband,

---

[1] Dick and Jane are the main characters in a series of elementary school readers introduced in the 1940s.

three children, a clean house, many wishes, and an occasional jar of fresh raspberry jelly held up to the sunlight to admire its color.

My mother died when I was eleven, so I cannot check with her about her feelings then, how she felt about being a wife and mother in the manner of the white middle class of the 1950s. She never said, outright, whether she wanted the same thing or something else for her daughters. But it always seemed as if something else was called for. My sister was older than me by almost ten years. Her response to my mother's limited portrait of the future for girls seemed to be to raise the ante of my mother's domestic heroinehood into outright martyrdom: she would marry very young and have six children, she would convert to Catholicism, she would take a night-school course in cake decorating, she would marry a poor but brilliant man, she would make brilliant stew from chicken backs, she would look just like Kim Novak.[2] I took the opposite track in my dreams: I would be a fireman, a cowboy, a doctor, anything clearly unlike a mother. I became a writer, a poet, a scholar, a professor, and a mother. I became the bad daughter of a good mother. But I am coming to believe that she wanted it that way, that many good mothers subverted their own culture in messages to their daughters, who would become the "bad" girls of the 1960s and beyond.

My mother seemed to behave like any other mother. She wore her hair curled away from her face, red lipstick, shirtwaist dresses, straight skirts, and V-neck blouses. Usually some kind of button-shaped earrings, white gloves in warm weather, and two-toned shoes. Pants were a rarity. Even when outdoors, she assumed a decorative posture, like the mothers in the school readers. If the family went fishing, she would not fish, but instead sat carefully in the brush, legs cast to the side in her skirt, writing letters on thin, watery-blue paper. She wrote to her sister in Iowa and to her aunt in California, with stories not about herself, but about her children.

When she went swimming, it was only for a "dip," and then in an absurd bathing cap that had fake bangs attached to it. Apparently, it was necessary to look pleasantly coiffed even when swimming. Once she was in, her arms looked like the fronds of palm or fern cutting quietly through the water—hers was a quiet sidestroke, nothing to do with kicking, thrashing, or splashing. Her house was almost barren in its neatness. There were no signs of disheveled books or newspapers, no crumbs from newly baked bread, no muddy shoes, no leaves the dog dragged in, no toys in the wake of children. I am not sure where these things were hidden. She cooked the food other mothers seemed to: chicken à la king, meat loaf, pancakes, tuna fish sandwiches improved with pickle juice, angel food cake. Our clothes were clean

---

[2] Movie actor.

and ironed. There were orange flowers dutifully planted in spots around the yard, but no riotous garden.

As in every other family I know of, my father was the household king. The unspoken rule which everyone understood was that he made the money, so he set the tone. All else followed from that—how bouncy or not we were in the house, whether we told any of our own stories at the dinner table, whether my mother had any success in pouring out her heart to him at midnight. Perhaps partly because of my father's leading role in this scenario, I could not tell you to this day much about my mother's likes and dislikes, about her passions, except for odd hints.

Every day she found her way to the piano—a cavernous old Chickering baby grand, which she had somehow squeezed into the demure proportions of a suburban brick house built in 1946. I only recently realized that everything she played had the tone and tempo of melancholy, even the folk songs and children's songs she played for us. The ones she picked for herself were full of loss. The refrain of longing was the same, whether the songs were American like "Shenandoah"—"I long to hear you / Away I'm bound to go, / 'Cross the wide [pause] Missouri"—or Eastern European love songs with doleful titles like "Bloom, My Little Bud of Rosemary." In her restrained and slightly too-slow rendition, even children's songs seemed tragic: "Go tell Aunt Lucy / Go tell Aunt Lu—u—cy / The old gray goose is dead." The plight of the three kittens who lost their mittens indeed seemed something of a lament. She was drawn to the piano at almost the same hour of every afternoon, and it was at these times that she seemed to get the closest to saying what was on her mind. But it was only close, an approximation, her song without words, which we noted the way you would note an afternoon sky changing to slate, or the color of moss.

I am ashamed to say that it seemed as if my mother were mainly another feature of the house, not any sort of passionate human being. She was the aproned person who went with the little brick house painted cool green and yellow, with primrose chintz curtains, white tiles in the kitchen, and two-toned linoleum. I see now that this one-dimensional perspective of her was not only because of my child's-eye view, that I was the center of the universe and my mother was there to serve me. It was also because my mother did not know how to name or speak her needs and desires, large or small. I do not really know if she felt most alive in a sooty city street or a woody ravine, yearned only for solitude or for a circle of admirers, liked chocolate definitely more than marzipan, would have died to be a ballerina or a brain surgeon. It seemed that the duty of mothers was not to have any desires, lost or fulfilled or not. Without desire, they were "good" mothers. This is what my mother strove to be, and it was what she was said to be.

However, it was known in our family that my mother had some unmet vocation—this strain was like a chronic illness—that she had some calling totally unrelated to making egg salad sandwiches. She had managed to graduate from college in the middle of the Depression at the young age of twenty. She went to Washington University, during the same years that Tennessee Williams came and left, but did not know this until later. After college she worked on the *St. Louis Star-Ledger,* in a secretarial job for an editor which included writing obituaries and checking the comic strips for continuity. She had trained to be an elementary-school teacher, but, according to my father, felt too ill at ease to stand up in front of a classroom. After marriage, she worked for a couple of years at the paper, and then gave it up.

My father had had to skip college, and the fact that he had a "college-educated" wife meant that he had to be vigilant in maintaining his position as the head of the house. He was always happy to tell the story about coming home one night from work and finding my mother at the kitchen table. The table was covered with little slips of paper and an opened copy of *The Joy of Cooking.* My mother had her head in her hands. She had tried to convert the fractions in a recipe for pot roast, and somehow, even with her college degree, the "poor dear" hadn't been able to manage it. "Well," he'd say, looking happy, "I pulled out my slide rule and had the matter settled in a minute or two." Apparently this endeared her to him. At the same time, this kind of moment in married life was corrosive—and eventually helped to make the idea of her other calling more and more faraway, more like an old sigh.

The refrain of my mother's longing joins in my memory with an image of her lying on the couch for an afternoon nap. Her pumps were tossed off, and she had curled herself around a bit. This was a private retreat where we clearly were not welcome. I think that sometimes, before she went off to this solitary place, before I went back to my room to play like a good child with bride dolls and puzzles in the shape of the United States, she told me a thing or two. She became slightly confidential, the way children do before they fall off to sleep. She might say something about wanting to go back to school or wanting to write some stories. Then she took a nap. For what was the good mother of the 1950s supposed to do about dreams, desires? Mine slept on them, the way the cat slept curled on the doorstep, daily. But she did tell her daughter about them first.

Despite her determination to look and act like the women in the Dick and Jane schoolbooks, I believe that my mother wanted to save something wild in me. Direct statement was beyond her—she'd be stepping too far out of role. Dick and Jane's mother did not lament the good old days at the newspaper office, or sigh about the book she wanted to write, or tell her daughters to forget about marriage. But my mother did forbid me to read fairly tales where they cut off a dancing girl's feet, or turned ambitious mermaids to sea foam. She stopped me from joining my friends in the race to become beauty queens and little mommies. She took me on a trip four-hundred miles from our house, to visit a woman who lived with books, not children. I think many of us must have such stories—moments when our mothers, seemingly frozen in the posture of silence, broke out, briefly, to tell us about some other life they hoped for. For themselves, or for us, or for some other woman, sometime.

It seems now that a very large amount of childhood time ticked away in the middle of the living-room floor—practicing cartwheels, waiting for Annette Funicello and the other Mouseketeers[3] to emerge from the little black dots on the TV screen, waiting for dinner, waiting for my father to read me the comics, waiting for my mother to finish paying bills, waiting to learn how to read, waiting until it was dark and the lightning bugs would come out.

One Sunday, after Sunday school and before Sunday dinner, I wore a pair of black patent-leather shoes with white anklet socks. The shoes had a strap across the top that buckled, Mary Jane-style.[4] The strap was "convertible"—attached to both sides of the shoe with a little hinge so you could flip it back behind your heel. What I wanted, absolutely more than anything else in life, was to be able to wear this strap in back, not over the top of my foot. That way they would look like "flats," a much more grown-up shoe than a Mary Jane.

If my shoes looked like flats, it would prove that I was grown-up, not just a child, and a girl, but a real girl like my teenage sister, who had hair spray and flats, and boyfriends with saddle shoes and cars with fins. From this shoe, the progression from childhood to full womanhood was clearly mapped out—Mary Janes to flats to pumps with a small tasteful heel, and finally to the realm of pure sex and authority, "spike" heels. We revered the sound high heels made clicking down a hallway, and vaguely knew that they also had something to do with men falling over their feet, for women. Some of the other girls in my Sunday-school class had been allowed to fix their shoes so that they looked like flats. As soon as they did this, they seemed to gain years in world-experience and expertise. I didn't think about the fact that their shoes would fall off their feet when they ran or jumped. I only thought of how sleek their feet looked, freed from childhood.

So standing in the middle of the living room, probably waiting for my grandmother to arrive carrying a basket of mending so she could keep busy waiting for Sunday dinner, I experimented with slinging the straps back. I admired the unbroken expanse of white sock. Without the strap, I felt

---

[3] Child actors on "The Mickey Mouse Club."
[4] Mary Janes were a style of little girls' shoes.

instantly transformed, now a sinful Cinderella with some new shoes of big-girl life. I slid up and down the rug on the smooth soles of my shoes. I tried kicking them off effortlessly, the way June Allyson or Doris Day[5] might have with their beautiful high-heeled shoes, and slipping them on again.

Somewhere in the middle of this reverie I must have run into the kitchen and asked my mother if I could now wear my shoes the convertible way all the time. All the other girls were, I'm sure I told her. No, she said quietly, you're not old enough. But Mom, I said. No, she said, you're not old enough for that, there's plenty of time for *that*. My ears burned with rage. Right then, I understood *that* to mean the whole journey to full-grown woman, from flats to pumps to high heels. To boyfriends to wedding cakes and babies crying. Something in her tone clearly meant that all of *that* was not all it was cooked up to be. Not worth sacrificing one moment of your native girlhood for, not worth changing the straps on your Mary Jane shoes.

My mother had an old friend. This in itself surprised me, since my mother seemed to me to have little history aside from taking me to parks and frying up bacon. Her friend's name was Hope West, which I knew from seeing it on the binding of one of the books in our house. She was an anthropologist, and she and my mother had been in college together at Washington University. In August of 1959, when I was seven, my family took a short trip to Chicago, to visit the Field Museum, to have lunch in the Marshall Field's tearoom,[6] and to visit Hope West. In the museum I was thrilled by displays of Kodiak bears, hunks of alabaster and chrysolite, and dinosaur bones. My other main concern on this trip was eating fried chicken as often as possible.

It seemed a little dreary to visit one of my mother's friends in the middle of all of this, and the August heat was thick. All of her "old college friends" I had met so far seemed to fall into one not very interesting category. They had given up their jobs, married, and had children. They had "luncheon," not lunch, with card parties once or twice a year, on card tables in their living rooms, were all very pleasant, and all seemed to be named Mary Helen or Helen Louise. But this old friend had no children, I was told, was not married, and worked as a writer. Never had I met a woman like this.

Further, she lived by herself in an apartment. In my limited experience as a girl growing up outside St. Louis in a suburban house with a scrubby field behind it, an apartment in the city seemed to be a shrine to one's own mind. Especially this woman's apartment, since she was the author of books. As far as I knew, she and my mother hadn't seen each other since college, and now it was more than twenty-five years later.

---

[5] Movie actors.

[6] Chicago Natural History Museum; Chicago department store.

So I knew, when we walked into her apartment at the end of a humid August afternoon, that some kind of moment had arrived for my mother. Our family—my sister, my brother, my mother and father, and myself—were much too large for Hope West's apartment. We were a bulky group that disturbed the streamlined serenity of this "modern" 1950s brick skyscraper. My parents tried to make us look spotless and presentable, dabbing at our collars or the corners of our mouths, catching stray strands of hair. But here was a seven-year-old with legs long like a young horse's, with scabby knees from falling in blackberry patches. A fourteen-year-old boy in wilted khaki pants, whose voice was changing, and who was obsessed with meteorology. And a sixteen-year-old girl with three or four crinoline petticoats and upswept blond hair so that she could look like Kim Novak in *Picnic*.

My father stood slightly aside in shirt sleeves because of the heat, and smoked a Pall Mall. His social bearing was a bit confused because this woman was a scholar and a writer. He didn't seem to know whether to adopt the polite, deferential mode reserved for elderly maiden aunts, or the more bossy, commandeering mode used with business friends. And there was my mother, a *mother* with white gloves, responsible for all of these children who were now either bumping into coffee tables, in danger of breaking the African artifacts, or rudely staring out the window at Lake Michigan. But I remember thinking, despite our gangliness, that Hope West was certainly the one to be pitied. She was "a woman without children"—a fate always presented in our family as a lifetime tragedy, a sadness to be avoided at any cost.

Yet, Hope West did not look sad. She did not look like any of the other women I had ever met, the mothers with comfortable tummies, generous upper arms, curly hair with a little breeze in it, wearing a print dress that puffed out at the waist. Mothers who actually spent time crisscrossing the prongs of a fork on top of cookies for decoration. Hope West was tall and wore a tubular green suit. Her whole face gathered toward her hair, which was pulled up in a French twist. Her face and her hair seemed to collect what she was seeing and thinking.

There were no cookies waiting for us on the coffee table. One side of the living room held a wall of books, more than I had ever seen in anyone's house. Most important, most amazing to me, was that all of these books were hers. On another side of the room was a huge picture window that overlooked Lake Michigan and the tops of buildings. Not flowers and a swing set. No one but Hope West enjoyed this view of Lake Michigan's endless blue tabletop—hard to imagine, when the five of us crowded around the kitchen window at our house to look at rabbits or possums traveling through the backyard. Her own view, and her own books—and some of them were undoubtedly hers, of her own writing. How would it feel, I wondered, to have your own book on your own bookshelf? Her bookshelves, her room, her Lake

Michigan. I had never met a woman who didn't share everything with everyone. Who didn't have to give up the best pork chop for the father or the children, who had more than a few private things in a bureau drawer that her children always raided. Hope West seemed strange and monumental, standing straight and gray-eyed in her French twist, in front of her books and a long vista outside.

Suddenly, the seemingly inevitable and unfortunate outlines of women's destinies fell into relief for me. You could be Hope West, alone, with your books, with no children. Or you could be my mother with children, and no book of your own. I felt that each of the old friends looked at the other and saw what she did not have. It seemed that I had to choose sides, then and there. Of course I thought, maybe in loyalty, that I would be like my mother, the one with children. But I had always wanted to write a book, to hold a book of my own in my hand. Did I have to choose?

We took Hope West out to dinner with us. I ate fried chicken again, and wondered what Hope West did for dinner, alone, on all those other nights, when we weren't there to take her out. My mother never did become Hope West, the writer of books, the mother of no children. But she did bring her impressionable children across four-hundred flat miles of Missouri and Illinois to visit her on an impossibly hot summer day in 1959.

How far could a woman walk? This question seemed to underlie another of my mother's rather odd strictures, besides the one about grown-up girl shoes. My mother was not one to forbid or censor very much. She had read Dr. Spock, after all, and was determined to be different from her mother, who was said to have been "severe." But she had been strong on the subject of those patent-leather shoes, and she was also very clear about not reading two particular fairy tales to me. This was puzzling. She believed in reading, and let me go through everything else in the house from *Mr. Dog* to photo essays on Czechoslovakia to *The Hunchback of Notre Dame*.

But there was a certain book with a languorous picture of a mermaid on the cover that I coveted. The book had a special mystique because it had belonged to my mother as a child, and because she had forbidden me to read two of the stories inside. It was a beginning-to-fall-apart edition of Andersen's fairy tales, from the 1920s, a "Washington Square Classic." The quality of the paper seemed to be just a cut above newsprint. There were only six color illustrations—the Snow Queen, Elise with the swans, a sleeping woman among water lilies, an angel with a child, the little mermaid, and a prince finding a sleeping princess in the garden of paradise. There were also two dozen other tales the illustrator could have chosen from, but he picked opportunities to paint mournful women. They were all long-haired, entwined in swans or water, and doomed.

I treasured this book because it was one of the few things my mother had kept from her own childhood. There were no favorite dolls, toys, or sweaters—just a few books. When she first brought the fairy-tale book up to my room—she must have kept it in some special part of the house, since I had never seen it with the other books—I was impressed by its age. Its yellow cover fell into the yellow light of my bedside lamp as dusk fell outside. It proved that my mother had been a child—and the fact that there were only six illustrations in a volume of so many stories further convinced me that life in the old days, my mother's old days, was deprived and strange indeed. I've carried this book with me through more than fifteen changes of address since I left home twenty years ago, carefully packing it, dusting it, yet sometimes ignoring it, letting its binding fall off. And thinking, so what if I finally lose it, knowing I would never forgive myself if I did.

Now this book brings back the feeling of what it was like in a Missouri bedroom with a view of a field of brush to be a child who thought she was safe. In flannel pajamas on ironed cotton sheets, with a wool blanket, a quilt embroidered by my aunts and grandmother that seemed to have purple asters blowing slightly in the wind, a chenille bedspread with peach and blue tufts, an oak table and chair next to the bed, and a mother who was probably even wearing a damp apron. You could pick up a little something about her when she read out loud. She did not read dramatically, or very humorously, even when it came to the burlesque parts of "The Three Bears"—but she read with feeling and thoughtfulness, the way she played the piano. You could hear more of the longing. It seemed as if she liked to be lost in the stories as much as her children did. Maybe she was a little sad, too. There was a lulling note in her voice, as if acknowledging that this story was something she could bring you for only a very short time of your life, this short time before you fell asleep and grew up.

We read all of the stories in the Hans Christian Andersen except two, "The Little Mermaid" and "The Red Shoes." I wanted to hear about them, but my mother said, "Don't read those stories. They're too sad." This was unusual for her—she made few direct statements and gave little forceful advice. So this directive coming from her stunned me. Besides, the best picture in the whole book, the cover picture even, was of the mermaid. She sat in profile, with her hair fanning out into seaweed, posed with her tail curled improbably under her at the bottom of the sea. She was so beautiful. But my mother would not read her story, in that golden light with the dusk falling outside.

Since they were forbidden, I wanted to read those stories all the more. My mother eventually gave in and read them to me. I found out that the little mermaid fell in love with a human prince, wanted to be human, and sold her tongue to a witch in order to have legs, like a princess. She got her legs, but they were a bad fit. My mother could barely choke out the line about the mermaid's legs: *they hurt like knives* whenever she walked.

It seemed to me that my mother, that many other women, who had ambitions that seemed as farfetched and unlikely as a mermaid having legs, if they wanted to roam, be a traveling writer or pursue some idea of their own making anywhere, were punished in the same way for their dreams. Maybe my mother had tried something like this once, but her *legs hurt like knives*. Why was the price for endeavor so dear? Why did the mermaid have to lose her voice, her tongue, just to be able to walk the same landscape as the prince? Another woman helped her toward what she wanted, but there was the terrible price of pain and silence. Was this helping woman a witch, a mother? Was this story just about growing up, a warning against trying to walk like a man? Or about making yourself fit for a man by becoming mute?

For all her terrible sacrifices, the mermaid fails to meet her prince. She struggles across the land in her bad legs, only in time to see, from afar, his wedding to a real princess taking place. She cannot even call out, since her voice is gone. This was more bad news for girls like me, the ones that might try to transform themselves into something else, to ask a witch, or a mother, sometime, for traveling legs. It implied that the real princess, the natural girl, the one who was born to this station, did not have to change herself. The princesses would marry the princes no matter what.

My mother was warning me that her own story and the story of my life to come might be "too sad." Would my legs turn to knives when I tried to walk? Would growing up like a girl cut my tongue out? Perhaps she thought in some primitive way that if I never read the story, none of this would happen to me. But I can tell you that for many years of my early childhood, I was awakened from sleep a few times every week by pains in my legs. I was told that they were called "growing" pains.

In the second story my mother wouldn't read, "The Red Shoes," a girl longs for a special pair of shoes. She gets them. She dances joyfully in the town square. But then her feet won't stop dancing. She's about to die from never stopping. A woodcutter cuts her feet off so that she can stop. So she stops, but she dies. It seemed to me that there was a special fate that this girl had really wanted with those red shoes. Wear red shoes. Dance and dance. But somehow this red desire for a girl was sickness. Desire will kill you eventually. You'll be cut off at the feet by some man, sooner or later.

The mermaid, too, was cut off by desire. When she finally glimpsed the prince from far off, and could not call out on her bad legs, she became so sad that she turned to sea foam. My mother made no instructive comments about my future, like get a job before a man, be a mother or not, forget marriage. This was years before the women's movement, before women looked twice at what happened to women in the stories handed down to us. But I do know, from the way she read these stories to me, in a bedroom in Missouri in 1959, that she did not want me, her daughter, ever to walk on legs that hurt like knives, to have my feet cut off if I tried to dance, or to have my life amount to sea foam.

STUDY AND DISCUSSION QUESTIONS

1. List several behaviors the narrator's mother engaged in that made her a "Dick and Jane" mother. Name several other behaviors that exhibited her "darker side."
2. Discuss the power dynamics between husband and wife in the narrator's family.
3. Why does the narrator want to flip back the straps on her black patent leather shoes and why does her mother not let her? Mention a parallel incident from your own childhood.
4. What is the significance to the narrator of the visit to her mother's friend, Hope West? Does the name itself have any significance?
5. What is Nekola's interpretation of (a) "The Little Mermaid" and (b) "The Red Shoes" in relation to the possibilities of her own life?
6. Looking back at the opening paragraph of the essay, notice that Nekola begins with a reference to a third fairy tale, "Sleeping Beauty." Why does she see her mother's face in the thirteenth fairy? Why might it be appropriate for Nekola to begin with this particular fairy tale? You might want to reread the Grimm Brothers' version of "Sleeping Beauty."
7. Consider the title. What do you think Nekola means by "good" and "bad" here?
8. Since the narrator grew up in the 1950s, she might be the age of your mother. Does the essay add to your understanding of your own mother? How are the dynamics between you and your mother like or unlike those the narrator describes? How and how much does your relationship depend on the different historical contexts in which you and your mother were raised?

SUGGESTIONS FOR WRITING

1. Think about your relation to your own mother if you are a woman or to your father if you are a man. What kind of messages do you remember receiving as you grew up about whether and how to be like that parent of the same gender? About what it means to be a woman or what it means to be a man?

2. Write a short essay discussing the significance of shoes in "Good Mothers, Bad Daughters."

3. Write a short essay discussing references to speech and silence in "Good Mothers, Bad Daughters."

4. Write a character sketch of your mother as you remember her from your childhood: how she dressed, how she acted, how she behaved toward you. What was important to her, do you think?

HE DEFIES YOU STILL: THE MEMOIRS OF A SISSY

Tommi Avicolli

Tommi Avicolli is the author of Magic Doesn't Live Here Anymore *(1976) and, under the name Tommi Avicolli Mecca, of* Between Little Rock and a Hard Place *(1993). His shorter writings have appeared in a variety of publications, including the book* Fuori: Essays by Italian/American Lesbians and Gays *(1996), edited by Anthony Julian Tamburri.*

Scene One:

A homeroom in a Catholic high school in South Philadelphia. The boy sits quietly in the first aisle, third desk, reading a book. He does not look up, not even for a moment. He is hoping no one will remember he is sitting there. He wishes he were invisible. The teacher is not yet in the classroom so the other boys are talking and laughing loudly.

Suddenly, a voice from beside him: "Hey, you're a faggot, ain't you?"

The boy does not answer. He goes on reading his book, or rather pretending he is reading his book. It is impossible to actually read now.

"Hey, I'm talking to you!"

The boy still does not look up. He is so scared his heart is thumping madly. But he can't look up.

"Faggot, I'm talking to you!"

To look up is to meet the eyes of the tormentor.

Suddenly a sharp pencil point is thrust into the boy's arm. He jolts, shaking off the pencil, aware that there is blood seeping from the wound.

"What did you do that for?" he asks timidly.

"Cause I hate faggots," the other boy says, laughing. Some other boys begin to laugh, too. A symphony of laughter. The boy feels as if he's going to cry. But he must not cry. Must not cry. So he holds back the tears and tries to read the book again. He must read the book. Read the book.

When the teacher arrives a few minutes later, the class quiets down. The boy does not tell the teacher what has happened. He spits on the wound to clean it, dabbing it with a tissue until the bleeding stops. For weeks he fears some dreadful infection from the lead in the pencil point.

Scene Two:

The boy is walking home from school. A group of boys (two, maybe three, he is not certain) grab him from behind, drag him into an alley and beat him up. When he gets home, he races up to his room, refusing dinner ("I don't feel well," he tells his mother through the locked door) and spends the night alone in the dark wishing he would die. . . .

These are not fictitious accounts—I *was* that boy. Having been branded a sissy by neighborhood children because I preferred jump rope to baseball and dolls to playing soldiers, I was often taunted with "hey sissy" or "hey faggot" or "yoo hoo, honey" when I left the house.

To avoid harassment, I spent many summers alone in my room. I went out on rainy days when the street was empty.

I came to like being alone. I didn't need anyone, I told myself over and over. I was an island. Contact with others meant pain. Alone, I was protected. I began writing poems, then short stories. There was no reason to go outside anymore. I had a world of my own.

> In the schoolyard today
> they'll single you out
> Their laughter will leave your ears ringing
> like the church bells
> that once awed you. . .[1]

School was one of the more painful experiences of my youth. The neighborhood bullies could be avoided. The taunts of the children living in those endless row houses could be evaded by staying in my room. But school was something I had to face day after day for some two hundred mornings a year.

---

[1] From the poem "Faggot," by Tommi Avicolli, published in *GPU News,* September 1979. [Author's note]

I had few friends in school. Some kids would talk to me, but few wanted to be known as my close friend. Afraid of labels. If I was a sissy, then they would be sissies, too. I was condemned to loneliness.

Fortunately, a new boy moved into our neighborhood and befriended me; he wasn't afraid of the labels. He protected me when the other guys threatened to beat me up. He walked me home from school; he broke through the terrible loneliness. We were in third or fourth grade at the time.

We spent a summer or two together. Then his parents sent him to camp and I was once again confined to my room.

Scene Three:

High school lunchroom. The boy sits at a table near the back of the room. Without warning, his lunch bag is grabbed and tossed to another table. Someone opens it and confiscates a package of Tastykakes; another boy takes the sandwich. The empty bag is tossed back to the boy who stares at it, dumbfounded. He should be used to this; it has happened before.

Someone says, "Faggot," laughing. There is always laughter. It does not annoy him anymore.

There is no teacher nearby. There is never a teacher around. And what would he say if there were? Could he report the crime? He would be jumped after school if he did. Besides, it would be his word against theirs. Teachers never noticed anything. They never heard the taunts. Never heard the word, "faggot." They were the great deaf mutes, pillars of indifference; a sissy's pain was not relevant to history and geography and god made me to love honor and obey him, amen.

The boy reaches into his pocket for some money, but there's only a few coins. Always just a few coins. He cleans windshields at his father's gas station on Saturdays and Sundays to earn money. But it's never much. Only enough now to buy a carton of milk and some cookies. Only enough to watch the other boys eat and laugh, hoping they'll choke on their food . . . .

Scene Four:

High school religion class. Someone has a copy of *Playboy*. Father N. is not in the room yet; he's late, as usual. Someone taps the boy roughly on the shoulder. He turns. A finger points to the centerfold model, pink fleshy body, thin and sleek. Almost painted. Not real. The other asks in a mocking voice, "Hey, does she turn you on? Look at those tits!"

The boy smiles, nodding meekly; turns away.

The other jabs him harder on the shoulder, "Hey, what'samatter, don't you like girls?"

Laughter. Thousands of mouths; unbearable din of laughter. In the arena: thumbs down. Don't spare the queer.

"Wanna suck my dick, huh? That turn you on, faggot!"

What did being a sissy really mean? It was a way of walking (from the hips rather than the shoulders); it was a way of talking (often with a lisp or in a high-pitched voice); it was a way of relating to others (gently, not wanting to fight, or hurt anybody's feelings). It was being intelligent ("an egghead" they called it sometimes); getting good grades. It meant not being interested in sports, not playing football in the street after school; not discussing teams and scores and playoffs. And it involved not showing a fervent interest in girls, not talking about scoring or tits or *Playboy* centerfolds. Not concealing pictures of naked women in your history book; or porno books in your locker.

On the other hand, anyone could be a "faggot." It was a catchall. If you did something that didn't conform to the acceptable behavior of the group, then you risked being called a faggot. It was the most commonly used putdown. It kept guys in line. They became angry when somebody called them a faggot. More fights started over calling someone a faggot than anything else. The word had power. It toppled the male ego, shattered his delicate facade, violated the image he projected. He was tough. Without feeling. Faggot cut through all this. It made him vulnerable. Feminine. And feminine was the worst thing he could possibly be. Girls were fine for fucking, but no boy in his right mind wanted to be like them. A boy was the opposite of a girl. He was not feminine. He was not feeling. He was not weak.

Just look at the gym teacher who growled like a dog; or the priest with the black belt who threw kids against the wall in rage when they didn't know their Latin. They were men, they got respect.

But not the physics teacher who preached pacificism during lectures on the nature of atoms. Everybody knew what he was—and why he believed in the antiwar movement.

Scene Five:

Father: I wanna see you walk, Mark.

Mark: What do you mean?

Father: Just walk, Mark.

Mark: (Starts to walk) I don't understand.

Father: That's it, just walk.

Mark: (Walks back and forth)

Father: Now come here.

         (Mark approaches; father slaps him across the face, hard)

Mark: What was that for?

Father: I want you to walk right now.

Mark: What do you mean?

Father: Stop fooling around, Mark, I want you to walk like a man.

Mark: Dad, I . . .

Father: (Interrupting) Don't say another word. Just get over there and walk right—walk like a man.[2]

My parents only knew that the neighborhood kids called me names. They begged me to act more like the other boys. My brothers were ashamed of me. They never said it, but I knew. Just as I knew that my parents were embarassed by my behavior.

At times, they tried to get me to act differently. Once my father lectured me on how to walk right. I'm still not clear on what that means. Not from the hips, I guess; don't "swish" like faggots do.

A nun in elementary school told my mother at open house that there was "something wrong with me." I had draped my sweater over my shoulders like a girl, she said. I was a smart kid, no complaints about my grades, but I should know better than to wear my sweater like a girl.

My mother stood there, mute. I wanted her to say something, to chastise the nun, to defend me. But how could she? This was a nun talking—representative of Jesus, protector of all that was good and decent.

An uncle once told me I should start "acting like a boy" instead of a girl. Everybody seemed ashamed of me. And I guess I was ashamed of myself, too. It was hard not to be.

Scene Six:

Priest: Do you like girls, Mark?

Mark: Uh-huh.

Priest: I mean REALLY like them?

Mark: Yeah—they're okay.

Priest: There's a role they play in your salvation. Do you understand it, Mark?

Mark: Yeah.

---

[2] From the play *Judgement of the Roaches,* by Tommi Avicolli, produced in Philadelphia at the Gay & Lesbian Coffee house, the Painted Bride Arts Center, and the University of Pennsylvania; aired over WXPN-FM in four parts; and presented at the Lesbian/Gay Conference in Norfolk, VA, July 1980. [Author's note]

Priest: You've got to like girls. Even if you should decide to enter the semi-nary, it's important to keep in mind God's plan for a man and a woman. . . .[3]

Catholicism of course condemned homosexuality. Effeminancy was tol-erated as long as the effeminate person did not admit to being gay. Thus, priests could be effeminate because they weren't gay.

As a sissy, I couldn't count on support from the church. A male's sole purpose in life was to father children—souls for the church to save. The only hope a homosexual had of attaining salvation was to remain totally celibate. Don't even think of touching another boy. To think of a sin was a sin. And to sin was to put a mark on the soul. Sin—led to hell. There was no way around it. If you sinned, you were doomed.

Realizing I was gay wasn't an easy task. Although I knew I was attracted to boys by the time I was about eleven, I didn't connect this attraction to homosexuality. I was not queer. Not I. I was merely appreciating a boy's good looks, his fine features, his proportions. It didn't seem to matter that I didn't appreciate a girl's looks in the same way. There was no twitching in my thighs when I gazed upon a beautiful girl. But I wasn't queer.

We sat through endless English classes, and history courses about the wars between men who were not allowed to love each other. No gay history was ever taught. You're just a faggot. Homosexuals had never contributed to the human race. God destroyed the queers in Sodom and Gommorrah.

I resisted that label—queer—for the longest time. Even when every-thing pointed to it, I refused to see it. I was certainly not queer. Not I.

Near the end of my junior year in high school, most of the teasing and taunting had let up. Now I was just ignored. Besides, I was getting a reputa-tion for being a hippie, since I spoke up in social studies classes against the war, and wore my hair as long as I could without incurring the wrath of the administration. When your hair reached a certain length, you were told to get a hair cut. If you didn't, you were sent down to the vice principal's office where you were given a hair cut.

I had a friend toward the end of junior year; his name was Joe. He in-troduced me to Jay at the bowling alley in South Philadelphia. I knew im-mediately I was in love with Jay.

A relationship developed. It was all very daring; neither of us under-stood what was happening. I still rejected the label. I wasn't queer. He wasn't queer. But I knew I was in love with him. I told myself that all the time. Yet I wasn't a homosexual.

---

[3] Ibid. [Author's note]

Franny was a queer. He lived a few blocks away. He used to dress in women's clothes and wait for the bus on the corner. Everybody laughed at Franny. Everybody knew he was queer.

Then, one night, Halloween, a chilly October night, Jay called:

Scene Seven:

. . . "What?"

"It's wrong."

"What's wrong."

Tossing in my sleep—sweating. It was the winter of '69. The heavy woolen cover became a thick shroud on top of me. The heat pricked me like so many needles.

"Why can't I see you tonight?"

"We can't see each other anymore. . . ."

My heart was an acrobat. It leaped like a frog. Landed in a deep puddle. Help, it shouted. It was going down for the third time.

"Why?" I felt nauseous. I was going to vomit.

"We can't. I've got to go."

"Wait—!"

"What?"

There were tears running down my cheeks in streams that left a salty residue at the corners of my lips. The record player in the background shut off, closing me in. The walls of the room collapsed. I was entombed.

"Please, talk to me. I can't let you go like this. I want to know what's wrong. Please . . ."

"I can't see you anymore. It's over. It was a mistake."

"It wasn't a mistake, Jay. I—I love you."

"Don't say that!" Voice quivering; don't force me to see things I don't want to see right now.

"But I do. And you love me. Admit it. Don't break it off now. Admit it. Admit that you love me."

"I've got to go."

"You can't go. Admit it!"

"Goodbye."

"Jay?"

Silence.[4]

We learned about Michelangelo, Oscar Wilde, Gertrude Stein—but never that they were queer. They were not queer. Walt Whitman, the "father of American poetry," was not queer. No one was queer. I was alone, totally

---

[4] From the novel *Deaf Mute's Final Dance,* by Tommi Avicolli. [Author's note]

unique. One of a kind. Except for Franny who wore dresses and makeup. Where did Franny go every night? Were there others like me somewhere? Another planet, perhaps?

In school, they never talked of queers. They did not exist. The only hint we got of this other species was in religion class. And even then it was clouded in mystery—never spelled out. It was a sin. Like masturbation. Like looking at *Playboy* and getting a hard-on. A sin.

Once a progressive priest in senior-year religion class actually mentioned homosexuals—he said the word, broke the silence—but he was talking about homosexuals as pathetic and sick. Fixated at some early stage; penis, anal, whatever. Only heterosexuals passed on to the nirvana of sexual development.

No other images from the halls of the Catholic high school except those the other boys knew: swishy faggot sucking cock in an alley somewhere, grabbing asses in the bathroom. Never mentioning how straight boys craved blow jobs, too.

It was all a secret. You were not supposed to talk about queers. Whisper maybe. Laugh about them, yes. But don't be open, honest; don't try to understand. Don't cite their accomplishments. No history faces you this morning. You're a faggot. No history—a faggot.

Epilogue:

The boy marching down Spruce Street. Hundreds of queers. Signs proclaiming gay pride. Speakers. Tables with literature from gay groups. A miracle, he is thinking. Tears are coming loose now. Someone hugs him.

> You could not control
> the sissy in me
> nor could you exorcise him
> nor electrocute him
> You declared him illegal illegitimate
> insane and immature
> but he defies you still.[5]

STUDY AND DISCUSSION QUESTIONS

1. List the eight scenes Avicolli presents to the reader.
2. What were the narrator's responses to being tormented by his classmates in elementary school?

---

[5] From the poem "Sissy Poem," published in *Magic Doesn't Live Here Anymore*, Spruce Street Press, 1976. [Author's note]

3. List the words and/or labels for homosexual used in this essay. Add others you know of. How does this list make you feel?

4. What is the distinction between "sissy" and "faggot," according to Avicolli?

5. How did the narrator's parents cope with his "difference"?

6. Most of us went through the experience of having our first teenage romance end in failure. Why is the narrator's experience of this common phenomenon even more devastating than most of ours?

7. Discuss the poem in the epilogue.

SUGGESTIONS FOR WRITING

1. How and why did the narrator resist accepting who he was? What mores in the Church, the school curriculum, and society in general guided him toward this resistance?

2. Describe an experience in which you were seen as different in some way.

3. Avicolli says no gay history or literature was taught when he was in school; for example, the fact that Michelangelo, Oscar Wilde, Gertrude Stein, and Walt Whitman were gay was never mentioned. Can you remember occasions in your own educational experience when homosexuality was a subject, even in passing? Discuss.

FROM *TALKING TO HIGH MONKS IN THE SNOW: AN ASIAN AMERICAN ODYSSEY*

Lydia Minatoya

Lydia Minatoya was born in Albany, New York, in 1950 and received a PhD from the University of Maryland. She works now as a community college counselor and teacher. Her memoir, Talking to High Monks in the Snow, was published in 1992.

Perhaps it begins with my naming. During her pregnancy, my mother was reading Dr. Spock. "Children need to belong," he cautioned. "An unusual name can make them the subject of ridicule." My father frowned when he heard this. He stole a worried glance at my sister. Burdened by her Japanese name, Misa played unsuspectingly on the kitchen floor.

The Japanese know full well the dangers of conspicuousness. "The nail that sticks out gets pounded down," cautions an old maxim. In America, Relocation[1] was all the proof they needed.

And so it was, with great earnestness, my parents searched for a conventional name. They wanted me to have the full true promise of America.

"I will ask my colleague Froilan," said my father. "He is the smartest man I know."

"And he has poetic soul," said my mother, who cared about such things.

In due course, Father consulted Froilan. He gave Froilan his conditions for suitability.

"First, if possible, the full name should be alliterative," said my father. "Like Misa Minatoya." He closed his eyes and sang my sister's name. "Second, if not an alliteration, at least the name should have assonantal rhyme."

"Like Misa Minatoya?" said Froilan with a teasing grin.

"Exactly," my father intoned. He gave an emphatic nod. "Finally, most importantly, the name must be readily recognized as conventional." He peered at Froilan with hope. "Do you have any suggestions or ideas?"

Froilan, whose own American child was named Ricardito, thought a while.

"We already have selected the name for a boy," offered my Father. "Eugene."

"Eugene?" wondered Froilan. "But it meets none of your conditions!"

"Eugene is a special case," said my father, "after Eugene, Oregon, and Eugene O'Neill. The beauty of the Pacific Northwest, the power of a great writer."

"I see," said Froilan, who did not but who realized that this naming business would be more complex than he had anticipated. "How about Maria?"

"Too common," said my father. "We want a *conventional* name, not a common one."

"Hmmm," said Froilan, wondering what the distinction was. He thought some more and then brightened. "Lydia!" he declared. He rhymed the name with media. "Lydia for *la bonita infanta!*"

And so I received my uncommon conventional name. It really did not provide the camouflage my parents had anticipated. I remained unalterably

---

[1] In 1942, the United States government forcibly removed over 100,000 Japanese Americans from their homes and interned them in camps for the duration of World War II.

alien. For Dr. Spock had been addressing *American* families, and in those days, everyone knew all real American families were white.

Call it denial, but many Japanese Americans never quite understood that the promise of America was not truly meant for them. They lived in horse stalls at the Santa Anita racetrack and said the Pledge of Allegiance daily. They rode to Relocation Camps under armed guard, labeled with numbered tags, and sang "The Star-Spangled Banner." They lived in deserts or swamps, ludicrously imprisoned—where would they run if they ever escaped—and formed garden clubs, and yearbook staffs, and citizen town meetings. They even elected beauty queens.

My mother practiced her okoto[2] and was featured in a recital. She taught classes in fashion design and her students mounted a show. Into exile she had carried an okoto and a sewing machine. They were her past and her future. She believed in Art and Technology.

My mother's camp was the third most populous city in the entire state of Wyoming. Across the barren lands, behind barbed wire, bloomed these little oases of democracy. The older generation bore the humiliation with pride. "*Kodomo no tame ni,*" they said. For the sake of the children. They thought that if their dignity was great, then their children would be spared. Call it valor. Call it bathos. Perhaps it was closer to slapstick: a sweet and bitter lunacy.

Call it adaptive behavior. Coming from a land swept by savage typhoons, ravaged by earthquakes and volcanoes, the Japanese have evolved a view of the world: a cooperative, stoic, almost magical way of thinking. Get along, work hard, and never quite see the things that can bring you pain. Against the tyranny of nature, of feudal lords, of wartime hysteria, the charm works equally well.

And so my parents gave me an American name and hoped that I could pass. They nourished me with the American dream: Opportunity, Will, Transformation.

When I was four and my sister was eight, Misa regularly used me as a comic foil. She would bring her playmates home from school and query me as I sat amidst the milk bottles on the front steps.

"What do you want to be when you grow up?" she would say. She would nudge her audience into attentiveness.

"A mother kitty cat!" I would enthuse. Our cat had just delivered her first litter of kittens and I was enchanted by the rasping tongue and soft mewings of motherhood.

"And what makes you think you can become a cat?" Misa would prompt, gesturing to her howling friends—wait for this; it gets better yet.

---

[2] Japanese stringed instrument.

"This is America," I stoutly would declare. "I can grow up to be anything that I want!"

My faith was unshakable. I believed. Opportunity. Will. Transformation.

When we lived in Albany, I always was the teachers' pet. "So tiny, so precocious, so prettily dressed!" They thought I was a living doll and this was fine with me.

My father knew that the effusive praise would die. He had been through this with my sister. After five years of being a perfect darling, Misa had reached the age where students were tracked by ability. Then, the anger started. Misa had tested into the advanced track. It was impossible, the community declared. Misa was forbidden entry into advanced classes as long as there were white children being placed below her. In her defense, before an angry rabble, my father made a presentation to the Board of Education.

But I was too young to know of this. I knew only that my teachers praised and petted me. They took me to other classes as an example. "Watch now, as Lydia demonstrates attentive behavior," they would croon as I was led to an empty desk at the head of the class. I had a routine. I would sit carefully, spreading my petticoated skirt neatly beneath me. I would pull my chair close to the desk, crossing my swinging legs at my snowy white anklets. I would fold my hands carefully on the desk before me and stare pensively at the blackboard.

This routine won me few friends. The sixth-grade boys threw rocks at me. They danced around me in a tight circle, pulling at the corners of their eyes. "Ching Chong Chinaman," they chanted. But teachers loved me. When I was in first grade, a third-grade teacher went weeping to the principal. She begged to have me skipped. She was leaving to get married and wanted her turn with the dolly.

When we moved, the greatest shock was the knowledge that I had lost my charm. From the first, my teacher failed to notice me. But to me, it did not matter. I was in love. I watched her moods, her needs, her small vanities. I was determined to ingratiate.

Miss Hempstead was a shimmering vision with a small upturned nose and eyes that were kewpie-doll blue. Slender as a sylph, she tripped around the classroom, all saucy in her high-heeled shoes. Whenever I looked at Miss Hempstead, I pitied the Albany teachers whom, formerly, I had adored. Poor old Miss Rosenberg. With a shiver of distaste, I recalled her loose fleshy arms, her mottled hands, the scent of lavender as she crushed me to her heavy breasts.

Miss Hempstead had a pet of her own. Her name was Linda Sherlock. I watched Linda closely and plotted Miss Hempstead's courtship. The key was the piano. Miss Hempstead played the piano. She fancied herself a musical star. She sang songs from Broadway revues and shaped her students' reactions. "Getting to know you," she would sing. We would smile at her in a staged manner and position ourselves obediently at her feet.

Miss Hempstead was famous for her ability to soothe. Each day at rest time, she played the piano and sang soporific songs. Linda Sherlock was the only child who succumbed. Routinely, Linda's head would bend and nod until she crumpled gracefully onto her folded arms. A tousled strand of blond hair would fall across her forehead. Miss Hempstead would end her song, would gently lower the keyboard cover. She would turn toward the restive eyes of the class. "Isn't she sweetness itself!" Miss Hempstead would declare. It made me want to vomit.

I was growing weary. My studiousness, my attentiveness, my fastidious grooming and pert poise: all were failing me. I changed my tactics. I became a problem. Miss Hempstead sent me home with nasty notes in sealed envelopes: Lydia is a slow child, a noisy child, her presence is disruptive. My mother looked at me with surprise, "*Nani desu ka?* Are you having problems with your teacher?" But I was tenacious. I pushed harder and harder, firmly caught in the obsessive need of the scorned.

One day I snapped. As Miss Hempstead began to sing her wretched lullabies, my head dropped to the desk with a powerful CRACK! It lolled there, briefly, then rolled toward the edge with a momentum that sent my entire body catapulting to the floor. Miss Hempstead's spine stretched slightly, like a cat that senses danger. Otherwise, she paid no heed. The linoleum floor was smooth and cool. It emitted a faint pleasant odor: a mixture of chalk dust and wax.

I began to snore heavily. The class sat electrified. There would be no drowsing today. The music went on and on. Finally, one boy could not stand it. "Miss Hempstead," he probed plaintively, "Lydia has fallen asleep on the floor!" Miss Hempstead did not turn. Her playing grew slightly strident but she did not falter.

I lay on the floor through rest time. I lay on the floor through math drill. I lay on the floor while my classmates scraped around me, pushing their sturdy little wooden desks into the configuration for reading circle. It was not until penmanship practice that I finally stretched and stirred. I rose like Sleeping Beauty and slipped back to my seat. I smiled enigmatically. A spell had been broken. I never again had a crush on a teacher.

STUDY AND DISCUSSION QUESTIONS

1. What's in a name? Why did the narrator's parents think her name would be so important?

2. What does the narrator characterize as the Japanese world view?

3. Minatoya writes that her parents hoped she could "pass." What does the concept of passing mean? Mention some examples of passing.

4. Discuss Lydia's specific version of the American Dream.

5. Why were Lydia and her older sister each teacher's pet for a few years? When and why does this stop?

6. List instances of discrimination on the basis of race/culture alluded to in this memoir.

SUGGESTIONS FOR WRITING

1. Research and write a brief history of the Relocation of Japanese Americans during the Second World War.

2. Analyze the story about Miss Hempstead's class. How, for Lydia, is this episode a practical exercise of her American Dream philosophy?

THE KITCHEN

Alfred Kazin

Alfred Kazin (b. 1915) was educated at the City College of New York and Columbia University and has taught at colleges and universities around the country. He is known best for his works of literary criticism—On Native Grounds (1942) and Bright Book of Life (1973) among them—but also for his autobiographical writing, in such books as A Walker in the City (1951), a chapter of which appears below, New York Jew (1978), and A Lifetime Burning in Every Moment (1996).

The last time I saw our kitchen this clearly was one afternoon in London at the end of the war, when I waited out the rain in the entrance to a music store. A radio was playing into the street, and standing there I heard a broadcast of the first Sabbath service from Belsen Concentration Camp. When the liberated Jewish prisoners recited the *Hear O Israel, the Lord Our God, the Lord is One,*

I felt myself carried back to the Friday evenings at home, when with the Sabbath at sundown a healing quietness would come over Brownsville.[1]

It was the darkness and emptiness of the streets I liked most about Friday evening, as if in preparation for that day of rest and worship which the Jews greet "as a bride"—that day when the very touch of money is prohibited, all work, all travel, all household duties, even to the turning on and off of a light—Jewry had found its way past its tormented heart to some ancient still center of itself. I waited for the streets to go dark on Friday evening as other children waited for the Christmas lights. Even Friday morning after the tests were over glowed in anticipation. When I returned home after three, the warm odor of a coffee cake baking in the oven and the sight of my mother on her hands and knees scrubbing the linoleum on the dining room floor filled me with such tenderness that I could feel my senses reaching out to embrace every single object in our household. One Friday, after a morning in school spent on the voyages of Henry Hudson, I returned with the phrase *Among the discoverers of the New World* singing in my mind as the theme of my own new-found freedom on the Sabbath.

My great moment came at six, when my father returned from work, his overalls smelling faintly of turpentine and shellac, white drops of silver paint still gleaming on his chin. Hanging his overcoat in the long dark hall that led into our kitchen, he would leave in one pocket a loosely folded copy of the New York *World;* and then everything that beckoned to me from that other hemisphere of my brain beyond the East River would start up from the smell of fresh newsprint and the sight of the globe on the front page. It was a paper that carried special associations for me with Brooklyn Bridge. They published the *World* under the green dome on Park Row overlooking the bridge; the fresh salt air of New York harbor lingered for me in the smell of paint and damp newsprint in the hall. I felt that my father brought the outside straight into our house with each day's copy of the *World*. The bridge somehow stood for freedom; the *World* for that rangy kindness and fraternalism and ease we found in Heywood Broun.[2] My father would read aloud from "It Seems To Me" with a delighted smile on his face. "A very clear and courageous man!" he would say. "Look how he stands up for our Sacco and Vanzetti! A real social conscience, that man! Practically a Socialist!" Then, taking off his overalls, he would wash up at the kitchen sink, peeling and gnawing the paint off his nails with Gold Dust Washing Powder as I poured it into his hands, smacking his lips and grunting with pleasure as he washed himself clean of the job at last, and making me feel that I was really helping him, that I, too, was contributing to the greatness of the evening and the coming day.

---

[1] Brooklyn, New York, neighborhood.

[2] Newspaper columnist.

By sundown the streets were empty, the curtains had been drawn, the world put to rights. Even the kitchen walls had been scrubbed and now gleamed in the Sabbath candles. On the long white tablecloth were the "company" dishes, filled for some with *gefillte* fish on lettuce leaves, ringed by red horseradish, sour and half-sour pickles, tomato salad with a light vinegar dressing; for others, with chopped liver in a bed of lettuce leaves and white radishes; the long white *khalleh*, the Sabbath loaf; chicken soup with noodles *and* dumplings; chicken, meat loaf, prunes, and sweet potatoes that had been baked all day into an open pie; compote of prunes and quince, apricots and orange rind; applesauce; a great brown nutcake filled with almonds, the traditional *lekakh;* all surrounded by glasses of port wine, seltzer bottles with their nozzles staring down at us waiting to be pressed; a samovar of Russian tea, *svetouchnee* from the little red box, always served in tall glasses, with lemon slices floating on top. My father and mother sipped it in Russian fashion, through lumps of sugar held between the teeth.

Afterwards we went into the "dining room" and, since we were not particularly orthodox, allowed ourselves little pleasures outside the Sabbath rule—an occasional game of Casino at the dining-room table where we never dined; and listening to the victrola. The evening was particularly good for me whenever the unmarried cousin who boarded with us had her two closest friends in after supper.

They were all dressmakers, like my mother; had worked with my mother in the same East Side sweatshops; were all passionately loyal members of the International Ladies Garment Workers Union; and were all unmarried. We were their only family. Despite my mother's frenzied matchmaking, she had never succeeded in pinning a husband down for any of them. As she said, they were all too *particular*—what a calamity for a Jewish woman to remain unmarried! But my cousin and her friends accepted their fate calmly, and prided themselves on their culture and their strong *progressive* interests. They felt they belonged not to the "kitchen world," like my mother, but to the enlightened tradition of the old Russian intelligentsia. Whenever my mother sighed over them, they would smile out of their greater knowledge of the world, and looking at me with a pointed appeal for recognition, would speak of novels they had read in Yiddish and Russian, of *Winesburg, Ohio*, of some article in the *Nation*.[3]

Our cousin and her two friends were of my parents' generation, but I could never believe it—they seemed to enjoy life with such outspokenness. They were the first grown-up people I had ever met who used the word *love* without embarrassment. "*Libbe! Libbe!*" my mother would explode

---

[3] *Winesburg, Ohio*, novel by Sherwood Anderson; *The Nation*, weekly magazine on politics, books, and the arts.

whenever one of them protested that she could not, after all, marry a man she did not love. "What is this love you make such a stew about? You do not like the way he holds his cigarette? Marry him first and it will all come out right in the end!" It astonished me to realize there was a world in which even unmarried women no longer young were simply individual human beings with lives of their own. *Our* parents, whatever affection might offhandedly be expressed between them, always had the look of being committed to something deeper than *mere* love. Their marriages were neither happy nor unhappy; they were arrangements. However they had met—whether in Russia or in the steerage or, like my parents, in an East Side boarding house—whatever they still thought of each other, *love* was not a word they used easily. Marriage was an institution people entered into—for all I could ever tell—only from immigrant loneliness, a need to be with one's own kind that mechanically resulted in the *family.* The *family* was a whole greater than all the individuals who made it up, yet made sense only in their untiring solidarity. I was perfectly sure that in my parents' minds *libbe* was something exotic and not wholly legitimate, reserved for "educated" people like their children, who were the sole end of their existence. My father and mother worked in a rage to put us above their level; they had married to make *us* possible. We were the only conceivable end to all their striving; we were their America.

So far as I knew, love was not an element admissible in my parents' experience. Any open talk of it between themselves would have seemed ridiculous. It would have suggested a wicked self-indulgence, a preposterous attention to one's own feelings, possible only to those who were free enough to choose. They did not consider themselves free. They were awed by us, as they were awed by their own imagined unworthiness, and looked on themselves only as instruments toward the ideal "American" future that would be lived by their children. As poor immigrants who had remained in Brownsville, painfully conscious of the *alrightniks*[4] on Eastern Parkway—oh, those successes of whom I was always hearing so much, and whom we admired despite all our socialism!—everything in their lives combined to make them look down on love as something *they* had no time for. Of course there was a deep resentment in this, and when on those Friday evenings our cousin or her two friends openly mentioned the unheard-of collapse of someone's marriage—

"Sórelle and Berke? I don't believe it?"

"But it's true."

"You must be joking!"

"No, it's true!"

---

[4] Well off or bourgeois people (Yiddish).

"You're joking! You're joking!"

"No, it's true!"

—I noticed that my parents' talk had an unnaturally hard edge to it, as if those who gave themselves up to love must inevitably come to grief. Love, they could have said, was not *serious*. Life was a battle to "make sure"; it had no place, as we had no time, for whims.

Love, in fact, was something for the movies, which my parents enjoyed, but a little ashamedly. They were the land of the impossible. On those few occasions when my mother closed her sewing machine in the evening and allowed herself a visit to the Supreme, or the Palace, or the Premier, she would return, her eyes gleaming with wonder and some distrust of the strangeness of it all, to report on erotic fanatics who were, thank God, like no one we knew. What heedlessness! What daring! What riches! To my mother riches alone were the gateway to romance, for only those who had money enough could afford the freedom, and the crazy boldness, to give themselves up to love.

Yet there they were in our own dining room, our cousin and her two friends—women, grown-up women—talking openly of the look on Garbo's face when John Gilbert took her in his arms, serenely disposing of each new *khayimyankel*,[5] poor wretch, my mother had picked for them, and arguing my father down on small points of Socialist doctrine. As they sat around the cut-glass bowl on the table—cracking walnuts, expertly peeling the skin off an apple in long even strips, cozily sipping at a glass of tea—they crossed their legs in comfort and gave off a deliciously musky fragrance of face powder that instantly framed them for me in all their dark coloring, brilliantly white teeth, and the rosy Russian blouses that swelled and rippled in terraces of embroidery over their opulent breasts.

They had a great flavor for me, those three women: they were the positive center of that togetherness that always meant so much to me in our dining room on Friday evenings. It was a quality that seemed to start in the prickly thickness of the cut-glass bowl laden with nuts and fruits; in the light from the long black-shaded lamp hanging over the table as it shimmered against the thick surfaces of the bowl and softened that room where the lace curtains were drawn against the dark and empty streets— and then found its unexpectedly tender voice in the Yiddish folksongs and Socialist hymns they taught me— *"Let's Now Forgive Each Other"; "Tsuzamen, Tsuzamen, All Together, Brothers!"* Those Friday evenings, I suddenly found myself enveloped in some old, primary Socialist idea that men could go beyond every barrier of race and nation and language, even of class! into some potential loving union of the whole human race. I was suddenly glad to be a Jew, as these women were Jews—simply and naturally glad of

---

[5] Tom, Dick, or Harry (Yiddish).

those Jewish dressmakers who spoke with enthusiastic familiarity of Sholem Aleichem and Peretz, Gorky and Tolstoy, who glowed at every reminiscence of Nijinsky, of Nazimova in *The Cherry Orchard,* of Pavlova in "The Swan."[6]

Often, those Friday evenings, they spoke of *der heym,* "Home," and then it was hard for me. *Heym* was a terrible word. I saw millions of Jews lying dead under the Polish eagle with knives in their throats. I was afraid with my mother's fears, thought I should weep when she wept, lived again through every pogrom whose terrors she chanted. I associated with that old European life only pain, mud, and hopelessness, but I was of it still, through her. Whenever she would call through the roll of her many brothers and sisters and their children, remembering at each name that this one was dead, that one dead, another starving and sure soon to die—who knew *how* they were living these days in that miserable Poland?—I felt there was some supernatural Polish eagle across the sea whose face I should never see, but which sent out dark electrical rays to hold me fast.

In many ways *der heym* was entirely dim and abstract, nothing to do with me at all, alien as the skullcap and beard and frock coat of my mother's father, whom I never saw, but whose calm orthodox dignity stared up at me from an old cracked photograph at the bottom of the bureau drawer. Yet I lived each of my mother's fears from Dugschitz to Hamburg to London to Hester Street to Brownsville through and through with such fidelity that there were times when I wished I had made that journey too, wished I could have seen Czarist Russia, since I had in any event to suffer it all over again. I often felt odd twinges of jealousy because my parents could talk about that more intense, somehow less *experimental* life than ours with so many private smiles between themselves. It was bewildering, it made me long constantly to get at some past nearer my own New York life, my having to live with all those running wounds of a world I had never seen.

Then, under cover of the talk those Friday evenings, I would take up *The Boy's Life of Theodore Roosevelt* again, and moodily call out to those strangers on the summer veranda in Oyster Bay until my father spoke *his* tale of arriving in America. That was hard, too, painful in another way—yet it always made him curiously lighthearted and left me swimming in space. For he had gone off painting box cars on the Union Pacific, had been as far west as Omaha, had actually seen Sidney Hillman toiling in Hart, Schaffner and Marx's Chicago

---

[6] Sholem Aleichem, Yiddish-language fiction writer; Isaac Loeb Peretz, Jewish poet and novelist; Maxim Gorky, Russian novelist and playwright; Leo Tolstoy, Russian novelist; Vaslav Nijinsky, Russian ballet dancer and choreographer; Alla Nazimova, Russian American actress; *The Cherry Orchard,* drama by Russian fiction writer and playwright Anton Chekhov; Anna Pavlova, Russian ballet dancer; "The Swan," dance from *Swan Lake,* a ballet by Russian composer Peter Ilyich Tchaikovsky.

factory,[7] had heard his beloved Debs making fools of Bryan and Taft in the 1908 campaign,[8] had been offered a homestead in Colorado! *Omaha* was the most beautiful word I had ever heard, *homestead* almost as beautiful; but I could never forgive him for not having accepted that homestead.

"What would I have done there? I'm no farmer."

"You should have taken it! Why do we always live here!"

"It would have been too lonely. Nobody I knew."

"What a chance!"

"Don't be childish. Nobody I knew."

"Why? Why?"

"Alfred, what do you want of us poor Jews?"

So it was: we had always to be together: believers and non-believers, we were a people; I was of that people. Unthinkable to go one's own way, to doubt or to escape the fact that I was a Jew. I had heard of Jews who pretended they were not, but could not understand them. We had all of us lived together so long that we would not have known how to separate even if we had wanted to. The most terrible word was *aleyn,* alone. I always had the same picture of a man desolately walking down a dark street, newspapers and cigarette butts contemptuously flying in his face as he tasted in the dusty grit the full measure of his strangeness. *Aleyn! Aleyn!* My father had been alone here in America as a boy. *His* father, whose name I bore, had died here at twenty-five of pneumonia caught on a garment workers' picket line, and his body flung in with thousands of other Jews who had perished those first years on the East Side. My father had never been able to find his father's grave. *Aleyn! Aleyn!* Did immigrant Jews, then, marry only out of loneliness? Was even Socialism just a happier way of keeping us together?

I trusted it to do that. Socialism would be one long Friday evening around the samovar and the cut-glass bowl laden with nuts and fruits, all of us singing *Tsuzamen, tsuzamen, ale tsuzamen!* Then the heroes of the Russian novel—*our* kind of people—would walk the world, and I—still wearing a circle-necked Russian blouse *"à la Tolstoy"*—would live forever with those I loved in that beautiful Russian country of the mind. Listening to our cousin and her two friends I, who had never seen it, who associated with it nothing but the names of great writers and my father's saying as we went through the Brooklyn Botanic Garden—"Nice! but you should have seen the Czar's summer palace at Tsarskoye-Selo!"—suddenly saw Russia as the grand antithesis of all bourgeois ideals, the spiritual home of all truly free people. I was perfectly sure that there was no literature in the world like the Russian; that the

---

[7] Union leader; men's clothing store.

[8] Socialist Eugene Debs, Democrat William Jennings Bryan, and Republican William Taft ran for President in 1908.

only warm hearts in the world were Russian, like our cousin and her two friends; that other people were always dully materialist, but that the Russian soul, like Nijinsky's dream of pure flight, would always leap outward, past all barriers, to a lyric world in which my ideal socialism and the fiery moodiness of Tchaikovsky's *Pathétique* would be entirely at home with each other. *Tsuzamen, alle tsuzamen!* How many millions would be with us! China was in our house those Friday evenings, Africa, the Indian masses. And it was those three unmarried dressmakers from the rank and file who fully wrapped me in that spell, with the worldly clang of their agate beads and the musky fragrance of their face powder and their embroidered Russian blouses, with the great names of Russian writers ringing against the cut-glass bowl under the black lamp. Never did the bowl look so laden, never did apples and tea smell so good, never did the samovar pour out with such steaming bounty, as on those Friday evenings when I tasted in the tea and the talk the evangelical heart of our cousin and her two friends, and realized that it was we—we!—who would someday put the world on its noblest course.

"*Kinder, kinder,*" my mother would say. "Enough *discusye.* Maybe now a little music? Alfred, play *Scheherazade!*"[9]

You could melt their hearts with it; the effect of the violin on almost everyone I knew was uncanny. I could watch them softening, easing, already on the brink of tears—yet with their hands at rest in their laps, they stared straight ahead at the wall, breathing hard, an unforeseen smile of rapture on their mouths. Any slow movement, if only it were played lingeringly and sagely enough, seemed to come to them as a reminiscence of a reminiscence. It seemed to have something to do with our being Jews. The depths of Jewish memory the violin could throw open apparently had no limit—for every slow movement was based on something "Russian," every plaintive melody even in Beethoven or Mozart was "Jewish." I could skip from composer to composer, from theme to theme, without any fear, ever, of being detected, for all slow movements fell into a single chant of *der heym* and of the great *Kol Nidre* sung in the first evening hours of the Day of Atonement, in whose long rending cry—of contrition? of grief? of hopeless love for the Creator?—I relived all of the Jews' bitter intimacy with death.

Then I cranked up the old brown Victor, took our favorite records out of the red velvet pleated compartments, and we listened to John McCormack singing *Ave Maria,* Amelita Galli-Curci singing *Caro Nome* ("How ugly she is!" my parents would say wonderingly. "Have you seen her picture? Incredible! But how she sings!"), and Alma Gluck singing *Comin' Thro' the Rye.* The high point was Caruso singing from *La Juive.* He inspired in my father and

---

[9] *Kinder, kinder,* Children, children (Yiddish); *discusye,* discussion (Yiddish); *Scheherezade,* symphonic suite by Russian composer Nikolay Rimsky-Korsakov.

mother such helpless, intimidated adoration that I came to think of what was always humbly referred to as his *golden voice* as the invocation of a god. The pleasure he gave us was beyond all music. When Mischa Elman played some well-known melody we sighed familiarly at each other—his tone was so *warm;* he bubbled slowly in my ears like the sound of chicken fat crackling in the pan. But Caruso, "that *Italyéner,*" seemed to me the echo of some outrageously pagan voice at the roof of the world. While I pushed at the hand-crank and the wheezy sounds of the orchestra in the background came to me as the whispered turnings, sighs and alarms of the crowd around the circus pit, there on high, and rising higher and higher with each note, that voice, that *golden voice,* leaped its way from one trapeze to another. We sat hunched in our wonder, our adoration, our fear. Would he make it? Could any human being find that last impossible rung?

> *Rachel! Quand du Seigneur la grâce tutélaire. . . .*

Then, suddenly bounding back to earth again, there he was before us again, secretly smiling, the tones welling out of him with such brazen strength, such irresistible energy, that he left us gasping. I could see him standing inside the victrola box—a centaur just out of the woods, not quite human, with that enigmatic, almost contemptuous smile on his face. "What a voice!" my father would say over and over, deeply shaken. "What a voice! It's not human! Never was there a voice like it! Only the other day I was reading that when they opened him up after he died they found his vocal chords were ab-solutely unique!" Then, his face white with pleasure, with amazement, with wonder: "Oh that *Italyéner!* Oh that *Italyéner!* What a power he has, that *Italyéner!*"

In Brownsville tenements the kitchen is always the largest room and the center of the household. As a child I felt that we lived in a kitchen to which four other rooms were annexed. My mother, a "home" dressmaker, had her workshop in the kitchen. She told me once that she had begun dress-making in Poland at thirteen; as far back as I can remember, she was always making dresses for the local women. She had an innate sense of design, a quick eye for all the subtleties in the latest fashions, even when she despised them, and great boldness. For three or four dollars she would study the fash-ion magazines with a customer, go with the customer to the remnants store on Belmont Avenue to pick out the material, argue the owner down—all remnants stores, for some reason, were supposed to be shady, as if the own-ers dealt in stolen goods—and then for days would patiently fit and baste and sew and fit again. Our apartment was always full of women in their housedresses sitting around the kitchen table waiting for a fitting. My little bedroom next to the kitchen was the fitting room. The sewing machine, an old nut-brown Singer with golden scrolls painted along the black arm and engraved along the two tiers of little drawers massed with needles and thread on each side of the treadle, stood next to the window and the great coal-black stove which up to my last year in college was our main source of heat. By December the two outer bedrooms were closed off, and used to chill bottles of milk and cream, cold borscht and jellied calves' feet.

The kitchen held our lives together. My mother worked in it all day long, we ate in it almost all meals except the Passover *seder*, I did my homework and first writing at the kitchen table, and in winter I often had a bed made up for me on three kitchen chairs near the stove. On the wall just over the table hung a long horizontal mirror that sloped to a ship's prow at each end and was lined in cherry wood. It took up the whole wall, and drew every object in the kitchen to itself. The walls were a fiercely stippled whitewash, so often rewhitened by my father in slack seasons that the paint looked as if it had been squeezed and cracked into the walls. A large electric bulb hung down the center of the kitchen at the end of a chain that had been hooked into the ceiling; the old gas ring and key still jutted out of the wall like antlers. In the corner next to the toilet was the sink at which we washed, and the square tub in which my mother did our clothes. Above it, tacked to the shelf on which were pleasantly ranged square, blue-bordered white sugar and spice jars, hung calendars from the Public National Bank on Pitkin Avenue and the Minsker Progressive Branch of the Workman's Circle;[10] receipts for the payment of insurance premiums, and household bills on a spindle; two little boxes engraved with Hebrew letters. One of these was for the poor, the other to buy back the Land of Israel. Each spring a bearded little man would suddenly appear in our kitchen, salute us with a hurried Hebrew blessing, empty the boxes (sometimes with a sidelong look of disdain if they were not full), hurriedly bless us again for remembering our less fortunate Jewish brothers and sisters, and so take his departure until the next spring, after vainly trying to persuade my mother to take still another box. We did occasionally remember to drop coins in the boxes, but this was usually only on the dreaded morning of "midterms" and final examinations, because my mother thought it would bring me luck. She was extremely superstitious, but embarrassed about it, and always laughed at herself whenever, on the morning of an examination, she counseled me to leave the house on my right foot. "I know it's silly," her smile seemed to say, "but what harm can it do? It may calm God down."

The kitchen gave a special character to our lives; my mother's character. All my memories of that kitchen are dominated by the nearness of my mother sitting all day long at her sewing machine, by the clacking of the treadle against

---

[10] The Workmen's [*sic*] Circle, a Jewish, labor-oriented fraternal order; Minsk, a city in Russia where presumably the members of this branch came from.

the linoleum floor, by the patient twist of her right shoulder as she automatically pushed at the wheel with one hand or lifted the foot to free the needle where it had got stuck in a thick piece of material. The kitchen was her life. Year by year, as I began to take in her fantastic capacity for labor and her anxious zeal, I realized it was ourselves she kept stitched together. I can never remember a time when she was not working. She worked because the law of her life was work, work and anxiety; she worked because she would have found life meaningless without work. She read almost no English; she could read the Yiddish paper, but never felt she had time to. We were always talking of a time when I would teach her how to read, but somehow there was never time. When I awoke in the morning she was already at her machine, or in the great morning crowd of housewives at the grocery getting fresh rolls for breakfast. When I returned from school she was at her machine, or conferring over *McCall's*[11] with some neighborhood woman who had come in pointing hopefully to an illustration—"Mrs. Kazin! Mrs. Kazin! Make me a dress like it shows here in the picture!" When my father came home from work she had somehow mysteriously interrupted herself to make supper for us, and the dishes cleared and washed, was back at her machine. When I went to bed at night, often she was still there, pounding away at the treadle, hunched over the wheel, her hands steering a piece of gauze under the needle with a finesse that always contrasted sharply with her swollen hands and broken nails. Her left hand had been pierced through when as a girl she had worked in the infamous Triangle Shirtwaist Factory[12] on the East Side. A needle had gone straight through the palm, severing a large vein. They had sewn it up for her so clumsily that a tuft of flesh always lay folded over the palm.

The kitchen was the great machine that set our lives running; it whirred down a little only on Saturdays and holy days. From my mother's kitchen I gained my first picture of life as a white, overheated, starkly lit workshop redolent with Jewish cooking, crowded with women in housedresses, strewn with fashion magazines, patterns, dress material, spools of thread—and at whose center, so lashed to her machine that bolts of energy seemed to dance out of her hands and feet as she worked, my mother stamped the treadle hard against the floor, hard, hard, and silently, grimly at war, beat out the first rhythm of the world for me.

Every sound from the street roared and trembled at our windows—a mother feeding her child on the doorstep, the screech of the trolley cars on Rockaway Avenue, the eternal smash of a handball against the wall of our

---

[11] Women's homemaking and fashion magazine.

[12] Clothing factory where, in 1911, 146 garment workers, mostly young Italian and Jewish immigrant women, died in a fire because of locked doors and inadequate fire escapes.

house, the clatter of *"der Italyéner"*'s cart packed with watermelons, the sing-song of the old-clothes men walking Chester Street, the cries *"Árbes! Árbes! Kinder! Kinder! Heyse gute árbes!"*[13] All day long people streamed into our apartment as a matter of course—"customers," upstairs neighbors, downstairs neighbors, women who would stop in for a half-hour's talk, salesmen, rela-tives, insurance agents. Usually they came in without ringing the bell—every-one knew my mother was always at home. I would hear the front door opening, the wind whistling through our front door, and then some familiar face would appear in our kitchen with the same bland, matter-of-fact inquiring look: no need to stand on ceremony: my mother and her kitchen were available to everyone all day long.

At night the kitchen contracted around the blaze of light on the cloth, the patterns, the ironing board where the iron had burned a black border around the tear in the muslin cover; the finished dresses looked so frilly as they jostled on their wire hangers after all the work my mother had put into them. And then I would get that strangely ominous smell of tension from the dress fabrics and the burn in the cover of the ironing board—as if each piece of cloth and paper crushed with light under the naked bulb might suddenly go up in flames. Whenever I pass some small tailoring shop still lit up at night and see the owner hunched over his steam press; whenever in some poorer neighborhood of the city I see through a window some small crowded kitchen naked under the harsh light glittering in the ceiling, I still smell that fiery breath, that warning of imminent fire. I was always holding my breath. What I must have felt most about ourselves, I see now, was that we ourselves were like kindling—that all the hard-pressed pieces of ourselves and all the hard-used objects in that kitchen were like so many slivers of wood that might go up in flames if we came too near the white-blazing filaments in that naked bulb. Our tension itself was fire, we ourselves were forever burning—to live, to get down the foreboding in our souls, to make good.

Twice a year, on the anniversaries of her parents' deaths, my mother placed on top of the ice-box an ordinary kitchen glass packed with wax, the *yortsayt,* and lit the candle in it. Sitting at the kitchen table over my home-work, I would look across the threshold to that mourning-glass, and sense that for my mother the distance from our kitchen to *der heym,* from life to death, was only a flame's length away. Poor as we were, it was not poverty that drove my mother so hard; it was loneliness—some endless bitter brood-ing over all those left behind, dead or dying or soon to die; a loneliness locked up in her kitchen that dwelt every day on the hazardousness of life and the

---

[13] Chick peas! Chick peas! Children! Children! Good, hot chick peas! (Yiddish).

nearness of death, but still kept struggling in the lock, trying to get us through by endless labor.

With us, life started up again only on the last shore. There seemed to be no middle ground between despair and the fury of our ambition. Whenever my mother spoke of her hopes for us, it was with such unbelievingness that the likes of us would ever come to anything, such abashed hope and readiness for pain, that I finally came to see in the flame burning on top of the ice-box death itself burning away the bones of poor Jews, burning out in us everything but courage, the blind resolution to live. In the light of that mourning-candle, there were ranged around me how many dead and dying—how many eras of pain, of exile, of dispersion, of cringing before the powers of this world!

It was always at dusk that my mother's loneliness came home most to me. Painfully alert to every shift in the light at her window, she would suddenly confess her fatigue by removing her pince-nez, and then wearily pushing aside the great mound of fabrics on her machine, would stare at the street as if to warm herself in the last of the sun. "How sad it is!" I once heard her say. "It grips me! It grips me!" Twilight was the bottommost part of the day, the chillest and loneliest time for her. Always so near to her moods, I knew she was fighting some deep inner dread, struggling against the returning tide of darkness along the streets that invariably assailed her heart with the same foreboding—Where? Where now? Where is the day taking us now?

Yet one good look at the street would revive her. I see her now, perched against the windowsill, with her face against the glass, her eyes almost asleep in enjoyment, just as she starts up with the guilty cry—"What foolishness is this in me!"—and goes to the stove to prepare supper for us: a moment, only a moment, watching the evening crowd of women gathering at the grocery for fresh bread and milk. But between my mother's pent-up face at the window and the winter sun dying in the fabrics—"Alfred, see how beautiful!"—she has drawn for me one single line of sentience.

The unmarried cousin who boarded with us had English books in her room—the only English books in our house I did not bring into it myself. Half an hour before supper, I liked nothing better than to stray into her room, and sitting on the India print spread of her bed next to the yellow wicker bookstand, look through her books and smell the musky face powder that filled her room. There was no closet: her embroidered Russian blouses and red velvet suits hung behind a curtain, and the lint seemed to float off the velvet and swim in multicolored motes through the air. On the wall over her bed hung a picture of two half-nude lovers fleeing from a storm, and an oval-framed picture of Psyche perched on a rock. On the wicker bookstand, in a star-shaped frame of thick glass, was a photograph of our cousin's brother, missing since the Battle of Tannenberg,[14] in the uniform of a Czarist Army private.

In that wicker bookstand, below the blue set of Sholem Aleichem in Yiddish and the scattered volumes of Russian novels, were the books I would never have to drag from the Stone Avenue Library myself—THE WORLD'S GREATEST SELECTED SHORT STORIES; a biography of Alfred E. Smith entitled *Up From the City Streets;* a Grosset and Dunlap edition of *The Sheik;* and in English, a volume of stories by Alexander Kuprin.[15] Day after day at five-thirty, half an hour before supper, I would sit myself carefully on the India print, and fondle those books with such rapture that they were actually *there,* for me to look through whenever I liked, that on some days I could not bear to open them at all, but sat as close to the sun in the windows as I could, breathing the lint in, and the sun still hot on the India spread.

On the roof just across the street, the older boys now home from work would spring their pigeons from the traps. You could see the feathers glistening faintly in the last light, beating thinly against their sides—they, too, sucking air as the birds leaped up from their wire cages. Then, widening and widening their flight each time they came over our roof again, they went round a sycamore and the spire of the church without stopping. The sun fell straight on the India spread—how the thin prickly material burned in my nostrils—and glowed along the bony gnarled bumps in the legs of the yellow wicker bookstand. Happiness was warmth. Beyond Chester Street, beyond even Rockaway, I could see to where the Italians lived on broken streets that rose up to a hill topped by a church. The church seemed to be thickly surrounded by trees. In his star-shaped glass on the bookstand, that Russian soldier missing since the Battle of Tannenberg looked steadily at me from under his round forage cap. His chest bulged against two rows of gold buttons up and down his black blouse. Where? Where now? Had they put him, too, into a great pit? Suddenly it did not matter. Happiness was the sun on the India spread, the hot languid sands lapping at the tent of the Sheik—*"Monseigneur! My desert prince!"*—the summer smell of the scum on the East River just off Oliver Street where Alfred E. Smith worked in the Fulton Fish Market. In the Kuprin stories an old man and a boy went wandering up a road in the Crimea. There was dust on the road, dust on the leaves—*hoo! hoo! my son! how it is hot!* But they were happy. It was summer in the Crimea, and just to walk along with them made me happy. When they got hungry they stopped at a spring, took black bread, salt, and tomatoes out of their knapsacks, and ate. The ripe open tomatoes gushed red from their mouths, the black bread

---

[14] Massive defeat for the Russian army during World War I.

[15] Governor of New York and 1928 Democratic Presidential candidate; 1921 novel by E. M. Hull; Russian novelist.

and salt were good, very good, and when they leaned over to drink at the spring, the water was so icy cold it made my teeth ache. I read that story over and over, sometimes skipping pages to get to the part about the bread, the salt, the tomatoes, the icy water. *I could taste that bread, that salt, those tomatoes, that icy spring.*

Now the light begins to die. Twilight is also the mind's grazing time. Twilight is the bottom of that arc down which we had fallen the whole long day, but where I now sit at our cousin's window in some strange silence of attention, watching the pigeons go round and round to the leafy smell of soupgreens from the stove. In the cool of that first evening hour, as I sit at the table waiting for supper and my father and the New York *World,* everything is so rich to overflowing, I hardly know where to begin.

STUDY AND DISCUSSION QUESTIONS

1. Why do you think Kazin chooses to begin this reminiscence of his childhood with a description of the beginning of the Jewish Sabbath on Friday night? List elements that are part of his description of these childhood Friday nights.

2. Pick out one specific aspect of Kazin's description of his Sabbath eves that particularly struck you and discuss it.

3. What time period would you say "The Kitchen" is set in? What clues do you have?

4. How do the narrator's parents feel about love? What do the narrator's cousin and her two friends think about it? Why does Kazin provide the contrast?

5. What does *heym* (home) mean to the narrator's immigrant parents? For Kazin, what does home have to do with being Jewish, and why could the father not accept a homestead in Colorado?

6. Though it is not the focus of this piece, there are references to the hard life Kazin's family has been leading. List two or three such references.

7. Why and how was the kitchen the center of this household?

8. What kinds of work are referred to in this memoir?

9. What was the narrator's mother like? What is her importance to this essay?

10. Discuss the importance of books and music in this family.

11. Pick one of the symbols Kazin uses—fire, twilight, food, the kitchen itself—and discuss what the symbol represents and what resonances it has.

12. Discuss the references to socialism in the essay.

SUGGESTIONS FOR WRITING

1. Kazin's writing here is full of vivid, sense-based description. Choose a paragraph and analyze how Kazin uses the senses of sight, taste, touch, smell, and hearing to move the remembered world of his childhood into the reader's experience.

2. What part of your home was the center of your own life while you were growing up? It could be your kitchen or some other room or even the back yard. Describe that space in vivid, sense-based images. Try to convey through the description a sense of who your family was and what your childhood was like.

3. Kazin ends "The Kitchen" with these words: "everything is so rich to overflowing, I hardly know where to begin." How are these words an appropriate (and not ironic) summation of what some readers might see as a deprived working-class childhood? What are the riches to which Kazin refers?

NOTES OF A NATIVE SON

James Baldwin

James Baldwin (1924–1987) was the son of a Harlem Pentecostal preacher and himself began preaching at fourteen, before turning to a life of writing. He lived in Europe for almost a decade but returned to the United States in 1957 and became an active civil rights spokesperson. Baldwin is known for his plays, including Blues for Mister Charlie *(1964); his essays, including the collection* Notes of a Native Son *(1955); and his novels, among them* Go Tell It on the Mountain *(1953) and* Giovanni's Room *(1956), the latter about gay male life in Paris.*

I

On the 29th of July, in 1943, my father died. On the same day, a few hours later, his last child was born. Over a month before this, while all our energies were concentrated in waiting for these events, there had been, in Detroit, one of the bloodiest race riots of the century. A few hours after my father's funeral, while he lay in state in the undertaker's chapel, a race riot broke out in Harlem. On the morning of the 3rd of August, we drove my father to the graveyard through a wilderness of smashed plate glass.

The day of my father's funeral had also been my nineteenth birthday. As we drove him to the graveyard, the spoils of injustice, anarchy, discontent, and hatred were all around us. It seemed to me that God himself had devised, to mark my father's end, the most sustained and brutally dissonant of codas. And it seemed to me, too, that the violence which rose all about us as my father left the world had been devised as a corrective for the pride of his eldest son. I had declined to believe in that apocalypse which had been central to my father's vision; very well, life seemed to be saying, here is something that will certainly pass for an apocalypse until the real thing comes along. I had inclined to be contemptuous of my father for the conditions of his life, for the conditions of our lives. When his life had ended I began to wonder about that life and also, in a new way, to be apprehensive about my own.

I had not known my father very well. We had got on badly, partly because we shared, in our different fashions, the vice of stubborn pride. When he was dead I realized that I had hardly ever spoken to him. When he had been dead a long time I began to wish I had. It seems to be typical of life in America, where opportunities, real and fancied, are thicker than anywhere else on the globe, that the second generation has no time to talk to the first. No one, including my father, seems to have known exactly how old he was, but his mother had been born during slavery. He was of the first generation of free men. He, along with thousands of other Negroes, came North after 1919 and I was part of that generation which had never seen the landscape of what Negroes sometimes call the Old Country.

He had been born in New Orleans and had been a quite young man there during the time that Louis Armstrong, a boy, was running errands for the dives and honky-tonks of what was always presented to me as one of the most wicked of cities—to this day, whenever I think of New Orleans, I also helplessly think of Sodom and Gomorrah. My father never mentioned Louis Armstrong, except to forbid us to play his records; but there was a picture of him on our wall for a long time. One of my father's strong-willed female relatives had placed it there and forbade my father to take it down. He never did, but he eventually maneuvered her out of the house and when, some years later, she was in trouble and near death, he refused to do anything to help her.

He was, I think, very handsome. I gather this from photographs and from my own memories of him, dressed in his Sunday best and on his way to preach a sermon somewhere, when I was little. Handsome, proud, and ingrown, "like a toe-nail," somebody said. But he looked to me, as I grew older, like pictures I had seen of African tribal chieftains: he really should have been naked, with war-paint on and barbaric mementos, standing among spears. He could be chilling in the pulpit and indescribably cruel in his personal life and he was certainly the most bitter man I have ever met; yet it must be said that there was something else in him, buried in him, which lent him his tremendous power and, even, a rather crushing charm. It had something to do with his blackness, I think—he was very black—with his blackness and his beauty, and with the fact that he knew that he was black but did not know that he was beautiful. He claimed to be proud of his blackness but it had also been the cause of much humiliation and it had fixed bleak boundaries to his life. He was not a young man when we were growing up and he had already suffered many kinds of ruin; in his outrageously demanding and protective way he loved his children, who were black like him and menaced, like him; and all these things sometimes showed in his face when he tried, never to my knowledge with any success, to establish contact with any of us. When he took one of his children on his knee to play, the child always became fretful and began to cry; when he tried to help one of us with our homework the absolutely unabating tension which emanated from him caused our minds and our tongues to become paralyzed, so that he, scarcely knowing why, flew into a rage and the child, not knowing why, was punished. If it ever entered his head to bring a surprise home for his children, it was, almost unfailingly, the wrong surprise and even the big watermelons he often brought home on his back in the summertime led to the most appalling scenes. I do not remember, in all those years, that one of his children was ever glad to see him come home. From what I was able to gather of his early life, it seemed that this inability to establish contact with other people had always marked him and had been one of the things which had driven him out of New Orleans. There was something in him, therefore, groping and tentative, which was never expressed and which was buried with him. One saw it most clearly when he was facing new people and hoping to impress them. But he never did, not for long. We went from church to smaller and more improbable church, he found himself in less and less demand as a minister, and by the time he died none of his friends had come to see him for a long time. He had lived and died in an intolerable bitterness of spirit and it frightened me, as we drove him to the graveyard through those unquiet, ruined streets, to see how powerful and overflowing this bitterness could be and to realize that this bitterness now was mine.

When he died I had been away from home for a little over a year. In that year I had had time to become aware of the meaning of all my father's bitter warnings, had discovered the secret of his proudly pursed lips and rigid carriage: I had discovered the weight of white people in the world. I saw that this had been for my ancestors and now would be for me an awful thing to live with and that the bitterness which had helped to kill my father could also kill me.

He had been ill a long time—in the mind, as we now realized, reliving instances of his fantastic intransigence in the new light of his affliction and endeavoring to feel a sorrow for him which never, quite, came true. We had not known that he was being eaten up by paranoia, and the discovery that his cruelty, to our bodies and our minds, had been one of the symptoms of his illness was not, then, enough to enable us to forgive him. The younger children felt, quite simply, relief that he would not be coming home anymore. My mother's observation that it was he, after all, who had kept them alive all these years meant nothing because the problems of keeping children alive are not real for children. The older children felt, with my father gone, that they could invite their friends to the house without fear that their friends would be insulted or, as had sometimes happened with me, being told that their friends were in league with the devil and intended to rob our family of everything we owned. (I didn't fail to wonder, and it made me hate him, what on earth we owned that anybody else would want.)

His illness was beyond all hope of healing before anyone realized that he was ill. He had always been so strange and had lived, like a prophet, in such unimaginably close communion with the Lord that his long silences which were punctuated by moans and hallelujahs and snatches of old songs while he sat at the living-room window never seemed odd to us. It was not until he refused to eat because, he said, his family was trying to poison him that my mother was forced to accept as a fact what had, until then, been only an unwilling suspicion. When he was committed, it was discovered that he had tuberculosis and, as it turned out, the disease of his mind allowed the disease of his body to destroy him. For the doctors could not force him to eat, either, and, though he was fed intravenously, it was clear from the beginning that there was no hope for him.

In my mind's eye I could see him, sitting at the window, locked up in his terrors; hating and fearing every living soul including his children who had betrayed him, too, by reaching towards the world which had despised him. There were nine of us. I began to wonder what it could have felt like for such a man to have had nine children whom he could barely feed. He used to make little jokes about our poverty, which never, of course, seemed very funny to us; they could not have seemed very funny to him, either, or else our all too feeble response to them would never have caused such rages. He spent great energy and achieved, to our chagrin, no small amount of success in keeping us away from the people who surrounded us, people who had all-night rent parties to which we listened when we should have been sleeping, people who cursed and drank and flashed razor blades on Lenox Avenue. He could not understand why, if they had so much energy to spare, they could not use it to make their lives better. He treated almost everybody on our block with a most uncharitable asperity and neither they, nor, of course, their children were slow to reciprocate.

The only white people who came to our house were welfare workers and bill collectors. It was almost always my mother who dealt with them, for my father's temper, which was at the mercy of his pride, was never to be trusted. It was clear that he felt their very presence in his home to be a violation: this was conveyed by his carriage, almost ludicrously stiff, and by his voice, harsh and vindictively polite. When I was around nine or ten I wrote a play which was directed by a young, white schoolteacher, a woman, who then took an interest in me, and gave me books to read and, in order to corroborate my theatrical bent, decided to take me to see what she somewhat tactlessly referred to as "real" plays. Theatergoing was forbidden in our house, but, with the really cruel intuitiveness of a child, I suspected that the color of this woman's skin would carry the day for me. When, at school, she suggested taking me to the theater, I did not, as I might have done if she had been a Negro, find a way of discouraging her, but agreed that she should pick me up at my house one evening. I then, very cleverly, left all the rest to my mother, who suggested to my father, as I knew she would, that it would not be very nice to let such a kind woman make the trip for nothing. Also, since it was a schoolteacher, I imagine that my mother countered the idea of sin with the idea of "education," which word, even with my father, carried a kind of bitter weight.

Before the teacher came my father took me aside to ask *why* she was coming, what *interest* she could possibly have in our house, in a boy like me. I said I didn't know but I, too, suggested that it had something to do with education. And I understood that my father was waiting for me to say something—I didn't quite know what; perhaps that I wanted his protection against this teacher and her "education." I said none of these things and the teacher came and we went out. It was clear, during the brief interview in our living room, that my father was agreeing very much against his will and that he would have refused permission if he had dared. The fact that he did not dare caused me to despise him: I had no way of knowing that he was facing in that living room a wholly unprecedented and frightening situation.

Later, when my father had been laid off from his job, this woman became very important to us. She was really a very sweet and generous woman and went to a great deal of trouble to be of help to us, particularly during one awful winter. My mother called her by the highest name she knew. She said she was a "christian." My father could scarcely disagree but during the four or five years of our relatively close association he never trusted her and was always trying to surprise in her open, Midwestern face the genuine, cunningly hidden, and hideous motivation. In later years, particularly when it began to be clear that this "education" of mine was going to lead me to perdition, he became more explicit and warned me that my white friends in high school were not really my friends and that I would see, when I was older, how white people would do anything to keep a Negro down. Some of them could be nice, he admitted, but none of them were to be trusted and most of them were not even nice. The best thing was to have as little to do with them as possible. I did not feel this way and I was certain, in my innocence, that I never would.

But the year which preceded my father's death had made a great change in my life. I had been living in New Jersey, working in defense plants, working and living among southerners, white and black. I knew about the south, of course, and about how southerners treated Negroes and how they expected them to behave, but it had never entered my mind that anyone would look at me and expect *me* to behave that way. I learned in New Jersey that to be a Negro meant, precisely, that one was never looked at but was simply at the mercy of the reflexes the color of one's skin caused in other people. I acted in New Jersey as I had always acted, that is as though I thought a great deal of myself—I had to *act* that way—with results that were, simply, unbelievable. I had scarcely arrived before I had earned the enmity, which was extraordinarily ingenious, of all my superiors and nearly all my co-workers. In the beginning, to make matters worse, I simply did not know what was happening. I did not know what I had done, and I shortly began to wonder what *anyone* could possibly do, to bring about such unanimous, active, and unbearably vocal hostility. I knew about jim-crow but I had never experienced it. I went to the same self-service restaurant three times and stood with all the Princeton boys before the counter, waiting for a hamburger and coffee; it was always an extraordinarily long time before anything was set before me; but it was not until the fourth visit that I learned that, in fact, nothing had ever been set before me: I had simply picked something up. Negroes were not served there, I was told, and they had been waiting for me to realize that I was always the only Negro present. Once I was told this, I determined to go there all the time. But now they were ready for me and, though some dreadful scenes were subsequently enacted in that restaurant, I never ate there again.

It was the same story all over New Jersey, in bars, bowling alleys, diners, places to live. I was always being forced to leave, silently, or with mutual imprecations. I very shortly became notorious and children giggled behind me when I passed and their elders whispered or shouted—they really believed that I was mad. And it did begin to work on my mind, of course; I began to be afraid to go anywhere and to compensate for this I went places to which I really should not have gone and where, God knows, I had no desire to be. My reputation in town naturally enhanced my reputation at work and my working day became one long series of acrobatics designed to keep me out of trouble. I cannot say that these acrobatics succeeded. It began to seem that the machinery of the organization I worked for was turning over, day and night, with but one aim: to eject me. I was fired once, and contrived, with the aid of a friend from New York, to get back on the payroll; was fired again, and bounced back again. It took a while to fire me for the third time, but the third time took. There were no loopholes anywhere. There was not even any way of getting back inside the gates.

That year in New Jersey lives in my mind as though it were the year during which, having an unsuspected predilection for it, I first contracted some dread, chronic disease, the unfailing symptom of which is a kind of blind fever, a pounding in the skull and fire in the bowels. Once this disease is contracted, one can never be really carefree again, for the fever, without an instant's warning, can recur at any moment. It can wreck more important things than race relations. There is not a Negro alive who does not have this rage in his blood—one has the choice, merely, of living with it consciously or surrendering to it. As for me, this fever has recurred in me, and does, and will until the day I die.

My last night in New Jersey, a white friend from New York took me to the nearest big town, Trenton, to go to the movies and have a few drinks. As it turned out, he also saved me from, at the very least, a violent whipping. Almost every detail of that night stands out very clearly in my memory. I even remember the name of the movie we saw because its title impressed me as being so patly ironical. It was a movie about the German occupation of France, starring Maureen O'Hara and Charles Laughton and called *This Land Is Mine.* I remember the name of the diner we walked into when the movie ended: it was the "American Diner." When we walked in the counterman asked what we wanted and I remember answering with the casual sharpness which had become my habit: "We want a hamburger and a cup of coffee, what do you think we want?" I do not know why, after a year of such rebuffs, I so completely failed to anticipate his answer, which was, of course, "We don't serve Negroes here." This reply failed to discompose me, at least for the moment. I made some sardonic comment about the name of the diner and we walked out into the streets.

This was the time of what was called the "brown-out," when the lights in all American cities were very dim. When we re-entered the streets something happened to me which had the force of an optical illusion, or a nightmare. The streets were very crowded and I was facing north. People were moving in every direction but it seemed to me, in that instant, that all of the people I could see, and many more than that, were moving toward me, against me, and that everyone was white. I remember how their faces gleamed. And I felt, like a physical sensation, a *click* at the nape of my neck as though some interior string connecting my head to my body had been cut. I began to walk. I heard my friend call after me, but I ignored him. Heaven only knows what was going on in his mind, but he had the good sense not to touch me—I don't know what would have happened if he had—and to keep me in sight. I don't know what was going on in my mind, either; I certainly had no conscious plan. I wanted to do something to crush these white faces, which were crushing me.

I walked for perhaps a block or two until I came to an enormous, glittering, and fashionable restaurant in which I knew not even the intercession of the Virgin would cause me to be served. I pushed through the doors and took the first vacant seat I saw, at a table for two, and waited.

I do not know how long I waited and I rather wonder, until today, what I could possibly have looked like. Whatever I looked like, I frightened the waitress who shortly appeared, and the moment she appeared all of my fury flowed towards her. I hated her for her white face, and for her great, astounded, frightened eyes. I felt that if she found a black man so frightening I would make her fright worthwhile.

She did not ask me what I wanted, but repeated, as though she had learned it somewhere, "We don't serve Negroes here." She did not say it with the blunt, derisive hostility to which I had grown so accustomed, but, rather, with a note of apology in her voice, and fear. This made me colder and more murderous than ever. I felt I had to do something with my hands. I wanted her to come close enough for me to get her neck between my hands.

So I pretended not to have understood her, hoping to draw her closer. And she did step a very short step closer, with her pencil poised incongruously over her pad, and repeated the formula: ". . . don't serve Negroes here."

Somehow, with the repetition of that phrase, which was already ringing in my head like a thousand bells of a nightmare, I realized that she would never come any closer and that I would have to strike from a distance. There was nothing on the table but an ordinary water-mug half full of water, and I picked this up and hurled it with all my strength at her. She ducked and it missed her and shattered against the mirror behind the bar. And, with that sound, my frozen blood abruptly thawed, I returned from wherever I had been, I *saw*, for the first time, the restaurant, the people with their mouths open, already, as it seemed to me, rising as one man, and I realized what I had done, and where I was, and I was frightened. I rose and began running for the door. A round, potbellied man grabbed me by the nape of the neck just as I reached the doors and began to beat me about the face. I kicked him and got loose and ran into the streets. My friend whispered, *"Run!"* and I ran.

My friend stayed outside the restaurant long enough to misdirect my pursuers and the police, who arrived, he told me, at once. I do not know what I said to him when he came to my room that night. I could not have said much. I felt, in the oddest, most awful way, that I had somehow betrayed him. I lived it over and over and over again, the way one relives an automobile accident after it has happened and one finds oneself alone and safe. I could not get over two facts, both equally difficult for the imagination to grasp, and one was that I could have been murdered. But the other was that I had been ready to commit murder. I saw nothing very clearly but I did see this: that my life, my *real* life, was in danger, and not from anything other people might do but from the hatred I carried in my own heart.

II

I had returned home around the second week in June—in great haste because it seemed that my father's death and my mother's confinement were both but a matter of hours. In the case of my mother, it soon became clear that she had simply made a miscalculation. This had always been her tendency and I don't believe that a single one of us arrived in the world, or has since arrived anywhere else, on time. But none of us dawdled so intolerably about the business of being born as did my baby sister. We sometimes amused ourselves, during those endless, stifling weeks, by picturing the baby sitting within in the safe, warm dark, bitterly regretting the necessity of becoming a part of our chaos and stubbornly putting it off as long as possible. I understood her perfectly and congratulated her on showing such good sense so soon. Death, however, sat as purposefully at my father's bedside as life stirred within my mother's womb and it was harder to understand why he so lingered in that long shadow. It seemed that he had bent, and for a long time, too, all of his energies towards dying. Now death was ready for him but my father held back.

All of Harlem, indeed, seemed to be infected by waiting. I had never before known it to be so violently still. Racial tensions throughout this country were exacerbated during the early years of the war, partly because the labor market brought together hundreds of thousands of ill-prepared people and partly because Negro soldiers, regardless of where they were born, received their military training in the south. What happened in defense plants and army camps had repercussions, naturally, in every Negro ghetto. The situation in Harlem had grown bad enough for clergymen, policemen, educators, politicians, and social workers to assert in one breath that there was no "crime wave" and to offer, in the very next breath, suggestions as to how to combat it. These suggestions always seemed to involve playgrounds, despite the fact that racial skirmishes were occurring in the playgrounds, too. Playground or not, crime wave or not, the Harlem police force had been augmented in March, and the unrest grew—perhaps, in fact, partly as a result of the ghetto's instinctive hatred of policemen. Perhaps the most revealing news item, out of the steady parade of reports of muggings, stabbings, shootings, assaults, gang wars, and accusations of police brutality is the item concerning six Negro girls who set upon a white girl in the subway because, as they all too accurately put it, she was stepping on their toes. Indeed she was, all over the nation.

I had never before been so aware of policemen, on foot, on horseback, on corners, everywhere, always two by two. Nor had I ever been so aware of small knots of people. They were on stoops and on corners and in doorways, and what was striking about them, I think, was that they did not seem to be talking. Never, when I passed these groups, did the usual sound of a curse or a laugh ring out and neither did there seem to be any hum of gossip. There was certainly, on the other hand, occurring between them communication extraordinarily intense. Another thing that was striking was the unexpected diversity of the people who made up these groups. Usually, for example, one would see a group of sharpies standing on the street corner, jiving the passing chicks; or a group of older men, usually, for some reason, in the vicinity of a barber shop, discussing baseball scores, or the numbers or making rather chilling observations about women they had known. Women, in a general way, tended to be seen less often together—unless they were church women, or very young girls, or prostitutes met together for an unprofessional instant. But that summer I saw the strangest combinations: large, respectable, churchly matrons standing on the stoops or the corners with their hair tied up, together with a girl in sleazy satin whose face bore the marks of gin and the razor, or heavy-set, abrupt, no-nonsense older men, in company with the most disreputable and fanatical "race" men, or these same "race" men with the sharpies, or these sharpies with the churchly women. Seventh Day Adventists and Methodists and Spiritualists seemed to be hobnobbing with Holyrollers and they were all, alike, entangled with the most flagrant disbelievers; something heavy in their stance seemed to indicate that they had all, incredibly, seen a common vision, and on each face there seemed to be the same strange, bitter shadow.

The churchly women and the matter-of-fact, no-nonsense men had children in the Army. The sleazy girls they talked to had lovers there, the sharpies and the "race" men had friends and brothers there. It would have demanded an unquestioning patriotism, happily as uncommon in this country as it is undesirable, for these people not to have been disturbed by the bitter letters they received, by the newspaper stories they read, not to have been enraged by the posters, then to be found all over New York, which described the Japanese as "yellow-bellied Japs." It was only the "race" men, to be sure, who spoke ceaselessly of being revenged—how this vengeance was to be exacted was not clear—for the indignities and dangers suffered by Negro boys in uniform; but everybody felt a directionless, hopeless bitterness, as well as that panic which can scarcely be suppressed when one knows that a human being one loves is beyond one's reach, and in danger. This helplessness and this gnawing uneasiness does something, at length, to even the toughest mind. Perhaps the best way to sum all this up is to say that the people I knew felt, mainly, a peculiar kind of relief when they knew that their boys were being shipped out of the south, to do battle overseas. It was, perhaps, like feeling that the most dangerous part of a dangerous journey had been passed and that now, even if death should come, it would come with honor and without the complicity of their countrymen. Such a death would be, in short, a fact with which one could hope to live.

It was on the 28th of July, which I believe was a Wednesday, that I visited my father for the first time during his illness and for the last time in his life. The moment I saw him I knew why I had put off this visit so long. I had told my mother that I did not want to see him because I hated him. But this was not true. It was only that I *had* hated him and I wanted to hold on to this hatred. I did not want to look on him as a ruin: it was not a ruin I had hated. I imagine that one of the reasons people cling to their hates so stubbornly is because they sense, once hate is gone, that they will be forced to deal with pain.

We traveled out to him, his older sister and myself, to what seemed to be the very end of a very Long Island. It was hot and dusty and we wrangled, my aunt and I, all the way out, over the fact that I had recently begun to smoke and, as she said, to give myself airs. But I knew that she wrangled with me because she could not bear to face the fact of her brother's dying. Neither could I endure the reality of her despair, her unstated bafflement as to what had happened to her brother's life, and her own. So we wrangled and I smoked and from time to time she fell into a heavy reverie. Covertly, I watched her face, which was the face of an old woman; it had fallen in, the eyes were sunken and lightless; soon she would be dying, too.

In my childhood—it had not been so long ago—I had thought her beautiful. She had been quick-witted and quick-moving and very generous with all the children and each of her visits had been an event. At one time one of my brothers and myself had thought of running away to live with her. Now she could no longer produce out of her handbag some unexpected and yet familiar delight. She made me feel pity and revulsion and fear. It was awful to realize that she no longer caused me to feel affection. The closer we came to the hospital the more querulous she became and at the same time, naturally, grew more dependent on me. Between pity and guilt and fear I began to feel that there was another me trapped in my skull like a jack-in-the-box who might escape my control at any moment and fill the air with screaming.

She began to cry the moment we entered the room and she saw him lying there, all shriveled and still, like a little black monkey. The great, gleaming apparatus which fed him and would have compelled him to be still even if he had been able to move brought to mind, not beneficence, but torture; the tubes entering his arm made me think of pictures I had seen when a child, of Gulliver, tied down by the pygmies on that island. My aunt wept and wept, there was a whistling sound in my father's throat; nothing was said; he could not speak. I wanted to take his hand, to say something. But I do not know what I could have said, even if he could have heard me. He was not really in that room with us, he had at last really embarked on his journey; and though my aunt told me that he said he was going to meet Jesus, I did not hear anything except that whistling in his throat. The doctor came back and we left, into that unbearable train again, and home. In the morning came the telegram saying that he was dead. Then the house was suddenly full of relatives, friends, hysteria, and confusion and I quickly left my mother and the children to the care of those impressive women, who, in Negro communities at least, automatically appear at times of bereavement armed with lotions, proverbs, and patience, and an ability to cook. I went downtown. By the time I returned, later the same day, my mother had been carried to the hospital and the baby had been born.

III

For my father's funeral I had nothing black to wear and this posed a nagging problem all day long. It was one of those problems, simple, or impossible of solution, to which the mind insanely clings in order to avoid the mind's real trouble. I spent most of that day at the downtown apartment of a girl I knew, celebrating my birthday with whiskey and wondering what to wear that night. When planning a birthday celebration one naturally does not expect that it will be up against competition from a funeral and this girl had anticipated taking me out that night, for a big dinner and a night club afterwards. Sometime during the course of that long day we decided that we would go out anyway, when my father's funeral service was over. I imagine *I* decided it, since, as the funeral hour approached, it became clearer and clearer to me that I would not know what to do with myself when it was over. The girl, stifling her very lively concern as to the possible effects of the whiskey on one of my father's chief mourners, concentrated on being conciliatory and practically helpful. She found a black shirt for me somewhere and ironed it and, dressed in the darkest pants and jacket I owned, and slightly drunk, I made my way to my father's funeral.

The chapel was full, but not packed, and very quiet. There were, mainly, my father's relatives, and his children, and here and there I saw faces I had not seen since childhood, the faces of my father's one-time friends. They were very dark and solemn now, seeming somehow to suggest that they had known all along that something like this would happen. Chief among the mourners was my aunt, who had quarreled with my father all his life; by which I do not mean to suggest that her mourning was insincere or that she had not loved him. I suppose that she was one of the few people in the world who had, and their incessant quarreling proved precisely the strength of the tie that bound them. The only other person in the world, as far as I knew, whose relationship to my father rivaled my aunt's in depth was my mother, who was not there.

It seemed to me, of course, that it was a very long funeral. But it was, if anything, a rather shorter funeral than most, nor, since there were no overwhelming, uncontrollable expressions of grief, could it be called—if I dare to use the word—successful. The minister who preached my father's funeral sermon was one of the few my father had still been seeing as he neared his end. He presented to us in his sermon a man whom none of us had ever seen—a man thoughtful, patient, and forbearing, a Christian inspiration to all who knew him, and a model for his children. And no doubt the children, in their disturbed and guilty state, were almost ready to believe this; he had been remote enough to be anything and, anyway, the shock of the incontrovertible, that it was really our father lying up there in that casket, prepared the mind for anything. His sister moaned and this grief-stricken moaning was taken as corroboration. The other faces held a dark, non-committal thoughtfulness. This was not the man they had known, but they had scarcely expected to be confronted with *him;* this was, in a sense deeper than questions of fact, the man they had not known, and the man they had not known may have been the real one. The real man, whoever he had been, had suffered and now he was dead: this was all that was sure and all that mattered now. Every man in the chapel hoped that when his hour came he, too, would be eulogized, which is to say forgiven, and that all of his lapses, greeds, errors, and strayings from the truth would be invested with coherence and looked upon with charity. This was perhaps the last thing human beings could give each other and it was what they demanded, after all, of the Lord. Only the Lord saw the midnight tears, only He was present when one of His children, moaning and wringing hands, paced up and down the room. When one slapped one's child in anger the recoil in the heart reverberated through heaven and became part of the pain of the universe. And when the children were hungry and sullen and distrustful and one watched them, daily, growing wilder, and further away, and running headlong into danger, it was the Lord who knew what the changed heart endured as the strap was laid to the backside; the Lord alone who knew what one *would* have said if one had had, like the Lord, the gift of the living word. It was the Lord who knew of the impossibility every parent in that room faced: how to prepare the child for the day when the child would be despised and how to *create* in the child—by what means?—a stronger antidote to this poison than one had found for oneself. The avenues, side streets, bars, billiard halls, hospitals, police stations, and even the playgrounds of Harlem—not to mention the houses of correction, the jails, and the morgue—testified to the potency of the poison while remaining silent as to the efficacy of whatever antidote, irresistibly raising the question of whether or not such an antidote existed; raising, which was worse, the question of whether or not an antidote was desirable; perhaps poison should be fought with poison. With these several schisms in the mind and with more terrors in the heart than could be named, it was better not to judge the man who had gone down under an impossible burden. It was better to remember: *Thou knowest this man's fall; but thou knowest not his wrassling.*

While the preacher talked and I watched the children—years of changing their diapers, scrubbing them, slapping them, taking them to school, and scolding them had had the perhaps inevitable result of making me love them, though I am not sure I knew this then—my mind was busily breaking out with a rash of disconnected impressions. Snatches of popular songs, indecent jokes, bits of books I had read, movie sequences, faces, voices, political issues—I thought I was going mad; all these impressions suspended, as it were, in the solution of the faint nausea produced in me by the heat and liquor. For a moment I had the impression that my alcoholic breath, inefficiently disguised with chewing gum, filled the entire chapel. Then someone began singing one of my father's favorite songs and, abruptly, I was with him, sitting on his knee, in the hot, enormous, crowded church which was the first church we attended. It was the Abyssinia Baptist Church on 138th Street. We had not gone there long. With this image, a host of others came. I had forgotten, in the rage of my growing up, how proud my father had been of me when I was little. Apparently, I had had a voice and my father had liked to show me off before the members of the church. I had forgotten what he had looked like when he was pleased but now I remembered that he had always been grinning with pleasure when my solos ended. I even remembered certain expressions on his face when he teased my mother—had he loved her? I would never know. And when had it all begun to change? For now it seemed that he had not always been cruel. I remembered being taken for a haircut and scraping my knee on the footrest of the barber's chair and I remembered my father's face as he soothed my crying and applied the stinging iodine. Then I remembered our fights, fights which had been of the worst possible kind because my technique had been silence.

I remembered the one time in all our life together when we had really spoken to each other.

It was on a Sunday and it must have been shortly before I left home. We were walking, just the two of us, in our usual silence, to or from church. I was in high school and had been doing a lot of writing and I was, at about this time, the editor of the high school magazine. But I had also been a Young Minister and had been preaching from the pulpit. Lately, I had been taking fewer engagements and preached as rarely as possible. It was said in the church, quite truthfully, that I was "cooling off."

My father asked me abruptly, "You'd rather write than preach, wouldn't you?"

I was astonished at his question—because it was a real question. I answered, "Yes."

That was all we said. It was awful to remember that that was all we had *ever* said.

The casket now was opened and mourners were being led up the aisle to look for the last time on the deceased. The assumption was that the family was too overcome with grief to be allowed to make this journey alone and I watched while my aunt was led to the casket and, muffled in black, and shaking, led back to her seat. I disapproved of forcing the children to look on their dead father, considering that the shock of his death, or, more truthfully, the shock of death as a reality, was already a little more than a child could bear, but my judgment in this matter had been overruled and there they were, bewildered and frightened and very small, being led, one by one, to the casket. But there is also something very gallant about children at such moments. It has something to do with their silence and gravity and with the fact that one cannot help them. Their legs, somehow, seem *exposed*, so that it is at once incredible and terribly clear that their legs are all they have to hold them up.

I had not wanted to go to the casket myself and I certainly had not wished to be led there, but there was no way of avoiding either of these forms. One of the deacons led me up and I looked on my father's face. I cannot say that it looked like him at all. His blackness had been equivocated by powder and there was no suggestion in that casket of what his power had or could have been. He was simply an old man dead, and it was hard to believe that he had ever given anyone either joy or pain. Yet, his life filled that room. Further up the avenue his wife was holding his newborn child. Life and death so close together, and love and hatred, and right and wrong, said something to me which I did not want to hear concerning man, concerning the life of man.

After the funeral, while I was downtown desperately celebrating my birthday, a Negro soldier, in the lobby of the Hotel Braddock, got into a fight with a white policeman over a Negro girl. Negro girls, white policemen, in or out of uniform, and Negro males—in or out of uniform—were part of the furniture of the lobby of the Hotel Braddock and this was certainly not the first time such an incident had occurred. It was destined, however, to receive an unprecedented publicity, for the fight between the policeman and the soldier ended with the shooting of the soldier. Rumor, flowing immediately to the streets outside, stated that the soldier had been shot in the back, an instantaneous and revealing invention, and that the soldier had died protecting a Negro woman. The facts were somewhat different—for example, the soldier had not been shot in the back, and was not dead, and the girl seems to have been as dubious a symbol of womanhood as her white counterpart in Georgia usually is, but no one was interested in the facts. They preferred the invention because this invention expressed and corroborated their hates and fears so perfectly. It is just as well to remember that people are always doing this. Perhaps many of those legends, including Christianity, to which the world clings began their conquest of the world with just some such concerted surrender to distortion. The effect, in Harlem, of this particular legend was like the effect of a lit match in a tin of gasoline. The mob gathered before the doors of the Hotel Braddock simply began to swell and to spread in every direction, and Harlem exploded.

The mob did not cross the ghetto lines. It would have been easy, for example, to have gone over Morningside Park on the west side or to have crossed the Grand Central railroad tracks at 125th Street on the east side, to wreak havoc in white neighborhoods. The mob seems to have been mainly interested in something more potent and real than the white face, that is, in white power, and the principal damage done during the riot of the summer of 1943 was to white business establishments in Harlem. It might have been a far bloodier story, of course, if, at the hour the riot began, these establishments had still been open. From the Hotel Braddock the mob fanned out, east and west along 125th Street, and for the entire length of Lenox, Seventh, and Eighth avenues. Along each of these avenues, and along each major side street—116th, 125th, 135th, and so on—bars, stores, pawnshops, restaurants, even little luncheonettes had been smashed open and entered and looted— looted, it might be added, with more haste than efficiency. The shelves really looked as though a bomb had struck them. Cans of beans and soup and dog food, along with toilet paper, corn flakes, sardines, and milk tumbled every which way, and abandoned cash registers and cases of beer leaned crazily out of the splintered windows and were strewn along the avenues. Sheets, blankets, and clothing of every description formed a kind of path, as though people had dropped them while running. I truly had not realized that Harlem *had* so many stores until I saw them all smashed open; the first time the word *wealth* ever entered my mind in relation to Harlem was when I saw it scattered in the streets. But one's first, incongruous impression of plenty was countered immediately by an impression of waste. None of this was doing anybody any good. It would have been better to have left the plate glass as it had been and the goods lying in the stores.

It would have been better, but it would also have been intolerable, for Harlem had needed something to smash. To smash something is the ghetto's chronic need. Most of the time it is the members of the ghetto who smash each other, and themselves. But as long as the ghetto walls are standing there will always come a moment when these outlets do not work. That summer, for example, it was not enough to get into a fight on Lenox Avenue, or curse out one's cronies in the barber shops. If ever, indeed, the violence which fills Harlem's churches, pool halls, and bars erupts outward in a more direct fashion, Harlem and its citizens are likely to vanish in an apocalyptic flood. That this is not likely to happen is due to a great many reasons, most hidden and powerful among them the Negro's real relation to the white American. This relation prohibits, simply, anything as uncomplicated and satisfactory as pure hatred. In order really to hate white people, one has to blot so much out of the mind—and the heart—that this hatred itself becomes an exhausting and self-destructive pose. But this does not mean, on the other hand, that love comes easily: the white world is too powerful, too complacent, too ready with gratuitous humiliation, and, above all, too ignorant and too innocent for that. One is absolutely forced to make perpetual qualifications and one's own reactions are always canceling each other out. It is this, really, which has driven so many people mad, both white and black. One is always in the position of having to decide between amputation and gangrene. Amputation is swift but time may prove that the amputation was not necessary—or one may delay the amputation too long. Gangrene is slow, but it is impossible to be sure that one is reading one's symptoms right. The idea of going through life as a cripple is more than one can bear, and equally unbearable is the risk of swelling up slowly, in agony, with poison. And the trouble, finally, is that the risks are real even if the choices do not exist.

"But as for me and my house," my father had said, "we will serve the Lord." I wondered, as we drove him to his resting place, what this line had meant for him. I had heard him preach it many times. I had preached it once myself, proudly giving it an interpretation different from my father's. Now the whole thing came back to me, as though my father and I were on our way to Sunday school and I were memorizing the golden text: *And if it seem evil unto you to serve the Lord, choose you this day whom you will serve; whether the gods which your fathers served that were on the other side of the flood, or the gods of the Amorites, in whose land ye dwell: but as for me and my house, we will serve the Lord.* I suspected in these familiar lines a meaning which had never been there for me before. All of my father's texts and songs, which I had decided were meaningless, were arranged before me at his death like empty bottles, waiting to hold the meaning which life would give them for me. This was his legacy: nothing is ever escaped. That bleakly memorable morning I hated the unbelievable streets and the Negroes and whites who had, equally, made them that way. But I knew that it was folly, as my father would have said, this bitterness was folly. It was necessary to hold on to the things that mattered. The dead man mattered, the new life mattered; blackness and whiteness did not matter; to believe that they did was to acquiesce in one's own destruction. Hatred, which could destroy so much, never failed to destroy the man who hated and this was an immutable law.

It began to seem that one would have to hold in the mind forever two ideas which seemed to be in opposition. The first idea was acceptance, the acceptance, totally without rancor, of life as it is, and men as they are: in the light of this idea, it goes without saying that injustice is a commonplace. But this did not mean that one could be complacent, for the second idea was of equal power: that one must never, in one's own life, accept these injustices as commonplace but must fight them with all one's strength. This fight begins, however, in the heart and it now had been laid to my charge to keep my own heart free of hatred and despair. This intimation made my heart heavy and, now that my father was irrecoverable, I wished that he had been beside me so that I could have searched his face for the answers which only the future would give me now.

STUDY AND DISCUSSION QUESTIONS

1. Baldwin opens his essay by providing the reader with both historical and biographical facts. Why do you think he chooses to begin in this way?

2. What was Baldwin's father's relation with his children like?

3. What does Baldwin say was the source of his father's bitterness?

4. Discuss the incident in the New Jersey restaurant. What does Baldwin learn from this experience? How is the experience connected to his assessment of his father?

5. Discuss the several kinds of waiting Baldwin explores in section two of the essay.

6. What is the poison Baldwin thinks about during his father's funeral? And how does the existence of this poison create a dilemma for parents?

7. Discuss Baldwin's metaphor of the choice between amputation and gangrene.

8. Why do race riots happen, according to Baldwin?

9. Analyze the meaning of Baldwin's title, "Notes of a Native Son."

10. Baldwin concludes that "one would have to hold in the mind forever two ideas which seemed to be in opposition." Why? What are these two ideas? How hard is it, or would it be, for you to perform this balancing act?

SUGGESTIONS FOR WRITING

1. Write a short essay analyzing the structure of this essay. What happens within the narrator, in his family, and in the community in each of the three sections? What concepts and metaphors recur?

2. Discuss the relationship between Baldwin and his father and, using specific references from the text, follow the development of Baldwin's understanding of his father and of himself.

3. Think about one of your own parents: what is a central lesson about life or philosophy of life that you have learned from him or her? Give specific incidents/examples that seem to embody this philosophy and how you have coped with it.

4. Why do you think riots and uprisings tend to stay in the rioters' own community?

THE DEATH OF FRED ASTAIRE

Leslie Lawrence

Leslie Lawrence's short stories have appeared in The Massachusetts Review, Sojourner, The Green Mountain Review, *and elsewhere. She received an MFA in fiction from Goddard College.*

In the summer of 1984 I lived for six weeks in Ludlow, Vermont, with my lover's cocker spaniel. I had known the lover (we'll call her Dale) and the dog (Coney) for about a year, and at this point I was fonder of the lover. Cockers were not my preferred breed, and this one was overweight and undertrained; prone to stomach, back, and ear aches; an obsessive humper; clingy and wimpy. I couldn't understand why he'd insist on sitting by the feet of a nearly motionless human tapping out the first draft of a novel when he could have been romping through the woods with the gang of more doggy dogs who lived up the road. I wasn't flattered. I felt crowded. And every time I shifted positions or sighed, his ears would perk and he would rise and wag in anticipation of an outing.

I suppose it snuck up on me slowly. I remember searching the Grand Union[1] parking lot for the shadiest spot, and then my pleasure at seeing his delight when I returned with my bundles. I worked hard trying to teach him to eat his biscuits from the kitchen floor instead of the living room Oriental— even harder trying to teach him to stick by my heels when we ran. On the dumb side, but with a frightening desire to please, he was eminently trainable; I felt my terrible power over him and struggled to use it responsibly. However it happened (clutching his silky fur through those middle-of-the-night thunderstorms, spying his motionless form waiting on the bank as I swam to shore), three, maybe four weeks into our enforced, often irksome intimacy, I found myself planning my afternoon outings with him in mind.

To be fair, his tastes and mine were similar; nevertheless, there were days I quit work early because he had been sitting so patiently, so glumly; days I chose to go one place rather than another because I knew he would enjoy it more. And when I realized this—that I had become a person capable

---

[1] Grocery store chain.

of making sacrifices, however minor, for a dog who wasn't mine and wasn't the kind of dog I would have chosen—and then when I realized it was no longer a question of putting his desires before mine, because his pleasure had become my own—then I knew I wanted a baby.

This wasn't exactly news. As a child, I always imagined I'd one day be a mother. And a friend recently reminded me of our first lunch in 1975, when I told her, "with great earnestness and passion," that what I most wanted was to get married and raise a family. Five years after that, sitting in the car with Karen, my first woman lover (Dale was my second), I told her that even though I loved her, had never felt more in love, never been happier in my life, I knew we wouldn't last more than a few months because I wanted to get married and have children. When Karen and I broke up two years later, I again began to search for a man to start a family with—despite the fact that when I encountered mothers with their children I had difficulty imagining myself so engaged with the tedium, so patient and loving. Only now, with Coney providing evidence (reliable or not) that I had what it takes, did my desire for children change from being a rather abstract assumption about some future I could not seem to catch up with to a yearning I could taste. This both pleased and panicked me. I was thirty-three. Dale and I were planning to live together in the fall, and this arrangement was not likely to lead to anyone's pregnancy.

I had heard of lesbians raising children together when one or both had given birth while married. I had heard of lesbians adopting children and even of conceiving them themselves through artificial insemination, but I felt sure these options were for other people: committed lesbians, women who had always known, or who didn't but once they came out realized the signs had been there all along; women who not only loved women but thought it better to love women; women who had great anger or bitterness about aspects of their own childhoods and thought raising children with women would be a better way to raise children and would result in better children, a better world, or rather, planet. I was none of these women.

Though none of my many relationships with men had lasted more than a couple of years, I considered them as happy and healthy as most I had seen. I had loved some of these men and was still attracted to men. I liked watching them play basketball, fiddle with car engines, hoist sails, dress wounds, argue in court. I had always enjoyed wearing my boyfriend's shirts—they made me feel thin and sexy; and nothing turned me on more than the sight of a man holding an infant in the crook of his arm or throwing a baby into the air.

Certainly I considered myself a feminist. I recognized ways in which I had compromised myself in my relationships with men; I had discovered that when I was with women I felt more fully myself and more deeply loved. Still, I had never been entirely comfortable with terms like "overthrowing the patriarchy," probably because in many ways that patriarchy had treated me well.

I remembered my childhood as happy, had only minor complaints about the way my parents had raised me, and perhaps most significant of all, I was a daddy's girl—a fact apparently so obvious that even though I never had much of a voice, in a camp production I was the one who sang "My Heart Belongs to Daddy." As a child, I was Daddy's little helper, trotting behind him with the rake, the caulking gun, the monkey wrench. He taught me to ride a two-wheeler, to keep my head throughout a geometry proof. His loves were my loves—invigorating music, the color red, veal parmigiana, Adlai Stevenson, the first forsythia; his values my values—naturalness, honesty, independence, persistence, daring, conversation, family. In my early twenties I began to discover the many things I admired in my mother (her graciousness, generosity, intuitive feminism, intelligence, love of art and literature—in short, her depth of feeling and understanding), but up until then, it was my father I held on high and aimed to please, and the thought that my little girl (for of course, I would have a little me) might not have a father at all, and certainly not in the same way I had mine, this was nothing I was ready to imagine.

Of course, as a child of the 1960s, I did not want to replicate my parents' lives, but my idea of doing things differently consisted of marrying a man with long hair, maybe an earring, most likely a non-Jew with an unimpressive income; of doing it not in a temple or country club but on some mountaintop, *sans* ice sculptures, *avec*[2] wildflowers. It was preferring chamber music to symphonies, sending my children to Quaker camps, never consulting an "interior decorator." It did not include, as the title of one of the books I eventually read on the subject put it, "Having a Baby Without a Man."

Perhaps if my mother had once been a night-club singer, or my sister had eloped with a goy, or my father had been married once before—if anyone in my immediate family had had just the tiniest secret or blemish. Or if I had frequently felt left out or had to endure taunts. But we were Jews who lived among Jews, and my experience with feeling different or oppressed went no further than having been briefly forced to wear shoes with protruding metal plates designed to correct my pigeon toes, no further than occasionally being the last to be chosen for a softball team. When my sister, who was studying physical therapy, discovered that (like many people) one of my legs is slightly longer than the other, I felt truly shaken. And when I was in my first lesbian relationship—well, on the one hand, accustomed as I was to approval, I told nearly everyone and was often bold, even cavalier. On the other hand, I had dreams about being corraled and branded, I lived in dread of so much as a raised eyebrow, I daily chose to look as straight—no straighter—than I always had. And when I knew, really knew, I wanted a baby, I thought: this

---

[2] *Sans,* without; *avec,* with (both French).

having-a-baby-without-a-man idea—it may be fine for lots of people, but not for me.

So why didn't I just tell Dale I couldn't move in with her? I guess because I loved her, loved the way she loved me. Because I had confidence in our ability to live together happily (a rare feeling for me). Because as much as I might lampoon those Be Here Now, Go with What You Feel folks, I knew they had something to teach ruminating planners like me. Or maybe (because I had climbed mountains, run races, written novels, gone to dark lesbian bars?) I faintly suspected I might someday be able to consider what, at present, felt beyond me (and when we first met and I casually asked Dale if she wanted children she had said yes).

What I know for sure is that I wanted a baby soon, but not immediately, and so when a visiting friend pointed out, while we picked raspberries to calm my nerves, "Just because you move in with someone doesn't mean you can't move out!"—even though I knew this was just the sort of thinking that simply traded bearable pain in the near future for agony later on—I found myself repeating the line in my head, even quoting it to friends, as if it contained some lifesaving truth.

No doubt the line was not far from my mind that late August morning I was readying the house for my departure. Coney, fearful of being left, was constantly at my heels, and "My Fair Lady"[3] was on the radio. Though I had long ago decided show music was too lowbrow for sophisticated me, I was singing along and loving it. But then "The Rain in Spain" came on, and around the time Professor Higgins's "no-no-no" talk gave way to his "yes-by-gosh-she's-got-it" song, I noticed my throat had clamped shut. I bore with it another round or two, but soon I dropped the sponge, slumped down, and gave in to the feeling. Then, just a minute or so later, after I had wiped the tears, I was left wondering: what was that all about?

The song was a happy one, not about anything that particularly hit home, except maybe that Higgins trained Eliza in much the same stern way I trained Coney and we both fell in love, but no, I didn't think that was it. Back to my scrubbing, I was remembering how we used to sing out at the tops of our lungs—my Daddy and I—mimicking Rex's haughty Britishness and howling along with Julie's triumphant "Spaaains" and "plaaains." I was remembering his black hair and red cheeks and my throat was tightening again as I thought (not without *some* amusement): well, maybe I'm sad because it looks like I'm *not* going to marry my father after all. Nor even a man like him. Nor any man at all.

Months later, when a friend asked, "If Dale were a man would you marry her?" I quickly said, "Yes." We loved being together, had together created a

---

[3] Broadway musical by Lerner and Loewe, starring Rex Harrison as Professor Higgins and Julie Andrews as Eliza.

beautiful home (with, come to think of it, much help from "our architect," the yuppie's interior decorator). One friend who had spent a weekend commented on the balance, the grace she saw in our lives. I was touched; I felt it, too. And Coney—he was healthier, happier, more disciplined, thinner, and, most important, equally wild about each of us.

And so, when I saw a notice about a discussion at the women's center on lesbian parenting, off I went—alone, for although Dale had said she was interested in raising children with me, she believed coming out or being found out would jeopardize her job, and unlike me who has a large appetite for hashing things out in groups, she tends to make her decisions in private.

I had expected the discussion to be geared to lesbians considering parenting; probably I had assumed it would be, like many feminist events, an upbeat, cheerleading sort of thing. What it turned out to be was a support group for women already doing it, women who clearly needed support. The children being discussed were all troubled in one way or another. One teenage daughter was so intent on proving her heterosexuality that she had become, according to her mother, a "slut." Another daughter's best friend's parents had prohibited their daughter from visiting. A boy avoided the problem by never inviting his friends home. One woman's ex-husband had threatened to sue for custody. Another woman, a "nonbiological mom," certain that no one at her job could handle her situation, lied when she needed to go home to tend her sick child. And another "coparent" (another new word for me) was tired of her lover's daughter hating her. They all seemed tired; and they all had money problems. Still, not wanting to feel daunted, I focused on how much I liked the women, how impressed I was by their strength, integrity, and resiliency. I reminded myself that in all cases, their children, born while the mother was married, had expectations of normalcy and a relatively recent relationship with the coparent. Finally, though I knew I ought not feel anything but guilt and outrage over my class privilege, I consoled myself with the observation that these women (or most of them) were not so privileged, and that perhaps I, with my sense of entitlement, not to mention my actual entitlement (a degree from an elite college, relatively wealthy and always generous parents), would be spared some of these women's difficulties.

It must have been that same winter (the first we lived together) that I attended (this time with my ex, Karen, and her new girlfriend) a local health clinic's introductory meeting on "artificial insemination," as it was called then, before they changed it to "alternative insemination," for "really, there's nothing artificial about it." I can't remember how I first heard about this meeting, but I had to call the clinic and, without mentioning my purpose, ask for a certain person. Only then was I told the time and place. I was shocked by all this secrecy. It had never occurred to me that what I was contemplating was risky in any realm other than the social or emotional. I still don't know what law I was breaking or what the clinic feared (loss of funding, bad press, chastisement from the archdiocese?), but as I entered the specified building and located the basement stairs, I felt like a novice member of some underground cadre meeting to plan their next bombing.

At this gathering, in addition to the three of us, were a straight single woman in her late thirties; a straight-looking, very-much-in-love-looking lesbian couple; a less straight-looking but also loving-looking interracial lesbian couple; and the two presenters, a nurse and a lawyer.

The nurse spoke first: The sperm was flown in from a bank in Oakland; someone met it at the airport with dry ice—even so, it was crucial that the client get to the clinic within a few hours (of course, all of this had to be carefully coordinated with one's cycle); each insemination cost fifty dollars, and usually one did two or three a cycle; on the average, pregnancy was achieved after about six months, but sometimes it took years; one's chances for a healthy pregnancy and baby were no better or worse with "AI"; the bank screened its donors carefully, but there were no guarantees—though their donors were not paid, which meant they were more likely to answer the questionnaire honestly; one received some basic information, including donor's height and weight, race and religion, hair and eye coloring, occupation, and special talents; there were two possible arrangements—either the father would stay forever unknown, though you could get certain medical information, or the father could become known when the child reached eighteen.

As for the news from the legal front: Yes, it was possible that your baby could be the half sibling of someone else's child and not know it and fall in love (heterosexual) with that person and perform incest and give birth to the kind of child born from such unions; yes, although they were very cautious in their labeling, names were never used and a mix-up wasn't impossible and you could end up with a baby who was of a different race than you had ordered; and yes, it was possible in the case of donors who never intended to identify themselves that the child could have a medical condition which necessitated genetic information beyond the basics on record and that information would be impossible to obtain; and no, she didn't know if there were copies of the records or what would happen if there was a fire in the building that housed them.

The above were answers to questions from the group, questions I would never have thought to ask. What I thought to ask but didn't was, What do I tell my child when she asks who her father is? What do I say when she is older and wants to know who I thought I was that I could choose to deprive her of a father? And will we—the child and I—spend the rest of our lives (or a mere eighteen years) walking down the street, into the supermarket, onto the airplane, searching the eyes of strangers for the man who was her father?

Such questions told me that neither the eighteen-year wait nor the life of eternal ignorance were the right routes for *me*. And artificial insemination, the actual process of racing to the clinic and climbing upon a cold metal table—well, there was nothing inherently horrible about it, unless a person had once had rather different images of conception. Which is all to say that although I dutifully took notes (for I could no longer assume that what was out of the question at the present would remain that way), when I got home I began the list in the back of my little black journal. It includes former lovers, men I had dated once or twice, old friends, husbands of friends, friends of friends, someone I once shared an office with, my car mechanic . . . I remember trying to maintain a brainstorming mentality, but I see now I must have censored from the start. Absent, for example, are the names of my one gay male friend (the HIV test wasn't out yet) and a straight man I came close to marrying—not because I felt this would be too sticky but because of his sister's colitis, his brother's asthma, his father's blood pressure. I remember thinking that if I had married him, none of this would have prevented me from wanting his child; I also remember realizing that if Dale and I could mate and I was applying the same strict standards to her family history, she would not have passed the test. Still, I told myself it was entirely appropriate that I should apply different standards to a donor than to a husband or mate, and when the word *eugenics* grazed my mind, I swallowed the bad taste and refused to be stymied.

Shortly after I entered the first round of names, I received a formal-looking envelope from someone on the list, an old college friend who had, for one night, been my lover. Though I had been sure this man wasn't for me (too intense, too wounded, too spiritual), when I saw the wedding invitation, I couldn't not, at least for a moment, think that I could have—*should* have—been the one to marry him. More lingering was the realization that his marriage would make it less likely—no, just about impossible—that he would want to father a child with me. It seemed to mock the whole plan, exposing its full ridiculousness, its inevitable failure. (I declined the invitation, never even sent a present.) And the longer I looked at my list, the clearer it became that really, there were hardly any genuine possibilities—certainly not the husbands of friends, especially not the one whose wife had just had a hysterectomy (and to think I had once viewed that as an auspicious sign!); not the ones I barely knew; or the one who had the horrible teeth; or the one who would insist on the kid going to his alma mater; or the one who might interpret a missing button or dirty face as a sign of bad mothering; or the one who once he had his "own" children would forget our kid's birthday; or the one who was probably still in love with me; or the one who worked in a lab with blood; or the ones who might not be absolutely, unequivocally okay on the lesbian issue.

That didn't leave many, but in the spring of 1985, after endless discussions with Dale (another story), I wrote Jim (one of the old friends, first on the list) and asked if he'd consider fathering my child. He promptly replied with an antique postcard, a photo of an elegantly dressed man and woman in a rowboat, its title something like "Lifelong Friendship." Jim's own words were brief: "Very flattered, very nervous, very interested."

How perfect! I thought. The photo, its title, his message. For a few minutes at least, this no longer seemed like such a crazy idea.

That summer, I was further spurred on when I visited a childhood friend, a lesbian who'd recently had a baby. Carol lived with her lover, her lover's teenaged son from her married years, and Carol's four-year-old daughter, conceived by AI. When I went to dinner, I was relieved to see that the daughter was a normal, pretty little girl (I don't know what I expected), adored by her older "brother," an unusually thoughtful and articulate sixteen-year-old. What I most remember from the evening was how at bedtime the daughter climbed into her coparent's lap and clung happily to her, in no way displaying confusion over her breasts and smooth cheeks.

Though normally I'm a sucker for crisp Yuppie cafés, when my parents were visiting from New York about a year later, I suggested a large, noisy deli I hoped would make them feel at ease (despite the small portions and inferior rye bread). I'd already given my parents three blows—that I was involved with a woman, involved with a second woman, moving in with the second— still, telling them my latest plan wasn't going to be easy: it would slam the door on any lingering hope that this was all just a phase. More important, it (or the baby, anyway) would slam that same door on me. Preparing for this moment in therapy, I often cried. I certainly didn't want to cry now—nor did I want to sound overly casual about the potential problems. In my previous comings out to my parents I had struggled with similar conflicts, and while proud to have shielded them from the depth of my pain and uncertainty, I also longed for them to know the real me.

In any case, they took the news calmly. (The Bloody Marys I suggested probably helped. Also, my mother wasn't entirely surprised—she knew I'd visited Carol and that had started her wondering.) Quickly getting into the spirit of the thing, they began arguing in favor of an unknown donor. This surprised and embarrassed me. I figured they, of all people, would share my desire for a live and involved father, that link to heterosexuality who could provide at least a whiff of normalcy. But they were more concerned about the possibility of "complications." And they were not alone. Dale had mixed feelings on the issue. My sister, her husband, and several friends with first-hand knowledge of disastrous situations involving a known father felt as my parents did. Nevertheless, I proceeded with my plans—albeit rather slowly, in part because I had my own anxieties, but also because I had started a new teaching job and didn't think it wise to get pregnant my first year, especially since I wasn't married.

About a year after our lunch at the deli and shortly after a weekend family party celebrating my father's sixty-fifth, I phoned my parents to discuss the latest baby news. I mention the celebration because it was in part responsible for my decision to view my folks as potentially helpful allies in this project. We'd all gotten along well over the weekend, and my parents had been particularly warm to Dale, who, for the first time, felt fully accepted into our clan. Also, the poem I'd written for my father had been a big success; and after my recitation, as my father walked toward me with open arms, oblivious to everyone else in the room, even his beloved brother who had traveled so far to be there, I could see that even after I had betrayed him (for that's how I thought of it—he'd given me his all so that I might become the perfect wife for a man a lot like himself), even now when it was becoming less and less likely that I'd ever come around, I was still his best girl, the apple of his eye.

Feeling more confident than I had in years, I called my parents and asked for their opinions on some serious legal and medical matters. Things seemed to be going well until my mother got off the phone to take another call and my father said, "Look, we've been dealing with this and will continue to, but I want you to know what a great disappointment it is."

I couldn't speak. Having always found my father's disappointment impossible to bear, I grunted a good-bye, hung up, and burst into tears.

A few minutes later the phone rang—my mother wanting to make sure I was all right. As we continued to talk, my mother began to speak of that Mother's Day when I was about six, maybe eight, and we went out for lunch at Tavern on the Green. Did I remember?

Yes, I said, I remembered (unless I was just remembering because she'd mentioned this not too long ago, shortly after I'd sent her a book that included a section on lesbian daughters coming out to their mothers—a section she said she found very moving). I remembered the lushness of Central Park, the horse-drawn carriages, the tables with linen cloths and pink flowers, the ladies with their pastel dresses, men in their dark suits, the roving violinists. And yes, I remembered what my mother most remembered: how I sat in my party dress with my legs wide apart, absolutely transfixed by the couples dancing. Once again, as my mother spoke of this, she choked up, and, lumpy-throated myself, I wondered just what was causing our emotion. Not the wide-apart legs adumbrating lesbianism—no, I'd always been, still was, on the feminine side—more likely it was that she could not find the thread connecting that little girl to the woman I've become, or even if she could (and once or twice she suggested an intuitive understanding of why a woman might choose a woman), it saddened her that I was never going to be a part of those handsome couples that so entranced me.

Later that night I watched "Eyes on the Prize"[4] on TV. There were Andrew Goodman's parents talking about him with pride and continued belief in his cause. There was Medgar Evers's wife just after her husband was killed by white supremacists. There was Fannie Lou Hamer, a poor uneducated woman speaking out so passionately, so articulately. All that hope and dignity, unity and courage—it moved me so, that night especially because it was my disappointed father who had taught me about Rosa Parks and *Brown* v. *Board of Education*[5] and had told me, again and again, how important it is to stand up for what you believe in.

The next morning, crossing the river in the ancient BMW my father had handed down to me, I heard Yehudi Menuhin playing Brahms's Violin Concerto, one of my father's favorites. Turning onto Storrow Drive I switched into fourth, and amidst the rising curlicue of strings I discovered I was crying yet again—from the memory of that music filling the house of my childhood, the order, the sunlight, the passion, the faith in the future.

A month later Jim and I met in a Mexican restaurant to discuss our wishes—those we'd agree on informally and those we'd put into a legal contract. How much should he see the child? How much should he pay? What if the child isn't normal? What if Jim marries and has other children? Should he be present at the birth? And just what is it I'm afraid of—too much involvement or not enough?

The answer: both.

That summer, Fred Astaire died. I heard the news on the radio and gasped. I'd always loved Fred; still, that didn't explain the grief I felt. On the radio they called it "the end of an era, the end of style, of dancing cheek to cheek."

In October 1987 I attended the gay rights march on Washington with Karen. I knew that if I ever did have a child, this would at times mask my lesbianism, at other times expose it. I knew it was important for my child as well as myself that I—Dale and I—be proud of who we are. Walking through a city overtaken by gay people, doing my habitual accounting of ways I was and was not like other gay people—I couldn't help noticing what seemed to be a particularly high proportion of people of both genders wearing red glasses. I wore red glasses, and I loved my red glasses, had always felt they were "me"; so maybe

[4] *Eyes on the Prize,* multipart television documentary about the civil rights movement; Andrew Goodman, Medgar Evers, Fannie Lou Hamer, and Rosa Parks were featured civil rights activists.

[5] 1954 Supreme Court ruling declaring segregated schools illegal.

that's what clinched it—all those red glasses: I was glad to be there, I identified, I belonged. I felt that way even at the mass gay wedding, a lengthy, hodgepodge ceremony full of Christian and pantheistic rhetoric, liberation politics, flowers, and kitsch, where all the very weirdest had gathered—the fattest, skinniest, hairiest, smoothest, queens, bull dykes, down-and-outest—even there I felt at home, like this was the appropriate, the logical place for me to be, given everything I was—a New York Jew, a graduate of a college known for its radical politics, a writer, my father's daughter, my mother's daughter. For old time's sake and for ongoing friendship, Karen and I married. We didn't have a ring, but we kissed; we threw rice.

A journal entry from late August 1988: "Last night I checked my mucous—stretchy. Jim called to say we're on for Saturday. Last session with M. helped me decide on AI as opposed to intercourse. It's more important for Dale to be there and in on this from the very beginning. I picture us making love first and me crying—for a change. But I can also imagine feeling happy, close, excited. And Labor Day weekend—how auspicious!"

What actually happened: It poured on our way to Vermont, but just as we drove up to Jim's funky farmhouse, the sun peeked out. On the oak kitchen table were pink and violet wildflowers. Jim appeared with a bottle of champagne. He took out the crystal glasses, and we sipped to I don't remember what. Soon after, Jim disappeared into his room and we sat out back with Coney. In ten minutes, maybe fifteen (it was beginning to seem like Jim might be running into difficulties), he walked out the back door and stuck up his thumb. We cheered. Dale and I (and Coney) headed into his cool, damp bedroom with its brass bed, white comforter, tree-graced window. The glass was on the night table, the sperm pearly, ample. I had my syringes (sans needles). Never very dexterous, I fumbled through the procedure. No time to make love even if we'd been so inclined. I suppose I had imagined Dale inserting it, in some pathetic imitation of intercourse, but she didn't want to. So I did it. And then, we waited the requisite twenty minutes, urging the miracle to occur.

It didn't.

Not that time. Nor the next few. But one Thursday afternoon in November (Veterans Day!) I drove up by myself feeling something in the air. Jim wasn't home yet when I arrived, and I'd had such a heady trip I took out my notebook and began writing:

I will call you A for beginning, and will tell you how it was—the ride up to Vermont for your conception. Late fall. Still filled with ambivalence, I imagined turning around—but midway or so, my mood changed. I saw men in their cars glancing at me and couldn't help feeling pleased. I heard Dvořák's American Quartet—long lines, full of melancholy and longing.

Maybe that was it, or the wind picking up. I felt a tenderness for this crazy life of mine. I imagined I was going up to see my lover to make a baby, you. Then, remembering it wasn't like that, I imagined how, many years from now, I would describe the night you were conceived. Funny I never asked my parents about my conception. Never asked my mother if she had any misgivings, and if she did, I'm not sure I'd want to know. But if you want to know whether you were born of love: you were. I think that's what I'm trying to say. Tonight I loved my life—the music, the sky, the journey, the freedom. I stopped for gas. Self-service was crowded so I splurged. I stopped to buy wine for later, coffee for now. It started to rain. I almost missed my exit. I felt a pain, near my right hip, thought I might be ovulating that very minute. Touched my breasts—not swollen yet. Threw my quarters into the basket and one fell. I thought about telling you all these little things. Stories with no point except that I had a life. I was here. It was ordinary and I was caressing it all—the ordinary, the strange, the way it was and wasn't what I wanted. I wanted you to know you had a mother who drove to Vermont, stopped for gas, wine, coffee, almost missed her exit, got teary-eyed with Dvořák and thoughts of you. Men looked at her, and she felt right in the middle of her life. She listened to the radio. "One quarter of the New York prisoners have AIDS. Texas will be the site for the $4.4 billion atom smasher. Bush, elected two days ago, is working to smooth out his transition to the White House." No, the world isn't going the way I'd like. Even my life—not the way I imagined. Harder. But I headed north off the highway. It got dark and began to rain. At Route 107, I made a sharp right, and there was Anabel's, a white colonial inn, all lit up. And somehow that was enough—sublime. And you.

I realize now I've been thinking of you as a boy.

Two dogs are curled up beside me now in front of the woodstove. Dale is home. I called her earlier. We had a nice talk. You are on your way.

And he was.

This is not, of course, the end of the story. That boy is now almost two, and there's much I could say about how it has been and how our unusual family puts us both on the margins of conventional society and, at the same time, smack in the middle of it. But I must stop soon. And in searching for a way to close, I remember a recent fantasy: It's Mother's Day years from now. We go to Tavern on the Green or some place like it, and Max sits with his knees apart and, enchanted, watches his two moms dance.

But who am I kidding. Even if Dale were the type, even if it became perfectly acceptable for two women to slow dance at Tavern on the Green—it's not just the dance that holds such sway over me. It's the tension between the dress and the suit, the smooth and the rough, the swinger and the one swung.

Or so I thought. Now I'm not sure.

A few weeks ago I went to a concert of ballroom dancers. To my surprise, I found all that cheek-to-cheek stuff rather dull and bloodless. At first I decided this was probably because the men were all gay. Then I read in the program that most of the couples were married (to each other); so I thought, well, maybe *that's* why it's so desexualized. Then the tangos began: first women tangoing with women, then men tangoing with men. (I leaned forward in my chair and sat with my legs apart, entranced.) And afterward even the straight woman I was with agreed this was by far the most exciting number. The odd thing was, nothing seemed odd about it. There was no cross-dressing; the women all wore tight black dresses, the men tight black suits; no partner seemed to lead the other; and yet—how they sizzled!

So who knows?

I write this from a cabin in the country. Here with Dale and Max, we have time and air and mountains. Sometimes we put on Max's red plastic Sony and dance in the kitchen—all three of us or some combination of two or Max alone—and then I catch Dale's eye and we smile and I think, *I'm not missing anything, this is the whole thing.*

STUDY AND DISCUSSION QUESTIONS

1. Discuss Lawrence's three-paragraph opening. Do you find the way she leads up to and introduces her thesis effective?

2. What is the narrator's history with men? With women? What point is Lawrence making through this biographical outline?

3. The narrator calls attention to her class privilege, her "sense of entitlement" and her "actual entitlement." How do these factors affect the way she makes decisions and the way events subsequently turn out?

4. By what method does the narrator finally choose to be inseminated? What were the other options available to her and why does she choose this way?

5. How do her parents react to her choices about her sexuality and about her maternity? Would you say this reaction is usual or unusual?

6. What kinds of feelings does the narrator experience during her three- to four-year journey toward becoming a mother? Give examples for each type.

7. How would you characterize Lawrence's writing style in "The Death of Fred Astaire"?

SUGGESTIONS FOR WRITING

1. So, what does becoming a mother as part of a lesbian couple have to do with the death of Fred Astaire? Discuss how Lawrence uses images of dance as a metaphorical structure in her essay.

2. Toward the end of her essay, Lawrence writes a letter to her unborn son. Write a letter from Max back to his mother, imagining that he is now somewhere between eighteen and twenty-five years old.

3. How might this story have been different if the narrator had been less privileged? What if she had not been middle class, or what if she had not been white?

HUMAN OBSOLESCENCE

Jules Henry

Anthropologist Jules Henry (1904–1969) taught at Washington University in St. Louis and studied cultures in Mexico and Brazil as well as in the United States. Among his books are Culture Against Man *(1963), from which the following is excerpted, and* Pathways to Madness *(1965), a study of five dysfunctional American families.*

This chapter is about three hospitals for the aged: Municipal Sanitarium ("Muni San"), Rosemont ("Hell's Vestibule") and Tower Nursing Home.[1] Though Muni San is supported by public funds, Rosemont and Tower Nursing Home are private, profit-making institutions. Tower is comfortable and humane, Rosemont is inhuman, and Muni San is somewhere in between.[2] Taken together these three institutions give a good picture of the kinds of fates that await most of the people who become sick and obsolete in our culture.

---

[1] The names Muni San, Tower, and Rosemont have been arbitrarily chosen and have no reference to any actual institutions that may bear the names. [Author's note]

[2] They were studied by trained graduate nurses under my direction. [Author's note]

MUNI SAN

Although Muni San has a vast number of beds, this study concerns only one part of it—a ward containing around a hundred patients and having male and female sections. For these patients there were a registered nurse and about a dozen attendants spread over three shifts. A doctor made regular rounds and patients were bathed twice a week. Linens were changed when the patients were bathed or were incontinent. The patients were adequately fed and kept clean, though it often took the help a long time to get around to it. Although Muni San does what it can within the limits of a penurious budget, the patients suffer psychologically from the impersonality and vastness of the setting.

A NOTE ON THE SOCIAL CONSCIENCE

Public institutions for sick "social security paupers"—those who have no income but their social security checks—are ruled by the social conscience; that is to say, obvious things that readily excite conventional feelings of right and wrong are taken account of within the limits of miserly budgets, but everything else is slighted. For example, an institution may have plenty of medicine and an abundance of sterile gauze, but the medicine is often administered by ignorant persons and the gauze contaminated by ill-trained aides. Bedding, even when sufficient, may be dingy grey because of penny-pinching on soap and bleach. Food may be adequate but distributed in assembly-line fashion and eaten within obligatory time limits. Every bed may have a thin blanket sufficient for the regulated temperature of the institution, but if the heating breaks down or the staff decides to open the windows when the outside temperature is freezing, the patients are unprotected. Thus, were the social conscience to inquire whether the inmates had enough of what they need, the answer would be "yes," and the social conscience, easily lulled by appearances and small expenditures, would sleep on.

Always interested more in outward seeming than inner reality, always eager not to be stirred or get involved too much, always afraid of "pampering" its public charges and more given to the expression of drives than of values, the social conscience cannot be stirred to a concern with "psychology" unless some terrible evil, like juvenile delinquency, rages across the land. Hence, the spiritual degradation and hopelessness of its obsolete charges seem none of its affair. The social conscience is affected by things having "high visibility," like clean floors, freshly painted walls, and plenty of medical supplies, rather than by those having "low visibility," like personal involvement. A nurse in a mental hospital once put it to me this way: "When you go off duty they can tell if you've got a clean dressing room, but they can't tell if you've talked to a patient." In an institution for obsolete social security paupers the supervisor can tell whether or not a patient has been bathed but not whether the aide who did it spent a little extra time bathing the patient as if he was a human being rather than something inanimate. Since too many minutes devoted to being human will make an aide late in getting her quota of patients "done," they are washed like a row of sinks, and their privacy is violated because there is no time to move screens around or to manipulate the bedclothes in a way that preserves the patient's sense of modesty.

In many primitive societies the soul is imagined to leave the body at death or just prior to it; here, on the other hand, society drives out the remnants of the soul of the institutionalized old person while it struggles to keep his body alive. Routinization, inattention, carelessness, and the deprivation of communication—the chance to talk, to respond, to read, to see pictures on the wall, to be called by one's name rather than "you" or no name at all—are ways in which millions of once useful but now obsolete human beings are detached from their selves long before they are lowered into the grave.

THE NATURE AND CAUSES OF STILLNESS

As one enters a public hospital for the aged the thing that first impresses him is the stillness. It is natural that a tomb for the living should be silent, and since those who work in such a depressing atmosphere need something to sustain them, the wards present the paradox of a tomblike hush pervaded by the rasping throb of rock 'n roll music:

> The patients in the first section sat quietly by their neatly made beds except for one bedfast patient. There was no conversation between patients. The windows were frosted over. The radio beat out rock 'n roll. One man was reading. The rest of the ambulatory patients were just sitting.

These patients are not silent because they are too sick to move but because hospital "life," as we shall see, does something to them. But let us continue on our way.

> Two men were sleeping and two were reading, one with his back to the ward. One sat in a chair at the end of his bed, just sitting. A third sat in a wheelchair holding his urinal, which he used as a spitoon. One patient walked through on his way out of the ward. That was the only activity on this section.
>
> The first section of the men's ward was still, with the exception of the rock 'n roll. By this I mean that there was absolutely no activity. Mr. Bergstrom and Mr. Xavier were not on the ward.
>
> Mr. Erik was sitting dressed on the side of his unmade bed. Mr. Quall sat in his chair by the window, facing the wall.

Mr. Anison lay propped up in bed watching Elsie, an aide who had come in and started to mop. She moved his bed, pulling and pushing it as she cleaned without a word to him.

"Noisy" patients who get into animated discussions are put into "noisy" sections, or are moved from place to place until they find patients who will not respond to them, and so settle down. One day the observer

asked the head nurse if there was a way of telling which patient was in which bed according to the chart in the hall. She took me out and showed me how and explained that it was often inaccurate because patients were moved frequently.

Since arguments among patients interfere with the smooth functioning of the hospital, the sensible thing is to interrupt communication between them and thus nip all possible disputes in the bud—or before the bud. Unruffled routine requires also that improbabilities be controlled and hence that all patients be perceived and treated as identical. In these circumstances the elimination of patients' individuality is first accomplished by dropping names:

The aides worked silently, speaking to the patients only to make requests such as "turn over," "sit down," and other remarks connected with the work at hand. The patients did what they were asked to do. The radio was playing rock 'n roll.

The aide Elsie walked over to Mr. Gratz who was sitting by his bedside table in a chair. She took him by the right shirt sleeve and said, "Get up." He got up and Elsie moved his chair across the aisle and then guided him over to sit down. He is blind.

Miss Jones, the aide, finished tucking the sheet around Mr. Stilter and went over to Mr. Sprocket's bed. She tugged him on the arm and said, "Sit over here—I want to make the bed." He looked at her and didn't say anything but got up and sat in the chair holding his head in his hands.

Gertrude Beck came into the room and went over to one of the beds and turned the patient on her side without saying anything except to another aide, Miss Jones. She pulled up the gown exposing the patient's buttocks and gave her an injection. I glanced back at the patient as Beck left the room and saw that the patient was still on her side, buttocks exposed, blood oozing from the injection site. Jones saw this about the same time I did and came over and pulled the sheet up and patted the blood with it without saying anything.

The patients, of course, know that they are not addressed by name not only because that's the way of the hospital but because often their names are not known—there are so many of them and they are moved around so much:

Miss Ruuzman, the head nurse, leaned over Mr. Cronach's bed to look at his name card at the head of his bed and then walked rapidly back up the ward and out. Mr. Cronach said indignantly, "If she looks at that bed-card much more she may remember my name." "Mr. Cronach, I presume," I said inanely.

Nameless, handled like things, deprived in the vast silences of the hospital of the opportunity to give and receive human response; without property, and reduced almost below the capacity to experience disgust by the hospital's enormous delay in cleaning up bedpans, commodes, and soiled bedclothes, the patient is like a wanderer in one of Piranesi's prisons.

THE PROBLEM OF FALSE HOPE

As I passed through one of the wards I saw Mr. Yarmouth. He waved and motioned for me to come over. The first thing he asked was, "Do you live near my brother near King Street?" It seems that Mr. Yarmouth wanted me to find out if his brother was going to bring Mr. Yarmouth's other shoe. He pointed to his feet and I could see that he had a shoe on his right foot but none on his left. Mr. Yarmouth continued to tell me that he hoped his brother wouldn't let him down; his brother was supposed to bring his other shoe. I told him I lived on Maple and he said, "No, that isn't near my brother." He said if he only had his other shoe he could get up and around. He said that if his brother didn't get the shoe for him Reverend Burr would. The Reverend had promised that he would see about it. Mr. Yarmouth said, "Let's see, today's Friday isn't it?" and I said, "Yes." He said, "Well, there is still Saturday and Sunday maybe. I won't give up hope, I never give up hope." I said, "No, don't ever give up."

The record does not tell whether or not Mr. Yarmouth ever got his other shoe; but his dependence on relatives and children—who often do not come—for even a shoe, his anguish of hope, his sense of being trapped, are repeated themes.

The history of Mr. Yarmouth's eyeglasses is more complete than the brief tale of his missing shoe.

First day.   Mr. Yarmouth waved at me and then motioned for me to come over to where he sat in a chair at the foot of his bed. I said, "Hi, how are you today?" He said "Fine," and then asked if I would make a phone call for him. I said I'd be glad to if I could. He then asked if I had a dime and I replied that I did not. It turned out that he wanted reading glasses that his brother had. He said that he had lost his and needed them badly. I told him that I would ask Miss Everson and left him to do so. I found her and told her that Mr. Yarmouth had asked me to call his brother about his glasses and she walked to the desk and wrote this down in a little green book. She was very friendly and said that sometimes the men didn't even have relatives and that then the hospital tried to take care of these things. I replied that I would tell him that

I'd talked with her about it and she said, "No" and wrote something in the book. I thanked her and went back to the ward. Mr. Yarmouth asked me if I had any money and I said no, and I told him I talked with Miss Everson, and he said, "Who's that?" I explained that she was the charge nurse and was going to take care of his glasses. He seemed satisfied.

Who is Miss Everson anyway, and what is Mr. Yarmouth to her? "Sometimes," says Miss Everson, "the men [those identityless hundreds] don't even have relatives." As for this particular man, lacking particular eyeglasses, Miss Everson does not know whether or not he has a brother. Like a figure in a dream, writing in a phantom book where all that is written washes away, the charge nurse notes Mr. Yarmouth's request. But the act of writing is an act of magic and an act of pseudo-communication: by writing him down she has done away with Mr. Yarmouth, and the fact that Miss Everson is a make-believe listener writing a make-believe message makes the transmission of the observer's message and the writing in the book a pseudo-communication.

But to Mr. Yarmouth the communication was real:

Third day.   Mr. Yarmouth, who was sitting in a chair at the foot of his bed, beckoned me to come over, "Did you get my brother about my glasses?" I was absolutely amazed. I told him that I hadn't been able to make the call but that Miss Everson had written the request down. "Who's Miss Everson?" he asked. "When does the mail come?" I said I didn't know but that I would go and ask Miss Everson about the mail and the glasses. He kept urging me to find out even though I assured him I would as soon as I could find Miss Everson. (Later) Mr. Yarmouth beckoned to me wildly. "You forgot me," he said, "I knew you would." "No I didn't really forget you, Mr. Yarmouth, I just haven't found Miss Everson yet, but she's here somewhere." "Well, you be sure and tell me." I promised I would.

Mr. Yarmouth is sick—sick with false hope, a grave illness in the hospital. Symptoms of this disease are noisiness, demandingness, and the delusion that something one wants desperately is going to happen. The inner function of the delusion is to prevent the patient from thinking he is dead. Patients afflicted with false hope may become difficult to manage: for example, Mr. Yarmouth had the observer running back and forth stupidly between him and Miss Everson.

When I found Miss Everson I told her that I had been amazed that Mr. Yarmouth had remembered me, and that he had asked me about his glasses. Miss Everson was very nice and seemed surprised too. She said, "Just tell him *you're* working on it."
    Then I went back to Mr. Yarmouth and told him "they're working on it—they're trying to get your glasses." He seemed satisfied and I left, waving at him as I went.

Miss Everson, who seems to understand the signs and symptoms well, handles the naive observer with sweet and consummate tact: "Just tell him *you're* working on it," she says. What else could she do? If the hospital were to call or write the patients' relatives for "every little thing" it would have to hire a special staff just to handle the phone calls and the correspondence.

The symptom that clinches the diagnosis of false hope is the anger of the staff at the patient.

> Fifth day.   I noticed that Mr. Yarmouth had been moved to the left corner of the ward in Mr. Worth's place. He saw me, waved and asked me, "Have they come yet?" I called back, "Not yet."

> Sixth day.   Mr. Yarmouth was still at his window. I went over to him and asked what he was doing in his new spot and he told me that they had moved him around, he didn't know why, and that he had nothing to do but look at the wall. I replied, "Don't do that, look out the window." "I'm trying to," he answered. He was very subdued today.

Mr. Yarmouth had been moved for being argumentative and noisy: frustration over the glasses was more than he could bear.

> Eighth day.   Mr. Yarmouth sat in exactly the same position he has been in since he was moved into this section. He was sitting by the window facing the wall by his bed. He is so subdued it is striking. . . . When he saw me Mr. Yarmouth beckoned to me to come over. He used to do this with a kind of devilishness but now he is almost lethargic, and when he asked me about his glasses and I told him I hadn't been able to find out about them he just accepted this, although in the past he has insisted that I let him know when I'll tell him. As I left he said, with a pathetic attempt to bolster his self-esteem, "Be sure to send the bill to me."

Mr. Yarmouth is "improving." He is giving up hope, yet his self-esteem still prods him into futile gestures of adequacy, as he clings to the idea and the memory of reading and of eyes that served him once:

> Tenth day.   Mr. Yarmouth with his back to the window. He asked me again about his glasses and I again told him that the order was written down. He knows he won't get them and so do I, so all of this is just a farce. I finally couldn't stand it any more and patting him on the shoulder told him I'd see him later.

> Twelfth day.   Mr. Yarmouth got out a Christian Science booklet to show me how he can read the larger headings but not the smaller print. "You know," he said, "I'm getting nervous, all I can do is sit here and read, and I have to have glasses." His request is only reasonable and I feel like a heel about it— how ineffectual can you be? Now he asks me about calling his nephew instead of his brother. We talked about Mr. Yarmouth's having been an oculist:

"All the doctors used to call me and tell what they wanted and then I'd see that it was done and out on time. They depended on me."

Thus ends the saga of Mr. Yarmouth's glasses. Not once in his false hope did he make contact directly with one of the staff; his only channel of communication—or shall we say, pseudo-communication—was the observer. To him the hospital was a remote impersonal "They," inexorable and inscrutable like the prosecution in Kafka's *The Trial*. With not enough money for even a phone call, with nobody coming to see him, Mr. Yarmouth is marooned, and being marooned he is "nervous." When in his anxiety he argues with those around him, he is moved around and away from the patients he knows by the same "They" that promise to get his glasses but never do. He is punished for remaining human.

THE FEELING OF BEING DISCARDED

As one comes to know these patients one develops a feeling of unreality about their relatives: do they exist or don't they? Take the case of Mrs. Kohn.

> She was sitting in her wheelchair beside her bed, embroidering. She showed me the pillow cases and showed me how to make French knots. At first she talked slowly, but when she got on the subject of her nieces she talked more rapidly. She took hold of my hand and held it. She said, "I have a niece living in town. Every year she goes to Wisconsin on vacation and sends me a card saying, 'I'll be seeing you soon,' and she never does come to see me."

The feeling of being discarded makes them cling to whoever shows a human interest. Holding on for dear life to their remnants of life and humanness is an idiosyncrasy of human obsolescence:

> I had only been in there for a few minutes when Mrs. Ramsey in her bed began calling out, "I'm cold, I'm cold. Cover me up." I walked over to her bed and she grabbed my hand and said, "Cover me, cover me up." I told her that her hands were cold and I pulled the covers up on them.

We have studied the process of becoming obsolete through the history of one man, Mr. Yarmouth; let us now observe a woman. Mrs. Prilmer was moved around, just like Mr. Yarmouth, because she was "noisy." Let us follow her for a few days:

> First day.   As I entered the ward Mrs. Prilmer who was sitting on the edge of her bed motioned for me to come over, calling, "Here, here." I went over to her and she took my hand and held on to my arm trying to pull herself up, saying, "Take me to the office, call me a cab, I want to go home. Help me, I

can't walk." I said, "I can't do that," but she said, "Yes you can." A patient walked up and said, "Are you her daughter?" and I said, "No." Then the patient said, "She has a daughter and three sons," and Mrs. Prilmer affirmed, "Yes, my daughter lives in Boston; my son comes to visit me every day." So I suggested that she talk to her son about going home, but she replied, "He isn't coming today." I asked, "But I thought you said he came to see you every day?" and Mrs. Prilmer answered, "But he isn't coming today." So I walked over to the aide Miss Jones who was making a bed on the other side of the ward and told her what had happened. She laughed and said, "She used to be so quiet. Tell her her son will be here this afternoon." But I mentioned what I had told her and what answer I had received. "Maybe it would be better if you told her." So Miss Jones went over. Meanwhile I started talking with Mrs. Kohn and she said, "I've been waiting for physiotherapy to come after me. Sometimes I sit here and wait all day and they don't come. I think I'd be just as well off sitting at home." I nodded and Mrs. Kohn pointed to Mrs. Prilmer, saying, "She goes on like that all the time, even during the night. She stops anybody who'll talk to her; I think she's a little feeble-minded." Just then the aide walked away and Mrs. Prilmer called after her and said she wanted to go home. Jones answered, "I'll tell you what, I'll call the superintendent of the hospital; I'll send him over to see you, O.K.?" When Mrs. Prilmer said, "Yes," Jones and several of the patients laughed.

The record reads further: Finally I left just as an attendant was entering with a heavy cloth strap. Alice (another nurse-observer) asked if Mrs. Prilmer was going to be restrained with that. I said I thought so but I didn't return to find out.

There prevails among us a nightmare *Dream of the Trap*, which is the opposite of the *Midsummer Night's Dream*.[3] In the *Dream of the Trap* we are imprisoned by a malevolent "They"; we struggle to escape; we yearn for friends who never come. In our midnight terror we sometimes whimper, sometimes scream without sound. This dream is fear of desertion, of failure, of loss of self to coercive "forces." The hospital is the dream come true. The benign observer, of course, was an intruder in the dream, and had she not spoken to Miss Jones about Mrs. Prilmer the old lady would have been ignored. Mrs. Prilmer, starring in her last role, performed it as if she had practiced it many times in dreams: she seized the observer, clung to her, and tried to escape, through her, back to the outer world that had buried her here.

The other patients, usually too ignorant or too much in need themselves, attack one another, so that instead of helping they make things worse. So Mrs. Kohn, who has clung to the observer herself, assails Mrs. Prilmer and, talking out loud as if she was not there to hear her, says, "I think she's a

---

[3] Play by William Shakespeare.

little feeble-minded." Mrs. Burns from her wheelchair tried to help Mrs. Prilmer, but it did little good: Mrs. Prilmer even antagonized Rosemary, a "good" aide:

> Eighth day.   From Mrs. Prilmer I could hear, "My son, my son." Mrs. Lorenz answered something and Mrs. Burns said, "You're mean." From her wheelchair she threw Mrs. Prilmer a rag saying, "Here, blow your nose."
>
> The aide Rosemary was around doing chores and Mrs. Burns said, "We need some more Rosemarys." I agreed. Rosemary helped Mrs. Kohn off the bedpan and passed out clean but badly wrinkled towels. As Mrs. Burns took one she observed, "It seems to me they could run these things through the mangle; it would be easier on these people's skins, but they don't care about them." As Rosemary took care of Mrs. Prilmer she called the old lady "squeaky," remarking that Mrs. Prilmer "squeaks" all the time. "Are you gonna be quiet now?" Mrs. Prilmer nodded assent, but made a face and motioned with her hand for Rosemary to go away. Rosemary said, "Don't you like me?" and when Mrs. Prilmer answered, "No," Rosemary said, "O.K., if you don't like me I don't like you either." Rosemary left and went into the next ward and Mrs. Prilmer, looking agitated, sat tapping with her hand on the arm of her chair.

After all, what is there in life for an ignorant, poorly paid helper in a human junkyard? A minority discover that what can save *their* lives is to be good to the patients within the limits of miserly budgets and pressure toward routine. But when an ungrateful patient turns and says, "I don't like you," it is too much. A week later Mrs. Prilmer had been moved in with the "noisy" patients.

> I noticed all the patients in this room have been changed since I was last in here. They moved all the "louder" patients into this room. Mrs. Prilmer sat over in the corner to the left. As soon as I entered the room she called "Nurse, nurse, nurse." I must say that I was slightly overwhelmed when I entered, but when I recovered I went over to Mrs. Prilmer and she seized my arm and pulled me down toward her, for she was sitting on a commode near her bed. Her stockings had fallen down to her ankles. She talked fast and furiously, "How is your mama? How is your papa?" She told me that her head hurt and that she wasn't feeling very good. As I talked to her she held my arm with one hand and stroked it with the other. She kept talking on and on: it seemed as though she would say anything just to keep me there.

Of course, one has to be sensible about these things: what are you going to do with noisy and distracted patients with phantom relatives? Where are you going to get the money to pay for enough help, let alone enough help skilled psychologically to deal with these people who have been cast aside like old fenders? An administrator threw up his hands:

I've got to remember that some of the help can't do anything but give bed baths: they were hired right off the streets and they just don't know. Of course, I've got some that can't learn either. Some can hardly read or write.

So you put the noisy ones all together to get them out of the way of the quiet ones, to isolate them so they won't disturb the help, but especially as an implied threat to anyone with noisy inclinations: if he doesn't keep quiet that's where he'll end up.

DEHUMANIZATION AND DEATH

If in every human contact something is communicated, something learned, and something felt, it follows that where nothing is communicated, learned, or felt there is nothing human either. The vast hospital silences, particularly on the men's side, tell us that humanness is ebbing there. The very quietness, however, informs the inmates—not so much because they think it, but rather because they feel it—that they are not human beings. As long as they remain physically alive, nevertheless, they seem never to lose the ability to feel: the primordial capacity for adaptive radiation which is lost only when the cells die remains, expressed, however feebly, in attitude and behavior:

> Mr. Unger sat in his wheelchair by the foot of his bed. He was dressed and wore a black corduroy cap. He was holding a urinal in his lap like a spitoon, and the neck of it was bloody. I said, "Good morning, Mr. Unger, how are you?" He looked up at me (he sits with his head down), smiled, and reached out to shake my hand. I get a warm feeling from Mr. Unger and am fond of him. Next to him sat Mr. Butler, dressed, in a chair: he was just staring. A bedpan with dried feces sat uncovered in front of Mr. Butler's bedside table on the floor.

So they feel they are not human, and from this comes anguish that expresses itself in clinging. But silence is not the only form of dehumanizing communication to which these people are exposed. Empty walls, rows of beds close together, the dreariness of their fellow inmates, the bedpans, the odors, the routinization, all tell them they have become junk. Capping it all is the hostility of the patients to one another and the arbitrary movement from place to place like empty boxes in a storeroom. At the end is a degraded death.

> I stopped at the desk to look at Mr. Naron's chart and noted what orders were written. The aide Myrtle saw me and told me, "He's going to die today. The priest[4] was up here this morning already." One of the orders I noted read, "Side rails to be applied," but on going back to the unit I saw that there were

---

[4] During the study no clergyman was seen on the wards. [Author's note]

no side rails on Mr. Naron's bed. He was turning from side to side and was quite restless. The aides Elizabeth and Frost were standing by his bed. Elizabeth was fingering the soiled adhesive tape that was keeping the nasal oxygen tube in place, and she asked Frost, "Can you change this?" and Frost responded very hostilely, "No, they won't let me do it; I'm not supposed to be bright enough." Then she nodded in the direction of Mr. Naron and remarked, "He's keeping me from doing my work; I'm behind now." Elizabeth shrugged her shoulders and walked on.

Frost looked at Mr. Naron and then went over to another bed and began making it. Mr. Naron was not screened off from the rest of the patients although there was a screen against the wall, not in use. The patients who were sitting in chairs would occasionally look in Mr. Naron's direction, and as I passed by them I heard these comments: "Ain't he dead yet? The priest already been here. I wonder how much longer he's going to be." Most of the patients who were in chairs were just staring down at the floor. There was no conversation among them except for an occasional whispered, "Is he dead?"

Thus passed Mr. Naron: a nuisance to the end, interfering with people's work; surrounded, perhaps, in his last moments, by his own phantom community of brothers, sisters, and children. He died as he had lived: he was just a "he" and a "him" without a name; people talked about him as if he were not there. To the end people did not do what they were supposed to do, and to the end he was tended by help who barely knew their jobs. No one held his hand, there were no tears, only a corroding irritation that he was taking so long to die—while the social conscience stood piously by, trying its respectable best to keep Mr. Naron alive with an oxygen tube fastened to his nose with a piece of dirty adhesive. Society is satisfied that it has "done its best" when it pours oxygen into a dying man. That he has first been degraded to the level of social junk is none of its affair.

STUDY AND DISCUSSION QUESTIONS

1. What, specifically, are the two sides of the dilemma a public institution for impoverished patients faces?

2. List several ways in which patients' individuality is taken away by such institutions.

3. From the point of view of the staff at Muni San, what is the rationale for the way the patients are treated?

4. Define what Henry means by "false hope." What are its symptoms? Why do patients engage in it?

5. What do you find particularly striking in the story of Mr. Yarmouth and his glasses?

6. What does the story about Mrs. Prilmer and Rosemary illustrate?

7. What are the ways in which Mr. Naron's death is less than dignified?

8. Why do you think Jules Henry structures his essay around stories of individual patients? What effect does this choice have on the reader? How does it help carry out Henry's purpose in this essay?

9. What is a "noisy" patient? Why are such patients noisy? What happens to them?

10. What does money have to do with the situation at Muni San? List some examples from the essay.

SUGGESTIONS FOR WRITING

1. Look up the words "obsolete" and "obsolescence." How are old people made to feel obsolete in Muni San?

2. Try this thought experiment: imagine that you are seventy-eight years old and in an institution like Muni San. Write in first-person narration about your day.

3. What do you think should be "done" about the elderly? Consider a range of possibilities and argue for one.

CARNAL ACTS

Nancy Mairs

Nancy Mairs was born in 1943 in Long Beach, California and studied at Wheaton College and the University of Arizona. Early in her career, she wrote several books of poetry, including Instead It Is Winter *(1977). She then turned to autobiographical essays, which have been collected in such volumes as* Plain Text *(1986),* Carnal Acts: Essays *(1990), where the following appeared,* Voice Lessons: On Becoming a (Woman) Writer *(1994), and* Waist-High in the World: A Life Among the Nondisabled *(1997).*

Inviting me to speak at her small liberal-arts college during Women's Week, a young woman set me a task: "We would be pleased," she wrote, "if you could talk on how you cope with your M.S. disability, and also how you discovered your voice as a writer." Oh, Lord, I thought in dismay, how am I going to pull this one off? How can I yoke two such disparate subjects into a coherent presentation, without doing violence to one, or the other, or both, or myself? This is going to take some fancy footwork, and my feet scarcely carry out the basic steps, let alone anything elaborate.

To make matters worse, the assumption underlying each of her questions struck me as suspect. To ask *how* I cope with multiple sclerosis suggests that I *do* cope. Now, "to cope," *Webster's Third* tells me, is "to face or encounter and to find necessary expedients to overcome problems and difficulties." In these terms, I have to confess, I don't feel like much of a coper. I'm likely to deal with my problems and difficulties by squawking and flapping around like that hysterical chicken who was convinced the sky was falling. Never mind that in my case the sky really *is* falling. In response to a clonk on the head, regardless of its origin, one might comport oneself with a grace and courtesy I generally lack.

As for "finding" my voice, the implication is that it was at one time lost or missing. But I don't think it ever was. Ask my mother, who will tell you a little wearily that I was speaking full sentences by the time I was a year old and could never be silenced again. As for its being a writer's voice, it seems to have become one early on. Ask Mother again. At the age of eight I rewrote the Trojan War, she will say, and what Nestor was about to do to Helen at the end doesn't bear discussion in polite company.

Faced with these uncertainties, I took my own teacherly advice, something, I must confess, I don't always do. "If an idea is giving you trouble," I tell my writing students, "put it on the back burner and let it simmer while you do something else. Go to the movies. Reread a stack of old love letters. Sit in your history class and take detailed notes on the Teapot Dome scandal.[1] If you've got your idea in mind, it will go on cooking at some level no matter what else you're doing." "I've had an idea for my documented essay on the back burner," one of my students once scribbled in her journal, "and I think it's just boiled over!"

I can't claim to have reached such a flash point. But in the weeks I've had the themes "disability" and "voice" sitting around in my head, they seem to have converged on their own, without my having to wrench them together and bind them with hoops of tough rhetoric. They *are* related, indeed interdependent, with an intimacy that has for some reason remained, until now, submerged below the surface of my attention. Forced to juxtapose them, I yank them out of the depths, a little startled to discover how they

---

[1] 1921 controversy in which the illegal sale of federal oil land in Teapot Dome, Wyoming caused the resignation of the Secretary of the Interior.

were intertwined down there out of sight. This kind of discovery can un-
nerve you at first. You feel like a giant hand that, pulling two swimmers out
of the water, two separate heads bobbling on the iridescent swells, finds the
two bodies below, legs coiled around each other, in an ecstasy of copulation.
You don't quite know where to turn your eyes.

Perhaps the place to start illuminating this erotic connection between
who I am and how I speak lies in history. I have known that I have multiple
sclerosis for about seventeen years now, though the disease probably started
long before. The hypothesis is that the disease process, in which the protective covering of the nerves in the brain and spinal cord is eaten away and replaced by scar tissue, "hard patches," is caused by an autoimmune reaction to
a slow-acting virus. Research suggests that I was infected by this virus, which
no one has ever seen and which therefore, technically, doesn't even "exist,"
between the ages of four and fifteen. In effect, living with this mysterious
mechanism feels like having your present self, and the past selves it embodies, haunted by a capricious and meanspirited ghost, unseen except for its
footprints, which trips you even when you're watching where you're going,
knocks glassware out of your hand, squeezes the urine out of your bladder before you reach the bathroom, and weights your whole body with a weariness
no amount of rest can relieve. An alien invader must be at work. But of course
it's not. It's your own body. That is, it's you.

This, for me, has been the most difficult aspect of adjusting to a chronic
incurable degenerative disease: the fact that it has rammed my "self" straight
back into the body I had been trained to believe it could, through high-
minded acts and aspirations, rise above. The Western tradition of distin-
guishing the body from the mind and/or the soul is so ancient as to have
become part of our collective unconscious, if one is inclined to believe in
such a noumenon, or at least to have become an unquestioned element in
the social instruction we impose upon infants from birth, in much the same
way we inculcate, without reflection, the gender distinctions "female" and
"male." I *have* a body, you are likely to say if you talk about embodiment at
all; you don't say, I *am* a body. A body is a separate entity possessable by the
"I"; the "I" and the body aren't, as the copula would make them, grammati-
cally indistinguishable.

To widen the rift between the self and the body, we treat our bodies as
subordinates, inferior in moral status. Open association with them shames us.
In fact, we treat our bodies with very much the same distance and ambivalence women have traditionally received from men in our culture. Sometimes
this treatment is benevolent, even respectful, but all too often it is tainted by
outright sadism. I think of the bodybuilding regimens that have become popular in the last decade or so, with the complicated vacillations they reflect
between self-worship and self-degradation: joggers and aerobic dancers and

weightlifters all beating their bodies into shape. "No pain, no gain," the saying goes. "Feel the burn." Bodies get treated like wayward women who have to be shown who's boss, even if it means slapping them around a little. I'm not for a moment opposing rugged exercise here. I'm simply questioning the spirit in which it is often undertaken.

Since, as Hélène Cixous points out in her essay on women and writing, "Sorties,"[2] thought has always worked "through dual, hierarchical oppositions" (p. 64), the mind/body split cannot possibly be innocent. The utterance of an "I" immediately calls into being its opposite, the "not-I" Western discourse being unequipped to conceive "that which is neither 'I' nor 'not-I,'" "that which is both 'I' and 'not-I'" or some other permutation which language doesn't permit me to speak. The "not-I" is, by definition, other. And we've never been too fond of the other. We prefer the same. We tend to ascribe to the other those qualities we prefer not to associate with ourselves: it is the hidden, the dark, the secret, the shameful. Thus, when the "I" takes possession of the body, it makes the body into another, direct object of a transitive verb, with all the other's repudiated and potentially dangerous qualities.

At the least, then, the body had best be viewed with suspicion. And a woman's body is particularly suspect, since so much of it is in fact hidden, dark, secret, carried about on the inside where, even with the aid of a speculum, one can never perceive all of it in the plain light of day, a graspable whole. I, for one, have never understood why anyone would want to carry all that delicate stuff around on the outside. It would make you awfully anxious, I should think, put you constantly on the defensive, create a kind of siege mentality that viewed all other beings, even your own kind, as threats to be warded off with spears and guns and atomic missiles. And you'd never get to experience that inward dreaming that comes when your flesh surrounds all your treasures, holding them close like a sturdy shuttered house. Be my personal skepticism as it may, however, as a cultural woman I bear just as much shame as any woman for my dark, enfolded secrets. Let the word for my external genitals tell the tale: my pudendum, from the Latin infinitive meaning "to be ashamed."

It's bad enough to carry your genitals like a sealed envelope bearing the cipher that, once unlocked, might loose the chaotic flood of female pleasure—*jouissance*, the French call it—upon the world-of-the-same. But I have an additional reason to feel shame for my body, less explicitly connected with its sexuality: it is a crippled body. Thus it is doubly other, not merely by the homosexual standards of patriarchal culture but by the standards of physical desirability erected for every body in our world. Men, who are by definition

---

[2] In *The Newly Born Woman*, translated by Betsy Wing (Minneapolis: University of Minnesota Press, 1986). [Author's note]

exonerated from shame in sexual terms (this doesn't mean that an individual man might not experience sexual shame, of course; remember that I'm talking in general about discourse, not folks), may—more likely must—experience bodily shame if they are crippled. I won't presume to speak about the details of their experience, however. I don't know enough. I'll just go on telling what it's like to be a crippled woman, trusting that, since we're fellow creatures who've been living together for some thousands of years now, much of my experience will resonate with theirs.

I was never a beautiful woman, and for that reason I've spent most of my life (together with probably at least 95 percent of the female population of the United States) suffering from the shame of falling short of an unattainable standard. The ideal woman of my generation was . . . perky, I think you'd say, rather than gorgeous. Blond hair pulled into a bouncing ponytail. Wide blue eyes, a turned-up nose with maybe a scattering of golden freckles across it, a small mouth with full lips over straight white teeth. Her breasts were large but well harnessed high on her chest; her tiny waist flared to hips just wide enough to give the crinolines under her circle skirt a starting outward push. In terms of personality, she was outgoing, even bubbly, not pensive or mysterious. Her milieu was the front fender of a white Corvette convertible, surrounded by teasing crewcuts, dressed in black flats, a sissy blouse, and the letter sweater of the Corvette owner. Needless to say, she never missed a prom.

Ten years or so later, when I first noticed the symptoms that would be diagnosed as MS, I was probably looking my best. Not beautiful still, but the ideal had shifted enough so that my flat chest and narrow hips gave me an elegantly attenuated shape, set off by a thick mass of long, straight, shining hair. I had terrific legs, long and shapely, revealed nearly to the pudendum by the fashionable miniskirts and hot pants I adopted with more enthusiasm than delicacy of taste. Not surprisingly, I suppose, during this time I involved myself in several pretty torrid love affairs.

The beginning of MS wasn't too bad. The first symptom, besides the pernicious fatigue that had begun to devour me, was "foot drop," the inability to raise my left foot at the ankle. As a consequence, I'd started to limp, but I could still wear high heels, and a bit of a limp might seem more intriguing than repulsive. After a few months, when the doctor suggested a cane, a crippled friend gave me quite an elegant wood-and-silver one, which I carried with a fair amount of panache. The real blow to my self-image came when I had to get a brace. As braces go, it's not bad: lightweight plastic molded to my foot and leg, fitting down into an ordinary shoe and secured around my calf by a Velcro strap. It reduces my limp and, more important, the danger of tripping and falling. But it meant the end of high heels. And it's ugly. Not as ugly as I think it is, I gather, but still pretty ugly. It signified for me, and perhaps still does, the permanence and irreversibility of my condition. The brace makes my MS concrete and forces me to wear it on the outside. As soon as I strapped the brace on, I climbed into trousers and stayed there (though not in the same trousers, of course). The idea of going around with my bare brace hanging out seemed almost as indecent as exposing my breasts. Not until 1984, soon after I won the Western States Book Award for poetry, did I put on a skirt short enough to reveal my plasticized leg. The connection between winning a writing award and baring my brace is not merely fortuitous; being affirmed as a writer really did embolden me. Since then, I've grown so accustomed to wearing skirts that I don't think about my brace any more than I think about my cane. I've incorporated them, I suppose: made them, in their necessity, insensate but fundamental parts of my body.

Meanwhile, I had to adjust to the most outward and visible sign of all, a three-wheeled electric scooter called an Amigo. This lessens my fatigue and increases my range terrifically, but it also shouts out to the world, "Here is a woman who can't stand on her own two feet." At the same time, paradoxically, it renders me invisible, reducing me to the height of a seven-year-old, with a child's attendant low status. "Would she like smoking or nonsmoking?" the gate agent assigning me a seat asks the friend traveling with me. In crowds I see nothing but buttocks. I can tell you the name of every type of designer jeans ever sold. The wearers, eyes front, trip over me and fall across my handlebars into my lap. "Hey!" I want to shout to the lofty world. "Down here! There's a person down here!" But I'm not, by their standards, quite a person anymore.

My self-esteem diminishes further as age and illness strip from me the features that made me, for a brief while anyway, a good-looking, even sexy, young woman. No more long, bounding strides: I shuffle along with the timid gait I remember observing, with pity and impatience, in the little old ladies at Boston's Symphony Hall on Friday afternoons. No more lithe, girlish figure: my belly sags from the loss of muscle tone, which also creates all kinds of intestinal disruptions, hopelessly humiliating in a society in which excretory functions remain strictly unspeakable. No more sex, either, if society had its way. The sexuality of the disabled so repulses most people that you can hardly get a doctor, let alone a member of the general population, to consider the issues it raises. Cripples simply aren't supposed to Want It, much less Do It. Fortunately, I've got a husband with a strong libido and a weak sense of social propriety, or else I'd find myself perforce practicing a vow of chastity I never cared to take.

Afflicted by the general shame of having a body at all, and the specific shame of having one weakened and misshapen by disease, I ought not to be able to hold my head up in public. And yet I've gotten into the habit of holding my head up in public, sometimes under excruciating circumstances. Recently, for instance, I had to give a reading at the University of Arizona.

Having smashed three of my front teeth in a fall onto the concrete floor of my screened porch, I was in the process of getting them crowned, and the temporary crowns flew out during dinner right before the reading. What to do? I wanted, of course, to rush home and hide till the dental office opened the next morning. But I couldn't very well break my word at this last moment. So, looking like Hansel and Gretel's witch, and lisping worse than the Wife of Bath,[3] I got up on stage and read. Somehow, over the years, I've learned how to set shame aside and do what I have to do.

Here, I think, is where my "voice" comes in. Because, in spite of my demurral at the beginning, I do in fact cope with my disability at least some of the time. And I do so, I think, by speaking about it, and about the whole experience of being a body, specifically a female body, out loud, in a clear, level tone that drowns out the frantic whispers of my mother, my grandmothers, all the other trainers of wayward childish tongues: "Sssh! Sssh! Nice girls don't talk like that. Don't mention sweat. Don't mention menstrual blood. Don't ask what your grandfather does on his business trips. Don't laugh so loud. You sound like a loon. Keep your voice down. Don't tell. Don't tell. Don't tell." Speaking out loud is an antidote to shame. I want to distinguish clearly here between "shame," as I'm using the word, and "guilt" and "embarrassment," which, though equally painful, are not similarly poisonous. Guilt arises from performing a forbidden act or failing to perform a required one. In either case, the guilty person can, through reparation, erase the offense and start fresh. Embarrassment, less opprobrious though not necessarily less distressing, is generally caused by acting in a socially stupid or awkward way. When I trip and sprawl in public, when I wet myself, when my front teeth fly out, I feel horribly embarrassed, but, like the pain of childbirth, the sensation blurs and dissolves in time. If it didn't, every child would be an only child, and no one would set foot in public after the onset of puberty, when embarrassment erupts like a geyser and bathes one's whole life in its bitter stream. Shame may attach itself to guilt or embarrassment, complicating their resolution, but it is not the same emotion. I feel guilt or embarrassment for something I've done; shame, for who I am. I may stop doing bad or stupid things, but I can't stop being. How then can I help but be ashamed? Of the three conditions, this is the one that cracks and stifles my voice.

I can subvert its power, I've found, by acknowledging who I am, shame and all, and, in doing so, raising what was hidden, dark, secret about my life into the plain light of shared human experience. What we aren't permitted to utter holds us, each isolated from every other, in a kind of solipsistic thrall. Without any way to check our reality against anyone else's, we assume that

---

[3] Hansel, Gretel, and witch, characters in the Grimm Brothers' fairy tale, "Hansel and Gretel"; Wife of Bath, character in Geoffrey Chaucer's narrative poem, *The Canterbury Tales.*

our fears and shortcomings are ours alone. One of the strangest consequences of publishing a collection of personal essays called *Plaintext* has been the steady trickle of letters and telephone calls saying essentially, in a tone of unmistakable relief, "Oh, me too! Me too!" It's as though the part I thought was solo has turned out to be a chorus. But none of us was singing loud enough for the others to hear.

Singing loud enough demands a particular kind of voice, I think. And I was wrong to suggest, at the beginning, that I've always had my voice. I have indeed always had *a* voice, but it wasn't *this* voice, the one with which I could call up and transform my hidden self from a naughty girl into a woman talking directly to others like herself. Recently, in the process of writing a new book, a memoir entitled *Remembering the Bone House*, I've had occasion to read some of my early writing, from college, high school, even junior high. It's not an experience I recommend to anyone susceptible to shame. Not that the writing was all that bad. I was surprised at how competent a lot of it was. Here was a writer who already knew precisely how the language worked. But the voice . . . oh, the voice was all wrong: maudlin, rhapsodic, breaking here and there into little shrieks, almost, you might say, hysterical. It was a voice that had shucked off its own body, its own homely life of Cheerios for breakfast and seventy pages of Chaucer to read before the exam on Tuesday and a planter's wart growing painfully on the ball of its foot, and reeled now wraithlike through the air, seeking incarnation only as the heroine who enacts her doomed love for the tall, dark, mysterious stranger. If it didn't get that part, it wouldn't play at all.

Among all these overheated and vaporous imaginings, I must have retained some shred of sense, because I stopped writing prose entirely, except for scholarly papers, for nearly twenty years. I even forgot, not exactly that I had written prose, but at least what kind of prose it was. So when I needed to take up the process again, I could start almost fresh, using the vocal range I'd gotten used to in years of asking the waiter in the Greek restaurant for an extra anchovy on my salad, congratulating the puppy on making a puddle outside rather than inside the patio door, pondering with my daughter the vageries of female orgasm, saying goodbye to my husband, and hello, and goodbye, and hello. This new voice—thoughtful, affectionate, often amused—was essential because what I needed to write about when I returned to prose was an attempt I'd made not long before to kill myself, and suicide simply refuses to be spoken of authentically in high-flown romantic language. It's too ugly. Too shameful. Too strictly a bodily event. And, yes, too funny as well, though people are sometimes shocked to find humor shoved up against suicide. They don't like the incongruity. But let's face it, life (real life, I mean, not the edited-for-television version) is a cacophonous affair from start to finish. I might have wanted to portray my suicidal self as a languishing maiden, too exquisitely sensitive to sustain life's wounding pressures on her soul. (I didn't want to, as a matter of fact, but I might have.) The truth remained, regardless of my desires, that when my husband lugged me into the emergency room, my hair matted, my face swollen and gray, my nightgown streaked with blood and urine, I was no frail and tender spirit. I was a body, and one in a hell of a mess.

I "should" have kept quiet about that experience. I know the rules of polite discourse. I should have kept my shame, and the nearly lethal sense of isolation and alienation it brought, to myself. And I might have, except for something the psychiatrist in the emergency room had told my husband. "You might as well take her home," he said. "If she wants to kill herself, she'll do it no matter how many precautions we take. They always do." *They* always do. I was one of "them," whoever they were. I was, in this context anyway, not singular, not aberrant, but typical. I think it was this sense of commonality with others I didn't even know, a sense of being returned somehow, in spite of my appalling act, to the human family, that urged me to write that first essay, not merely speaking out but calling out, perhaps. "Here's the way I am," it said. "How about you?" And the answer came, as I've said: "Me too! Me too!"

This has been the kind of work I've continued to do: to scrutinize the details of my own experience and to report what I see, and what I think about what I see, as lucidly and accurately as possible. But because feminine experience has been immemorially devalued and repressed, I continue to find this task terrifying. "Every woman has known the torture of beginning to speak aloud," Cixous writes, "heart beating as if to break, occasionally falling into loss of language, ground and language slipping out from under her, because for woman speaking—even just opening her mouth—in public is something rash, a transgression" (p. 92).

The voice I summon up wants to crack, to whisper, to trail back into silence. "I'm sorry to have nothing more than this to say," it wants to apologize. "I shouldn't be taking up your time. I've never fought in a war, or even in a schoolyard free-for-all. I've never tried to see who could piss farthest up the barn wall. I've never even been to a whorehouse. All the important formative experiences have passed me by. I was raped once. I've borne two children. Milk trickling out of my breasts, blood trickling from between my legs. You don't want to hear about it. Sometimes I'm too scared to leave my house. Not scared *of* anything, just scared: mouth dry, bowels writhing. When the fear got really bad, they locked me up for six months, but that was years ago. I'm getting old now. Misshapen, too. I don't blame you if you can't get it up. No one could possibly desire a body like this. It's not your fault. It's mine. Forgive me. I didn't mean to start crying. I'm sorry . . . sorry . . . sorry. . . ."

An easy solace to the anxiety of speaking aloud: this slow subsidence beneath the waves of shame, back into what Cixous calls "this body that has been worse than confiscated, a body replaced with a disturbing stranger, sick or dead, who so often is a bad influence, the cause and place of inhibitions. By censuring the body," she goes on, "breath and speech are censored at the same time" (p. 97). But I am not going back, not going under one more time. To do so would demonstrate a failure of nerve far worse than the depredations of MS have caused. Paradoxically, losing one sort of nerve has given me another. No one is going to take my breath away. No one is going to leave me speechless. To be silent is to comply with the standard of feminine grace. But my crippled body already violates all notions of feminine grace. What more have I got to lose? I've gone beyond shame. I'm shameless, you might say. You know, as in "shameless hussy"? A woman with her bare brace and her tongue hanging out.

I've "found" my voice, then, just where it ought to have been, in the body-warmed breath escaping my lungs and throat. Forced by the exigencies of physical disease to embrace my self in the flesh, I couldn't write bodiless prose. The voice is the creature of the body that produces it. I speak as a crippled woman. At the same time, in the utterance I redeem both "cripple" and "woman" from the shameful silences by which I have often felt surrounded, contained, set apart; I give myself permission to live openly among others, to reach out for them, stroke them with fingers and sighs. No body, no voice; no voice, no body. That's what I know in my bones.

STUDY AND DISCUSSION QUESTIONS

1. Western tradition, says Mairs, teaches us that the body is separate from the mind and/or the soul. List some beliefs and/or behaviors that follow from this assumption, according to Mairs.

2. How is the body "other"?

3. What are a couple of ways in which the mind/body duality has been particularly problematic for women?

4. How is their relation to the body particularly problematical for people with a "chronic incurable degenerative disease" or, more generally, for those whose body is not functioning the way they feel it should— through illness, disability, or age?

5. What are the differences between guilt, embarrassment, and shame?

6. How does Mairs try to overcome shame?

7. How does Mairs's writing voice change during the twenty years she does not write prose?

8. What does Mairs say she does as a writer? Do you feel, having read this essay, that she accomplishes her aims? Give an example.

9. Mairs quotes French philosopher Hélène Cixous several times in this essay. Discuss the connections between body and voice that Cixous advances and that Mairs illustrates with her own experience.

10. How and why does Mairs become a "shameless hussy"?

11. Discuss the aptness of the title Mairs chose for this essay: "Carnal Acts."

SUGGESTIONS FOR WRITING

1. Nancy Mairs chooses to begin her essay by sharing the process by which she thought about the topic. Analyze what she does in each of the first six paragraphs of the essay. Where would you say she states its thesis?

2. Do you feel that you *have* a body or that you *are* a body? What kind of behavior in your own life would follow from each premise?

3. Discuss the psychology of shame as it relates to one's body and to one's voice, according to Mairs's essay. How might social factors like gender, race, age, class status, and physical capability affect the workings of shame?

4. What are the "rules of polite discourse" Mairs refers to? Can you recall occasions when you felt the pressure of those rules? What are the benefits, on the one hand, and the negative consequences, on the other, of following those rules?

EDUCATION

"Education is not preparation for life; education is life itself." If John Dewey is right in this, life, for many, is pretty bad. Education may hold out the promise of freeing the individual and alleviating social ills, but the reality for many students is more repressive than liberating and schools themselves are often counted today among our worst social ills.

Death at an Early Age is the title Jonathan Kozol gave to his book detailing the experience of poor, black children in Boston's public schools. In the chapter included here, we meet Stephen, age eight, a boy quite troubled but possessed of an enthusiasm and a talent for drawing; we also meet his tyrannical art teacher, whose only concerns are neatness and obedience. The subject may be art, but the lesson is something else entirely: that students like Stephen are not cut out for creative and independent work, that in fact they don't matter. What's sometimes called the "hidden curriculum" is preparing these children for their assigned place in the social order.

Santha Rama Rau and her sister Premila, though not poor, also encounter an educational system that seeks not to nourish but to diminish them. "By Any Other Name," a chapter from Rau's autobiography, describes their experience in India in the late 1920s. The headmistress of the Anglo-Indian school they attend changes their Indian names to "pretty" English ones and a teacher insists that "Indians cheat" on exams. Whatever else they may learn at school, Santha and Premila certainly learn what their status is under British colonial rule.

Fortunately, education can take place outside of school. In "The Paterson Public Library," Judith Ortiz Cofer remembers the thrill she felt visiting the library as a child. School was a place of "ritual humiliation" for some and of violence for many, including Cofer, but the library offered her freedom and endless possibility. Even today, Cofer finds a library exhilarating: "Everything that is is mine for the asking. Because I can read about it."

But not all books give us what we want. In "Trusting the Words," Michael Dorris describes a troubling experience he had while reading aloud to his seven- and eight-year-old daughters from Laura Ingalls Wilder's *Little House in the Big Woods,* a novel he remembered loving as a child. Dorris, himself of Native American ancestry, becomes aware, as he reads, of Wilder's "Eurocentric" point of view, in which Indians, when not invisible, appear as racist caricatures. But his daughters are enjoying the story. Figuring out how to handle this delicate situation proves quite educational for Dorris.

The relation of "minority" to dominant culture is problematic in higher education as well as in children's bedtime reading. In "The Politics of Remediation," Mike Rose describes his work at UCLA's Tutorial Center, where students of color with strong potential but weak preparation struggle to adapt to an alien institution. Many have come from schools not unlike that described in *Death at an Early Age.* Although sympathetic teachers at the Tutorial Center may help, for some students, the academic culture of the university remains almost inaccessible.

College promises those who do succeed a rewarding career after graduation. But what kind of career should a college student prepare for? An idealistic one? A lucrative one? (It's the rare career that's both.) In "Premature Pragmatism," Barbara Ehrenreich, much influenced by the idealistic and activist 1960s, expresses her disappointment with contemporary college students, who are running to majors like management and finance. An increasingly harsh and competitive world outside college seems to be shaping life within.

The ills of the larger society have a particularly powerful impact on the college students June Jordan writes about in "Nobody Mean More to Me Than You and the Future Life of Willie Jordan." They have come to understand the importance of a course in "The Art of Black English," which teaches them the very culture that education and other social forces are undermining, and they are flourishing in Jordan's class. But then the world outside intrudes in a very immediate way, as they learn that police have killed the brother of a fellow student. The picture is grim, but in the passion of their response to this crisis there is cause for hope as well as a glimpse of education's continuing potential as a positive force for personal liberation and social change.

FROM *DEATH AT AN EARLY AGE*

Jonathan Kozol

As the subtitles of his books suggest, Jonathan Kozol (b. 1936) has written passionately on the consequences for individual human beings of major social problems. His work includes Death at an Early Age: The Destruction of the Hearts and Minds of Negro Children in the Boston Public Schools *(1967), the first chapter of which appears below,* Rachel and Her Children: Homeless Families in America *(1988),* Savage Inequalities: Children in America's Schools *(1991), and* Amazing Grace: The Lives of Children and the Conscience of a Nation *(1995).* Death at an Early Age *won the National Book Award.*

Stephen is eight years old. A picture of him standing in front of the bulletin board on Arab bedouins shows a little light-brown person staring with unusual concentration at a chosen spot upon the floor. Stephen is tiny, desperate, unwell. Sometimes he talks to himself. He moves his mouth as if he were talking. At other times he laughs out loud in class for no apparent reason. He is also an indescribably mild and unmalicious child. He cannot do any of his school work well. His math and reading are poor. In Third Grade he was in a class that had substitute teachers much of the year. Most of the year before that, he had a row of substitute teachers too. He is in the Fourth Grade now but his work is barely at the level of the Second. Nobody has complained about the things that have happened to Stephen because he does not have any mother or father. Stephen is a ward of the State of Massachusetts and, as such, he has been placed in the home of some very poor people who do not want him now that he is not a baby any more. The money that they are given for him to pay his expenses every week does not cover the other kind of expense—the more important kind which is the immense emotional burden that is continually at stake. Stephen often comes into school badly beaten. If I ask him about it, he is apt to deny it because he does not want us to know first-hand what a miserable time he has. Like many children, and many adults too, Stephen is far more concerned with hiding his abased condition from the view of the world than he is with escaping that condition. He lied to me first when I asked him how his eye got so battered. He said it happened from being hit by accident when somebody opened up the door. Later, because it was so bruised and because I questioned him, he admitted that it was his foster mother who had flung him out onto the porch. His eye had struck the banister and it had closed and purpled. The children in the class were frightened to see him. I thought that they also felt some real compassion, but perhaps it was just shock.

Although Stephen did poorly in his school work, there was one thing he could do well. He was a fine artist. He made delightful drawings. The thing about them that was good, however, was also the thing that got him into trouble. For they were not neat and orderly and organized but entirely random and casual, messy, somewhat unpredictable, seldom according to the instructions he had been given, and—in short—real drawings. For these drawings, Stephen received considerable embarrassment at the hands of the Art Teacher. This person was a lady no longer very young who had some rather fixed values and opinions about children and about teaching. Above all, her manner was marked by unusual confidence. She seldom would merely walk into our class but seemed always to sweep into it. Even for myself, her advent, at least in the beginning of the year, used to cause a wave of anxiety. For she came into our class generally in a mood of self-assurance and of almost punitive restlessness which never made one confident but which generally made me wonder what I had done wrong. In dealing with Stephen, I thought she could be quite overwhelming.

The Art Teacher's most common technique for art instruction was to pass out mimeographed designs and then to have the pupils fill them in according to a dictated or suggested color plan. An alternate approach was to stick up on the wall or on the blackboard some of the drawings on a particular subject that had been done in the previous years by predominantly white classes. These drawings, neat and ordered and very uniform, would be the models for our children. The art lesson, in effect, would be to copy what had been done before, and the neatest and most accurate reproductions of the original drawings would be the ones that would win the highest approval from the teacher. None of the new drawings, the Art Teacher would tell me frequently, was comparable to the work that had been done in former times, but at least the children in the class could try to copy good examples. The fact that they were being asked to copy something in which they could not believe because it was not of them and did not in any way correspond to their own interests did not occur to the Art Teacher, or if it did occur she did not say it. Like a number of other teachers at my school and in other schools of the same nature, she possessed a remarkable self-defense apparatus, and anything that seriously threatened to disturb her point of view could be effectively denied.

How did a pupil like Stephen react to a teacher of this sort? Alone almost out of the entire class, I think that he absolutely turned off his signals while she was speaking and withdrew to his own private spot. At his desk he would sit silently while the Art Teacher was talking and performing. With a pencil, frequently stubby and end-bitten, he would scribble and fiddle and cock his head and whisper to himself throughout the time that the Art Teacher was going on. At length, when the art lesson officially began, he would perhaps push aside his little drawing and try the paint and paper that he had been given, usually using the watercolors freely and the paintbrush sloppily and a little bit defiantly and he would come up with things that certainly were delightful and personal and private, and full of his own nature.

If Stephen began to fiddle around during a lesson, the Art Teacher generally would not notice him at first. When she did, both he and I and the children around him would prepare for trouble. For she would go at his desk with something truly like a vengeance and would shriek at him in a way that carried terror. "Give me that! Your paints are all muddy! You've made it a mess. Look at what he's done! He's mixed up the colors! I don't know why we waste good paper on this child!" Then: "Garbage! Junk! He gives me garbage and junk! And garbage is one thing I will not have." Now I thought that that garbage and junk was very nearly the only real artwork in the class. I do not know very much about painting, but I know enough to know that the Art Teacher did not know much about it either and that, furthermore, she did not know or care anything at all about the way in which you can destroy a human being. Stephen, in many ways already dying, died a second and third and fourth and final death before her anger.

Sometimes when the Art Teacher was not present in our classroom, and when no other supervisory person happened to be there, Stephen would sneak up to me, maybe while I was sitting at my desk and going over records or totaling up the milk money or checking a paper, so that I would not see him until he was beside me. Then, hastily, secretly, with mystery, with fun, with something out of a spy movie, he would hand me one of his small drawings. The ones I liked the most, to be honest, were often not completely his own, but pictures which he had copied out of comic books and then elaborated, amended, fiddled with, and frequently added to by putting under them some kind of mock announcement ("I AM THE GREATEST AND THE STRONGEST") which might have been something he had wished. I think he must have seen something special and valuable about comic books, because another thing that he sometimes did was just cut out part of a comic book story that he liked and bring it in to me as a present. When he did this, as with his paintings and drawings, he usually would belittle his gift by crumpling it up or folding it up very tiny before he handed it to me. It was a way, perhaps, of saying that he didn't value it too much (although it was clear that he did value it a great deal) in case I didn't like it.

If the Art Teacher came upon us while he was slipping me a picture he had drawn, both he and I were apt to get an effective lashing out. Although she could be as affectionate and benevolent as she liked with other children, with Stephen she was almost always scathing in her comments and made no attempt at seeming mild. "He wants to show you his little scribbles because he wants to use you and your affection for him and make you pity him but we don't have time for that. Keep him away. If you don't, I'll do it. I don't want him getting near you during class."

For weeks after that outburst, when we had been caught in the act of friendship, he stopped coming near me. He stopped bringing me his draw-ings. He kept to his seat and giggled, mumbled, fiddled. Possibly he felt that he was doing this for my sake in order not to get me into further trouble. Then one day for a brief second he got up his nerve and darted forward. He crumpled up some paper in his fist and handed it to me quickly and got back into his chair. The crumpled paper turned out to be more funnies that he had painstakingly cut out. Another time he dropped a ball of crunched-up math paper on my desk. On the paper he had written out his age—eight years old—and his birthday—which I seem to remember came at Christ-mas. I also remember that once he either whispered to me or wrote to me on a note that he weighed sixty pounds. This information, I thought, came al-most a little boastfully, even though it obviously isn't a lot to weigh if you are almost nine, and I wondered about it for a time until it occurred to me that maybe it was just one of very few things that he knew about himself, one of the half dozen measurable facts that had anything to do with him in the world, and so—like all people, using as best they can whatever they've got—he had to make the most of it.

I think that much of his life, inwardly and outwardly, must have involved a steady and, as it turned out, inwardly at least, a losing battle to survive. He battled for his existence and, like many defenseless humans, he had to use whatever odd little weapons came to hand. Acting up at school was part of it. He was granted so little attention that he must have panicked repeatedly about the possibility that, with a few slight mistakes, he might simply stop existing or being seen at all. I imagine this is one reason why he seemed so often to in-vite or court a tongue-lashing or a whipping. Doing anything at all that would make a teacher mad at him, scream at him, strike at him, would also have been a kind of ratification, even if it was painful, that he actually was there. Other times, outside of school, he might do things like pulling a fire alarm lever and then having the satisfaction of hearing the sirens and seeing the fire engines and knowing that it was all of his own doing and to his own credit, so that at least he would have proof in that way that his hands and his arm muscles and his mischievous imagination actually did count for something measurable in the world. Maybe the only way in which he could ever impinge upon other people's lives was by infuriating them, but that at least was something. It was better than not having any use at all.

I remember that the Art Teacher once caught him out in the back, in the hallway, in front of a big floor-length coat-closet mirror. She grabbed him by the arm and pulled him into the classroom and announced to me and to the children in the classroom that he was "just standing there and making faces at himself and staring." While she talked, he looked away and examined the floor with his eyes, as he did so often, because he was embarrassed by being exposed like that. I thought it was needlessly cruel of her to have hauled him before the children in that manner, and surely a little hesitation on her part might have given her a moment to think why he might *like* to see himself in a mirror, even if it was only to see a scratched reflection. I didn't think it was shameful for him to be doing that, even to be making funny faces. It seemed rather normal and explicable to me that he might want to check up on his existence. Possibly it was a desperate act, and certainly a curious one, but I do not think it was unnatural. What did seem to me to be unnatural was the unusual virulence of the Art Teacher's reaction.

Another time, seeing him all curled up in one of the corners, I went over to him and tried to get him to look up at me and smile and talk. He would not do that. He remained all shriveled up there and he would not cry and would not laugh. I said to him: "Stephen, if you curl up like that and will not even look up at me, it will just seem as if you wanted to make me think you were a little rat." He looked down at himself hurriedly and then he looked up at me and he chuckled grotesquely and he said, with a pitiful little laugh: "I *know* I couldn't be a rat, Mr. Kozol, because a rat has got to have a little tail!" I never forgot that and I told it later to a child psychiatrist, whose answer to me made it more explicit and more clear: "It is the absence of a tail which convinces him that he has not yet become a rat." Perhaps that is overly absolute and smacks a bit of the psychiatric dogmatism that seems so difficult to accept because it leaves so little room for uncertainty or doubt; yet in this one instance I do not really think that it carries the point too far. For it is the Boston schoolteachers themselves who for years have been speaking of the Negro children in their charge as "animals" and the school building that houses them as "a zoo." And it is well known by now how commonly the injustices and depredations of the Boston school system have compelled its Negro pupils to regard themselves with something less than the dignity and respect of human beings. The toll that this took was probably greater upon Stephen than it might have been upon some other children. But the price that it exacted was paid ultimately by every child, and in the long run I am convinced that the same price has been paid by every teacher too.

STUDY AND DISCUSSION QUESTIONS

1. Stephen is being beaten at home. Why does he try to hide this?

2. The Art Teacher wants her students to copy other drawings neatly, not create their own. How might her desire relate to the children's race and social class?

3. What are some of the reasons the Art Teacher reacts so strongly to Stephen?

4. Why does Kozol begin his essay by describing a photograph of Stephen? What might this beginning suggest about Kozol himself?

5. When the other children see Stephen's bruised eye, Kozol is not sure if they feel "real compassion." What does this doubt add to the essay's indictment of the school system and of the larger society?

SUGGESTIONS FOR WRITING

1. Kozol writes that "the injustices and depredations of the Boston school system have compelled its Negro pupils to regard themselves with something less than the dignity and respect of human beings." For this, he adds, a "price has been paid by every teacher." What is the price?

2. Write a letter to the Boston school board explaining your reactions to what Kozol describes and making recommendations for action.

3. What might be done to help Stephen?

BY ANY OTHER NAME

Santha Rama Rau

Santha Rama Rau was born in Madras, India in 1923 and moved to England at age six, when her father, a diplomat, was dispatched there. Among her writings are the novels Remember the House *(1956) and* The Adventuress *(1971). The following is from* Gifts of Passage *(1961), her autobiography, parts of which originally appeared in the* New Yorker *magazine.*

At the Anglo-Indian day school in Zorinabad to which my sister and I were sent when she was eight and I was five and a half, they changed our names.

On the first day of school, a hot, windless morning of a north Indian September, we stood in the headmistress's study and she said, "Now you're the *new* girls. What are your names?"

My sister answered for us. "I am Premila, and she"—nodding in my direction—"is Santha."

The headmistress had been in India, I suppose, fifteen years or so, but she still smiled her helpless inability to cope with Indian names. Her rimless half-glasses glittered, and the precarious bun on the top of her head trembled as she shook her head. "Oh, my dears, those are much too hard for me. Suppose we give you pretty English names. Wouldn't that be more jolly? Let's see, now—Pamela for you, I think." She shrugged in a baffled way at my sister. "That's as close as I can get. And for *you*," she said to me, "how about Cynthia? Isn't that nice?"

My sister was always less easily intimidated than I was, and while she kept a stubborn silence, I said, "Thank you," in a very tiny voice.

We had been sent to that school because my father, among his responsibilities as an officer of the civil service, had a tour of duty to perform in the villages around that steamy little provincial town, where he had his headquarters at that time. He used to make his shorter inspection tours on horseback, and a week before, in the stale heat of a typically postmonsoon day, we had waved good-by to him and a little procession—an assistant, a secretary, two bearers, and the man to look after the bedding rolls and luggage. They rode away through our large garden, still bright green from the rains, and we turned back into the twilight of the house and the sound of fans whispering in every room.

Up to then, my mother had refused to send Premila to school in the British-run establishments of that time, because, she used to say, "you can bury a dog's tail for seven years and it still comes out curly, and you can take a Britisher away from his home for a lifetime and he still remains insular." The examinations and degrees from entirely Indian schools were not, in those days, considered valid. In my case, the question had never come up, and probably never would have come up if Mother's extraordinary good health had not broken down. For the first time in my life, she was not able to continue the lessons she had been giving us every morning. So our Hindi books were put away, the stories of the Lord Krishna as a little boy were left in mid-air, and we were sent to the Anglo-Indian school.

That first day at school is still, when I think of it, a remarkable one. At that age, if one's name is changed, one develops a curious form of dual personality. I remember having a certain detached and disbelieving concern in the actions of "Cynthia," but certainly no responsibility. Accordingly, I followed the thin, erect back of the headmistress down the veranda to my classroom feeling, at most, a passing interest in what was going to happen to me in this strange, new atmosphere of School.

The building was Indian in design, with wide verandas opening onto a central courtyard, but Indian verandas are usually whitewashed, with stone floors. These, in the tradition of British schools, were painted dark brown and had matting on the floors. It gave a feeling of extra intensity to the heat.

I suppose there were about a dozen Indian children in the school—which contained perhaps forty children in all—and four of them were in my class. They were all sitting at the back of the room, and I went to join them. I sat next to a small, solemn girl who didn't smile at me. She had long, glossy-black braids and wore a cotton dress, but she still kept on her Indian jewelry—a gold chain around her neck, thin gold bracelets, and tiny ruby studs in her ears. Like most Indian children, she had a rim of black kohl around her eyes. The cotton dress should have looked strange, but all I could think of was that I should ask my mother if I couldn't wear a dress to school, too, instead of my Indian clothes.

I can't remember too much about the proceedings in class that day, except for the beginning. The teacher pointed to me and asked me to stand up. "Now, dear, tell the class your name."

I said nothing.

"Come along," she said, frowning slightly. "What's your name, dear?"

"I don't know," I said, finally.

The English children in the front of the class—there were about eight or ten of them—giggled and twisted around in their chairs to look at me. I sat down quickly and opened my eyes very wide, hoping in that way to dry them off. The little girl with the braids put out her hand and very lightly touched my arm. She still didn't smile.

Most of that morning I was rather bored. I looked briefly at the children's drawings pinned to the wall, and then concentrated on a lizard clinging to the ledge of the high, barred window behind the teacher's head. Occasionally it would shoot out its long yellow tongue for a fly, and then it would rest, with its eyes closed and its belly palpitating, as though it were swallowing several times quickly. The lessons were mostly concerned with reading and writing and simple numbers—things that my mother had already taught me—and I paid very little attention. The teacher wrote on the easel blackboard words like "bat" and "cat," which seemed babyish to me; only "apple" was new and incomprehensible.

When it was time for the lunch recess, I followed the girl with braids out onto the veranda. There the children from the other classes were assembled. I saw Premila at once and ran over to her, as she had charge of our lunchbox. The children were all opening packages and sitting down to eat sandwiches. Premila and I were the only ones who had Indian food—thin wheat chapatties, some vegetable curry, and a bottle of buttermilk. Premila thrust half of it into my hand and whispered fiercely that I should go and sit with my class, because that was what the others seemed to be doing.

The enormous black eyes of the little Indian girl from my class looked at my food longingly, so I offered her some. But she only shook her head and plowed her way solemnly through her sandwiches.

I was very sleepy after lunch, because at home we always took a siesta. It was usually a pleasant time of day, with the bedroom darkened against the harsh afternoon sun, the drifting off into sleep with the sound of Mother's voice reading a story in one's mind, and, finally, the shrill, fussy voice of the ayah waking one for tea.

At school, we rested for a short time on low, folding cots on the veranda, and then we were expected to play games. During the hot part of the afternoon we played indoors, and after the shadows had begun to lengthen and the slight breeze of the evening had come up we moved outside to the wide courtyard.

I had never really grasped the system of competitive games. At home, whenever we played tag or guessing games, I was always allowed to "win"— "because," Mother used to tell Premila, "she is the youngest, and we have to allow for that." I had often heard her say it, and it seemed quite reasonable to me, but the result was that I had no clear idea of what "winning" meant.

When we played twos-and-threes that afternoon at school, in accordance with my training, I let one of the small English boys catch me, but was naturally rather puzzled when the other children did not return the courtesy. I ran about for what seemed like hours without ever catching anyone, until it was time for school to close. Much later I learned that my attitude was called "not being a good sport," and I stopped allowing myself to be caught, but it was not for years that I really learned the spirit of the thing.

When I saw our car come up to the school gate, I broke away from my classmates and rushed toward it yelling. "Ayah! Ayah!" It seemed like an eternity since I had seen her that morning—a wizened, affectionate figure in her white cotton sari, giving me dozens of urgent and useless instructions on how to be a good girl at school. Premila followed more sedately, and she told me on the way home never to do that again in front of the other children.

When we got home we went straight to Mother's high, white room to have tea with her, and I immediately climbed onto the bed and bounced gently up and down on the springs. Mother asked how we had liked our first day in school. I was so pleased to be home and to have left that peculiar Cynthia behind that I had nothing whatever to say about school, except to ask what "apple" meant. But Premila told Mother about the classes, and added that in her class they had weekly tests to see if they had learned their lessons well.

I asked, "What's a test?"

Premila said, "You're too small to have them. You won't have them in your class for donkey's years." She had learned the expression that day and was using it for the first time. We all laughed enormously at her wit. She also told

Mother, in an aside, that we should take sandwiches to school the next day. Not, she said, that *she* minded. But they would be simpler for me to handle.

That whole lovely evening I didn't think about school at all. I sprinted barefoot across the lawns with my favorite playmate, the cook's son, to the stream at the end of the garden. We quarreled in our usual way, waded in the tepid water under the lime trees, and waited for the night to bring out the smell of the jasmine. I listened with fascination to his stories of ghosts and demons, until I was too frightened to cross the garden alone in the semidarkness. The ayah found me, shouted at the cook's son, scolded me, hurried me in to supper—it was an entirely usual, wonderful evening.

It was a week later, the day of Premila's first test, that our lives changed rather abruptly. I was sitting at the back of my class, in my usual inattentive way, only half listening to the teacher. I had started a rather guarded friendship with the girl with the braids, whose name turned out to be Nalini (Nancy, in school). The three other Indian children were already fast friends. Even at that age it was apparent to all of us that friendship with the English or Anglo-Indian children was out of the question. Occasionally, during the class, my new friend and I would draw pictures and show them to each other secretly.

The door opened sharply and Premila marched in. At first, the teacher smiled at her in a kindly and encouraging way and said, "Now, you're little Cynthia's sister?"

Premila didn't even look at her. She stood with her feet planted firmly apart and her shoulders rigid, and addressed herself directly to me. "Get up," she said. "We're going home."

I didn't know what had happened, but I was aware that it was a crisis of some sort. I rose obediently and started to walk toward my sister.

"Bring your pencils and your notebook," she said.

I went back for them, and together we left the room. The teacher started to say something just as Premila closed the door, but we didn't wait to hear what it was.

In complete silence we left the school grounds and started to walk home. Then I asked Premila what the matter was. All she would say was "We're going home for good."

It was a very tiring walk for a child of five and a half, and I dragged along behind Premila with my pencils growing sticky in my hand. I can still remember looking at the dusty hedges, and the tangles of thorns in the ditches by the side of the road, smelling the faint fragrance from the eucalyptus trees and wondering whether we would ever reach home. Occasionally a horse-drawn tonga passed us, and the women, in their pink or green silks, stared at Premila and me trudging along on the side of the road. A few coolies and a line of women carrying baskets of vegetables on their heads smiled at us. But it was nearing the hottest time of day, and the road was almost deserted. I walked more and more slowly, and shouted to Premila, from time to time, "Wait for me!" with increasing peevishness. She spoke to me only once, and that was to tell me to carry my notebook on my head, because of the sun.

When we got to our house the ayah was just taking a tray of lunch into Mother's room. She immediately started a long, worried questioning about what are you children doing back here at this hour of the day.

Mother looked very startled and very concerned, and asked Premila what had happened.

Premila said, "We had our test today, and She made me and the other Indians sit at the back of the room, with a desk between each one."

Mother said, "Why was that, darling?"

"She said it was because Indians cheat," Premila added. "So I don't think we should go back to that school."

Mother looked very distant, and was silent a long time. At last she said, "Of course not, darling." She sounded displeased.

We all shared the curry she was having for lunch, and afterward I was sent off to the beautifully familiar bedroom for my siesta. I could hear Mother and Premila talking through the open door.

Mother said, "Do you suppose she understood all that?"

Premila said, "I shouldn't think so. She's a baby."

Mother said, "Well, I hope it won't bother her."

Of course, they were both wrong. I understood it perfectly, and I remember it all very clearly. But I put it happily away, because it had all happened to a girl called Cynthia, and I never was really particularly interested in her.

STUDY AND DISCUSSION QUESTIONS

1. "Suppose we give you pretty English names," the headmistress says to Santha and Premila. What are the implications of this statement?

2. What does the description of the school building reveal (in the eighth paragraph) about the British in India?

3. How do we learn that Premila is more eager than her sister to fit in at school? Why do you think she is? How does this difference contribute to the difference in their reactions to the incident at the end?

4. What indications are there of the social class of Santha's family? Does their class position in any way help explain Premila's insistence that she and her sister are not returning to the school?

5. What does the last sentence mean?

6. What are the possible meanings of the essay's title?

SUGGESTIONS FOR WRITING

1. The events described take place in the late 1920s. If you can, read about life in India under British colonial rule at that time. What more do you now understand about the experience of Santha's family?

2. Write the letter Premila might write to the headmistress explaining why she isn't coming back to the school.

THE PATERSON
PUBLIC LIBRARY

Judith Ortiz Cofer

Judith Ortiz Cofer was born in Puerto Rico in 1952 and moved to the United States as a small girl. She studied at Augusta College, at Florida Atlantic University, and at Oxford, and she now teaches at the University of Georgia at Athens. Cofer has published several books of poetry, including Terms of Survival *(1987), as well as the essay collection* Silent Dancing *(1990). Her novel* The Line of the Sun *(1989) was nominated for a Pulitzer Prize. The following appeared in* The Latin Deli: Prose and Poetry *(1993).*

It was a Greek temple in the ruins of an American city. To get to it I had to walk through neighborhoods where not even the carcasses of rusted cars on blocks nor the death traps of discarded appliances were parted with, so that the yards of the borderline poor, people who lived not in a huge building, as I did, but in their own decrepit little houses, looked liked a reversed archaeological site, incongruous next to the pillared palace of the Paterson Public Library.

The library must have been built during Paterson's boom years as the model industrial city of the North. Enough marble was used in its construction to have kept several Michelangelos busily satisfied for a lifetime. Two roaring lions, taller than a grammar school girl, greeted those brave enough to seek answers there. Another memorable detail about the façade of this important place to me was the phrases carved deeply into the walls—perhaps the immortal words of Greek philosophers—I could not tell, since

I was developing astigmatism at that time and could only make out the lovely geometric designs they made.

All during the school week I both anticipated and feared the long walk to the library because it took me through enemy territory. The black girl Lorraine, who had chosen me to hate and terrorize with threats at school, lived in one of the gloomy little houses that circled the library like beggars. Lorraine would eventually carry out her violence against me by beating me up in a confrontation formally announced through the school grapevine so that for days I lived with a panic that has rarely been equaled in my adult life, since now I can get grown-ups to listen to me, and at that time disasters had to be a fait accompli for a teacher or a parent to get involved. Why did Lorraine hate me? For reasons neither one of us fully understood at the time. All I remember was that our sixth grade teacher seemed to favor me, and her way of showing it was by having me tutor "slow" students in spelling and grammar. Lorraine, older and bigger than myself, since she was repeating the grade, was subjected to this ritual humiliation, which involved sitting in the hallway, obviously separated from the class—one of us for being smart, the other for the opposite reason. Lorraine resisted my efforts to teach her the basic rules of spelling. She would hiss her threats at me, addressing me as *You little spic.* Her hostility sent shudders through me. But baffling as it was, I also accepted it as inevitable. She would beat me up. I told my mother and the teacher, and they both reassured me in vague adult terms that a girl like Lorraine would not dare get in trouble again. She had a history of problems that made her a likely candidate for reform school. But Lorraine and I knew that the violence she harbored had found a target: me—the skinny Puerto Rican girl whose father was away with the navy most of the time and whose mother did not speak English; I was the perfect choice.

Thoughts like these occupied my mind as I walked to the library on Saturday mornings. But my need for books was strong enough to propel me down the dreary streets with their slush-covered sidewalks and the skinny trees of winter looking like dark figures from a distance: angry black girls waiting to attack me.

But the sight of the building was enough to reassure me that sanctuary was within reach. Inside the glass doors was the inexhaustible treasure of books, and I made my way through the stacks like the beggar invited to the wedding feast. I remember the musty, organic smell of the library, so different from the air outside. It was the smell of an ancient forest, and since the first books that I read for pleasure were fairy tales, the aroma of transforming wood suited me as a prop.

With my pink library card I was allowed to check out two books from the first floor—the children's section. I would take the full hour my mother had given me (generously adding fifteen minutes to get home before she sent my brother after me) to choose the books I would take home for the week. I made my way first through the world's fairy tales. Here I discovered that there is a Cinderella in every culture, that she didn't necessarily have the white skin and rosy cheeks Walt Disney had given her, and that the prince they all waited for could appear in any color, shape, or form. The prince didn't even have to be a man.

It was the way I absorbed fantasy in those days that gave me the sense of inner freedom, a feeling of power and the ability to fly that is the main reward of the writer. As I read those stories I became not only the characters but their creator. I am still fascinated by the idea that fairy tales and fables are part of humankind's collective unconscious—a familiar theory that acquires concreteness in my own writing today, when I discover over and over that the character I create or the themes that recur in my poems and in my fiction are my own versions of the "types" I learned to recognize very early in my life in fairy tales.

There was also violence in these stories: villains decapitated in honorable battle, goblins and witches pursued, beaten, and burned at the stake by heroes with magic weapons, possessing the supernatural strength granted to the self-righteous in folklore. I understood those black-and-white duels between evil and justice. But Lorraine's blind hatred of my person and my knee-liquefying fear of her were not so clear to me at that time. It would be many years before I learned about the politics of race, before I internalized the awful reality of the struggle for territory that underscored the lives of blacks and Puerto Ricans in Paterson during my childhood. Each job given to a light-skinned Hispanic was one less job for a black man; every apartment leased to a Puerto Rican family was one less place available to blacks. Worst of all, though the Puerto Rican children had to master a new language in the schools and were often subjected to the scorn and impatience of teachers burdened with too many students making too many demands in a classroom, the blacks were obviously the ones singled out for "special" treatment. In other words, whenever possible they were assigned to special education classes in order to relieve the teacher's workload, mainly because their black English dialect sounded "ungrammatical" and "illiterate" to our white Seton Hall University and City College-educated instructors. I have on occasion become angry at being treated like I'm mentally deficient by persons who make that prejudgment upon hearing an unfamiliar accent. I can only imagine what it must have been like for children like Lorraine, whose skin color alone put her in a pigeonhole she felt she had to fight her way out of every day of her life.

I was one of the lucky ones; as an insatiable reader I quickly became more than adept at the use of the English language. My life as a navy brat, moving with my family from Paterson to Puerto Rico every few months as my father's tours of duty demanded, taught me to depend on knowledge as my main source of security. What I learned from books borrowed from the Greek temple among the ruins of the city I carried with me as the lightest of carry-on luggage. My teachers in both countries treated me well in general. The easiest way to become a teacher's pet, or *la favorita,* is to ask the teacher for books to read—and I was always looking for reading material. Even my mother's romantic novels by Corín Tellado and her *Buenhogar* (Spanish *Good Housekeeping* magazine) were not safe from my insatiable word hunger.

Since the days when I was stalked by Lorraine, libraries have always been an adventure for me. Fear of an ambush is no longer the reason why I feel my pulse quicken a little when I approach a library building, when I enter the stacks and inhale the familiar smell of old leather and paper. It may be the memory of the danger that heightens my senses, but it is really the expectation that I felt then and that I still feel now about books. They contained most of the information I needed to survive in two languages and in two worlds. When adults were too busy to answer my endless questions, I could always *look it up;* when I felt unbearably lonely, as I often did during those early gypsy years traveling with my family, I read to escape and also to connect: you can come back to a book as you cannot always to a person or place you miss. I read and reread favorite books until the characters seemed like relatives or friends I could see when I wanted or needed to see them.

I still feel that way about books. They represent my spiritual life. A library is my sanctuary, and I am always at home in one. It is not surprising that in recalling my first library, the Paterson Public Library, I have always described it as a temple.

Lorraine carried out her threat. One day after school, as several of our classmates, Puerto Rican and black, circled us to watch, Lorraine grabbed a handful of my long hair and forced me to my knees. Then she slapped my face hard enough that the sound echoed off the brick walls of the school building and ran off while I screamed at the sight of blood on my white knee socks and felt the throbbing on my scalp where I would have a bald spot advertising my shame for weeks to come.

No one intervened. To this crowd, it was one of many such violent scenes taking place among the adults and the children of people fighting over a rapidly shrinking territory. It happens in the jungle and it happens in the city. But another course of action other than "fight or flight" is open to those of us lucky enough to discover it, and that is channeling one's anger and energy into the development of a mental life. It requires something like obsessiveness for a young person growing up in an environment where physical labor and physical endurance are the marks of a survivor—as is the case with minority peoples living in large cities. But many of us do manage to discover books. In my case, it may have been what anthropologists call a cultural adaptation. Being physically small, non-English-speaking, and always the new kid on the block, I was forced to look for an alternative mode to survival in Paterson. Reading books empowered me.

Even now, a visit to the library recharges the batteries in my brain. Looking through the card catalog reassures me that there is no subject that I cannot investigate, no world I cannot explore. Everything that is is mine for the asking. Because I can read about it.

STUDY AND DISCUSSION QUESTIONS

1. Why are books so important to Cofer as a young girl?

2. Why does Lorraine hate Cofer?

3. Lorraine and Cofer see each other as enemies. Do they have anything in common?

4. Lorraine's "skin color alone put her in a pigeonhole she felt she had to fight her way out of every day of her life." Explain.

5. Cofer writes that Lorraine lived in "one of the gloomy little houses that circled the library like beggars." What are the implications of this description? Later, she tells of her visits to the library: "I made my way through the stacks like the beggar invited to the wedding feast." What is she saying?

6. Why is Cofer now able to be so sympathetic towards a girl who terrorized her?

SUGGESTIONS FOR WRITING

1. Cofer says little about the school she and Lorraine attended. Describe what you imagine life was like inside that school.

2. In the library, Cofer "discovered that there is a Cinderella in every culture, that she didn't necessarily have the white skin and rosy cheeks Walt Disney had given her." Why do you think Cofer mentions this discovery?

3. What do you guess Lorraine's life is like today? Imagine the encounter that might take place between her and Cofer as adults.

TRUSTING THE WORDS

Michael Dorris

Michael Dorris (1945–1997), who was part Modoc Indian, founded the Native American Studies Program at Dartmouth College, where he taught for many years. His fiction includes the novels A Yellow Raft in Blue Water *(1987) and* Cloud Chamber *(1997), as well as the story collection* Working Men *(1993). The* Broken Cord, *which won the 1989 National Book Award, chronicled the life of his adopted son Abel, who suffered from fetal alcohol syndrome. Dorris and his wife, Louise Erdrich, cooperated closely on a number of books, including the novel* The Crown of Columbus *(1991). The following appeared in his collection* Paper Trail: Essays *(1994).*

On the Banks of Plum Creek was the first brand-new hard-back book I ever bought for myself. It was not a casual or impulse purchase—such a luxury was beyond a family of our economic level—but a considered acquisition. Two summers before, during my daily browse in the small neighborhood library a short walk from where I lived, I had stumbled upon the shelf of Laura Ingalls Wilder novels. With their pastel covers, gentle illustrations, large type, and homey titles, they were appealing, inviting, but which one to try first? In the manner of Goldilocks, I decided that *Farmer Boy* looked too long, *Little House in the Big Woods* too short. *Plum Creek*, though, was just right. More than just right: by an amazing coincidence I had just an hour before consumed a plum for lunch!

Naturally, like thousands of other readers over the past fifty years, I was captured from page one. The snug little dwelling dug into the side of a creek bank was as irresistible to me at age eight as Bilbo Baggins's[1] similar den proved to be some ten years later. The ever-mobile Ingalls family—adaptable, affectionate Pa; conventional, resourceful Ma; pretty, good-girl Mary; baby Carrie—were the Swiss Family Robinson[2] next door, the us-against-the-world American ideal of underdogs who, through grit and wit and optimism, prevailed over every natural disaster and took advantage of every available resource in their inexorable path toward increased creature

---

[1] Hero of *The Hobbit,* a novel by J. R. R. Tolkien.
[2] Title of children's adventure story.

comforts and status. As linchpin and leading protagonist, second child Laura was full-swing into the adventure of growing up, and as such she was not just like me, but like me the way I aspired to be: plucky and brave, composed of equal parts good will and self-interest. Her life was a constantly unfolding tapestry, its events intricately connected and stitched with affectionate detail. The cast of human and animal players auxiliary to the central family was limited and manageable enough for a reader to grasp as distinct individuals, and within the balanced, safe context of ultimate parental protection, even a week-long blizzard was the occasion for a chapter titled "A Day of Games."

I doubt if any of today's powerful publishing marketing committees would project the young me as a likely target audience for the Wilder books. Superficially, Laura and I had so little in common, so few intersections of experience with which I should logically have been able to identify. Those experts would probably conclude that I—as a mixed-blood, male, only child of a single-parent, mostly urban, fixed-income family—would prefer novels more reflective of myself. True, I wasn't immune to "boy books." I dutifully followed every scrape that Frank and Joe Hardy fell into, worked my way through James Fenimore Cooper, Charles Dickens, and Alexandre Dumas, and had a stack of *D.C. Comics* in which both Superman and Batman figured prominently. But when the time came to buy a real book, to receive the first volume in what has become an extensive personal collection of literature, I didn't hesitate: *On the Banks of Plum Creek* was an old friend I was sure I'd want to read many more times in the years to come, as indeed I have.

The nine Little House books—*Little House in the Big Woods, Little House on the Prairie, On the Banks of Plum Creek, By the Shores of Silver Lake, The Long Winter, Farmer Boy, Little Town on the Prairie, These Happy Golden Years,* and *The First Four Years*—together with two subsequent collections of Laura Ingalls Wilder's diary entries *(On the Way Home)* and letters *(West from Home),* supplemented by related songbooks and cookbooks, chronicle and particularize like no other source the mythic American frontier journey from precarious adversity into middle-class security. If, as it appears from *The Ghost in the Little House,* William Holtz's new and convincing life of Rose Wilder Lane (Laura's only child, who grew up to be a thoroughly modern woman and one of the most far-flung and daring journalists of the 1920s and 1930s), the novels are more collaborative biography than home-spun autobiography, their power is in no way diminished. That the characters are crafted verisimilitudes rather than drawn word-for-word upon fact only contributes to the readability of the series. The belated discovery that the generous, self-taught, talented, and complicated daughter shaped the rough yet keenly precise recollections of her farmer mother into art is an intriguing surprise—but certainly does not undermine either the historical or the humanistic value of a saga that at its heart depicts the universal struggle of a child growing to adulthood and independence.

Far more problematic, at least for me, were the issues raised when, with the enthusiasm of a father who had long looked forward to sharing a favorite tale, I set down last year to begin reading the books to my two daughters, ages seven and eight. Not one page into *Little House in the Big Woods,* I heard my own voice saying, "As far as a man could go to the north in a day, or a week, or a whole month, there was nothing but woods. There were no houses. There were no roads. There were no people. There were only trees and the wild animals who had their homes among them."

Say what? Excuse me, but weren't we forgetting the Chippewa branch of my daughters' immediate ancestry, not to mention the thousands of resident Menominees, Potawatomis, Sauks, Foxes, Winnebagos, and Ottawas who inhabited mid-nineteenth-century Wisconsin, as they had for many hundreds of years? Exactly upon whose indigenous land was Grandma and Grandpa's cozy house constructed? Had they paid for the bountiful property, teeming with wild game and fish? This fun-filled world of extended Ingallses was curiously empty, a pristine wilderness in which only white folks toiled and cavorted, ate and harvested, celebrated and were kind to each other.

My dilemma, as raconteur, was clear. My little girls looked up to me with trusting eyes, eager to hear me continue with the first of these books I had promised with such anticipation. I had made "an event" out of their reading, an intergenerational gift, and now in the cold light of an adult perspective I realized that I was, in my reluctance to dilute the pleasure of a good story with the sober stuff of history, in the process of perpetuating a Eurocentric attitude that was still very much alive. One had only to peruse newspaper accounts of contemporary Wisconsin controversies over tribal fishing rights, bingo emporia, and legal and tax jurisdiction to realize that many of Grandpa and Grandma's descendants remained determined that there could be "no people" except those who were just like them.

Okay, I admit it. I closed the book rather than be politically correct at 8 P.M. in my daughters' bedroom. I'd save the cold water of reality for the light of day, and anyway, I seemed to remember that once Ma and Pa pushed west they had encountered native people.

"Let's start instead tomorrow with *Little House on the Prairie,*" I suggested. This idea went over well, since it evoked in my girls the visual image of the pretty, if often saccharine, TV series of the same name.

Fast forward to the next evening, paragraph two: "*They were going to the Indian country.*"

Good sign! The packing up and the journey west were lovingly and minutely related. The sense of space and sky found on the plains was gloriously rendered. The pages turned, my daughters' eyes stayed bright long past their usual bedtime, the book was everything I remembered—realistic, lyrical, exciting in all the right ways. And then, page 46.

> Laura chewed and swallowed, and she said, "I want to see a papoose."
>
> "Mercy on us!" Ma said, "Whatever makes you want to see Indians? We will see enough of them. More than we want to, I wouldn't wonder."
>
> "They wouldn't hurt us, would they?" Mary asked. Mary was always good; she never spoke with her mouth full.
>
> "No!" Ma said. "Don't get such an idea into your head."
>
> "Why don't you like Indians, Ma?" Laura asked, and she caught a drip of molasses with her tongue.
>
> "I just don't like them, and don't lick your fingers, Laura," said Ma.
>
> "This is Indian country, isn't it?" Laura said. "What did we come to their country for, if you don't like them?"
>
> Ma said she didn't know whether this was Indian country or not. She didn't know where the Kansas line was. But whether or no, the Indians would not be here long. Pa had word from a man in Washington that the Indian Territory would be open to settlement soon.

What was a responsible father to do? Stop the narrative, explain that Ma was a know-nothing racist? Describe the bitter injustice of unilateral treaty abridgment? Break into a chorus of "Oklahoma!"[3] and then point out how American popular culture has long covered up the shame of the Dawes Act[4] by glossing it over with Sooner folklore?

This time, I simply invented an extra line of dialogue.

"That's awful, Ma," I had Laura say. "I'm ashamed to hear such a thing."

But the fantasy of the 1990s-enlightened Laura evaporated not ten pages later.

> That night by the fire Laura asked again when she would see a papoose, but Pa didn't know. He said you never saw Indians unless they wanted you to see them. He had seen Indians when he was a boy in New York State, but Laura never had. She knew they were wild men with red skins, and their hatchets were called tomahawks.
>
> Pa knew all about wild animals, so he must know about wild men, too. Laura thought he would show her a papoose some day, just as he had shown her fawns, and little bears, and wolves.

That part, I confess, I simply skipped, edited right out, blipped. In no time flat Pa was back to his fiddle, Ma was doing something deft and culinary with cornmeal. Nature was nature.

---

[3] Song from Broadway musical *Oklahoma!*, by Rodgers and Hammerstein.

[4] 1877 Legislation that converted tribal lands into individually owned small properties, with unassigned land to be sold to non-Indians.

Only the wind rustled in the prairie grasses. The big, yellow moon was sailing high overhead. The sky was so full of light that not one star twinkled in it, and all the prairie was a shadowy mellowness.

And there were no Indians, no cholera-ridden, starving reservations, no prohibitions to the practice of native religion, no Wounded Knee a few hundred miles to the north, no Sand Creek[5] an equal distance to the west. Manifest Destiny protected its own, and family values prevailed, staunchly Calvinist and oblivious to any ethical messiness that might interfere with the romance.

The next chapter, "Moving In," was heralded by a drawing of tipis. I closed the book and kissed the girls goodnight, then retreated to my office to preview on my own. For a while, beyond Ma's offhand disparaging comments about not wanting to "live like Indians," the Ingalls family contented itself with building a house and fending off a wolf pack. Good clean fun, character-building hard work, the grist that made this country great.

Until . . .

suddenly [Jack, the bulldog] stood up and growled a fierce, deep growl. The hair on his neck stood straight up and his eyes glared red.

Laura was frightened. Jack had never growled at her before. Then she looked over her shoulder where Jack was looking, and she saw two naked wild men coming, one behind the other, on the Indian trail.

"Mary! Look!" she cried. Mary looked and saw them, too.

They were tall, thin, fierce-looking men. Their skin was brownish-red. Their head seemed to go up to a peak, and the peak was a tuft of hair that stood straight up and ended in feathers. Their eyes were black and still and glittering, like snake's eyes.

The Indians went into the new house and Laura worried for the safety of Ma and baby Carrie. "I'm going to let Jack loose," Laura whispered, hoarsely. "Jack will kill them."

But no, the Indians only wanted some of Ma's cornbread and Pa's tobacco. They were wearing skunk skins, which didn't smell good, and their eyes glittered some more, but otherwise they were perfectly benign. When Pa came home he at first dealt with news of the visit with laudable equanimity, but then went on, before stopping himself, to add, "The main thing is to be on good terms with the Indians. We don't want to wake up some night with a band of the screeching dev—."

The concluding chapters of *Little House on the Prairie* are full of Indians—some threatening, some noble. The settlers worry over the possibility of

---

[5] Wounded Knee, South Dakota and Sand Creek, Colorado were sites of Native American massacres by United States Army troops in the 1890s.

being attacked and driven out, but it doesn't transpire. Instead, inevitably, the Indians are forced to evacuate in an endless line that trails past the family home. Pa takes this banishment as a given.

> "When white settlers come into a country, the Indians have to move on. The government is going to move these Indians farther west, any time now. That's why we're here, Laura. White people are going to settle all this country, and we get the best land because we get here first and take our pick. Now do you understand?"
>
> "Yes, Pa," Laura said. "But Pa, I thought this was Indian Territory. Won't it make the Indians mad to have to—"
>
> "No more questions, Laura," Pa said firmly. "Go to sleep."

Pa never felt as guilty as I would have liked him to, though he did disagree with his friend Mr. Scott who maintained that "the only good Indian is a dead Indian." Ma, on the other hand, remained an unreconstructed bigot—as late as *The Long Winter,* three novels and many years later, the very mention of even friendly, helpful Indians set her off.

> "What Indian?" Ma asked [Pa]. She looked as if she were smelling the smell of an Indian whenever she said the word. Ma despised Indians. She was afraid of them, too.
>
> For her part, Laura seemed typically open-minded, wanting at one point to adopt an Indian baby.
>
> "Its eyes are so black," Laura sobbed. She could not say what she meant.

At last, the Ingalls family, emblematic of all those like them who went west with the blithe assumption that resident tribes had no title rights to the country they had occupied from time immemorial, witnessed the realization of their dream: a vanishing native population. Surprisingly, it was not a jubilant moment.

> It was dinner-time, and no one thought of dinner. Indian ponies were still going by, carrying bunches of skins and tent-poles and dangling baskets and cooking pots. There were a few more women and a few more naked Indian children and Laura and Mary still stayed in the doorway, looking, till that long line of Indians slowly pulled itself over the western edge of the world. And nothing was left but silence and emptiness. All the world seemed very quiet and lonely.

As it turned out, I didn't read aloud the Little House books to my daughters because, quite frankly, I realized I couldn't have kept my mouth shut at the objectionable parts. I would have felt compelled to interrupt the story constantly with editorial asides, history lessons, thought questions, critiques of the racism or sexism embedded in the text. I would have studiously purified those novels, treated them as sociology or fixed them up to suit a contemporary and, I firmly believe, more enlightened sensibility.

Certainly they could be used that way, but, I wonder, would my daughters then grow up with the selective fond memories of each volume that I myself carried? Or would they learn from me that every page of a book had to pass a test in order for the whole to entertain? Would reading with me become a chore, a "learning experience," a tension, and not the pleasure I wished it?

Laura Ingalls Wilder and her daughter, Rose Wilder Lane, created a series peopled by characters who were, for better or worse, true to the prevailing attitudes of their day. Resisting the temptation to stereotype or sensationalize beyond the often ill-informed opinions of both adults and children, the actual incidents that involve Indians are portrayed as invariably anticlimactic—more ordinary and less dramatic than anyone, even Pa, expects them to be. Distilled from the aura of mystery and danger, the Indians on the periphery of the Ingalls family's vision are thin, unfortunate, and determinedly honest. Their journey is the sad underside of the bright pioneer coin, and their defeat and expulsion brings no one any glory. Ma and Pa's self-serving lack of compassion was probably no worse than most and much better than that of those who filed claims west of the Mississippi 150 years ago, and to create them otherwise and still present them as "typical" would be wishful thinking.

Ruminating on my own various interactions with the Little House books, I remembered that I had never much cared for Ma—even when I was a young boy she had struck me as prudish and cautious and uptight, with untested prejudices and unexamined rules that fairly cried out for rebellion. I remembered that I had Ma to thank, possibly more than anyone else in real life or in literature, for my first startling awareness that an adult authority figure could actually be dense and narrow minded. I remembered that those nagging, unanswered questions about what *did* happen to Indians in the nineteenth century (and why) had engendered an indignant pride in the Modoc part of my ethnic heritage. They had sent me to elderly relatives and to the history section of the library and that in turn had led to school research projects and maps, activism in the 1960s, and support of the American Indian Movement and, ultimately, no doubt, contributed heavily to my founding of the Native American Studies Program at Dartmouth College in 1972 and teaching there for the next fifteen years. Take that, Ma!

Books, important as they can and should be, are after all but a part of the much larger context that informs them. They illuminate our experience but at the same time our experience sheds light back upon their ideas and theories. A book converts less than it nudges us toward what we otherwise already think. The existence of characters who are distasteful or complicated merely reflects the world as it is.

I placed the Little House novels on the top shelf of the bookcase and told my daughters I thought it would be better if they read them, when and if they wanted to, to themselves. I trust that they will not be corrupted into Indianophobes even as they thrill to description of a runaway buggy or warm to the first blush of young love when Laura and Almanzo go courting. I trust that they will be able to differentiate courage from pettiness, justice from exploitation. I'll bide my time, and when, eventually, each of my girls bursts through a door, eyes ablaze with outrage, waving a book in her hand, furious . . . then we'll talk about it.

STUDY AND DISCUSSION QUESTIONS

1. Why, according to Dorris, are the Little House books so appealing?

2. Reading Wilder's work to his daughters, Dorris feared he was "perpetuating a Eurocentric attitude that was still very much alive." What does this mean?

3. Dorris describes the "family values" of *Little House on the Prairie* as "oblivious to any ethical messiness that might interfere with the romance." What is he saying?

4. Why does Dorris decide not to keep reading Wilder's books aloud to his daughters? Why doesn't he simply continue reading and explain his objections as he goes?

5. Why is Dorris now thankful to Ma, that "unreconstructed bigot"?

6. Why does Dorris title his essay, "Trusting the Words"? Why not, say, "Trusting the Kids"?

SUGGESTIONS FOR WRITING

1. If you are familiar with the television series "Little House on the Prairie," compare it to Wilder's novels as Dorris describes them. Would you recommend the series to children?

2. To what extent do you think Dorris's reaction depends upon his own and his daughters' Native American ancestry? Would his dilemma have been different otherwise? Should it have been?

3. Can you remember a book (or movie or television show) that you enjoyed as a child but whose perspective you now find distasteful? If you had children (perhaps you do), would you keep them away from it?

THE POLITICS OF REMEDIATION

Mike Rose

Mike Rose (b. 1944) teaches in the Writing Program and in the Graduate School of Education at the University of California at Los Angeles. What follows is an excerpt from a chapter of his book Lives on the Boundary: The Struggles and Achievements of America's Underprepared *(1989). Rose has also written* Possible Lives: The Promise of Public Education in America *(1995).*

The students are taking their seats in the large auditorium, moving in two streams down the main aisles, entering from a side exit to capture seats in the front. You're a few minutes late and find a seat somewhere in the middle. There are a couple of hundred students around you and in front of you, a hundred or so behind. A youngish man walks onto the stage and lays a folder and a book on the podium. There are track lights above him, and in back of him there's a system of huge blackboards that rise and descend on rollers in the wall. The man begins talking. He raises his voice and taps the podium and sweeps his hand through the air. Occasionally, he'll turn to the moving boards and write out a phrase or someone's name or a reference to a section of the textbook. You begin writing these things down. He has a beard and smiles now and then and seems wrapped up in what he's talking about.

This is Introductory Sociology. It's one of the courses students can elect to fulfill their general education requirements. The catalogue said that Introductory Sociology would deal with "the characteristics of social life" and "the processes of social interaction." It also said that the course would cover the "tools of sociological investigation," but that came last and was kind of general and didn't seem too important. You're curious about what it is that makes people tick and curious, as well, about the causes of social problems, so a course on social interaction sounded interesting. You filled Sociology 1 in on some cards and sent them out and eventually got other cards back that told you you were enrolled.

"These are the social facts that are reflected in the interpretations we make of them," says the man on the stage and then extends his open hand toward the audience. "Now, this is not the place to rehearse the arguments between Kantian idealists and Lockean realists, but . . ." You're still writing down, ". . .

reflected in the interpretations we make of them . . ." and he continues: "But let us stop for a moment and consider what it means to say 'social fact.' What is a fact? And in considering this question, we are drawn into hermeneutics." He turns to write that last word on the board, and as he writes you copy it down in your notes. He refers the class to the textbook, to a "controlling metaphor" and to "microanalyses"—and as you're writing this down, you hear him stressing "constructivist interpretations" and reading a quotation from somebody and concluding that "in the ambiguity lies the richness."

People are taking notes and you are taking notes. You are taking notes on a lecture you don't understand. You get a phrase, a sentence, then the next loses you. It's as though you're hearing a conversation in a crowd or from another room—out of phase, muted. The man on the stage concludes his lecture and everyone rustles and you close your notebook and prepare to leave. You feel a little strange. Maybe tomorrow this stuff will clear up. Maybe by tomorrow this will be easier. But by the time you're in the hallway, you don't think it will be easier at all.

When I was in the Teacher Corps, I saw daily the effects of background on schooling. Kids came into the schools with hand-me-down skirts and pants, they didn't have lunch money, they were failing. The connections between neighborhood and classroom were striking. This was true, though in different ways, with the veterans. The Tutorial Center also served low-income white and low- and middle-income minority students, but because the kind of students who make it to a place like UCLA enter with a long history of success and, to varying degrees, have removed superficial indicators of their lineage, it's harder, at first glance, to see how profoundly a single assignment or a whole academic career can be affected by background and social circumstance—by interactions of class, race, and gender. But as I settled into Campbell Hall, I saw illustrations continually, ones that complicated easy judgment and expectation.

Sometimes issues of economics and race were brought up by the students themselves. Such issues were also raised by the existence of the Ethnic Studies Centers, the perennial posters in the hallways, or the lobbying of older, politically active students, and they emerged in some of the students' classes. There was wide variation in the students' responses. Some had grown up watching their parents deal with insult, had heard slurs in their schools about skin color and family and language. A young woman writes in her placement exam for Freshman English:

> I could not go into the restroom, the cafeteria, or any place of the high school area alone, without having some girl following me and calling me names or pushing me around. Some of their favorite names for me were "wetback,"

"beaner," or "illegal alien." I did not pay much attention to the name calling, but when they started pulling my hair, pushing me, or throwing beans
at me, I reacted.

Students like her were drawn to issues of race, read the walls of Campbell
with understanding, saw connections between the messages on green paper
and the hurt in their own past. They had been sensitized to exclusion as they
were growing up.

But there were those who came to Campbell Hall with a different past
and a different outlook. Some of those who grew up with the protections of
middle-class life knew of the wrongs done to their people, but slavery and
Nisei internment and agricultural camps seemed distant to them, something
heard in their grandmothers' stories—a hazy film playing in an incomprehensible past. Their own coming of age had been shaped by their parents'
hard-won assimilation, the irony of that achievement being an erasure of history for the children of the assimilated. These students had passed through
a variety of social and religious clubs and organizations in which they saw
people of their race exercise power. They felt at the center of things themselves, optimistic, forward-looking, the force of their own personal history
leading them to expect an uncomplicated blending into campus life. I think
that many of them were ambivalent about Campbell Hall—it was good to
have the services, but they felt strange about being marked as different.

"Why are we reading this junk? This is just junk!" Denise was tapping
the page and looking at me, then off across the room, then back at me. Underneath the light strikes of her finger was a passage her history professor
had excerpted from the Lincoln-Douglas debates[1]:

> . . . there is a physical difference between the white and black races which I
> believe will forever forbid the two races living together on terms of social and
> political equality. And inasmuch as they cannot so live, while they do re-
> main together there must be the position of superior and inferior, and I as
> much as any other man am in favor of having the superior position assigned
> to the white race.

"Yeah," I said, "Abraham Lincoln. Pretty upsetting, isn't it? Why do you think
the professor gave it to the class?" "Well," she said, still angry, "that's not the
point. The point is, why do we have to read stuff like this?" The week before,
Denise and I had the following exchange. She had to write a paper for her composition class. It was built on an excerpt from Henry Roth's immigrant novel,
Call It Sleep, and the assignment required her to write about the hardships current immigrants face. Our discussion worked its way around to attitudes, so I

---

[1] Series of debates between 1858 Senate candidates Abraham Lincoln and Stephen A. Douglas.

suggested to Denise that she write on the things she'd heard said about Hispanic immigrants in Southern California. She looked at me as though I'd whispered something obscene in her ear. "No!" she said emphatically, pulling back her head, "that's rude." "Rude," I said. "Explain to me what's—" She cut in. "You don't want to put that in a paper. That doesn't belong." Some things were better left unsaid. Decent people, Denise had learned, just don't say them. There is a life to lead, and it will be a good life. Put the stuff your grandmother lived and your father saw behind you. It belongs in the past. It need not be dredged up if we're to move on. And, in fact, Denise could not dredge it up—the flow of her writing stopped cold by an ugly historical text that was both confusing and painful for her to see.

The counselor's office was always dusky, the sun blocked by thick trees outside the windows. There was an oversize easy chair by his desk. In it sat Marita, thin, head down, hands in her lap, her shiny hair covering her face. The counselor spoke her name, and she looked up, her eyes red in the halflight. The counselor explained that the graduate student who taught her English had accused Marita of plagiarism and had turned her paper over to the director of Freshman English. He asked her to continue, to tell me the story herself.

Marita had been at UCLA for about three weeks. This was her first writing assignment. The class had read a discussion of creativity by Jacob Bronowski and were supposed to write papers agreeing or disagreeing with his discussion. What, Marita wondered, would she say? "What is the insight with which the scientist tries to see into nature?" asked Bronowski. Marita wasn't a scientist, and she didn't consider herself to be a particularly creative person, like an artist or an actress. Her father had always been absolute about the expression of opinion, especially with his daughters: "Don't talk unless you know." "All science is the search for unity in hidden likenesses," asserted Bronowski. "The world is full of fools who speak in ignorance," Marita's father would say, and Marita grew up cautious and reticent. Her thoughts on creativity seemed obvious or, worse yet, silly next to this man Bronowski. What did it mean anyway when he said: "We remake nature by the act of discovery, in the poem or in the theorem"? She wanted to do well on the assignment, so she went to the little library by her house and looked in the encyclopedia. She found an entry on creativity and used some selections from it that had to do with mathematicians and scientists. On the bottom of the last page of her paper, she listed the encyclopedia and her English composition textbook as her references. What had she done wrong? "They're saying I cheated. I didn't cheat." She paused and thought. "You're supposed to use other people, and I did, and I put the name of the book I used on the back of my paper."

The counselor handed me the paper. It was clear by the third sentence that the writing was not all hers. She had incorporated stretches of old encyclopedia prose into her paper and had quoted only some of it. I couldn't know if she had lifted directly or paraphrased the rest, but it was formal and dated and sprinkled with high-cultural references, just not what you'd find in freshman writing. I imagined that it had pleased her previous teachers that she cared enough about her work to go find sources, to rely on experts. Marita had come from a tough school in Compton—an area to the southeast of where I'd grown up—and her conscientiousness and diligence, her commitment to the academic way, must have been a great joy to those who taught her. She shifted, hoisting herself back up from the recesses of the counselor's chair. "Are they going to dismiss me? Are they going to kick me out of school?"

Marita was adrift in a set of conventions she didn't fully understand; she offended without knowing why. Virtually all the writing academics do is built on the writing of others. Every argument proceeds from the texts of others. Marita was only partially initiated to how this works: She was still unsure as to how to weave quotations in with her own prose, how to mark the difference, how to cite whom she used, how to strike the proper balance between her writing and someone else's—how, in short, to position herself in an academic discussion.

I told Marita that I would talk with her teacher and that I was sure we could work something out, maybe another chance to write the paper. I excused myself and walked slowly back to my office, half lost in thought, reading here and there in the Bronowski excerpt. It was typical fare for Freshman English anthologies, the sort of essay you'd originally find in places like *The New Yorker*.[2] Bronowski, the eminent scientist, looking back on his career, weaving poetry in with cybernetics, quoting *Faust* in German, allusive, learned, reflective.

The people who put together those freshman anthologies are drawn to this sort of thing: It's in the tradition of the English essay and reflects rich learning and polished style. But it's easy to forget how difficult these essays can be and how developed a taste they require. When I was at Loyola, someone recommended I buy Jacques Barzun's *The Energies of Art,* a collection of "fifteen striking essays on art and culture." I remember starting one essay and stopping, adrift, two or three pages later. Then another, but no go. The words arose from a depth of knowledge and a developed perception and a wealth of received ways to talk about art and a seemingly endless reserve of allusions. I felt like a janitor at a gallery opening, silent, intimidated, little flecks of knowledge—Bagehot, Stendhal, baroque ideology—sticking to the fiber of my broom.

---

[2] Upscale weekly magazine.

Marita's assignment assumed a number of things: an ability to slip into Bronowski's discussion, a reserve of personal experiences that the writer herself would perceive as creative, a knowledge of and facility with—confidence with, really—the kinds of stylistic moves you'd find in those *New Yorker* essays. And it did *not* assume that someone, by family culture, by gender, would be reluctant to engage the reading on its own terms. Marita was being asked to write in a cognitive and social vacuum. I'm sure the other students in her class had a rough time of it as well. Many competent adult writers would too. But the solution Marita used marked her as an outsider and almost tripped the legal switches of the university.

STUDY AND DISCUSSION QUESTIONS

1. Why does Rose address the first section directly to *"you,"* the reader?

2. The second paragraph ends: *"You filled Sociology 1 in on some cards and sent them out and eventually got other cards back that told you you were enrolled."* What is Rose trying to say here?

3. Of middle-class students of color, Rose writes: "Their own coming of age had been shaped by their parents' hard-won assimilation, the irony of that achievement being an erasure of history for the children of the assimilated." What does he mean?

4. Why is Denise so angry at being asked to read the quote from Abraham Lincoln? What do you think the history professor's purpose was in assigning it? Was he or she wrong to do so?

5. What are some of the reasons Marita had such a hard time with her assignment?

6. How do the three sections of this excerpt fit together? What light do they shed on one another?

SUGGESTIONS FOR WRITING

1. Have you ever had an experience in college like the one Rose describes in the first section of "The Politics of Remediation"? What can be done to help avoid such situations?

2. Suppose Marita's teacher had said, "If she can't write a paper without plagiarizing, maybe she doesn't belong in college." How might you reply?

PREMATURE PRAGMATISM

Barbara Ehrenreich

Barbara Ehrenreich (b. 1941) has a PhD in biology and was an early critic of the health care system in the United States. A wide-ranging social critic, she has also written about economic globalism, welfare, sexism, and war, and she is active in Democratic Socialists of America. Among her books are For Her Own Good: One Hundred Fifty Years of the Experts' Advice to Women *(1978),* The Hearts of Men: American Dreams and the Flight from Commitment *(1983),* Fear of Falling: The Inner Life of the Middle Class *(1989),* Blood Rites: Origins and History of the Passion of War *(1997), and several essay collections. The following essay originally appeared in* Ms. *magazine in 1986.*

The setting was one of those bucolic Ivy League campuses where the tuition exceeds the average American annual income and the favorite sport is white-water rafting—as far, in other words, as one might hope to get from the banal economic worries that plague the grown-up world. The subject, among the roomful of young women who had come to meet with me, turned to "life after college"—"if there is one" (nervous giggles). "My dream was to go into psychiatric social work," offered a serious young woman in overalls and a "Divest Now"[1] button, "but I don't think I could live on that, so I'm going into banking instead." When I protested that she should hold on to her ideals and try to get by on the $30,000 or so a year psychiatric social workers earn, she looked baffled, as if I were recommending an internship with Mother Teresa.[2]

"Ideals are all right when you're young," declared another woman, a campus activist who certainly seemed to fit the age group for which she found idealism appropriate, "but you do have to think of earning a living." Well, yes, I thought to myself, we older feminists have been saying for some time that the goal of higher education for women is not the "MRS" degree, but when did we ever say that it was *banking?*

---

[1] Slogan of movement of American college students and others who worked to pressure their institutions to stop investing in companies doing business in apartheid South Africa.

[2] Nun known for working with the poor in India.

Not that a little respect for the dollar isn't a fine thing in the young, and a useful antidote, in my day anyway, for the effects of too much Hesse or Kahlil Gibran. But no one in the room had gone so far as to suggest a career in alms-giving, washing lepers' feet, or doing literacy training among the Bushmen. "Idealism," to these undergraduates, was defined as an ordinary, respectable profession in the human services. "Realism" meant plunging almost straight from pubescence into the stone-hearted world of finance capitalism.

I call this mind-set, which you will find on almost any campus today, "premature pragmatism," and I am qualified to comment because I, too, was once a victim of it. I had gone to college with an intellectual agenda that included solving the mind-body problem, discovering the sources of human evil, and getting a tentative reading on the purpose of life. But within a few months I had dropped all that and become a chemistry major—partly because I had figured out that there are only meager rewards, in this world, for those who know the purpose of life and the source of all evil.

The result, twenty-odd years later, is more or less what you'd expect: I'm an ex-science major with no definite occupation (unless you count "writing," that universal cover for those who avoid wage slavery at all costs), and I am still obsessed by the Ultimate Questions, such as What It's All About and Whether the Universe Will Expand Forever. I could have turned out much worse; I could have stayed in chemistry and gone into something distinctly unidealistic like nerve gas or plastics, in which case I might have become rich and would almost certainly also have become an embittered alchoholic or a middle-aged dropout. The point is that premature pragmatism didn't work for me, and I doubt that it will work for any young person intending to set aside a "Divest Now" button for one reading "You Have a Friend at Chase Manhattan."[3]

Yet premature pragmatism has become as popular on campuses as, in past eras, swallowing goldfish to impress one's friends or taking over the administration building to demand a better world. There has been a precipitous decline, just since the seventies, in the number of students majoring in mind-expanding but only incidentally remunerative fields like history and mathematics. Meanwhile, business—as an academic pursuit—is booming: almost one-fourth of all college graduates were business majors in 1983, compared to about one-seventh in 1973, while the proportions who major in philosophy or literature have vanished beyond the decimal point to less than 1 percent.

Even more alarming, to anyone whose own life has been scarred by premature pragmatism, is the decline in "idealism" as expressed by undergraduates and measured by pollsters. In 1968, 85 percent of college students said

---

[3] Advertising slogan of New York City bank.

that they hoped their education would help them "develop a philosophy of life," etc., etc. In 1985, only 44 percent adhered to such lofty goals, while the majority expected that education would help them "earn a lot of money." There has been, in other words, almost a 50 percent decline in idealism and a 100 percent increase in venality, or to put it less judgmentally, premature pragmatism.

I concede, though, that there are good reasons for the hard-nosed pragmatism of today's college students. They face rougher times, economically, than did my generation or the generation before mine. As economists Frank Levy and Richard Michel have recently shown, today's baby boomers (and especially the younger ones) are far less likely than their own parents to be able to buy a home, maintain a family on one income, or to watch their standard of living improve as they grow older.

So the best comeback for the young woman in overalls would have been for her to snap at me, "You think I should live on thirty thousand dollars a year! Well, perhaps you hadn't noticed that the National Association of Homebuilders now estimates that it takes an income of thirty-seven thousand dollars a year to be able to afford a modest, median-priced home. Or that if I want to send my own eventual children to a college like this I will need well over fifty thousand dollars a year. Or are you suggesting I rely on a rich husband?" And she would have been dead on the mark: in today's economy, idealism is a luxury that most of us are likely to enjoy only at the price of simple comforts like housing and education. The mood on campus isn't so much venality as it is *fear*.

But still, premature pragmatism isn't necessarily a winning strategy. In the first place, what looks like "realism" at age eighteen may become sheer folly by age thirty-eight. Occupations go in and out of corporate favor, so that chemistry, for example—which seemed to be a safe bet two decades ago—has become one of those disciplines that prepare people for a life in the retail end of the newspaper business. The same may eventually happen to today's campus favorites—like law, management, and finance. At least it seems to me that there must be an ecological limit to the number of paper pushers the earth can sustain, and that human civilization will collapse when the number of, say, tax lawyers exceeds the world's total population of farmers, weavers, fisherpersons, and pediatric nurses.

Furthermore, with any luck at all, one becomes a rather different person at age thirty-eight than one was at eighteen. The list of famous people who ended up in a different line of work than the one they first embarked on includes Clark Gable (former lumberjack), artist Henri Rousseau (postal clerk), Elvis Presley (truck driver), St. Augustine (playboy), Walt Disney (ambulance driver), and Che Guevara (physician). Heads of state are notoriously ill prepared for their mature careers; think of Adolph Hitler (landscape painter),

Ho Chi Minh (seaman), and our own Ronald Reagan. Women's careers are if anything even more unpredictable, to judge from my own friends: Barbara (a biochemist turned novelist), Sara (French literature professor, now a book editor), cousin Barb (anthropology to medicine).

But the saddest thing about today's premature pragmatists is not that they will almost certainly be unprepared for their midlife career destinations, but that they will be unprepared for Life, in the grand sense, at all. The years between eighteen and twenty-two were not given to us to be frittered away in contemplation of future tax shelters and mortgage payments. In fact, it is almost a requirement of developmental biology that these years be spent in erotic reverie, metaphysical speculation, and schemes for universal peace and justice. Sometimes, of course, we lose sight of the heroic dreams of youth later on, as overdue bills and carburetor problems take their toll. But those who never dream at all start to lose much more—their wit, empathy, perspective, and, for lack of a more secular term, their immortal souls.

Then what about the fact that it takes nearly a six-figure income to achieve what used to be known as a "middle-class" lifestyle? What about my young Ivy League friend, forced to choose between a career in human service and what she believes, perhaps realistically, to be an adequate income? All I can say is that there is something grievously wrong with a culture that values Wall Street sharks above social workers, armament manufacturers above artists, or, for that matter, corporate lawyers above homemakers. Somehow, we're going to have to make the world a little more habitable for idealists, whether they are eighteen or thirty-eight. In fact, I suspect that more and more young people, forced to choose between their ideals and their economic security, will start opting instead for a career in social change. "The pay is lousy," as veteran writer-historian-social-change-activist Irving Howe likes to say, "but it's steady work."

STUDY AND DISCUSSION QUESTIONS

1. At the end of the second paragraph, Ehrenreich poses *"banking"* as the epitome of the unidealistic occupation. Why banking?

2. What are Ehrenreich's *pragmatic* arguments against premature pragmatism?

3. How does Ehrenreich become increasingly sympathetic to the premature pragmatist as her essay proceeds?

4. Ehrenreich writes: "All I can say is that there is something grievously wrong with a culture that values Wall Street sharks above social workers, armament manufacturers above artists, or, for that matter,

corporate lawyers above homemakers." What is her point in making the third comparison?

5. Ehrenreich focuses on a group of students at an Ivy League college. Are the issues different for students at, say, a community college?

SUGGESTIONS FOR WRITING

1. Find out the number of students in each of the majors at your school. Can you draw any conclusions?

2. Consider your own academic major and career plans, if you've already decided. To what extent are they idealistic and to what extent "pragmatic"?

NOBODY MEAN MORE TO ME THAN YOU AND THE FUTURE LIFE OF WILLIE JORDAN

June Jordan

June Jordan was born in Harlem in 1936 and studied at Barnard College and the University of Chicago. She has worked at a number of colleges and now teaches African American studies at the University of California at Berkeley. Her poetry includes Some Changes *(1971),* Passion *(1980),* Naming Our Destiny *(1989), and* Haruko/Love Poems *(1994). Her essays have been collected in* Civil Wars *(1981),* Moving Towards Home: Political Essays *(1989),* Technical Difficulties: African-American Notes on the State of the Union *(1994), and other volumes. The following was written in 1985.*

Black English is not exactly a linguistic buffalo; as children, most of the thirty-five million Afro-Americans living here depend on this language for our discovery of the world. But then we approach our maturity inside a larger social body that will not support our efforts to become anything other than the clones of those who are neither our mothers nor our fathers. We begin to grow up in a house where every true mirror shows us the face of somebody who does not belong there, whose walk and whose talk will never look or sound 'right,' because that house was meant to shelter a family that is alien and hostile to us. As we learn our way around this environment, either we hide our original word habits, or we completely surrender our own voice, hoping to please those who will never respect anyone different from themselves: Black English is not exactly a linguistic buffalo, but we should understand its status as an endangered species, as a perishing, irreplaceable system of community intelligence, or we should expect its extinction, and, along with that, the extinguishing of much that constitutes our own proud, and singular identity.

What we casually call 'English,' less and less defers to England and its 'gentlemen.' 'English' is no longer a specific matter of geography or an element of class privilege; more than thirty-three countries use this tool as a means of 'intranational communication.' Countries as disparate as Zimbabwe and Malaysia, or Israel and Uganda, use it as their non-native currency of convenience. Obviously, this tool, this 'English,' cannot function inside thirty-three discrete societies on the basis of rules and values absolutely determined somewhere else, in a thirty-fourth other country, for example.

In addition to that staggering congeries of non-native users of English, there are five countries, or 333,746,000 people, for whom this thing called 'English' serves as a native tongue. Approximately 10 percent of these native speakers of 'English' are Afro-American citizens of the USA. I cite these numbers and varieties of human beings dependent on 'English' in order, quickly, to suggest how strange and how tenuous is any concept of 'Standard English.' Obviously, numerous forms of English now operate inside a natural, an uncontrollable, continuum of development. I would suppose 'the standard' for English in Malaysia is not the same as 'the standard' in Zimbabwe. I know that standard forms of English for Black people in this country do not copy that of whites. And, in fact, the structural differences between these two kinds of English have intensified, becoming more Black, or less white, despite the expected homogenizing effects of television and other mass media.

Nonetheless, white standards of English persist, supreme and unquestioned, in these United States. Despite our multi-lingual population, and despite the deepening Black and white cleavage within that conglomerate, white standards control our official and popular judgments of verbal proficiency and correct, or incorrect, language skills, including speech. In contrast to India, where at least fourteen languages co-exist as legitimate Indian languages, in contrast to Nicaragua, where all citizens are legally entitled to formal school instruction in their regional or tribal languages, compulsory education in America compels accommodation to exclusively white forms of 'English.' White English, in America, is 'Standard English.'

This story begins two years ago. I was teaching a new course, 'In Search of the Invisible Black Woman,' and my rather large class seemed evenly divided between young Black women and men. Five or six white students also sat in attendance. With unexpected speed and enthusiasm we had moved through historical narratives of the nineteenth century to literature by and about Black women, in the twentieth. I had assigned the first forty pages of Alice Walker's *The Color Purple,* and I came, eagerly, to class that morning:

'So!' I exclaimed, aloud. 'What did you think? How did you like it?'

The students studied their hands, or the floor. There was no response. The tense, resistant feeling in the room fairly astounded me.

At last, one student, a young woman still not meeting my eyes, muttered something in my direction.

'What did you say?' I prompted her.

'Why she have them talk so funny. It don't sound right.'

'You mean the language?'

Another student lifted his head: 'It don't look right, neither. I couldn't hardly read it.'

At this, several students dumped on the book. Just about unanimously, their criticisms targeted the language. I listened to what they wanted to say and silently marvelled at the similarities between their casual speech patterns and Alice Walker's written version of Black English.

But I decided against pointing to these identical traits of syntax; I wanted not to make them self-conscious about their own spoken language—not while they clearly felt it was 'wrong.' Instead I decided to swallow my astonishment. Here was a negative Black reaction to a prize winning accomplishment of Black literature that white readers across the country had selected as a best seller. Black rejection was aimed at the one irreducibly Black element of Walker's work: the language—Celie's Black English. I wrote the opening lines of *The Color Purple* on the blackboard and asked the students to help me translate these sentences into Standard English:

> *You better not never tell nobody but God. It'd kill your mammy.*
> Dear God,
>   I am fourteen years old. I have always been a good girl. Maybe you can give me a sign letting me know what is happening to me.
>   Last spring after Little Lucious come I heard them fussing. He was pulling on her arm. She say it too soon, Fonso. I aint well. Finally he leave her alone. A week go by, he pulling on her arm again. She say, Naw, I ain't gonna. Can't you see I'm already half dead, an all of the children.

Our process of translation exploded with hilarity and even hysterical, shocked laughter. The Black writer, Alice Walker, knew what she was doing! If rudimentary criteria for good fiction include the manipulation of language so that the syntax and diction of sentences will tell you the identity of speakers, the probable age and sex and class of speakers, and even the locale— urban/rural/southern/western—then Walker had written, perfectly. This is the translation into Standard English that our class produced:

> *Absolutely, one should never confide in anybody besides God. Your secrets could prove devastating to your mother.*
> Dear God,
>   I am fourteen years old. I have always been good. But now, could you help me to understand what is happening to me?
>   Last spring, after my little brother, Lucious, was born, I heard my parents fighting. My father kept pulling at my mother's arm. But she told him, 'It's too soon for sex, Alfonso. I am still not feeling well.' Finally, my father left her alone. A week went by, and then he began bothering my mother, again: Pulling her arm. She told him, 'No, I won't! Can't you see I'm already exhausted from all of these children?'

(Our favorite line was 'It's too soon for sex, Alfonso.')

Once we could stop laughing, once we could stop our exponentially wild improvisations on the theme of Translated Black English, the students pushed me to explain their own negative first reactions to their spoken language on the printed page. I thought it was probably akin to the shock of seeing yourself in a photograph for the first time. Most of the students had never before seen a written facsimile of the way they talk. None of the students had ever learned how to read and write their own verbal system of communication: Black English. Alternatively, this fact began to baffle or else bemuse and then infuriate my students. Why not? Was it too late? Could they learn how to do it, now? And, ultimately, the final test question, the one testing my sincerity: Could I teach them? Because I had never taught anyone Black English and, as far as I knew, no one, anywhere in the United States, had ever offered such a course, the best I could say was 'I'll try.'

He looked like a wrestler.
    He sat dead center in the packed room and, every time our eyes met, he quickly nodded his head as though anxious to reassure, and encourage, me.
    Short, with strikingly broad shoulders and long arms, he spoke with a surprisingly high, soft voice that matched the soft bright movement of his eyes. His name was Willie Jordan. He would have seemed even more unlikely in the context of Contemporary Women's Poetry, except that ten or twelve other Black men were taking the course, as well. Still, Willie was conspicuous. His extreme fitness, the muscular density of his presence underscored the riveted, gentle attention that he gave to anything anyone said. Generally, he did not join the loud and rowdy dialogue flying back and forth, but there could be no doubt about his interest in our discussions. And, when he stood

to present an argument he'd prepared, overnight, that nervous smile of his vanished and an irregular stammering replaced it, as he spoke with visceral sincerity, word by word.

That was how I met Willie Jordan. It was in between 'In Search of the Invisible Black Woman' and 'The Art of Black English.' I was waiting for Departmental approval and I supposed that Willie might be, so to speak, killing time until he, too, could study Black English. But Willie really did want to explore Contemporary Women's poetry and, to that end, volunteered for extra research and never missed a class.

Towards the end of that semester, Willie approached me for an independent study project on South Africa. It would commence the next semester. I thought Willie's writing needed the kind of improvement only intense practice will yield. I knew his intelligence was outstanding. But he'd wholeheartedly opted for 'Standard English' at a rather late age, and the results were stilted and frequently polysyllabic, simply for the sake of having more syllables. Willie's unnatural formality of language seemed to me consistent with the formality of his research into South African apartheid. As he projected his studies, he would have little time, indeed, for newspapers. Instead, more than 90 percent of his research would mean saturation in strictly historical, if not archival, material. I was certainly interested. It would be tricky to guide him into a more confident and spontaneous relationship both with language and apartheid. It was going to be wonderful to see what happened when he could catch up with himself, entirely, and talk back to the world.

September, 1984: Breezy fall weather and much excitement! My class, 'The Art of Black English,' was full to the limit of the fire laws. And, in Independent Study, Willie Jordan showed up, weekly, fifteen minutes early for each of our sessions. I was pretty happy to be teaching, altogether!

I remember an early class when a young brother, replete with his ever present pork-pie hat, raised his hand and then told us that most of what he'd heard was 'all right' except it was 'too clean.' 'The brothers on the street,' he continued, 'they mix it up more. Like "fuck" and "motherfuck." Or like "shit."' He waited. I waited. Then all of us laughed a good while, and we got into a brawl about 'correct' and 'realistic' Black English that led to Rule 1.

Rule 1: *Black English is about a whole lot more than mothafuckin.*

As a criterion, we decided, 'realistic' could take you anywhere you want to go. Artful places. Angry places. Eloquent and sweetalkin places. Polemical places. Church. And the local Bar & Grill. We were checking out a language, not a mood or a scene or one guy's forgettable mouthing off.

It was hard. For most of the students, learning Black English required a fallback to patterns and rhythms of speech that many of their parents had beaten out of them. I mean *beaten.* And, in a majority of cases, correct Black English could be achieved only by striving for *incorrect* Standard English, something they were still pushing at, quite uncertainly. This state of affairs led to Rule 2.

Rule 2: *If it's wrong in Standard English it's probably right in Black English, or, at least, you're hot.*

It was hard. Roommates and family members ridiculed their studies, or remained incredulous. 'You *studying* that shit? At school?' But we were beginning to feel the companionship of pioneers. And we decided that we needed another rule that would establish each one of us as equally important to our success. This was Rule 3.

Rule 3: *If it don't sound like something that come out somebody mouth then it don't sound right. If it don't sound right then it ain't hardly right. Period.*

This rule produced two weeks of compositions in which the students agonizingly tried to spell the sound of the Black English sentence they wanted to convey. But Black English is, pre-eminently, an oral/spoken means of communication. *And spelling don't talk.* So we needed Rule 4.

Rule 4: *Forget about the spelling. Let the syntax carry you.*

Once we arrived at Rule 4 we started to fly because syntax, the structure of an idea, leads you to the world view of the speaker and reveals her values. The syntax of a sentence equals the structure of your consciousness. If we insisted that the language of Black English adheres to a distinctive Black syntax, then we were postulating a profound difference between white and Black people, *per se*. Was it a difference to prize or to obliterate?

There are three qualities of Black English—the presence of life, voice, and clarity—that testify to a distinctive Black value system that we became excited about and self-consciously tried to maintain.

1. Black English has been produced by a pre-technocratic, if not anti-technological, culture. More, our culture has been constantly threatened by annihilation or, at least, the swallowed blurring of assimilation. Therefore, our language is a system constructed by people constantly needing to insist that we exist, that we are present. Our language devolves from a culture that abhors all abstraction, or anything tending to obscure or delete the fact of the human being who is here and now/the truth of the person who is speaking or listening. Consequently, *there is no passive voice construction possible in Black English.* For example, you cannot say, 'Black English is being eliminated.' You must say, instead, 'White people eliminating Black English.' The assumption of the presence of life governs all of Black English. Therefore, overwhelmingly, *all action takes place in the language of the present indicative.* And every sentence assumes the living and active participation of at least two human beings, the speaker and the listener.

2. A primary consequence of the person-centered values of Black English is the delivery of voice. If you speak or write Black English, your ideas will necessarily possess that otherwise elusive attribute, *voice.*

3. One main benefit following from the person-centered values of Black English is that of *clarity*. If your idea, your sentence, assumes the presence of at least two living and active people, you will make it understandable because the motivation behind every sentence is the wish to say something real to somebody real.

As the weeks piled up, translation from Standard English into Black English or vice versa occupied a hefty part of our course work.

> Standard English (hereafter S.E.): 'In considering the idea of studying Black English those questioned suggested—'
> (What's the subject? Where's the person? Is anybody alive in there, in that idea?)
> Black English (hereafter B.E.): 'I been asking people what you think about somebody studying Black English and they answer me like this:'

But there were interesting limits. You cannot 'translate' instances of Standard English preoccupied with abstraction or with nothing/nobody evidently alive, into Black English. That would warp the language into uses antithetical to the guiding perspective of its community of users. Rather you must first change those Standard English sentences, themselves, into ideas consistent with the person-centered assumptions of Black English.

Guidelines For Black English

1. Minimal number of words for every idea: This is the source for the aphoristic and/or poetic force of the language; eliminate every possible word.

2. Clarity: If the sentence is not clear it's not Black English.

3. Eliminate use of the verb *to be* whenever possible. This leads to the deployment of more descriptive and, therefore, more precise verbs.

4. Use *be* or *been* only when you want to describe a chronic, ongoing state of things.

> He *be* at the office, by 9. (He is always at the office by 9.)
> He *been* with her since forever.

5. Zero copula: Always eliminate the verb *to be* whenever it would combine with another verb, in Standard English.

> S.E.: She is going out with him.
> B.E.: She going out with him.

6. Eliminate *do* as in:

> S.E.: What do you think? What do you want?
> B.E.: What you think? What you want?

Rules number 3, 4, 5, and 6 provide for the use of the minimal number of verbs per idea and, therefore, greater accuracy in the choice of verb.

7. In general, if you wish to say something really positive, try to formulate the idea using emphatic negative structure.

> S.E.: He's fabulous.
> B.E.: He bad.

8. Use double or triple negatives for dramatic emphasis.

> S.E.: Tina Turner sings out of this world.
> B.E.: Ain nobody sing like Tina.

9. Never use the *-ed* suffix to indicate the past tense of a verb.

> S.E.: She closed the door.
> B.E.: She close the door. Or, she have close the door.

10. Regardless of intentional verb time, only use the third person singular, present indicative, for use of the verb *to have,* as an auxiliary.

> S.E.: He had his wallet then he lost it.
> B.E.: He have him wallet then he lose it.
> S.E.: He had seen that movie.
> B.E.: He seen that movie. Or, he have see that movie.

11. Observe a minimal inflection of verbs. Particularly, never change from the first person singular forms to the third person singular.

> S.E.: Present Tense Forms: He goes to the store.
> B.E.: He go to the store.
> S.E.: Past Tense Forms: He went to the store.
> B.E.: He go to the store. Or, he gone to the store. Or, he been to the
>   store.

12. The possessive case scarcely ever appears in Black English. Never use an apostrophe ('s) construction. If you wander into a possessive case component of an idea, then keep logically consistent: *ours, his, theirs, mines.* But, most likely, if you bump into such a component, you have wandered outside the underlying world-view of Black English.

> S.E.: He will take their car tomorrow.
> B.E.: He taking they car tomorrow.

13. Plurality: Logical consistency, continued: If the modifier indicates plurality then the noun remains in the singular case.

> S.E.: He ate twelve doughnuts.
> B.E.: He eat twelve doughnut.
> S.E.: She has many books.
> B.E.: She have many book.

14. Listen for, or invent, special Black English forms of the past tense, such as: 'He losted it. That what she felted.' If they are clear and readily understood, then use them.

15. Do not hesitate to play with words, sometimes inventing them: e.g. 'astropotomous' means huge like a hippo plus astronomical and, therefore, signifies real big.

16. In Black English, unless you keenly want to underscore the past tense nature of an action, stay in the present tense and rely on the overall context of your ideas for the conveyance of time and sequence.

17. Never use the suffix *-ly* form of an adverb in Black English.

> S.E.: The rain came down rather quickly.
> B.E.: The rain come down pretty quick.

18. Never use the indefinite article *an* in Black English.

> S.E.: He wanted to ride an elephant.
> B.E.: He want to ride him a elephant.

19. Invariant syntax: in correct Black English it is possible to formulate an imperative, an interrogative, and a simple declarative idea with the same syntax:

> B.E.: You going to the store?
> You going to the store.
> You going to the store!

Where was Willie Jordan? We'd reached the mid-term of the semester. Students had formulated Black English guidelines, by consensus, and they were now writing with remarkable beauty, purpose, and enjoyment.

'I ain hardly speakin for everybody but myself so understan that.'—Kim Parks

Samples from student writings:

'Janie have a great big ole hole inside her. Tea Cake the only thing that fit that hole . . .

'That pear tree beautiful to Janie, especial when bees fiddlin with the blossomin pear there growin large and lovely. But personal speakin, the love she get from starin at that tree ain the love what starin back at her in them relationship.' (Monica Morris)

'Love is a big theme in, *They Eye Was Watching God*. Love show people new corners inside theyself. It pull out good stuff and stuff back bad stuff . . . Joe worship the doing uh his own hand and need other people to worship him too. But he ain't think about Janie that she a person and ought to live like anybody common do. Queen life not for Janie.' (Monica Morris)

'In both life and writin, Black womens have varietous experience of love that be cold like a iceberg or fiery like a inferno. Passion got for the other partner involve, man or woman, seem as shallow, ankle-deep water or the most profoundest abyss.' (Constance Evans)

'Family love another bond that ain't never break under no pressure.' (Constance Evans)

'You know it really cold/When the friend you/Always get out the fire/Act like they don't know you/When you in the heat.' (Constance Evans)

'Big classroom discussion bout love at this time. I never take no class where us have any long arguin for and against for two or three day. New to me and great. I find the class time talkin a million time more interestin than detail bout the book.' (Kathy Esseks)

As these examples suggest, Black English no longer limited the students, in any way. In fact, one of them, Philip Garfield, would shortly 'translate' a pivotal scene from Ibsen's *Doll's House,* as his final term paper:

> Nora: I didn't gived no shit. I thinked you a asshole back then, too, you make it so hard for me save mines husband life.
>
> Krogstad: Girl, it clear you ain't any idea what you done. You done exact what I once done, and I losed my reputation over it.
>
> Nora: You asks me believe you once act brave save you wife life?
>
> Krogstad: Law care less why you done it.
>
> Nora: Law must suck.
>
> Krogstad: Suck or no, if I wants, judge screw you wid dis paper.
>
> Nora: No way, man. (Philip Garfield)

But where was Willie? Compulsively punctual, and always thoroughly prepared with neatly typed compositions, he had disappeared. He failed to show up for our regularly scheduled conference, and I received neither a note nor a phone call of explanation. A whole week went by. I wondered if

Willie had finally been captured by the extremely current happenings in South Africa: passage of a new constitution that did not enfranchise the Black majority, and militant Black South African reaction to that affront. I wondered if he'd been hurt, somewhere. I wondered if the serious workload of weekly readings and writings had overwhelmed him and changed his mind about independent study. Where was Willie Jordan?

One week after the first conference that Willie missed, he called: 'Hello, Professor Jordan? This is Willie. I'm sorry I wasn't there last week. But something has come up and I'm pretty upset. I'm sorry but I really can't deal right now.'

I asked Willie to drop by my office and just let me see that he was okay. He agreed to do that. When I saw him I knew something hideous had happened. Something had hurt him and scared him to the marrow. He was all agitated and stammering and tense and incoherent. At last, his sadly jumbled account let me surmise, as follows: Brooklyn police had murdered his unarmed, twenty-five year old brother, Reggie Jordan. Neither Willie nor his elderly parents knew what to do about it. Nobody from the press was interested. His folks had no money. Police ran his family around and around, to no point. And Reggie was really dead. And Willie wanted to fight, but he felt helpless.

With Willie's permission, I began to try to secure legal counsel for the Jordan family. Unfortunately Black victims of police violence are truly numerous while the resources available to prosecute their killers are truly scarce. A friend of mine at the Center for Constitutional Rights estimated that just the preparatory costs for bringing the cops into court normally approaches $180,000. Unless the execution of Reggie Jordan became a major community cause for organizing, and protest, his murder would simply become a statistical item.

Again, with Willie's permission, I contacted every newspaper and media person I could think of. But the William Bastone feature article in *The Village Voice* was the only result from that canvassing.

Again, with Willie's permission, I presented the case to my class in Black English. We had talked about the politics of language. We had talked about love and sex and child abuse and men and women. But the murder of Reggie Jordan broke like a hurricane across the room.

There are few 'issues' as endemic to Black life as police violence. Most of the students knew and respected and liked Jordan. Many of them came from the very neighborhood where the murder had occurred. All of the students had known somebody close to them who had been killed by police, or had known frightening moments of gratuitous confrontation with the cops. They wanted to do everything at once to avenge death. Number One: They decided to compose personal statements of condolence to Willie Jordan and his family written in Black English. Number Two: They decided to compose individual messages to the police, in Black English. These should be prefaced by an explanatory paragraph composed by the entire group. Number Three: These individual messages, with their lead paragraph, should be sent to *Newsday*.

The morning after we agreed on these objectives, one of the young women students appeared with an unidentified visitor, who sat through the class, smiling in a peculiar, comfortable way.

Now we had to make more tactical decisions. Because we wanted the messages published, and because we thought it imperative that our outrage be known by the police, the tactical question was this: Should the opening, group paragraph be written in Black English or Standard English?

I have seldom been privy to a discussion with so much heart at the dead heat of it. I will never forget the eloquence, the sudden haltings of speech, the fierce struggle against tears, the furious throwaway, and useless explosions that this question elicited.

That one question contained several others, each of them extraordinarily painful to even contemplate. How best to serve the memory of Reggie Jordan? Should we use the language of the killers—Standard English—in order to make our ideas acceptable to those controlling the killers? But wouldn't what we had to say be rejected, summarily, if we said it in our own language, the language of the victim, Reggie Jordan? But if we sought to express ourselves by abandoning our language wouldn't that mean our suicide on top of Reggie's murder? But if we expressed ourselves in our own language wouldn't that be suicidal to the wish to communicate with those who, evidently, did not give a damn about us/Reggie/police violence in the Black community?

At the end of one of the longest, most difficult hours of my own life, the students voted, unanimously, to preface their individual messages with a paragraph composed in the language of Reggie Jordan. *'At least we don't give up nothing else. At lease we stick to the truth: Be who we been. And stay all the way with Reggie.'*

It was heartbreaking to proceed, from that point. Everyone in the room realized that our decision in favor of Black English had doomed our writings, even as the distinctive reality of our Black lives always has doomed our efforts to 'be who we been' in this country.

I went to the blackboard and took down this paragraph, dictated by the class:

'. . . YOU COPS!

WE THE BROTHER AND SISTER OF WILLIE JORDAN, A FELLOW STONY BROOK STUDENT WHO THE BROTHER OF THE DEAD REGGIE JORDAN. REGGIE, LIKE MANY BROTHER AND SISTER, HE A VICTIM OF BRUTAL RACIST POLICE, OCTOBER 25, 1984. US APPALL, FED

UP, BECAUSE THAT ANOTHER SENSELESS DEATH WHAT OCCUR IN OUR COMMUNITY. THIS WHAT WE FEEL, THIS, FROM OUR HEART, FOR WE AIN'T STAYIN' SILENT NO MORE.'

With the completion of this introduction, nobody said anything. I asked for comments. At this invitation, the unidentified visitor, a young Black man, ceaselessly smiling, raised his hand. He was, it so happens, a rookie cop. He had just joined the force in September and, he said, he thought he should clarify a few things. So he came forward and sprawled easily into a posture of barroom, or fireside, nostalgia:

'See,' Officer Charles enlightened us, 'Most times when you out on the street and something come down you do one of two things. Over-react or under-react. Now, if you under-react then you can get yourself kilt. And if you over-react then maybe you kill somebody. Fortunately it's about nine times out of ten and you will over-react. So the brother got kilt. And I'm sorry about that, believe me. But what you have to understand is what kilt him: over-reaction. That's all. Now you talk about Black people and white police but see, now, I'm a cop myself. And (big smile) I'm Black. And just a couple months ago I was on the other side. But see it's the same for me. You a cop, you the ultimate authority: the Ultimate Authority. And you on the street, most of the time you can only do one of two things: over-react or under-react. That's all it is with the brother. Over-reaction. Didn't have nothing to do with race.'

That morning Officer Charles had the good fortune to escape without being boiled alive. But barely. And I remember the pride of his smile when I read about the fate of Black policemen and other collaborators, in South Africa. I remember him, and I remember the shock and palpable feeling of shame that filled the room. It was as though that foolish, and deadly, young man had just relieved himself of his foolish, and deadly, explanation, face to face with the grief of Reggie Jordan's father and Reggie Jordan's mother. Class ended quietly. I copied the paragraph from the blackboard, collected the individual messages and left to type them up.

Newsday rejected the piece.

The Village Voice could not find room in their 'Letters' section to print the individual messages from the students to the police.

None of the tv news reporters picked up the story.

Nobody raised $180,000 to prosecute the murder of Reggie Jordan.

Reggie Jordan is really dead.

I asked Willie Jordan to write an essay pulling together everything important to him from that semester. He was still deeply beside himself with frustration and amazement and loss. This is what he wrote, un-edited, and in its entirety:

'Throughout the course of this semester I have been researching the effects of oppression and exploitation along racial lines in South Africa and its neighboring countries. I have become aware of South African police brutalization of native Africans beyond the extent of the law, even though the laws themselves are catalyst affliction upon Black men, women and children. Many Africans die each year as a result of the deliberate use of police force to protect the white power structure.

'Social control agents in South Africa, such as policemen, are also used to force compliance among citizens through both overt and covert tactics. It is not uncommon to find bold-faced coercion and cold-blooded killings of Blacks by South African police for undetermined and/or inadequate reasons. Perhaps the truth is that the only reasons for this heinous treatment of Blacks rests in racial differences. We should also understand that what is conveyed through the media is not always accurate and may sometimes be construed as the tip of the iceberg at best.

'I recently received a painful reminder that racism, poverty, and the abuse of power are global problems which are by no means unique to South Africa. On October 25, 1984 at approximately 3:00 p.m. my brother, Mr. Reginald Jordan, was shot and killed by two New York City policemen from the 75th precinct in the East New York section of Brooklyn. His life ended at the age of twenty-five. Even up to this current point in time the Police Department has failed to provide my family, which consists of five brothers, eight sisters, and two parents, with a plausible reason for Reggie's death. Out of the many stories that were given to my family by the Police Department, not one of them seems to hold water. In fact, I honestly believe that the Police Department's assessment of my brother's murder is nothing short of ABSOLUTE BULLSHIT, and thus far no evidence had been produced to alter perception of the situation.

'Furthermore, I believe that one of three cases may have occurred in this incident. First, Reggie's death may have been the desired outcome of the police officer's action, in which case the killing was premeditated. Or, it was a case of mistaken identity, which clarifies the fact that the two officers who killed my brother and their commanding parties are all grossly incompetent. Or, both of the above cases are correct, i.e., Reggie's murderers intended to kill him and the Police Department behaved insubordinately.

'Part of the argument of the officers who shot Reggie was that he had attacked one of them and took his gun. This was their major claim. They also said that only one of them had actually shot Reggie. The facts, however, speak for themselves. According to the Death Certificate and autopsy report, Reggie was shot eight times from point-blank range. The Doctor who performed the autopsy told me himself that two bullets entered the side of my brother's head, four bullets were sprayed into his back, and two bullets struck him in the back of his legs. It is obvious that unnecessary force was used by the police and that it is extremely difficult to shoot someone in his back when he is attacking or approaching you.

'After experiencing a situation like this and researching South Africa I believe that to a large degree, justice may only exist as rhetoric. I find it difficult to talk of true justice when the oppression of my people both at home and abroad attests to the fact that inequality and injustice are serious problems whereby Blacks and Third World people are perpetually short-changed by society. Something has to be done about the way in which this world is set up. Although it is a difficult task, we do have the power to make a change.'

Willie J. Jordan Jr
EGL 487, Section 58, November 14, 1984

STUDY AND DISCUSSION QUESTIONS

1. What point is Jordan making in her discussion of the use of English around the world? How does this point relate to what follows in the essay?

2. Why did the Black students initially dislike Alice Walker's use of Black English in her novel? Why did they change their minds?

3. Why was it difficult at first for the Black students to learn Black English?

4. What does Jordan mean by "the person-centered assumptions of Black English"?

5. Why might it be important to have a *course* in Black English?

6. Why does Jordan keep emphasizing that she acted "with Willie's permission" in responding to Reggie's murder?

7. Jordan writes of "Willie's unnatural formality of language." Where might this formality have come from?

SUGGESTIONS FOR WRITING

1. Whatever your race/ethnicity, do you react at all negatively when you hear Black English? If so, why do you think that is?

2. What was the effect on you of seeing the "Guidelines For Black English" in print?

3. Do you agree with the class's decision to write their "explanatory paragraph" in Black English?

THREE

MASS CULTURE

Mass culture, folk or popular culture, high culture: what do these terms mean? High culture is what people traditionally have gone to college to learn—the classics in literature and the arts. However, what is considered a classic can change over time. The mutability of the literary canon is suggested by the fact that only a few decades ago, American students studied a list of great works of literature in which the literary productions of their own country played a minor role. Folk or popular culture is what people who share for example race, class, ethnicity, or a work environment produce to communicate with each other: quilts made to be passed down in a family, union songs or songs to sing while picking cotton, an anthology of your writing which you and your classmates might produce for and with each other. In contrast, mass culture, the subject we are offering for your serious consideration in this section of *Against the Current,* is produced as a commodity by the few for the many. It is increasingly the type of culture that is most readily available to the mass of people. We might ask ourselves why that is so. Jerry Mander, writing in this section, might answer that television, to take one example, "is uniquely suited to implant and continuously reinforce dominant ideologies." The essays in this section look at several significant forms of mass culture: advertising, television, mail-order catalogs, Hollywood films, department store mannequins, and children's toys. What other forms of mass culture occur to you?

To what extent is mass culture a reflection of what the masses believe and to what extent is mass culture used to manipulate and to dictate what people believe? Stuart and Elizabeth Ewen's essay "In the Shadow of the

Image" reminds us that forms of "mass produced and mass distributed images" have had a great impact on people since before the arrival of television. These images affect the way we feel, the way we think and believe, and the way we behave, even though we are not generally conscious of their power. The Ewens' essay takes the form of juxtaposed verbal "snapshots," underscoring the randomness, the complexity, and the pervasiveness of the process by which mass culture imprints itself in our minds. How to guard against this flood of information, intended to motivate and to manipulate its recipients, is a major worry for all of us. It is easy to imagine this flood of information becoming increasingly dangerous. Some science fiction novelists, extrapolating from the current situation into the future, already have imagined advertising projectors which flash images directly into the brains of passersby.

Today, however, we have television. "For most human beings in the Western world," begins Jerry Mander in "Television: Audiovisual Training for the Modern World," "watching television has become the principal means of interaction with the new world now under construction, as well as a primary activity of everyday life." The average American adult watches television five hours a day; the average child between the ages of two and five is glued to the set three-and-a-half hours per day. In spite of many research studies and analytical articles such as Mander's, people go on watching television copiously and allowing their children to do the same. Is it simply that television is addictive, so that the occasional family that goes cold turkey and turns off the set is unusual enough to be worth a newspaper feature? Or is there something about the stress of contemporary life in the United States, where it is generally necessary for all adults in a family to work, that turns the television into the babysitter of choice? Are workers too tired to do anything but sink into a stew of mass-produced images when they get home in the evening? For Mander, the technological capacities of the medium and its impact on human neurology are the prime sources of danger. He is also concerned about the extent to which whoever controls the transmission of images controls what people perceive as reality.

Taking *The Cosby Show* as his example, Henry Louis Gates, Jr. explores how social stereotyping is alive and well in television depictions of black people. In "TV's Black World Turns—But Stays Unreal," Gates traces the evolution of racial character types in American literature onto the small screen. With the rise in popularity of depictions of upper-middle-class black families supplanting depictions of poor, unsuccessful black people, the picture grows more confusing but no more accurate, suggests Gates. Who are these people? What relation do they have to everyday reality? If they can make it, asks the viewer, why can't I? Here Americans' tendency to deny the importance of social class mixes with their stereotyped production of racial images. Gates worries that the consumption of fabricated and often fantastic images of black Americans might obscure in American minds the actual facts of widespread poverty and lack of choice that many working-class black people in North America have to face.

In "Class Struggle in Hollywood," Benjamin DeMott, who has written extensively about class in the United States, analyzes several popular Hollywood films that purport to be seriously about the working class and about relations between social classes: *Working Girl, White Palace, Pretty Woman, Driving Miss Daisy, Platoon,* and *Dirty Dancing.* He finds that filmmakers continually undercut, dismiss, or deny the very concept of class division and of power inequity in the United States as they add to a national tradition that prefers Horatio Alger myths of upward mobility for the deserving to the reality of economic inequality. The American belief in a meritocracy means first, that if you don't achieve at least middle-class status, it is your own individual failure; and second, that if you cannot identify as a member of, say, the working class, then you cannot join together with others in collective action to improve your own condition and that of others in your group.

While Gates looks at the appealing middle-class fantasy of *The Cosby Show* and DeMott marks the ways in which class division is undercut in Hollywood films, Barbara Ehrenreich analyzes what she calls our other favorite television show, *Roseanne.* Unabashedly working class, overweight, and feminist, Roseanne challenges viewers' sensibilities while the Huxtable family soothes them. Ehrenreich suggests this sitcom takes the depiction of the working-class family far beyond Archie Bunker and other television representations of working-class life. Through Roseanne's female perspective, we see a complex view of the family as refuge from capitalism that is, nevertheless, flawed by patriarchy. While many of the essays in this section analyze the dangers of mass culture, its tendency towards the lowest common denominator, and its role as purveyor of mass ideology, Ehrenreich seems to find in *Roseanne* some subversive and potentially revolutionary messages about women, the working class, and the stressed American family which have managed to sneak past the corporate censors. Or, wait a minute, is there a conservative message lurking under the apparent subversion?

Also focusing on women, Susan Faludi investigates the beauty industry, which has become a multi-billion-dollar conglomerate composed of businesses ranging from clothing manufacturers to cosmetics purveyors to plastic surgeons. Faludi explains the way this industry maneuvers women's images from decade to decade. The action-oriented, wholesome-looking woman of the World War II period, for example, segues into the passive and palely glamorous female of the early 1950s. The effect this manipulation of image has on women's self-esteem, as their expectations of beauty become ever more difficult to reach, has been well documented in studies of eating disorders and of the medical consequences of plastic surgery. Faludi begins her article by interviewing a man who sculpts the department store mannequins whose plastic proportions set the standard real women then feel they have to meet. In 1988, she reports, those proportions were 34–23–36.

Lisa Jones marks the advent of mass marketing of mail-order catalogs, which she calls "designer advert-zines," as some time in the 1980s. These days, catalogs make up the biggest bulk of our daily mail and we are profoundly sympathetic to the mailperson who has to trudge around the neighborhood hauling them on her shoulder. Most likely, the catalogs will go right into our recycling bins, if we have them. But let's be honest. Most of us do sneak a glance at those catalogs. We do sit down at the kitchen table to flip through pages full of down comforters, miracle uplift bras, terra-cotta garlic roasters, kids' corduroy pants, ecologically correct t-shirts imprinted with representatives of near-extinct species, and solar powered mosquito repellers, as well as the WASPy look with which African American writer Lisa Jones is doing her own complicated dance. And sometimes they do lasso us: we pick up the phone and dial 1–800—. So perhaps the cost to the catalog producers is worth it. The cost to the consumer, after we subtract the occasional convenience of not having to get in the car and drive to the mall, is one more unneeded tug at the credit card and the time we lose while we review the day's take of 'logs. One more time, we are overloaded with image information about who we should be, and we despair because, darn it, we do not look like these models, white or black.

We pass on our cultural and human legacy by the way we socialize our children, our next generation. In the modern era in the West, control over this socialization has gradually transferred from the hearts and hands of families to the shelves of toy stores at malls (or to the toy of the week accompanying your child's Happy Meal). Actually, the emergence of toys as a major and lucrative industry is fairly recent and parallels advertisers' definition of children as big-time consumers worthy of special targeting-note the predatory word. Roland Barthes, French philosopher of contemporary culture, makes a case for how the meanings and possibilities of toys have become increasingly delimited or static. In function, form, and material construction, suggests Barthes, contemporary commercial toys condition our children to an adult world of diminished possibility. We might connect Barthes's comments on the material nature, the function, and the effect of toys to Jerry Mander's comments about children and television, including his conclusion that "television effectively produces a new form of human being—less creative, speedier, and more interested in *things*—albeit better able to handle, appreciate, and approve of the new technological world."

Reading and thinking about the essays in this section may increase your awareness of the number, the complexity, and the subtlety of mass images and their accompanying messages in the contemporary western world. As American and other western corporations penetrate less "developed" regions, those regions too become drawn into a sticky and possibly sinister "world wide web." Given the pervasiveness of mass culture which is driven by increasingly sophisticated technology, what are our possible responses? Is technology itself problematic, or only the uses to which the technology is put? Ought we simply to accept that we are Mander's "new form of human being" and enjoy what we can of our new identity? If we do wish to resist mass culture, how can we go about doing so? Certainly there is a long, though often derided, tradition of resistance both to mass culture and the technology which makes it possible—from the Luddite destruction of machinery in the nineteenth century to back-to-the-land movements today. Living a conscious life, trying to pick and choose for oneself and with one's children what images to take in, is a middle way that requires much work. The next decision you make, ask yourself what mass-produced images influenced it.

IN THE SHADOW
OF THE IMAGE

Stuart Ewen and Elizabeth Ewen

Stuart Ewen (b. 1945) teaches media studies at Hunter College and the City University of New York Graduate Center and is the author of Captains of Consciousness: Advertising and the Social Roots of the Consumer Culture *(1976),* All Consuming Images: The Politics of Style in Contemporary Culture *(1990), and* PR! A Social History of Spin *(1996). Elizabeth Ewen (b. 1943) teaches American Studies at the State University of New York at Old Westbury and is the author of* Immigrant Women in the Land of Dollars: Life and Culture on the Lower East Side, 1890–1925 *(1985). The following is the introduction to their collaborative work,* Channels of Desire: Mass Images and the Shaping of American Consciousness *(1982).*

Maria Aguilar was born twenty-seven years ago near Mayagüez, on the island of Puerto Rico. Her family had lived off the land for generations. Today she sits in a rattling IRT[1] subway car, speeding through the iron-and-rock guts of Manhattan. She sits on the train, her ears dazed by the loud outcry of wheels against tracks. Surrounded by a galaxy of unknown fellow strangers, she looks up at a long strip of colorful signboards placed high above the bobbing heads of the others. All the posters call for her attention.

Looking down at her, a blond-haired lady cabdriver leans out of her driver's side window. Here is the famed philosopher of this strange urban world, and a woman she can talk to. The tough-wise eyes of the cabby combine with a youthful beauty, speaking to Maria Aguilar directly:

Estoy sentada 12 horas al dia.
Lo último que necesito son hemorroides.

(I sit for twelve hours a day. The last thing I need are hemorrhoids.)

Under this candid testimonial lies a package of Preparation H ointment, and the promise "Alivia dolores y picasonas. Y ayuda a reducir la

---

[1] Interborough Rapid Transit.

hinchazón." (Relieves pain and itching. And helps reduce swelling.) As her mind's eye takes it all in, the train sweeps into Maria's stop. She gets out; climbs the stairs to the street; walks to work where she will spend her day sitting on a stool in a small garment factory, sewing hems on pretty dresses.

* * *

Every day, while Benny Doyle drives his Mustang to work along State Road Number 20, he passes a giant billboard along the shoulder. The billboard is selling whisky and features a woman in a black velvet dress stretching across its brilliant canvas.

As Benny Doyle downshifts by, the lounging beauty looks out to him. Day after day he sees her here. The first time he wasn't sure, but now he's convinced that her eyes are following him.

* * *

The morning sun shines on the red-tan forehead of Bill O'Conner as he drinks espresso on his sun deck, alongside the ocean cliffs of La Jolla, California. Turning through the daily paper, he reads a story about Zimbabwe.

"Rhodesia," he thinks to himself.

The story argues that a large number of Africans in Zimbabwe are fearful about black majority rule, and are concerned over a white exodus. Two black hotel workers are quoted by the article. Bill puts this, as a fact, into his mind.

Later that day, over a business lunch, he repeats the story to five white business associates, sitting at the restaurant table. They share a superior laugh over the ineptitude of black African political rule. Three more tellings, children of the first, take place over the next four days. These are spoken by two of Bill O'Conner's luncheon companions; passed on to still others in the supposed voice of political wisdom.[2]

* * *

Barbara and John Marsh get into their seven-year-old Dodge pickup and drive twenty-three miles to the nearest Sears in Cedar Rapids. After years of breakdowns and months of hesitation they've decided to buy a new washing machine. They come to Sears because it is there, and because they believe that their new Sears machine will be steady and reliable. The Marshes will pay for their purchase for the next year or so.

Barbara's great-grandfather, Elijah Simmons, had purchased a cream-separator from Sears, Roebuck in 1897 and he swore by it.

* * *

---

[2] This newspaper article was brought to our attention by journalist Les Payne, speaking at the American Writers Congress, New York City, October 10, 1981. [Author's note]

When the clock-radio sprang the morning affront upon him, Archie Bishop rolled resentfully out of his crumpled bed and trudged slowly to the john. A few moments later he was unconsciously squeezing toothpaste out of a mess of red and white Colgate packaging. A dozen scrubs of the mouth and he expectorated a white, minty glob into the basin.

Still groggy, he turned on the hot water, slapping occasional palmfuls onto his gray face.

A can of Noxzema shave cream sat on the edge of the sink, a film of crud and whiskers across its once neat label. Archie reached for the bomb and filled his left hand with a white creamy mound, then spread it over his beard. He shaved, then looked with resignation at the regular collection of cuts on his neck.

Stepping into a shower, he soaped up with a soap that promised to wake him up. Groggily, he then grabbed a bottle of Clairol Herbal Essence Shampoo. He turned the tablet-shaped bottle to its back label, carefully reading the "Directions."

"Wet hair."

He wet his hair.

"Lather."

He lathered.

"Rinse."

He rinsed.

"Repeat if necessary."

Not sure whether it was altogether necessary, he repeated the process according to directions.

Late in the evening, Maria Aguilar stepped back in the subway train, heading home to the Bronx after a long and tiring day. This time, a poster told her that "The Pain Stops Here!"

She barely noticed, but later she would swallow two New Extra Strength Bufferin tablets with a glass of water from a rusty tap.

*   *   *

Two cockroaches in cartoon form leer out onto the street from a wall advertisement. The man cockroach is drawn like a hipster, wearing shades and a cockroach zoot-suit. He strolls hand-in-hand with a lady cockroach, who is dressed like a floozy and blushing beet-red. Caught in the midst of their cockroach-rendezvous, they step sinfully into a Black Flag Roach Motel. Beneath them, in Spanish, the words:

> Las Cucarachas entran . . . pero non pueden salir. (In the English version: Cockroaches check in . . . but they don't check out.)

The roaches are trapped; sin is punished. Salvation is gauged by one's ability to live roach-free. The sinners of the earth shall be inundated by roaches. Moral tales and insects encourage passersby to rid their houses of sin. In their homes, sometimes, people wonder whether God has forsaken them.

* * *

Beverly Jackson sits at a metal and tan Formica table and looks through the *New York Post.* She is bombarded by a catalog of horror. Children are mutilated . . . subway riders attacked. . . . Fanatics are marauding and noble despots lie in bloody heaps. Occasionally someone steps off the crime-infested streets to claim a million dollars in lottery winnings.

Beverly Jackson's skin crawls; she feels a knot encircling her lungs. She is beset by immobility, hopelessness, depression.

Slowly she walks over to her sixth-floor window, gazing out into the sooty afternoon. From the empty street below, Beverly Jackson imagines a crowd yelling "Jump! . . . Jump!"

* * *

Between 1957 and 1966 Frank Miller saw a dozen John Wayne movies, countless other westerns and war dramas. In 1969 he led a charge up a hill without a name in Southeast Asia. No one followed; he took a bullet in the chest.

Today he sits in a chair and doesn't get up. He feels that images betrayed him, and now he camps out across from the White House while another movie star cuts benefits for veterans. In the morning newspaper he reads of a massive weapons buildup taking place.

* * *

Gina Concepcion now comes to school wearing the Jordache look. All this has been made possible by weeks and weeks of afterschool employment at a supermarket checkout counter. Now, each morning, she tugs the decorative denim over her young legs, sucking in her lean belly to close the snaps.

These pants are expensive compared to the "no-name" brands, but they're worth it, she reasons. They fit better, and she fits better.

* * *

The theater marquee, stretching out over a crumbling, garbage-strewn sidewalk, announced "The Decline of Western Civilization."[3] At the ticket window a smaller sign read "All Seats $5.00."

* * *

It was ten in the morning and Joyce Hopkins stood before a mirror next to her bed. Her interview at General Public Utilities, Nuclear Division, was only four hours away and all she could think was "What to wear?"

---

[3] 1981 movie directed by Penelope Spheeris.

A half hour later Joyce stood again before the mirror, wearing a slip and stockings. On the bed, next to her, lay a two-foot-high mountain of discarded options. Mocking the title of a recent bestseller, which she hadn't read, she said aloud to herself, "Dress for Success. . . . What *do* they like?"

At one o'clock she walked out the door wearing a brownish tweed jacket; a cream-colored Qiana blouse, full-cut with a tied collar; a dark beige skirt, fairly straight and hemmed (by Maria Aguilar) two inches below the knee; sheer fawn stockings, and simple but elegant reddish-brown pumps on her feet. Her hair was to the shoulder, her look tawny.

When she got the job she thanked her friend Millie, a middle manager, for the tip not to wear pants.

*   *   *

Joe Davis stood at the endless conveyor, placing caps on a round-the-clock parade of automobile radiators. His nose and eyes burned. His ears buzzed in the din. In a furtive moment he looked up and to the right. On the plant wall was a large yellow sign with THINK! printed on it in bold type. Joe turned back quickly to the radiator caps.

Fifty years earlier, in another factory, in another state, Joe's grandfather, Nat Davis, had looked up and seen another sign:

A *Clean* Machine Runs Better.
Your Body is a Machine.
KEEP IT CLEAN.

Though he tried and tried, Joe Davis' grandfather was never able to get the dirt out from under his nails. Neither could his great-grandfather, who couldn't read.

*   *   *

In 1952 Mary Bird left her family in Charleston to earn money as a maid in a Philadelphia suburb. She earned thirty-five dollars a week, plus room and board, in a dingy retreat of a ranch-style tract house.

Twenty-eight years later she sits on a bus, heading toward her small room in North Philly. Across from her, on an advertising poster, a sumptuous meal is displayed. Golden fried chicken, green beans glistening with butter and flecked by pimento, and a fluffy cloud of rice fill the greater part of a calico-patterned dinner plate. Next to the plate sit a steaming boat of gravy, and an icy drink in an amber tumbler. The plate is on a quilted blue placemat, flanked by a thick linen napkin and colonial silverware.

As Mary Bird's hungers are aroused, the wording on the placard instructs her: *"Come Home to Carolina."*

*   *   *

SHOPPING LIST

paper towels
milk
eggs
rice crispies
chicken
snacks for kids (twinkies, chips, etc.)
potatoes
coke, ginger ale, plain soda
cheer
brillo
peanut butter
bread
ragu (2 jars)
spagetti
saran wrap
salad
get cleaning, bank, *must pay electric!!!*

* * *

On his way to Nina's house, Sidney passed an ad for Smirnoff vodka. A sultry beauty with wet hair and beads of moisture on her smooth, tanned face looked out at him. *"Try a Main Squeeze."* For a teenage boy the invitation transcended the arena of drink; he felt a quick throb-pulse at the base of his belly and his step quickened.

In October of 1957, at the age of two and a half, Aaron Stone was watching television. Suddenly, from the black screen, there leaped a circus clown, selling children's vitamins, and yelling "Hi! boys and girls!" He ran, terrified, from the room, screaming.

For years after, Aaron watched television in perpetual fear that the vitamin clown would reappear. Slowly his family assured him that the television was just a mechanical box and couldn't really hurt him, that the vitamin clown was harmless.

Today, as an adult, Aaron Stone takes vitamins, is ambivalent about clowns, and watches television, although there are occasional moments of anxiety.

These are some of the facts of our lives; disparate moments, disconnected, dissociated. Meaningless moments. Random incidents. Memory traces. Each is an unplanned encounter, part of day-to-day existence. Viewed alone, each by itself, such spaces of our lives seem insignificant, trivial. They are the decisions and reveries of survival; the stuff of small talk; the chance preoccupations of our eyes and minds in a world of images—soon forgotten.

Viewed together, however, as an ensemble, an integrated panorama of social life, human activity, hope and despair, images and information, another tale unfolds from these vignettes. They reveal a pattern of life, the structures of perception.

As familiar moments in American life, all of these events bear the footprints of a history that weighs upon us, but is largely untold. We live and breathe an atmosphere where mass images are everywhere in evidence; mass produced, mass distributed. In the streets, in our homes, among a crowd, or alone, they speak to us, overwhelm our vision. Their presence, their messages are givens; unavoidable. Though their history is still relatively short, their prehistory is, for the most part, forgotten, unimaginable.

The history that unites the seemingly random routines of daily life is one that embraces the rise of an industrial consumer society. It involves explosive interactions between modernity and old ways of life. It includes the proliferation, over days and decades, of a wide, repeatable vernacular of commercial images and ideas. This history spells new patterns of social, productive, and political life.

STUDY AND DISCUSSION QUESTIONS

1. Why do you suppose the authors of "In the Shadow of the Image" give the reader a long series of anecdotes/stories/examples before telling you what their point is?

2. Sort the anecdotes/stories/examples into categories or types and discuss what you have found.

3. How conscious of the images which enter their minds are the people illustrated here?

4. How, in these examples, do the images affect the people who take them in? Discuss the consequences of image intake in two or three of the anecdotes.

5. Why do the authors include the shopping list?

6. Only the last story, about two-and-a-half-year-old Aaron Stone, mentions television. Is this surprising to you in an article about mass-produced images? Why do you suppose the Ewens do not focus primarily on television?

SUGGESTIONS FOR WRITING

1. For one day, be aware of as many incoming images as you can, especially *intentional* images such as commercial and political images. Carry a notebook with you and note each. Append to your list an analysis of the overall or cumulative message(s) and your response.

2. Discuss a behavior pattern of your own that is or may be influenced by commercial images.

TELEVISION: AUDIOVISUAL TRAINING FOR THE MODERN WORLD

Jerry Mander

Jerry Mander (b. 1936) was the president of a commercial public relations company and later of an advertising agency, but left in the 1970s to work in nonprofit organizations devoted to social change and the environment. He has written Four Arguments for the Elimination of Television *(1978) and* In the Absence of the Sacred: The Failure of Technology and the Survival of the Indian Nations *(1991), from which the following chapter is taken and, with Edward Goldsmith, he has edited* The Case Against the Global Economy *(1996).*

People who have read *Four Arguments for the Elimination of Television* will recognize much of the information in this chapter. I am restating certain points in the present context because of the critical role television plays in the larger technological web.

For most human beings in the Western world, watching television has become the principal means of interaction with the new world now under construction, as well as a primary activity of everyday life. At the same time, the institutions at the fulcrum of the process use television to train human beings in what to think, what to feel, and how to be in the modern world.

In the chapter that follows this one, which deals with satellite television, we examine additional impacts of television in the less-developed countries, where it serves as an instrument of cultural cloning.

LIVING INSIDE MEDIA

Let's start with some 1990 statistics. They are of such monumental importance, and yet are so infrequently discussed, that I try to include them whenever I write about television.

- According to the U.S. Department of Commerce, 99.5 percent of the homes in the United States that have electricity have television sets. Electronically speaking, we are all wired together as a single entity. An electronic signal sent from a single source can now reach nearly every person in the country—250 million people across 3 million square miles—at exactly the same time. When such figures first appeared in the sixties, Marshall McLuhan hailed them as a portent of a new "global village," but he missed an important political point. The autocratic potential—the power of the one speaking into the brains of the many—is unprecedented. Its consequences are only discussed adequately in science fiction, by such people as Orwell and Huxley. The consequences are also keenly appreciated by those institutions large enough to attempt to control the medium: corporations, government, religion.
- According to the A. C. Nielsen Company, 95 percent of the U.S. population watches some TV every day. No day goes by without a "hit" of television, which indicates the level of engagement, or addiction, that people feel for the medium.
- Nielsen reports that the average American home has a television on for nearly eight hours per day. The average American adult watches TV nearly five hours per day. The average child between ages two and five watches about three and a half hours per day. The average adult over fifty-five watches nearly six hours.

Consider the situation of the average adult who watches for almost five hours daily. This person spends more time watching television than he or she spends doing anything else in life except sleeping or working or going to school. But if the *average* person is watching five hours per day, then roughly half of the U.S. population is watching *more* than five hours. (In practice, this means watching through most of each weekend, plus three or four hours each weeknight.)

It is hardly an exaggeration to say that the main activity of life for Americans, aside from work or sleep, has become watching television. Television has effectively replaced the diverse activities of previous generations, such as community events, cultural pursuits, and family life.

Ours is the first society in history of which it can be said that life has moved *inside* media. The average person, watching television for five hours per day, is physically engaged with—looking at and experiencing—a *machine.* To that extent, the person is not relating to anything else in the environment. But the environment of TV is not static, it is aggressive. It enters people's minds and leaves images within, which people then carry permanently. So television is an external environment that becomes an internal, mental environment.

The situation is really so odd that it lends itself well to science fiction descriptions. Imagine, for example, that a research team of anthropologists from Andromeda Galaxy is sent to Earth. Hovering above our country, the researchers might report back to their home base something like this:

"We are scanning the Americans now. Night after night they sit still in dark rooms, not talking to each other, barely moving except to eat. Many of them sit in separate rooms, but even those sitting in groups rarely speak to one another. They are staring at a light! The light flickers on and off many times per second [from the AC current]. The humans' eyes are not moving, and since we know that there is an association between eye movement and thought, we have measured their brain waves. Their brains are in 'alpha,' a noncognitive, passive-receptive mode. The humans are *receivers.*

"As for the light, it comes in the form of images, sent from only a few sources, thousands of miles from where the humans are gathering them in. The images are of places and events that are not, for the most part, related to the people's lives. Once placed into their heads, the images seem to take on permanence. We have noted that people use these images in their conversations with other people, and that they begin to dress and act in a manner that imitates the images. They also choose their national leaders from among the images.

"In summary, this place seems to be engaged in some kind of weird mental training akin to brainwashing."

If this is a fair description of the situation in the United States, it is also becoming a description of many other parts of the world. Right now, about 60 percent of the world population has access to television. In many places where television has recently arrived—remote villages in Africa, South America, Indonesia, northern Canada; places where there are not even roads—satellite communications have made it possible for people to ingest the dominant external society. In grass houses, on the frozen tundra, on tiny tropical islands, in the jungles of Brazil and Africa, people are sitting in their traditional homes of logs or mud or grass, and they are watching "Dallas" and "The Edge of Night" and "Bonanza."

More than 50 percent of the television watched outside the U.S. consists of reruns of popular American-made shows. Satellite communications, introduced as yet another democratic breakthrough for technology, are being used to place imagery of American-style commodity life, American values, American commercials, American-style experience in the heads of everyone, wherever they are. The end result will be worldwide monoculture.

FREEDOM OF SPEECH FOR THE WEALTHY

We think of television as a democratic medium, since we all get to watch it in our homes. But if it is "democratic" on the receiving end, it is surely not that on the sending end.

According to *Advertising Age,* about 75 percent of commercial network television time is paid for by the 100 largest corporations in the country. Many people do not react to this statistic as being important. But consider that there are presently 450,000 corporations in the United States, and some 250 million people, representing extremely diverse viewpoints about lifestyle, politics, and personal and national priorities. Only 100 corporations get to decide what will appear on television and what will not. These corporations do not overtly announce their refusal to finance programs that contain views disconsonant with their own; their control is far more subtle. It works in the minds of television producers who, when thinking about what programs to produce, have to mitigate their desires by their need to sell the programs to corporate backers. An effective censorship results.

While a small number of corporations pay for 75 percent of commercial broadcast time, and thereby dominate that medium, they now also pay for more than 50 percent of public television. During the Reagan years, federal support for noncommercial television was virtually eliminated, leaving a void that public television filled by appealing to corporations. As corporate influence has grown in public TV, so has the quality and length of the corporate commercial tags before and after the shows they sponsor. Whereas public television once featured such messages as "This program has been brought to you through a grant by Exxon," now we see the Exxon logo, followed by an added advertising phrase or two and an audio slogan.

The reason why only the largest corporations in the world dominate the broadcast signals is obvious: They are the only ones who can afford it. According to the present structure of network TV, a half-minute of prime time sells for about $200,000 to $300,000; during events such as the Super

Bowl, the price is more like $700,000. Very few medium-sized corporations or businesses, and even fewer individuals, could pay $200,000 for a single message broadcast to the world.

If you and your friends decided that you had a very important statement to make about an issue—let's say the cutting down of old-growth redwoods in the Pacific Northwest—and if you were very fortunate (and rich), perhaps you could manage to raise sufficient money to actually place your message on the airwaves—*once*. Meanwhile, the multinational corporation doing the logging could buy the spot that appears before yours, and the one immediately after, and then three more later in the evening, and then five more tomorrow and the next day and the day after, and so on throughout the month. Some corporations have advertising budgets ranging from 100 million to over one billion dollars per year. Television is effectively a "private medium," for their use only.

That television is a private system in the hands of the largest corporations is difficult for most Americans to grasp. This is because we believe that freedom of speech is an inalienable right that we all enjoy equally. Nothing could be further from the truth. As A. J. Liebling said, "Freedom of the press is available only to those who own one." Similarly, freedom of speech is more available to some than to others, namely, to the people who can purchase it on national television. This leads to certain kinds of information dominating the airwaves.

The 100 largest corporations manufacture drugs, chemicals, cosmetics, packaged-processed foods, cars, and oil, and are involved in other extractive industries. But whether you are viewing a commercial for aspirin, cars, or cosmetics, the message is exactly the same. *All* advertising is saying this: Whether you buy this commodity or that one, satisfaction in life comes from commodities.

So we have the most pervasive and powerful communications medium in history, and it is totally financed by people with identical views of how life should be lived. They express this view unabashedly. Which brings us to the most shocking statistic: *The average American who watches five hours of television per day sees approximately 21,000 commercials per year.* That's 21,000 repetitions of essentially identical messages about life, aggressively placed into viewers' minds, all saying, *Buy something—do it now!*

So an entire nation of people is sitting night after night in their rooms, in a passive condition, receiving information from faraway places in the form of imagery placed in their brains, repeated 21,000 times per year, telling them how to live their lives. If the instrument responsible for this activity weren't TV, our familiar companion, then you, like the Andromeda scientists, would probably call it a system of mass brainwashing and political control, and would be damned worried about it.

THE TECHNOLOGY OF PASSIVITY

Economics is not the only reason why television is such a suitable medium for corporate control. Equally important is the nature of the television-viewing experience; how television affects human beings. From a corporate point of view, the effect is beneficial.

*   *   *

Even in the absence of chemical evidence of addiction, the amount of time people spend daily in front of their TV, and the way lives are scheduled around it, ought to be sufficient, *de facto* proof of TV's hypnotic and addictive abilities. In fact, when I interviewed people for *Four Arguments,* interviewees consistently used terms such as "hypnotic," "mesmerizing," or "addictive" to describe their experiences of television viewing. And many used the term "zombie" to describe how their kids looked while watching television.

Eventually, I sought scientific evidence about the validity of these anecdotal descriptions, and found some researchers ready to validate such characterizations.

For example, scientists who study brain-wave activity found that the longer one watches television, the more likely the brain will slip into "alpha" level: a slow, steady brain-wave pattern in which the mind is in its most receptive mode. It is a noncognitive mode; i.e., information can be placed into the mind *directly,* without viewer participation. When watching television, people are receiving images into their brains without thinking about them. Australian National University researchers call this a kind of "sleep-teaching." So if you look at your child in front of the TV and think of him or her as "zonked," that is apparently an apt description.

There are many reasons why the brain slips into this passive-receptive alpha condition. One reason is the lack of eye movement when watching TV, because of the small size of the screen. Sitting at a normal distance, the eye can gather most of the image without scanning the screen for it. The image comes in whole. This lack of *seeking* images disrupts the normal association between eye movement and thought stimulation, which is a genetically provided safety valve for human beings. Before modern times, any unusual event in the environment would attract instant attention; all the senses would immediately turn to it, including the vision sense and its "feeler," the eyes. But when an image doesn't have to be sought, an important form of mental stimulation is absent.

A second factor causing the brain to slip into alpha-wave activity is that, with the eyes not moving and the screen flickering on and off sixty times per second, an effective hypnosis is induced, at lest in the view of psychologists who use hypnotism. Looking at the flickering light of a TV screen is akin to staring at the hypnotist's candle.

I think the third factor is the most important. The information on the TV screen—the images—come at their own speed, outside of the viewer's control; an image *stream*. One doesn't "pull out" and contemplate TV images, as if they were still photographs or images described in a written passage. If you attempted to do that you would fall behind the image stream. So there are two choices: surrender to the images, or withdrew from the experience. But if you are going to watch television (or film) at all, you *must* allow the images to enter you at their own speed. So, the nature of the experience makes you passive to its process, in body and mind. (More complete discussions of this process can be found in *The Plug-In Drug* by Marie Winn, and Australian National University's *Choice of Futures* by Fred and Merrylyn Emery, as well as in *Four Arguments for the Elimination of Television*.)

Does this problem also exist with other media? Not to the same degree. Take film, for example. The nature of the film-going experience is that one usually goes with a friend. That, in itself, stimulates the mind. And since film is shown in a public place, with other people present, there are many more stimuli and feelings accompanying the experience; a mood envelops the room.

Also, film imagery is much more refined and detailed than television imagery. The TV image, composed of tiny dots, is very coarse compared with film. A lot is lost in the television picture. Film, on the other hand, can bring out great background detail, much better images of nature, much greater subtlety. The richer the detail of the image, the more involving it is to the viewer. (This comparative advantage for film imagery over TV will only be partially mitigated when "high-definition TV" is introduced in a few years.)

Films are almost always shown on a much larger screen than are television programs, thus requiring considerably more eye movement. And when the film is over, the theater lights come up, people react, and finally rise to leave. They don't just sit there as the next stream of imagery invades them. The act of leaving, and then perhaps going to a café and talking it over, combined with the other elements of film-going, serve to bring the images up from the lower right brain (where images would otherwise reside, like dreams) into greater consciousness. The images come out of the unconscious, unusable realms into the conscious, where they can be examined to some extent.

Radio is a medium that does not impose images at all; in fact, radio stimulates the imagination in much the way books do. A situation is described and the listener actively visualizes. This very act suppresses alpha. When watching television, on the other hand, one's own image-making goes into dormancy.

Print media are by far the most engaging and participatory of any media. Since there is no inherent time limitation with books and newspapers, they can offer much more complex detail and background than any so-called visual medium. If I should now ask you to imagine a lush green field with a trickling stream, billowy clouds above, two great white dogs lying in the grass, lovers on a nearby hillside . . . you can certainly imagine that scene in great detail and color. You created these pictures in your own mind; they do not necessarily match the image I have in my mind of the same scene. If a similar image were shown on television, it would be flatter than the one you created. Meanwhile you would not be engaged in your own image-making; you would be passive to the process, relatively uninvolved.

No medium is as effective as print for providing information in detail. Since it does not have the limitations of time, it can deliver to the reader whatever it takes to achieve understanding, from one or two sentences to multiple volumes. But most importantly, gathering data from print is an active, not passive, process.

To read successfully, you must apply conscious mental effort. It is impossible to be in alpha level while reading, at least not if you want to understand what you read. We have all had the experience of reading a paragraph on a page, then realizing that we hadn't actually read it, then having to read the same material a second time. In doing this, we apply conscious effort to the process; we put our brain into a cognitive mode in order to grasp the information.

Also, when reading, one has the opportunity to review the material, underline it, write notes in the margin, tear out a page, Xerox it, send copies to friends, and reread at will, fast or slow. The reader controls most elements of the process and can create the conditions for accepting the information. All of this is impossible with TV-viewing. The information must be taken as it comes, without resistance. As a result, researchers at Australian National University described the TV-viewing experience as inherently pacifying. San Francisco brain researcher Erik Peper said, "The word 'zombie' is the best way to describe the experience." And Cornell University professor Rose Goldsen called television viewing "mnemonic learning"; that is, "learning without the conscious participation of the learner." It is sleep-teaching.

So television-viewing, if it can be compared to a drug experience, seems to have many of the characteristics of Valium and other tranquilizers. But that is only half of the story. Actually, if television is a drug, it is not really Valium; it is *speed*.

ACCELERATION OF THE NERVOUS SYSTEM

In their famous study of the effects of television, researchers at Australian National University predicted that as television became more popular in

Australia, there would be a corresponding increase in hyperactivity among children. I found this prediction alarming because many parents of hyperactive children place their kids in front of the television set, where they seem to calm down. Apparently, the opposite effect is what finally results.

Here's how it works: While sitting quietly in front of the TV, the child sees people punching each other on the screen. There is the impulse to react—the fight-or-flight instinct is activated—but since it would be absurd to react to a television fight, the child suppresses the emotion. As the fighting continues, so does the cycle of impulse and suppression. Throughout the television-viewing experience, the child is drawn back and forth on this seesaw of action and suppression, all the while appearing zapped and inactive. When the set goes off, this stored-up energy bursts forth in the disorganized, frantic behavior that we associate with hyperactivity. Often, the only calming act is to again put the set on, which starts the cycle anew. But there are also more subtle ways that television speeds humans up.

*   *   *

I am a member of the pre-television generation. Until I was in my late teens, there wasn't any television. So as a child my after-school activities were different from those of the average child today.

I can recall how it felt coming home from school every day. First, I would look in the refrigerator to see if my mother had left me any snacks. I would quickly take care of those. Then, I might play with the dog. I would go up to my room. I would lie on the living room floor. I would become bored. Nothing to do.

Slowly I would slip into a state that I have lately begun to call "downtime" (not in the computer sense)—a kind of deadly boredom. A bottom of feeling, as it were. It was connected with a gnawing anxiety in the stomach. It was so unpleasant that I would eventually decide to *do something*. I would call a friend. I would go outdoors. I would play ball. I would read.

I think that the downtime I am describing was the norm for kids during the 1940s, when life was slower than it is today. Looking back, I view that time of nothingness as serving an important creative function. Out of this nothing-to-do condition some activity would eventually emerge. You got to the bottom of your feelings, you let things slide to their lowest state, and *then* you took charge. You experienced yourself in movement, with ideas. Taking all young people in the country as a group, this downtime could be considered a national genetic pool of creativity.

Today, however, after teenagers come home and begin to slip into downtime with its accompanying unpleasant feeling, they reach for the television knob. This stops the slide. Used this way, television is a mood-alteration system, like a drug. As the mood comes on, they reach for the drug, just as adults reach for the drink—or the TV—at the end of the day. So television for young-sters, in addition to *being* a drug, can be understood as early training for "harder" drugs.

Obviously, we all have ways of altering our moods. However, I don't think most of us see our TV-watching as a mood-altering device. Under-standing it in such terms gives new meaning to the fact that the average young person watches for nearly four hours per day. By reaching for the TV drug, a generation of young people are short-circuiting their own down-time. They are not allowing themselves to live through the pits of their own experience, or to feel their own creative response to it. The net result, I think, will be a generation of young people who are less able to act on their own, or to be creative. Educators are already telling us that this is so. This habit may also be depriving young people of the fundamental self-knowledge that dealing with one's feelings produces. And it leaves this new drugged gener-ation feeling that they can't experience life without technological and chem-ical props. So TV not only trains them for drug dependency, it also trains them for commodity dependency.

PERCEPTUAL SPEEDUP AND CONFUSION

When watching television, the viewer is moved into a perceptual uni-verse that is much, much faster than ordinary life. To get an idea of how this works, I suggest that you turn on your television set now and switch to a com-mercial network. (This is an especially useful exercise to do during prime time, when more money is spent on production values.) Count the number of times something happens in the image that could not happen in ordinary life. One moment the camera puts you in front of the image, in another moment you are behind it or above it or rolling around it. Then you are out on the street; then it is tomorrow, or yesterday. A commercial appears on the screen with dancers, music, and cartoons. A couple walks on a hillside hundreds of yards away, but you can hear them speaking as though you were next to them. Words flash on and off the screen. There are suddenly two simultaneous images, or three. You are looking at a face, then suddenly at hands, then suddenly you are outdoors. Long periods of historical time are jammed together. You move from landscape, to sky, to humans in rapid succession. Young people are run-ning toward you—*Cut.* Now they are on a beach—*Cut.* Now you are watch-ing beer poured into a glass—*Cut.* Now music is playing—*Cut.* An announcer speaks from somewhere. Now you are in Europe. Now in Asia. There is a war, there is a commercial . . . All of this is jammed together in a steady stream of imagery, fracturing your attention while condensing time and mixing cate-gories of reality, nonreality, and semireality.

These image fluctuations and technical changes, as well as hundreds of other kinds not mentioned, are what I have called technical events in television imagery. These alterations of the image could not happen in ordinary life; they are *technical* alterations only possible within moving-image media: films, video, or television.

If you actually counted these technical events as I suggested above, you would find that during commercials—especially during prime time—the image changes at an average of ten to fifteen times per thirty-second commercial. During a regular program on a commercial channel, camera movements or technical events occur about seven to ten times per minute. On public television programs, there are probably three to four camera movements or technical events per minute. (There are fewer on public television than commercial television simply because commercial television can afford more cameras, more edits, and more technology. Similarly, advertisers can spend more than any television program can afford. This is one reason why people pay attention to advertising despite the lack of real content. It is visually more engaging. When people say that "advertising is the most interesting thing on television" they are not aware they are speaking about the *technology* of advertising.)

This hyperactivated imagery continues for as long as a viewer is watching the screen. For heavy viewers of television it means five or six (or more) hours living within a perceptual universe that is constantly fractured, and in which time and events are both condensed and accelerated.

Finally, the set goes off. The viewers are back in their rooms. Nothing is moving. The room does not rise up or whirl around. People do not suddenly flash on and off in front of them. It doesn't become tomorrow or yesterday in a flash. Actually, nothing at all is happening. There is simply the same room as before: walls, windows, furniture. Ordinary life and ordinary feelings and thoughts. Very slow, by comparison. Too slow. Anxiety sets in.

Having lived in the amazingly rapid world of television imagery, ordinary life is dull by comparison, and far too slow. But consider how it affects one's ability to be in nature. The natural world is *really* slow. Save for the waving of trees in the wind, or the occasional animal movement, things barely happen at all. To experience nature, to feel its subtleties, requires human perceptual ability that is capable of slowness. It requires that human beings approach the experience with patience and calm. Life in the modern world does not encourage that; it encourages the opposite. Cars, planes, video games, faxes, Walkmans, television, computers, working and traveling on schedules dictated by assembly lines and offices—we in the Western world have attuned ourselves to rhythms that are outside of nature. We are trained to seek satisfaction in the packaging that technology provides. Big "hits." We live in a world of constant catharsis, constant change, constant unrest. While out in the *real* world, in nature, we become anxious and uncomfortable. We desire to get back indoors, to get that TV set back on, to get "up to speed."

For children, this change is very serious, and has been well noted by educators. Countless teachers have told me how young people are utterly unable to maintain attention. They become bored after only a few minutes of the same subject. They need constant change. And they need the teacher to "perform" rather then teach, to deliver material with snappy punch lines. As for reading, very few young people are now patient enough to get through a book such as *The Hunchback of Notre Dame,* where events move slowly and where detail, rather than constant explosive content, is what matters.

But not only children are affected by this replacement of our living environment with television. All human beings are changing. We are all being sped up. The natural world has retreated beyond our awareness. We hear people say that nature is boring, and it is clear why they say this. We don't know how to be with it. We are not slow enough. Caring about what happens to nature is not part of our emotional world, which helps pave the way for the exploitation of nature and native people. Simultaneously, it makes us think that our future is on some other planet out there in space.

Television synchronizes our internal processes with the new world of concrete, computers, space travel, and acceleration. It makes our insides—brain and nervous system—compatible with the world outside ourselves. For human beings, it is the worst possible combination of influences. It puts our brains into a passive alpha state, zapping our thinking processes and destroying our creative impulses. Simultaneously, it speeds up our nervous systems, making us too fast to feel calm, too fast to read, almost too fast to relate meaningfully to other human beings, and too fast for nature. From this alienation training, a new human emerges. Speed junkie. Videovoid. Technovoid.

THE POLITICS OF CONFUSED REALITY

When people spend the greatest part of their lives relating to television imagery, then television imagery becomes the greatest part of people's lives. It begins to seem like life itself. Television images define the terms of people's understanding, the boundaries of human awareness. Without an offsetting system of imagery in people's lives, television images take on a quality of reality that they do not deserve.

The political consequences of such a situation, where a population becomes isolated within an artificial information environment, has been a favorite subject of many science-fiction writers over the years.

George Orwell's *1984* describes an information environment so monolithic and aggressive that it became the total source and absolute limit of human knowledge. Every room had a two-way "telescreen" that could not be turned off; its nonstop programming consisted of official music, economic data, and constant reports of military victories.

In *1984*, television became the instrument of daily training sessions for human emotions via constant juxtapositions of the images of Good vs. Evil: the benevolent, beloved Big Brother versus the hated, loathsome enemy, Goldstein. "Two Minutes Hate" periods would be regularly scheduled each day; the "disgusting" image of Goldstein on the TV screen, amid streams of official invective, caused the entire populace to join frenzied mass rages, "a hideous ecstasy of fear and vindictiveness."

Print media—books, documents, diaries—were virtually eliminated. Without such written records, the past became a manufactured creation of the present. Anything that differed from the telescreen version of reality existed solely in the memories of a few individuals, who would eventually be found out. Earlier languages were destroyed, and it was forbidden to visit the wilderness, which was itself the past.

The effect of the total control of imagery was to unify mass consciousness within a single-media version of reality. With all information coming disembodied via the telescreen, and with the whole population receiving this monolithic information at the same time, and with no verifiable points of comparison, how was one to know what was true and real and what was not? Did Goldstein even exist? Did Big Brother? How could anyone know? Reality was up for grabs. Resistance to information was pointless. All minds merged with the official imagery. Eventually, people accepted even utterly contradictory "doublethink" statements: "WAR IS PEACE," "HATE IS LOVE," "IGNORANCE IS STRENGTH."

Obviously, there are big differences between the scenario depicted in *1984* and present-day America, but as television-viewing statistics indicate, the differences may be less significant than the similarities. Television has become the primary world we relate to. Like Orwell's nonstop broadcasts, TV enters and occupies our minds and causes similar results, as we will discuss.

In his science-fiction book *Fahrenheit 451*, Ray Bradbury tells of a society in which human relationships are less important than the relationships people have with characters in television shows. Every home has a wall-sized television screen. And the characters on the screen are programmed to address the viewers personally. The TV characters, therefore, become the primary characters in people's lives.

You have only to listen to conversations these days—on buses, in restaurants, or even at the office—to observe that many people discuss the characters in sitcoms and soaps as if they were neighbors or friends. People in our society often follow the lives of TV people with greater care and interest than they follow the lives of their own family members. For many people—especially heavy television viewers—life and television have already merged.

There are bizarre consequences to this. Years ago, 250,000 people wrote to Marcus Welby, M.D.,[1] asking for medical advice. Performers in soaps have often been assaulted and verbally abused by people on the street for their characters' behavior. Many researchers—most notably, Gerbner and Gross of the University of Pennsylvania—have established that Americans tend to take even fictional TV shows as true and believable. Recently, people such as Nancy Reagan, Henry Kissinger, and Michael Jordan have made guest appearances on sitcoms. Does this make the other characters, or the show itself, more real? Or does it make Kissinger less real? Fiction and reality have lost their boundaries.

People who immerse themselves in the surrogate reality of television life deal on a daily basis with a reality totally unlike any that has preceded it. For example, when watching television news, you are presumably taking in actual world events, happening before *you* as they happen in real-time. But actually, most of what you see happened earlier; you are viewing edited tapes of these events. Sometimes the events being described are not presented as images, but are verbal descriptions by the announcer. Then the news is interrupted by a commercial. The commercial is not happening in the same place as the event that just preceded it, nor is the announcer in that place. Yet they are all somehow within this image stream. Soon after this, you may be watching a fictional dramatic program, which uses real people performing scripted events, in an accelerated time frame, also interrupted by commercials that may feature well-known stars relating to unreal situations in a realistic manner. Then you watch a docudrama, which is a fictionalized re-creation of a real event, in which you are asked to grasp both the realistic elements and the re-created semifictional elements in the same plane of understanding. (In 1989, ABC News was discovered to have *simulated* a contact between an alleged U.S. spy and a Soviet agent; this was the first known case of "re-created actuality" within a format that claimed reality.)

In other instances, you may be watching the future, which looks real, but is actually a scripted drama. Or talk shows, in which real people, usually actors (who normally play fictional roles), talk about real events in their actual lives. Then again commercials appear, which have "real" actors who are playing roles, as well as real people like John Madden or Chuck Yeager (the test pilot) in acting roles, and so on.

I have not even scratched the surface of the numbers of categories of reality that come and go every few minutes on television. Meanwhile, however, *you* are actually sitting home in your room and all of this imagery enters your mind without vivid distinction. When you see Henry Kissinger in a drama you may say to yourself, "This is Henry Kissinger; he is not in the same category of reality as the other actors; there is another level of reality operating

---

[1] Hero of television drama.

here," but probably you don't. You just accept the stream as it comes. For heavy viewers of television, practiced in this acceptance, distinctions become extremely blurred.

Whereas the fictional presentations of television take on a kind of reality, the real events of the political world, which are also fitted into the image flow, take on the characteristics of the fictional material on the screen. Wars, riots, international spying, and electoral contests all begin to be viewed as the latest exciting TV series or, in the case of presidential contests, as sporting events. They come and go as frequently as sitcoms or drama, and are just as dependent on the ratings. (The choice of subjects for TV news is often based upon what will attract and maintain viewers. See Edward J. Epstein's *News From Nowhere.*) And so each great tragedy or world crisis—even those as monumental as the Philippines revolution, or the democratic uprisings in China and Eastern Europe, or the Chernobyl disaster, or the Salman Rushdie death threat,[2] or the war between the U.S. and Iraq—each news event dominates the tube for a short while, and then is put on the back burner or totally forgotten. Each of the productions fit nicely into evening-news formats; they run steadily for two to eight weeks, depending on the subject and the attention span of the viewers, and then are dropped.

They all deal with "real" world events, but they come to us in the steady, mixed-up stream of real, unreal, and semireal events that is everyday television. In our minds, these real news events merge with other material, becoming just another set of stored imagery that all have similar reality values. They enter and leave our lives with the accelerated rhythms of the rest of television events, eventually dissolving into the past. We become engaged, enraged, entertained, involved, and then they are over. We feel we have been experiencing our lives as we watch these world events, but really all that happened is that we sat home in our living rooms and watched television. This is true whether we are watching news, or Cousteau's whales, or our "friends" on the late-night talk shows or in the soaps. They are all part of the same pulsating stream of imagery and so they become equal in our minds. J. R. Ewing, John Madden, Johnny Carson, Imelda Marcos, Sylvester Stallone, Madonna, Roseanne, Moammar Khadafy, Bart Simpson, Michael Jordan, Michael Jackson, Laura Palmer, Sadam Hussein, Charlton Heston, Manuel Noriega, Clint Eastwood . . . (As you read each of these names, did you get a visual picture of each of them? You did! Did you realize that there were pictures of these people living in your mind? Or that you hold all these images, which represent wildly

---

[2] In 1989, Iranian Muslim leader Ayatollah Khomeini called for the execution of Rushdie, a British writer, for publishing his allegedly blasphemous novel *The Satanic Verses,* and Rushdie went into hiding for years.

different categories of "real life," from politician to athlete to performer to fictional character, to cartoon, on more or less the same plane of reality?)

Though we can distinguish among the categories of reality that the television stream delivers to us, we rarely do. We let the images flow and lodge into our brains without distinction. That the resultant wipe-out of the lines between real and not real might lead us to some distortion in our political reality should have been obvious to us many years ago.

THE TELEVISION PRESIDENT

Comedians have often suggested that Ronald Reagan's immense popularity might have been helped by television-induced confusion. But I would like to make the case that this was concretely true, and that it's not so funny.

Ronald Reagan spent his adult life being an image, sometimes fictional—as when performing in films—and sometimes in that odd semi-reality that performers obtain in commercials. For his career combined film acting and, perhaps more important, spokesperson roles for General Electric Company advertising.

Because of his background, Reagan handled television as president with astonishing skill and power. He understood, as no one did before, that on television, style supersedes content: The way you behave and look is more important than what you say or do. He knew that complexity and historical perspective do not come across on TV as well as simplicity, bald assertion, the heavy use of symbolic content, and the appeal to formulaic values, deeply imbedded in Americans by previous decades of television and film: Good vs. Evil, America vs. The Enemy, Revere the Flag. (Reagan's protégé, George Bush, also learned these lessons; he was elected in 1988 because of his embrace of TV symbolism—the flag, the pledge of allegiance, black rapists—mixed with spots about Dukakis[3] and pollution, which turned out to be lies.)

Reagan's most remarkable achievement was to incorporate in his own persona an amazing set of archetypes from the popular movies of the 1940s and 1950s. In the *real* role of president, Ronald Reagan re-created a set of images that had been reinforced by standard story lines since World War II; he was making real what was previously just imagery held in the minds of the population.

Ronald Reagan became the World War II hero, standing tall. He became the admiral on the bridge of the ship, taking on the hated Nazis and Japanese, though it became the Commies and the Iranians. He was the western hero,

---

[3] Michael Dukakis, Massachusetts governor and 1988 Democratic candidate for President.

slow to anger, but push him too far and he became fierce in his response. He was not Rambo, a contemporary unfeeling slaughterer. He had morals. He was John Wayne. He was Gary Cooper in *High Noon.*

Reagan was also the family man of the 1950s: affable, homey, a little bit sexy, and in love with his adoring wife. He was kindly and grandfatherly, with a few personality quirks. He didn't remember things so good. He pronounced some of them fancy French names wrong. He meant Camus, but he said "Kaymus." But his fallabilities made us love him more; they gave him an unthreatening, comedic aspect, sort of like Jimmy Stewart.

Yet he was also the authoritative spokesperson—the same one he used to be for General Electric. He believed in the technological dream and was willing to sell it hard. He believed in the American vision of the good life. He knew technology could achieve anything. He loved the challenge of the future. "Progress is our most important product."[4]

All of these characteristics were stereotypes from popular movies of the forties and fifties, and they remained in the minds of the millions of people who saw them. They conjured memories of a simpler time, when solutions were clear, when America was on top, and heroes and ordinary people could change things.

Ronald Reagan could reach into those memories of a generation, and incorporate them into himself. He appealed to the collective media unconscious to produce an almost alchemical result, making real what was previously fiction.

Reagan also grasped the antihistorical nature of TV reality, its *nowness.* He was very aggressive in his attempts to create historical truth. He understood that when a population is confined to a single information source, especially one that speaks imagery directly into the brain, that source has unprecedented power as a tool to control human minds. As in *1984,* real and unreal, truth and fiction, become equally arbitrary, for there is no way to clarify or check what TV asserts. And so Reagan could call his invasion of Grenada a "rescue" of students who were never in danger. He could assert that the Soviets knew that Korean Air flight 007 was a passenger plane before they shot it down, though subsequent stories suggested that Reagan *knew* that the Soviets did *not* know. (The initial image stuck, and the event is still understood in those terms today.) By asserting that Libya was behind the Berlin disco bombing, Reagan made *that* true for millions of Americans, and we supported his bloody retaliation, though later evidence showed that Syria had most likely created that event.

---

[4] General Electric advertising slogan.

Ronald Reagan called MX missiles "peacekeepers." He said that low-ering taxes on the wealthy benefited the poor, and he unabashedly claimed that massive rearming was the way to disarm. A few years later, George Bush said "the last best chance for peace" was to declare war against Iraq, and then said "the goal of the war is peace." All these statements qualify as ad-vanced "doublespeak."

Reagan and Bush also understood the important Orwellian lesson in fo-cusing public hatred on the repeated images of the enemy. Orwell had used the loathsome TV visage of Goldstein in "Two Minutes Hate" periods through-out the day. Reagan used Khomeni, then Khadafy, then Ortega.[5] Bush contin-ued the tendency, focusing American hatred on images of Willie Horton, then Manuel Noriega, then Saddam Hussein.[6]

The degree to which the public has accepted such presidential behav-ior without rebellion, and has enthusiastically supported both Reagan and Bush, is the degree to which George Orwell's predictions have proven accu-rate, and that television's political importance has been realized.

LATE NEWS: VIDEO WAR

February 4, 1991. As I write these words we are three weeks into the Iraq-U.S. war. My friends tell me they are "glued" to their TV screens, and ask if I am too.

In fact, I have watched some TV, more in amazement and disgust than for any useful information. Radio news, notably from National Public Radio and the Pacifica Network, has been far more detailed, informative, historical, wide-ranging, multifaceted, and faster in covering important events.

As with other news in the past, television's ability to deliver has been highly overrated. From the first day of the war, when CNN's Baghdad corre-spondents reported bombing in the city, TV delivered very little in the way of actual war footage. This was partly due to Pentagon censorship, which pro-hibited reporters from going into the field except under controlled condi-tions, prohibited images of American dead or of body bags, permitted only scant contact with outside sources, and censored all military communiqués.

---

[5] Muammar Khadafy, leader of Libya since 1970; Daniel Ortega, leader of the 1979 Sandinista rev-olution in Nicaragua and the country's elected president 1984–1990.

[6] In TV ads that many saw as racist, George Bush's 1988 Presidential campaign featured Willie Horton, a Black Massachusetts prison inmate who raped a woman while on prison furlough; the ads blamed Bush's opponent, Massachusetts governor Michael Dukakis. Manuel Noriega was leader of Panama 1983–1989. Saddam Hussein has been leader of Iraq since 1979.

Reporters were essentially confined to official versions of the story. Former *New York Times* political correspondent Richard Reeves characterized the TV industry, because of its submissive performance, as "PNN, the Pentagon News Network."

Also important were the technical limits of television. To get near the action, TV requires that relatively cumbersome, sometimes heavy video and sound equipment make its way across difficult terrain, and back. Radio and telephone transmission is far less difficult, more mobile, less expensive, and quicker under many circumstances. The net effect was that people who were at home glued to their TV screens were seeing mainly still photographs of CNN's or other correspondents, held on the screen for many minutes, while the story was actually reported by a telephone linkup. The only other images were occasional maps of the Middle East, or Pentagon stock footage of missiles or planes, or "talking head" shots of generals and commentators. Any usable, concrete information came almost exclusively in words, not images. So, while 100 million people believed themselves to be experiencing television, what they were really getting was radio, with a lit screen.

Throughout this massive barrage of military talking, there was scarcely one alternative viewpoint on television. Antiwar opinion was limited to an occasional twenty-second shot of a peace march, grossly underestimated rally counts, and no presentation of what marchers actually had to say. While there were many hours of interviews with military strategists, and loving details about weaponry, there were no serious interviews with antiwar leaders, or with people who could have provided a variety of viewpoints: leaders of women's organizations, artists, humanists, native people, environmentalists (except in reaction to the oil spill), pacifists, or, for that matter, people skilled in the arts of negotiation rather than war. Then, when poll results came in, everyone was surprised at the degree to which the public supported the war. How could the public do otherwise? What information were they given to perceive any alternative?

To their immense credit, noncommercial radio, and occasional newspaper reports, did provide some broader perspectives, but the monolithic power and domination of television made those voices, in those media, less significant than they should have been.

Television was essentially an instrument of official policy during the first weeks of the war. It adopted the role of cheerleader for the military-government viewpoint. The high point was probably the 1991 Super Bowl, which was indistinguishable from a multimedia pro-war extravaganza. The fans were shown waving American flags while sitting on red, white, and blue cushions. The players and coaches were interviewed about their hopes for our side in the larger game of war. The halftime show was a patriotic Disney display of the superiority of American values. And there were several intercuts to

George and Barbara Bush, watching the game at home, and speaking to us about how their thoughts, like ours, were on the righteousness of our "just cause" in the Persian Gulf. And then, Peter Jennings[7] showed us—oh no!—*those videos.*

Now it was time for television to really strut its stuff. The video images of the laser- and radar-guided missiles striking their targets with precision were made-in-heaven for television. It brought us, the viewers, into the cockpit of the plane; we could see the same screen the pilot saw. It demonstrated the unique artistic capability of the medium, equal to its delivery of multifaceted and multidimensional advertising imagery.

The laser-bomb images also revealed the natural symbiosis among video, computer, broadcast satellite, radar, and laser technologies, which stimulated 100 million people to glory in the miraculous technical superiority of our society. No other medium had ever been able to create such a brilliant advertisement, and instill such awe, for technology itself.

Of course, this so-called war footage that we were seeing—virtually the only war footage we saw during those first three weeks—had a familiar look to it. It was precisely the kind of imagery we had been trained to accept and to love, from a decade of playing video games. When Mr. Reagan said that video games were good training for bomber pilots, he failed to mention that it was also good training for *us;* it enabled us to truly identify with the bomber pilots, and brought us closer to them.

That the two sources of imagery—video games and war—became intertwined in our minds, and that the war itself became something of a giant video game, was so apparent that it was even noted by mass media pundits. What was not sufficiently noted was how amazingly odd this was.

I have described how Ronald Reagan had become a human presidential replay of previously implanted film and TV imagery. The images of high-tech war were also replays of previously implanted video imagery. They produced an instant hit of recognition, familiarity, and support for this utterly unprecedented technological merger. It was so neat, somehow, that all our favorite toys—computers, television, video games, and war games—had merged this way into something we could all experience right up there with our real pilots.

Nonetheless, there remained one area of confusion. For unlike the video-game wars in video parlors, the actual bombs had a final outcome that was not merely electronic: It was metal against flesh. This we did not experience.

Psychologist Robert Jay Lifton has written eloquently about the effects of high-technology warfare, which distances our society from the awareness of

---

[7] Television newscaster.

our acts. He calls it "psychic numbing." Our society remains appalled at the continuous acts of violence on our streets, where a killer so often acts impersonally, without feeling. And yet, says Lifton, through the collaboration and merging of the new technologies into TV imagery, we participate in the acts of violence performed by our military without actually experiencing them. And rather than being appalled by these acts, we like them. We are thrilled and excited by "the kill," as our military puts it, but are numb to the death that is involved. Rather than bringing us pain, it brings us pleasure. (The same is also true of the actual killers, the pilots.)

Finally what is revealed by television's performance in the war is its amazing efficiency when controlled by central authority. Of course we've already observed that efficiency over the last decades of television's control by corporations, which also train the population to view reality in a predetermined fashion, while minimizing alternative views. In times of war, the corporate role recedes temporarily. In fact, many advertisers withdrew their commercials for a time when war broke out, allowing the military issues to take center stage. Anyway, the celebration of high-tech war images ultimately supports corporate goals, which makes another neat symbiosis.

The main point to understand in all this is that the efficiency of television in influencing and controlling the populace does not result so much from any premeditated conspiracy by the military or corporations as it does from a *de facto* conspiracy of technical factors. As is the case with computers, TV technology is more efficient and more effective as an instrument of centralized control than it is for any other use.

The factors that conspire to create this inevitable condition include TV's incredible reach into every home in the country, and someday, every home in the world, combined with the power of the imagery it places in our brains. In addition, in more individual terms, it encourages passivity, isolation, confusion, addiction, and alienation; it homogenizes values and shuts out alternative visions.

Television is uniquely suited to implant and continuously reinforce dominant ideologies. And, while it hones our minds, it also accelerates our nervous systems into a form that matches the technological reality that is upon us. Television effectively produces a new form of human being—less creative, less able to make subtle distinctions, speedier, and more interested in *things*—albeit better able to handle, appreciate, and approve of the new technological world. High-speed computers, faxes, lasers, satellites, robotics, high-tech war, space travel, and the further suppression of nature are more palatable and desirable for us because of our involvement with TV. The ultimate result, in high-tech terms, is that television redesigns us to be compatible with the future.

STUDY AND DISCUSSION QUESTIONS

1. What are the three main points Mander makes in his introductory paragraphs? Note where he restates those points in the first section, "Living Inside Media."

2. How would you describe Mander's writing style: metaphorical or non-metaphorical? Elliptical or direct? How else might you characterize this style? Do you find that this style makes his argument effectively? Why or why not?

3. How many hours a day (on average) do you watch television? Be honest now.

4. Why does Mander use words like "brainwashing" and "censorship" in the section "Freedom of Speech for the Wealthy"? Who controls the mass images television transmits and why do they do so? What point is Mander trying to make about these people?

5. What points does Mander make by referring to science fiction novels? (Those he mentions, by the way, were published in the late 1940s, when television was just becoming widely available in the United States.)

6. List reasons why the brain goes into a "passive receptive alpha condition" in front of a television.

7. Discuss the following experiences: watching television, going to a film, listening to the radio, reading. What does Mander say about each? Do you agree or disagree?

8. How does television viewing accelerate people?

9. How does television viewing erode creativity?

10. Why, according to Mander, do we (adults as well as children) tend to get bored so easily now? Discuss what Mander has to say about technology and perception.

11. Why was Reagan such a popular president, according to Mander? How did Reagan (and subsequently Bush) realize some of George Orwell's *1984* extrapolations?

SUGGESTIONS FOR WRITING

1. Do you think that watching television is addictive? Argue for or against the addictiveness of television by citing Mander, by referring to your own experience through example and anecdote, and perhaps by doing some further reading on the subject.

2. Given Mander's view of the present relation between image technology and the human mind, what would an extrapolation of his argument into the future, say fifty years from now, look like?

3. Where were you during the Gulf War? How did you experience it?

4. Respond to Mander's three-paragraph conclusion about television's *de facto* technical conspiracy and about its ability to "implant and continuously reinforce dominant ideologies." Has Mander made his case in this extensive article? Come up with two or three questions you would ask Jerry Mander if he came to visit your class.

TV'S BLACK WORLD TURNS— BUT STAYS UNREAL

Henry Louis Gates, Jr.

Born in 1950 in Keyser, West Virginia, Henry Louis Gates, Jr. was educated at Yale University and at Cambridge, and is now Chair of the Afro-American Studies Department at Harvard. He is the editor of numerous books and series, including The Schomburg Library of Nineteenth-Century Black Women Writers *and, with Nellie Y. McKay,* The Norton Anthology of African American Literature *(1997). Among his other works are* The Signifying Monkey: Towards a Theory of Afro-American Literary Criticism *(1988),* Loose Cannons: Notes on the Culture Wars *(1992),* Colored People: A Memoir *(1994), and* Thirteen Ways of Looking at a Black Man *(1997). The following appeared in the* New York Times *in 1989.*

There is a telling moment in the 1986 film "Soul Man" when a young man explains to a friend why he has decided to down a bottle of tanning pills and turn himself black. The friend is skeptical: What's it actually going to be like, being black?

"It's gonna be great," the hero assures him. "These are the 80's, man. This is the 'Cosby' decade. America *loves* black people."

Alas, he soon discovers the gulf that separates the images of black people he sees on television and the reality that blacks experience every day.

Even black Americans sometimes need to be reminded about the deceptiveness of television. Blacks retain their fascination with black characters on TV: Many of us buy Jet magazine primarily to read its weekly television feature, which lists *every* black character (major or minor) to be seen on the screen that week. Yet our fixation with the presence of black characters on TV has blinded us to an important fact that "Cosby," which began in 1984, and its offshoots over the years demonstrate convincingly: There is very little connection between the social status of black Americans and the fabricated images of black people that Americans consume each day. Moreover, the representation of blacks on TV is a very poor index to our social advancement or political progress.

But the young man is right about one thing: This is the "Cosby" decade. The show's unprecedented success in depicting the lives of affluent blacks has exercised a profound influence on television in the last half of the 80's. And, judging from the premiere of this season's new black series—"Family Matters," "Homeroom" and "Snoops," as well as "Generations," an interracial soap opera—"Cosby's" success has led to the flow of TV sitcoms that feature the black middle class, each of which takes its lead from the "Cosby" show.

Historically blacks have always worried aloud about the image that white Americans harbor of us, first because we have never had control of those images and, second, because the greater number of those images have been negative. And given television's immediacy, and its capacity to reach so many viewers so quickly, blacks, at least since "Amos 'n' Andy"[1] back in the early 50's, have been especially concerned with our images on the screen. I can remember as a child sitting upstairs in my bedroom and hearing my mother shout at the top of her voice that someone *colored . . . colored!* was on TV and that we had all better come downstairs at once. And, without fail, we did, sitting in front of our TV, nervous, full of expectation and dread, praying that our home girl or boy would not let the race down.

"WHITE" MONEY VS. "COLORED" MONEY

Later, when American society could not successfully achieve the social reformation it sought in the 60's through the Great Society,[2] television solved the problem simply by inventing symbols of that transformation in the 80's, whether it was Cliff Huxtable—whom we might think of as the grandson

---

[1] Television comedy featuring two stereotyped black characters.

[2] President Lyndon Johnson's program of domestic reform, which included civil rights legislation and a "War on Poverty."

of Alexander Scott (played by Mr. Cosby in "I Spy," 1965–68)—or Benson (1979–86), the butler who transforms himself into a lieutenant governor.

Today, blacks are doing much better on TV than they are in real life, an irony underscored by the use of black public figures (Mr. Cosby, Michael Jackson, Michael Jordan, Bobby McFerrin[3]) as spokesmen for major businesses. When Mr. Cosby, deadpan, faces the camera squarely and says, "E. F. Hutton.[4] Because it's my money," the line blurs between Cliff Huxtable's successful career and Mr. Cosby.

This helps to explain why "Cosby" makes some people uncomfortable. As the dominant representation of blacks on TV, it suggests that blacks are solely responsible for their social conditions, with no acknowledgment of the severely constricted life opportunities that most black people face. What's troubling about the phenomenal success of "Cosby," then, is what was troubling about the earlier popularity of "Amos 'n' Andy": it's not the representation itself (Cliff Huxtable, a child of college-educated parents, is altogether believable), but the role it begins to play in our culture, the status it takes on as being, well, truly representative.

As long as *all* blacks were represented in demeaning or peripheral roles, it was possible to believe that American racism was, as it were, indiscriminate. The social vision of "Cosby," however, reflecting the minuscule integration of blacks into the upper middle class (having "white money," my mother used to say, rather than "colored" money) reassuringly throws the blame for black poverty back onto the impoverished.

This is the subliminal message of America's weekly dinner date with the Huxtables, played out to a lesser extent in other weekly TV encounters with middle-class black families, such as "227," "A Different World," "Amen" (Sherman Helmsley is a lawyer), and with isolated black individuals, such as the dashing Blair Underwood on "L. A. Law" and Philip Michael Thomas on "Miami Vice." One principal reason for the failure of Flip Wilson's "Charlie & Company" was the ambiguity of his class status; Wilson's character, Charlie Richmond, was an office worker at the Department of Highways, his wife (Gladys Knight) a schoolteacher. Wilson once joked, acidly, that he was the star of the black version of "The Cosby Show," which may have been true in ways that he did not intend.

---

[3] Michael Jackson, pop singer and dancer; Michael Jordan, professional basketball player; Bobby McFerrin, pop, jazz, and classical singer.

[4] Brokerage firm.

THE GREAT "AMOS 'N' ANDY" DEBATE

In 1933, Sterling Brown, the great black poet and critic, divided the full range of black character types in American literature into seven categories: the contented slave; the wretched freeman; the comic Negro; the brute Negro; the tragic mulatto; the local color Negro; and the exotic primitive. It was only one small step to associate our public negative image in the American mind with the public negative social roles that we were assigned and to which we were largely confined. "If only they could be exposed to the *best* of the race," the sentiment went, "then they would see that we were normal human beings and treat us better."

Such a burdensome role for the black image led, inevitably, to careful monitoring and, ultimately, to censorship of our representations in literature, film, radio and later television. The historian W. E. B. Du Bois summarized this line of thinking among blacks: "We want," he said in 1925, "everything that is said about us to tell of the best and highest and noblest in us. We insist that our Art and Propaganda be one. We fear that the evil in us will be called racial while in others it is viewed as individual. We fear that our shortcomings are not merely human but foreshadowings and threatenings of disaster and failure." And the genre about which we were most sensitive, Du Bois wrote, was comedy. "The more highly trained we become," he wrote in 1921, "the less we can laugh at Negro comedy."

One of my favorite pastimes is screening episodes of "Amos 'n' Andy" for black friends who think that the series was both socially offensive and politically detrimental. After a few minutes, even hard-liners have difficulty restraining their laughter. "It's still racist," is one typical comment, "but it was funny."

The performance of those great black actors—Tim Moore, Spencer Williams and Ernestine Wade—transformed racist stereotypes into authentic black humor. The dilemma of "Amos 'n' Andy," however, was that these were the *only* images of blacks that Americans could see on TV. The political consequences for the early civil rights movement were thought to be threatening. The N.A.A.C.P. helped to have the series killed.

What lies behind these sorts of arguments is a belief that social policies affecting black Americans were largely determined by our popular images in the media. But the success of the "Cosby" show has put the lie to that myth: "Cosby" exposes more white Americans than ever before to the most nobly idealized blacks in the history of entertainment, yet social and economic conditions for the average black American have not been bleaker in a very long time.

To make matters worse, "Cosby" is also one of the most popular shows in apartheid South Africa, underscoring the fact that the relationship between how whites treat us and their exposure to "the best" in us is far from straight-forward. (One can hear the Afrikaaner speaking to his black servants: "When you people are like Cliff and Clare, *then* we will abandon apartheid.")

There are probably as many reasons to like the "Cosby" show as there are devoted viewers—and there are millions of them. I happen to like it because my daughters (ages 9 and 7) like it, and I enjoy watching them watch themselves in the depictions of middle-class black kids, worrying about school, sibling rivalries and family tradition. But I also like "Cosby" because its very success has forced us to rethink completely the relation between black social progress and the images of blacks that American society fabricates, projects and digests.

But the "Cosby" vision of upper-middle-class blacks and their families is comparatively recent. And while it may have constituted the dominant image of blacks for the last five years, it is a direct reaction against the lower-class ghetto comedies of the 70's, such as "Sanford and Son" (1972–77), "Good Times" (1974–79), "That's My Mama" (1974–75) and "What's Happening!!" (1976–79). The latter three were single-mother-dominated sitcoms. Although "Good Times" began with a nuclear family, John Amos—who had succeeded marvelously in transforming the genre of the black maternal household—was soon killed off, enabling the show to conform to the stereotype of a fatherless black family.

Even "The Jeffersons" (1975–85) conforms to this mold. George and Louise began their TV existence as Archie Bunker's working-class neighbors, saved their pennies, then "moved on up," as the theme song says, to Manhattan's East Side. "The Jeffersons" also served as a bridge between sitcoms depicting the ghetto and those portraying the new black upper class.

In fact, in the history of black images on television, character types have distinct pasts and, as is also the case with white shows, series seem both to lead to other series and to spring from metaphorical ancestors.

PURE STREET IN A BROOKS BROTHERS SUIT

Let's track the evolution of the "Cosby" type on television. While social engineering is easier on the little screen than in the big city, Sterling Brown's list of black stereotypes in American literature proves quite serviceable as a guide to the images TV has purveyed for the last two decades. Were we writing a new sitcom using these character types, our cast might look like this—contented slave: Andy, Fred Sanford, J.J. ("Good Times"); wretched freeman: George Jefferson; comic Negro: Flip Wilson; brute Negro: Mr. T ("The A-Team"), Hawk ("Spenser: for Hire"); tragic mulatto: "Julia," Elvin ("Cosby"), Whitley ("A Different World"); local color Negro: Meschach Taylor ("Designing Women");

exotic primitive: Link ("Mod Squad" 1968–73), most black characters on MTV. If we add the category of Noble Negro (Cliff Huxtable, Benson), our list might be complete.

We can start with George Jefferson, who we might think of as a King-fish ("Amos 'n' Andy") or as a Fred Sanford ("Sanford and Son") who has fi-nally made it. Jefferson epitomized Richard Nixon's version of black capitalism, bootstrap variety, and all of its terrifying consequences. Jefferson was anything but a man of culture: Unlike the "Cosby" living room, his East Side apartment had no painting by Jacob Lawrence or Charles White, Ro-mare Bearden or Varnette Honeywood. Despite his new-found wealth, Jef-ferson was pure street, draped in a Brooks Brothers suit. You did not want to live next to a George Jefferson, and you most certainly did not want your daughter to marry one.

"The Jeffersons" was part of a larger trend in television in the depic-tion of black men. We might think of this as their domestication, in direct re-action to the questing, macho images of black males shown in the 60's news clips of the civil rights movement, the Black Panthers and the black power movement. While Jefferson (short, feisty, racist, rich, vulgar) represents one kind of domestication, a more curious kind was the cultural dwarfism rep-resented by "Diff'rent Strokes" (1978–86) and "Webster" (1983–87), in which small black "boys" (arrested adolescents who were much older than the char-acters they played) were adopted by tall, successful white males. These es-tablishment figures represented the myth of the benevolent paternalism of the white upper class, an American myth as old as the abolitionist movement.

Indeed, one central motif of 19th-century American art is a sculpted tall white male (often Lincoln) towering above a crouched or kneeling adult or adolescent slave, in the act of setting them free. "Webster" and "Diff'rent Strokes" depict black orphans who are rescued from blackness and poverty, adopted and raised just like any other upper-middle-class white kid, prep schools and all. These shows can be thought of as TV's fantasy of Lyndon Johnson's "Great Society" and the war on poverty rolled into one.

The formula was not as successful with a female character: An attempt to use the same format with a black woman, Shirley Hemphill ("One in a Million," 1980) lasted only six months. "The White Shadow" (1978–81) was a variation of this paternal motif, in which wild and unruly ghetto kids were tamed with a basketball.

These small black men signaled to the larger American audience that the very idea of the black male could be, and had been, successfully domesti-cated. Mr. T—whose 1983–87 "A-Team" run paralleled that of "Webster"—might appear to be an exception. We are forced to wonder, however, why such an important feature of his costume—and favorite fetish—was those dazzling gold chains, surely a subliminal suggestion of bondage.

This process of paternal domestication, in effect, made Cliff Huxtable's character a logical next step. In fact, I think of the evolution of the Huxtable character, generationally, in this way: imagine if George Jefferson owned the tenement building in which Florida and her family from "Good Times" lived. After John Amos dies, Jefferson evicts them for nonpayment of rent. Florida, destitute and distraught, tries to kill George. The state puts her children up for adoption.

They are adopted by Mr. Drummond ("Diff'rent Strokes") and graduate from Dalton, Exeter and Howard.[5] Gary Coleman's grandson becomes an obstetrician, marries a lovely lawyer named Clare, and they move to Brooklyn Heights. And there you have it: the transformation of the character type of the black male on television.

And while Clare Huxtable is a refreshingly positive depiction of an intelligent, successful black woman, she is clearly a descendant of "Julia" (1968–71), though a Julia with sensuality and sass. The extent of typecasting of black women as mammy figures, descended from the great Hollywood "Mammy" of "Gone with the Wind," is astonishing: Beulah, Mama in "Amos 'n' Andy," Geraldine ("Flip Wilson," 1970–75), Florida, Nel in "Gimme a Break" (1981-88), Louise ("The Jeffersons"), Eloise ("That's My Mama," 1974–75).

And what is the measure of the Huxtables' nobility? One of the reasons "Cosby" and its spin-off, "A Different World," are so popular is that the black characters in them have finally become, in most respects, just like white people.

While I applaud "Cosby's" success at depicting (at long last) the everyday concerns of black people (love, sex, ambition, generational conflicts, work and leisure) far beyond reflex responses to white racism, the question remains: Has TV managed to depict a truly "different world"? As Mark Crispin Miller puts it, "By insisting that blacks and whites are entirely alike, television denies the cultural barriers that slavery necessarily created; barriers that have hardened over years and years, and that still exist"—barriers that produced different cultures, distinct worlds.

And while "Cosby" is remarkably successful at introducing most Americans to traditional black cultural values, customs and norms, it has not succeeded at introducing America to a truly different world. The show that came closest—that presented the fullest range of black character types—was the 1987–88 series "Frank's Place," starring Tim Reid and his wife Daphne Maxwell Reid and set in a Creole restaurant in New Orleans.

---

[5] Dalton, private school in New York City; Exeter, secondary boarding school in Exeter, New Hampshire; Howard University, primarily black university in Washington, D.C.

Unfortunately, Mr. Reid apparently has learned his lesson: His new series, "Snoops," in which his wife also stars, is a black detective series suggestive of "The Thin Man." The couple is thoroughly middle class: He is a professor of criminology at Georgetown; she is head of protocol at the State Department. "Drugs and murder and psychotic people," Mr. Reid said in a recent interview. "I think we've seen enough of that in real life."

But it is also important to remember that the early 70's ghetto sitcoms ("Good Times" and "Sanford") were no more realistic than "Cosby" is. In fact, their success made the idea of ghetto life palatable for most Americans, robbing it of its reality as a place of exile, a place of rage, and frustration, and death. And perhaps with "Cosby's" success and the realization that the very structure of the sitcom (in which every character is a type) militates against its use as an agent of social change, blacks will stop looking to TV for our social liberation. As a popular song in the early 70's put it, "The revolution will not be televised."

STUDY AND DISCUSSION QUESTIONS

1. Why does Gates begin his article with the "Soul Man" anecdote and how does the anecdote lead into his thesis?

2. Gates remarks on the way 1970s sitcoms often featured working-class black families. The focus switched to middle and upper-middle-class families in the 1980s. Why do you think this change happened? What, so far, is the stereotypical 1990s representation of African American culture?

3. Compare/contrast the old Cosby show, which Gates discusses, and the recent one.

4. Discuss Gates's comment that *The Cosby Show's* "very success has forced us to rethink completely the relation between black social progress and the images of blacks that American society fabricates, projects and digests."

5. What are the seven black character types categorized by Sterling Brown in 1933? Do you concur with Gates's use of those types to categorize sitcom characters? Can you add further examples of character types?

6. What is the relation between social policy and images in the media? What does Gates imply? What do you think? Pick any example of this relation from your own observation and discuss.

7. Discuss the intersection of race and social class in this article.

SUGGESTIONS FOR WRITING

1. How, in your own experience, do television images fail to work either as a depiction of reality or, as Gates puts it, as "an agent of social change"? Pick a group of people with which you are familiar—women, the elderly, Jews, Italians, the working class, to name a few examples—and analyze the depiction of that group of people on television. Choose one program and analyze it in detail or find commonalities across several programs.

2. Why might mass culture (in this case, television) have presented in the 1980s so many images of the black middle class? How does Gates suggest that this presentation is simultaneously confusing and dangerous, both for black and for white viewers?

3. Analyze one television show about African Americans. You might or might not use Sterling Brown's character typology. What assumptions and fantasies about black Americans are embedded in the program?

CLASS STRUGGLE
IN HOLLYWOOD

Benjamin DeMott

Benjamin DeMott was born in 1924 and educated at Johns Hopkins, George Washington, and Harvard Universities. He served in the infantry during World War II and has worked as a journalist. Since 1951, he has taught at Amherst College, where he is now Mellon Professor of Humanities. DeMott has written novels and books of cultural criticism, including The Imperial Middle: Why Americans Can't Think Straight About Class *(1990) and* The Trouble with Friendship: Why Americans Can't Think Straight About Race *(1996). The essay below appeared in the* New York Times *in 1991.*

Increasingly in recent years movies have been dealing with power issues and class relationships—interactions between masters and servants, executives and underlings, yuppies and waitresses, millionaires and hookers, rich aristocrats and social-nobody lawyers. Think of "Reversal of Fortune" and "The

Bonfire of the Vanities." Think of "White Palace" and "Pretty Woman." Think of Michael Corleone's struggle for social acceptance in "The Godfather Part III." Think of "Working Girl," or "Driving Miss Daisy" or "Dirty Dancing." Script after script links up clout and cloutlessness, often to stunning box-office effect.

Not every movie version of the power theme speaks specifically about class relationships, and some versions are only loosely linked to social reality. The two worlds of "Edward Scissorhands," for example—hilltop mansion and tract house; solitary helpless artist versus artist-baiting mob—are derived less from everyday experience than from fairy tales, allegory and satire.

Usually, though, conventional realism is the chosen mode, and class skirmishes are sketched. The camera in "White Palace" studies St. Louis's fancier suburbs and its rundown Dog Town; class conflict erupts at the movie's crisis point. Nora, the waitress-heroine (Susan Sarandon), listens smolderingly to her yuppie lover's upper-middle friends and relations uttering their hypocritical socio-political pieties, and explodes. Storming her way out, she cries: "*I'm* working class!"

At first glance the angry explicitness of her outcry and the movie's declaration of difference look promising. They could signify that Hollywood is reaching toward maturity, trying to teach itself and the nation how to think straight about social hierarchy—the realities of class and class power. The need for such instruction is patent. This country has an ignoble tradition of evading social facts—pretending that individual episodes of upward mobility obviate grappling with the hardening socio-economic differences in our midst. Movies that deal responsibly with class relationships could, in theory, moderate the national evasiveness.

But, regrettably, contemporary "class movies" don't deal responsibly with class. The tone of their treatment of rich and poor is new; it is harsher and meaner than that of Frank Capra's "little guy" sagas or George Cukor's social comedies or John Ford's populism that were pleasing to our parents and grandparents in the 30's, 40's and 50's.

The harsher tone, however, doesn't bespeak fundamental change. At their best, Hollywood's new-style "class movies" nod at realities of social difference—and then go on to obfuscate them. At their worst these films are driven by near-total dedication to a scam—the maddeningly dangerous deceit that there are no classes in America.

One favorite story line stresses discovery: people who think firm class lines exist come to discover, by the end of the tale, that they're mistaken; everybody's really the same.

In the 1988 blockbuster "Working Girl," Tess McGill (Melanie Griffith), initially a bottom-dog secretary-gofer, is positive she can make it to the top. But her peers in the word-processing pool regard her aspirations as foolish.

They tell her, flat out, that the real world has lines and distinctions and that her daydreams of glory and business power are foolish. "I sing and dance in my underwear," says one pal, "but I'm not Madonna." The implicit message: Get real, Tess. Accept the reality of levels.

But Tess, of course, accepts no such thing. She reads W,[1] takes classes to improve her accent, seizes her boss's office when the latter breaks her leg skiing—and winds up not only doing deals but ordering the boss (Sigourney Weaver) to get her bony bottom out of sight. What does it take to get to the top? Desire, period. Tess's desire flies her straight up to a managerial perch, allowing her to become, almost effortlessly, all she can be: no problem, few barriers, class dismissed. In the final frame the doubters in the secretarial pool acknowledge their error; they rise to applaud the heroine who proved them wrong.

A second familiar story line involves upendings: characters theoretically on the social bottom shake the cages of characters who try to use their position to humiliate those below. The top dogs are so stupid they don't realize that socioeconomic power only lasts for a second and that they can be overcome by any intrepid underling.

Consider "Pretty Woman," the 1990 film that became one of the highest-grossing movies ever and is now near the top of video best-seller and rental charts. The would-be humiliators in this movie are snobbish salespeople on chic Rodeo Drive. Vivian (Julia Roberts), a hooker, runs afoul of them when she is sent on a shopping spree by the corporate raider (Richard Gere) who has hired her for a week. The raider wants elegance and the hooker aims to oblige—but on her first pass at the Drive she's suited up in hooker garb, and the salespeople are offended. "I don't think we have anything for you. *Please leave.*" Quickly the snobs are undone. The corporate raider flashes plastic and tells a shop manager that they'll be spending big and need appropriate cosseting. In minutes—through instruction in fork-tine-counting, for instance—the raider effects the few alterations of manners required to transform Vivian the street hooker into grandeur.

Regally togged, her arms filled with sleek clothes boxes, Vivian returns to the salespeople who were mean to her and sticks it to them in economic not moral terms. If they had been nice to her, they would have made a killing. ("You work on commission, don't you?")

Power is temporary and snobs are dopes—so goes the message. Ostracize a hooker in midmorning and she'll ruin you before tea. *Class dismissed.*

Comparable dismissals occur in movies drawing huge audiences of high school students. They usually have plot lines showing bottom dogs gliding smoothly and painlessly to the top. In "Dirty Dancing" (1987), Patrick Swayze,

---

[1] High-fashion magazine.

playing a talented working-class dancer (he has a card in the "housepainters and plasterers union"), competes for esteem with a Yale medical school student—and wins in a breeze.

In John Hughes's "Some Kind of Wonderful" (1987) and "Pretty in Pink" (1986), working-class heroes or heroines become romantically interested in classmates who rank above them, in terms of money and status, in the school society. As the attachments develop, the poor students commence to display gifts and talents that prove them equal to or intrinsically superior to the arrogant, insecure characters in whom they've become interested.

Once the nonclass, merit-based order or hierarchy has been established, and superficial, class-based gradations have been eliminated, the poor boy or girl chooses whether to continue the relationship with the pseudo-superior as an equal or to end it. Either way, the experience bolsters the belief that, in school and out, social strata are evanescent and meaningless.

But what is truly striking is the array of ploys and devices by which movie makers bring off escapes from significant confrontation with class realities. The Vietnam War film "Platoon" (1986), for example, lets on at the beginning that it will show us an upper-middle-class white soldier learning about differences between himself and the sons of the working class who compose the majority of his comrades in arms.

But in place of the experience of learning, we're offered liberal platitudes and star turns. The hero writes his grandmother that his fellow soldiers are the salt of the earth (little corroboration supplied); the soldiers themselves—particularly the blacks among them—are brought on for a succession of amusing monologues, following which they disappear, shipped out dead or alive; at no point is the gritty stuff of class difference even momentarily engaged.

In the much-acclaimed "Driving Miss Daisy" (1989), the early intimation is that the focus will be on relations between white employers and black servants. But almost immediately the outlines of that social difference are blurred. The white employer is Jewish and her synagogue is bombed; poor black and rich white become one, joint victims of discriminatory violence. ("You're my best friend, Hoke.") Class dismissed once more.

The story is nearly the same even in those unusual movies that focus solely on minority communities. Social difference is glanced at, defined in a few snippets of dialogue—and then trashed, often by means of a joke. In "House Party," Reginald Hudlin's 1990 film about teen-age life, the joke is about sex. Through establishing shots and talk, two girlfriends are placed at a social distance from each other. One lives in "the projects," the other in an expensively middle-class suburban home.

The film offers a single moment of reflection on the social difference in question; a young man points out that there is plenty of space for making out in the rich girl's house, none where the projects girl lives. Yet once more, class dismissed.

It's hardly surprising that the notion of America as a classless society emerges at its most schematic in movies aimed at relatively youthful, unsophisticated audiences. But the same impulse to paper over social differences surfaces in many more ambitious films purporting to raise subjects considered controversial by Hollywood standards (social injustice, war, the treatment of minorities).

And not infrequently that impulse drives film makers—such as Francis Ford Coppola in "The Godfather Part III" and Barry Levinson in "Avalon"—to overplay ethnic influence and underplay class influence on character.

The reason all this matters is simple. Treating class differences as totally inconsequential strengthens the national delusion that class power and position are insignificant. It encourages the middle-class—those with the clearest shot at upward mobility—to assume, wrongly, that all citizens enjoy the same freedom of movement that they enjoy. And it makes it easier for political leaders to speak as though class power had nothing to do with the inequities of life in America. ("Class is for European democracies or something else," says George Bush. "It isn't for the United States of America. We are not going to be divided by class.")

Movies that deal responsibly with class relationships might help to embolden leaders to begin talking candidly about real as opposed to phony issues of "fairness." But movies obviously can't do this as long as their makers are in terror of allowing class permanently out of the closet.

It's true that occasional moments occur when movie audiences can grasp the substantive dimensions of social difference. A person reached toward from above or below is seen to possess inner, mysterious resources (or limits) about which someone differently placed on the social scale can have no inkling, and can't conceivably lay claim.

There is one such moment in "Working Girl." Following orders, Tess, as secretarial underling, books her boss, Katharine Parker (Ms. Weaver), into a chalet for a ski weekend. She is helping Katharine fasten her new ski boots in the office when she is asked where in the chalet the room is located. Tess doesn't know; Katharine dials the resort and at once a flood of flawless German fills the room.

The camera angle shows us Tess's awe; we gaze up with her (from the glossy white boots that she, as footman, is buckling) to this animated, magical, Ivy-educated mistress of the world, self-transformed into Europe, performing in another language. Katharine is demonstrating quite casually that bottom dogs have no exact knowledge of what lies between them and their ideal, that top dogs possess secret skills nobody learns overnight, as in charm class, or by changing hairstyles—skills traceable to uncounted indulgent hours of tutoring, study and travel.

The bottom dog's eyes widen as frightening truth dawns. If a talent so mesmerizing—this poured-forth foreign self—can be invisible until now, must there not be others equally well-concealed? Maybe this dream to be her *is* foolish. What unimaginable barriers stand between me and my desire?

In the movie culture the answer to such questions is, of course: no real barriers, none. "Be all you can be" means, at the bottom as at the top, "Be whatever you wish," fear no obstacle, see no obstacle, there are no obstacles. "Working Girl" is, finally, a story about how ambitious working girls just can't lose—one more movie that obliterates class.

"White Palace," for all its initial explicitness about the reality of social differences, is, finally, a story asserting that such differences simply don't matter; pure passion erases them every time.

The other week Senator Daniel Patrick Moynihan told a Wall Street Journal reporter that the fundamental issue in this country is "class, not race." It's essential, he said, "to at least start thinking about it, start talking about it. Let's be honest. We're not doing that."

One reason we're not is that movies remain firmly resolved against letting us.

STUDY AND DISCUSSION QUESTIONS

1. What is the traditional stance of the United States toward class and class power? How do contemporary films that treat social class carry on this tradition, according to DeMott?

2. What is the difference, for DeMott, between contemporary films that treat social class and films that did so in the 1930s, 40s, and 50s? Why do you think there is an increasing number of films dealing with this subject?

3. Name the types of story line DeMott mentions and show how he uses film examples to back up his arguments.

4. What happens, according to DeMott, when class combines in film with race, ethnicity, or gender? Give some examples from the essay.

5. What are the consequences of downplaying or dismissing class difference?

6. What other films can you add to DeMott's list of films that have class and power, relations between classes, or working-class life as their subject?

7. Why does DeMott come back to *Working Girl* at the end of his essay? How is this effective?

SUGGESTIONS FOR WRITING

1. Choose a film made in the past decade that purportedly deals with social class and analyze the film using DeMott's approach. What is the overall story line? Does the film ultimately dismiss social class as important? Find one or two significant scenes about class relationships in the film that illustrate your thesis and discuss them in detail.

2. Write a plot outline for, and/or a scene from, a film you might make that would deal responsibly with the deep and increasing gulf between social classes in the United States.

3. DeMott ends his essay with the remark by Senator Moynihan that the fundamental issue in this country is class, not race. Do you agree or disagree? Why?

THE WRETCHED
OF THE HEARTH

Barbara Ehrenreich

Barbara Ehrenreich (b.1941) has a PhD in biology and was an early critic of the health care system in the United States. A wide-ranging social critic, she has also written about economic globalism, welfare, sexism, and war, and she is active in Democratic Socialists of America. Among her books are For Her Own Good: One Hundred Fifty Years of the Experts' Advice to Women *(1978),* The Hearts of Men: American Dreams and the Flight from Commitment *(1983),* Fear of Falling: The Inner Life of the Middle Class *(1989),* Blood Rites: Origins and History of the Passion of War *(1997), and several essay collections, including* The Snarling Citizen *(1995), where the following appeared.*

In the second half of the 1980s, when American conservatism had reached its masochistic zenith with the reelection of Ronald Reagan, when women's liberation had been replaced by the more delicate sensibility known as post-feminism, when everyone was a yuppie and the heartiest word of endorsement in our vocabulary was "appropriate," there was yet this one paradox: our favorite TV personages were a liberal black man and a left-wing white feminist. Cosby could be explained as a representative of America's officially pro-family mood, but Roseanne is a trickier case. Her idea of humor is to look down on her sleeping family in the eponymous sitcom and muse, "Mmmm, I wonder where we could find an all-night taxidermist."

If zeitgeist were destiny, Roseanne would never have happened. Only a few years ago, we learn from her autobiography, *Roseanne: My Life As a Woman*, Roseanne Arnold was just your run-of-the-mill radical feminist mother-of-three, writing poems involving the Great Goddess, denouncing all known feminist leaders as sellout trash, and praying for the sixties to be born again in a female body. Since the entertainment media do not normally cast about for fat, loudmouthed feminists to promote to superstardom, we must assume that Roseanne has something to say that many millions of people have been waiting to hear. Like this, upon being told of a woman who stabbed her husband thirty-seven times: "I admire her restraint."

Roseanne is the neglected underside of the American female experience, bringing together the great themes of poverty, obesity, and defiance. The overside is handled well enough by Candice Bergen *(Murphy Brown)* and Madonna, who exist to remind us that talented women who work out are bound to become fabulously successful. Roseanne works a whole different beat, both in her sitcom and in the movie *She-Devil*, portraying the hopeless underclass of the female sex: polyester-clad, overweight occupants of the slow track; fast-food waitresses, factory workers, housewives, members of the invisible pink-collar army; the despised, the jilted, the underpaid.

Not that *Roseanne* is free of class stereotyping. The Connors must bear part of the psychic burden imposed on all working-class people by their economic and occupational betters: they inhabit a zone of glad-handed gemeinschaft, evocative, now and then, of the stock wedding scene *(The Godfather, The Deer Hunter, Working Girl)* that routinely signifies lost old-world values. They indulge in a manic physicality that would be unthinkable among the more controlled and genteel Huxtables. They maintain a traditional, low-fiber diet of white bread and macaroni. They are not above a fart joke.

Still, in *Roseanne* I am willing to forgive the stereotypes as markers designed to remind us of where we are: in the home of a construction worker and his minimum-wage wife. Without the reminders, we might not be aware of how thoroughly the deeper prejudices of the professional class are being challenged. Roseanne's fictional husband Dan (played by the irresistibly cuddly John Goodman) drinks domestic beer and dedicates Sundays to football;

but far from being a Bunkeresque[1] boor, he looks to this feminist like the fabled "sensitive man" we have all been pining for. He treats his rotund wife like a sex goddess. He picks up on small cues signaling emotional distress. He helps with homework. And when Roseanne works overtime, he cooks, cleans, and rides herd on the kids without any of the piteous whining we have come to expect from upscale males in their rare, and lavishly documented, encounters with soiled Pampers.

Roseanne Connor has her own way of defying the stereotypes. Variously employed as a fast-food operative, a factory worker, a bartender, and a telephone salesperson, her real dream is to be a writer. When her twelve-year-old daughter Darlene (brilliantly played by Sara Gilbert) balks at a poetry-writing assignment, Roseanne gives her a little talking-to involving Sylvia Plath: "She inspired quite a few women, including *moi*."[2] In another episode, a middle-aged friend thanks Roseanne for inspiring her to dump her chauvinist husband and go to college. We have come a long way from the dithering, cowering Edith Bunker.[3]

Most of the time the Connors do the usual sitcom things. They have the little domestic misunderstandings that can be patched up in twenty-four minutes with wisecracks and a round of hugs. But *Roseanne* carries working-class verisimilitude into a new and previously taboo dimension—the workplace. In the world of employment, Roseanne knows exactly where she stands: "All the good power jobs are taken. Vanna turns the letters. Leona's got hotels. Margaret's running England[4] . . . 'Course she's not doing a very good job . . ."

And in the workplace as well as the kitchen, Roseanne knows how to dish it out. A friend of mine, herself a denizen of the low-wage end of the work force, claims to have seen an episode in which Roseanne led an occupational-health-and-safety battle at Wellman Plastics. I missed that one, but I have seen her, on more than one occasion, reduce the boss's ego to rubble. At Chicken Divine, for example, she is ordered to work weekends—an impossibility for a working mother—by an officious teenage boss who confides that he doesn't like working weekends either. In a sequence that could have been crafted by Michael Moore,[5] Roseanne responds: "Well, that's real good 'cause you never do. You sit in your office like a little

---

[1] Archie Bunker, the main character of the television sitcom "All in the Family."

[2] Me (French).

[3] Archie Bunker's wife.

[4] Vanna White, assistant to the host on the television game show "Wheel of Fortune"; Leona Helmsley, owner of hotels in New York City; Margaret Thatcher, British Prime Minister 1979–1990.

[5] Satirical writer and director.

Napoleon, making up schedules and screwing up people's lives." To which he says, "That's what they pay me for. And you are paid to follow my orders." Blah blah blah. To which she says, after staring at him fixedly for several seconds: "You know, you got a little prize hanging out of your nose there."

All family sitcoms, of course, teach us that wisecracks and swift put-downs are the preferred modes of affectionate discourse. But *Roseanne* takes the genre a step further—over the edge, some may say. In the era of big weddings and sudden man shortages, she describes marriage as "a life sentence, without parole." And in the era of the biological time clock and the petted yuppie midlife baby, she can tell Darlene to get a fork out of the drawer and "stick it through your tongue." Or she can say, when Dan asks "Are we missing an offspring?" at breakfast, "Yeah. Where do you think I got the bacon?"

It is *Roseanne*'s narrow-eyed cynicism about the family, even more than her class consciousness, that gives *Roseanne* its special frisson. Archie Bunker got our attention by telling us that we (blacks, Jews, "ethnics," WASPs, etc.) don't really like each other. Roseanne's message is that even within the family we don't much like each other. We *love* each other (who else do we have?); but The Family, with its lopsided division of labor and its ancient system of age-graded humiliations, just doesn't work. Or rather, it doesn't work unless the contradictions are smoothed out with irony and the hostilities are periodically blown off as humor. Coming from Mom, rather than from a jaded teenager or a bystander dad, this is scary news indeed.

So *Roseanne*'s theoretical outlook is, in the best left-feminist tradition, dialectical. On the one hand, she presents the family as a zone of intimacy and support, well worth defending against the forces of capitalism, which drive both mothers and fathers out of the home, scratching around for paychecks. On the other hand, the family is hardly a haven, especially for its grown-up females. It is marred from within by—among other things—the patriarchal division of leisure, which makes Dad and the kids the "consumers" of Mom's cooking, cleaning, nurturing, and (increasingly) her earnings. Mom's job is to keep the whole thing together—to see that the mortgage payments are made, to fend off the viperish teenagers, to find the missing green sock—but Mom is no longer interested in being a human sacrifice on the altar of "profamily values." She's been down to the feminist bookstore; she's been reading Sylvia Plath.

This is a bleak and radical vision. Not given to didacticism, Roseanne offers no programmatic ways out. Surely, we are led to conclude, pay equity would help, along with child care, and so on. But Roseanne leaves us hankering for a quality of change that goes beyond mere reform: for a world in which even the lowliest among us—the hash slinger, the sock finder, the factory hand—will be recognized as the poet she truly is.

STUDY AND DISCUSSION QUESTIONS

1. Define: postfeminism, yuppie, eponymous, zeitgeist, gemeinschaft, dialectical, patriarchy.

2. What stereotypes about the working class does the *Roseanne* sitcom perpetuate? What stereotypes about the working class does it challenge?

3. What view of the family is presented on *Roseanne*? How is it, as Ehrenreich suggests, dialectical?

4. In what ways does *Roseanne*, the program and the character, challenge our sensibilities?

5. What is Ehrenreich's main point and how does she use evidence in this essay? Give some examples.

6. Do you find *Roseanne* funny? Pick a scene from the program and analyze it. What is the humor based on? How and why does it appeal to you? Or, if it doesn't seem funny to you, analyze why not.

SUGGESTIONS FOR WRITING

1. Compare/contrast an episode of *Murphy Brown* and of *Roseanne*. You might want to look at home life/family, at the workplace, at issues of gender and social class, and at setting, as well as at the personalities of the two main characters.

2. Read a few of Sylvia Plath's poems. Why might Plath be both a surprising and an appropriate role model for Roseanne?

BEAUTY AND THE BACKLASH

Susan Faludi

Susan Faludi (b. 1959) has worked as a reporter for a number of newspapers, including the Wall Street Journal. *She won a Pulitzer Prize in 1991 for her article on the consequences for ordinary people of a leveraged buyout of a supermarket chain. Her book* Backlash: The Undeclared War Against American Women *won the National Book Critics Circle Award in 1991. The following is an excerpt from a chapter of* Backlash.

With the aid of a metal rod, the first woman of "the New Generation" stands in Robert Filoso's Los Angeles workshop, her feet dangling a few inches off the floor. Her clay arms are bandaged in gauze strips and her face hooded in a plastic bag, knotted at the neck to keep out dust motes. A single speck could cause a blemish.

"There are no imperfections in my models," the thirty-eight-year-old mannequin sculptor explains. "They all have to be taken out."[1] The dank environment inside the bag, however, has bred its own facial flaws. Between the woman's parted lips, a green mold is growing.

On this April morning in 1988, Filoso is at work on the model that will set the standard for the following year. Ever since he brought "the new realism" to female mannequins—chiseling detailed vertebrae, toes, and nipples—Filoso has led the $1.2 billion dummy industry, serving all the better retailers. This year, he is making some major changes. His New Generation woman has shrunk in height, gained almost three inches on her breasts, shed an inch from her waist, and developed three sets of eyelashes. The new vital statistics, 34-23-36, are voluptuous by mannequin standards,[2] but the Lacroix[3] era of strapless gowns and bone-tight bodices requires bigger busts and wasp waists. "Fashion," Filoso says, "determines the shape of my girls."

---

[1] Personal interview with Robert Filoso and personal observations, April 1988. (Subsequent Filoso quotes are from personal interview.) [Author's note]

[2] At the same time, sculptors of male mannequins were producing more macho models. Pucci Manikins, for example, was elevating its male dummies' height from six feet to six-two and inflating forty-inch chests to forty-two-inch pectorals. See Sam Allis, "What Do Men Really Want?" *Time,* Special Issue, Fall 1990, p. 80. [Author's note]

[3] Christian Lacroix, high-fashion French designer.

The sculptor gingerly unwinds the cloth strips and hands them to his assistant and model, Laurie Rothey. "It seems like so many of the girls are getting breast implants," Rothey is saying as they work, and she isn't referring to the mannequins. "It's the only way you can get jobs because big breasts are all the [modeling] agencies are hiring now. . . ."[4]

Filoso interrupts her with a curse. The clay hasn't dried yet and the mannequin's arm has flopped off its metal bone. The sculptor tries to reattach the limb but now one arm is shorter than the other. "Look at her now, she's a disaster," Filoso cries, throwing his towel on the floor and departing in a huff.

Later that day, his composure regained, Filoso describes his vision for the New Generation. He pictures an in-shape upscale Marilyn Monroe, a "curvey but thin" society lady who can "afford to go to Bergdorf Goodman's and buy anything." Their poses, too, he says, will be "more feminine, more contained. . . . In the 1970s, mannequins were always out there, reaching for something. Now they are pulling into themselves." That's the way it is for real women in the '80s, too, he says: "Now you can be yourself, you can be a lady. You don't have to be a powerhouse."

In Filoso's opinion, these developments are a big improvement over the '70s, when women "didn't care" about their appearance. "The stores didn't want beautiful mannequins, because they were afraid women customers would look at them and say, 'God, I could never look like that in a million years.'" That era, Filoso is happy to report, has passed. "Now, mannequins are really coming to life. They are going to start getting prettier again—more like the fashion photography you'd see in old magazines from the 1950s." And what of female customers who might say, as he put it, "God, I could never look like that in a million years"? But that's the good news, Filoso says. "Today, women can look at a beautiful mannequin in a store and say, 'I want to look like her,' and they actually can! They can go to their doctor and say, 'Doc, I want these cheekbones.' 'Doc, I want these breasts.'"

He sighs. "If I were smart, I would have become a plastic surgeon."

* * *

During the '80s, mannequins set the beauty trends—and real women were expected to follow. The dummies were "coming to life," while the ladies were breathing anesthesia and going under the knife. The beauty industry promoted a "return to femininity" as if it were a revival of natural womanhood—a flowering of all those innate female qualities supposedly suppressed in the feminist '70s. Yet the "feminine" traits the industry celebrated most

---

[4] Personal interview with Laurie Rothey, April 1988. [Author's note]

were grossly unnatural—and achieved with increasingly harsh, unhealthy, and punitive measures.

The beauty industry, of course, has never been an advocate of feminist aspirations. This is not to say that its promoters have a conscious political program against women's rights, just a commercial mandate to improve on the bottom line. And the formula the industry has counted on for many years—aggravating women's low self-esteem and high anxiety about a "feminine" appearance—has always served them well. (American women, according to surveys by the Kinsey Institute,[5] have more negative feelings about their bodies than women in any other culture studied.) The beauty makers' motives aren't particularly thought out or deep. Their overwrought and incessant instructions to women are more mindless than programmatic; their frenetic noise generators create more static than substance. But even so, in the '80s the beauty industry belonged to the cultural loop that produced backlash feedback. Inevitably, publicists for the beauty companies would pick up on the warning signals circulating about the toll of women's equality, too—and amplify them for their own purposes.

"Is your face paying the price of success?" worried a 1988 Nivea skin cream ad, in which a business-suited woman with a briefcase rushes a child to day care—and catches a glimpse of her career-pitted skin in a store window.[6] If only she were less successful, her visage would be more radiant. "The impact of work stress . . . can play havoc with your complexion," *Mademoiselle* warned; it can cause "a bad case of dandruff," "an eventual loss of hair" and, worst of all, weight gain. Most at risk, the magazine claimed, are "high-achieving women," whose comely appearance can be ravaged by "executive stress."[7] In ad after ad, the beauty industry hammered home its version of the backlash thesis: women's professional progress had downgraded their looks; equality had created worry lines and cellulite. This message was barely updated from a century earlier, when the late Victorian beauty press had warned women that their quest for higher education and employment was causing "a general lapse of attractiveness" and "spoiling complexions."[8]

The beauty merchants incited fear about the cost of women's occupational success largely because they feared, rightly, that that success had cost *them*—in profits. Since the rise of the women's movement in the '70s, cosmetics and fragrance companies had suffered a decade of flat-to-declining sales, hair-product merchandisers had fallen into a prolonged slump, and

---

[5] Center for study of sexual attitudes and behavior.

[6] Ad for Nivea Visage, 1988. [Author's note]

[7] Jeanne M. Toal, "Stress and the Single Girl," *Mademoiselle*, Sept. 1987, p. 293. [Author's note]

[8] Cynthia D. Kinnard, ed., *Antifeminism in American Thought: An Annotated Bibliography* (Boston: G.K. Hall & Co., 1986) pp. 307, 20. [Author's note]

hairdressers had watched helplessly as masses of female customers who were opting for simple low-cost cuts defected to discount unisex salons. In 1981, Revlon's earnings fell for the first time since 1968; by the following year, the company's profits had plunged a record 40 percent.[9] The industry aimed to restore its own economic health by persuading women that *they* were the ailing patients—and professionalism their ailment. Beauty became medicalized as its lab-coated army of promoters, and real doctors, prescribed physician-endorsed potions, injections for the skin, chemical "treatments" for the hair, plastic surgery for virtually every inch of the torso.[10] (One doctor even promised to reduce women's height by sawing their leg bones.[11]) Physicians and hospital administrators, struggling with their own financial difficulties, joined the industry in this campaign. Dermatologists faced with a shrinking teen market switched from treating adolescent pimples to "curing" adult female wrinkles. Gynecologists and obstetricians frustrated with a sluggish birthrate and skyrocketing malpractice premiums traded their forceps for liposuction scrapers. Hospitals facing revenue shortfalls opened cosmetic-surgery divisions and sponsored extreme and costly liquid-protein diet programs.[12]

The beauty industry may seem the most superficial of the cultural institutions participating in the backlash, but its impact on women was, in many respects, the most intimately destructive—to both female bodies and minds. Following the orders of the '80s beauty doctors made many women literally ill. Antiwrinkle treatments exposed them to carcinogens. Acid face peels burned their skin. Silicone injections left painful deformities. "Cosmetic" liposuction caused severe complications, infections, and even death. Internalized, the decade's beauty dictates played a role in exacerbating an epidemic of eating disorders. And the beauty industry helped to deepen the psychic isolation that so many women felt in the '80s, by reinforcing the representation of women's problems as purely personal ills, unrelated to

---

[9] "Charlie's Back," *Barron's*, May 13, 1985, p. 34. [Author's note]

[10] A medically oriented and physically punishing beauty standard is another backlash hallmark. Late Victorian doctors conducted the first "face skinning" operations and breast enlargements—called "breast piercing" because they inserted a metal ring to irritate and swell the flesh. In the '30s, face-lifts were popularized; in the "feminine mystique" era, silicone injections were introduced and intensively promoted. See Marjorie Rosen, *Popcorn Venus: Women, Movies, and the American Dream* (New York: Coward, McCann & Geoghegan, 1973) p. 181.; Maggie Angeloglou, *A History of Makeup* (London: The Macmillan Co., 1970) p. 103. [Author's note]

[11] Ann Louise Bardach, "The Dark Side of Cosmetic Surgery," *The Good Health Magazine, New York Times*, April 17, 1988, p. 24. [Author's note]

[12] By 1988, hospital weight-loss programs were generating $5.5 billion a year and diet clinics $10 billion—not bad for an industry with a 95 percent failure rate. See Molly O'Neill, "Dieters Craving Balance, Are Battling Fears of Food," *New York Times*, April 1, 1990, p. 1. [Author's note]

social pressures and curable only to the degree that the individual woman succeeded in fitting the universal standard—by physically changing herself.

The emblems of pulchritude marketed in the '80s—frailty, pallor, puerility—were all beauty marks handed down by previous backlash eras. Historically, the backlash Venus has been an enervated invalid recovering on the chaise longue, an ornamental and genteel lady sipping tea in the drawing room, a child bride shielded from the sun.[13] During the late Victorian era, the beauty industry glorified a cult of invalidism—and profited from it by promoting near-toxic potions that induced a chalky visage.[14] The wasting-away look helped in part to unleash the nation's first dieting mania and the emergence of anorexia in young women.[15] In times of backlash, the beauty standard converges with the social campaign against wayward women, allying itself with "traditional" morality; a porcelain and unblemished exterior becomes proof of a woman's internal purity, obedience, and restraint.[16] The beautiful backlash woman is controlled in both senses of the word. Her physique has been domesticated, her appearance tamed and manicured as the grounds of a gentleman's estate.

By contrast, athleticism, health, and vivid color are the defining properties of female beauty during periods when the culture is more receptive to women's quest for independence. In the late 1910s and early 1920s, female athletes began to eclipse movie stars as the nation's beauty archetypes; Coco Chanel's tan launched a nationwide vogue in ruddy outdoor looks; and Helena Rubinstein's brightly tinted cosmetics made loud and flamboyant colors acceptable.[17] By the late 1920s and '30s, however, the beauty press denounced women who tanned their faces and companies fired women who showed up at work sporting flashy makeup colors. Again, during World War II, invigorated and sun-tanned beauties received all the praise.[18] *Harper's Bazaar*

---

[13] See, for example, Bram Dijkstra, *Idols of Perversity: Fantasies of Feminine Evil in Fin de Siecle Culture* (New York: Oxford University Press, 1986) pp. 25–29. [Author's note]

[14] Dijkstra, *Idols of Perversity,* p. 29; Lois W. Banner, *American Beauty* (New York: Alfred A. Knopf, 1983) p. 41. [Author's note]

[15] Banner, *American Beauty,* p. 47; Joan Jacobs Brumberg, *Fasting Girls: The Emergence of Anorexia Nervosa as a Modern Disease* (Cambridge, Mass: Harvard University Press, 1988) pp. 101–140. [Author's note]

[16] This was an equation John Ruskin made explicit in his 1864 lecture on female beauty, "Of Queens' Gardens": "What the woman is to be within her gates, as the centre of order, the balm of distress, and the mirror of beauty; that she is also to be without her gates, where order is more difficult, distress more imminent, loveliness more rare." See Banner, *American Beauty,* p. 12; Valerie Steele, *Fashion and Eroticism: Ideals of Feminine Beauty from the Victorian Era to the Jazz Age* (New York: Oxford University Press, 1985) pp. 104–105. [Author's note]

[17] Banner, *American Beauty,* p. 277; Angeloglou, *History of Makeup,* pp. 109, 116–17, 119. [Author's note]

[18] See, for example, "The Changing Face of the American Beauty," *McCall's,* April 1976, p. 174. [Author's note]

described "the New American Look of 1943" this way: "Her face is out in the open and so is she. Her figure is lithe and strong. Its lines are lines of action. The glamour girl is no more."[19] With the war over, however, the beauty industry restored that girl—encouraged by a new breed of motivational research consultants who advised cosmetics companies to paint more passive images of femininity. Beauty publicists instructed women to inflate their breasts with padding or silicone, to frost their hair with carcinogenic dyes, to make themselves look paler by whitening their face and lips with titanium—to emulate, in short, that most bleached and medicalized glamour girl of them all, Marilyn Monroe.[20]

Under the '80s backlash, the pattern would repeat, as "Action Beauty," as it was so labeled and exalted in '70s women's magazines,[21] gave way to a sickbed aesthetic. It was a comprehensive transformation carried out at every level of the beauty culture—from the most superficially applied scent to the most invasive and dangerous operations.

STUDY AND DISCUSSION QUESTIONS

1. Why do you suppose Susan Faludi begins this chapter with a view of fashion mannequins?

2. When a writer employs *irony,* the meaning she literally expresses, or the event or situation she depicts, is the opposite of what the reader expects, and the result may be ridicule, humor, or sarcasm. List some of the ironies in the essay's opening section on Robert Filoso and his mannequins.

3. According to the beauty industry, what is the cost to women of "professional progress"?

4. What was the message to women in the 1980s about how they should look, according to Faludi?

5. What are some of the dangers to women which Faludi outlines of trying to look the way fashion decrees?

6. What does "backlash" mean and what is the backlash to which this essay refers?

7. How has beauty become "medicalized"?

---

[19] Tina Sutton and Louise Tutelian, "Play It Again, Roz," *Savvy,* April 1985, p. 60. [Author's note]

[20] Angeloglou, *History of Makeup,* p. 131; Kathryn Weibel, *Mirror Mirror: Images of Women Reflected in Popular Culture* (Garden City, N.Y.: Anchor Books, 1977) p. 161. [Author's note]

[21] See, for example, "Action Beauty," *Mademoiselle,* April 1979. The beauty magazines of the '70s are filled with editorial and advertising tributes to athletic, tanned, and all-natural looks. [Author's note]

SUGGESTIONS FOR WRITING

1. Trace the notions of beauty decreed by fashion from the Victorian era through the 1980s "backlash" and note how each corresponds to a view of who women essentially are and how they should behave. What do you see as the 90s "look" and what social implications does that look carry with it?

2. Although Faludi's article is about women, men are also affected by standards of beauty, both in terms of how men themselves are expected to look and in terms of their view of what is attractive in women. Whether you are a man or a woman, how have the dictates of the "looks" industry affected you personally, as you were growing up and now?

1-800-WASP

Lisa Jones

Lisa Jones, daughter of writers Amiri Baraka and Hettie Jones, was born in 1961. She studied at Yale and New York Universities and has worked as a staff writer for The Village Voice. *She has written several books with director Spike Lee and has published a collection of her essays,* Bulletproof Diva: Tales of Race, Sex, and Hair *(1994), where the following appeared.*

If you dropped dead tonight and were reborn in a mail order catalog, you'd say, "Please Lord, let it be J. Crew." So even in the next life, you could be seen, says the new fall catalog, "placing bids at Christie's[1]" or "huddled in the stands at the Army-Navy game.[2]" Nouvelle prep, it is. Roll-neck sweaters dyed java ("the new black"), flannel blazers in basil or dijon. Working in the city, though bound for Cos Cob.[3] Not as straitlaced Yankee as L.L. Bean, but urbanely WASP (more a state of dress, a wallet size, than a rigid racial criterion). Even Afrocentric iconoclast-bohème[4]-girl writers hunger for some

---

[1] High-priced auction house.

[2] Annual football game between the United States Military Academy at West Point and the United States Naval Academy at Annapolis.

[3] Affluent Connecticut suburb.

[4] Bohemian (French).

version of it. We mix the felt bowlers and peg-leg wool pants with kente[5] knapsacks and MAKE BLACK FILM T-shirts. It's a look we can't resist: Zora Neale Hurston meets George Sand and Jessie Fauset at Emily Dickinson's cabin in Amherst.[6] Our kind of weekend.

Catalogs are mighty image banks these days. The top trendies—Lands' End, Tweeds, and J. Crew—together mail millions of books each year to potential customers in fifty states. One quarter of J. Crew buyers are college students. (The catalogs are dropped in dorms by the pound.) Like MTV,[7] these designer advert-zines arrived in the eighties; they seemed to enter our lives in a new way (in the mail and largely unsolicited) and they fed our national lore. We look for ourselves in their cultural display cases. When people of color are missing as models—and they are for the most part—they're "disappeared" as ideal consumers, as sample citizens.

J. Crew, born in 1983, is not really a catalog at all, but a life-style guide with full-page photos and commentary (low boots to take you from "Park Ave. to Patagonia"). Stores and magazines have lost their point of view, gloats company creative director Jim Nevins, but not J. Crew. What that p.o.v. is is not too hard to suss out: Class. The name's a dead giveaway: "Crew" for the Ivy League trademark sport. And "J.": possibly borrowed from J. G. Hook, which packages "well-bred, classical apparel for women with an upscale lifestyle," recites a company spokesperson. One of J. Crew's retail stores arrived in New York City two years ago at, where else, that yuppie theme park, South Street Seaport.

J. Crew sells its WASP fantasies not from a converted farmhouse in Greenwich, but from Manhattan, a few blocks above Fourteenth Street. (Their warehouse, in Lynchburg, Virginia, has a prefab elite address: One Ivy Crescent.) Perhaps it's a small irony, but Crew's customers are 60 percent urban, and California is one of their strongest market bases. Being a WASP these days may carry some modest stigma in name, though not in name brand. Everyone, so it seems, wants to wear WASP clothes. Or, more to the point, fill their shoes, confiscate their myth and power.

Flipping through J. Crew's aisles this fall, you'll notice more black models peppered throughout. More, but not many: four—three women and one man—out of more than fifty total. (One black model per catalog had been their running standard.) September's male model has an eerie resemblance

---

[5] Woven cloth made by the Ashanti people of Ghana.

[6] Zora Neale Hurston, twentieth-century African American folklorist and fiction writer; George Sand, pseudonym of nineteenth-century French novelist Amandine Aurore Lucie Dupin; Jessie Redmon Fauset, novelist and key figure in the Harlem Renaissance; Emily Dickinson, nineteenth-century American poet.

[7] The Music Television cable channel.

to actor Courtney Vance in John Guare's *Six Degrees of Separation*. (The play's based on the true story of a young black man who—armed with nothing but an oxford shirt—ran a con game on rich whites.) With so much banking on image, since the consumer can't touch or try on, every choice designers make is carefully considered. The decision to use black models, especially in a catalog like J. Crew that oozes Anglo out of every 100 percent cotton pore, must be no exception. Were J. Crew's black models a nod to the racial rainbow seen in fashion mags or liberal window dressing? Or, better yet, a conscious effort to attract African Americans in what may be the waning days of the catalog boom? With annual postal rate hikes, catalogers can't afford to prospect randomly for new customers, why not target blacks?

"We don't do race-oriented marketing," said Adrienne Perkov, J. Crew's director of new market development. "We try to make the product available to everyone." That's an old standby: We don't market to a particular racial/ethnic group (i.e., whites, when we use all-white models), we sell a life-style. As if whites are "everyone," because it's assumed they have no race, and blacks can't signify this "everyone," because we do have one. "We always use a few," offered creative director Nevins, but he didn't have a clue why there would be more black models this fall. Although the company did a customer survey last year, according to Rae Slyper, director of marketing, race wasn't queried. "We wouldn't think of asking anything like that," Slyper yelped, nearly horror-struck. "Is this article about MINORITIES?!?"

"Invisible People" is the title of a new study of "minorities" (whatever that means in these times of shifting demographics) in magazine ads and mail-order catalogs, compiled by New York City's Department of Consumer Affairs. The meager representation of nonwhites is supported by two industry myths: that blacks in particular don't have disposable income (black consumer spending, the study says, will max out at four hundred billion dollars this year); and that when blacks appear in ads, companies experience "white flight" (a falsehood disproven by market studies since the sixties. If anything, putting black models in ads increases sales because blacks identify with them and buy more). Of the 157 catalogs reviewed, blacks made up less than 5 percent of 22,685 models pictured, despite the fact that blacks buy from catalogs at nearly the same rate as whites. (And a disproportionate number of the black models used were juveniles or light-complexion adults.) Several high-circulation catalogs, such as L.L. Bean and Laura Ashley, were whites-only.

Courting black consumers could mean better business for a catalog like J. Crew than the company might realize or be willing to acknowledge. Black people spend a good deal of their disposable income, says African-American consumer-market specialist Persephone Miller, on "image-enhancement" products, which include designer-label clothing from "upscale retailers." We tend to have poor images of ourselves, and through these products we seek to belong, to be accepted.

For those of us who don't "belong" in stores, the idea of shopping in the privacy of our own homes has a double meaning. Mailorder catalogs—toll-free, twenty-four-hour hotlines—are a racially stress-free shopping encounter, no more hassles, no more watchful eyes. All you need is a major credit card (which you might not have, since a lower percentage of black folks have them), and you're guaranteed unconditional acceptance. No one has to know your race, just buy. Or as some might say, buy in.

STUDY AND DISCUSSION QUESTIONS

1. Why does Jones pick J. Crew as the prime example for her essay on mail-order catalogs? What is the article's thesis and how does the J. Crew catalog illustrate that thesis?

2. When she talks about the J. Crew catalog as "not really a catalog at all, but a life-style guide," what does she mean? Do you agree: About J. Crew? About other mail-order catalogs?

3. What are the mail order catalogs' myths about blacks, according to Jones?

4. What is Jones's argument directed at catalog producers *for* including more representation of black people?

5. Why would anyone want to look WASP?

SUGGESTIONS FOR WRITING

1. For a week or so, save the catalogs that come to you in the mail. List them. Write a short humorous essay on who you are, according to the catalogs you've received.

2. Choose one mail order catalog and analyze it. Look at its images, text, and layout. What assumptions about class, race, gender, ethnicity, politics, and lifestyle are embedded in the catalog?

TOYS

Roland Barthes

French social and literary critic Roland Barthes (1915–1980) was a central figure in establishing the field of semiotics, the systematic study of signs and symbols. Among his most important books are Writing Degree Zero *(1953),* Mythologies *(1957), in which "Toys" appeared, and* Elements of Semiology *(1967).*

French toys: one could not find a better illustration of the fact that the adult Frenchman sees the child as another self. All the toys one commonly sees are essentially a microcosm of the adult world; they are all reduced copies of human objects, as if in the eyes of the public the child was, all told, nothing but a smaller man, a homunculus to whom must be supplied objects of his own size.

Invented forms are very rare: a few sets of blocks, which appeal to the spirit of do-it-yourself, are the only ones which offer dynamic forms. As for the others, French toys *always mean something,* and this something is always entirely socialized, constituted by the myths or the techniques of modern adult life: the Army, Broadcasting, the Post Office, Medicine (miniature instrument-cases, operating theatres for dolls), School, Hair-Styling (driers for permanent-waving), the Air Force (Parachutists), Transport (trains, Citroëns, Vedettes, Vespas,[1] petrol-stations), Science (Martian toys).

The fact that French toys *literally* prefigure the world of adult functions obviously cannot but prepare the child to accept them all, by constituting for him, even before he can think about it, the alibi of a Nature which has at all times created soldiers, postmen and Vespas. Toys here reveal the list of all the things the adult does not find unusual: war, bureaucracy, ugliness, Martians, etc. It is not so much, in fact, the imitation which is the sign of an abdication, as its literalness: French toys are like a Jivaro head, in which one recognizes, shrunken to the size of an apple, the wrinkles and hair of an adult. There exist, for instance, dolls which urinate; they have an oesophagus, one gives them a bottle, they wet their nappies; soon, no doubt, milk will turn to water in their stomachs. This is meant to prepare the little girl for the causality of house-keeping, to 'condition' her to her future role as mother. However, faced with this world of faithful and complicated objects, the child can only

---

[1] Citroëns, French-made cars; Vedettes, French-made boats; Vespas, Italian-made motor scooters.

identify himself as owner, as user, never as creator; he does not invent the world, he uses it: there are, prepared for him, actions without adventure, without wonder, without joy. He is turned into a little stay-at-home house-holder who does not even have to invent the mainsprings of adult causality; they are supplied to him ready-made: he has only to help himself, he is never allowed to discover anything from start to finish. The merest set of blocks, provided it is not too refined, implies a very different learning of the world: then, the child does not in any way create meaningful objects, it matters lit-tle to him whether they have an adult name; the actions he performs are not those of a user but those of a demiurge. He creates forms which walk, which roll, he creates life, not property: objects now act by themselves, they are no longer an inert and complicated material in the palm of his hand. But such toys are rather rare: French toys are usually based on imitation, they are meant to produce children who are users, not creators.

The bourgeois status of toys can be recognized not only in their forms, which are all functional, but also in their substances. Current toys are made of a graceless material, the product of chemistry, not of nature. Many are now moulded from complicated mixtures; the plastic material of which they are made has an appearance at once gross and hygienic, it destroys all the pleasure, the sweetness, the humanity of touch. A sign which fills one with consternation is the gradual disappearance of wood, in spite of its being an ideal material because of its firmness and its softness, and the natural warmth of its touch. Wood removes, from all the forms which it supports, the wound-ing quality of angles which are too sharp, the chemical coldness of metal. When the child handles it and knocks it, it neither vibrates nor grates, it has a sound at once muffled and sharp. It is a familiar and poetic substance, which does not sever the child from close contact with the tree, the table, the floor. Wood does not wound or break down; it does not shatter, it wears out, it can last a long time, live with the child, alter little by little the relations be-tween the object and the hand. If it dies, it is in dwindling, not in swelling out like those mechanical toys which disappear behind the hernia of a broken spring. Wood makes essential objects, objects for all time. Yet there hardly remain any of these wooden toys from the Vosges, these fretwork farms with their animals, which were only possible, it is true, in the days of the crafts-man. Henceforth, toys are chemical in substance and colour; their very ma-terial introduces one to a coenaesthesis of use, not pleasure. These toys die in fact very quickly, and once dead, they have no posthumous life for the child.

STUDY AND DISCUSSION QUESTIONS

1. For Barthes, "French toys *always mean something,* and this something is always entirely socialized." What does he mean by this and what effect

does this have on the children who play with these toys? Is what Barthes says in this article also true of toys in the United States?

2. Define: homonculus, prefigure, demiurge, bourgeois, coenaesthesis.

3. How and why do contemporary toys stifle creativity?

4. Discuss the differences between wood and plastic.

SUGGESTIONS FOR WRITING

1. Imagine and list any set of assumptions or beliefs (positive or negative, utopian or dystopian) that a society might want to instill in its children. Now imagine and describe some toys which would encourage those values or that ideology.

2. Discuss a couple of your favorite childhood playthings. What were they, what age were you when you played with them, and what did they teach you and fail to teach you?

3. If you have children (or plan to have children), what kind of toys will you want them to play with, and why?

FOUR

GENDER

"**A**natomy is destiny," wrote Sigmund Freud—a daunting pronouncement indeed. Acceptable roles for women, and for men, have no doubt expanded significantly since Freud's day, but a quick look around—at who usually cooks dinner, whose legs get more attention, who runs the country—should convince you that *something* is still shaping our destinies. A useful distinction in discussing these matters is between "sex" and "gender." Our "sex" exists from the beginning; except in very rare cases, we are born either female or male. "Gender," on the other hand, refers to the role we're socialized to play, the ways of thinking, feeling, and behaving deemed appropriate for us as female or as male. Sex is biological, gender social.

In the traditional social division of personality traits, the tendency towards strong emotions is given to women. What ought to be a positive quality—after all, how can we be fully human without feeling things deeply?—becomes, as part of the female gender stereotype, a flaw. As Susan Brownmiller writes in "Emotion," women are generally seen as "tossed and buffeted on the high seas of emotion, while men have the tough mental fiber, the intellectual muscle, to stay in control." (That men are far more likely than women to burst into violence oddly fails to shake this stereotype.) This pervasive image of how women are, and should be, not only justifies the unequal distribution of power in a sexist society, but also pressures women to conform.

"A woman's body *is* the woman," American writer Ambrose Bierce proclaimed a century ago. The pressure to conform in this realm, too, the pressure on a woman to look "right," can be especially intense, today more than ever in some ways. But if a woman is her body, what is a woman with part of her body missing? In "Breast Cancer: Power vs. Prosthesis," Audre Lorde recounts her experiences after the surgical removal of her right breast. She was angered at the emphasis by those around her on breast cancer as a "cosmetic problem," as if the alteration in her appearance were more serious than the threat to her life. The negative reactions to her decision not to wear a prosthesis, not to cover up the change in her body, not to hide her "difference" as if it were shameful reminded her of how much a woman's worth is still measured by how she looks.

The cruelty of reducing a woman to her emotions, to her appearance, or in any way to less than her full humanity is dramatized in "Lalita Mashi," by Chitra Banerjee Divakaruni. Born in a small village in India, Mashi, the author's aunt, was married off as a young girl to a man she did not know (a "stranger . . . now her master") and widowed at fifteen. Lacking a husband, the main thing that gave a woman value in this traditional society, and prohibited from ever marrying again, she lived "on sufferance" in her father's house, a despised servant and, as a widow, the embodiment of bad luck and shame. For Divakaruni, whose mother still wishes to erase her sister from memory, Lalita Mashi matters a great deal, for though she came to a tragic end (which you'll have to read the essay to learn), she did rebel and by doing so asserted that she was more than what a patriarchal society had tried to reduce her to.

But what about the suffering of men? Scott Russell Sanders writes in "The Men We Carry in Our Minds" of his bewilderment when women he met in college insisted that men held all the power, that women were oppressed. Growing up in rural poverty, he'd seen men coming home from factories or coal mines looking "as though somebody had been whipping them." The work women did at home was more varied and more human; women seemed to live richer and longer lives. Sanders does acknowledge that as a boy he might have been blind to women's suffering, to "what a prison a house could be," and to men's "bullying" of their wives. The men of whom Sanders writes, one could argue, were exploited not by their wives but by the owners of those factories and mines. Sanders's essay, finally, does not so much challenge the concept of sexism as suggest that we need to understand it in connection with social class.

To Dave Barry, the male gender role is not oppressive, just ridiculous. His comic essay "Why Sports Is a Drag" describes the heights of insanity men can reach in their enthusiasm for sports, an insanity that, even today, women rarely share. For example, he tells of a woman on his amateur softball team who, though an excellent player, is still not trusted by her male teammates: "They know that if she had to choose between catching a fly ball and saving an infant's life, deep in her soul, she would probably elect to save the infant's life, without even considering whether there were men [sic] on base." Even men who never play sports, whose athletic activity consists of working the remote while the game is on television, define themselves *as men* in part through their relationship to sports; sports enthusiasm can indeed be a kind of "drag," a costume men put on to create, for themselves and for others, a reassuringly macho image that may not represent who they really are.

To Leonard Kriegel, author of "On the Beach at Noordwijk," masculinity is a very serious matter. Stricken by polio at eleven, he now gets around with crutches and braces. If to be a man is to be strong, active, "capable," Kriegel must struggle ceaselessly to prove his manhood. He criticizes "the false pieties, the dead rituals, in which men enclose themselves," but so deeply ingrained in men and so pervasive in our culture is the traditional conception of masculinity that Kriegel can't help but cling to it and try to define himself within it. His essay powerfully dramatizes how difficult it can be, for men no less than for women, to escape the pressures of gender expectations. But, for all the pain men may feel, we need to remember that the male role, inflexible and limiting as it can be, involves power, not submission, strength not vulnerability—whether we look at who holds what jobs or who batters whom at home.

The seriousness of gender role expectations is also apparent in attitudes towards those who violate them fundamentally by loving people of the same sex. In "Huck Finn, Dan Quayle and the Value of Acceptance," Richard Rodriguez offers us the ruminations of a middle-aged man about to tell his parents that he's gay. Rodriguez is particularly distressed by attacks on "deviants" coming from political ideologues who preach "family values." As a challenge to traditional gender roles, gay men and lesbians are an irresistible target for those who fear recent changes in families and wish to return American life to an imagined glorious past where every man supported a family and every woman stayed happily at home with the kids. When there is only one acceptable way to be a man or to be a woman, homophobia is inevitable.

If we wish to break down these traditional roles, which have so often proved so oppressive, perhaps hope lies in supporting those who suffer most for challenging them. In "Marriage as a Restricted Club," Lindsy Van Gelder describes what it means to her and her lover, Pamela, that they cannot legally marry. Lesbian and gay couples are not only denied social approval—her relationship with Pamela is "simply not considered *authentic*," Van Gelder writes—but also joint health coverage, tax breaks, and other material benefits that heterosexual married couples take for granted. She urges her straight friends to "commit themselves to fighting for [her] rights." But in doing so, some might also be fighting for themselves, helping to dismantle the rigid structure of gender roles that prescribes what a woman should be and what a man should be. Anatomy will be destiny only if we let society make it so.

EMOTION

Susan Brownmiller

Susan Brownmiller was born in Brooklyn, New York in 1935 and studied at Cornell University. She has worked as an actress, a journalist, and a television newswriter and she was a founder of the New York Radical Feminists in the late 1960s. Among her books are Against Our Will: Men, Women, and Rape *(1975),* Femininity *(1984), a chapter of which appears below,* Waverly Place *(1989), a novel, and* Seeing Vietnam: Encounters of the Road and Heart *(1995).*

A 1970 landmark study, known in the field as *Broverman and Broverman,* reported that "Cries very easily" was rated by a group of professional psychologists as a highly feminine trait. "Very emotional," "Very excitable in a minor crisis" and "Feelings easily hurt" were additional characteristics on the femininity scale. So were "Very easily influenced," "Very subjective," "Unable to separate feelings from ideas," "Very illogical" and "Very sneaky." As might be expected, masculinity was defined by opposing, sturdier values: "Very direct," "Very logical," "Can make decisions easily," "Never cries." The importance of *Broverman and Broverman* was not in nailing down a set of popular assumptions and conventional perceptions—masculine-feminine scales were well established in the literature of psychology as a means of ascertaining normality and social adjustment—but in the authors' observation that stereotypic femininity was a grossly negative assessment of the female sex and, furthermore, that many so-called feminine traits ran counter to clinical descriptions of maturity and mental health.

Emotional femininity is a tough nut to crack, impossible to quantify yet hard to ignore. As the task of conforming to a specified physical design is a gender mission that few women care to resist, conforming to a prepackaged emotional design is another imperative task of gender. To satisfy a societal need for sexual clarification, and to justify second-class status, an emblematic constellation of inner traits, as well as their outward manifestations, has been put forward historically by some of the world's great thinkers as proof of the "different" feminine nature.

"Woman," wrote Aristotle, "is more compassionate than man, more easily moved to tears. At the same time, she is more jealous, more querulous, more apt to scold and to strike. She is, furthermore, more prone to despondency and less hopeful than man, more void of shame or self-respect, more false of speech, more deceptive and of more retentive memory. She is also more wakeful, more shrinking, more difficult to rouse to action, and she requires a smaller amount of nutriment."

Addressing a suffrage convention in 1855, Ralph Waldo Emerson had kindlier words on the nature of woman, explicating the nineteenth-century view that her difference was one of superior virtue. "Women," he extolled, "are the civilizers of mankind. What is civilization? I answer, the power of good women. . . . The starry crown of woman is in the power of her affection and sentiment, and the infinite enlargements to which they lead." (In less elevated language, the Emersonian view was perhaps what President Reagan had in mind when he cheerfully stated, "Why, if it wasn't for women, we men would still be walking around in skin suits carrying clubs.")

A clarification is in order. Are women believed to possess a wider or deeper emotional range, a greater sensitivity, say, to the beauties of nature or to the infinite complexities of feeling? Any male poet, artist, actor, marine biologist or backpacker would strenuously object. Rather, it is commonly agreed that women are tossed and buffeted on the high seas of emotion, while men have the tough mental fiber, the intellectual muscle, to stay in control. As for the civilizing influence, surely something more is meant than sophistication, culture and taste, using the correct fork or not belching after dinner. The idealization of emotional femininity, as women prefer to see themselves affirmed, is more exquisitely romantic: a finer temperament in a more fragile vessel, a gentler nature ruled by a twin need to love and to be protected: one who appreciates—without urgency to create—good art, music, literature and other public expressions of the private soul; a flame-bearer of spiritual values by whose shining example the men of the world are inspired to redemption and to accomplish great things.

Two thousand years ago *Dominus flevit*,[1] Jesus wept as he beheld Jerusalem. "Men ceased weeping," proposed Simone de Beauvoir, "when it became unfashionable." Now it is Mary, *Mater Dolorosa*,[2] who weeps with compassion for mankind. In mystical visions, in the reliquaries of obscure churches and miraculous shrines, the figure of the Virgin, the world's most feminine woman, has been seen to shed tears. There are still extant cultures in which men are positively lachrymose (and kissy-kissy) with no seeming detriment to their masculine image, but the Anglo-Saxon tradition, in particular, requires keeping a stiff upper lip. Weeping, keening women shrouded in black are an established fixture in mourning rites in many

---

[1] The Lord wept (Latin).

[2] The sorrowful mother (Latin).

nations. Inconsolable grief is a feminine role, at least in its unquiet representations. In what has become a stock photograph in the national news magazines, women weep for the multitudes when national tragedy (a terrorist bombing, an air crash, an assassination) strikes.

The catharsis of tears is encouraged in women—"There, there, now, let it all out"—while a man may be told to get a grip on himself, or to gulp down a double Scotch. Having "a good cry" in order to feel better afterward is not usually recommended as a means of raising the spirits of men, for the cathartic relief of succumbing to tears would be tempered by the uncomfortable knowledge that the loss of control was hardly manly. In the 1972 New Hampshire Presidential primary, Senator Edmund Muskie, then the Democratic front-runner, committed political suicide when he publicly cried during a campaign speech. Muskie had been talking about some harsh press comments directed at his wife when the tears filled his eyes. In retrospect it was his watershed moment: Could a man who became tearful when the going got rough in a political campaign be expected to face the Russians? To a nation that had delighted in the hatless, overcoatless macho posturing of John F. Kennedy, the military successes of General Ike and the irascible outbursts of "Give 'em hell" Harry Truman, the answer was No. Media accounts of Muskie's all-too-human tears were merciless. In the summer of 1983 the obvious and unshakable grief displayed by Israeli prime minister Menachem Begin after the death of his wife was seized upon by the Israeli and American press as evidence that a tough old warrior had lost his grip. Sharing this perception of his own emotional state, perhaps, Begin shortly afterward resigned.

Expressions of anger and rage are not a disqualifying factor in the masculine disposition. Anger in men is often understood, or excused, as reasonable or just. Anger in men may even be cast in a heroic mold—a righteous response to an insult against honor that will prelude a manly, aggressive act. Because competitive acts of personal assertion, not to mention acts of outright physical aggression, are known to flow from angry feelings, anger becomes the most unfeminine emotion a woman can show.

Anger in a woman isn't "nice." A woman who seethes with anger is "unattractive." An angry woman is hard, mean and nasty; she is unreliably, unprettily out of control. Her face contorts into unpleasant lines: the jaw juts, the eyes are narrowed, the teeth are bared. Anger is a violent snarl and a hostile threat, a declaration of war. The endless forbearance demanded of women, described as the feminine virtue of patience, prohibits an angry response. Picture a charming old-fashioned scene: The mistress of the house bends low over her needlework, cross-stitching her sampler: "Patience is a virtue, possess it if you can/Seldom seen in women, never seen in man." Does the needle jab through the cloth in uncommon fury? Does she prick her thumb in frustration?

Festering without a permissible release, women's undissolved anger has been known to seep out in petty, mean-spirited ways—fits of jealousy, fantasies of retaliation, unholy plots of revenge. Perhaps, after all, it is safer to cry. "Woman's aptitude for facile tears," wrote Beauvoir, "comes largely from the fact that her life is built upon a foundation of impotent revolt."[3]

Beauvoir hedged her bet, for her next words were these: "It is also doubtless true that physiologically she has less nervous control than a man." Is this "doubtless true," or is it more to the point, as Beauvoir continues, that "her education has taught her to let herself go more readily"?

Infants and children cry out of fear, frustration, discomfort, hunger, anxiety at separation from a parent, and rage. Surveying all available studies of crying newborns and little children, psychologists Eleanor Maccoby and Carol Jacklin found no appreciable sexual difference. If teenage girls and adult women are known to cry more than men—and there is no reason to question the popular wisdom in this regard—should the endocrine changes of adolescence be held to account? What of those weepy "blue days" of premenstrual tension that genuinely afflict so many women? What about mid-life depression, known in some circles as "the feminine malady"? Are these conditions, as some men propose, a sign of "raging hormonal imbalance" that incapacitates the cool, logical functioning of the human brain? Or does feminine depression result, as psychiatrist Willard Gaylin suggests, when confidence in one's coping mechanism is lost?

Belief in a biological basis for the instability of female emotions has a notorious history in the development of medical science. Hippocrates the physician held that hysteria was caused by a wandering uterus that remained unfulfilled. Discovery in the seventeenth century that the thyroid gland was larger in women inspired that proposition that the thyroid's function was to give added grace to the feminine neck, but other beliefs maintained that the gland served to flush impurities from the blood before it reached the brain. A larger thyroid "was necessary to guard the female system from the influence of the more numerous causes of irritation and vexation" to which the sex was unfortunately disposed. Nineteenth-century doctors averred that womb-related disorders were the cause of such female complaints as "nervous prostration." For those without money to seek out a physician's care, Lydia E. Pinkham's Vegetable Compound and other patent medicines were available to give relief. In the 1940s and '50s, prefrontal lobotomy was briefly and tragically in vogue for a variety of psychiatric disorders, particularly among

---

[3] "Facile" is the English translator's match for the French *facile*, more correctly rendered as "easy." Beauvoir did not mean to ascribe a stereotypic superficiality to women in her remark. [Author's note]

women, since the surgical procedure had a flattening effect on raging emotions. Nowadays Valium appears to suffice.

Beginning in earnest in the 1960s, one line of research has attempted to isolate premenstrual tension as a contributing cause of accidents, suicide, admittance to mental hospitals and the commission of violent crimes. Mood swings, irritability and minor emotional upsets probably do lead to more "acting out" by females at a cyclical time in the month, but what does this prove beyond the increasingly accepted fact that the endocrine system has a critical influence on the human emotional threshold? Suicide, violent crime and dangerous psychiatric disorders are statistically four to nine times more prevalent in men. Should we theorize, then, that "raging hormonal imbalance" is a chronic, year-round condition in males? A disqualifying factor? By any method of calculation and for whatever reason—hormonal effects, the social inhibitions of femininity, the social pleasure of the masculine role, or all of these—the female gender is indisputably less prone to irrational, antisocial behavior. The price of inhibited anger and a nonviolent temperament may well be a bucketful of tears.

Like the emotion of anger, exulting in personal victory is a harshly unfeminine response. Of course, good winners of either sex are supposed to display some degree of sportsmanlike humility, but the merest hint of gloating triumph—"Me, me, me, I did it!"—is completely at odds with the modesty and deference expected of women and girls. Arm raised in a winner's salute, the ritualized climax of a prizefight, wrestling match or tennis championship, is unladylike, to say the least. The powerful feeling that victory engenders, the satisfaction of climbing to the top of the heap or clinching a deal, remains an inappropriate emotion. More appropriate to femininity are the predictable tears of the new Miss America as she accepts her crown and scepter. Trembling lip and brimming eyes suggest a Cinderella who has stumbled upon good fortune through unbelievable, undeserved luck. At her moment of victory the winner of America's favorite pageant appears overcome, rather than superior in any way. A Miss America who raised her scepter high like a trophy would not be in keeping with the feminine ideal.

The maidenly blush, that staple of the nineteenth-century lady's novel, was an excellent indicator of innocent virginal shyness in contrast to the worldliness and sophistication of men. In an age when a variety of remarks, largely sexual, were considered uncouth and not for the ears of virtuous women, the feminine blush was an expected response. On the other side of the ballroom, men never blushed, at least not in romantic fiction, since presumably they were knowledgeable and sexually practiced. Lowered eyes, heightened color, breathlessness and occasional swooning were further proofs of a fragile and innocent feminine nature that required protection in the rough, indelicate masculine world. (In the best-selling Harlequin and

Silhouette books devoured by romance addicts who need the quick fix, the maidenly blush is alive and well.)

In a new age of relative sexual freedom, or permissiveness, at any rate, squeals and moans replace the blush and the downcast eye. Screaming bob-bysoxers who fainted in the aisle at the Paramount Theater when a skinny young Frank Sinatra crooned his love ballads during the 1940s (reportedly, the first wave of fainting girls was staged by promoters) presaged the whim-pering orgasmic ecstasy at rock concerts in huge arenas today. By contrast, young men in the audience automatically rise to their feet and whistle and shout when the band starts to play, but they seldom appear overcome.

Most emphatically, feminine emotion has gotten louder. The ribald squeal of the stereotypic serving wench in Elizabethan times, a supposed in-dicator of loose, easy ways, seems to have lost its lower-class stigma. One byproduct of our media-obsessed society, in which privacy is considered a quaint and rather old-fashioned human need, has been the reproduction of the unmistakable sounds of female orgasm on a record (Donna Summer's "Love to Love You Baby," among other hits). More than commercialization of sex is operative here. Would the sounds of male orgasm suffice for a record-ing, and would they be unmistakable? Although I have seen no studies on this interesting sex difference, I believe it can be said that most women do vocalize more loudly and uncontrollably than men in the throes of sexual passion. Is this response physiological, compensatory or merely symptomatic of the feminine mission to display one's feelings (and the corresponding mas-culine mission to keep their feelings under control)?

Feminine emotion specializes in sentimentality, empathy and admis-sions of vulnerability—three characteristics that most men try to avoid. Link-ing these traits to female anatomy became an article of faith in the Freudian school. Erik Erikson, for one, spoke of an "inner space" (he meant the womb) that yearns for fulfillment through maternal love. Helene Deutsch, the grande dame of Freudian feminine psychology, spoke of psychic acceptance of hurt and pain; menstrual cramps, defloration and the agonies of childbirth called for a masochistic nature she believed was innate.

Love of babies, any baby and all babies, not only one's own, is a cele-brated and anticipated feminine emotion, and a woman who fails to ooh and ahh at the snapshot of a baby or cuddle a proffered infant in her arms is in-stantly suspect. Evidence of a maternal nature, of a certain innate competence when handling a baby or at least some indication of maternal longing, becomes a requirement of gender. Women with no particular feeling for babies are ex-tremely reluctant to admit their private truth, for the entire weight of women's place in the biological division of labor, not to mention the glorification of motherhood as woman's greatest and only truly satisfactory role, has kept alive the belief that all women yearn to fulfill their biological destiny out of a deep emotional need. That a sizable number of mothers have no genuine aptitude for the job is verified by the records of hospitals, family courts and social agencies where cases of battery and neglect are duly entered—and perhaps also by the characteristic upper-class custom of leaving the little ones to the care of the nanny. But despite this evidence that day-to-day motherhood is not a suitable or a stimulating occupation for all, the myth persists that a woman who prefers to remain childless must be heartless or selfish or less than complete.

Books have been written on maternal guilt and its exploitation, on the endemic feeling that whatever a mother does, her loving care may be inadequate or wrong, with consequences that can damage a child for life. Trends in child care (bottle feeding, demand feeding, not picking up the crying baby, delaying the toilet training or giving up an outside job to devote one's entire time to the family) illuminate the fear of maternal inadequacy as well as the variability of "expert" opinion in each generation. Advertising copywriters successfully manipulate this feminine fear when they pitch their clients' products. A certain cereal, one particular brand of packaged white bread, must be bought for the breakfast table or else you have failed to love your child sufficiently and denied him the chance to "build a strong body twelve ways." Until the gay liberation movement began to speak for itself, it was a commonplace of psychiatric wisdom that a mother had it within her power to destroy her son's heterosexual adjustment by failing to cut his baby curls, keep him away from dance class or encourage his interest in sports.

A requirement of femininity is that a woman devote her life to love— to mother love, to romantic love, to religious love, to amorphous, undifferentiated caring. The territory of the heart is admittedly a province that is open to all, but women alone are expected to make an obsessional career of its exploration, to find whatever adventure, power, fulfillment or tragedy that life has to offer within its bounds. There is no question that a woman is apt to feel most feminine, most confident of her interior gender makeup, when she is reliably within some stage of love—even the girlish crush or the stage of unrequited love or a broken heart. Men have suffered for love, and men have accomplished great feats in the name of love, but what man has ever felt at the top of his masculine form when he is lovesick or suffering from heartache?

Gloria Steinem once observed that the heart is a sex-distinctive symbol of feminine vulnerability in the marketing of fashion. Heart-shaped rings and heart-shaped gold pendants and heart-shaped frames on red plastic sunglasses announce an addiction to love that is beyond the pale of appropriate design for masculine ornamentation. (A man does not wear his heart on his sleeve.) The same observation applies a little less stringently to flowers.

Rare is the famous girl singer, whatever her age, of popular music (blues, country, Top Forty, disco or rock) who is not chiefly identified with some expression of love, usually its downside. Torchy bittersweet ballads and sad, suffering laments mixed with vows of eternal fidelity to the rotten bastard who done her wrong communicate the feminine message of love at any cost. Almost unique to the female singer, I think, is the poignant anthem of battered survival, from Fanny Brice's "My Man" to Gloria Gaynor's "I Will Survive," that does not quite shut the door on further emotional abuse if her man should return.

But the point is not emotional abuse (except in extreme, aberrant cases); the point is feeling. Women are instructed from childhood to be keepers of the heart, keepers of the sentimental memory. In diaries, packets of old love letters and family albums, in slender books of poetry in which a flower is pressed, a woman's emotional history is preserved. Remembrance of things past—the birthday, the anniversary, the death—is a feminine province. In the social division of labor, the wife is charged with maintaining the emotional connection, even with the husband's side of the family. Her thoughtful task is to make the long-distance call, select the present and write the thank-you note (chores that secretaries are asked to do by their bosses). Men are busy; they move forward. A woman looks back. It is significant that in the Biblical parable it was Lot's wife who looked back for one last precious glimpse of their city, their home, their past (and was turned into a pillar of salt).

Love confirms the feminine psyche. A celebrated difference between men and women (either women's weakness or women's strength, depending on one's values) is the obstinate reluctance, the emotional inability of women to separate sex from love. Understandably. Love makes the world go round, and women are supposed to get dizzy—to rise, to fall, to feel alive in every pore, to be undone. In place of a suitable attachment, an unlikely or inaccessible one may have to do. But more important, sex for a woman, even in an age of accessible contraception, has reproductive consequences that render that act a serious affair. Casual sex can have a most uncasual resolution. If a young girl thinks of love and marriage while a boy thinks of getting laid, her emotional commitment is rooted not only in her different upbringing but in her reproductive biology as well. Love, then, can become an alibi for thoughtless behavior, as it may also become an identity, or a distraction, à la Emma Bovary or Anna Karenina,[4] from the frustrations of a limited life.[5]

---

[4] Heroines of Gustave Flaubert's novel *Madame Bovary* and of Leo Tolstoy's novel *Anna Karenina*.

[5] The overwhelming influence of feminine love is frequently offered as a mitigating explanation by women who do unfeminine things. Elizabeth Bentley, the "Red Spy Queen" of the cold war Fifties, attributed her illegal activities to her passion for the Russian master spy Jacob Golos. Judith Coplon's defense for stealing Government documents was love for another Russian, Valentin Gubichev. More recently, Jean Harris haplessly failed to convince a jury that her love for "Scarsdale diet" Doctor Herman Tarnower was so great that she could not possibly have intended to kill him. [Author's note]

Christian houses of worship, especially in poor neighborhoods, are filled disproportionately by women. This phenomenon may not be entirely attributable to the historic role of the Catholic and Protestant religions in encouraging the public devotions of women (which Judaism and Islam did not), or because women have more time for prayer, or because in the Western world they are believed to be more religious by nature. Another contributing factor may be that the central article of Christian faith, "Jesus loves you," has particular appeal for the gender that defines itself through loving emotions.

Women's special interest in the field of compassion is catered to and promoted. Hollywood "weepies," otherwise known as four-handkerchief movies, were big-studio productions that were tailored to bring in female box-office receipts. Columns of advice to the lovelorn, such as the redoubtable "Dear Dorothy Dix" and the current "Dear Abby," were by tradition a woman's slot on daily newspapers, along with the coverage of society births and weddings, in the days when females were as rare in a newsroom as they were in a coal mine. In the heyday of the competitive tabloids, sob-sister journalism, that newsroom term for a human-interest story told with heart-wrenching pathos (usually by a tough male reporter who had the formula down pat), was held in contempt by those on the paper who covered the "hard stuff" of politics, crime and war. (Nathaneal West's famous antihero labored under the byline of Miss Lonelyhearts.) Despite its obvious audience appeal, "soft stuff" was, and is, on the lower rungs of journalism—trivial, weak and unmanly.

In Government circles during the Vietnam war, it was considered a sign of emotional softness, of lily-livered liberals and nervous nellies, to suggest that Napalmed babies, fire-bombed villages and defoliated crops were reason enough to pull out American forces. The peace movement, went the charge, was composed of cowards and fuzzy thinkers. Suspicion of an unmanly lack of hard practical logic always haunts those men who espouse peace and nonviolence, but women, the weaker sex, are permitted a certain amount of emotional leeway. Feminine logic, after all, is reputedly governed by the heartstrings. Compassion and sentiment are the basis for its notorious "subjectivity" compared to the "objectivity" of men who use themselves as the object standard.

As long as the social division of labor ordains that women should bear the chief emotional burden of caring for human life from the cradle to the grave while men may demonstrate their dimorphic difference through competitive acts of physical aggression, emblematic compassion and fear of violence are compelling reasons for an aversion to war and other environmental hazards. When law and custom deny the full range of public expression and economic opportunity that men claim for themselves, a woman must place much of her hopes, her dreams, her feminine identity and her social importance in the private sphere of personal relations, in the connective tissue of marriage, family, friendship and love. In a world out of balance, where men are taught to value toughness and linear vision as masculine traits that enable them to think strategically from conquest to conquest, from campaign to campaign without looking back, without getting sidetracked by vulnerable feelings, there is, and will be, an emotional difference between the sexes, a gender gap that may even appear on a Gallup poll.

If a true shape could emerge from the shadows of historic oppression, would the gender-specific experience of being female still suggest a range of perceptions and values that differ appreciably from those of men? It would be premature to offer an answer. Does a particular emotion ultimately resist separation from its historic deployment in the sexual balance of power? In the way of observation, this much can be said: The entwining of anatomy, history and culture presents such a persuasive emotional argument for a "different nature" that even the best aspects of femininity collaborate in its perpetuation.

SOURCES

Broverman and Broverman: Inge K. Broverman, Donald M. Broverman *et al.,* "Sex-Role Stereotypes and Clinical Judgments of Mental Health," *Journal of Consulting and Clinical Psychology* (Vol. 34, No. 1), 1970. See also Jacob Orlofsky, "Relationship Between Sex Role Attitudes and Personality Traits and the Sex Role Behavior Scale—1: A New Measure of Masculine and Feminine Role Behaviors and Interests," *Journal of Personality and Social Psychology* (Vol. 40, No. 5), 1981.

Selections from Aristotle and Ralph Waldo Emerson appear in Rosemary Agonito, ed., *History of Ideas on Woman: A Source Book,* New York: Putnam, 1977.

President Reagan's remark: *Time,* Sept. 12, 1983.

Jesus wept: Luke 19:41.

Mary as *Mater Dolorosa:* Marina Warner, *Alone of All Her Sex: The Myth and the Cult of the Virgin Mary,* New York: Knopf, 1976.

Muskie's tears: "Campaign Teardrops," *Time,* March 13, 1972.

Begin's grief: "Begin's Deep Depression," *Newsweek,* Sept. 26, 1983; "Begin's Clouds of Gloom," *Newsweek,* Aug. 1, 1983.

Beauvoir on crying: Simone de Beauvoir, *The Second Sex* (1949), trans. from the French by H. M. Parshley, New York: Knopf, 1953.

Studies on crying newborns and little children: Eleanor Maccoby and Carol Jacklin, *The Psychology of Sex Differences,* Stanford University Press, 1974.

Raging hormonal imbalance: Edgar Berman, *The Compleat Chauvinist: A Guide for the Bedeviled Male,* New York: Macmillan, 1981.

Depression: Willard Gaylin, *Feelings,* New York: Harper and Row, 1979; Pauline Bart, "Depression in Middle-Aged Women," in Gornick and Moran, eds., *Woman in Sexist Society,* New York: Basic Books, 1971.

Hippocrates and the wandering uterus: Joanna B. Rohrbaugh, *Women: Psychology's Puzzle,* New York: Basic Books, 1979.

Thyroid gland theories: Louis S. Goodman and Alfred Gilman, *The Pharmacological Basis of Therapeutics,* New York: Macmillan, 1975.

Nervous prostration: Sarah Stage, *Female Complaints: Lydia Pinkham and the Business of Women's Medicine,* New York: Norton, 1979.

Premenstrual tension: The pioneer in the field is Katharina Dalton, *The Menstrual Cycle,* New York: Pantheon, 1969.

Inner space: Erik Erikson, *Identity, Youth and Crisis,* New York: Norton, 1968.

Female masochism: Helene Deutsch, *The Psychology of Women* (2 vols.), New York: Grune and Stratton, 1944, 1945.

Maternal guilt is discussed in Shirley Radl, *Mother's Day Is Over,* New York: Charterhouse, 1973; Angela Barron McBride, *The Growth and Development of Mothers,* New York: Harper and Row, 1973; Adrienne Rich, *Of Woman Born,* New York: Norton, 1976; Jane Lazarre, *The Mother Knot,* New York: McGraw-Hill, 1976.

Feminine emotions in popular music: Aida Pavletich, *Rock-a-Bye, Baby,* New York: Doubleday, 1980.

Gender gap in Gallup poll: *Newsweek,* Sept. 19, 1983.

STUDY AND DISCUSSION QUESTIONS

1. Why does Brownmiller quote Aristotle at such length?

2. Emerson called women "the civilizers of mankind." What's wrong with that idea, according to Brownmiller?

3. Why are women discouraged from showing anger?

4. What point is Brownmiller making about "the maidenly blush"?

5. Why don't men's fashions incorporate hearts and flowers the way women's fashions do?

6. Why has there been such a persistent effort to find biological explanations for male-female differences? Why is it so important for Brownmiller to criticize these explanations?

7. How does the way Brownmiller writes about her subject challenge the gender role expectations she analyzes?

8. Explain the last sentence of "Emotion."

SUGGESTIONS FOR WRITING

1. Consider a woman whom you know well, perhaps your mother. To what extent does she fulfill the gender role expectations that Brownmiller describes? If she's deviated from them, how have those around her responded?

2. How well do you yourself meet the societal expectations Brownmiller analyzes? What pressures to conform have you experienced? What problems have you encountered when you haven't conformed?

BREAST CANCER: POWER VS. PROSTHESIS

Audre Lorde

Audre Lorde (1934–1992) was born in Harlem and studied at Hunter College and Columbia University. Her identity as a black lesbian feminist was central to her writing, which included poetry, such as The First Cities *(1968),* The Black Unicorn *(1978),* Our Dead Behind Us *(1986), and* The Marvelous Arithmetics of Distance *(1993), as well as nonfiction, among it the autobiography* Zami: A New Spelling of My Name *(1982),* The Cancer Journals *(1980), in which the following essay appeared, and* Sister Outsider *(1984).*

On Labor Day, 1978, during my regular monthly self-examination, I discovered a lump in my right breast which later proved to be malignant. During my following hospitalization, my mastectomy and its aftermath, I passed through many stages of pain, despair, fury, sadness and growth. I moved through these stages, sometimes feeling as if I had no choice, other times recognizing that I could choose oblivion—or a passivity that is very close to oblivion—but did not want to. As I slowly began to feel more equal to processing and examining the different parts of this experience, I also began to feel that in the process of losing a breast I had become a more whole person.

After a mastectomy, for many women including myself, there is a feeling of wanting to go back, of not wanting to persevere through this experience to whatever enlightenment might be at the core of it. And it is this feeling, this nostalgia, which is encouraged by most of the post-surgical counseling for women with breast cancer. This regressive tie to the past is emphasized by the concentration upon breast cancer as a cosmetic problem, one which can be solved by a prosthetic pretense. The American Cancer Society's Reach For Recovery Program, while doing a valuable service in contacting women immediately after surgery and letting them know they are not alone, nonetheless encourages this false and dangerous nostalgia in the mistaken belief that women are too weak to deal directly and courageously with the realities of our lives.

The woman from Reach For Recovery who came to see me in the hospital, while quite admirable and even impressive in her own right, certainly did not speak to my experience nor my concerns. As a 44 year old Black Lesbian Feminist, I knew there were very few role models around for me in this situation, but my primary concerns two days after mastectomy were hardly about what man I could capture in the future, whether or not my old boyfriend would still find me attractive enough, and even less about whether my two children would be embarrassed by me around their friends.

My concerns were about my chances for survival, the effects of a possibly shortened life upon my work and my priorities. Could this cancer have been prevented, and what could I do in the future to prevent its recurrence? Would I be able to maintain the control over my life that I had always taken for granted? A lifetime of loving women had taught me that when women love each other, physical change does not alter that love. It did not occur to me that anyone who really loved me would love me any less because I had one breast instead of two, although it did occur to me to wonder if they would be able to love and deal with the new me. So my concerns were quite different from those spoken to by the Reach For Recovery volunteer, but not one bit less crucial nor less poignant.

Yet every attempt I made to examine or question the possibility of a real integration of this experience into the totality of my life and my loving and my work, was ignored by this woman, or uneasily glossed over by her as not looking on "the bright side of things." I felt outraged and insulted, and weak as I was, this left me feeling even more isolated than before.

In the critical and vulnerable period following surgery, self-examination and self-evaluation are positive steps. To imply to a woman that yes, she can be the 'same' as before surgery, with the skillful application of a little puff of lambswool, and/or silicone gel, is to place an emphasis upon prosthesis which encourages her not to deal with herself as physically and emotionally real, even though altered and traumatized. This emphasis upon the cosmetic after surgery re-inforces this society's stereotype of women, that we are only what we look or appear, so this is the only aspect of our existence we need to address. Any woman who has had a breast removed because of cancer knows she does not feel the same. But we are allowed no psychic time or space to examine what our true feelings are, to make them our own. With quick cosmetic reassurance, we are told that our feelings are not important, our appearance is all, the sum total of self.

I did not have to look down at the bandages on my chest to know that I did not feel the same as before surgery. But I still felt like myself, like Audre, and that encompassed so much more than simply the way my chest appeared.

The emphasis upon physical pretense at this crucial point in a woman's reclaiming of her self and her body-image has two negative effects:

1. It encourages women to dwell in the past rather than a future. This prevents a woman from assessing herself in the present, and from coming to terms with the changed planes of her own body. Since these then remain alien to her, buried under prosthetic devices, she must mourn the loss of her breast in secret, as if it were the result of some crime of which she were guilty.

2. It encourages a woman to focus her energies upon the mastectomy as a cosmetic occurrence, to the exclusion of other factors in a constellation that could include her own death. It removes her from what that constellation means in terms of her living, and from developing priorities of usage for whatever time she has before her. It encourages her to ignore the necessity for nutritional vigilance and psychic armament that can help prevent recurrence.

I am talking here about the need for every woman to live a considered life. The necessity for that consideration grows and deepens as one faces directly one's own mortality and death. Self scrutiny and an evaluation of our lives, while painful, can be rewarding and strengthening journeys toward a deeper self. For as we open ourselves more and more to the genuine conditions of our lives, women become less and less willing to tolerate those conditions unaltered, or to passively accept external and destructive controls over our lives and our identities. Any short-circuiting of this quest for self-definition and power, however well-meaning and under whatever guise, must be seen as damaging, for it keeps the post-mastectomy woman in a position of perpetual and secret insufficiency, infantilized and dependent for her identity upon an external definition by appearance. In this way women are kept from expressing the power of our knowledge and experience, and through that expression, developing strengths that challenge those structures within our lives that support the Cancer Establishment. For instance, why hasn't the American Cancer Society publicized the connections between animal fat and breast cancer for our daughters the way it has publicized the connection between cigarette smoke and lung cancer? These links between animal fat, hormone production and breast cancer are not secret. (See G. Hems, in *British Journal of Cancer,* vol. 37, no. 6, 1978.)

Ten days after having my breast removed, I went to my doctor's office to have the stitches taken out. This was my first journey out since coming home from the hospital, and I was truly looking forward to it. A friend had washed my hair for me and it was black and shining, with my new grey hairs glistening in the sun. Color was starting to come back into my face and around my eyes. I wore the most opalescent of my moonstones, and a single floating bird dangling from my right ear in the name of grand assymmetry. With an African kente-cloth tunic and new leather boots, I knew I looked fine, with that brave new-born security of a beautiful woman having come through a very hard time and being very glad to be alive.

I felt really good, within the limits of that grey mush that still persisted in my brain from the effects of the anesthesia.

When I walked into the doctor's office, I was really rather pleased with myself, all things considered, pleased with the way I felt, with my own flair, with my own style. The doctor's nurse, a charmingly bright and steady woman of about my own age who had always given me a feeling of quiet no-nonsense support on my other visits, called me into the examining room. On the way, she asked me how I was feeling.

"Pretty good," I said, half-expecting her to make some comment about how good I looked.

"You're not wearing a prosthesis," she said, a little anxiously, and not at all like a question.

"No," I said, thrown off my guard for a minute. "It really doesn't feel right," referring to the lambswool puff given to me by the Reach For Recovery volunteer in the hospital.

Usually supportive and understanding, the nurse now looked at me urgently and disapprovingly as she told me that even if it didn't look exactly right, it was "better than nothing," and that as soon as my stitches were out I could be fitted for a "real form."

"You will feel so much better with it on," she said. "And besides, we really like you to wear something, at least when you come in. Otherwise it's bad for the morale of the office."

I could hardly believe my ears! I was too outraged to speak then, but this was to be only the first such assault on my right to define and to claim my own body.

Here we were, in the offices of one of the top breast cancer surgeons in New York City. Every woman there either had a breast removed, might have to have a breast removed, or was afraid of having to have a breast removed. And every woman there could have used a reminder that having one breast did not mean her life was over, nor that she was less a woman, nor that she was condemned to the use of a placebo in order to feel good about herself and the way she looked.

Yet a woman who has one breast and refuses to hide that fact behind a pathetic puff of lambswool which has no relationship nor likeness to her own breasts, a woman who is attempting to come to terms with her changed landscape and changed timetable of life and with her own body and pain and beauty and strength, that woman is seen as a threat to the "morale" of a breast surgeon's office!

Yet when Moishe Dayan, the Prime Minister of Israel, stands up in front of parliament or on TV with an eyepatch over his empty eyesocket, nobody tells him to go get a glass eye, or that he is bad for the morale of the office. The world sees him as a warrior with an honorable wound, and a loss of a piece of himself which he has marked, and mourned, and moved beyond. And if you have trouble dealing with Moishe Dayan's empty eye socket, everyone recognizes that it is your problem to solve, not his.

Well, women with breast cancer are warriors, also. I have been to war, and still am. So has every woman who has had one or both breasts amputated because of the cancer that is becoming the primary physical scourge of our time. For me, my scars are an honorable reminder that I may be a casualty in the cosmic war against radiation, animal fat, air pollution, McDonald's hamburgers and Red Dye No. 2,[1] but the fight is still going on, and I am still a part of it. I refuse to have my scars hidden or trivialized behind lambswool or silicone gel. I refuse to be reduced in my own eyes or in the eyes of others from warrior to mere victim, simply because it might render me a fraction more acceptable or less dangerous to the still complacent, those who believe if you cover up a problem it ceases to exist. I refuse to hide my body simply because it might make a woman-phobic world more comfortable.

As I sat in my doctor's office trying to order my perceptions of what had just occurred, I realized that the attitude towards prosthesis after breast cancer is an index of this society's attitudes towards women in general as decoration and externally defined sex object.

Two days later I wrote in my journal:

> I cannot wear a prosthesis right now because it feels like a lie more than merely a costume, and I have already placed this, my body under threat, seeking new ways of strength and trying to find the courage to tell the truth.

For me, the primary challenge at the core of mastectomy was the stark look at my own mortality, hinged upon the fear of a life-threatening cancer. This event called upon me to reexamine the quality and texture of my entire life, its priorities and commitments, as well as the possible alterations that might be required in the light of that re-examination. I had already faced my own death, whether or not I acknowledged it, and I needed now to develop that strength which survival had given me.

Prosthesis offers the empty comfort of "Nobody will know the difference." But it is that very difference which I wish to affirm, because I have

---

[1] Food coloring made from petroleum or coal.

lived it, and survived it, and wish to share that strength with other women. If we are to translate the silence surrounding breast cancer into language and action against this scourge, then the first step is that women with mastectomies must become visible to each other.[2] For silence and invisibility go hand in hand with powerlessness. By accepting the mask of prosthesis, one-breasted women proclaim ourselves as insufficients dependent upon pretense. We reinforce our own isolation and invisibility from each other, as well as the false complacency of a society which would rather not face the results of its own insanities. In addition, we withhold that visibility and support from one another which is such an aid to perspective and self-acceptance. Surrounded by other women day by day, all of whom appear to have two breasts, it is very difficult sometimes to remember that I AM NOT ALONE. Yet once I face death as a life process, what is there possibly left for me to fear? Who can every really have power over me again?

As women, we cannot afford to look the other way, nor to consider the incidence of breast cancer as a private nor secret personal problem. It is no secret that breast cancer is on the increase among women in America. According to the American Cancer Society's own statistics on breast cancer survival, of the women stricken, only 50% are still alive after three years. This figure drops to 30% if you are poor, or Black, or in any other way part of the underside of this society. We cannot ignore these facts, nor their implications, nor their effect upon our lives, individually and collectively. Early detection and early treatment is crucial in the management of breast cancer if those sorry statistics of survival are to improve. But for the incidence of early detection and early treatment to increase, american women must become free enough from social stereotypes concerning their appearance to realize that losing a breast is infinitely preferable to losing one's life. (Or one's eyes, or one's hands. . . .)

Although breast self-examination does not reduce the incidence of breast cancer, it does markedly reduce the rate of mortality, since most early tumors are found by women themselves. I discovered my own tumor upon a monthly breast exam, and so report most of the other women I know with a good prognosis for survival. With our alert awareness making such a difference in the survival rate for breast cancer, women need to face the possibility and the actuality of breast cancer as a reality rather than as myth, or retribution, or terror in the night, or a bad dream that will disappear if ignored. After surgery, there is a need for women to be aware of the possibility of bilateral recurrence, with vigilance rather than terror. This is not a spread of cancer, but a new occurrence in the other breast. Each woman must be

---

[2] Particular thanks to Maureen Brady for the conversation which developed this insight. [Author's note]

aware that an honest acquaintanceship with and evaluation of her own body is the best tool of detection.

Yet there still appears to be a conspiracy on the part of Cancer, Inc. to insist to every woman who has lost a breast that she is no different from before, if with a little skillful pretense and a few ounces of silicone gel she can pretend to herself and the watching world—the only orientation toward the world that women are supposed to have—that nothing has happened to challenge her. With this orientation a woman after surgery is allowed no time or space within which to weep, rage, internalize, and transcend her own loss. She is left no space to come to terms with her altered life, not to transform it into another level of dynamic existence.

The greatest incidence of breast cancer in american women appears within the ages of 40 to 55. These are the very years when women are portrayed in the popular media as fading and desexualized figures. Contrary to the media picture, I find myself as a woman of insight ascending into my highest powers, my greatest psychic strengths, and my fullest satisfactions. I am freer of the constraints and fears and indecisions of my younger years, and survival throughout these years has taught me how to value my own beauty, and how to look closely into the beauty of others. It has also taught me to value the lessons of survival, as well as my own perceptions. I feel more deeply, value those feelings more, and can put those feelings together with what I know in order to fashion a vision of and pathway toward true change. Within this time of assertion and growth, even the advent of a life-threatening cancer and the trauma of a mastectomy can be integrated into the life-force as knowledge and eventual strength, fuel for a more dynamic and focussed existence. Since the supposed threat of self-actualized women is one that our society seeks constantly to protect itself against, it is not coincidental that the sharing of this knowledge among women is diverted, in this case by the invisibility imposed by an insistence upon prosthesis as a norm for post-mastectomy women.

There is nothing wrong, per se, with the use of prostheses, if they can be chosen freely, for whatever reason, after a woman has had a chance to accept her new body. But usually prostheses serve a real function, to approximate the performance of a missing physical part. In other amputations and with other prosthetic devices, function is the main point of their existence. Artificial limbs perform specific tasks, allowing us to manipulate or to walk. Dentures allow us to chew our food. Only false breasts are designed for appearance only, as if the only real function of women's breasts were to appear in a certain shape and size and symmetry to onlookers, or to yield to external pressure. For no woman wearing a prosthesis can even for one moment believe it is her own breast, any more than a woman wearing falsies can.

Yet breast prostheses are offered to women after surgery in much the same way that candy is offered to babies after an injection, never mind that the end effect may be destructive. Their comfort is illusory; a transitional period can be provided by any loose-fitting blouse. After surgery, I most certainly did not feel better with a lambswool puff stuck in the front of my bra. The real truth is that certain other people feel better with that lump stuck into my bra, because they do not have to deal with me nor themselves in terms of mortality nor in terms of difference.

Attitudes toward the necessity for prostheses after breast surgery are merely a reflection of those attitudes within our society towards women in general as objectified and depersonalized sexual conveniences. Women have been programmed to view our bodies only in terms of how they look and feel to others, rather than how they feel to ourselves, and how we wish to use them. We are surrounded by media images portraying women as essentially decorative machines of consumer function, constantly doing battle with rampant decay. (Take your vitamins every day and he *might* keep you, if you don't forget to whiten your teeth, cover up your smells, color your grey hair and iron out your wrinkles. . . .) As women, we fight this depersonalization every day, this pressure toward the conversion of one's own self-image into a media expectation of what might satisfy male demand. The insistence upon breast prostheses as 'decent' rather than functional is an additional example of that wipe-out of self in which women are constantly encouraged to take part. I am personally affronted by the message that I am only acceptable if I look 'right' or 'normal,' where those norms have nothing to do with my own perceptions of who I am. Where 'normal' means the 'right' color, shape, size, or number of breasts, a woman's perception of her own body and the strengths that come from that perception are discouraged, trivialized, and ignored. When I mourn my right breast, it is not the appearance of it I mourn, but the feeling and the fact. But where the superficial is supreme, the idea that a woman can be beautiful and one-breasted is considered depraved, or at best, bizarre, a threat to 'morale.'

In order to keep me available to myself, and able to concentrate my energies upon the challenges of those worlds through which I move, I must consider what my body means to me. I must also separate those external demands about how I look and feel to others, from what I really want for my own body, and how I feel to my selves. As women we have been taught to respond with a guilty twitch at any mention of the particulars of our own oppression, as if we are ultimately guilty of whatever has been done to us. The rape victim is accused of enticing the rapist. The battered wife is accused of having angered her husband. A mastectomy is not a guilty act that must be hidden in order for me to regain acceptance or protect the sensibilities of others. Pretense has never brought about lasting change or progress.

Every woman has a right to define her own desires, make her own choices. But prostheses are often chosen, not from desire, but in default. Some women complain it is too much effort to fight the concerted pressure exerted by the fashion industry. Being one-breasted does not mean being unfashionable; it means giving some time and energy to choosing or constructing the proper clothes. In some cases, it means making or remaking clothing or jewelry. The fact that the fashion needs of one-breasted women are not currently being met doesn't mean that the concerted pressure of our demands cannot change that.[3]

There was a time in America not long ago when pregnant women were supposed to hide their physical realities. The pregnant woman who ventured forth into public had to design and construct her own clothing to be comfortable and attractive. With the increased demands of pregnant women who are no longer content to pretend non-existence, maternity fashion is now an established, flourishing and particular sector of the clothing field.

The design and marketing of items of wear for one-breasted women is only a question of time, and we who are now designing and wearing our own asymmetrical patterns and New Landscape jewelry are certainly in the vanguard of a new fashion!

Some women believe that a breast prosthesis is necessary to preserve correct posture and physical balance. But the weight of each breast is never the same to begin with, nor is the human body ever exactly the same on both sides. With a minimum of exercises to develop the habit of straight posture, the body can accommodate to one-breastedness quite easily, even when the breasts were quite heavy.

Women in public and private employment have reported the loss of jobs and promotions upon their return to work after a mastectomy, without regard to whether or not they wore prostheses. The social and economic discrimination practiced against women who have breast cancer is not diminished by pretending that mastectomies do not exist. Where a woman's job is at risk because of her health history, employment discrimination cannot be fought with a sack of silicone gel, nor with the constant fear and anxiety to which such subterfuge gives rise. Suggesting prosthesis as a solution to employment discrimination is like saying that the way to fight race prejudice is for Black people to pretend to be white. Employment discrimination against post-mastectomy women can only be fought in the open, with head-on attacks by strong and self-accepting women who refuse to be relegated to an inferior position, or to cower in a corner because they have one breast.

---

[3] Particular thanks to Frances Clayton for the conversations that developed this insight. [Author's note]

When post-mastectomy women are dissuaded from any realistic evaluation of themselves, they spend large amounts of time, energy, and money in following any will-o-wisp that seems to promise a more skillful pretense of normality. Without the acceptance of difference as part of our lives, and in a guilty search for illusion, these women fall easy prey to any shabby confidence scheme that happens along. The terror and silent loneliness of women attempting to replace the ghost of a breast leads to yet another victimization.

The following story does not impugn the many reputable makes of cosmetic breast forms which, although outrageously overpriced, can still serve a real function for the woman who is free enough to choose when and why she wears one or not. We find the other extreme reported upon in *The New York Times,* December 28, 1978:

ARTIFICIAL BREAST CONCERN
CHARGED WITH CHEATING

> A Manhattan concern is under inquiry for allegedly having victimized cancer patients who had ordered artificial breasts after mastectomies. . . . The number of women allegedly cheated could not be determined. The complaints received were believed to be "only a small percentage of the victims" because others seemed *too embarrassed to complain.* (italics mine)

Although the company in question, Apres Body Replacement, founded by Mrs. Elke Mack, was not a leader in the field of reputable makers of breast forms, it was given ample publicity on the ABC-TV program, "Good Morning, America" in 1977, and it is here that many women first heard of Apres. What was so special about the promises of this product that it enticed such attention, and so much money out of the pockets of women from New York to Maine? To continue from *The New York Times* article:

> Apres offered an "individually designed product that is a total duplicate of the remaining breast," and "worn on the body by use of a synthetic adhesive" supposedly formulated by a doctor.

It is reported that in some cases, women paid up to $600, sight unseen, for this article which was supposedly made from a form cast from their own bodies. When the women arrived to pick up the prosthesis, they received something having no relation or kinship to their own breasts, and which failed to adhere to their bodies, and which was totally useless. Other women received nothing at all for their money.

This is neither the worst nor the most expensive victimization, however. Within the framework of superficiality and pretense, the next logical step of a depersonalizing and woman-devaluating culture is the advent of the atrocity euphemistically called "breast reconstruction." This operation is now being pushed by the plastic surgery industry as the newest "advance" in breast surgery. Actually it is not new at all, being a technique previously used to augment or enlarge breasts. It should be noted that research being done on this potentially life-threatening practice represents time and research money spent—not on how to prevent the cancers that cost us our breasts and our lives—but rather upon how to pretend that our breasts are not gone, nor we as women at risk with our lives.

The operation consists of inserting silicone gel implants under the skin of the chest, usually shortly after a mastectomy and in a separate operation. At an approximate cost of $1500 to $3000 an implant (in 1978), this represents a lucrative piece of commerce for the cancer and plastic surgery industries in this country. There are now plastic surgeons recommending the removal of the other breast at the same time as the mastectomy is done, even where there is no clinically apparent reason.

> It is important when considering subcutaneous mastectomy to plan to do both breasts at the same time. . . . it is extremely difficult to attain the desired degree of symmetry under these circumstances with a unilateral prosthesis.
>
> R.K. Snyderman, M.D.
> in "What The Plastic Surgeon Has To Offer
> in the Management of Breast Tumors"

In the same article appearing in *Early Breast Cancer, Detection and Treatment,* edited by Stephen Gallegher, M.D., the author states:

> The companies are working with us. They will make prostheses to practically any design we desire. Remember that what we are doing in the reconstruction of the female breast is by no means a cosmetic triumph. What we are aiming for is to *allow women to look decent in clothes.* (italics mine). . . . The aim is for the patient to *look normal and natural when she has clothes on her body.*

Is it any coincidence that the plastic surgeons most interested in pushing breast reconstruction and most involved in the superficial aspects of women's breasts speak the language of sexist pigs? What is the positive correlation?

The American Cancer Society, while not openly endorsing this practice, is doing nothing to present a more balanced viewpoint concerning the dangers of reconstruction. In covering a panel on Breast Reconstruction held by the American Society of Plastic and Reconstructive Surgeons, the Spring, 1978 issue of the ACS *Cancer News* commented:

> Breast reconstruction will not recreate a perfect replica of the lost breast, but it will enable many women who have had mastectomies *to wear a normal bra or bikini.* (italics mine)

So, even for the editor of the ACS *Cancer News,* when a woman has faced the dread of breast cancer and triumphed, for whatever space of time, her primary concern should still be whether or not she can wear a *normal bra or bikini.* With unbelieveable cynicism, one plastic surgeon reports that for patients with a lessened likelihood of cure—a poor prognosis for survival—*he waits two years before implanting silicone gel into her body.* Another surgeon adds,

> Even when the patient has a poor prognosis, she wants a *better quality of life.* (italics mine)

In his eyes, obviously, this better quality of life will come, not through the woman learning to come to terms with her living and dying and her own personal power, but rather through her wearing a 'normal' bra.

Most of those breast cancer surgeons who oppose this practice being pushed by the American Society of Plastic and Reconstructive Surgeons either are silent, or tacitly encourage its use by their attitude toward the woman whom they serve.

On a CBS-TV Evening News Special Report on breast reconstruction in October, 1978, one lone doctor spoke out against the use of silicone gel implantations as a potentially carcinogenic move. But even he spoke of women as if their appearance and their lives were equally significant. "It's a real shame," he said, "when a woman has to choose between her life or her femininity." In other words, with a sack of silicone implanted under her skin, a woman may well be more likely to die from another cancer, but without that implant, according to this doctor, she is not 'feminine.'

While plastic surgeons in the service of 'normal bras and bikinis' insist that there is no evidence of increase in cancer recurrence because of breast reconstructions, Dr. Peter Pressman, a prominent breast cancer surgeon at Beth Israel Medical Center in New York City, has raised some excellent points. Although silicone gel implants have been used in enough nonmalignant breast augmentations to say that the material probably is not, in and of itself, carcinogenic, Dr. Pressman raises a number of questions which still remain concerning these implants after breast cancer.

1. There have been no large scale studies with matched control groups conducted among women who have had post-mastectomy reconstruction. Therefore, we cannot possibly have sufficient statistics available to demonstrate whether reconstruction has had any negative effect upon the recurrence of breast cancer.

2. It is possible that the additional surgery necessary for insertion of the prosthesis could stir up cancer cells which might otherwise remain dormant.

3. In the case of a recurrence of breast cancer, the recurrent tumor can be masked by the physical presence of the implanted prosthesis under

the skin. When the nipple and skin tissue is preserved to be used later in 'reconstruction,' minute cancer cells can hide within this tissue undetected.

Any information about the prevention or treatment of breast cancer which might possibly threaten the vested interests of the american medical establishment is difficult to acquire in this country. Only through continuing scrutiny of various non-mainstream sources of information, such as alternative and women's presses, can a picture of new possibilities for prevention and treatment of breast cancer emerge.

Much of this secrecy is engineered by the American Cancer Society, which has become "the loudest voice of the Cancer Establishment."[4] The ACS is the largest philanthropic institution in the United States and the world's largest nonreligious charity. Peter Chowka points out that the National Information Bureau, a charity watchdog organization, listed the ACS among the groups which do not meet its standards. During the past decade, the ACS collected over $1 billion from the american public.[5] In 1977 it had a $176 million fund balance, yet less than 15% of its budget was spent on assisting cancer patients.[6]

Any holistic approach to the problem of cancer is viewed by ACS with suspicion and alarm. It has consistently focussed upon treatment rather than prevention of cancer, and then only upon those treatments sanctioned by the most conservative branches of western medicine. We live in a profit economy and there is no profit in the prevention of cancer; there is only profit in the treatment of cancer. In 1976, 70% of the ACS research budget went to individuals and institutions with whom ACS board members were affiliated.[7] And of the 194 members of its governing board, one is a labor representative and one is Black. Women are not even mentioned.

The ACS was originally established to champion new research into the causes and the cure of cancer. But by its black-listing of new therapies without testing them, the ACS spends much of its remaining budget suppressing new and unconventional ideas and research.[8] Yet studies from other countries have shown interesting results from treatments largely ignored by ACS. European medicine reports hopeful experiments with immunotherapy, diet, and treatment with hormones and enzymes such as trypsin.[9] Silencing and

[4] Chowka, Peter, "Checking Up On the ACS." *New Age Magazine,* April '80, p. 22. [Author's note]

[5] *Ibid.* [Author's note]

[6] Epstein, Samuel, *The Politics of Cancer.* Anchor Books, New York. 1979. p. 456. [Author's note]

[7] *Ibid.* [Author's note]

[8] Chowka, Peter. p. 23. [Author's note]

[9] Martin, Wayne. "Let's Cut Cancer Deaths in Half." *Let's Live Magazine,* August, 1978. p. 356. [Author's note]

political repression by establishment medical journals keep much vital information about breast cancer underground and away from the women whose lives it most affects. Yet even in the United States, there are clinics waging alternative wars against cancer and the medical establishment, with varying degrees of success.[10]

Breast cancer is on the increase, and every woman should add to her arsenal of information by inquiring into these areas of 'underground medicine.' Who are its leaders and proponents, and what are their qualifications? Most important, what is their rate of success in the control of breast cancer,[11] and why is this information not common knowledge?

The mortality for breast cancer treated by conventional therapies has not decreased in over 40 years.[12] The ACS and its governmental partner, the National Cancer Institute, have been notoriously indifferent, if not hostile, to the idea of general environmental causes of cancer and the need for regulation and prevention.[13] Since the american medical establishment and the ACS are determined to suppress any cancer information not dependent upon western medical bias, whether this information is ultimately useful or not, we must pierce this silence ourselves and aggressively seek answers to these questions about new therapies. We must also heed the unavoidable evidence pointing toward the nutritional and environmental aspects of cancer prevention.

Cancer is not just another degenerative and unavoidable disease of the ageing process. It has distinct and identifiable causes, and these are mainly exposures to chemical or physical agents in the environment.[14] In the medical literature, there is mounting evidence that breast cancer is a chronic and systemic disease. Post-mastectomy women must be vigilantly aware that, contrary to the 'lightning strikes' theory, we are the most likely of all women to develop cancer somewhere else in the body.[15]

Every woman has a militant responsibility to involve herself actively with her own health. We owe ourselves the protection of all the information we can acquire about the treatment of cancer and its causes, as well as about the recent findings concerning immunology, nutrition, environment, and stress. And we owe ourselves this information *before* we may have a reason to use it.

---

[10] Null, Gary. "Alternative Cancer Therapies." *Cancer News Journal,* vol. 14, no. 14, December, 1979. (International Association of Cancer Victims and Friends, Inc. publication). [Author's note]

[11] *Ibid.* p. 18. [Author's note]

[12] Kushner, Rose. *Breast Cancer.* Harcourt, Brace & Jovanovitch. 1975. p. 161.[Author's note]

[13] Epstein, Samuel. p. 462. [Author's note]

[14] *Ibid.* pp. xv–xvi. [Author's note]

[15] Kushner, Rose. p. 163. [Author's note]

It was very important for me, after my mastectomy, to develop and encourage my own internal sense of power. I needed to rally my energies in such a way as to image myself as a fighter resisting rather than as a passive victim suffering. At all times, it felt crucial to me that I make a conscious commitment to survival. It is physically important for me to be loving my life rather than to be mourning my breast. I believe it is this love of my life and my self, and the careful tending of that love which was done by women who love and support me, which has been largely responsible for my strong and healthy recovery from the effects of my mastectomy. But a clear distinction must be made between this affirmation of self and the superficial farce of "looking on the bright side of things."

Like superficial spirituality, looking on the bright side of things is a euphemism used for obscuring certain realities of life, the open consideration of which might prove threatening or dangerous to the status quo. Last week I read a letter from a doctor in a medical magazine which said that no truly happy person ever gets cancer. Despite my knowing better, and despite my having dealt with this blame-the-victim thinking for years, for a moment this letter hit my guilt button. Had I really been guilty of the crime of not being happy in this best of all possible infernos?

The idea that the cancer patient should be made to feel guilty about having had cancer, as if in some way it were all her fault for not having been in the right psychological frame of mind at all times to prevent cancer, is a monstrous distortion of the idea that we can use our psychic strengths to help heal ourselves. This guilt trip which many cancer patients have been led into (you see, it *is* a shameful thing because you could have prevented it if only you had been more . . .) is an extension of the blame-the-victim syndrome. It does nothing to encourage the mobilization to our psychic defenses against the very real forms of death which surround us. It is easier to demand happiness than to clean up the environment. The acceptance of illusion and appearance as reality is another symptom of this same refusal to examine the realities of our lives. Let us seek 'joy' rather than real food and clean air and a saner future on a liveable earth! As if happiness alone can protect us from the results of profit-madness.

Was I wrong to be working so hard against the oppressions afflicting women and Black people? Was I in error to be speaking out against our silent passivity and the cynicism of a mechanized and inhuman civilization that is destroying our earth and those who live upon it? Was I really fighting the spread of radiation, racism, woman-slaughter, chemical invasion of our food, pollution of our environment, the abuse and psychic destruction of our young, merely to avoid dealing with my first and greatest responsibility—to be happy? In this disastrous time, when little girls are still being stitched shut between their legs, when victims of cancer are urged to court more cancer in order to be attractive to men, when 12 year old Black boys are shot down in the street at random by uniformed men who are cleared of any wrong-doing, when ancient and honorable citizens scavenge for food in garbage pails, and the growing answer to all this is media hype or surgical lobotomy; when daily gruesome murders of women from coast to coast no longer warrant mention in *The N. Y. Times,* when grants to teach retarded children are cut in favor of more billion dollar airplanes, when 900 people commit mass suicide rather than face life in america,[16] and we are told it is the job of the poor to stem inflation; what depraved monster could possibly be always happy?

The only really happy people I have ever met are those of us who work against these deaths with all the energy of our living, recognizing the deep and fundamental unhappiness with which we are surrounded, at the same time as we fight to keep from being submerged by it. But if the achievement and maintenance of perfect happiness is the only secret of a physically healthy life in america, then it is a wonder that we are not all dying of a malignant society. The happiest person in this country cannot help breathing in smokers' cigarette fumes, auto exhaust, and airborne chemical dust, nor avoid drinking the water, and eating the food. The idea that happiness can insulate us against the results of our environmental madness is a rumor circulated by our enemies to destroy us. And what Woman of Color in america over the age of 15 does not live with the knowledge that our daily lives are stitched with violence and with hatred, and to naively ignore that reality can mean destruction? We are equally destroyed by false happiness and false breasts, and the passive acceptance of false values which corrupt our lives and distort our experience.

The idea of having a breast removed was much more traumatic for me before my mastectomy than after the fact, but it certainly took time and the loving support of other women before I could once again look at and love my altered body with the warmth I had done before. But I did. In the second week after surgery, on one of those tortuous night rounds of fitful sleep, dreams, and exercises, when I was moving in and out of physical pain and psychic awareness of fear for my life and mourning for my breast, I wrote in my journal:

> In a perspective of urgency, I want to say now that I'd give anything to have done
> it differently—it being the birth of a unique and survival-worthy, or survival-
> effective, perspective. Or I'd give anything not to have cancer and my beautiful

---

[16] In 1978, Jim Jones and nine hundred of his People's Temple followers committed mass suicide in Jonestown, Guyana.

breast gone, fled with my love of it. But then immediately after I guess I have to qualify that—there really are some things I wouldn't give. I wouldn't give my life, first of all, or else I wouldn't have chosen to have the operation in the first place, and I did. I wouldn't give Frances, or the children, or even any one of the women I love. I wouldn't give up my poetry, and I guess when I come right down to it I wouldn't give my eyes, nor my arms. So I guess I do have to be careful that my urgencies reflect my priorities.

Sometimes I feel like I'm the spoils in a battle between good and evil, right now, or that I'm both sides doing the fighting, and I'm not even sure of the outcome nor the terms. But sometimes it comes into my head, like right now, what would you really give? And it feels like, even just musing, I could make a terrible and tragic error of judgement if I don't always keep my head and my priorities clear. It's as if the devil is really trying to buy my soul, and pretending that it doesn't matter if I say yes because everybody knows he's not for real anyway. But I don't know that. And I don't think this is all a dream at all, and no, I would not give up love.

Maybe this is the chance to live and speak those things I really do believe, that power comes from moving into whatever I fear most that cannot be avoided. But will I ever be strong enough again to open my mouth and not have a cry of raw pain leap out?

I think I was fighting the devil of despair within myself for my own soul.

When I started to write this article, I went back to the books I had read in the hospital as I made my decision to have a mastectomy. I came across pictures of women with one breast and mastectomy scars, and I remembered shrinking from these pictures before my surgery. Now they seemed not at all strange or frightening to me. At times, I miss my right breast, the actuality of it, its presence, with a great and poignant sense of loss. But in the same way, and just as infrequently, as I sometimes miss being 32, at the same time knowing that I have gained from the very loss I mourn.

Right after surgery I had a sense that I would never be able to bear missing that great well of sexual pleasure that I connected with my right breast. That sense has completely passed away, as I have come to realize that that well of feeling was within me. I alone own my feelings. I can never lose that feeling because I own it, because it comes out of myself. I can attach it anywhere I want to, because my feelings are a part of me, my sorrow and my joy.

I would never have chosen this path, but I am very glad to be who I am, here.

30 March 1979

STUDY AND DISCUSSION QUESTIONS

1. How do breast prostheses differ from other prostheses, according to Lorde? What is the significance of the difference?

2. Why is there such a push for women who've had mastectomies to wear prostheses? In what ways is this pressure destructive?

3. Lorde subtitles her essay "Power vs. Prosthesis." How are these two things antithetical?

4. What is Lorde's attitude towards women who do choose to wear prostheses? Is she condemning them?

5. "In the process of losing a breast I had become a more whole person." How so?

6. What are Lorde's criticisms of the American Cancer Society?

7. In footnotes, Lorde twice thanks women whose conversation has helped her develop specific ideas, not a common practice among writers. How does doing this relate to the themes of her essay?

8. Lorde describes herself as "a 44 year old Black Lesbian Feminist." How does each component of this description affect her experience with breast cancer?

SUGGESTIONS FOR WRITING

1. Imagine a discussion or argument between Lorde and the nurse who pushes her to wear a prosthesis to the doctor's office. How might such a discussion have gone? Write it out as if it were a scene in a play. If you'd like, bring in the doctor, who perhaps told the nurse what to say.

2. Why does Lorde move out from her own personal story to such diverse issues as poverty, military spending, and environmental pollution? Pick one and spell out its meaning to Lorde and its relation to her experiences.

LALITA MASHI

Chitra Banerjee Divakaruni

Born in India in 1956, Chitra Banerjee Divakaruni lives now in San Francisco and teaches creative writing at Foothill College. Among her books are the poetry volume Leaving Yuba City *(1997), the story collection* Arranged Marriages *(1995), and the novel* The Mistress of Spices *(1997). "Lalita Mashi" originally appeared in* Under Western Eyes: Personal Essays from Asian America *(1995), edited by Garret Hongo.*

The other day I saw Lalita Mashi, my mother's oldest sister. Suddenly, shockingly. But I should have expected it. In recent years she has always come to me this way.

I was standing on the platform of the Oakland BART[1] station, my attaché case filled with slides and spreadsheets, on my way to the City, where a committee of heavy-jowled old men were waiting for me to try to persuade them to change the way they do things. Dressed in my power outfit—navy-blue skirt and jacket, deep red silk blouse, pearls, stiletto heels—I felt confident, ready for them. I knew my presentation would go perfectly.

Then I saw her. She was sitting by the window of a train going in the other direction, her hair caught back loosely in a knot, her chin propped by her palm. It was a posture I knew so well my breath caught in my throat. And suddenly I was six years old again, back in my grandfather's house in a tiny Bengal village.

"Mashi," I called, "Lalita Mashi!" although I knew she couldn't possibly hear me through the double-layered glass. I waved frantically, trying to make her look up. But she was intent on something in the sky that only she could see. The warning beeps sounded, the doors closed, the train began to pull away. I dropped my case and started running along the platform, the gleaming electric tracks separating me from her. People stared. Still I ran, stumbling in my high heels, throwing out an arm for balance. Perhaps that desperate movement finally caught her eye, because she looked up. She was too far for me to read the expression on her face—recognition? bewilderment?—but the face itself I knew without a doubt. It was her face, yes, just

---

[1] Bay Area Rapid Transit: the San Francisco area subway.

the way it had been the last time I saw it. Except, of course, it couldn't be, even if by some unaccountable magic she had remained unchanged by time. Because Lalita Mashi died twenty-four years ago, halfway around the world, in the village of her father, where she had lived (except for one brief year) all her life.

Still, I couldn't shake off the woman's face, the angle of her chin tilted toward a wonder in the sky visible only to her. It haunted me like no face has the right to. And now I was hearing her voice. "*Shona*," it called, "golden child," the special name that Lalita Mashi gave me on those long-ago summers when I used to visit her. The voice caught in a sob—or was it a laugh? It tugged at me as I climbed onto my train. I knew it would stay with me for days, weeks. Forever.

Of the many women in my family that I've known and loved, who have shaped my life and thinking, whose legacies of pain and shame and courage I carry within, why is it I remember Lalita Mashi so clearly? I only knew her for a few years—she died when I was six—and after her death her name was never mentioned in the family. Perhaps it is the mystery that clings to her story, the faint odor of disgrace. Perhaps it is because I, the defiant daughter who left the protection of the family to come to America, who faced their bewilderment and fought their anger, know that she and I are two of a kind.

Mashi was born in the early years of the twentieth century in the village of Mashagram in Bengal, the first child of the Mukherjee household. Hers was a respected family; not only was her father—my grandfather—a Brahmin, but he also owned a good amount of fertile paddy land. His was one of the few homes in the village built of brick instead of black mud.

No one knows the exact year of Mashi's birth. Few people kept track of such things in those days, especially for girl-children. And her parents, who might have recalled it by the calamities of nature that marked most rural lives—the year the Basumati River flooded, the year the too heavy rains ruined the crops—have chosen to forget. So I am free to place her where I want—in the 1930s, when the Independence movement against the British was beginning to sweep the land.

It was the beginning, many would say, of women's independence as well. A lot of women came out of purdah to take part in the battle for their country's freedom. For the first time in their lives, they stood shoulder to shoulder with men (the threat of the British being considered more dangerous than the loss of tradition). They shouted *Jai Hind* and carried the bright new Indian flag, saffron and green and white. They faced the *lathi* charges of the troops and went to jail and died with smiles on their faces. They became national heroines, Sarojini Naidu, Matangini Hazra. Traveling minstrels made up songs about their courage and glory.

But back in Mashagram, my grandfather's village, the winds of change were slow in arriving. Maybe they were held back by the thick bamboo forests that surrounded the village on every side, where even in the daytime one might come across a wild boar or a cheetah. Maybe they spent themselves crossing the miles and miles of fields—mustard and paddy and jute—which farmers tilled and watered patiently, with the help of their buffaloes, as they had for thousands of years. At any rate, they did not ruffle even the edges of my aunt's life.

Lalita Mashi grew up in the big house surrounded by a high wall, like girls of good family were supposed to. I imagine she was taught needlework and cooking by my grandmother. Much like my own mother a few years later, she must have sat in the courtyard (under the thick shade of the pipal tree, so her skin would not turn dark) and stitched quilts decorated with the elaborate tamarind leaf design. On feast days she must have helped Grandmother cook the sweet *kheer* that took hours to prepare, stirring the thickening milk over the slow coal fire patiently, learning at once a skill and a womanly virtue. In addition—and this was unusual—she was taught to read and write by an old Brahmin, for my grandfather was a progressive man. For a while another old Brahmin came by every week to give her singing lessons—religious *bhajans* only, of course, not the modern *gazals* or *rabindra sangeet* that could give a young girl the wrong kinds of ideas. Mashi had a natural skill for song, a sweet clear voice that rose as unapologetically into the air as any bird's—I remember it from vacations I would later spend at my grandfather's. But the old women whispered it was too loud, shameless. And when she turned twelve, all lessons were stopped, for it wasn't fitting that a daughter of the Mukherjee household should be taught by a man, even if he was white-bearded and hobbled around on a cane. There might be talk, and it might affect her chances of making a good marriage.

Did Lalita Mashi cry when the lessons were stopped? Did she shout her anger at her mother (she would not have dared to do so with her father)? When asked to fetch water, did she throw down the earthenware *kalash*, smashing it to smithereens? Did she burn the curries so that the family would have in their mouths the same taste of bitterness that was in hers? But it is more likely that she put away her songbooks and grammar texts sadly but without surprise—for they were, after all, childish things which would not help her in her future life—and busied herself learning more appropriate skills. She knew what the true purpose of her life, the life of all women, was—she had been told it every day since she was old enough to understand.

And that purpose was fulfilled soon enough for Mashi. The flower of marriage, as they call it in our language, bloomed for her as soon as her menstrual blood proclaimed her a woman. My grandfather, a practical man, saw no point in waiting. A daughter was only born to a family as a loan. Unlike a son, she couldn't carry forth the family name. Nor could she, at the yearly memorial services, offer rice and water to the spirits of departed ancestors. One might as well return her to her true home, her husband's house, as soon as possible. Grandfather knew that a woman's fragile beauty tarnishes soon, her good name even sooner. A grown daughter in the house is more dangerous than a firebrand in a field of ripe grain. Besides, he had two other daughters he needed to find husbands for.

This does not mean my grandfather didn't love Lalita Mashi. She was a girl-child, yes, but his oldest, the first baby he had held in his arms, on whose forehead he had pressed the kiss of blessing. Perhaps he had walked up and down with her on nights when his wife was too tired to do so, whispering to quieten her crying. *Hush, my moonbeam, my little bird.* Even to an Indian father that would count for something.

I imagine my grandfather sparing no efforts to find Lalita Mashi a suitable husband, sending matchmakers to all the nearby villages to inquire after young men whose families were of the same standing as his, whose horoscopes matched his daughter's. And when he discovered such a man, he spared no expense for the wedding, inviting people from three villages to admire the style with which a daughter of the Mukherjee house was sent off to her in-laws.

I see Mashi being brought into the marriage courtyard, under the silk canopy where the bridegroom is sitting. Red-veiled, wrapped in a red-gold Banarasi silk (the color of married bliss), she keeps her eyes tightly closed, for it would be bad luck to see her husband's face before the priest had recited the proper mantras. Is she frightened at the thought of leaving her familiar world behind? Does she struggle to hold back tears as she walks around the fire with the stranger who is now her master, to whom society has given every right over her body and her spirit?

The next morning the bride and groom start on their journey home at the exact auspicious moment specified by the family astrologer. Conches sound, women strew their path with flowers and rice and prayers for strong sons, and five bullock carts filled with dowry follow their painted palanquin along the dusty village road.

But the old astrologer must have read the signs wrong. For soon my aunt is back again. Only this time she returns weeping, stripped of her jewelry and dressed in the coarse white cloth that widows wear. The servant who brings her back carries a letter from her in-laws. The letter states that they never want to see her face again, for surely it is her bad luck that caused their son to die of typhoid within a year of his marriage.

Back in the house where she was born, Lalita Mashi must have slipped easily enough into the grooves of her old life. Everything was still the same—the lowing of the cows at dawn as they waited to be milked, the blind *baul* who came by each morning to sing the 108 names of Krishna, the women gathered in the hot afternoons of the mango season on the downstairs veranda, salting the hard green fruit for pickles. Yet everything was different.

Mashi would have known—though her parents were too kind, I hope, to ever let anyone say it—that she was in her father's house on sufferance. From the moment her parents give her away at the wedding with a handful of puffed rice, a married woman's place is with her in-laws. This house with the familiar high ocher wall she had looked back at, weeping, from the bridal palanquin, the green shutters through the cracks of which the women could look out and not be seen, the cool marble-floored dining room where the men were served dinner (the women ate in the kitchen, afterward)—she had dreamed about it many times while in her husband's house. Longed for it when her mother-in-law scolded her for a task not done correctly, an imagined slight. But it belonged to her brothers, and their sons, and theirs. She had no real place in it, and every so often—in case she was in any danger of forgetting—her brothers' wives would remind her of it with the twist of a lip, a silent, meaningful look.

So Mashi made herself useful. She milked the cows and scoured the heavy brass and copper *puja* dishes with coal ash and did all of the vegetarian cooking (a widow was not supposed to touch meat). She picked the red hibiscus flowers that grew against the wall and made garlands every morning for the family deity, the goddess Kali. On auspicious days, Durga Puja or a wedding or a naming ceremony, she stayed out of sight so that her ill luck wouldn't taint the others.

She took care of the babies that were being born to her brothers' wives, dressing them in the tiny clothes she had hand-stitched, feeding them, bathing them, singing to them through the hot afternoons when their mothers slept. After the men had eaten, she served dinner to the women, and sat down to her cold, solitary meal only after they had finished. When I visited during vacations, it would be very late—the moon disappeared behind the bamboo trees by the pond—before she finished cleaning the kitchen and came up to bed.

She certainly didn't have to work so hard. No one ever asked her to, and there were servants. Perhaps she kept herself busy to stay sane, to not dwell on the fact that since the age of fifteen her life had effectively been over.

Was she unhappy? Most will say she had no cause to be. She was better off than many other widows who, not coming from such affluent families, are shunned as burdens by both in-laws and parents, who have to throw themselves on village charity and live by doing odd jobs—roasting puffed rice for festivals, making painted fans out of palm leaves—who in desperation run away to the cities and blacken, forever, the family name.

My actual memories of Lalita Mashi are few, and so many of my own feelings have been superimposed on them—hurt and hate and hope—that I am no longer sure that this is how it was. But here is one:

It is a June night in Mashagram, pitch dark and very hot. A girl of five, I have been sent to Grandfather's because a cholera epidemic is raging in Calcutta. Sweaty and fretful, I toss and turn under the coarse mosquito netting, push restlessly at the sleeping body next to mine.

"I'm thirsty, Lalita Mashi. I feel itchy all over."

"Hush, *shona*, don't cry. Mashi will get you water."

Through the haze of the netting, my eyes follow my aunt across the room, which is lit only by the sliver of moon hanging low outside the barred window. A glimmer of white in her cotton sari, Mashi bends over the earthen *kalash* in the corner of the room. (As far back as I can remember, she has always worn white, and always the same thick, cheap handloom that no one else in the house would touch. Even my grandmother, who seems very old to me with her crushed velvet skin, wears beautiful *tangails* with brilliant maroon and gold borders and *dhakais* so fine they can be pulled through her gold ring.) Mashi's long hair, which she pulls back into a tight bun during the day, as widows should, swings softly about her face. Before I fall asleep, I like to weave my fingers through its silky darkness, to press my face against it as I would never dare to with my own stricter mother. It smells faintly of hibiscus flowers, because although widows are not supposed to, sometimes Aunt puts the fragrant red oil in her hair. She does it at night after the others have gone to bed, after she has bolted the door of her room. But I know because I sleep with her whenever I come to Grandfather's house. She lets me rub in the sweet oil, shows me how to curve the fingertips to massage the scalp. *You have such gentle fingers, shona.* Sometimes she sings very softly, eyes closed, while I am rubbing. *O Krishna, I've given up all for your love. Don't forsake me now.* It is a traditional religious song, such as the traveling *bauls* sing, but Mashi transforms it with her longing. Mashi has the sweetest voice, I think, even nicer than Mother's. The note of sadness in it makes me shiver a little. If I had the words, I would say that it haunts me. I take great care not to pull on Mashi's hair, not to snarl its smoothness in any way. I would die before I give away Mashi's secret.

But Mashi is the one who dies, in between vacations, so I am not there when it happens. Mother looks up from a letter and her eyes are red-rimmed. A sob bursts out of her. It is the first time I remember seeing my mother cry. Lalita Mashi has drowned, she tells me, in the *dighi*, the women's lake.

I cannot believe it. I picture the *dighi*, its dark waters stretching all the way to the horizon. So many times when we've been there to bathe, I've seen Mashi swim toward the middle, where people say it is deeper than a ten-story building, her powerful strokes parting the masses of mauve water hyacinths. She would swim until her body became a tiny bobbing speck, until I, waiting on the worn stone steps with the hand-spun *gamchahs* with which we dried ourselves, was afraid that surely this time she wouldn't be able to get back. But she always did, smiling and not even out of breath, her slim, gleaming body cutting effortlessly through the rippling water.

"It can't be," I tell Mother. I want to do something terrible to express the baffled rage I feel—throw myself at her, snatch the letter from her hand, take the edge of her sari between my teeth and pull until it rips. But of course I don't.

She wipes at her swollen eyes and tells me she doesn't want to talk about it. She tells me to go to my room.

No one at Grandfather's will talk about it either when I visit them next summer. They change the subject adroitly whenever I ask. "Have some of this nice *nimbu* pickle," they say. Or "Go see Mangli-cow's new calf, so cute you won't believe it." In the steamy afternoons when the women gather in the downstairs hall to sew and talk, Mashi's name is never spoken. Her photographs have all been removed from albums. Her clothes have disappeared. Her room is filled with dusty old trunks that look like they've always been there. It is as though Mashi had never lived.

It is the ultimate punishment.

Death in our Indian culture is not necessarily a tragedy. Too much of it happens every day for us to think of it as such, if we are to keep ourselves from going crazy. We devise heavens for our dead—the seven *lokas* where they go to enjoy the fruits of their karma, until they are born again. And on earth we cherish them by keeping them in our thoughts. Even daughters have photographs hung in the corner of their parents' bedroom. On the anniversary of their deaths, jasmine garlands are placed around them, incense lighted. Food is offered to beggars and cows, and Brahmins are paid to pray for their souls.

But what when you are forgotten, deliberately, your name plucked out from the hearts of those you loved best and sent wandering over the void? I am not a believer in spirits, but sometimes I dream of my aunt, a tiny white wraith, palms outstretched, mouth open in supplication. She winds about the house, about her mother's bed, for surely a mother wouldn't want her daughter—no matter what she had done—to be doomed forever to the terrible mists that are worse than darkness, where after a while even her own face is taken from her.

My grandmother too must have dreamed of her daughter. Startled awake in her high mahogany bed, under the thin mosquito netting, she must have lain in half-shadow, listening to Grandfather's heavy breath, and felt that wrench in her belly, that ripping of the umbilical cord that mothers know whenever their children are in despair. Perhaps she thought of going down to the *dighi* secretly, with a little boat made out of plantain leaves and filled with my aunt's favorite foods. Perhaps she could send money to a Brahmin in faraway Kashi, by the holy Ganges that cleanses all sins, to pray for Mashi? A small photo, hidden in her dresser drawer under the velvet boxes filled with jewels she would give to her daughters-in-law to give to theirs—who would know of it? But she did none of these things. For the sake of her other children, for the good name of the family she had taken as hers when she walked around the wedding fire—so long ago she hardly remembered she'd had another life before it—she kept hidden whatever was inside her. At *pujas* and harvest festivals she wore her red-bordered silks as always and smiled as she served scented betel leaves to the women who visited. Who can blame her? The choices a mother has to make are often hard, heartbreaking.

But they couldn't stop the mouth of rumor. Even I heard things when I visited—snatches of servant gossip, neighbor ladies whispering. Something about a man. A drowning that wasn't quite an accident. A too quick funeral. Family dishonor.

Here is another wisp of memory: I am playing out in the courtyard with the children of the neighborhood. Something happens and a girl yells that I'm a slut, just like my aunt was. I wrestle the girl, whose name I have long forgotten, to the dirt, claw at her face till the blood comes. Later, when Mother, shamed and angry, brings the switch down on the backs of my legs, demanding *why, why did you do it?* I stand tearless, silent with an animal stubbornness, unable to explain.

It would take me years to discover the circumstances of Lalita Mashi's death—to even begin to discover them—though perhaps "uncover" would be a more accurate word. I was handicapped by the double disadvantage of my youth and my femaleness. The questions I did dare to bring up, suitably polite, oblique enough not to offend anyone's sensibility, could always be brushed aside by adults. The foolish fancies of teenage girls, everyone knows, need not be taken seriously. Perhaps I could have pressed harder, but I think a part of me was afraid of what I might find.

It was only when I was done with college and the family was looking to arrange a suitable match for me—against my wishes, for I wanted to go abroad to continue my studies—that I got up the courage to confront my mother. Perhaps it was out of a desperation I didn't know how to put into words, a desperation that I was being pushed toward disaster, just as Lalita Mashi had been.

It is late at night, but the June air is still moist and heavy with heat. It presses down upon my sweating skin like a premonition as I watch Mother go through the bedtime rituals she must have learned as a girl. At the marble basin she sprinkles warm water on her face, then rubs in the lentil-and-turmeric-paste that is supposed to lighten the skin. When it dries into a yellow crust, she washes it off, first with hot, then cold water. She pats on a glycerine-and-rosewater solution from a bottle that I recognize because I have seen a similar one for years on Grandmother's dressing table. She takes the ivory comb carved with her initials and runs it through hair that is fragrant with *amla* and that is, even at her age, softer and thicker than mine. Unhurried and deliberate, her movements belong to a different generation, a simpler, more elegant age when women had the time to indulge in beauty. But I am wrong to call it an indulgence. The color of a woman's skin, the length of her silk-black uncut hair, the way her eyes glowed when underlined with *kajal*—these could make all the difference between a good match and a second-rate one. They could hold fast a husband whose roving eye might otherwise turn toward a second marriage, a younger wife. Is the age I live in that different?

As I observe the long, languorous strokes of Mother's comb it strikes me that Mashi must have performed the same rituals until widowhood deprived her of the right—and, according to all who kept watch on her, the reason. She was not even allowed to keep a mirror in her room. For what? people would have asked in genuine bewilderment had anyone suggested it. For birthdays she was given vellum-bound copies of the *Ramayana* and the *Puranas,* which assert that the body is a thing of vanity, a poor garment to be cast off at death. What accompanies us into the beyond are our virtuous deeds, our ability to sacrifice. If Mashi had any doubts as to how to achieve this, she had only to look at the examples of the many good women—Sita, Savitri, Gandhari—provided by the good books. I remember again how Mashi had to hide behind her locked bedroom door even to apply a little hibiscus oil to her hair, and suddenly I am so angry that the question I had rehearsed so carefully tumbles out of me, stopping my mother in mid-motion.

What really happened to Mashi?

My mother looks at me, then away. I wait for her to make the usual excuses. I am ready to fight them today—something in the air, the smell of a far rain falling on the great brown Ganges, the smell of my coming departure, gives me strength. Perhaps my mother senses it too, for she says with a sigh, "It's a long story." And as we sit on her high mahogany bed, where as a child I had spent many nights of illness, with her cool hand on my brow, soothing away my fevered nightmares, she tells me.

Mashi's story is ordinary enough—the story, I think, of many young widows of the time. She had the misfortune to fall in love. It was a misfortune because though in far-off Calcutta changes had begun to take place, in the villages a widow of good family would never be allowed to remarry—if marriage was at all what the man Mashi loved had in his mind.

Who it was my mother never knew. Lalita Mashi had whispered a few words to her on Mother's last visit, feverish and hasty, not making total sense. But it was Durga Puja, the busiest time of the year. New clothes had to be stitched for the children and dyed in auspicious colors, sweet coconut-and-jaggery balls to be ground and cooked, the floors decorated with traditional good-luck designs painted with rice paste. My mother's place was with the other married women, stirring enormous pots of *khichuri*, the thick lentil-rice soup with which all visitors would be fed, frying *brinjals* and yellow squash and fresh-picked sweet potatoes. She wouldn't have had much of an opportunity to be alone with her widow-sister—who was expected to keep to her room—to ask her questions, or even to warn.

"But who do you think it might have been?" I ask.

She shrugs. The identity of the man is not important. All that matters is the enormity of Mashi's crime, her betrayal of the family.

Nevertheless I imagine him—I need to—this man who charmed my aunt as bird catchers charm the red-throated bulbuls from their safe nests. He must have come from the city—Burdwan, Jamshedpur, maybe even Calcutta—wearing a white tailored kurta over his starched dhoti, the dark sleeveless Nehru jacket that the freedom fighters favored. Perhaps he sported a pencil-thin mustache like I've seen in the oil paintings of my uncles that hang along the dark corridors of grandfather's house.

The man stood outside the high ocher walls, singing one of the patriotic songs so popular at the time—*break the shackles, light the fire, the time for sleep is over*—exhorting listeners to join the revolution. Lalita Mashi would have peeped through the green shutters of her bedroom, felt that fervent young voice rising up at her like flame, stirring emotions she thought she was long done with. She fought them, for she knew that was the way to heartbreak—or worse. But when her brothers invited the man in to drink a glass of tea and tell them news of the big city, she couldn't resist joining the other women of the house behind the curtain to listen. At dinnertime—for he stayed on, this man with his magnet voice that held even the men in thrall—she served him the biggest, best pieces of dessert, the sweet, cloud-light *rasogollahs* she had spent all afternoon making. And when he looked up to thank her, she did not glance down as was proper, but held his eyes with the bright black flash in her own.

But I could be mistaken. He could well have been one of the village men, someone Mashi had known for years, a friend of her brothers who came by evenings to play a game of chess or read the Calcutta newspaper my grandfather subscribed to. Someone who had helped to carry the *piri*, the ornamental wooden plank on which the bride sat, at her wedding. Someone she had called "older brother" as village custom demanded. Someone who had watched with pity as, her bowed, white-veiled head glimmering in the failing light, she now silently served them thin, salty *namkeens* and tall stainless-steel glasses of cardamon tea. Watched and pondered until one day the pity had turned to something else, and he had waited in the shadows of the plantain trees beside the pond to speak to her when she came to fetch water.

Finding a place to meet would not have been difficult, but arranging a time when she would not be missed by the household would take a lot of care. Perhaps they met when she went to the women's lake for her bath, very early in the morning before the sun had dried the dew from the tiny blue moss flowers. She would look around to make sure no one was in sight, then turn into a dark bamboo grove—a different one each time for safety's sake—and there he would be, waiting, his kurta shining through the gloom of the trees as bright as the armor of any knight. They would come together urgently, lips seeking lips, fingers pulling at clothing, hot breath on naked skin that shivered with the cold and the excitement and the guilt, the knowledge that time was surely running out. For her sake I hope there was more. I hope they talked, sitting side by side, her head resting on his shoulder, his arm around her waist. He described to her life in the city—horse-drawn *tangas* driven by turbanned men from the north; the red-faced British guards standing at attention in their starched white uniforms outside the Governor's House; restaurants where you could walk in and order whatever you wanted to eat; the freedom of living on a street where no one knew your name. Promised to take her with him when he went—soon, soon now. She sang for him in a windy whisper that caught in her throat, *O Krishna, I've given up all for your love. Don't forsake me now.*

Lalita Mashi must have known how it would end. All the ancient tales of doomed lovers she—and I—had grown up on would have left no doubts in her mind. Why then did she rush toward destruction, like the rain flies that flung themselves into our kerosene lamps on monsoon nights? Why did she choose to bring shame on the family I know she loved? Why did she risk their hatred, their stern forgetting—not just in this life but even after, into the eternities? I cannot believe it was for the sex, or even for romantic passion. It was, I think, something more complex and deliberate, rising from a deeper, more urgent need. But for proof I can offer, once again, only a brief and tenuous memory:

Those nights in Grandfather's house, before we went to bed, Lalita Mashi would extinguish the oil lamp by pinching the flaming wick with her fingers.

"But doesn't it hurt?" I had asked her once, distressed.

Mashi had smiled. Only now, years later, I can gauge the sadness of that smile.

"Sometimes the pain is the only way I know I'm alive, *shona*."

*   *   *

All that month while the family was trying to arrange a match for Susheela, her youngest sister, Lalita Mashi was restless and distracted. She would burst into tears for no reason at all. She burnt the simplest curries, scolded the children for the littlest pranks. Even her mother, busy as she was putting together jewelry and saris for the dowry, noticed the change in her and dosed her with the juice of *tulsi* leaves in case she was coming down with *kalajor*, the black fever. *Jealousy*, whispered the sisters-in-law behind their veils. *Pure jealousy of Susheela.*

Was Mashi counting the days with terror until it was well past her time of month, until the nausea and tiredness and aching breasts left no doubts in her mind of her body's betrayal? Was she trying to decide whether to wrench herself away from all that was loved and familiar for an uncertain future from which there was no turning back? Or was the man—tired with waiting or afraid of reprisal—gone already, so that she was contemplating the final choice he had left to her?

Sitting face to face with my mother as she braids her hair into tight obedience, I remember another day. It is late summer, almost the end of my vacation. Barefoot from play, I run into the dim living room decorated with old-fashioned oil lamps and clouded mirrors in mahogany frames. Heavy shades of *khush-khush* grass, dampened against the heat, cover the windows. Yes, here's Grandfather, just as I hoped, reclining in his favorite easy chair, immaculate in his ivory kurta, his hookah in his hand. Maybe I can climb onto his lap and get him to finish the story of the evil magician and the princess of the gold mountain.

Then I notice the young woman standing in front of him, twisting the edge of her widow's sari.

"Please, Father," she pleads, looking down at her hands.

"No," says the old man, his voice dispassionate. "I've made my decision already."

He closes his eyes and draws on the hookah as though the woman in front of him did not exist. Lalita Mashi makes a small, choking sound and runs from the room, holding her hands to her face. The rush of her white sari stirs the air of the room so that I can smell for a moment the faint, damp fragrance of the *khush-khush* curtains.

What could she have wanted so much? What could have been so forbidden that her father, usually so loving, would deny her this ruthlessly?

"Mashi," I cry, but there is no reply, only the British clock painted with happy shepherds and shepherdesses that ticks and ticks on the wall behind Grandfather's head.

It is the last memory I have of Mashi.

It is the memory that will finally give me the courage to leave Calcutta, to tear through the protective, suffocating cocoon of family in which we had both always lived, and strike out for the unknown.

Three weeks after Mashi disappeared, my mother told me, they found the body in the *dighi*. It had floated up among the *shapla* flowers on the far end, naked and bloated. No one was sure how long it had been in the water.

"There was a lot of bad talk," Mother said, "and the marriage the family had arranged for Susheela fell through." There is no anger in her voice, or blame. Only a mild sorrow.

Even now, years later, I dream of Lalita Mashi on that last night. The air is still, as before a storm, and only the cry of a lone jackal, eerily like a woman's, wavers along it. Before she steps over the threshold of the house to which there is no coming back, Mashi stops for a moment outside the new baby's room, listens for a cry. Hesitates, pressing a hand to the growing curve of her belly. Then she is running, her shadow long and trembly behind her, yearning backward to those ocher walls. At the edge of the lake she stops to pick up the stones, choosing the smoothest, roundest ones. The water gleams faintly in the light of the waning moon. When she steps in, it is not cold like she had feared but warm, warm, a lover's kiss. She pushes off without sound, as gracefully as though she were a white-plumed waterbird.

But what when her arms and legs grow too tired to carry her further, when the stones tied to her sari begin to weigh her down? And the water itself becomes a black hand squeezing her lungs, pulling her under. Does she struggle then, does she cry out her lover's name? Does she try to untie the stones and swim back to shore because the worst life is better than this breathless, choking end?

I am not sure. The dream always grows murky at this point, a swirl of rain and wind and dank, black lake mud, the smell of which will persist in my nostrils long after I wake. But her face—I sometimes see it in the last moments of the dream, framed by a bare arm flailing in wet moonlight, its mouth opening in a furious, futile cry. Sometimes it is my face.

One time when I wake, weeping, I call my mother in Calcutta.

"You killed Mashi, all of you," I cry, liberated from the usual filial courtesies by darkness and fear and pain. "You left her no other course of action."

A moment of silence at the other end. Then my mother's voice, calm as always. "She knew the rules, Lalita, the dangers." The edge of warning in her voice is meant for me too—the wayward niece of a wayward aunt. "She made the first choice. After that there was nothing anyone else could do."

Much as I wish to, I cannot deny her words, the truth in them. What is truth except that which we have made so by believing in it, generation after generation? And so a new dream is added to my old one. In it the wheel of karma[2] rises, enormous, inexorable, the color of thunder. With a grating roar it rolls forward, gaining on the tiny figure of my aunt, who has set it in motion. She makes no effort to run, to escape it. She believes in it too.

But a few weeks later a brief note reaches me. It is in my mother's hand, unsigned—perhaps her attempt at consolation, for a mother must take part in the heartaches of her daughter, even a wayward one.

"There were no identifying marks on the body," says the note. "The face was completely eaten by fish. It could have been any young woman."

I've seen Lalita Mashi many times since then, in the airport as I rush toward my gate, in a crowded vegetable market, at the other end of a dimly lit restaurant filled with elegant diners. I no longer try to go to her. I know from experience that when I get close enough, she will turn into someone else and give me a polite, inquiring glance.

But it doesn't matter. Because I have another picture now inside my head to counter the dream of drowning, the dream of the crushing wheel. In it a young woman is leaving her father's home at night. She stops for a moment outside the new baby's room, listens for a cry. Presses her hand to the growing curve of her belly. Then she steps resolutely over the threshold and begins to walk. She is going to the station at the edge of the bamboo forest where a night train will stop in an hour's time. She will meet her lover there, and together they will travel to their new life.

Or perhaps the woman is alone. There is no man. He left a long time ago, as all men ultimately do. But the woman doesn't care. She knows now that she has always been alone. It is the nature of her condition, of being female, though throughout her life she has tried to hide it—in wish-dreams, in gossip, in frenzied activity—like her mother, and her mother, and her mother before her. The realization makes her feel translucent, weightless, as though she could lift off the ground at any moment.

The woman's arms swing freely by her side, for she is carrying no baggage. She knows that nothing from her old life will fit into her new one, the one she—and I—cannot quite imagine yet. Not the taboos, not the memories. She will have to create all anew, out of herself, as the mother goddess,

---

[2] The Hindu conception of destiny, which is often portrayed as a wheel that rolls inexorably once set in motion.

Prakriti, does after the end of the world. The bamboo trees rustle like footsteps in the rising wind. She doesn't look back. She walks lightly, this woman, having shed her fears along with her hopes, and, as she makes her way across the moonlit land, I hear her sing.

STUDY AND DISCUSSION QUESTIONS

1. "A daughter was only born to a family as a loan." What does this statement mean? What view of women does it embody?

2. What is life like for widows in Lalita Mashi's village? Why?

3. At one point, Divakaruni imagines that Lalita Mashi served dinner at her family's house to the man who was to become her lover and that she "did not glance down as was proper." Why would she be expected not to look him in the eye?

4. Why does the identity of Lalita Mashi's lover matter to Divakaruni but not to her mother?

5. "Lalita Mashi must have known how it would end. . . . Why then did she rush toward destruction . . . ?" What's the answer?

6. Near the end of the essay, Divakaruni remembers overhearing her grandfather denying Lalita Mashi a request. What do you think the request might have been?

7. We learn in the second paragraph that it is on her way to a meeting that the author thinks she sees Lalita Mashi. How does this relate to Mashi's story?

8. Not until more than half way through the essay do we begin to get a more-or-less straightforward account of Lalita Mashi's story. Why doesn't the author just tell it this way from the start?

SUGGESTIONS FOR WRITING

1. "You killed Mashi, all of you," Divakaruni yells at her mother. Is this accusation true?

2. Is Lalita Mashi's story just a story about long ago and far away?

THE MEN WE
CARRY IN OUR MINDS

Scott Russell Sanders

Scott Russell Sanders was born in 1945 in Memphis, Tennessee, studied at Brown University and Cambridge, and now teaches at Indiana University. He has written fiction, including science fiction, as well as literary criticism and personal essays. Among his books are The Paradise of Bombs *(1987), from which the following is taken,* Staying Put: Making a Home in a Restless World *(1993), and* Writing from the Center *(1995).*

"This must be a hard time for women," I say to my friend Anneke. "They have so many paths to choose from, and so many voices calling them."

"I think it's a lot harder for men," she replies.

"How do you figure that?"

"The women I know feel excited, innocent, like crusaders in a just cause. The men I know are eaten up with guilt."

"Women feel such pressure to be everything, do everything," I say. "Career, kids, art, politics. Have their babies and get back to the office a week later. It's as if they're trying to overcome a million years' worth of evolution in one lifetime."

"But we help one another. And we have this deep-down sense that we're in the *right*—we've been held back, passed over, used—while men feel they're in the wrong. Men are the ones who've been discredited, who have to search their souls."

I search my soul. I discover guilty feelings aplenty—toward the poor, the Vietnamese, Native Americans, the whales, an endless list of debts. But toward women I feel something more confused, a snarl of shame, envy, wary tenderness, and amazement. This muddle troubles me. To hide my unease I say, "You're right, it's tough being a man these days."

"Don't laugh," Anneke frowns at me. "I wouldn't be a man for anything. It's much easier being the victim. All the victim has to do is break free. The persecutor has to live with his past."

How deep is that past? I find myself wondering. How much of an inheritance do I have to throw off?

When I was a boy growing up on the back roads of Tennessee and Ohio, the men I knew labored with their bodies. They were marginal farmers, just scraping by, or welders, steelworkers, carpenters; they swept floors, dug ditches, mined coal, or drove trucks, their forearms ropy with muscle; they trained horses, stoked furnaces, made tires, stood on assembly lines wrestling parts onto cars and refrigerators. They got up before light, worked all day long whatever the weather, and when they came home at night they looked as though somebody had been whipping them. In the evenings and on weekends they worked on their own places, tilling gardens that were lumpy with clay, fixing broken-down cars, hammering on houses that were always too drafty, too leaky, too small.

The bodies of the men I knew were twisted and maimed in ways visible and invisible. The nails of their hands were black and split, the hands tattooed with scars. Some had lost fingers. Heavy lifting had given many of them finicky backs and guts weak from hernias. Racing against conveyor belts had given them ulcers. Their ankles and knees ached from years of standing on concrete. Anyone who had worked for long around machines was hard of hearing. They squinted, and the skin of their faces was creased like the leather of old work gloves. There were times, studying them, when I dreaded growing up. Most of them coughed, from dust or cigarettes, and most of them drank cheap wine or whiskey, so their eyes looked bloodshot and bruised. The fathers of my friends always seemed older than the mothers. Men wore out sooner. Only women lived into old age.

As a boy I also knew another sort of men, who did not sweat and break down like mules. They were soldiers, and so far as I could tell they scarcely worked at all. But when the shooting started, many of them would die. That was what soldiers were *for*, just as a hammer was for driving nails.

Warriors and toilers: those seemed, in my boyhood vision, to be the chief destinies for men. They weren't the only destinies, as I learned from having a few male teachers, from reading books, and from watching television. But the men on television—the politicians, the astronauts, the generals, the savvy lawyers, the philosophical doctors, the bosses who gave orders to both soldiers and laborers—seemed as remote and unreal to me as the figures in Renaissance tapestries. I could no more imagine growing up to become one of these cool, potent creatures than I could imagine becoming a prince.

A nearer and more hopeful example was that of my father, who had escaped from a red-dirt farm to a tire factory, and from the assembly line to the front office. Eventually he dressed in a white shirt and tie. He carried himself as if he had been born to work with his mind. But his body, remembering the earlier years of slogging work, began to give out on him in his fifties, and it quit on him entirely before he turned 65.

A scholarship enabled me not only to attend college, a rare enough feat in my circle, but even to study in a university meant for the children of the rich. Here I met for the first time young men who had assumed from birth that they would lead lives of comfort and power. And for the first time I met women who told me that men were guilty of having kept all the joys and privileges of the earth for themselves. I was baffled. What privileges? What joys? I thought about the maimed, dismal lives of most of the men back home. What had they stolen from their wives and daughters? The right to go five days a week, 12 months a year, for 30 or 40 years to a steel mill or a coal mine? The right to drop bombs and die in war? The right to feel every leak in the roof, every gap in the fence, every cough in the engine as a wound they must mend? The right to feel, when the layoff comes or the plant shuts down, not only afraid but ashamed?

I was slow to understand the deep grievances of women. This was because, as a boy, I had envied them. Before college, the only people I had ever known who were interested in art or music or literature, the only ones who read books, the only ones who ever seemed to enjoy a sense of ease and grace were the mothers and daughters. Like the menfolk, they fretted about money, they scrimped and made do. But, when the pay stopped coming in, they were not the ones who had failed. Nor did they have to go to war, and that seemed to me a blessed fact. By comparison with the narrow, ironclad days of fathers, there was an expansiveness, I thought, in the days of mothers. They went to see neighbors, to shop in town, to run errands at school, at the library, at church. No doubt, had I looked harder at their lives, I would have envied them less. It was not my fate to become a woman, so it was easier for me to see the graces. I didn't see, then, what a prison a house could be, since houses seemed to be brighter, handsomer places than any factory. I did not realize—because such things were never spoken of—how often women suffered from men's bullying. Even then I could see how exhausting it was for a mother to cater all day to the needs of young children. But if I had been asked, as a boy, to choose between tending a baby and tending a machine, I think I would have chosen the baby. (Having now tended both, I know I would choose the baby.)

So I was baffled when the women at college accused me and my sex of having cornered the world's pleasures. I think something like my bafflement has been felt by other boys (and by girls as well) who grew up in dirt-poor farm country, in mining country, in black ghettos, in Hispanic barrios, in the shadows of factories, in Third World nations—any place where the fate of men is just as grim and bleak as the fate of women.

When the women I met at college thought about the joys and privileges of men, they did not carry in their minds the sort of men I had known in my childhood. They thought of their fathers, who were bankers, physicians, architects, stockbrokers, the big wheels of the big cities. They were never laid off, never short of cash at month's end, never lined up for welfare. These fathers made decisions that mattered. They ran the world.

The daughters of such men wanted to share in this power, this glory. So did I. They yearned for a say over their future, for jobs worthy of their abilities, for the right to live at peace, unmolested, whole. Yes, I thought, yes yes. The difference between me and these daughters was that they saw me, because of my sex, as destined from birth to become like their fathers, and therefore as an enemy to their desires. But I knew better. I wasn't an enemy, in fact or in feeling. I was an ally. If I had known, then, how to tell them so, would they have believed me? Would they now?

STUDY AND DISCUSSION QUESTIONS

1. As a boy, Sanders "envied" women. Why?

2. Why did the men Sanders saw as he grew up feel "not only afraid but ashamed" when they were laid off?

3. Is Sanders saying that feminism has nothing to offer poor women?

4. Why does Sanders begin his essay with a description of his discussion with Anneke? How does this discussion relate to the story he tells of his life?

5. In his last paragraph, Sanders writes: "I wasn't an enemy, in fact or in feeling. I was an ally." How so?

SUGGESTIONS FOR WRITING

1. Sanders paints a stark contrast between the world of the "dirt poor" men he saw when a child and that of the well-to-do fathers of the women he knew at college. In terms of gender roles, are there any commonalities between these two worlds?

2. In what ways has your social class affected your views on gender roles? Write a brief autobiographical sketch that offers an explanation of where your present views come from.

WHY SPORTS IS A DRAG

Dave Barry

Dave Barry (b. 1947) attended Haverford College and worked as a journalist for a local newspaper, where he began writing a humor column. He moved on to the Miami Herald and in 1988 won a Pulitzer Prize for his commentary. Among his numerous books are: Babies and Other Hazards of Sex: How to Make a Tiny Person in Only Nine Months, with Tools You Probably Have Around the Home *(1984),* Stay Fit and Healthy Until You're Dead *(1985), and* Dave Barry's Complete Guide to Guys: A Fairly Short Book *(1995).*

Mankind's yearning to engage in sports is older than recorded history, dating back to the time, millions of years ago, when the first primitive man picked up a crude club and a round rock, tossed the rock into the air, and whomped the club into the sloping forehead of the first primitive umpire. What inner force drove this first athlete? Your guess is as good as mine. Better, probably, because you haven't had four beers. All I know is, whatever the reason, Mankind is still nuts about sports. As Howard Cosell,[1] who may not be the most likable person in the world but is certainly one of the most obnoxious, put it: "In terms of Mankind and sports, blah blah blah blah the 1954 Brooklyn Dodgers."

Notice that Howard and I both use the term "Mankind." Womankind really isn't into sports in the same way. I realize things have changed since my high-school days, when sports were considered unfeminine and your average girls' gym class consisted of six girls in those gym outfits colored Digestive Enzyme Green running around waving field-hockey sticks and squealing, and 127 girls on the sidelines in civilian clothing, claiming it was That Time of the Month. I realize that today you have a number of top female athletes such as Martina Navratilova who can run like deer and bench-press Chevrolet pickup trucks. But to be brutally frank, women as a group have a long way to go before they reach the level of intensity and dedication to sports that enables men to be such incredible jerks about it.

If you don't believe me, go to your local racquetball club and observe the difference between the way men and women play. Where I play, the

---

[1] Radio and television sportscaster.

women tend to gather on the court in groups of random sizes—sometimes three, sometimes five, as if it were a Jane Fonda workout—and the way they play is, one of them will hit the ball at the wall and the rest of them will admire the shot and compliment her quite sincerely, and then they all sort of relax, as if they're thinking, well, thank goodness *that's* over with, and they always seem very surprised when the ball comes *back*. If one of them has the presence of mind to take another swing, and if she actually hits the ball, everybody is *very* complimentary. If she misses it, the others all tell her what a *good* try she made, really, then they all laugh and act very relieved because they know they have some time to talk before the ball comes bouncing off that darned *wall* again.

Meanwhile, over in the next court, you will have two males wearing various knee braces and wrist bands and special leatheroid racquetball gloves, hurling themselves into the walls like musk oxen on Dexedrine, and after every single point one or both them will yell "S—!" in the self-reproving tone of voice you might use if you had just accidentally shot your grandmother. American men tend to take their sports seriously, much more seriously than they take family matters or Asia.

This is why it's usually a mistake for men and women to play on teams together. I sometimes play in a coed slow-pitch softball league, where the rules say you have to have two women on the field. The teams always have one of the women play catcher, because in slow-pitch softball the batters hit just about every pitch, so it wouldn't really hurt you much if you had a deceased person at catcher. Our team usually puts the other woman at second base, where the maximum possible number of males can get there on short notice to help out in case of emergency. As far as I can tell, our second basewoman is a pretty good baseball player, better than I am anyway, but there's no way to know for sure because if the ball gets anywhere near her, a male comes barging over from, say, right field, to deal with it. She's been on the team for three seasons now, but the males still don't trust her. They know that if she had to choose between catching a fly ball and saving an infant's life, deep in her soul, she would probably elect to save the infant's life, without even considering whether there were men on base.

This difference in attitude between men and women carries over to the area of talking about sports, especially sporting events that took place long ago. Take the 1960 World Series. If we were to look at it objectively, we would have to agree that the outcome of the 1960 World Series no longer matters. You could make a fairly strong case that it didn't really matter in 1960. Women know this, which is why you almost never hear them mention the 1960 World Series, whereas you take virtually any male over age 35 and even if he can't remember which of his children has diabetes, he can remember exactly how Pirates shortstop Bill Mazeroski hit the ninth-inning home run that beat the Yankees, and he will take every available opportunity to discuss it at length with other males.

See that? Out there in Readerland, you females just read right through that last sentence, nodding in agreement, but you males leaped from your chairs and shouted: "Mazeroski wasn't a SHORTSTOP! Mazeroski played SECOND BASE!" Every male in America has millions of perfectly good brain cells devoted to information like this. We can't help it. We have no perspective. I have a friend named Buzz, a successful businessman and the most rational person you ever want to meet, and the high point of his entire life is the time he got Stan Albeck, the coach of the New Jersey Nets, to look directly at him during a professional basketball game and make a very personal remark rhyming with "duck shoe." I should explain that Buzz and I have season tickets to the Philadelphia 76ers, so naturally we hate the Nets a great deal. It was a great honor when Albeck singled Buzz out of the crowd for recognition. The rest of us males congratulated Buzz as if he'd won the Nobel Prize for Physics.

It's silly, really, this male lack of perspective, and it can lead to unnecessary tragedy, such as soccer-riot deaths and the University of Texas. What is even more tragic is that women are losing perspective, too. Even as you read these words, women are writing vicious letters to the editor, expressing great fury at me for suggesting they don't take their racquetball seriously. Soon they will be droning on about the importance of relief pitching.

STUDY AND DISCUSSION QUESTIONS

1. What is the main target of Barry's satire?
2. Why does he mention that the "second basewoman" is a better player than he is?
3. Barry puts men and women in very different worlds. Where is he?
4. In the picture Barry paints, what kinds of things do women value instead of sports?
5. Is this essay sexist?

SUGGESTIONS FOR WRITING

1. *Why* are so many men nuts about sports?
2. Write a sketch of someone you know, male or female, who either fits or challenges the stereotypes Barry plays with.

On the Beach at Noordwijk

Leonard Kriegel

Leonard Kriegel (b. 1933) taught American literature at the City College of New York and directed its Workers' Center. He has written the novel Quitting Time *(1982) as well as a number of works of nonfiction, including* Working Through: A Teacher's Journey in the Urban University *(1972),* On Men and Manhood *(1979), where the following appeared, and* Falling Into Life *(1992).*

Someone once lauded to him Franz Rosenzweig's courageous tolerance of his total paralysis, and Freud responded "What else can he do?" The same remark can be turned on Freud, as it can on all of us who suffer from illness.
　　　　　　　　　　—Ernest Becker, The Denial of Death

I

Above the beach at Noordwijk, I push forward on my crutches, push against the salt-splayed North Sea wind, marshalling my determination to fight the wind and the bleak nature it embodies. My two-year-old son pulls at my hand, reminding me of how vulnerable I still am. For even here, in this alien Holland, the past can never be laid to rest: It can only be placated. Not the kind of lesson a thirty-one-year-old American man can afford to ignore. For between a man and his son stands the man's past, the confused struggles and momentary victories of his own coming-of-age. Like all sons, my two-year-old holds his father's past and future rolled into a single storehouse of memory and expectation. And like all American sons, he will eventually be trapped by the ambiguities of his own manhood.

I stare down at him, proud but reflective. In my mind, I shape his future. No matter how much I might try to deny it, I know that I am American enough to want this child to vindicate my life here on earth, to justify even the accident of a childhood attack of polio which has left me with lifeless brace-bound legs. I approach the dimensions which I want him to know. A healthy American father, a hero for a time which mocks heroes, distrusts the heroic—father, husband, lover, teacher, man. An example, a presence. I have come through—and to come through in the twentieth century is a kind of heroism: We Americans can still admire endurance, at least as much as a time grown meretricious with self-consciousness permits. Mark and I stand on the concrete embankment above the beach and stare out at the hammering North Sea surf. For the moment, I feel at peace with the world. Mark's fingers curl around the pinky that juts out from the handle of the crutch I hold in my right hand. The weight of my body comes down on my left hand. I feel significant.

I have acquitted myself well: American man. Not an important fate, but not trivial either. Both the struggles and the ambiguities I have known have made up my own manhood. And yet, the process of claiming one's personal manhood is like this North Sea wind, curling around each of us, enfolding us, isolating the individual against his struggles. Men in America share the testing, the need to prove the individual's capacity. This America of ours is, after all, a country of the mind.

My own testing was a war with the virus that entered my body when I was eleven and might easily have proved terminal. From that event, I now etch a coherent past. I want to bank that past as greedily as a miser hoards his dollars, draw upon it for a sense of self, frame an *I* from it, hammer out my manhood from it. My pride is in having survived as a cripple and man: This two-year-old son holding on to my outstretched pinky is proof enough of that. At least for me he is. In America, men steal their manhood from such tests. A son remains an insurance policy who measures the reality of his father's own emergence.

So I stand here, holding my son's hand, and as if I were standing before a fun-house mirror, my past undulates before me. It reflects triumphs, defeats, anxieties, hesitations, distortions, courage, fear, recklessness. I want to see my future reflected in Mark's eyes, but I see only the horizon stretching toward America. Still, I own this moment as I own my manhood. I have paid the prices demanded of me and will settle for no other category than American man.

Mark lets go of my pinky and pulls away. I watch him waddle toward the incline leading down to the beach without fearing for his safety. He is bright, and he accepts the limits we have imposed on him, just as he accepts my crutches, or the patched and peeling leather jacket I have been wearing with the devotion of an acolyte to his surplice ever since my father gave it to me as a present when I was seventeen. "Be careful!" I call to him. But I know he can take care of himself. A herring seller pushing his cart passes me, his eyes following mine to Mark's tiny form which stands alone. He stops the cart, stirs the brine barrel hanging in front. "He wants to be his own man," the herring seller says to me in Dutch. "A little man on the beach at Noordwijk."

To be his own man. To possess the power of manhood, the self-assurance—this promise had been held out to each of us, to me, to Mark, as it would be held out to his own unborn sons, from the very first squalling cries that announce a man's entrance into this world. A man's character is his fate, says Heraclitus. But an American man's fate is first seen in the way he approaches manhood, the way he moves, loves, provides for others. It is a truth sensed at the heart of his being, the dead center of his manliness. He will be what he demands of himself. What would I teach this son whose arrival had announced a passing in my own life, a turning of the corner in my quest for manhood? How would I tell him what he had to know if he, too, were to be a survivor? How equip him to exist in a culture growing increasingly suspicious of the very idea of manhood, even while it threatened to up the ante of the demands it would make upon him?

He wants to be his own man. Well, there were no sureties. No more for my son than for me. To be your own man in America meant that you learned to trust nothing beyond your own capacity, that you stamped your endurance on the only world you knew. I want to teach my son how to maneuver his way through the false pieties, the dead rituals, in which men enclose themselves. I want to hold on to him and then to cut him loose. I stand on the concrete embankment above the beach at Noordwijk and watch, hesitant but approving, as he creates distance between us.

"Come daddy!" he calls from the beach, the shrill childish voice floating into the wind, so that I am not sure of the words but only of the figure of my son. The herring seller leans across his cart and smiles at me, showing a mouth filled with gold-crowned teeth. "Come daddy!" Mark repeats. I am filled with fresh pride at his boldness. I have been put on earth to feel just this. The herring seller points in Mark's direction. "He wants his father," he laughs, nodding, as if he were giving me his permission to go to my son.

Images of manhood. Streetcorner cripple, now a father, still sucking on my adolescent dream. I will myself to immense prowess; I move toward my son. I must create my man again. Father this time. Lover, provider, teacher the next. But for now, between myself and my son, a demonstration of the authority of manhood is required. I have won the self I claim. There is nothing I cannot do. At thirty-one, I still expect to conquer. No one can accuse me of being resigned or accepting. A man is the sum total of his resistance and he must prove himself. There is no rest when we struggle for manhood. Not even before our sons. For a son is a witness.

"I'm coming," I call. He stands now about twenty yards into the beach, waiting for me. I walk down the incline that leads from the embankment to the beach. The herring seller disappears, the buildings fronting the embankment evaporate, there is nothing but the wind and the clouds and my son waiting for me on the beach and this incredible power that floods my body. I feel an absolute physical sense of myself—potent, naked, alone, certain. Adolescent illusions hang in the air like ripe pears from the Dutch sky. I snatch at them, approaching my son as I knock the very world apart. Mine is a willing surrender to illusion. The desire fathered by manhood leads to my revolt against reality. *The child is father to the man,* I recall. The child I had been, the child I had fathered. Illusion devouring reality. I follow my son, my visible other self. I am going to pick him up, saddle his legs around my neck. Together, we will run across this foreign beach, an American father with his American son.

Habits and dreams and will pick me up, make me new again. I need nothing, no one, other than this son, this emerging self. I am in the movies, in the books. I am absolutely self-sufficient. For there is nothing else to be given to me other than the prerogative of being an American man. The cripple within dies, and a fierce clarity seizes me. Men choose their moments. And in this particular moment, nothing is left to prove because there is no other man to judge me but myself.

My dream of power is pulled from the very heart of America along with the need not to give in to fate alone. At the age of eleven, a virus severs legs from will. I am forced to fall back upon illusion for the first time. For there is no other way to breathe life into the dream I had inherited by being born a man in America. I drift into what my imagination has absorbed and clear a path for myself. Walk where the road can still be cut, and ignore the surrounding trees.

Still, I had to differentiate between my dreams and the actual conditions in which I existed. The fact remained that I could not run, could not even walk without the braces strapped to my legs and the crutches I gripped. But as I approach my son on the beach at Noordwijk, the braces and crutches disappear. For one hallucinatory moment, I can run again. I believe that literally. For that one moment, I negate the reality of the virus, all the reminders of my *condition*. Aspirations of the uncrippled cripple, ghosts of my own past floating free in Vermeer's sky.

I reach the bottom of the incline. My crutches slice the sand, sink. I push up on shoulders liberated by the power of myth now, pushing like Moby Dick[1] himself rising from the sea. And then sink, Ahab again. The dream evaporates as suddenly as it has seized me. I can barely walk towards my son, the crutches sink deeper and deeper into the sand with each step I take. I will drown in sand before I reach him. I will die of rage unless I can smash it against something. I caricature illusion now. Nonfather, nonrunner, nonhusband, nonman—the vision has popped, I want to scream.

The wind howls against the beach, chokes off the scream in my throat. Mark's face is pensive with fear, recognition. I feel exposed to his glance,

---

[1] The great white whale pursued by Ahab in Herman Melville's novel, *Moby Dick*.

betrayed by his eyes. The manhood game has caught me, tricked me, hurled me to the ground leaving only the murderous rage in my heart. I want to destroy, to prove my presence. But to whom? I will not seek understanding, nor sympathy. Just this need to declare a finish, this murder in the heart. Only the manhood game is never finished.

Mark retreats before the puzzle of this other father. It is evident, even to his two-year-old mind, that he must be his own man now. I can feel the herring seller's eyes stabbing my back. The past breaks loose from its moorings, reality floats free. There was never a man who did not desire to get even.

"Mark go?" my son asks hesitantly. He edges deeper into the beach, away from me. *He wants to be his own man. A little man on the beach at Noordwijk.*

"No. Wait for me." Before I can try again, my wife is suddenly at my side, staring first at our son, then at me, her face puzzled, then overwhelmed by the rage in my eyes. Mark ferrets himself away from me, glancing at her.

I turn, throwing myself out of the sand trap, exaggerating the very difficulties that threaten. "Please!" I hear her insist. "Don't do that to yourself." I ignore the voice. I want to recapture the illusion. I want to run again. In the very calm she wants for me lies the risk of madness. I do not want to surrender to passivity, to acquiesce to reality.

I manage to get back to the incline and move up the embankment, humiliated but still filled with rage. The herring seller is still there, watching. When my eyes meet his, he turns and pushes his cart before him, leaving me to myself and the sharpness of the wind from the North Sea. He has witnessed my failure: I would like to kill him.

II

Why does that memory pulsate for me even today with all the pressures and contradictions of being both a man and an American? I still find myself checked by that memory, stopped hard on my way, as if I had left some particle of the man I was on the beach with my son. I inevitably drift back to that scene and go through the process of coupling my American manhood first to illusion, and then to rage. And I wonder, finally, whether this is not the pattern for each of us. I do not want to presume to offer that moment, or any moment of my life, as a paradigm for anyone else's struggles but my own. And yet, that is exactly what I do. I stake a claim for each of us, for each American man. I stand once again before my two-year-old son and discover that the first hurdle is allowing what one loves most in this world to create and then to destroy illusion. A man should be the impresario of his own illusions, and only then, he discovers, will he be able to open himself to the judgement of what he most loves on this earth. A child is one's substance, but a son in America is a judge, the barometer of whether or not a man has measured up. But the burden of that expectation is too great, both for the son and for the father.

Ultimately, mine was the rage of the witness who stands back and sees himself drowning. And what I saw was that everything I had struggled for would be taken from my grasp. I saw the inevitability of what Mark would face in his time and my rage hardened into permanence.

Even today, I want what I wanted on that beach—to set myself right with my past. To run again, to live out the very fantasies that we know are adolescent, to catch my manhood as it is being formed: an American legacy. I want to re-create my past, to get even with accident, to move into that darkness which harbors my courage and my power and my selfhood and all the other shaman names we give to those qualities we hunger after.

I know that something is missing. I have been tricked, lied to, have given in to illusion. And above all else I have been tested. For the self pressed to its aspirations declares what a man is, and what he can be, here in America. In my resistance to what actually occurred on that beach in Noordwijk, I discover what my dreams of manhood are.

This, then, accounts for the violence of my reaction to what must be considered a minor event. It wasn't that I could not run on the beach with my son. I had long since made a highly successful "adjustment" to what the virus had left. Compensation was easy enough, demanding merely the substitution of one kind of performance for another. No, what had been called into question here was the endurance I had grafted on myself, that virtue I most highly valued. For endurance was critical in the confrontation with the myths that had been bequeathed to me long before I thrust my individual *I* into the American battle.

No American man could afford to be anything less than capable—this was the price of being an American. The world as it was issued its challenge; the American man as he was offered his answer. He lived in the midst of a siege where each man was bound to an isolation that denied the possibility of any solidarity with others, particularly other men. To be both American and man was to be man alone—and to lack even the belief in the *absurd* with which European men had tempered their condition. The self was demanding because it could be nothing else and could turn nowhere else—not even to a philosophy like existentialism, whose very threat of emptiness became a source of comfort.

Isolation in America was man's natural state. To be alone was necessary, perhaps even enviable. There was no other recourse but in one's own living consciousness. As a cripple, I was deeply aware of those boundaries the world had set for me. I would not have been conscious if I failed to grasp them. I knew from the beginning that I would be classified as both pariah and victim, to be pitied, shunned, praised, labelled, and classified. I knew that for as long as I remained alive, I would find myself admired for my "courage," for my "toughness," for my "determination." I knew also that I existed within the peculiar paradox of manhood's American forms: that a man had to learn to accept defeat as irremediable and yet pretend that he was actually asserting his freedom in fighting against such acceptance. To go to your fate was unavoidable; to go quiescently was disgraceful. Expect nothing, but act as if you want everything. You broke the harmony of nature with crutches and prostheses, then employed them with the subtle daring that made them accoutrements of survival. For when the odds against a man's claiming his own existence are great enough, then existence itself could be transformed into defiance. You could seize selfhood from those who insisted on being blind or indifferent to your manhood. My struggle was real—perhaps it was the normal man who had to look over his shoulder, wondering whether or not he was good enough to survive.

"Man is nothing else but what he makes of himself!" cries Sartre. Even if I were to be defeated, to sink in the sand, I could still carve my manhood out of that agony and doubt. I had at least earned my survival. In the normal's language, I had "overcome my handicap." In my view, he still had to earn *his* survival. And so it was that he would shadow me, always nervous in my presence; so it was he would clothe me in the pious sentimentality of Tiny Tim.[2] Occasionally, however, he would discover that we were brothers under the bone: Each of us would be forced to recognize the man within. We had to see each other. And then I began to wonder whether my manhood was better than his, just because mine had been tested and his had not. The threat of my visibility demands my dismissal; the fact of his presence inspires my contempt. We are even for the moment.

I remember the wind cutting against my face. I no longer want to murder the herring seller, a man who could not understand my rage. After all I am still alive. I sit in the bar, sheltered from the North Sea wind, and stare out at the empty beach. In a world filled with success, I still have to set an example for my son. No disguises, no pretense, just imposing myself on my time. I do not want to serve as inspiration for other men. I am satisfied with this fatherhood, difficult as it is.

"I will set my life upon a cast / And I will stand the hazard of the die." Villain or not, I sympathize with the pain of Shakespeare's Richard.[3] It is a pain absorbed in a defiance that is vital to his crooked nature and to my unsated rage. Richard is human, recognizable—I see myself in him. A man

---

[2] Child with crutch and braces in *A Christmas Carol*, by Charles Dickens.
[3] In *Richard III*.

stands up before the measure that has been meted out to him. Richard, too, is an adolescent. Only there is more to the adolescent's desire to prove himself, to call the limit on what he can endure, than mature men are willing to admit. Richard is a model. Spawned by the indifference of accident, he imposes his scars, his unrepentant evil on the world. But just as Shakespeare and the world insist that he acknowledge his evil, Richard insists that they acknowledge his presence. To be a man is to demand an accounting for your life, even when that accounting leads to death.

I wish to match the man within to the challenge outside. Like other American men, I enclose myself within dreams of dominance. Each of us harbors a secret self, a man thrust upon earth to shape it to his will. The world's reality snatches at you, but you respond by seeking a way in which you can exert a solitary pressure for change, gathering momentum from the clear harsh limitations of your own existence. There is something awkward, brittle, about such fantasies. But there is something heroic, something manly about them, too.

III

I struggle to match the fantasy with my performance. *Performance* is an embarrassing word; *manhood* is an embarrassing word. Notches on our contemporary belts. It is so much easier to make the idea of manhood humorous. Only to be a man is to commit yourself to the need for performance. No amount of humor can disguise that. A man performs in order to set the terms of his life beyond his limitations. He performs to affirm the idea that accident is a form of opportunity. Mere physical survival may never quite be reward enough for the agony it demands, but it remains, nonetheless, an immense source of pride for those of us who have pulled our survival from the ashes of our being. "Illness is an object," writes Ernest Becker. "We transfer to our own body as if it were a friend on whom we can lean for strength or an enemy who threatens us with danger. At least it makes us feel real and gives us a little purchase on our fate."[4]

My body is a constant reminder of my fate. To have come through is every American man's dream; for me, it is the very integrity of my existence. Every time I take a step, every time I make love, every time I hold my son, I translate death into capacity. Always, performance is central—it would be nonsense to deny that. And I do not hesitate to admit that I want the quality

---

[4] Ernest Becker, *The Denial of Death* (New York, 1973), p. 144. My debt to Becker is extensive particularly to this book. Few thinkers have handled the problem of coming to terms with the need for the heroic so well. [Author's note]

of my performance to be recognized by others. For unless manhood is acknowledged by others, it counts for little.

It would be so easy, I think, to blame *alienation* or *technology* or any of the hundred other modern soporifics for every question. In every age, not just our own, manhood was something that had to be won. Were men in the past any more certain of how to respond to the demands made upon them? I tell myself they were, but how can I know? Our options today are abundant. Why, then, do the choices we make seem forced upon us?

I look at American men and I see the reflection of the cripple's perennial struggle to measure performance when the rules of the game are constantly shifting. One simply must learn to live with the lack of surety. No matter what I did, no matter what the quality of my performance—as father, as teacher, as provider, as lover—what haunted me was the recognition that my triumphs could so easily be seized by others. To what extent is performance the measure? Men deny its validity, but it dominates our consciousness; it bestows the gift of self. The trouble is that none of us is ever quite certain of where performance ends and the parody of that performance begins.

I am comfortable with the need for challenge, the dream of a heroic existence, perhaps more so than other men, simply because I have had to struggle for the trappings of manhood in a world grown increasingly indifferent to it. In the works of Bellow, of Lowell, of Mailer, life is most immediate when it forces the individual into a corner, heightening the possibilities that it opens for him. As if when the trap springs, the man emerges. Manhood demands that each of us defy categorization. We each live with the intimate dread of our own incapacity. We each need to accept the tests of our performance while we learn to deny the legitimacy of those who set the standards.

I knew the tests I gave myself. I knew how consumed with ambition I could actually become, I knew how easily my desire to seek affirmation from a world indifferent to my fate could be broken off, twisted away from its fulfillment. Like most American men, I had learned to behave as if I had created myself: a man alone. And like all American men, I often found myself hounded by hesitation, secret doubts, confusion over what was expected of me. Balanced against these was the need to force myself over whatever obstacles stood in my way. I accepted the necessity of action as I did the limitations declared by the virus. And yet, I could still ask a reckoning of that virus. My difficulty came in controlling reality before it passed into illusion, particularly when I grew tired of the close-in combat, the everyday drudgery of strapping braces to legs and moving out.

No one, I discovered, lived more consistently with the manhood he sought than did the cripple. It was simply impossible for me have come through, to have claimed a self, without accepting the need for courage. How many times did the cripple in me have to place his body next to that which threatened it? Another notch on the belt. Even nature was a field mined with booby traps, an explosion of destructive possibilities, demanding a stealth and measurement disproportionate to what normal men had to muster. You had to learn to accept ice and snow and rain as enemies, you had to walk the streets with eyes alerted to the sidewalk debris, searching for oil slicks or dead leaf clusters or pieces of paper or patches of sand with the wary potential for imminent encounter of a soldier in a World War II movie scouting a Pacific atoll.

Such enemies were real, they were intimate. They taught me that it was possible, as Becker writes, to look at the enemy within my body as "an *object*, an adversary, something against which to marshal one's courage; disease and dying are still *living* processes in which one is engaged."[5] They taught me that in order to survive, I simply had to be better—better as performer, better as man. And they fed me a sense of my own singularity that became the "dirty little secret" of my life. Of all confessions, this is the most difficult to make: I came to feel a certain contempt for other men who did not or could not match my prowess with their own fallibility.

Having lived with pain as a simple cipher, in much the same manner as a man learns to live with his appetites, how was I to accommodate myself to a culture in which grown men rhapsodized over the *courage* of an athlete who earned his living on aching knees? Only immediacies were entitled to respect. If we really are nothing else but what we make of ourselves, then the man who made himself a man also made legitimate the traditional "masculine" virtues, the very virtues which ultimately became his embarrassment. His needs could not be analyzed out of existence, not when he gambled so much of himself to legitimatize those needs.

As long as I was conscious of the pressures on my particular existence, I could claim a place for myself in this world. I would reverse the concept of *stigmatization* so that it put me beyond the range of the normal man but did so on terms which I chose.[6] I would not settle for a drifting lesser normalcy. To be a man was to make demands upon others as well as upon myself. To be a man was to seek out ways in which the existence of others was an encounter with my own ambitions. Invariably, however, the challenges I had to handle were not necessarily those I sought out—they would continually creep up and catch me unawares. Always I would experience that momentary surprise

---

[5] Ibid., p. 104. [Author's note]

[6] I have taken the idea of *stigmatization* from Erving Goffman's *Stigma: Notes on the Management of Spoiled Identity* (Englewood Cliffs, N.J., 1963). I have, however, turned Goffman's argument around, since I believe that stigmatization can prove to be liberating through the very distance it provides from the world of the *normals*. [Author's note]

as the element of exposure slipped into consciousness and jabbed some naked nerve. I would lie there, amazed at the intensity of the pain, defenseless. As it is in sex. A momentary release. And then back into consciousness, like a spotlight snapping on my poised body.

IV

She goes to shut the window and the man, myself at nineteen, watches the way her naked body moves across the room. I think I am detached. But I am disturbed because I see myself watching her movements. I do not want to expose this stopping and starting, this feeling that I am lying in bed in the midst of a fever, although certainly not sick. While fucking, I square myself with time. I want the bronze medal. I stare at my toes that peep out of a thin sheet. Dead legs of a lover. *For a gimp you performed well.* My mind laughs soundlessly. "Want a drink?" she asks. She opens the blinds to let in streams of afternoon sun. She is naked at the window but oblivious to her body.

"No thank you." I want to say something sharp, quick-witted. Language leaves its mark. She returns to the bed and sits down on the edge, but I say nothing. She reaches across me and takes her cigarettes from the night table. Irritated with her, I narrow my life to questions of purpose. I do not know why I am irritated with this woman, and so I grow irritated with myself. I know what I am going to ask her. What men want to know, whether they ask or not. How do I measure up? It does not matter that my legs do not function; that is simply an additional challenge. "How was it?" I ask. And hate myself for asking. And hate her for not anticipating, for making it necessary.

Her eyes sweep my prone body. "Join the ranks," she says. "Do you want to be graded?"

I shrug. This woman is all right; she knows more than I do. She is perhaps thirty, older than I am, and that, too, irritates me. Sex is like everything else a man does. The need to be graded. Good, better, best. A grammar for the body.

"Why make it a trial?" she asks. "Why can't pleasure just be?" She puffs on the cigarette. "When I first started, I used to think it was more difficult for us, only it's men who have the curse. Why can't you just have a good time instead of all making it such a contest? God, you must hate each other."

"No," I insist, "it's not hate." I am afraid of saying too much. Women seem self-possessed, competent. I am afraid that she is mocking me. She possesses a distance from herself that I cannot afford. I wonder whether manhood itself is simply a disease, like the other one I know so well. Well, we grow comfortable with our diseases. And the morning comes when you wake to discover that it is even more difficult to live without them than it is to live with them. "It's just. . . ."

"That you have to cast your shadow on some piece of ground," she interrupts. And laughs. "Each of you is always wondering how much of a liar the other is. How much does he know that you don't?"

"About you? About women?" She is a divorcée and I wonder now what her husband was like. It is the first time I have ever thought of him, although this is our third time together.

"About everything. About each other, most of all. Men create virgins and men create studs." She touches my foot. "Can you feel that?"

"I can feel everything," I say quickly.

"I don't know what that's like," she says, as if she were talking to herself, alone in the room.

I wonder whether it is what men have created or what has been created for us. The other side of performance. What begins as pleasure turns in on itself. Still, it was easy enough to brand performance "macho," even then, in 1953. And yet, it is difficult to ignore it, to bury it beneath its strutting artificiality. After all, performance has its specific commitments, and it provides the exhilaration of letting you prove that you remain superior to your circumstances.

Even the gamesmanship with which you manipulate the environment has its place. All right, grade me, lady. Are my hands caressing enough? my tongue quick enough? my cock hard enough? my eyes aware enough? Casanova, Lord Byron, P. T. Barnum, Rusty the Prong, lascivious monks from de Sade, Paul Bunyan—love rides us down into life. How many did you fuck? Incessant buzz buzz buzz on streetcorners all over the nation. A world full of women tones the very impossibility of the thing. The fantasy pulls at our deepest instincts, shapes the future, overwhelms fear with the greater fear of being left behind.

She turns away again and sits with her back to me on the edge of the bed. Suddenly, she seems small, almost childlike, and I wonder why what I do with this woman, with any woman, counts for so much. Why do I have this self-conscious need to reveal no weakness, to translate weakness into strength, to succeed in her eyes? After all, she will never be more than a stranger to me. The necessity of taking risks in pursuit of my own substance irritates me now. All right, and in my mind I say it to her: "Lady, I want more than pleasure. I want a certain standing in your eyes. It is not necessary to be a sexual outlaw to know that much."

Men communicate their fears through their efforts to control sex. She has caught me waiting to be patted on the head and she has kicked me in the balls. I stare at her back and feel the fool. No man ever quite rids himself of the anxiety of performance. I feel it at nineteen, I will feel it forever. Even if I deserve it, I am aware of the shame, the haunting sense of a scene that is to be played over and over again in any man's lifetime. And I cannot even take refuge in "the cripple."

The performance is like the death you grow to anticipate with all its inherent terrors and obligations. But I enjoy it now, play with it. Challenge and response—Darwinian legacies. I do not really believe this enjoyment is unhealthy. It does not leave me uncomfortable, and I do not think it leaves most men uncomfortable. No, it leaves us eager. There is a certain sense of risk in sex. This is, after all, the area in a man's life in which he is most completely exposed, most open and alone, wanting approval from the women who come to weigh his style and pass judgement on the prince or pauper within his heart. Sex was meant to engage a man's energies, direct his strategies, meant to heighten existence itself.

Years have passed, and all the memories seem to fuse into a single vision. I find myself looking back, wondering whether the greatest sin we have left the generations that follow us was making sex, too, a tepid affair. In place of performance, we bequeathed a passive fantasy. After all, a man runs risks with himself only when he does the hard-nosed grubbing that reality demands, only when he is willing to express power and vulnerability in the same gesture. But a fantasy that is never put to the test has neither quality. The gift of passivity, in itself, demands no payment, just as it demands neither physical nor psychological contact. If performance can be branded macho, then fantasy is masturbatory.[7]

V

The beach at Noordwijk haunts me; I search for different openings into the past, for the man working into himself. Space is all around me. It heals. Illusion, I have discovered, can carry you too far. I want a different balance.

It is New Year's Eve and I see myself riding the subway down to the Lower East Side.[8] The party is in an old dimly lit tenement in a neighborhood which will soon be known as the East Village. But this is the night in which 1955 will become 1956 and the neighborhood is still the Lower East Side. The party is in an apartment that is up four steep flights of stairs. I enter the building in the cold darkness. The corners of the narrow hallway dipped in urine, and dried, like a smell from a Bowery shelter. Sweating walls, clotted paint—the poverty is so exaggerated as to seem almost staged. I examine the staircase—the first thing I do whenever I enter a strange building, since

---

[7] Where masturbation had once offered no more than a kind of mechanical satisfaction, it now seems to have become an end in itself, at least if one listens to many of the voices around us. For a sense of how widespread this view of masturbation has apparently grown, the reader should consult Natalie Gittelson's *Dominus: A Woman Looks at Men's Lives* (New York, 1978). [Author's note]

[8] Manhattan neighborhood.

each staircase is unpredictable, a new challenge for me, a different threat. This one is sectioned off into three parts, each of six steps, with a landing between, so that a corridor of space, around four feet wide, runs from the roof above the fifth floor to the black-and-white tiled entrance landing on which I am standing.

The stairs are scratched, chipped, the banister of cast iron. It has been painted over a dark forest green which blends to near-black in the dim light provided by the forty-watt bulbs pinned to each landing. I maneuver my way upstairs, pausing to look down at each landing. As I approach the fourth floor, where the party is already under way, I feel as if I am staring down an unused mine shaft. The dim light makes the space below me stretch out, then disappear into shadow so that by the time I reach the apartment landing it is as if I am hundreds of feet above the entrance. I know that it is actually no more than forty feet, but the impression remains, nonetheless.

Hours pass, the year changes, I drink to it. I am with a woman I do not know who tells me that I look like her English lover who died in Korea. I drink, I did not even know the English had been in Korea, I am interested in her, but not interested enough. During the four hours that I remain at the party, I think about the staircase. I am looking forward to descending the staircase and the expectation heightens as the evening goes on. The woman is talkative, intelligent. I think about the angles of descent, about the empty mine shaft plunging to the dimly lit bottom. Going up, the banister was on the left. I will have to descend the stairs backwards. I am afraid. The woman keeps talking. I plan my descent. I will have to hold one crutch in my right hand, brace the other crutch against the banister with my left thumb, and maneuver my legs into the blackness behind me as I seek the solidity of the step below. The weak light will shadow the landings. My mind plays with the potential for disaster. I see my body falling through blank space—I can think of little else. Fear and anticipation mingle, then the fear disappears and there is only anticipation. Like sex. A need for the specific gesture.

Just before 2:00 A.M. I decide to leave. The woman is puzzled; she would like to come with me. I am sober enough to know that I do not want her to. I stand alone at the head of the staircase. In order to gain leverage, I must lift my body by straightening the right arm until all my weight is on the triceps and forearm. Then I shift my weight to my left arm, which pushes up from the banister, while I pin the other crutch against the banister with my thumb. I float in space, lean out and over the banister, so that the body in which I have invested my future moves into the emptiness, four stories above the tiled floor, staring down into the muted distance of the mine shaft, staring into its mouth. My awareness is absolute, clear, my head thickens not with the liquor I have drunk but with the grip of my vanity. No one else on the staircase, either coming or going. Shrouded in the dim light, I seize the moment. Life is immediate, tensile with the immensity of its own promise, as I lean out across the banister into hostile space. Suspended, almost frozen, I meet the virus head on, a spectator at my own performance.

The *only* thing keeping the virus from claiming the rest of me is the power in *my* body, *my* arms, a power I have laboriously built up, doing hundreds of pushups and parallel bar dips each day, soaking my hands in brine to toughen the thick callouses even more, working with weights, springs, coils, dumbbells. Stubborn insistence seizes my mind and tells me that I can now determine the course of my fate. I have captured the man within, have stolen him from the virus, and I want to laugh with the pleasure of it. I am filled with a surge of joy so great that its intensity is frightening, my hand begins to slip down the banister, and then a voice cries out from somewhere inside, "Not now! Don't give it the victory! Be the man you've made!" My fingers cramp, dig hard against the cast iron, hold, until I understand that it is over—I have claimed my body once again. A man must be a man. A man must be better than himself.

VI

Another surprise confrontation with my manhood, this one embarrassing for what it reminds me of. That night, I recall, it was still possible to believe. I had a moment in which I felt myself suspended in space, beyond the reach of circumstance, free to choose, to embrace the possibility of death and then to dismiss it as an inadequate alternative. Never again would I fuse my existence with the ability to choose the course of my life. It was through the acceptance of risk, the legacy of accident embodied in the cripple's condition, that I broke through to manhood, hanging four stories above the dingy tiled entrance of an East Side tenement.

Men clutch at manhood to control the anguish and turmoil of their lives. And yet, I knew that I was not a better man for the virus' having slipped into my blood. Suffering can neither dominate nor transform a man's life. But it does create choices, possibilities. And choices, finally, imply acknowledging risks. If you allow yourself to be categorized, you are accepting the ways in which society chooses to eliminate risks, to subdue the realities they impose.

And is not this the very condition that threatens men today? For men have discovered that they have been assigned a variety of new classifications. They are suddenly frozen into a new time, they must be both passive and spontaneous at once—all in the cause of liberating themselves! New times bring new demands, and men now chart the dead ends and blind alleys in which they find themselves trapped. And men discover that *liberation*, too, is only a word, like *courage* and *manliness* and *strength*.

"I want to screw the world now as much as I did then," the forty-five-year-old businessman-turned-dropout says as we nurse our drinks in a Village bar. "They got you coming and going and you're supposed to pretend that it feels good, that you've never felt better in your life. Jesus, this is no world to be a man. Maybe it once was, but it's been dipped in shit since."

He wants something real to struggle against. "Like you," he insists. "Disease is something real." What he means is that he thinks that I have learned the cost, that I understand that only the man who defines himself is capable of meeting that cost. He is not talking about suffering or even about disease. Suffering is rarely more than a question of how much you can take, and he knows that as well as I do. A certain turn of the screw will elicit pain from each of us. No, the source of pride is in having come through, in having managed to transform even disease into a performance.

A man learns to adapt his vulnerability, his pain, to his needs as a man. In his quest for a usable self, a meaningful manhood, he struggles to put his moments to use. I stare at myself on the beach at Noordwijk and I catch the fantasy as it catches me. There is the man I once dreamed of being—and then my body sinks into the sand, my very being buried in the lost vision. But now I am myself once again and I lean across the banister above the tiled floor, aware of the choice before me. If that was the man I once dreamed of being, then here is the man I am yet going to be, the process hard but malleable. Past and future solidify here, are made one. Both demand resistance.

A man has to fight against the power of accident. To face the world as it presents itself, to respond honestly to each new situation—men have been asked to do this from the beginnings of time. "Let a man then know his worth," writes Emerson, "and keep things under his feet." A man's dignity finally consists of the terms of the struggle he declares. To live with that struggle is to be man enough—for himself and for all those sons still waiting on the beach.

STUDY AND DISCUSSION QUESTIONS

1. Why does Kriegel think he will be able to walk across the sand and reach his son?

2. Why is Kriegel so angry at the herring seller? If the herring seller were a woman, would Kriegel's feelings be different?

3. What is the significance of "performance" in Kriegel's conception of manhood?

4. "Why can't you just have a good time instead of all making it such a contest?" asks the woman Kriegel goes to bed with. What's the answer?

5. "For unless manhood is acknowledged by others, it counts for little." Explain.

6. Why do you think Kriegel uses the word "cripple" and even, at one point, the word "*gimp*"?

7. Has Kriegel gained anything from his disability?

8. What exactly is Kriegel's attitude towards "manhood"?

SUGGESTIONS FOR WRITING

1. "On the Beach at Noordwijk" is a difficult essay, often quite abstract. Write a one-paragraph summary of Kriegel's main points.

2. "Men clutch at manhood to control the anguish and turmoil of their lives." Does this statement shed light on anyone you know?

3. What might a female version of Kriegel's essay look like? If not physical disability, what condition might force a woman to focus intensely on the meaning of "womanhood"? Outline what she might say.

HUCK FINN, DAN QUAYLE AND THE VALUE OF ACCEPTANCE

Richard Rodriguez

Richard Rodriguez was born in San Francisco in 1944 and studied at Stanford, Columbia, and the University of California, Berkeley. He has published Hunger of Memory: The Education of Richard Rodriguez *(1987) and* Days of Obligation: An Argument with My Mexican Father *(1992). The essay below originally appeared in the* Los Angeles Times Magazine *in 1992.*

I am sitting alone in my car, in front of my parents' house—a middle-aged man with a boy's secret to tell. What words will I use to tell them? I hate the word *gay,* find its little affirming sparkle more pathetic than assertive. I am happier with the less polite *queer.* But to my parents I would say *homosexual,* avoid the Mexican slang *joto* (I had always heard it said in our house with hints of condescension), though *joto* is less mocking than the sissy-boy *maricón.*

The buzz on everyone's lips now: Family values. The other night on TV, the vice president of the United States, his arm around his wife, smiled into the camera and described homosexuality as "mostly a choice." But how would he know? Homosexuality never felt like a choice to me.

A few minutes ago Rush Limbaugh, the radio guy with a voice that reminds me, for some reason, of a butcher's arms, was banging his console and booming a near-reasonable polemic about family values. Limbaugh was not very clear about which values exactly he considers to be family values. A divorced man who lives alone in New York?

My parents live on a gray, treeless street in San Francisco not far from the ocean. Probably more than half of the neighborhood is immigrant. India lives next door to Greece, who lives next door to Russia. I wonder what the Chinese lady next door to my parents makes of the politicians' phrase *family values.*

What immigrants know, what my parents certainly know, is that when you come to this country, you risk losing your children. The assurance of family—continuity, inevitability—is precisely what America encourages its children to overturn. *Become your own man.* We who are native to this country know this too, of course, though we are likely to deny it. Only a society so guilty about its betrayal of family would tolerate the pieties of politicians regarding family values.

On the same summer day that Republicans were swarming in Houston[1] (buzzing about family values), a friend of mine who escaped family values awhile back and who now wears earrings resembling intrauterine devices, was complaining to me over coffee about the Chinese. The Chinese will never take over San Francisco, my friend said, because the Chinese do not want to take over San Francisco. The Chinese do not even *see* San Francisco! All they care about is their damn families. All they care about is double-parking smack in front of the restaurant on Clement Street and pulling granny out of the car—and damn anyone who happens to be in the car behind them or the next or the next.

Politicians would be horrified by such an American opinion, of course. But then, what do politicians, Republicans or Democrats, really know of our family life? Or what are they willing to admit? Even in that area where they could reasonably be expected to have something to say—regarding the relationship of family life to our economic system—the politicians say nothing. Republicans celebrate American economic freedom, but Republicans don't seem to connect that economic freedom to the social breakdown they find

---

[1] Site of 1992 Republican National Convention.

appalling. Democrats, on the other hand, if more tolerant of the drift from familial tradition, are suspicious of the very capitalism that creates social freedom.

How you become free in America: Consider the immigrant. He gets a job. Soon he is earning more money than his father ever made (his father's authority is thereby subtly undermined). The immigrant begins living a life his father never knew. The immigrant moves from one job to another, changes houses. His economic choices determine his home address—not the other way around. The immigrant is on his way to becoming his own man.

When I was broke a few years ago and trying to finish a book, I lived with my parents. What a thing to do! A major theme of America is leaving home. We trust the child who forsakes family connections to make it on his own. We call that the making of a man.

Let's talk about this man stuff for a minute. America's ethos is anti-domestic. We may be intrigued by blood that runs through wealth—the Kennedys or the Rockefellers—but they seem European to us. Which is to say, they are movies. They are Corleones.[2] Our real pledge of allegiance: We say in America that nothing about your family—your class, your race, your pedigree—should be as important as what you yourself achieve. We end up in 1992 introducing ourselves by first names.

What authority can Papa have in a country that formed its identity in an act of Oedipal rebellion against a mad British king? Papa is a joke in America, a stock sitcom figure—Archie Bunker or Homer Simpson. But my Mexican father went to work every morning, and he stood in a white smock, making false teeth, oblivious of the shelves of grinning false teeth mocking his devotion.

The nuns in grammar school—my wonderful Irish nuns—used to push Mark Twain on me. I distrusted Huck Finn,[3] he seemed like a gringo kid I would steer clear of in the schoolyard. (He was too confident.) I realize now, of course, that Huck is the closest we have to a national hero. We trust the story of a boy who has no home and is restless for the river. (Huck's Pap is drunk.) Americans are more forgiving of Huck's wildness than of the sweetness of the Chinese boy who walks to school with his mama or grandma. (There is no worse thing in America than to be a mama's boy, nothing better than to be a real boy—all boy—like Huck, who eludes Aunt Sally, and is eager for the world of men.)

There's a bent old woman coming up the street. She glances nervously as she passes my car. What would you tell us, old lady, of family values in America?

---

[2] Italian crime family in *The Godfather,* novel by Mario Puzo and film by Francis Ford Coppola.

[3] Hero of Mark Twain's novel, *The Adventures of Huckleberry Finn.*

America is an immigrant country, we say. Motherhood—parenthood—is less our point than adoption. If I had to assign gender to America, I would note the consensus of the rest of the world. When America is burned in effigy, a male is burned. Americans themselves speak of Uncle Sam.

Like the Goddess of Liberty, Uncle Sam has no children of his own. He steals children to make men of them, mocks all reticence, all modesty, all memory. Uncle Sam is a hectoring Yankee, a skinflint uncle, gaunt, uncouth, unloved. He is the American Savonarola—hater of moonshine, destroyer of stills, burner of cocaine. Sam has no patience with mamas' boys.

You betray Uncle Sam by favoring private over public life, by seeking to exempt yourself, by cheating on your income taxes, by avoiding jury duty, by trying to keep your boy on the farm.

Mothers are traditionally the guardians of the family—against America—though even Mom may side with America against queers and deserters, at least when the Old Man is around. Premature gray hair. Arthritis in her shoulders. Bowlegged with time, red hands. In their fiercely flowered housedresses, mothers are always smarter than fathers in America. But in reality they are betrayed by their children who leave. In a thousand ways. They end up alone.

We kind of like the daughter who was a tomboy. Remember her? It was always easier to be a tomboy in America than a sissy. Americans admired Annie Oakley more than they admired Liberace[4] (who, nevertheless, always remembered his mother). But today we do not admire Annie Oakley when we see Mom becoming Annie Oakley.

The American household now needs two incomes, everyone says. Meaning: Mom is *forced* to leave home out of economic necessity. But lots of us know lots of moms who are sick and tired of being mom, or only mom. It's like the nuns getting fed up, teaching kids for all those years and having those kids grow up telling stories of how awful Catholic school was! Not every woman in America wants her life's work to be forgiveness. Today there are moms who don't want their husbands' names. And the most disturbing possibility: What happens when Mom doesn't want to be Mom at all? Refuses pregnancy?

Mom is only becoming an American like the rest of us. Certainly, people all over the world are going to describe the influence of feminism on women (all over the world) as their "Americanization." And rightly so.

Nothing of this, of course, will the politician's wife tell you. The politician's wife is careful to follow her husband's sentimental reassurances that nothing has changed about America except perhaps for the sinister influence of deviants. Like myself.

---

[4] Annie Oakley, sharpshooter; Liberace, pianist and entertainer.

I contain within myself an anomaly at least as interesting as the Republican Party's version of family values. I am a homosexual Catholic, a communicant in a tradition that rejects even as it upholds me.

I do not count myself among those Christians who proclaim themselves protectors of family values. They regard me as no less an enemy of the family than the "radical feminists." But the joke about families that all homosexuals know is that we are the ones who stick around and make families possible. Call on us. I can think of 20 or 30 examples. A gay son or daughter is the only one who is "free" (married brothers and sisters are too busy). And, indeed, because we have admitted the inadmissible about ourselves (that we are queer)—we are adepts at imagination—we can even imagine those who refuse to imagine us. We can imagine Mom's loneliness, for example. If Mom needs to be taken to church or to the doctor or ferried between Christmas dinners, depend on the gay son or lesbian daughter.

I won't deny that the so-called gay liberation movement, along with feminism, undermined the heterosexual household, if that's what politicians mean when they say family values. Against churchly reminders that sex was for procreation, the gay bar as much as the birth-control pill taught Americans not to fear sexual pleasure. In the past two decades—and, not coincidentally, parallel to the feminist movement—the gay liberation movement moved a generation of Americans toward the idea of a childless adulthood. If the women's movement was ultimately more concerned about getting out of the house and into the workplace, the gay movement was in its way more subversive to Puritan America because it stressed the importance of play.

Several months ago, the society editor of the morning paper in San Francisco suggested (on a list of "must haves") that every society dame must have at least one gay male friend. A ballet companion. A lunch date. The remark was glib and incorrect enough to beg complaints from homosexual readers, but there was a truth about it as well. Homosexual men have provided women with an alternate model of masculinity. And the truth: The Old Man, God bless him, is a bore. Thus are we seen as preserving marriages? Even Republican marriages?

For myself, homosexuality is a deep brotherhood but does not involve domestic life. Which is why, my married sisters will tell you, I can afford the time to be a writer. And why are so many homosexuals such wonderful teachers and priests and favorite aunts, if not because we are freed from the house? On the other hand, I know lots of homosexual couples (male and female) who model their lives on the traditional heterosexual version of domesticity and marriage. Republican politicians mock the notion of a homosexual marriage, but ironically such marriages honor the heterosexual marriage by imitating it.

"The only loving couples I know," a friend of mine recently remarked, "are all gay couples."

This woman was not saying that she does not love her children or that she is planning a divorce. But she was saying something about the sadness of American domestic life: the fact that there is so little joy in family intimacy. Which is perhaps why gossip (public intrusion into the private) has become a national industry. All day long, in forlorn houses, the television lights up a freakish parade of husbands and mothers-in-law and children upon the stage of Sally or Oprah or Phil.[5] They tell on each other. The audience ooohhhs. Then a psychiatrist-shaman appears at the end to dispense prescriptions—the importance of family members granting one another more "space."

The question I desperately need to ask you is whether we Americans have ever truly valued the family. We are famous, or our immigrant ancestors were famous, for the willingness to leave home. And it is ironic that a crusade under the banner of family values has been taken up by those who would otherwise pass themselves off as patriots. For they seem not to understand America, nor do I think they love the freedoms America grants. Do they understand why, in a country that prizes individuality and is suspicious of authority, children are disinclined to submit to their parents? You cannot celebrate American values in the public realm without expecting them to touch our private lives. As Barbara Bush remarked recently, family values are also neighborhood values. It may be harmless enough for Barbara Bush to recall a sweeter America—Midland, Texas, in the 1950s. But the question left begging is why we chose to leave Midland, Texas. Americans like to say that we can't go home again. The truth is that we don't want to go home again, don't want to be known, recognized. Don't want to respond in the same old ways. (And you know you will if you go back there.)

Little 10-year-old girls know that there are reasons for getting away from the family. They learn to keep their secrets—under lock and key—addressed to Dear Diary. Growing up queer, you learn to keep secrets as well. In no place are those secrets more firmly held than within the family house. You learn to live in closets. I know a Chinese man who arrived in America about 10 years ago. He got a job and made some money. And during that time he came to confront his homosexuality. And then his family arrived. I do not yet know the end of this story.

The genius of America is that it permits children to leave home, it permits us to become different from our parents. But the sadness, the loneliness of America, is clear too.

---

[5] Sally Jessy Raphael, Oprah Winfrey, and Phil Donahue, television talk show hosts.

Listen to the way Americans talk about immigrants. If, on the one hand, there is impatience when today's immigrants do not seem to give up their family, there is also a fascination with this reluctance. In Los Angeles, Hispanics are considered people of family. Hispanic women are hired to be at the center of the American family—to babysit and diaper, to cook and to clean and to ease the dying. Hispanic attachment to family is seen by many Americans, I think, as the reason why Hispanics don't get ahead. But if Asians privately annoy us for being so family oriented, they are also stereotypically celebrated as the new "whiz kids" in school. Don't Asians go to college, after all, to honor their parents?

More important still is the technological and economic ascendancy of Asia, particularly Japan, on the American imagination. Americans are starting to wonder whether perhaps the family values of Asia put the United States at a disadvantage. The old platitude had it that ours is a vibrant, robust society for being a society of individuals. Now we look to Asia and see team effort paying off.

In this time of national homesickness, of nostalgia, for how we imagine America used to be, there are obvious dangers. We are going to start blaming each other for the loss. Since we are inclined, as Americans, to think of ourselves individually, we are disinclined to think of ourselves as creating one another or influencing one another.

But it is not the politician or any political debate about family values that has brought me here on a gray morning to my parents' house. It is some payment I owe to my youth and to my parents' youth. I imagine us sitting in the living room, amid my mother's sentimental doilies and the family photographs, trying to take the measure of the people we have turned out to be in America.

A San Francisco poet, when he was in the hospital and dying, called a priest to his bedside. The old poet wanted to make his peace with Mother Church. He wanted baptism. The priest asked why. "Because the Catholic Church has to accept me," said the poet. "Because I am a sinner."

Isn't willy-nilly inclusiveness the point, the only possible point to be derived from the concept of family? Curiously, both President Bush and Vice President Quayle got in trouble with their constituents recently for expressing a real family value. Both men said that they would try to dissuade a daughter or granddaughter from having an abortion. But, finally, they said they would support her decision, continue to love her, never abandon her.

There are families that do not accept. There are children who are forced to leave home because of abortions or homosexuality. There are family secrets that Papa never hears. Which is to say there are families that never learn the point of families.

But there she is at the window. My mother has seen me and she waves me in. Her face asks: Why am I sitting outside? (Have they, after all, known my secret for years and kept it, out of embarrassment, not knowing what to say?) Families accept, often by silence. My father opens the door to welcome me in.

STUDY AND DISCUSSION QUESTIONS

1. Why does Rodriguez's essay open with him sitting by himself in his car outside his parents' house? Why does it close with his father opening the door for him to come in?

2. Why does Rodriguez want to tell his parents that he is gay?

3. What is Rodriguez's criticism of politicians who preach "family values"? Why does this topic matter to him so much?

4. Rodriguez discusses what seem like two very different issues: American attitudes towards immigrants and towards gays. What connections is he making?

5. In his second paragraph, Rodriguez challenges Dan Quayle's assertion that homosexuality is a choice. What is the political significance of this question?

6. "It was always easier to be a tomboy in America than a sissy." Why might that be?

SUGGESTIONS FOR WRITING

1. Describe the conversation you imagine Rodriguez will have with his parents about his sexual orientation.

2. Write a letter to one or both of your parents (or to anyone else very close to you) announcing that you are gay or lesbian.

MARRIAGE AS A RESTRICTED CLUB

Lindsy Van Gelder

Lindsy Van Gelder was born in 1942 in Plainfield, New Jersey. She studied at Northwestern University and Sarah Lawrence College, and she has worked as a reporter and television news commentator. She has written Are You Two Together: A Gay and Lesbian Grand Tour of Europe *(1991) and, with Pamela Robin Brandt,* The Girls Next Door: Into the Heart of Lesbian America *(1996). The following essay appeared in* Ms. *magazine in 1984.*

Several years ago, I stopped going to weddings. In fact, I no longer celebrate the wedding anniversaries or engagements of friends, relatives, or anyone else, although I might wish them lifelong joy in their relationships. My explanation is that the next wedding I attend will be my own—to the woman I've loved and lived with for nearly six years.

Although I've been legally married to a man myself (and came close to marrying two others), I've come, in these last six years with Pamela, to see heterosexual marriage as very much a restricted club. (Nor is this likely to change in the near future, if one can judge by the recent clobbering of what was actually a rather tame proposal to recognize "domestic partnerships" in San Francisco.) Regardless of the *reason* people marry—whether to save on real estate taxes or qualify for married students housing or simply to express love—lesbians and gay men can't obtain the same results should they desire to do so. It seems apparent to me that few friends of Pamela's and mine would even join a club that excluded blacks, Jews, or women, much less assume that they could expect their black, Jewish, or female friends to toast their new status with champagne. But probably no other stand of principle we've ever made in our lives has been so misunderstood, or caused so much bad feeling on both sides.

Several people have reacted with surprise to our views, it never having occurred to them that gay people *can't* legally marry. (Why on earth did they think that none of us had bothered?) The most common reaction, however, is acute embarrassment, followed by a denial of our main point—that the about-to-be-wed person is embarking on a privileged status. (One friend of Pamela's insisted that lesbians are "lucky" not to have to agonize over whether or not to get married.) So wrapped in gauze is the institution of marriage, so ingrained the expectation that brides and grooms can enjoy the world's delighted approval, that it's hard for me not to feel put on the defensive for being so mean-spirited, eccentric, and/or politically rigid as to boycott such a happy event.

Another question we've fielded more than once (usually from our most radical friends, both gay and straight) is why we'd want to get married in the first place. In fact, I have mixed feelings about registering my personal life with the state, but—and this seems to me to be the essence of radical politics—I'd prefer to be the one making the choice. And while feminists in recent years have rightly focused on puncturing the Schlaflyite[1] myth of the legally protected homemaker, it's also true that marriage does confer some very real dollars-and-cents benefits. One example of inequity is our inability to file joint tax returns, although many couples, both gay and straight, go through periods when one partner in the relationship is unemployed or makes considerably less money than the other. At one time in our relationship, Pamela—who is a musician—was between bands and earning next to nothing. I was making a little over $37,000 a year as a newspaper reporter, a salary that put me in the 42 percent tax bracket—about $300 a week taken out of my paycheck. If we had been married, we could have filed a joint tax return and each paid taxes on half my salary, in the 25 or 30 percent bracket. The difference would have been nearly $100-a-week in our pockets.

Around the same time, Pamela suffered a months'-long illness which would have been covered by my health insurance if she were my spouse. We were luckier than many; we could afford it. But on top of the worry and expense involved (and despite the fact that intellectually we believe in the ideal of free medical care for everyone), we found it almost impossible to avoid internalizing a sense of personal failure—the knowledge that *because of who we are, we can't take care of each other.* I've heard of other gay people whose lovers were deported because they couldn't marry them and enable them to become citizens; still others who were barred from intensive-care units where their lovers lay stricken because they weren't "immediate family."

I would never begrudge a straight friend who got married to save a lover from deportation or staggering medical bills, but the truth is that I no longer sympathize with most of the less tangible justifications. This includes the oft-heard "for the sake of the children" argument, since (like many gay people, especially women) I *have* children, and I resent the implication that some families are more "legitimate" than others. (It's important to safeguard one's children's rights to their father's property, but a legal contract will do the same thing as marriage.)

But the single most painful and infuriating rationale for marriage, as far as I'm concerned, is the one that goes: "We wanted to stand up and show the world that we've made a *genuine* commitment." When one is gay, such

---

[1] Follower of Phyllis Schlafly, an antifeminist activist.

sentiments are labeled "flaunting." My lover and I almost never find our-selves in public settings outside the gay ghetto where we are (a) perceived to be a couple at all (people constantly ask us if we're sisters, although we look nothing like each other), and (b) valued as such. Usually we're forced to choose between being invisible and being despised. "Making a genuine com-mitment" in this milieu is like walking a highwire without a net—with most of the audience not even watching and a fair segment rooting for you to fall. A disproportionate number of gay couples do.

I think it's difficult for even my closest, most feminist straight women friends to empathize with the intensity of my desire to be recognized as Pamela's partner. (In fact, it may be harder for feminists to understand than for others; I know that when I was straight, I often resented being viewed as one half of a couple. My struggle was for an independent identity, not the cojoined one I now crave.) But we are simply not considered *authentic,* and the reminders are constant. Recently at a party, a man I'd known for years spied me across the room and came over to me, arms outstretched, big happy-to-see-you grin on his face. Pamela had a gig that night and wasn't at the party; my friend's wife was there but in another room, and I hadn't seen her yet. "How's M____?" I asked the man. "Oh, she's fine," he replied, continu-ing to smile pleasantly. "Are you and Pam still together?"

Our sex life itself is against the law in many states, of course, and like all lesbians and gay men, we are without many other rights, both large and small. (In Virginia, for instance, it's technically against the law for us to buy liquor.) But as a gay couple, we are also most likely to be labeled and dis-criminated against in those very settings that, for most heterosexual Ameri-cans, constitute the most relaxed and personal parts of life. Virtually every tiny public act of togetherness—from holding hands on the street to renting a hotel room to dancing—requires us constantly to risk humiliation (I think, for example, of the two California women who were recently thrown out of a restaurant that had special romantic tables for couples), sexual harassment (it's astonishing how many men can't resist coming on to a lesbian couple), and even physical assault. A great deal of energy goes into just expecting pos-sible trouble. It's a process which, after six years, has become second nature for me—but occasionally, when I'm in Provincetown or someplace else with a large lesbian population, I experience the *absence* of it as a feeling of virtual weightlessness.

What does all this have to do with my friends' weddings? Obviously, I can't expect my friends to live my life. But I do think that lines are being drawn in this "profamily" Reagan era, and I have no choice about what side I'm placed on. My straight friends do, and at the very least, I expect them to acknowledge that. I certainly expect them to understand why I don't want to be among the rice-throwers and well-wishers at their weddings; beyond that, I would hope that they would commit themselves to fighting for my rights—preferably in personally visible ways, like marching in gay pride parades. But I also wish they wouldn't get married, period. And if that sounds hard-nosed, I hope I'm only proving my point—that not being able to marry isn't a minor issue.

Not that my life would likely be changed as the result of any individual straight person's symbolic refusal to marry. (Nor, for that matter, do all gay couples want to be wed.) But it's a political reality that heterosexual live-together couples are among our best tactical allies. The movement to repeal state sodomy laws has profited from the desire of straight people to keep the government out of *their* bedrooms. Similarly, it was a heterosexual New York woman who went to court several years ago to fight her landlord's demand that she either marry her live-in boyfriend or face eviction for violating a lease clause prohibiting "unrelated" tenants—and whose struggle led to the recent passage of a state rent law that had ramifications for thousands of gay couples, including Pamela and me.

The right wing has seized on "homosexual marriage" as its bottom-line scare phrase in much the same way that "Would you want your sister to marry one?" was brandished twenty-five years ago. *They* see marriage as their turf. And so when I see feminists crossing into that territory of respectability and "sinlessness," I feel my buffer zone slipping away. I feel as though my friends are taking off their armbands, leaving me exposed.

STUDY AND DISCUSSION QUESTIONS

1. What material benefits of marriage are lesbians and gays denied? What nonmaterial ones?

2. Why are Van Gelder and Pamela so frequently asked if they are sisters?

3. Why is Van Gelder so annoyed that an old friend asked if she and Pamela were still together?

4. Explain the essay's last sentence.

SUGGESTIONS FOR WRITING

1. Imagine that you are lesbian or gay (perhaps you are). Write a letter accepting or rejecting a wedding invitation from a very close heterosexual friend.

2. Imagine that you are heterosexual (perhaps you are) and that a very close lesbian or gay friend has written to you that she or he will not be attending your wedding for reasons similar to Van Gelder's. Write a reply.

RACE AND ETHNICITY

What is race? We tend to think of it as something very fundamental about a person, rooted in physical characteristics, and genetically determined. From birth, it would seem, each of us is a member of one (usually it's one) of three groups, which have been carefully mapped out by biologists and anthropologists, who have endlessly studied humanity's origins and development. But why is someone with three white grandparents and one black grandparent considered black in the United States? If race is simply a biological category, surely such a person is more "white" than "black." Or why, say, were Italian and Jewish immigrants, today called "white ethnics," once considered members of other races? Or why are people as different looking as Swedes and Greeks, for example, both labeled white? Clearly, racial categorization is messier than we tend to think.

In fact, many scientists today question the notion of distinct, separate human races altogether. They point out that there's more genetic variety within each "race" than, on average, between "races"; that human diversity is too complex and peoples too intermingled to sort it all into the three broad categories of Asian, Caucasian, and Negro; and that, while physical characteristics such as skin color, nose size, and body shape obviously vary, they do not always cluster together in the neat packages earlier racial theorists thought they found.

Yet, obviously, as the readings in this section illustrate, race does matter. However problematic it may be as a scientific concept, race certainly plays an essential *social* role, central to human history if not to human biology.

(And, therefore, it's really not so different from that complicated categorization by geographical origin, religion, language, and culture that we tend to call "ethnicity.") If Americans call the person with one black and three white grandparents black, perhaps we ought to look at race as a political category. Efforts to divide people neatly into black and white, to call these groups two distinct races when clearly there is a continuum, and (as is often done) to exaggerate the differences between blacks and whites—perhaps we should ask whether all this has more to do with justifying discrimination than with understanding nature. However shaky the scientific foundations of these racial categories, they have serious repercussions. Race matters because racism continues.

Why are black people (however defined) significantly poorer on average than white people in the United States? One possible answer is that African Americans have suffered and continue to suffer discrimination, even oppression, that this inequality represents an injustice. For many, a more comforting answer is that black people are simply different, inferior in some way to people of other races, that their condition is their own fault. The first answer demands that we do something, demands change; the second tells us that the way things are is just fine, or at least inevitable. In "Racist Arguments and IQ," Stephen Jay Gould analyzes the work of Arthur Jensen, who, in the late 1960s, claimed that IQ test scores proved American blacks less intelligent than whites. Gould methodically disassembles and debunks Jensen's case, demonstrating its flimsiness. Yet twenty-five years after Jensen, similar claims arose and were given wide and serious attention, with the publication of *The Bell Curve*, by Richard J. Herrnstein and Charles Murray. Why do such theories refuse to die? Gould considers race-based IQ comparisons to be of negligible scientific interest and believes that a truer measure of intelligence might just as likely reveal blacks to be superior. But none of these comparisons should matter, he insists, for a decent society would offer adequate opportunity for "the realization of valued potential in all individuals."

One effort to begin to do that has been affirmative action. In "The Great White Myth," Anna Quindlen defends this attempt to begin to redress past and present discrimination against people of color and against women from claims that it represents "the systematic oppression of white men." In a country whose income inequality surpasses that of most other advanced industrial nations, it is not surprising that many feel insecure about their own position and find the beneficiaries of affirmative action, especially if of another "race," convenient scapegoats. But why can't a nation as rich as the United States provide the means for developing that "valued potential in all individuals"?

What it means to be an individual while also a member of a group is a tough question for Henry Louis Gates, Jr. The preface to his memoir, *Colored*

People, offers us a glimpse into his struggles with racial identity, his complex connection to a "race" of people that he loves dearly and that the wider society does not. Gates's experiences suggest that in American society black people belong to a race in a way that white people do not. Jeffrey Dahmer, for example, is usually regarded as a mass murderer, not as a *white* mass murderer. So why does Gates, eminent professor and literary critic, feel "implicated" by the criminal behavior of boxer Mike Tyson? How come he so often feels reduced to his race? "I rebel at the notion," he writes, ". . . that race must be the most important thing about me."

Race seems at first to be just about the least important thing about Barbara Ehrenreich, author of "Cultural Baggage." Not even very "ethnic"— her Scottish, English, and Irish ancestry makes her practically a WASP— she answers "none" when asked her ethnic background. In a society so obsessed with race and ethnicity, she feels rootless. Her humorous essay describes her search for a meaningful heritage and how she finally finds one she can cherish in her family's long history of atheism, skepticism, and tolerance. Ehrenreich shares some of Gates's discomfort with the imposition of identity by others, but, being white, she has much greater freedom to create her own identity.

Amy Tan, author of "Mother Tongue," also possesses ways of shaping her own identity. As a novelist, she chooses to embrace her Chinese heritage; the "different Englishes" she has learned contribute richly to her creativity. But things have been quite different for her immigrant mother, whose Chinese-inflected English can be a disability. Tan sees her mother's speech as "vivid, direct, full of observation and imagery," but native speakers of English—people in banks, stores, hospitals; people with power over her mother's life—hear only "broken English." Growing up, Tan observed the reactions to her mother's English, felt ashamed of her, and assumed, with the others, that her thinking was as "broken" as her speech. Tan's mother once seemed like a stereotype even to her own daughter.

The power and tenacity of racial and ethnic stereotypes never cease to anger Puerto Rican writer Judith Ortiz Cofer. All too frequently, her ethnicity, to borrow Gates's phrase, appears to be "the most important thing" about her; in fact, it's often the only thing people see. "The Myth of the Latina Woman: I Just Met a Girl Named María" relates a number of unnerving incidents: a drunken stranger on a bus spots Cofer and begins singing "María" from *West Side Story* in her face, a man in a hotel screams an obscene version of the song "La Bamba" at her, and so on. The accumulation of such affronts, if nothing else, is simply exhausting. Yet Cofer, as she puts it, is "one of the lucky ones." The stereotype of the Latina as "Hot Tamale" or "good domestic" hits those who lack Cofer's education and position far harder, and seriously hurts their chances for getting ahead.

White ethnics can also find themselves straitjacketed by the attitudes of others. In "Luigi, Tony, and the Family," Michael Parenti analyzes the stereotypes of Italian Americans and the media images that help keep those stereotypes alive. As we watch television and go to the movies, it's hard to remember that not every Italian is a mobster, greaser, or sauce-stirring mama. Parenti is particularly distressed when he finds Italian Americans themselves embracing these stereotypes—their cars sporting "Mafia Staff Car, Keepa You Hands Off" bumper stickers—as if, in our media-obsessed culture, recognition of *any* kind should be welcomed. To Parenti, such cartoon-like images play an ideological role, distracting from the real problems faced by "working-class ethnics": "the demoralizing hardships of underemployment, layoffs, low wages, high taxes, job-connected disabilities, and staggering living costs."

The stereotyped imagery of one group has even been incorporated into a national holiday, Thanksgiving. In order for American culture to celebrate what was, in effect, a major step along the road to the virtual extermination of Native Americans, it's had to turn them into our friends, guests at the dinner table who, as Michael Dorris writes, "did not question the enforced exchange of their territories for a piece of pie." In "For Indians, No Thanksgiving," Dorris argues that the myth and pageantry of this cozy family holiday represent a national denial not only of the history of brutal racism against Native Americans but of the desperate poverty of their few remaining descendants.

Acknowledgement of past injustices may not guarantee a better future, but certainly the kind of denial that Dorris condemns can only make things worse. Is it possible to recognize the full damage that has been created out of our racial and ethnic differences and still remain hopeful? Writing in the bicentennial year of 1976, Toni Morrison tried to envision America's future. The title of her essay, "A Slow Walk of Trees (as Grandmother Would Say), Hopeless (as Grandfather Would Say)," suggests her uncertainty about the potential for progress in relations between blacks and whites. With dismay she watched violent racial conflict over busing in Boston, which she viewed as yet another "pitched battle between the children of slaves and the children of immigrants." As we look at today's events, whatever they may be, we may find it as hard as Morrison did to imagine a better future. But if we can remember that the differences among us are rooted not in biology but in history, not in nature but in the society we ourselves help to shape, then perhaps some day we will honestly be able to celebrate our diversity.

RACIST ARGUMENTS AND IQ

Stephen Jay Gould

Stephen Jay Gould (b. 1941) teaches geology, zoology, and paleon-
tology at Harvard University. Aside from his technical work in evo-
lutionary theory, Gould is known for his popular science writing,
much of it collected in such volumes as Ever Since Darwin *(1977),*
where the following appeared, The Panda's Thumb *(1980),* Hen's
Teeth and Horse's Toes *(1983),* Bully for Brontosaurus *(1991),*
and Dinosaur in a Haystack *(1996).*

Louis Agassiz, the greatest biologist of mid-nineteenth-century America, argued that God had created blacks and whites as separate species. The de-
fenders of slavery took much comfort from this assertion, for biblical
prescriptions of charity and equality did not have to extend across a species
boundary. What could an abolitionist say? Science had shone its cold and dispassionate light upon the subject; Christian hope and sentimentality could
not refute it.

Similar arguments, carrying the apparent sanction of science, have been
continually invoked in attempts to equate egalitarianism with sentimental
hope and emotional blindness. People who are unaware of this historical pattern tend to accept each recurrence at face value: that is, they assume that
each statement arises from the "data" actually presented, rather than from
the social conditions that truly inspire it.

The racist arguments of the nineteenth century were based primarily on
craniometry, the measurement of human skulls. Today, these contentions
stand totally discredited. What craniometry was to the nineteenth century, intelligence testing has been to the twentieth. The victory of the eugenics movement in the Immigration Restriction Act of 1924 signaled its first unfortunate
effect—for the severe restrictions upon non-Europeans and upon southern
and eastern Europeans gained much support from results of the first extensive and uniform application of intelligence tests in America—the Army
Mental Tests of World War I. These tests were engineered and administered
by psychologist Robert M. Yerkes, who concluded that "education alone will
not place the negro *[sic]* race on a par with its Caucasian competitors." It is
now clear that Yerkes and his colleagues knew no way to separate genetic

from environmental components in postulating causes for different performances on the tests.

The latest episode of this recurring drama began in 1969, when Arthur Jensen published an article entitled, "How Much Can We Boost IQ and Scholastic Achievement?" in the *Harvard Educational Review*. Again, the claim went forward that new and uncomfortable information had come to light, and that science had to speak the "truth" even if it refuted some cherished notions of a liberal philosophy. But again, I shall argue, Jensen had no new data; and what he did present was flawed beyond repair by inconsistencies and illogical claims.

Jensen assumes that IQ tests adequately measure something we may call "intelligence." He then attempts to tease apart the genetic and environmental factors causing differences in performance. He does this primarily by relying upon the one natural experiment we possess: identical twins reared apart—for differences in IQ between genetically identical people can only be environmental. The average difference in IQ for identical twins is less than the difference for two unrelated individuals raised in similarly varied environments. From the data on twins, Jensen obtains an estimate of environmental influence. He concludes that IQ has a heritability of about 0.8 (or 80 percent) *within* the population of American and European whites. The average difference between American whites and blacks is 15 IQ points (one standard deviation). He asserts that this difference is too large to attribute to environment, given the high heritability of IQ. Lest anyone think that Jensen writes in the tradition of abstract scholarship, I merely quote the first line of his famous work: "Compensatory education has been tried, and it apparently has failed."

I believe that this argument can be refuted in a "hierarchical" fashion—that is, we can discredit it at one level and then show that it fails at a more inclusive level even if we allow Jensen's argument for the first two levels:

Level 1: The equation of IQ with intelligence. Who knows what IQ measures? It is a good predictor of "success" in school, but is such success a result of intelligence, apple polishing, or the assimilation of values that the leaders of society prefer? Some psychologists get around this argument by defining intelligence operationally as the scores attained on "intelligence" tests. A neat trick. But at this point, the technical definition of intelligence has strayed so far from the vernacular that we can no longer define the issue. But let me allow (although I don't believe it), for the sake of argument, that IQ measures some meaningful aspect of intelligence in its vernacular sense.

Level 2: The heritability of IQ. Here again, we encounter a confusion between vernacular and technical meanings of the same word. "Inherited," to a layman, means "fixed," "inexorable," or "unchangeable." To a geneticist, "inherited" refers to an estimate of similarity between related individuals based on genes held in common. It carries no implications of inevitability or of immutable entities beyond the reach of environmental influence. Eyeglasses correct a variety of inherited problems in vision; insulin can check diabetes.

Jensen insists that IQ is 80 percent heritable. Princeton psychologist Leon J. Kamin has done the dog-work of meticulously checking through details of the twin studies that form the basis of this estimate. He has found an astonishing number of inconsistencies and downright inaccuracies. For example, the late Sir Cyril Burt, who generated the largest body of data on identical twins reared apart, pursued his studies of intelligence for more than forty years. Although he increased his sample sizes in a variety of "improved" versions, some of his correlation coefficients remain unchanged to the third decimal place—a statistically impossible situation.[1] IQ depends in part upon sex and age; and other studies did not standardize properly for them. An improper correction may produce higher values between twins not because they hold genes for intelligence in common, but simply because they share the same sex and age. The data are so flawed that no valid estimate for the heritability of IQ can be drawn at all. But let me assume (although no data support it), for the sake of argument, that the heritability of IQ is as high as 0.8.

Level 3: The confusion of within- and between-group variation. Jensen draws a causal connection between his two major assertions—that the within-group heritability of IQ is 0.8 for American whites, and that the mean difference in IQ between American blacks and whites is 15 points. He assumes that the black "deficit" is largely genetic in origin because IQ is so highly heritable. This is a *non sequitur* of the worst possible kind—for there is no necessary relationship between heritability within a group and differences in mean values of two separate groups.

A simple example will suffice to illustrate this flaw in Jensen's argument. Height has a much higher heritability within groups than anyone has ever claimed for IQ. Suppose that height has a mean value of five feet two inches and a heritability of 0.9 (a realistic value) within a group of nutritionally deprived Indian farmers. High heritability simply means that short farmers will tend to have short offspring, and tall farmers tall offspring. It says nothing whatever against the possibility that proper nutrition could raise the mean height to six feet (taller than average white Americans). It only means that, in this improved status, farmers shorter than average (they may now be five feet ten inches) would still tend to have shorter than average children.

---

[1] I wrote this essay in 1974. Since then, the case against Sir Cyril has progressed from an inference of carelessness to a spectacular (and well-founded) suspicion of fraud. Reporters for the London *Times* have discovered, for example, that Sir Cyril's coauthors (for the infamous twin studies) apparently did not exist outside his imagination. In the light of Kamin's discoveries, one must suspect that the data have an equal claim to reality. [Author's note]

I do not claim that intelligence, however defined, has no genetic basis—I regard it as trivially true, uninteresting, and unimportant that it does. The expression of any trait represents a complex interaction of heredity and environment. Our job is simply to provide the best environmental situation for the realization of valued potential in all individuals. I merely point out that a specific claim purporting to demonstrate a mean genetic deficiency in the intelligence of American blacks rests upon no new facts whatever and can cite no valid data in its support. It is just as likely that blacks have a genetic advantage over whites. And, either way, it doesn't matter a damn. An individual can't be judged by his group mean.

If current biological determinism in the study of human intelligence rests upon no new facts (actually, no facts at all), then why has it become so popular of late? The answer must be social and political. The 1960s were good years for liberalism; a fair amount of money was spent on poverty programs and relatively little happened. Enter new leaders and new priorities. Why didn't the earlier programs work? Two possibilities are open: (1) we didn't spend enough money, we didn't make sufficiently creative efforts, or (and this makes any established leader jittery) we cannot solve these problems without a fundamental social and economic transformation of society; or (2) the programs failed because their recipients are inherently what they are—blaming the victims. Now, which alternative will be chosen by men in power in an age of retrenchment?

I have shown, I hope, that biological determinism is not simply an amusing matter for clever cocktail party comments about the human animal. It is a general notion with important philosophical implications and major political consequences. As John Stuart Mill wrote, in a statement that should be the motto of the opposition: "Of all the vulgar modes of escaping from the consideration of the effect of social and moral influences upon the human mind, the most vulgar is that of attributing the diversities of conduct and character to inherent natural differences."

STUDY AND DISCUSSION QUESTIONS

1. Why does Gould bother to tell us that Louis Agassiz is "the greatest biologist of mid-nineteenth century America"?

2. In his second paragraph, Gould mentions "egalitarianism." Define this concept and explain how it relates to his arguments.

3. What is Gould's purpose in tracing racial theories of IQ back to nineteenth-century craniometry?

4. Explain Gould's critique of "the equation of IQ with intelligence."

5. How does Gould dispute Jensen's assertion of "the heritability of IQ."

6. What does Gould mean by "the confusion of within- and between-group variation"?

7. Explain in detail Gould's use of the example of "nutritionally deprived Indian farmers"?

8. What is Gould's "social and political" explanation for the interest in racial theories of intelligence?

SUGGESTIONS FOR WRITING

1. Read about the eugenics movement, which Gould mentions in his third paragraph. How does its history relate to Gould's essay?

2. Pick a group in our society other than African Americans whose lower (or higher) social and economic status you've heard attributed to inborn differences. How convinced are you?

3. Suppose it were proved (even to Gould's satisfaction) that left-handed people are, on average, less intelligent than right-handers. What use, in your view, should society make of this finding?

THE GREAT WHITE MYTH

Anna Quindlen

Anna Quindlen (b. 1953) worked as a reporter for the New York Post *and the* New York Times *before becoming a regular columnist at the* Times. *Her columns, which won her a Pulitzer Prize in 1992, are collected in* Living Out Loud *(1988) and* Thinking Out Loud *(1993), where the following appeared. Quindlen has also written the novels* Object Lessons *(1991) and* One True Thing *(1994).*

In a college classroom a young white man rises and asks about the future. What, he wants to know, can it possibly hold for him when most of the jobs, most of the good positions, most of the spots in professional schools are being given to women and, most especially, to blacks?

The temptation to be short, sarcastic, incredulous in reply is powerful. But you have to remember that kids learn their lessons from adults. That's what the mother of two black children who were sprayed with white paint in the Bronx said last week about the assailants, teenagers who called her son and daughter "nigger" and vowed they would turn them white. "Can you imagine what they are being taught at home?" she asked.

A nation based on laws, we like to believe that when they are changed, attitudes will change along with them. This is naive. America continues to be a country whose people are obsessed with maintaining some spurious pecking order. At the bottom are African-Americans, taught at age twelve and fourteen through the utter humiliation of having their faces cleaned with paint thinner that there are those who think that even becoming white from a bottle is better than not being white at all.

Each generation finds its own reasons to hate. The worried young white men I've met on college campuses in the last year have internalized the newest myth of American race relations, and it has made them bitter. It is called affirmative action, a.k.a. the systematic oppression of white men. All good things in life, they've learned, from college admission to executive position, are being given to black citizens. The verb is ubiquitous: given.

Never mind that you can walk through the offices of almost any big company and see a sea of white faces. Never mind that with all that has been written about preferential treatment for minority law students, only about 7,500 of the 127,000 students enrolled in law school last year were African-American. Never mind that only 3 percent of the doctors in this country are black.

Never mind that in the good old days preferential treatment was routinely given to brothers and sons of workers in certain lines of work. Perceptions of programs to educate and hire more black citizens as, in part, an antidote to decades of systematic exclusion have been inflated to enormous proportions in the public mind. Like hot-air balloons, they fill up the blue sky of the American landscape with the gaudy stripes of hyperbole. Listen and you will believe that the construction sites, the precinct houses, the investment banks are filled with African-Americans.

Unless you actually visit them.

The opponents of affirmative action programs say they are opposing the rank unfairness of preferential treatment. But there was no great hue and cry when colleges were candid about wanting to have geographic diversity, perhaps giving the kid from Montana an edge. There has been no national outcry when legacy applicants whose transcripts were supplemented by Dad's alumnus status—and cash contributions to the college—were admitted over more qualified comers. We somehow discovered that life was not fair only when the beneficiaries happened to be black.

And so the chasm widens. The old myth was the black American incapable of prosperity. It was common knowledge that welfare was purely a benefits program for blacks; it was common knowledge although it was false.

The percentage of whites on public assistance is almost identical with the percentage of blacks.

The new myth is that the world is full of black Americans prospering unfairly at white expense, and anecdotal evidence abounds. The stories about the incompetent black co-worker always leave out two things: the incompetent white co-workers and the talented black ones. They also leave out the tendency of so many managers to hire those who seem most like themselves when young.

"It seems like if you're a white male you don't have a chance," said another young man on a campus where a scant 5 percent of his classmates were black. What the kid really means is that he no longer has the edge, that the rules of a system that may have served his father well have changed. It is one of those good-old-days constructs to believe it was a system based purely on merit, but we know that's not true. It is a system that once favored him, and others like him. Now sometimes—just sometimes—it favors someone different.

STUDY AND DISCUSSION QUESTIONS

1. How do Quindlen's first and second paragraphs relate to each other? What is her point in these paragraphs?

2. Why does Quindlen emphasize the word "given" in her fourth paragraph?

3. What is Quindlen's main approach in challenging "the newest myth of American race relations"?

4. Why, according to Quindlen, is affirmative action necessary?

5. Quindlen writes that "only 3 percent of the doctors in this country are black." What percentage of the American population as a whole is black? What are some of the possible consequences of this disparity?

6. Why does Quindlen focus on white men and not white women?

SUGGESTIONS FOR WRITING

1. Quindlen writes that Americans are "obsessed with maintaining some spurious pecking order." Do you agree? If so, what signs do you see of this?

2. The author of "The Great White Myth" is herself white. Does this make her arguments more persuasive or less persuasive to you? What are the possible implications of your answer?

FROM *COLORED PEOPLE*

Henry Louis Gates, Jr.

Born in 1950 in Keyser, West Virginia, Henry Louis Gates, Jr. was educated at Yale University and at Cambridge, and is now Chair of the Afro-American Studies Department at Harvard. He is the editor of numerous books and series, including The Schomburg Library of Nineteenth-Century Black Women Writers *and, with Nellie Y. McKay,* The Norton Anthology of African American Literature *(1997). Among his other works are* The Signifying Monkey: Towards a Theory of Afro-American Literary Criticism *(1988),* Loose Canons: Notes on the Culture Wars *(1992),* Colored People: A Memoir *(1994), the preface to which appears below, and* Thirteen Ways of Looking at a Black Man *(1997).*

Dear Maggie and Liza:

I have written to you because a world into which I was born, a world that nurtured and sustained me, has mysteriously disappeared. My darkest fear is that Piedmont, West Virginia, will cease to exist, if some executives on Park Avenue decide that it is more profitable to build a completely new paper mill elsewhere than to overhaul one a century old. Then they would close it, just as they did in Cumberland with Celanese, and Pittsburgh Plate Glass, and the Kelly-Springfield Tire Company. The town will die, but our people will not move. They will not *be* moved. Because for them, Piedmont—snuggled between the Allegheny Mountains and the Potomac River Valley—is life itself.

I have written to you because of the day when we were driving home and you asked your mother and me just exactly what the civil rights movement had been all about and I pointed to a motel on Route 2 and said that at one time I could not have stayed there. Your mother could have stayed there, but your mother couldn't have stayed there with me. And you kids looked at us like we were telling you the biggest lie you had ever heard. So I thought about writing to you.

I have written for another reason, as well. I remember that once we were walking in Washington, D.C., heading for the National Zoo, and you asked me if I had known the man to whom I had just spoken. I said no. And, Liza, you volunteered that you found it embarrassing that I would speak to a complete stranger on the street. It called to mind a trip I'd made to Pittsburgh with my father. On the way from his friend Mr. Ozzie Washington's sister's house, I heard Daddy speak to a colored man, then saw him tip his hat to the man's wife. (Daddy liked nice hats: Caterpillar hats for work, Dobbs hats[1] for Sunday.) It's just something that you do, he said, when I asked him if he had known those people and why had he spoken to them.

Last summer, I sat at a sidewalk café in Italy, and three or four "black" Italians walked casually by, as well as a dozen or more blacker Africans. Each spoke to me; rather, each nodded his head slightly or acknowledged me by a glance, ever so subtly. When I was growing up, we always did this with each other, passing boats in a sea of white folk.

Yet there were certain Negroes who would avoid acknowledging you in this way in an integrated setting, especially if the two of you were the ones doing the integrating. Don't go over there with those white people if all you're going to do is Jim Crow yourselves—Daddy must have said that to me a thousand times. And by that I think he meant we shouldn't *cling* to each other out of habit or fear, or use protective coloration to evade the risks of living like any other human being, or use clannishness as a cop-out for exploring ourselves and possibly making new selves, forged in the crucible of integration. Your black ass, he'd laugh, is integrated already.

But there are other reasons that people distrust the reflex—the nod, the glance, the murmured greeting.

One reason is a resentment at being lumped together with thirty million African Americans whom you don't know and most of whom you will never know. Completely by the accident of racism, we have been bound together with people with whom we may or may not have something in common, just because we are "black." Thirty million Americans are black, and thirty million is a lot of people. One day you wonder: What do the misdeeds of a Mike Tyson[2] have to do with me? So why do I feel implicated? And how can I not feel racial recrimination when I can feel racial pride?

Then, too, there were Negroes who were embarrassed about *being* Negroes, who didn't want to be bothered with race and with other black people. One of the more painful things about being colored was being colored in public around other colored people, who were embarrassed to be colored and embarrassed that we *both* were colored and in public together. As if to say: "Negro, will you *pul-lease* disappear so that I can get my own white people?" As if to say: "I'm not a Negro like other Negroes." As if to say: "I am a human being—let me be!"

---

[1] Caterpillar, manufacturer of construction machinery; Dobbs, manufacturer of dress hats.
[2] Heavyweight boxing champion convicted of rape.

For much of my adolescence and adulthood, I thought of these people as having betrayed the race. I used to walk up to them and call them *Brother* or *Sister,* loud and with a sardonic edge, when they looked like they were trying to "escape." When I went off to college, I would make the "conversion" of errant classmates a serious project, a political commitment.

I used to reserve my special scorn for those Negroes who were always being embarrassed by someone else in the race. Someone too dark, someone too "loud," someone too "wrong." Someone who dared to wear red in public. Loud and wrong: we used to say that about each other. Nigger is loud and wrong. "Loud" carried a triple meaning: speaking too loudly, dressing too loudly, and just *being* too loudly.

I do know that, when I was a boy, many Negroes would have been the first to censure other Negroes once they were admitted into all-white neighborhoods or schools or clubs. "An embarrassment to the race"—phrases of that sort were bandied about. Accordingly, many of us in our generation engaged in strange antics to flout those strictures. Like eating watermelon in public, eating it loudly and merrily, and spitting the seeds into the middle of the street, red juice running down the sides of our cheeks, collecting under our chins. Or taking the greatest pride in the Royal Kink.[3] Uncle Harry used to say he didn't *like* watermelon, which I knew was a lie because I saw him wolf down slices when I was a little kid, before he went off to seminary at Boston University. But he came around, just like he came around to painting God and Jesus black, and all the seraphim and the cherubim, too. And I, from another direction, have gradually come around, also, and stopped trying to tell other Negroes how to be black.

Do you remember when your mother and I woke you up early on a Sunday morning, just to watch Nelson Mandela walk out of prison, and how it took a couple of hours for him to emerge, and how you both wanted to go back to bed and, then, to watch cartoons? And how we began to worry that something bad had happened to him on the way out, because the delay was so long? And when he finally walked out of that prison, how we were so excited and teary-eyed at Mandela's nobility, his princeliness, his straight back and unbowed head? I think I felt that there walked the Negro, as Pop might have said; there walked the whole of the African people, as regal as any king. And that feeling I had, that gooseflesh sense of identity that I felt at seeing Nelson Mandela, listening to Mahalia Jackson sing, watching Muhammad Ali fight, or hearing Martin Luther King speak, is part of what I mean by being colored. I realize the sentiment may not be logical, but I want to have my cake and eat it, too. Which is why I still nod or speak to black people on the

---

[3] Probably a reference to kinky hair, worn proudly.

streets and why it felt so good to be acknowledged by the Afro-Italians who passed my table at the café in Milan.

I want to be able to take special pride in a Jessye Norman aria, a Muhammad Ali shuffle, a Michael Jordan slam dunk, a Spike Lee movie, a Thurgood Marshall opinion, a Toni Morrison novel, James Brown's Camel Walk. Above all, I enjoy the unselfconscious moments of a shared cultural intimacy, whatever form they take, when no one else is watching, when no white people are around. Like Joe Louis's fights, which my father still talks about as part of the fixed repertoire of stories that texture our lives. You've seen his eyes shining as he describes how Louis hit Max Schmeling so many times and so hard, and how some reporter asked him, after the fight: "Joe, what would you have done if that last punch hadn't knocked Schmeling out?" And how ole Joe responded, without missing a beat: "I'da run around behind him to see what was holdin' him up!"

Even so, I rebel at the notion that I can't be part of other groups, that I can't construct identities through elective affinity, that race must be the most important thing about me. Is that what I want on my gravestone: Here lies an African American? So I'm divided. I want to be black, to know black, to luxuriate in whatever I might be calling blackness at any particular time—but to do so in order to come out the other side, to experience a humanity that is neither colorless nor reducible to color. Bach *and* James Brown. Sushi *and* fried catfish. Part of me admires those people who can say with a straight face that they have transcended any attachment to a particular community or group . . . but I always want to run around behind them to see what holds them up.

I am not Everynegro. I am not native to the great black metropolises: New York, Chicago, or Los Angeles, say. Nor can I claim to be a "citizen of the world." I am from and of a time and a place—Piedmont, West Virginia—and that's a world apart, a world of difference. So this is not a story of a race but a story of a village, a family, and its friends. And of a sort of segregated peace. What hurt me most about the glorious black awakening of the late sixties and early seventies is that we lost our sense of humor. Many of us thought that enlightened politics excluded it.

In your lifetimes, I suspect, you will go from being African Americans, to "people of color," to being, once again, "colored people." (The linguistic trend toward condensation is strong.) I don't mind any of the names myself. But I have to confess that I like "colored" best, maybe because when I hear the word, I hear it in my mother's voice and in the sepia tones of my childhood. As artlessly and honestly as I can, I have tried to evoke a colored world of the fifties, a Negro world of the early sixties, and the advent of a black world of the later sixties, from the point of view of the boy I was. When you are old enough to read what follows, I hope that it brings you even a small measure of understanding, at long last, of why we see the world with such different eyes . . . and why that is for me a source both of gladness and of regret. And I hope you'll understand why I continue to speak to colored people I pass on the streets.

Love,
Daddy

STUDY AND DISCUSSION QUESTIONS

1. Starting in his second paragraph, Gates offers several anecdotes in an effort to explain why he is writing. What answer do they suggest?

2. "What do the misdeeds of a Mike Tyson have to do with me?" Gates asks rhetorically. "So why do I feel implicated?" he continues. Why does he?

3. Explain exactly what Gates is saying in his eighth paragraph, the one that begins, "Then, too . . . ."

4. What does Gates mean when he says, "I want to have my cake and eat it, too"?

5. Why does Joe Louis still mean so much to Gates's father?

6. "I rebel at the notion . . . that race must be the most important thing about me." What does Gates mean? Is race the most important thing about a white person?

7. At the end of his preface, Gates writes to his children: "we see the world with such different eyes . . . [and] that is for me a source both of gladness and of regret." Explain.

SUGGESTIONS FOR WRITING

1. Whatever your race or ethnicity, explore to what extent and in what ways you view individual African Americans as members of a group.

2. Trace the various terms ("colored," "black," etc.) that Gates uses to name his people. What is he doing?

CULTURAL BAGGAGE

Barbara Ehrenreich

Barbara Ehrenreich (b. 1941) has a PhD in biology and was an early critic of the health care system in the United States. A wide-ranging social critic, she has also written about economic globalism, welfare, sexism, and war and she is active in Democratic Socialists of America. Among her books are For Her Own Good: One Hundred Fifty Years of the Experts' Advice to Women *(1978),* The Hearts of Men: American Dreams and the Flight from Commitment *(1983),* Fear of Falling: The Inner Life of the Middle Class *(1989),* Blood Rites: Origins and History of the Passion of War *(1997), and several essay collections. The following originally appeared in the* New York Times *in 1992.*

An acquaintance was telling me about the joys of rediscovering her ethnic and religious heritage. "I know exactly what my ancestors were doing 2,000 years ago," she said, eyes gleaming with enthusiasm, "and I can do the same things now." Then she leaned forward and inquired politely, "And what is your ethnic background, if I may ask?"

"None," I said, that being the first word in line to get out of my mouth. Well, not "none," I backtracked. Scottish, English, Irish—that was something, I supposed. Too much Irish to qualify as a WASP; too much of the hated English to warrant a "Kiss Me, I'm Irish" button; plus there are a number of dead ends in the family tree due to adoptions, missing records, failing memories and the like. I was blushing by this time. Did "none" mean I was rejecting my heritage out of Anglo-Celtic self-hate? Or was I revealing a hidden ethnic chauvinism in which the Britannically derived serve as a kind of neutral standard compared with the ethnic "others"?

Throughout the 1960s and '70s I watched one group after another—African Americans, Latinos, Native Americans—stand up and proudly reclaim their roots while I just sank back ever deeper into my seat. All this excitement over ethnicity stemmed, I uneasily sensed, from a past in which their ancestors had been trampled upon by my ancestors, or at least by people who looked very much like them. In addition, it had begun to seem almost un-American not to have some sort of hyphen at hand, linking one to more venerable times and locales.

But the truth is, I was raised with none. We'd eaten ethnic foods in my childhood home, but these were all borrowed, like the pasties, or Cornish meat pies, my father had picked up from his fellow miners in Butte, Montana. If my mother had one rule, it was militant ecumenism in all matters of food and experience. "Try new things," she would say, meaning anything from sweet-breads to clams, with an emphasis on the "new."

As a child, I briefly nourished a craving for tradition and roots. I immersed myself in the works of Sir Walter Scott. I pretended to believe that the bagpipe was a musical instrument. I was fascinated to learn from a grandmother that we were descended from certain Highland clans and longed for a pleated skirt in one of their distinctive tartans.

But in *Ivanhoe*, it was the dark-eyed "Jewess" Rebecca I identified with, not the flaxen-haired bimbo Rowena. As for clans: Why not call them tribes—those bands of half-clad peasants and warriors whose idea of cuisine was stuffed sheep gut washed down with whisky? And then there was the sting of Disraeli's remark—which I came across in my early teens—to the effect that his ancestors had been leading orderly, literate lives when my ancestors were still rampaging through the Highlands daubing themselves with blue paint.

Motherhood put the screws on me, ethnicity-wise. I had hoped that by marrying a man of Eastern European Jewish ancestry I would acquire for my descendants the ethnic genes that my own forebears so sadly lacked. At one point I even subjected the children to a seder of my own design, including a little talk about the flight from Egypt and its relevance to modern social issues. But the kids insisted on buttering their matzos and snickering through my talk. "Give me a break, Mom," the older one said. "You don't even believe in God."

After the tiny pagans had been put to bed, I sat down to brood over Elijah's wine.[1] What had I been thinking? The kids knew that their Jewish grandparents were secular folks who didn't hold seders themselves. And if ethnicity eluded me, how could I expect it to take root in my children, who are not only Scottish English Irish, but Hungarian Polish Russian to boot?

But, then, on the fumes of Manischewitz,[2] a great insight took form in my mind. It was true, as the kids said, that I didn't "believe in God." But this could be taken as something very different from an accusation—a reminder of a genuine heritage. My parents had not believed in God either, nor had my grandparents or any other progenitors going back to the great-great level. They had become disillusioned with Christianity generations ago—just as, on the in-law side, my children's other ancestors had shaken off their Orthodox

---

[1] At the Passover seder, an extra cup of wine is poured in case the prophet Elijah arrives.

[2] Brand of kosher wine.

Judaism. This insight did not exactly furnish me with an "identity," but it was at least something to work with: We are the kind of people, I realized—whatever our distant ancestors' religions—who do not believe, who do not carry on traditions, who do not do things just because someone has done them before.

The epiphany went on: I recalled that my mother never introduced a procedure for cooking or cleaning by telling me, "Grandma did it this way." What did Grandma know, living in the days before vacuum cleaners and disposable toilet mops? In my parents' general view, new things were better than old and the very fact that some ritual had been performed in the past was a good reason for abandoning it now. Because what was the past, as our forebears knew it? Nothing but poverty, superstition and grief. "Think for yourself," Dad used to say. "Always ask why."

In fact, this may have been the ideal cultural heritage for my particular ethnic strain—bounced as it was from the Highlands of Scotland across the sea, out to the Rockies, down into the mines and finally spewed out into high-tech, suburban America. What better philosophy, for a race of migrants, than "think for yourself"? What better maxim, for a people whose whole world was rudely inverted every 30 years or so, than "try new things"?

The more tradition-minded, the newly enthusiastic celebrants of Purim and Kwanzaa and Solstice, may see little point to survival if the survivors carry no cultural freight—religion, for example, or ethnic tradition. To which I would say that skepticism, curiosity and wide-eyed ecumenical tolerance are also worthy elements of the human tradition and are at least as old as such notions as "Serbian" or "Croatian," "Scottish" or "Jewish." I make no claims for my personal line of progenitors except that they remained loyal to the values that may have induced all of our ancestors, long, long ago, to climb down from the trees and make their way into the open plains.

A few weeks ago I cleared my throat and asked the children, now mostly grown and fearsomely smart, whether they felt any stirrings of ethnic or religious identity, which might have been, ahem, insufficiently nourished at home. "None," they said, adding firmly, "and the world would be a better place if nobody else did, either." My chest swelled with pride, as would my mother's, to know that the race of "none" marches on.

STUDY AND DISCUSSION QUESTIONS

1. Why did Ehrenreich feel the need for an ethnic identity?

2. What does Ehrenreich mean when she writes, in the second paragraph, of "a hidden ethnic chauvinism in which the Britannically derived serve as a kind of neutral standard compared with the ethnic 'others'"?

3. Why do you think Ehrenreich tells us that her father was a miner?

4. What does the essay's title mean?

5. What is the tone of "Cultural Baggage"? Is it effective?

SUGGESTIONS FOR WRITING

1. Ehrenreich views her atheism and her "skepticism, curiosity and wide-eyed ecumenical tolerance" as "a genuine heritage." What do you think?

2. How do you identify yourself in terms of "ethnic background"? How do you feel about that identification?

MOTHER TONGUE

Amy Tan

Amy Tan was born in Oakland in 1952, attended college in California, and worked as a technical writer before beginning to write fiction. Her first novel, The Joy Luck Club (1989), *was an instant success, and she has since written* The Kitchen God's Wife *(1991) and* The Hundred Secret Senses *(1995). "Mother Tongue" first appeared in the* Threepenny Review *in 1990.*

I am not a scholar of English or literature. I cannot give you much more than personal opinions on the English language and its variations in this country or others.

I am a writer. And by that definition, I am someone who has always loved language. I am fascinated by language in daily life. I spend a great deal of my time thinking about the power of language—the way it can evoke an emotion, a visual image, a complex idea, or a simple truth. Language is the tool of my trade. And I use them all—all the Englishes I grew up with.

Recently, I was made keenly aware of the different Englishes I do use. I was giving a talk to a large group of people, the same talk I had already given to half a dozen other groups. The nature of the talk was about my writing, my life, and my book, *The Joy Luck Club.* The talk was going along well enough, until I remembered one major difference that made the whole talk sound wrong. My mother was in the room. And it was perhaps the first time she had heard me give a lengthy speech, using the kind of English I have never used with her. I was saying things like, "The intersection of memory upon imagination" and "There is an aspect of my fiction that relates to thus-and-thus"—a speech filled with carefully wrought grammatical phrases, burdened, it suddenly seemed to me, with nominalized forms, past perfect tenses, conditional phrases, all the forms of standard English that I had learned in school and through books, the forms of English I did not use at home with my mother.

Just last week, I was walking down the street with my mother, and I again found myself conscious of the English I was using, the English I do use with her. We were talking about the price of new and used furniture and I heard myself saying this: "Not waste money that way." My husband was with us as well, and he didn't notice any switch in my English. And then I realized why. It's because over the twenty years we've been together I've often used that same kind of English with him, and sometimes he even uses it with me. It has become our language of intimacy, a different sort of English that relates to family talk, the language I grew up with.

So you'll have some idea of what this family talk I heard sounds like, I'll quote what my mother said during a recent conversation which I videotaped and then transcribed. During this conversation, my mother was talking about a political gangster in Shang-hai who had the same last name as her family's, Du, and how the gangster in his early years wanted to be adopted by her family, which was rich by comparison. Later, the gangster became more powerful, far richer than my mother's family, and one day showed up at my mother's wedding to pay his respects. Here's what she said in part:

"Du Yusong having business like fruit stand. Like off the street kind. He is Du like Du Zong—but not Tsung-ming Island people. The local people call putong, the river east side, he belong to that side local people. That man want to ask Du Zong father take him in like become own family. Du Zong father wasn't look down on him, but didn't take seriously, until that man big like become a mafia. Now important person, very hard to inviting him. Chinese way, came only to show respect, don't stay for dinner. Respect for making big celebration, he shows up. Mean gives lots of respect. Chinese custom. Chinese social life that way. If too important won't have to stay too long. He come to my wedding. I didn't see, I heard it. I gone to boy's side, they have YMCA dinner. Chinese age I was nineteen."

You should know that my mother's expressive command of English belies how much she actually understands. She reads the *Forbes* report, listens to *Wall Street Week*, converses daily with her stockbroker, reads all of Shirley MacLaine's books with ease[1]—all kinds of things I can't begin to understand.

---

[1] *Forbes*, a business magazine; "Wall Street Week," a television show about economic trends and the stock market; Shirley MacLaine, an actor.

Yet some of my friends tell me they understand 50 percent of what my mother says. Some say they understand 80 to 90 percent. Some say they understand none of it, as if she were speaking pure Chinese. But to me, my mother's English is perfectly clear, perfectly natural. It's my mother tongue. Her language, as I hear it, is vivid, direct, full of observation and imagery. That was the language that helped shape the way I saw things, expressed things, made sense of the world.

Lately, I've been giving more thought to the kind of English my mother speaks. Like others, I have described it to people as "broken" or "fractured" English. But I wince when I say that. It has always bothered me that I can think of no way to describe it other than "broken," as if it were damaged and needed to be fixed, as if it lacked a certain wholeness and soundness. I've heard other terms used, "limited English," for example. But they seem just as bad, as if everything is limited, including people's perceptions of the limited English speaker.

I know this for a fact, because when I was growing up, my mother's "limited" English limited *my* perception of her. I was ashamed of her English. I believed that her English reflected the quality of what she had to say. That is, because she expressed them imperfectly her thoughts were imperfect. And I had plenty of empirical evidence to support me: the fact that people in department stores, at banks, and at restaurants did not take her seriously, did not give her good service, pretended not to understand her, or even acted as if they did not hear her.

My mother has long realized the limitations of her English as well. When I was fifteen, she used to have me call people on the phone to pretend I was she. In this guise, I was forced to ask for information or even to complain and yell at people who had been rude to her. One time it was a call to her stockbroker in New York. She had cashed out her small portfolio and it just so happened we were going to go to New York the next week, our very first trip outside California. I had to get on the phone and say in an adolescent voice that was not very convincing, "This is Mrs. Tan."

And my mother was standing in the back whispering loudly, "Why he don't send me check, already two weeks late. So mad he lie to me, losing me money."

And then I said in perfect English, "Yes, I'm getting rather concerned. You had agreed to send the check two weeks ago, but it hasn't arrived."

Then she began to talk more loudly. "What he want, I come to New York tell him front of his boss, you cheating me?" And I was trying to calm her down, make her be quiet, while telling the stockbroker, "I can't tolerate any more excuses. If I don't receive the check immediately, I am going to have to speak to your manager when I'm in New York next week." And sure enough, the following week there we were in front of this astonished stockbroker, and I was sitting there red-faced and quiet, and my mother, the real Mrs. Tan, was shouting at his boss in her impeccable broken English.

We used a similar routine just five days ago, for a situation that was far less humorous. My mother had gone to the hospital for an appointment, to find out about a benign brain tumor a CAT scan had revealed a month ago. She said she had spoken very good English, her best English, no mistakes. Still, she said, the hospital did not apologize when they said they had lost the CAT scan and she had come for nothing. She said they did not seem to have any sympathy when she told them she was anxious to know the exact diagnosis, since her husband and son had both died of brain tumors. She said they would not give her any more information until the next time and she would have to make another appointment for that. So she said she would not leave until the doctor called her daughter. She wouldn't budge. And when the doctor finally called her daughter, me, who spoke in perfect English—lo and behold—we had assurances the CAT scan would be found, promises that a conference call on Monday would be held, and apologies for any suffering my mother had gone through for a most regrettable mistake.

I think my mother's English almost had an effect on limiting my possibilities in life as well. Sociologists and linguists probably will tell you that a person's developing language skills are more influenced by peers. But I do think that the language spoken in the family, especially in immigrant families which are more insular, plays a large role in shaping the language of the child. And I believe that it affected my results on achievement tests, IQ tests, and the SAT. While my English skills were never judged as poor, compared to math, English could not be considered my strong suit. In grade school I did moderately well, getting perhaps B's, sometimes B-pluses, in English and scoring perhaps in the sixtieth or seventieth percentile on achievement tests. But those scores were not good enough to override the opinion that my true abilities lay in math and science, because in those areas I achieved A's and scored in the ninetieth percentile or higher.

This was understandable. Math is precise; there is only one correct answer. Whereas, for me at least, the answers on English tests were always a judgment call, a matter of opinion and personal experience. Those tests were constructed around items like fill-in-the-blank sentence completion, such as, "Even though Tom was _____ , Mary thought he was _____ ." And the correct answer always seemed to be the most bland combinations of thoughts, for example, "Even though Tom was shy, Mary thought he was charming," with the grammatical structure "even though" limiting the correct answer to some sort of semantic opposites, so you wouldn't get answers like, "Even though Tom was foolish, Mary thought he was ridiculous." Well, according to my mother, there were very few limitations as to what Tom could have been and what Mary might have thought of him. So I never did well on tests like that.

The same was true with word analogies, pairs of words in which you were supposed to find some sort of logical, semantic relationship—for example, "*Sunset* is to *nightfall* as _____ is to _____ ." And here you would be presented with a list of four possible pairs, one of which showed the same kind of relationship: *red* is to *stoplight, bus* is to *arrival, chills* is to *fever, yawn* is to *boring.* Well, I could never think that way. I knew what the tests were asking, but I could not block out of my mind the images already created by the first pair, "*sunset* is to *nightfall*"—and I would see a burst of colors against a darkening sky, the moon rising, the lowering of a curtain of stars. And all the other pairs of words—red, bus, stoplight, boring—just threw up a mass of confusing images, making it impossible for me to sort out something as logical as saying: "A sunset precedes nightfall" is the same as "a chill precedes a fever." The only way I would have gotten that answer right would have been to imagine an associative situation, for example, my being disobedient and staying out past sunset, catching a chill at night, which turns into feverish pneumonia as punishment, which indeed did happen to me.

I have been thinking about all this lately, about my mother's English, about achievement tests. Because lately I've been asked, as a writer, why there are not more Asian Americans represented in American literature. Why are there few Asian Americans enrolled in creative writing programs? Why do so many Chinese students go into engineering? Well, these are broad sociological questions I can't begin to answer. But I have noticed in surveys—in fact, just last week—that Asian students, as a whole, always do significantly better on math achievement tests than in English. And this makes me think that there are other Asian-American students whose English spoken in the home might also be described as "broken" or "limited." And perhaps they also have teachers who are steering them away from writing and into math and science, which is what happened to me.

Fortunately, I happen to be rebellious in nature and enjoy the challenge of disproving assumptions made about me. I became an English major my first year in college, after being enrolled as pre-med. I started writing nonfiction as a freelancer the week after I was told by my former boss that writing was my worst skill and I should hone my talents toward account management.

But it wasn't until 1985 that I finally began to write fiction. And at first I wrote using what I thought to be wittily crafted sentences, sentences that would finally prove I had mastery over the English language. Here's an example from the first draft of a story that later made its way into *The Joy Luck Club,* but without this line: "That was my mental quandary in its nascent state." A terrible line, which I can barely pronounce.

Fortunately, for reasons I won't get into today, I later decided I should envision a reader for the stories I would write. And the reader I decided upon was my mother, because these were stories about mothers. So with this reader in mind—and in fact she did read my early drafts—I began to write stories using all the Englishes I grew up with: the English I spoke to my mother, which for lack of a better term might be described as "simple"; the English she used with me, which for lack of a better term might be described as "broken"; my translation of her Chinese, which could certainly be described as "watered down"; and what I imagined to be her translation of her Chinese if she could speak in perfect English, her internal language, and for that I sought to preserve the essence, but neither an English nor a Chinese structure. I wanted to capture what language ability tests can never reveal: her intent, her passion, her imagery, the rhythms of her speech and the nature of her thoughts.

Apart from what any critic had to say about my writing, I knew I had succeeded where it counted when my mother finished reading my book and gave me her verdict: "So easy to read."

STUDY AND DISCUSSION QUESTIONS

1. Growing up, Tan thought that her mother's English "reflected the quality of what she had to say." How come?

2. What's Tan's point in telling the story about her mother's CAT scan? Why exactly did the hospital staff behave the way they did?

3. What, besides academic aptitude, is measured by standardized test questions like the two Tan discusses?

4. What's wrong with the sentence Tan quotes from her first draft of *The Joy Luck Club*? What might have led her to write such a sentence?

5. What does her mother's verdict—"So easy to read"—tell Tan about her novel?

SUGGESTION FOR WRITING

1. If you are a native speaker of English, how do you react to someone who speaks "broken" English? Or, if English is not your first language and people can tell, how do they react to you? Describe a specific incident or two.

THE MYTH OF THE LATINA WOMAN: I JUST MET A GIRL NAMED MARÍA

Judith Ortiz Cofer

Judith Ortiz Cofer was born in Puerto Rico in 1952 and moved to the United States as a small girl. She studied at Augusta College, at Florida Atlantic University, and at Oxford, and she now teaches at the University of Georgia at Athens. Cofer has published several books of poetry, including Terms of Survival *(1987), as well as the essay collection* Silent Dancing *(1990). Her novel* The Line of the Sun *(1989) was nominated for a Pulitzer Prize. The following appeared in* The Latin Deli: Prose and Poetry *(1993).*

On a bus trip to London from Oxford University where I was earning some graduate credits one summer, a young man, obviously fresh from a pub, spotted me and as if struck by inspiration went down on his knees in the aisle. With both hands over his heart he broke into an Irish tenor's rendition of "María" from *West Side Story*.[1] My politely amused fellow passengers gave his lovely voice the round of gentle applause it deserved. Though I was not quite as amused, I managed my version of an English smile: no show of teeth, no extreme contortions of the facial muscles—I was at this time of my life practicing reserve and cool. Oh, that British control, how I coveted it. But María had followed me to London, reminding me of a prime fact of my life: you can leave the Island, master the English language, and travel as far as you can, but if you are a Latina, especially one like me who so obviously belongs to Rita Moreno's[2] gene pool, the Island travels with you.

This is sometimes a very good thing—it may win you that extra minute of someone's attention. But with some people, the same things can make *you* an island—not so much a tropical paradise as an Alcatraz, a place nobody wants to visit. As a Puerto Rican girl growing up in the United States and

---

[1] Broadway musical by Leonard Bernstein and Steven Sondheim about two New York City gangs, one Puerto Rican, the other "American."

[2] Puerto Rican actor who played the female lead, María, in *West Side Story*.

wanting like most children to "belong," I resented the stereotype that my Hispanic appearance called forth from many people I met.

Our family lived in a large urban center in New Jersey during the sixties, where life was designed as a microcosm of my parents' *casas* on the island. We spoke in Spanish, we ate Puerto Rican food bought at the *bodega*, and we practiced strict Catholicism complete with Saturday confession and Sunday mass at a church where our parents were accommodated into a one-hour Spanish mass slot, performed by a Chinese priest trained as a missionary for Latin America.

As a girl I was kept under strict surveillance, since virtue and modesty were, by cultural equation, the same as family honor. As a teenager I was instructed on how to behave as a proper *señorita*. But it was a conflicting message girls got, since the Puerto Rican mothers also encouraged their daughters to look and act like women and to dress in clothes our Anglo friends and their mothers found too "mature" for our age. It was, and is, cultural, yet I often felt humiliated when I appeared at an American friend's party wearing a dress more suitable to a semiformal than to a playroom birthday celebration. At Puerto Rican festivities, neither the music nor the colors we wore could be too loud. I still experience a vague sense of letdown when I'm invited to a "party" and it turns out to be a marathon conversation in hushed tones rather than a fiesta with salsa, laughter, and dancing—the kind of celebration I remember from my childhood.

I remember Career Day in our high school, when teachers told us to come dressed as if for a job interview. It quickly became obvious that to the barrio girls, "dressing up" sometimes meant wearing ornate jewelry and clothing that would be more appropriate (by mainstream standards) for the company Christmas party than as daily office attire. That morning I had agonized in front of my closet, trying to figure out what a "career girl" would wear because, essentially, except for Marlo Thomas[3] on TV, I had no models on which to base my decision. I knew how to dress for school: at the Catholic school I attended we all wore uniforms; I knew how to dress for Sunday mass, and I knew what dresses to wear for parties at my relatives' homes. Though I do not recall the precise details of my Career Day outfit, it must have been a composite of the above choices. But I remember a comment my friend (an Italian-American) made in later years that coalesced my impressions of that day. She said that at the business school she was attending the Puerto Rican girls always stood out for wearing "everything at once." She meant, of course, too much jewelry, too many accessories. On that day at school, we were simply made the negative models by the nuns who were themselves not credible

---

[3] Actor who starred in "That Girl," television sitcom about a young career woman.

fashion experts to any of us. But it was painfully obvious to me that to the others, in their tailored skirts and silk blouses, we must have seemed "hopeless" and "vulgar." Though I now know that most adolescents feel out of step much of the time, I also know that for the Puerto Rican girls of my generation that sense was intensified. The way our teachers and classmates looked at us that day in school was just a taste of the culture clash that awaited us in the real world, where prospective employers and men on the street would often misinterpret our tight skirts and jingling bracelets as a come-on.

Mixed cultural signals have perpetuated certain stereotypes—for example, that of the Hispanic woman as the "Hot Tamale" or sexual firebrand. It is a one-dimensional view that the media have found easy to promote. In their special vocabulary, advertisers have designated "sizzling" and "smoldering" as the adjectives of choice for describing not only the foods but also the women of Latin America. From conversations in my house I recall hearing about the harassment that Puerto Rican women endured in factories where the "boss men" talked to them as if sexual innuendo was all they understood and, worse, often gave them the choice of submitting to advances or being fired.

It is custom, however, not chromosomes, that leads us to choose scarlet over pale pink. As young girls, we were influenced in our decisions about clothes and colors by the women—older sisters and mothers who had grown up on a tropical island where the natural environment was a riot of primary colors, where showing your skin was one way to keep cool as well as to look sexy. Most important of all, on the island, women perhaps felt freer to dress and move more provocatively, since, in most cases, they were protected by the traditions, mores, and laws of a Spanish/Catholic system of morality and machismo whose main rule was: *You may look at my sister, but if you touch her I will kill you.* The extended family and church structure could provide a young woman with a circle of safety in her small pueblo on the island; if a man "wronged" a girl, everyone would close in to save her family honor.

This is what I have gleaned from my discussions as an adult with older Puerto Rican women. They have told me about dressing in their best party clothes on Saturday nights and going to the town's plaza to promenade with their girlfriends in front of the boys they liked. The males were thus given an opportunity to admire the women and to express their admiration in the form of *piropos:* erotically charged street poems they composed on the spot. I have been subjected to a few piropos while visiting the Island, and they can be outrageous, although custom dictates that they must never cross into obscenity. This ritual, as I understand it, also entails a show of studied indifference on the woman's part; if she is "decent," she must not acknowledge the man's impassioned words. So I do understand how things can be lost in translation. When a Puerto Rican girl dressed in her idea of what is attractive meets a man from the mainstream culture who has been trained to react to certain types of clothing as a sexual signal, a clash is likely to take place. The line I first heard based on this aspect of the myth happened when the boy who took me to my first formal dance leaned over to plant a sloppy overeager kiss painfully on my mouth, and when I didn't respond with sufficient passion said in a resentful tone: "I thought you Latin girls were supposed to mature early"—my first instance of being thought of as a fruit or vegetable— I was supposed to *ripen,* not just grow into womanhood like other girls.

It is surprising to some of my professional friends that some people, including those who should know better, still put others "in their place." Though rarer, these incidents are still commonplace in my life. It happened to me most recently during a stay at a very classy metropolitan hotel favored by young professional couples for their weddings. Late one evening after the theater, as I walked toward my room with my new colleague (a woman with whom I was coordinating an arts program), a middle-aged man in a tuxedo, a young girl in satin and lace on his arm, stepped directly into our path. With his champagne glass extended toward me, he exclaimed, "Evita!"[4]

Our way blocked, my companion and I listened as the man half-recited, half-bellowed "Don't Cry for Me, Argentina."[5] When he finished, the young girl said: "How about a round of applause for my daddy?" We complied, hoping this would bring the silly spectacle to a close. I was becoming aware that our little group was attracting the attention of the other guests. "Daddy" must have perceived this too, and he once more barred the way as we tried to walk past him. He began to shout-sing a ditty to the tune of "La Bamba"[6]—except the lyrics were about a girl named María whose exploits all rhymed with her name and gonorrhea. The girl kept saying "Oh, Daddy" and looking at me with pleading eyes. She wanted me to laugh along with the others. My companion and I stood silently waiting for the man to end his offensive song. When he finished, I looked not at him but at his daughter. I advised her calmly never to ask her father what he had done in the army. Then I walked between them and to my room. My friend complimented me on my cool handling of the situation. I confessed to her that I really had wanted to push the jerk into the swimming pool. I knew that this same man—probably a corporate executive, well educated, even worldly by most standards—would not have been likely to regale a white woman with a dirty song in public. He would perhaps have checked his impulse by assuming that she could be somebody's wife or mother, or at least *somebody*

---

[4] Eva Duarte de Perón, wife of Argentinean president Juan Domingo Perón and inspiration for the Broadway musical *Evita,* by Andrew Lloyd Webber and Tim Rice.

[5] Song from *Evita.*

[6] Popular song recorded by Chicano singer, Ritchie Valens.

who might take offense. But to him, I was just an Evita or a María: merely a character in his cartoon-populated universe.

Because of my education and my proficiency with the English language, I have acquired many mechanisms for dealing with the anger I experience. This was not true for my parents, nor is it true for the many Latin women working at menial jobs who must put up with stereotypes about our ethnic group such as: "They make good domestics." This is another facet of the myth of the Latin woman in the United States. Its origin is simple to deduce. Work as domestics, waitressing, and factory jobs are all that's available to women with little English and few skills. The myth of the Hispanic menial has been sustained by the same media phenomenon that made "Mammy" from *Gone with the Wind*[7] America's idea of the black woman for generations; María, the housemaid or counter girl, is now indelibly etched into the national psyche. The big and the little screens have presented us with the picture of the funny Hispanic maid, mispronouncing words and cooking up a spicy storm in a shiny California kitchen.

This media-engendered image of the Latina in the United States has been documented by feminist Hispanic scholars, who claim that such portrayals are partially responsible for the denial of opportunities for upward mobility among Latinas in the professions. I have a Chicana friend working on a Ph.D. in philosophy at a major university. She says her doctor still shakes his head in puzzled amazement at all the "big words" she uses. Since I do not wear my diplomas around my neck for all to see, I too have on occasion been sent to that "kitchen," where some think I obviously belong.

One such incident that has stayed with me, though I recognize it as a minor offense, happened on the day of my first public poetry reading. It took place in Miami in a boat-restaurant where we were having lunch before the event. I was nervous and excited as I walked in with my notebook in my hand. An older woman motioned me to her table. Thinking (foolish me) that she wanted me to autograph a copy of my brand new slender volume of verse, I went over. She ordered a cup of coffee from me, assuming that I was the waitress. Easy enough to mistake my poems for menus, I suppose. I know that it wasn't an intentional act of cruelty, yet of all the good things that happened that day, I remember that scene most clearly, because it reminded me of what I had to overcome before anyone would take me seriously. In retrospect I understand that my anger gave my reading fire, that I have almost always taken doubts in my abilities as a challenge—and that the result is, most times, a feeling of satisfaction at having won a convert when I see the cold, appraising eyes warm to my words, the body language change, the smile that

---

[7] Novel by Margaret Mitchell.

indicates that I have opened some avenue for communication. That day I read to that woman and her lowered eyes told me that she was embarrassed at her little faux pas, and when I willed her to look up at me, it was my victory, and she graciously allowed me to punish her with my full attention. We shook hands at the end of the reading, and I never saw her again. She has probably forgotten the whole thing but maybe not.

Yet I am one of the lucky ones. My parents made it possible for me to acquire a stronger footing in the mainstream culture by giving me the chance at an education. And books and art have saved me from the harsher forms of ethnic and racial prejudice that many of my Hispanic *compañeras*[8] have had to endure. I travel a lot around the United States, reading from my books of poetry and my novel, and the reception I most often receive is one of positive interest by people who want to know more about my culture. There are, however, thousands of Latinas without the privilege of an education or the entrée into society that I have. For them life is a struggle against the misconceptions perpetuated by the myth of the Latina as whore, domestic or criminal. We cannot change this by legislating the way people look at us. The transformation, as I see it, has to occur at a much more individual level. My personal goal in my public life is to try to replace the old pervasive stereotypes and myths about Latinas with a much more interesting set of realities. Every time I give a reading, I hope the stories I tell, the dreams and fears I examine in my work, can achieve some universal truth which will get my audience past the particulars of my skin color, my accent, or my clothes.

I once wrote a poem in which I called us Latinas "God's brown daughters." This poem is really a prayer of sorts, offered upward, but also, through the human-to-human channel of art, outward. It is a prayer for communication, and for respect. In it, Latin women pray "in Spanish to an Anglo God / with a Jewish heritage," and they are "fervently hoping / that if not omnipotent, / at least He be bilingual."

STUDY AND DISCUSSION QUESTIONS

1. What *is* the myth of the Latina woman?

2. Why was choosing what to wear for Career Day in high school so difficult for Cofer?

3. "It is custom, however, not chromosomes, that leads us to choose scarlet over pale pink." What is Cofer's point here? Why does she mention chromosomes?

---

[8] Companions, sisters (Spanish).

4. Why does Cofer tell us that the man who shouted songs at her in the hotel seemed like "a corporate executive, well educated, even worldly by most standards"?

5. Cofer told the man's daughter "never to ask her father what he had done in the army." What did she mean?

6. How does social class enter into the myth of the Latina woman and its consequences?

7. Why did it bother Cofer so much to be mistaken for a waitress at her poetry reading? Is she saying it's shameful to be a waitress?

8. What is the meaning of the poetry quoted at the end?

SUGGESTIONS FOR WRITING

1. Write the letter that the woman who mistook Cofer for a waitress might have written to her the next day.

2. Near the end, Cofer says: "Yet I am one of the lucky ones." What kinds of stories might a Latina who doesn't possess Cofer's education have to tell?

3. Cofer occasionally discusses media images. Analyze the portrayal of "the Latina" in a film or television show.

LUIGI, TONY, AND THE FAMILY

Michael Parenti

Michael Parenti was born in New York City in 1933, studied at City College there and at Brown and Yale Universities, and has taught at colleges around the country. Among his books are Democracy for the Few *(1974),* Power and the Powerless *(1978),* The Sword and the Dollar *(1988), and* Make-Believe Media *(1992), from which the following chapter is taken.*

Throughout the 1960s, social scientists predicted that White ethnic identities were becoming a thing of the past, as various national groups blended into the great American melting pot. No sooner had this opinion become part of the conventional wisdom than there developed in the early seventies a marked resurgence of ethnic consciousness. Sometimes in emulation of the Black struggle and sometimes in competitive response to it, the White ethnics began to make themselves heard.

This resurgence was partly a reaction to a dominant social order that had imposed a program of "Americanization" upon the immigrants and their children. The White ethnics began to resist the homogenization of identity and culture that were the long-standing goals of a society that on other days called itself "pluralistic." In addition, many White ethnic demands, like Black ones, were politico-economic in nature, calling for greater access to political office, improved community services, housing, jobs and job advancement, better schools, and a more equitable tax burden.

By the 1970s, ethnicity was no longer an embarrassment. If anything, it had become a subject of popular interest, enough so to attract the attention of the mass media. Ethnic characters and explicit ethnic references soon became common fare in television situation comedies, cop and crime shows, commercials, and Hollywood films.

To illustrate how the media handle or mishandle the ethnic experience, I will concentrate on Italian-Americans. The screen treatment of this group provides one of the many unfortunate examples of what the make-believe media are capable of doing. In the late 1970s, the Italians were "discovered" by Hollywood. With stars like Al Pacino, Robert De Niro, Sylvester Stallone, and John Travolta shouting, shooting, punching, or dancing their way across the screen, the Italians had become one of Hollywood's favorite ethnic groups. But at what price?[1]

The Stages of Stereotype

How have Italian-Americans been represented in the media? In ways not unlike other ethnic groups:

The Invisible Man. To use the title of Ralph Ellison's book about Blacks, for a long time the Italian, like every other ethnic, was invisible, nonexistent. Be it radio, movies, television dramas, popular literature, or the Dick-and-Jane readers of grade school, the world was inhabited by middle- and upper-middle-class WASPs, creamy-faced suburban youngsters with executive-looking fathers and trim American-beauty mothers, visions of Anglo-Protestant affluence and gentility.

---

[1] For an earlier, shorter version of this treatment of Italian Americans see Michael Parenti, "The Media Are the Mafia," *Monthly Review,* March 1979, pp. 20–26. [Author's note]

Minor Stock Characters. In the early days of movies and radio when Italians did make an appearance in the Anglo-American world, it was usually as minor stock characters: the cheerful waiter, the talkative barber, the simple pushcart vendor, human scenery on the urban landscape with no lives of their own—or certainly no lives deemed worthy of narrative treatment. As unassimilated oddities, Italians were treated no differently than other ethnic stand-ins, such as the Irish cleaning lady, the Jewish shopkeeper, and the Black domestic.

The Grateful Immigrant. One of the stock characters of the late 1940s and early 1950s became a featured personality in a radio series and subsequently a television series called *Life with Luigi.* Played by an Irish-American actor, J. Carroll Naish, Luigi was the cloyingly sweet immigrant who spent his time gratefully exclaiming, "Mama mia, I'm-a love-a deese-a bootifull-a country, Amerrreeca!" Naish's understanding of an Italian immigrant's looks, accent, and mannerisms, painfully reminiscent of Chico Marx (another caricature), bore little resemblance to the real thing. Luigi was a creature conjured up by the make-believe media as a confirmation of the goodness of the existing American social order. In Luigi and characters like him, we had evidence that the immigrant was not a victim but a joyful, appreciative beneficiary of his adopted country.

The Mafia Gangster. In the fearful imagination of nativistic America, crime was always associated with the big city and the swarthy foreigner. In the 1930s and 1940s, the Italian mobster had to share the Hollywood screen with his Irish and Jewish counterparts. In later years, with television series like "The Untouchables" and movies like *The Godfather,* the Italian was fashioned into the archetypal gangster, so that eventually the association of Italian-Americans with crime was instantaneous and international. One can travel throughout Europe and most other lands where Hollywood films are shown and encounter the stereotype. While in Lisbon during the revolutionary ferment of 1975, I talked to a Portuguese army lieutenant who, upon discovering I was Italian-American, commented gleefully "Ah, mafioso!" A half-hour later, the exact same response was accorded me by a Portuguese army captain. The lieutenant had right-wing sympathies and the captain was leftist—which demonstrates how Hollywood can cut its swath across the ideological spectrum.

With the help of the media, a few thousand hoodlums in the organized rackets who are of Italian origin, representing a tiny fraction of the Italian-American population, became representative of an entire ethnic group. In one of his stand-up feature films, the comedian Richard Pryor joked: "Not all Italians are in the Mafia. They just all *work* for the Mafia." The Mafia association became one of those respectable forms of bigotry.

There have been Irish, Jewish, Black, Latino, Italian, and even Anglo-Protestant mobsters in our history. None of these hoodlums is representative of the larger ethnic formations from which they happened to originate. Needless to say, none of the movies dealing with such characters has ever provided an authentic rendition of the rich cultural heritages and working-class histories of these groups.

The Respectables. Partly in response to protests launched against the gangland shows, Italian surnames began appearing in movies and television dramas attached to characters other than mobsters and thugs; they were mostly police, criminal lawyers, and private investigators such as Columbo, Baretta, Del Vecchio, D'Angelo, and Petrocelli. The Italian crimebuster, of course, was still closely associated with crime and violence; and like all media lawmen, his operational methods were sometimes difficult to distinguish from those of the criminals against whom he was pitted.

The Jivy Proletarian. In the 1970s, the media discovered commercial success in a new working-class, streetwise Italian who was neither a cop nor a crook, but sometimes a comedy character like Henry Winkler's "the Fonz" or John Travolta's Vinnie Barbarino (unschooled even when going to school), and sometimes a Cinderella as in *Rocky* (I, II, III, IV, V) or in *Saturday Night Fever* (1978). The frequent appearance of this Italian proletariat type, action-prone, noncerebral, at home with sex and violence, was a flashy variation of an older stereotype—not only of Italians but of working-class people in general: loud-mouthed, visceral, nonintellectual, acting on their emotions, living a life worth escaping. The media's ethnic bigotry is also a class bigotry.

The intertwining of class and ethnic bigotry is clearly displayed in the popular film *Saturday Night Fever.* The lead character, Tony Manero (John Travolta), is a working-class Italian-American from Bay Ridge, Brooklyn, whose life, the film seems to say, will—and should—never amount to much. His family is composed of three generations of Italian stereotypes who gather around the dinner table to scold, shout, and whack each other on the head. Tony spends his days working in a neighborhood hardware store and his nights dancing in the local disco. He and his buddies also pass their time ogling women, riding around in an old car, and speaking Hollywood's super-slurry version of Brooklynese. For a change of pace, they do such things as gang-rape a local woman and launch a violent attack on a rival Puerto Rican gang whose members are referred to throughout the film as "spics." "We hit them Italian style—where they live," one of Tony's cohorts proudly exclaims after they almost kill several people by driving a car through the window of the storefront that serves as the Puerto Ricans' clubhouse.

Tony, who is made out to be a shade less Neanderthal than his chums, is finally shaken from his desolate neighborhood life when one member of his group accidentally slips off the Verrazano Bridge during a playful interlude. In the last scene, Tony, rattled by the death of his friend, crosses the bridge, both literally and symbolically, to find his way to the better, finer world:

specifically, the middle-class Manhattan apartment of a girlfriend. She herself was originally from a somewhat more respectable part of Bay Ridge, but she knows enough to fix up her place as might any West Village intellectual, complete with bohemian art fixtures and a bare brick wall in the living room. She asks the thoroughly chastised Tony if he is ready to redo his worthless life. With bowed head, he sobbingly announces his desire for personal gentrification. So the movie ends, presumably with our hero preparing himself for voice and diction lessons and evening courses at the New School.[2] Somehow changing one's class is volitional, a mere matter of choosing the right attitude.

The moral is clear: proletariat Bay Ridge is not only a tough place to live, but it offers a morally inferior way of life. The middle-class life is not only economically more secure and comfortable, it is ethically superior.

Five years later, Hollywood inflicted upon us a sequel to *Saturday Night Fever*, entitled *Staying Alive* (1983), with John Travolta still playing Tony Manero, who now is going to dance school after permanently moving to Manhattan. On a visit home, his mother praises him by saying: "You must have something if you could escape from this neighborhood." On another occasion, he excuses his boorish behavior to an upper-crust prospective girlfriend by saying: "The people I lived with didn't know how to be nice." And, "There's a gentleman inside me waiting to come out." So there's hope for the uncouth working-class Italian boy if only he can put enough space between himself and Brooklyn.

The choosing-between-two-worlds theme is explored with somewhat more intelligence in *Bloodbrothers* (1978). Stony De Coco must decide whether he is going to stick with the parochial, male-bonded world of Italian-American construction workers with their pride in their work and barroom camaraderie or become a middle-class professional of sorts, a recreation assistant who deals with children. He really prefers the latter occupation, but his father sees it as "woman's work." Pop says things like: "The blood that runs in your veins—that's De Coco blood. You're ours!" Stony's family turns out to be pathological. Mom is a hysteric who induces anorexia nervosa in his younger brother, and Pop is a macho maniac who beats Mom senselessly because of a suspected infidelity. Once more, working-class Italians are depicted as screaming screwballs. So Stony heads for the kinder, gentler, middle-class Anglo world.[3]

Not so the Italian boy in *The Wanderers* (1979). Engaged to a neighborhood girl, he bolts from his own engagement party when he sees his true

---

[2] The New School for Social Research, an institution of higher education in New York City.

[3] Peter Biskind and Barbara Ehrenreich, "Machismo and Hollywood's Working Class," in Donald Lazere (ed.), *American Media and Mass Culture* (Berkeley: University of California Press, 1987), pp. 208–209. [Author's note]

love stroll by. Of course, she is a "better-class" lass. He follows her for two blocks, and suddenly he's out of the Bronx and in Greenwich Village, probably not far from where Tony Manero and Stony De Coco have settled down with *their* upper-class women. But some people just don't want to better themselves. He soon realizes he can never fit into his lady's "faintly androgynous, bohemian world. It's back to the trattoria under the wing of his Hawaiian-shirted, mafioso father-in-law."[4]

Sempre Mafia

Of the various Italian stereotypes in the media, the Mafia image is the most enduring. By 1985, *Prizzi's Honor* offered us a new twist in gangster depravity, a romance between a mafioso and a lovely lady who herself turns out to be a gangland hit woman. At one point she refers to her Polish antecedents as "polack," thereby demonstrating Hollywood's inability to recognize the existence of one of America's most defamed ethnic groups in anything but defamatory terms. Prizzi and his Polish-American woman get along swimmingly at first. After a whirlwind romance, they marry. Eventually, however, their relationship comes into conflict with the interests of "the family." It's all resolved when Prizzi beats his wife to the draw, putting a knife through her neck as she is about to blow him away with one of her favorite work tools. The movie actually ends happily after Prizzi stuffs her body in the trunk of a car and returns to an earlier Mafia sweetheart who has all along been plotting to get him back. Done by one of Hollywood's leading directors, John Huston, this comic-book flick was treated as a serious cinematic effort by critics.

Almost forty years after television first featured the Italian mobster in "The Untouchables," Mafia characters continued in abundant supply in films and TV series. As if to demonstrate that nothing changes, in 1990 alone Hollywood gave us *The Freshman, My Blue Heaven, King of New York, Miller's Crossing, Godfather III,* and *GoodFellas.* The first two are comedies. In all of them, Italian mobsters either are the central characters or play important supporting roles. *King of New York* manages to offend women, African-Americans, Chinese, Latinos, and Irish—as well as Italians. *Godfather III* is a dreary imitation of the two previous *Godfather* films, again elevating the don to a kind of admirable patriarchal deity. Distinct among these films was *GoodFellas,* a well-made Martin Scorsese film. Based on a true story, it divests the mobsters of any romantic or glorified aura, revealing them to be the vicious petty hoods, cutthroats, and victimizers they really are.

---

[4] Ibid. [Author's note]

The image of the Italian as gangster even permeates gangster movies about other groups. *Once Upon a Time in America* (1984), a movie about Jewish mobsters, and *Year of the Dragon* (1985), about Chinese mobsters, were amply offensive to these respective groups. Each also included Italian racketeers as an ethno-criminal element that competes with the Jewish and Chinese mobsters. For an added twist, the hero in *Year of the Dragon* is a slightly crazed Polish-American detective named White, who describes himself repeatedly as a "polack" and even a "dumb polack." On one occasion, he informs an antagonist, "You made one mistake: I'm not an Italian, I'm a polack. I can't be bribed." Detective White refers to the Chinese legacy of a "thousand-year history" of crime—which the Chinese have now brought to this country. He draws feverish comparisons between Vietnam's jungles and Chinatown's streets. "This is Vietnam all over again—nobody wants to win."

The film's Chinese mobsters are in a long line of Asian criminal stereotypes from the old Dr. Fu Manchu movies down to the James Bond flicks and "Hawaii Five-O" television series. The only Asian female of note in this movie is the Chinese-American newscaster who, of course, becomes a compliant appendage to Supercop White once the action moves from the streets to the bed.[5] *Year of the Dragon* offers some intriguing glimpses into life in New York's Chinatown, leaving one to wonder what interesting movies could be made about the Chinese-American experience were the make-believe media ever to pay attention to Chinese who don't shoot people in the face.

In comedy films, too, Italians have often appeared as mobsters, as in *The Ritz* (1976), in which a Mafia-related son-in-law goes to a gay bathhouse to avoid extermination by his family. Similarly, in *Some Like It Hot* (1959), *Broadway Danny Rose* (1984), and *The Freshman* (1990) the protagonists have scary and humorous encounters with Italian mobsters.

Italian-American women are almost nonexistent as central characters in the entertainment media, portrayed mostly as homebound acolytes. A typical representation was offered on "Wiseguy," a CBS weekly serial running in the late 1980s, featuring a Federal agent named Vinnie Terranova along with assorted mob figures, some of whom happen to be his relatives. In the final episode of the 1988–89 season, Vinnie's mother, who talks with what is supposed to be an Italian accent, rushes from her vacation in Italy because she senses correctly that her Vinnie has a "girl-a." "Oh, he looks-a awful. I shudden-a left-a him alone," the protective mama says when she reunites with him. Sounding like Luigi in drag, she asks anxiously if Vinnie's new girlfriend, Amber, is Italian. "No? well-a is-a she Catholeec?" Thank goodness, yes. A third of a loaf is better than none. But Vinnie's mom is offended when she

---

[5] Eric Dittus, "A Review of 'Year of the Dragon,'" *Hawaii Herald*, September 20, 1985, pp. 1–2. [Author's note]

pops over to Vinnie's apartment unannounced and finds him in bed with Amber. "And they-a no yet-a married." Later she comes around and kisses Amber when their engagement is announced. "You-a are engaged and-a I am-a happy." Mama herself married a reformed Mafia don who had renounced his life of crime.

A seemingly refreshing departure from this kind of mama-mia stereotype was the 1986 NBC autobiographical film about Antoinette Giancana, a young woman who loves her father but rebels against his domination and seeks to be herself in a male-ruled household. Here is one of those rare instances where the struggles of an Italian-American woman are given respectful treatment. There is one catch, however: Papa Giancana is a notorious Mafia don and the title of the film is *Mafia Princess*. To the extent that the media can explore new and worthwhile themes, it seems they must still be packaged in an old casement.

After being fed enough of this fare, we need to remind ourselves that not all Italians are gangsters and not all gangsters are Italian. As with other ethnic groups, in the last several decades Italians have moved in noticeable numbers into government service, political life, the professions, and the arts. It can be argued that these people usually do less sensationally horrifying things than mobsters and are therefore less likely to win the attention of an image industry that specializes in violence and other forms of sensationalism. Still, noncriminal characters do appear in films and television shows; it would not be unrealistic to portray ethnics more frequently engaged in normal social activities and in positions of responsibility and empowerment. And the introduction of ethnic themes into story lines other than those occupied by Hollywood stereotypes might represent a refreshing and appealing departure from the usual fare. To prove the point, one need only recall *Marty* (1955), originally a television drama and later an Oscar-winning Hollywood film that portrayed a love affair involving a lonely Italian-American butcher. Marty is a likeable, hardworking guy, who lives with his mother and hangs out with his buddies, cruising the neighborhood dance halls in the evenings. Doubting that he is very lovable, he nevertheless wins the heart of a local lass, who is intelligent, sensitive, and supposedly of plain appearance. Marty's mother is a first-generation Italian immigrant, who struggles to remain active and useful in her old age. She is concerned about the Americanizing influences that might induce her son "to give up the house" and move into an apartment. The characterizations are touching and readily recognizable without being stereotypic or slighting.

Moonstruck (1987) is another example of that rare genre: a movie about Italians who are not gangsters. The humor is sometimes overly slick in that silly, heavy-handed TV sitcom way. The characters are broadly drawn; occasionally overdrawn. For instance, the grandfather—played by an actor with an odd Eastern European accent—is predictably quaint as he herds his dogs into the park so that they might bay at the moon. The mother oozes familial integrity. The daughter—and heroine of the story—falls in love with the brooding brother of her fiancé, a love consummated to the wonderful music of *La Boheme.*[6] Whatever its flaws, *Moonstruck* is an entertaining film that portrays Brooklyn working-class and petty bourgeois ethnics as warm, engaging—and law-abiding—human beings.

A film done with more intelligence and realism is *Dominic and Eugene* (1988), which tells the story of fraternal twins who plan on sharing a house together. One brother is being helped through medical school by the other, who is a sanitation worker. The story focuses on how they resolve the contradictions that face them while managing to remain close and stay committed to each other. *Dominic and Eugene* is well-acted; it is touching but not oversentimentalized or overdone. The Italian-American identities of the brothers and some neighbors are established early and easily and do not figure in the plot in any prominent way, except to leave us with an impression that Italian working-class people are human and decent, capable of living lives that are worthy of narrative treatment—without the assistance of a single mafioso thug.

Free of Mafia thugs but not of other threadbare ethnic stereotypes is "The Fanelli Boys," an NBC 1990 television situation comedy series about four working-class, Italian-American brothers who are trying to get their lives into shape. Lucky for them, their mama decides not to move to Florida. Instead she stays in Brooklyn to help them through their difficulties. The show's sitcom humor is abrasive and overdone and the Italian working-class characters are loud and harsh. Having discovered an ethnic group, NBC demonstrates it has nothing better to offer us than the same old hackneyed standbys.

Spaghetti Benders from Madison Avenue

Once ethnicity became an acceptable media topic, it was not long before ethnic types were worked into television ads. The TV commercial is the quintessential propaganda message: single-minded, brief, simple, slick, and repetitive. Ethnic stereotypes offer their own instant image recognition: Parsimonious Scots offer us wise counsel regarding bargain-priced gasoline; elegant and snobbish French recommend the best wines, perfumes, and mustards; sweaty, robust Irishmen endorse the right deodorant soap; rotund

---

[6] Opera by Giacomo Puccini.

Germans offer up the best beer; while Japanese prove their love for the extra light beer in the way they supposedly know best—by smashing a barroom table in half with a karate blow.

The Italian has appeared in a variety of advertising roles. There is the Latin lover who wins his lady, less with his amorous overtures than with his right choice of beverage; the Mafia don ready to start a gang-land massacre if the lasagna isn't *magnifico;* the nearly inarticulate disco dimwit who can barely say "Trident" as he twirls his partners around the dance floor.[7] The ethnic characters in commercials are literally caricatures of caricatures.

In the world of commercials, Italians tend to be simple-minded oral creatures. They taste, sip, eat, chew, and offer exclamations such as "Mama mia! Datza spicy meatball!" The stereotypic linking of Italians with food so predominates as to preclude this ethnic group's association with other realms (except crime, of course). Thus, a 1986 PBS documentary mini-series on the English language, narrated by Robert MacNeil, noted how various foreign languages have enriched the English language. However, Italian was something of an exception, MacNeil said, since the Italian words that have passed into English "all relate to food." (Overlooked were such inedibles as cognoscenti, literati, illuminati, ghetto, crescendo, aggiornamento, gambado, inamorata, vendetta, virtuoso, paparazzi, impresario, rotunda, chiaroscuro, buffo, brio, bravo, bravado, divertimento, and imbroglio, along with musical terms like contralto, soprano, fortissimo, basso, pizzicato, piano, and viola.)

Their days taken up with runs to and from the kitchen, Italians, no doubt, would be a poor choice when it comes to chairing a board meeting, offering medical advice, or conducting a scientific experiment, notes Marco Ciolli. "Certainly, no commercial has ever shown an Italian-American involved in any professional activity."[8] A leader of the National Italian-American Foundation complained that "commercials are outdated and subconsciously give a negative image to people who have never had any personal contacts with Italians."[9] One advertising executive concedes the point: "What the hell do I know about Italians? I mean, outside the fact that they like to eat spaghetti, drink wine, and the men chase after women. What more am I supposed to know?"[10]

To say that the media merely reflect reality (after all, there *are* Italian gangsters and Italians *do* drink wine and eat spaghetti) is to overlook the distorted dimension of the "reality" presented. The media's tactic, finding its highest (or lowest) articulation in television ads, is to move *with* the cheap,

---

[7] Marco Ciolli, "Exploring the Italian Image," *Attenzione,* September 1979, p. 16. [Author's note]

[8] Ibid. [Author's note]

[9] Frank Rotondaro, quoted in ibid. [Author's note]

[10] Ibid. [Author's note]

facile notions about one group or another, rather than against them. If there are misconceptions that can easily be made plausible, amusing, or sensational, then the media will use them. Madison Avenue's goal is to manipulate rather than educate, to reach as many people as quickly as possible with readily evocative images. So the media merchandisers pander to the crudest impressions of ethnics held by the public, encouraging each group to embrace the prefabricated images of other groups—and even of its own.

Internalizing the False Image

The make-believe media's treatment of Italian-Americans provides dramatic illustration of how commercially produced stereotypes become accepted by the entire society, including many members of the ethnic group itself. "The ethnic becomes part of the world that is stigmatizing his very self," notes the writer Joseph Papaleo.[11] More than once, on strolls through Italian neighborhoods in New York, I have spotted cars with bumper stickers that read, "Mafia Staff Car, Keepa You Hands Off." While in Philadelphia, my attention was directed to a musical rock group of Italian-American youths who billed themselves as "The Godfathers." In 1981 at the feast of St. Anthony of Padua in New York, the neighborhood band played as its opening number the theme from *The Godfather.* As of the early 1990s, there even existed a "Godfather's" chain of pizzerias.

While many Italians find the association with crime offensive, some are finding a kind of group recognition in it—especially when the movies in question tell us nothing about the mob's role in union-busting, extortion, and shakedowns, and nothing about its victimization of workers, consumers, women (as wives or prostitutes), and small-business owners—including many Italians. Instead, hoodlums are transformed into folk heroes, loveable patriarchs who want nothing more than a decent life for their families and a steady income from their often unspecified "business" ventures.

Just as many African-Americans avidly watched "Amos 'n' Andy,"[12] so Mafia movies "play to audiences just as large in the theaters of Italian-American neighborhoods as they do elsewhere."[13] Like other ethnic groups, Italians have been starved for acknowledgment from the dominant culture, from that prosperous, powerful Other World. The feeling of being shut out,

---

[11] Joseph Papaleo, "Ethnic Pictures and Ethnic Fate," in Randall Miller (ed.), *Ethnic Images in American Film and Television* (Philadelphia: Balch Institute, 1978), p. 94. [Author's note]

[12] Television comedy featuring two stereotyped black characters.

[13] Richard Juliani, "The Image of the Italian in American Film and Television," in Miller, *Ethnic Images*, p. 102. [Author's note]

a stranger in one's own land, is part of what makes many ethnics so responsive to any kind of media representation, even a derogatory one.

The ethnics are always looking for signs that they count for something, that they *exist*—in a society that usually ignores their existence. A starving person will eat junk food. Better to be represented as a buffoon or even a murderous thug than not to exist at all. Like other ethnics, the Italians are still fighting the "invisible man" burden.

Mafia movies also offer the appeal of empowerment; they portray Italians in positions of strength and dominance, able to get things done as they want, in direct and forceful ways, not unlike the frontier cowboy hero. For powerless people, the Mafia don, with his army of hit men and network of lawyers, obliging politicians, and big-business friends, becomes an appealing figure. For these same reasons, I suspect, did some Chinese-Americans enjoy *Year of the Dragon*. That Chinese were being portrayed as thugs, extortionists, narcotic smugglers, and murderers weighed less than that they were finally being portrayed at all. No longer quaint and comic laundrymen and waiters, they were conducting serious conversations with each other in Chinese in the middle of an American movie, displaying shrewdness and resourcefulness (as well as homicidal ruthlessness)—and occupying positions of power and leadership.

The above observations might also help explain the popularity of ethnic mobster films to the public in general. Here are a breed of people who live outside the law with a powerful law of their own, who kowtow to no one, who are powerful and effective, who show cruelty to competitors and kindness to family and friends—except when family and friends become competitors. Here are the real urban cowboys, Jesse James with a machine gun, the Sicilian Robin Hoods—all as American as pizza pie. The Mafia has achieved a kind of folklore status, "rooted in a foreignness that makes it so much more mysteriously titillating than the same activities of organized crime by old-line American thugs might be."[14]

Finally, it must be noted that the media deny the seriousness of the ethnic experience and thereby evade the larger, more taboo question of class struggle. The ethnics' attention is directed toward irrelevant caricatures of themselves that serve as objects of either emulation or insult or both. The ethnics—of whom the Italians are only a more obvious example—are told what to think of themselves by the make-believe media. Controversies about ethnic "identity," group "dignity," and "assimilation" continue endlessly. Ignored by the make-believe media are the pressing problems of working-class ethnics: the demoralizing hardships of underemployment, layoffs, low wages, high taxes, job-connected disabilities, and staggering living costs.

---

[14] Television critic Richard Shepard in the *New York Times*, January 18, 1986. [Author's note]

Having their identities suppressed or falsified is but one manifestation of a larger violation that ethnics are made to suffer. What has been stolen from many of them is their labor, their health, their communities, and their ability to live with a sufficient measure of ease and security. So the ethnics are distracted from their own struggle and their own experience by the daily psychological muggings of Hollywood and television, by fabricated images of the world and of themselves. The medium is the message, and the media are the Mafia.

STUDY AND DISCUSSION QUESTIONS

1. Is Parenti saying that the media portrayal of Italian Americans is entirely false? If not, then what is he saying?

2. Why do you think Parenti so often quotes the pseudo-Italian American dialogue from the media he analyzes?

3. "The media's ethnic bigotry is also a class bigotry." How so?

4. What is the typical media image of the Italian American woman?

5. In what ways do the media images Parenti analyzes affect Italian Americans themselves?

6. What does Parenti like about the few movies he approves of?

7. Parenti writes that "the media deny the seriousness of the ethnic experience and thereby evade the larger, more taboo question of class struggle." Explain.

8. What does Parenti mean when he says, at the very end, that "the media are the Mafia."

SUGGESTIONS FOR WRITING

1. Pick a recent movie or television series that features Italian Americans and analyze how they are portrayed.

2. What images do *you* have of Italian Americans, male and female? (Maybe you are Italian American yourself.) What do you think some of the sources of these images are? Be as specific as you can.

For Indians, No Thanksgiving

Michael Dorris

*Michael Dorris (1945–1997), who was part Modoc Indian, founded
the Native American Studies Program at Dartmouth College, where
he taught for many years. His fiction includes the novels* A Yellow
Raft in Blue Water *(1987) and* Cloud Chamber *(1997) as well as
the story collection* Working Men *(1993). The Broken Cord, which
won the 1989 National Book Award, chronicled the life of his adopted
son Abel, who suffered from fetal alcohol syndrome. Dorris and his
wife, Louise Erdrich, cooperated closely on a number of books, including the novel* The Crown of Columbus *(1991). The following
appeared in his collection* Paper Trail: Essays *(1994).*

Maybe those Pilgrims and Wampanoags actually got together for a November picnic, maybe not. It matters only as an ironical footnote.

For the former group, it would have been a celebration of a precarious
hurdle successfully crossed on the path to the political domination, first of a
continent and eventually of a planet. For the latter, it would have been, at
best, a naive extravaganza—the last meeting as equals with invaders who,
within a few years, would win King Philip's War[1] and decorate the entrances
to their towns with rows of stakes, each topped with an Indian head.

The few aboriginal survivors of the ensuing violence were either sold
into Caribbean slavery by their better-armed, erstwhile hosts or ruthlessly
driven from their Cape Cod homes. Despite the symbolic idealism of the first
potluck, New England—from the emerging European point of view—simply
wasn't big enough for two sets of societies.

An enduring benefit of success, when one culture clashes with another,
is that the victorious group controls the record. It owns not only the immediate spoils but also the power to edit, embellish, and concoct the facts of the
original encounter for the generations to come. Events, once past, reside at the
small end of the telescope, the vague and hazy antecedents to accepted reality.

---

[1] War, 1675–1676, in which King Philip, a Pokunoket chief, led an effort to drive English settlers
off Indian land.

Our collective modern fantasy of Thanksgiving is a case in point. It has evolved into a ritual pageant that almost every one of us, as children, either acted in or were forced to watch—a seventeenth-century vision that we can conjure whole in the blink of an eye.

The cast of stock characters is as recognizable as those in any Macy's parade[2]: dour-faced Pilgrim men, right-to-bear-arms muskets at their sides, sitting around a rude outdoor table while their wives, dressed in long dresses, aprons, and linen caps, bustle about lifting the lids off steaming kettles— pater- and materfamilias of New World hospitality.

They dish out the turkey to a scattering of shirtless Indian invitees. But there is no ambiguity as to who is in charge of the occasion, who could be asked to leave, whose protocol prevails.

Only "good" Indians are admitted into this tableau, of course, as in those who accept the Manifest Destiny of a European presence and are prepared to adopt English dining customs and, by inference, English everything else.

These compliant Hollywood extras are, naturally enough, among the blessings the Pilgrims are thankful for—and why not? Holiday Indians are colorful, bring the food, and vanish after dessert. They are something exotic to write home about, like a visit to Frontierland.[3] In the sound bite of national folklore, they have metamorphosed into totems of America as evocative, and ultimately as vapid, as a flag factory.

And members of this particular make-believe tribe did not all repair to the happy hunting grounds during the first Christmas rush. They lived on, smoking peace pipes and popping up at appropriate crowd-pleasing moments.

They lost mock battles from coast to coast in Wild West shows. In nineteenth-century art, they sat bareback on their horses and stoically watched a lot of sunsets. Entire professional sports teams of them take the home field every Sunday afternoon in Cleveland, Atlanta, or Washington, D.C.

They are the sources of merit badges for Boy Scouts and the emblem of purity for imitation butter. They are, and have been from the beginning, predictable, manageable, domesticated inventions without depth or reality apart from that bestowed by their creators.

These appreciative Indians, as opposed to the pesky flesh and blood native peoples on whom they are loosely modeled, did not question the enforced exchange of their territories for a piece of pie. They did not protest when they died by the millions from European diseases.

---

[2] Thanksgiving parade sponsored by a New York City department store.

[3] One of six thematically-oriented sections of Disneyland.

They did not resist—except for the "bad" ones, the renegades—when solemn pacts made with them were broken or when their religions and customs were declared illegal. They did not make a fuss in courts in defense of their sovereignty. They never expected all the fixings anyway.

As for Thanksgiving 1988, the descendants of those first party-goers sit at increasingly distant tables, the pretense of equity all but abandoned. Against great odds, Native Americans have maintained political identity, but, in a country so insecure about heterogeneity that it votes its dominant language as "official," this refusal to melt into the pot has been an expensive choice.

A majority of reservation Indians reside in the most impoverished counties in the nation. They constitute the ethnic group at the wrong extreme of every scale: most under-nourished, most short-lived, least educated, least healthy. For them, Thanksgiving was perhaps their last square meal.

STUDY AND DISCUSSION QUESTIONS

1. Dorris writes, at the end of his fourth paragraph: "Events, once past, reside at the small end of the telescope, the vague and hazy antecedents to accepted reality." What does he mean?

2. What is the "collective modern fantasy of Thanksgiving"? What function does it serve?

3. Dorris seems to object to the use of Indian names and images by sports teams, advertisers, and the Boy Scouts. Why?

4. Why does it matter that the Thanksgiving "fantasy" distorts reality?

SUGGESTIONS FOR WRITING

1. What do you remember of elementary school Thanksgiving celebrations? What did they teach?

2. Plan an elementary school Thanksgiving lesson or celebration rooted in the realities Dorris describes.

A Slow Walk of Trees (As Grandmother Would Say), Hopeless (As Grandfather Would Say)

Toni Morrison

Toni Morrison (b. 1931) grew up in Lorain, Ohio and studied at Howard and Cornell Universities. She has worked as a senior editor at Random House and has taught at a number of colleges. Her novels include The Bluest Eye *(1969),* Sula *(1973),* Song of Solomon *(1977),* Beloved *(1987), and* Jazz *(1992). She has also published a volume of literary criticism,* Playing in the Dark: Whiteness and the Literary Imagination *(1992), and edited books on the meanings of the Clarence Thomas hearings and the O. J. Simpson trial. In 1993, she won the Nobel Prize for Literature. The following appeared in the* New York Times Magazine *in 1976.*

His name was John Solomon Willis, and when at age 5 he heard from the old folks that "the Emancipation Proclamation was coming," he crawled under the bed. It was his earliest recollection of what was to be his habitual response to the promises of white people: horror and an instinctive yearning for safety. He was my grandfather, a musician who managed to hold on to his violin but not his land. He lost all 88 acres of his Indian mother's inheritance to legal predators who built their fortunes on the likes of him. He was an unreconstructed black pessimist who, in spite of or because of emancipation, was convinced for 85 years that there was no hope whatever for black people in this country. His rancor was legitimate, for he, John Solomon, was not only an artist but a first-rate carpenter and farmer, reduced to sending home to his family money he made playing the violin because he was not able to find work. And this during the years when almost half the black male population were skilled craftsmen who lost their jobs to white ex-convicts and immigrant farmers.

His wife, however, was of a quite different frame of mind and believed that all things could be improved by faith in Jesus and an effort of the will.

So it was she, Ardelia Willis, who sneaked her seven children out of the back window into the darkness, rather than permit the patron of their sharecropper's existence to become their executioner as well, and headed north in 1912, when 99.2 percent of all black people in the U.S. were native-born and only 60 percent of white Americans were. And it was Ardelia who told her husband that they could not stay in the Kentucky town they ended up in because the teacher didn't know long division.

They have been dead now for 30 years and more and I still don't know which of them came closer to the truth about the possibilities of life for black people in this country. One of their grandchildren is a tenured professor at Princeton. Another, who suffered from what the Peruvian poet[1] called "anger that breaks a man into children," was picked up just as he entered his teens and emotionally lobotomized by the reformatories and mental institutions specifically designed to serve him. Neither John Solomon nor Ardelia lived long enough to despair over one or swell with pride over the other. But if they were alive today each would have selected and collected enough evidence to support the accuracy of the other's original point of view. And it would be difficult to convince either one that the other was right.

Some of the monstrous events that took place in John Solomon's America have been duplicated in alarming detail in my own America. There was the public murder of a President in a theater in 1865 and the public murder of another President on television in 1963. The Civil War of 1861 had its encore as the civil-rights movement of 1960. The torture and mutilation of a black West Point Cadet (Cadet Johnson Whittaker) in 1880 had its rerun with the 1970's murders of students at Jackson State College, Texas Southern and Southern University in Baton Rouge. And in 1976 we watch for what must be the thousandth time a pitched battle between the children of slaves and the children of immigrants—only this time, it is not the New York draft riots of 1863, but the busing turmoil in Paul Revere's home town, Boston.[2]

Hopeless, he'd said. Hopeless. For he was certain that white people of every political, religious, geographical and economic background would band together against black people everywhere when they felt the threat of our progress. And a hundred years after he sought safety from the white man's "promise," somebody put a bullet in Martin Luther King's brain. And not long before that some excellent samples of the master race demonstrated their

---

[1] César Vallejo.

[2] The New York City draft riots broke out in response to the Civil War draft, which the rich could avoid by paying the then large sum of $300; "busing turmoil": violent response by some whites to court-ordered busing to integrate Boston public schools in the 1970s.

courage and virility by dynamiting some little black girls to death.[3] If he were here now, my grandfather, he would shake his head, close his eyes and pull out his violin—too polite to say, "I told you so." And his wife would pay attention to the music but not to the sadness in her husband's eyes, for she would see what she expected to see—not the occasional historical repetition, but, like the slow walk of certain species of trees from the flatlands up into the mountains, she would see the signs of irrevocable and permanent change. She, who pulled her girls out of an inadequate school in the Cumberland Mountains, knew all along that the gentlemen from Alabama who had killed the little girls would be rounded up. And it wouldn't surprise her in the least to know that the number of black college graduates jumped 12 percent in the last three years; 47 percent in 20 years. That there are 140 black mayors in this country; 14 black judges in the District Circuit, 4 in the Courts of Appeals and one on the Supreme Court. That there are 17 blacks in Congress, one in the Senate; 276 in state legislatures—223 in state houses, 53 in state senates. That there are 112 elected black police chiefs and sheriffs; 1 Pulitzer Prize winner; 1 winner of the Prix de Rome; a dozen or so winners of the Guggenheim;[4] 4 deans of predominently white colleges. . . . Oh, her list would go on and on. But so would John Solomon's sweet sad music.

While my grandparents held opposite views on whether the fortunes of black people were improving, my own parents struck similarly opposed postures, but from another slant. They differed about whether the moral fiber of white people would ever improve. Quite a different argument. The old folks argued about how and if black people could improve themselves, who could be counted on to help us, who would hinder us and so on. My parents took issue over the question of whether it was possible for white people to improve. They assumed that black people were the humans of the globe, but had serious doubts about the quality and existence of white humanity. Thus my father, distrusting every word and every gesture of every white man on earth, assumed that the white man who crept up the stairs one afternoon had come to molest his daughters and threw him down the stairs and then our tricycle after him. (I think my father was wrong, but considering what I have seen since, it may have been very healthy for me to have witnessed that as my first black-white encounter.) My mother, however, *believed* in them—their possibilities. So when the meal we got on relief was bug-ridden, she wrote a long letter to Franklin Delano Roosevelt. And when white bill collectors came

---

[3] Four young girls were killed in 1963 when a Baptist church in Birmingham, Alabama was bombed.

[4] Prix de Rome, prestigious scholarship for young artists; Guggenheim, award to support scholarly research.

to our door, it was she who received them civilly and explained in a sweet voice that we were people of honor and that the debt would be taken care of. Her message to Roosevelt got through—our meal improved. Her message to the bill collectors did not always get through and there was occasional violence when my father (self-exiled to the bedroom for fear he could not hold his temper) would hear that her reasonableness had failed. My mother was always wounded by these scenes, for she thought the bill collector knew that she loved good credit more than life and that being in arrears on a payment horrified her probably more than it did him. So she thought he was rude because he was white. For years she walked to utility companies and department stores to pay bills in person and even now she does not seem convinced that checks are legal tender. My father loved excellence, worked hard (he held three jobs at once for 17 years) and was so outraged by the suggestion of personal slackness that he could explain it to himself only in terms of racism. He was a fastidious worker who was frightened of one thing: unemployment. I can remember now the doomsday-cum-graveyard sound of "laid off" and how the minute school was out he asked us, "Where you workin'?" Both my parents believed that all succor and aid came from themselves and their neighborhood, since "they"—white people in charge and those not in charge but in obstructionist positions—were in some way fundamentally, genetically corrupt.

So I grew up in a basically racist household with more than a child's share of contempt for white people. And for each white friend I acquired who made a small crack in that contempt, there was another who repaired it. For each one who related to me as a person, there was one who in my presence at least, became actively "white." And like most black people of my generation, I suffer from racial vertigo that can be cured only by taking what one needs from one's ancestors. John Solomon's cynicism and his deployment of his art as both weapon and solace, Ardelia's faith in the magic that can be wrought by sheer effort of the will; my mother's openmindedness in each new encounter and her habit of trying reasonableness first; my father's temper, his impatience and his efforts to keep "them" (throw them) out of his life. And it is out of these learned and selected attitudes that I look at the quality of life for my people in this country now.

These widely disparate and sometimes conflicting views, I suspect, were held not only by me, but by most black people. Some I know are clearer in their positions, have not sullied their anger with optimism or dirtied their hope with despair. But most of us are plagued by a sense of being worn shell-thin by constant repression and hostility as well as the impression of being buoyed by visible testimony of tremendous strides. There *is* repetition of the grotesque in our history. And there *is* the miraculous walk of trees. The question is whether our walk is progress or merely movement. O. J. Simpson leaning on a Hertz car *is* better than the Gold Dust Twins on the back of a soap box.[5] But is "Good Times" better than Stepin Fetchit?[6] Has the first order of business been taken care of? Does the law of the land work for us?

Are white people who murder black people punished with at least the same dispatch that sends black teen-age truants to Coxsackie?[7] Can we relax now and discuss "The Jeffersons"[8] instead of genocide? Or is the difference between the two only the difference between a greedy pointless white life-style and a messy pointless black death? Now that Mr. Poitier and Mr. Belafonte have shot up all the racists in "Buck and the Preacher," have they all gone away? Can we really move into better neighborhoods and not be set on fire? Is there anybody who will lay me a $5 bet on it?

The past decade is a fairly good index of the odds at which you lay your money down.

Ten years ago in Queens, as black people like me moved into a neighborhood 20 minutes away from the Triborough Bridge, "for sale" signs shot up in front of white folks' houses like dandelions after a hot spring rain. And the black people smiled. "Goody, goody," said my neighbor. "Maybe we can push them on out to the sea. You think?"

Now I live in another neighborhood, 20 minutes away from the George Washington Bridge, and again the "for sale" signs are pushing up out of the ground. Fewer, perhaps, and for different reasons, perhaps. Still the Haitian lady and I smile at each other. "My, my," she says "they goin' on up to the hills? Seem like they just come from there." "The woods," I say. "They like to live in the woods." She nods with infinite understanding, then shrugs. The Haitians have already arranged for one mass in the church to be said in French, already have their own newspaper, stores, community center. That's not movement. That's progress.

But the decade has other revelations. Ten years ago, young, bright, energetic blacks were sought out, pursued and hired into major corporations, major networks and onto the staffs of newspapers and national magazines. Many survived that courtship, some even with their souls intact. Newscasters, corporate lawyers, marketing specialists, journalists, production managers, plant foremen, college deans. But many more spend a lot of time on the telephone these days, or at the typewriter preparing résumés, which they send out (mostly to friends now) with little notes attached: "Is there anything you

---

[5] Racist caricature of two black children in a tub used as the logo for Gold Dust Washing Powder, popular in the early 1900s.

[6] Television sitcom about a black family in Chicago; black movie actor known for his stereotypical roles.

[7] Prison in New York State.

[8] Television sitcom about a black family in New York City.

know of?" Or they think there is a good book in the story of what happened to them, the great hoax that was played on them. They are right, of course, about the hoax, for many of them were given elegant executive jobs with the work drained out. Work minus power. Work minus decision-making. Work minus dominion. Affirmative Action Make Believe that a lot of black people *did* believe because they also believed that the white people in those nice offices were not like the ones in the general store or in the plumbers' union— that they were fundamentally kind, or fair, or something. Anything but the desperate prisoners of economics they turned out to be, holding on to their dominion with a tenacity and sang-froid that can only be described as Nixonian. So the bright and the black (architects, reporters, vice-presidents in charge of public relations) walk the streets right along with that astounding 38 percent of the black teen-aged female work force that does not have and never has had a job. So the black female college graduate earns two-thirds of what a white male high-school dropout earns. So the black people who put everything into community-action programs supported by Government funds have found themselves bereft of action, bereft of funds and all but bereft of community.

This decade has been rife with disappointment in practically every place where we thought we saw permanent change: Hostos, CUNY,[9] and the black-studies departments that erupted like minivolcanoes on campuses all over the nation; easy integrations of public-school systems; acceleration of promotion in factories and businesses. But now when we describe what has happened we cannot do it without using the verbs of upheaval and destruction: Open admission *closes;* minority-student quotas *fall* or *discontinue;* salary gaps between blacks and whites *widen;* black-studies departments *merge.* And the only growth black people can count on is in the prison population and the unemployment line. Even busing, which used to be a plain, if emotional, term at best, has now taken on an adjective normally reserved for rape and burglary—it is now called "forced" busing.

All of that counts, but I'm not sure that in the long haul it matters. Maybe Ardelia Willis had the best idea. One sees signs of her vision and the fruits of her prophecy in spite of the dread-lock statistics. The trees *are* walking, albeit slowly and quietly and without the fanfare of a cross-country run. It seems that at last black people have abandoned our foolish dependency on the Government to do the work that we once thought all of its citizenry would be delighted to do. Our love affair with the Federal Government is over. We misjudged the ardor of its attention. We thought its

---

[9] Hostos Community College, in the Bronx, known for its Spanish/English bilingual programs; the City University of New York (CUNY), a public higher education system.

majority constituency would *prefer* having their children grow up among happy, progressive, industrious, contented black children rather than among angry, disenchanted and dangerous ones. That the profit motive of industry alone would keep us employed and therefore spending, and that our poverty was bad for business. We thought landlords wanted us to have a share in our neighborhoods and therefore love and care for them. That city governments wanted us to control our schools and therefore preserve them.

We were wrong. And now, having been eliminated from the lists of urgent national priorities, from TV documentaries and the platitudes of editorials, black people have chosen, or been forced to seek safety from the white man's promise, but happily not under a bed. More and more, there is the return to Ardelia's ways: the exercise of the will, the recognition of obstacles as only that—obstacles, not fixed stars. Black judges are fixing appropriate rather than punitive bail for black "offenders" and letting the rest of the community of jurisprudence scream. Young black women are leaving plush Northern jobs to sit in their living rooms and teach black children, work among factory women and spend months finding money to finance the college education of young blacks. Groups of blacks are buying huge tracts of land in the South and cutting off entirely the dependency of whole communities on grocery chains. For the first time, significant numbers of black people are returning or migrating to the South to focus on the acquisition of land, the transferral of crafts and skills, and the sharing of resources, the rebuilding of neighborhoods.

In the shambles of closing admissions, falling quotas, widening salary gaps and merging black-studies departments, builders and healers are working quietly among us. They are not like the heroes of old, the leaders we followed blindly and upon whom we depended for everything, or the blacks who had accumulated wealth for its own sake, fame, medals or some public acknowledgment of success. These are the people whose work is real and pointed and clear in its application to the race. Some are old and have been at work for a long time in and out of the public eye. Some are new and just finding out what their work is. But they are unmistakably the natural aristocrats of the race. The ones who refuse to imitate, to compromise, and who are indifferent to public accolade. Whose work is free or priceless. They take huge risks economically and personally. They are not always popular, even among black people, but they are the ones whose work black people respect. They are the healers. Some are nowhere near the public eye: Ben Chavis, preacher and political activist languishing now in North Carolina prisons; Robert Moses, a pioneering activist; Sterling Brown, poet and teacher; Father Al McKnight, land reformer; Rudy Lombard, urban sociologist; Lerone Bennett, historian; C. L. R. James, scholar; Alyce Gullattee, psychologist and organizer. Others are public legends: Judge Crockett, Judge Bruce Wright, Stevie Wonder, Ishmael

Reed, Miles Davis, Richard Pryor, Muhammad Ali, Fannie Lou Hamer, Eubie Blake, Angela Davis, Bill Russell[10] . . .

But a complete roll-call is neither fitting nor necessary. They know who they are and so do we. They clarify our past, make livable our present and are certain to shape our future. And since the future is where our immortality as a race lies, no overview of the state of black people at this time can ignore some speculation on the only ones certain to live it—the children.

They are both exhilarating and frightening, those black children, and a source of wonderment to me. Although statistics about black teen-age crime and the "failure" of the courts to gut them are regularly printed and regularly received with outrage and fear, the children I know and see, those born after 1960, do not make such great copy. They are those who have grown up with nothing to prove to white people, whose perceptions of themselves are so new, so different, so focused they appear to me to be either magnificent hybrids or throwbacks to the time when our ancestors were called "royal." They are the baby sisters of the sit-in generation, the sons of the neighborhood blockbusters, the nephews of jailed revolutionaries, and a huge number who have had college graduates in their families for three and four generations. I thought we had left them nothing to love and nothing to want to know. I thought that those who exhibited some excitement about their future had long ago looked into the eyes of their teachers and were either saddened or outraged by the death of possibility they found there. I thought that those who were interested in the past had looked into the faces of their parents and seen betrayal. I thought the state had deprived them of a land and the landlords and banks had deprived them of a turf. So how is it that, with nothing to love, nothing they need to know, landless, turfless, minus a future and a past, these black children look us dead in the eye? They seem not to know how to apologize. And even when they are wrong they do not ask for forgiveness. It is as though they are waiting for us to apologize to them, to beg their pardon, to seek their approval. What species of black is this that not only does not choose to grovel, but doesn't know how? How will they keep jobs? How will they live? Won't they be killed before they reproduce? But they are unafraid. Is it because they refuse to see the world as we did? Is it because they have rejected both land and turf to seek instead a world? Maybe they finally got the message that we had been shouting into their faces; that they *live* here, *belong* here on this planet earth and that it is *theirs*. So they watch us with the eyes of poets and carpen-

---

[10] George W. Crockett, Jr., civil rights activist and Detroit criminal court judge; Judge Bruce Wright, New York State Supreme Court justice; Stevie Wonder, singer, musician, and songwriter; Ishmael Reed, novelist and essayist; Miles Davis, jazz trumpeter and composer; Richard Pryor, stand-up comedian and actor; Muhammad Ali, heavyweight boxing champion; Fannie Lou Hamer, civil rights activist; Eubie Blake, pianist and composer; Angela Davis, political activist and writer; Bill Russell, professional basketball player and coach.

ters and musicians and scholars and other people who know who they are because they have invented themselves and know where they are going because
they have envisioned it. All of which would please Ardelia—and John Solomon,
too, I think. After all, he did hold on to his violin.

STUDY AND DISCUSSION QUESTIONS

1. Compare Morrison's grandmother's and grandfather's views. How do
   the views of Morrison's mother and father mirror and differ from them?

2. Why does Morrison point out that, in 1912, "99.2 percent of all black
   people in the U.S. were native-born and only 60 percent of white
   Americans were"?

3. "And like most black people of my generation, I suffer from racial vertigo." Explain.

4. What are some of the reasons for optimism that Morrison points to?
   For pessimism?

5. What does Morrison mean by "Affirmative Action Make Believe"?
   Does she oppose affirmative action?

6. Why are black children "both exhilarating and frightening" to Morrison? What does she see in them?

7. How is this essay organized? How does its organization relate to its
   theme?

SUGGESTIONS FOR WRITING

1. Morrison says she still doesn't know which of her grandparents "came
   closer to the truth about the possibilities of life for black people in this
   country." Does her essay reveal *any* tilt towards either one's outlook?

2. This essay was published in 1976. Discuss some of the reasons to despair
   and some of the reasons to hope *today* about "the possibilities of life
   for black people in this country."

MONEY, WORK, AND SOCIAL CLASS

The working class possesses no economic or occupational independence, is employed by capital and its offshoots, possesses no access to
the labor process or the means of production outside that employment,
and must renew its labors for capital incessantly in order to subsist.

—Harry Braverman
*Labor and Monopoly Capital: The
Degradation of Work in the Twentieth Century*

Despite attention in the national media in recent years to the increasing
gap between rich and poor in the United States, most Americans 1) believe
that the country is basically a meritocracy and 2) identify themselves as middle class. This tendency to ignore that a class system exists here, as it does
everywhere else in the world, has numerous consequences. On the positive
side, social class is, relatively speaking, more fluid in the United States than
in many countries. People can, through hard work, a lot of luck, and the acquisition of an education, improve their prospects of having more choices
and material comforts. One is not necessarily locked into the class status of
one's parents, and parents like steelworker Mike LeFevre, whose oral history
is included here, dream of their children surpassing them. On the negative
side, the pull-yourself-up-by-your-own-bootstraps mentality means that failure to rise from one social class to another is often attributed to some innate
lack of drive, intelligence, or even worthiness on the part of the individual.
Americans tend to discount the fact that there are many applicants for few
places in the middle class or upper-middle class.

The structure and appearance of social classes in postindustrial societies are currently in transition, which further confuses the discussion of social class in the United States. Traditional working-class jobs such as those held by the assembly line workers Barbara Garson interviews in "Whistle While You Work" are in decline. Unionized factory work is being replaced by nonunionized service and low-level computer-punching work. The gender composition of the workforce is changing as well. Men traditionally have held the industrial jobs that are now disappearing. Meanwhile, women looking for jobs to maintain family incomes that can no longer keep up with rising costs take the new low-paying work. The livelihood of people in the middle class is changing as well, as information technology creates new occupations. Workers in these new technology-based occupations must be able to grasp the symbolic knowledge of computer languages, and aspirants to the middle class are more dependent than ever upon a traditional education. As the quote from *Labor and Monopoly Capital* suggests, most people, whatever their class status, are held more and more tightly by the grip of corporations (see Jerry Mander's article, "Corporations as Machines," for a structural analysis of why this is so); even people who have been "downsized" from the payrolls of corporations now work as their "consultants" or "casual workers." This section offers a variety of perspectives on people's relation to money, to how we make a living, and to how we identify ourselves in the class structure.

Social class and money come together in a bitingly ironic way in the opening chapter of Jamaica Kincaid's *A Small Place,* a memoir of her native Antigua. Here Kincaid brilliantly describes the island from the perspective of the newly arrived tourist who has escaped from the dreariness of a northern winter to bask in the sun of a Carribean island. But, however modest the means of the tourist, however well deserved the vacation, however nice the tourist is, that tourist is ugly in the eyes of the island's inhabitants. The vast majority of Antiguans are too poor to take a vacation, and what tourists perceive to be picturesque for Antiguans translates into a lived experience of misery. Unlike the tourist, they are "too poor to escape the reality of their lives," writes Kincaid. Thus the tourist's vacation is the islander's prison. Kincaid shows the gulf between social classes in several ways: 1) between the few rich and many poor on Antigua itself; 2) between the tourists from the developed West and the natives of the "undeveloped" island; and 3) between whites and blacks (for it just so happens that her tourist is white and her natives are black). Later in *A Small Place,* Kincaid will talk about the uneasiness of her own return as a middle-class black professional to the poverty stricken island of her birth.

What is work, anyway? How do you define work? As unpleasant, tedious activity? As activity of any kind for which you get paid? As activity which, whether or not it is pleasant and whether or not you are paid for it, produces something? This last category might include writing a song, reading a bedtime story with your child, or stacking a cord of wood for those deep winter log fires. Both Mike LeFevre, subject of Studs Terkel's interview, and Barbara Garson, author of "Whistle While You Work," focus on monotonous, tedious, alienating work, work which has been stripped of meaning because the connection between worker and final product has been severed. Capitalism attempts to transfer control of the work process from worker to management and therefore to effectively remove volition and meaning from the labor of the worker. Both LeFevre and the workers Garson writes of cope with this situation in a variety of inventive ways: by setting minigoals of productivity, by daydreaming, by slowing down and speeding up, occasionally by sabotaging production. And yet what Garson concludes from her interviews with workers, much to her surprise, is that work is crucial to a human being's self-definition, that meaningful work is in fact "a basic human need."

Jesus Colón's account of his early years as a dock and trainyard worker just after World War I suggests that he feels less alienated from his work than LeFevre or Garson's subjects. Colón describes in detail three different jobs—all of them difficult, dangerous, and performed in the cold. He in no way sentimentalizes the work, yet his tone is almost nostalgic, especially as he remembers his first foreman, Mr. Clark. Colón's commitment to the American working class is evident, and as the tone of this piece differs markedly from LeFevre's oral history, you might find it interesting to compare these two first-person worker's accounts.

The first four pieces of nonfictional prose in this section focus on the personal experience of the author or of interviewees; the next pair of essays demonstrate that satire is likewise an effective means of discussing money, work, and social class. Judy Brady's humorous "I Want a Wife" uses the technique of *reversal*. The speaker of "I Want a Wife" is a woman, and therein lies some of the essay's biting humor. She observes just what it is a wife traditionally is called upon to do, notes the meager rewards for being a good wife ("If, by chance, I find another person more suitable as a wife than the wife I already have, I want the liberty to replace my present wife with another one," muses the self-satisfied *persona* of this essay), and concludes that whoever has got a wife has got a pretty good deal. How does being a wife in Brady's terms parallel some of the observations made about other types of workers described in this section?

While several of the pieces included in this section look at working-class jobs, Ellen Goodman's "The Company Man" satirically chronicles the damage work can produce at the middle- or upper-middle-class level of society. Some people might say that Phil, whose extended obituary this essay is, was very successful; he had a very good job, made good money, possessed status, was able to provide much for his family materially, could send his children to good schools, and, in short, had a very privileged existence. Still, it killed him at age fifty-one and apparently damaged the quality of his life long before his death. One question to ask is whether the responsibility lies in Phil—was he insensitive, overly ambitious, simply a "Type A" (a popular concept about biology and personality, by the way, that has been disproven since Goodman's article was written), or does the responsibility lodge in the current economic system in the West—corporate or monopoly capitalism?

Jerry Mander's extensive analysis in "Corporations as Machines" suggests that many problematic qualities we ascribe to individuals are inherent in the nature and structure of corporations. "Though human beings work inside corporations," writes Mander, "a corporation is not a person, and does not have feelings." Corporate actions might spill tons of oil into the ocean and onto beaches, destroying delicately balanced ecologies; they might sell millions of cigarettes, causing hundreds of thousands of deaths through lung and throat cancer; but because corporations have no "feelings," they refuse to take responsibility, since taking responsibility would "impact on" profitability.

Shifting perspective for a moment, consider that we in the West are increasingly defined as "consumers" and that the word "consumer" is used at least as often now as the word "citizen." Increasingly, not only our work life but our life outside of work is being defined by the vast web of corporate influence. It is very difficult to escape corporate influence in this country. To test that hypothesis, you might try listing the ways in which corporations affect your life on a daily basis, from what you eat and where you live to how you amuse yourself.

FROM *A SMALL PLACE*

Jamaica Kincaid

*Jamaica Kincaid was born Elaine Potter Richardson in St. John's, An-
tigua in 1949. At sixteen she came to the United States to work as an
au pair and after a number of years became a staff writer for the* New
Yorker *magazine and changed her name. Her fiction includes* At the
Bottom of the River *(1983),* Annie John *(1985),* Lucy *(1990),
and* The Autobiography of My Mother *(1996). The following is the
opening of* A Small Place *(1988), a work of nonfiction.*

If you go to Antigua as a tourist, this is what you will see. If you come by
aeroplane, you will land at the V. C. Bird International Airport. Vere Cornwall
(V. C.) Bird is the Prime Minister of Antigua. You may be the sort of tourist
who would wonder why a Prime Minister would want an airport named after
him—why not a school, why not a hospital, why not some great public monument? You are a tourist and you have not yet seen a school in Antigua, you
have not yet seen the hospital in Antigua, you have not yet seen a public monument in Antigua. As your plane descends to land, you might say, What a
beautiful island Antigua is—more beautiful than any of the other islands you
have seen, and they were very beautiful, in their way, but they were much too
green, much too lush with vegetation, which indicated to you, the tourist,
that they got quite a bit of rainfall, and rain is the very thing that you, just
now, do not want, for you are thinking of the hard and cold and dark and
long days you spent working in North America (or, worse, Europe), earning
some money so that you could stay in this place (Antigua) where the sun always shines and where the climate is deliciously hot and dry for the four to
ten days you are going to be staying there; and since you are on your holiday,
since you are a tourist, the thought of what it might be like for someone who
had to live day in, day out in a place that suffers constantly from drought,
and so has to watch carefully every drop of fresh water used (while at the
same time surrounded by a sea and an ocean—the Caribbean Sea on one
side, the Atlantic Ocean on the other), must never cross your mind.

You disembark from your plane. You go through customs. Since you
are a tourist, a North American or European—to be frank, white—and not
an Antiguan black returning to Antigua from Europe or North America with
cardboard boxes of much needed cheap clothes and food for relatives, you

move through customs swiftly, you move through customs with ease. Your bags are not searched. You emerge from customs into the hot, clean air: immediately you feel cleansed, immediately you feel blessed (which is to say special); you feel free. You see a man, a taxi driver; you ask him to take you to your destination; he quotes you a price. You immediately think that the price is in the local currency, for you are a tourist and you are familiar with these things (rates of exchange) and you feel even more free, for things seem so cheap, but then your driver ends by saying, "In U.S. currency." You may say, "Hmmmm, do you have a formal sheet that lists official prices and destinations?" Your driver obeys the law and shows you the sheet, and he apologises for the incredible mistake he has made in quoting you a price off the top of his head which is so vastly different (favouring him) from the one listed. You are driven to your hotel by this taxi driver in his taxi, a brand-new Japanese-made vehicle. The road on which you are travelling is a very bad road, very much in need of repair. You are feeling wonderful, so you say, "Oh, what a marvellous change these bad roads are from the splendid highways I am used to in North America." (Or, worse, Europe.) Your driver is reckless; he is a dangerous man who drives in the middle of the road when he thinks no other cars are coming in the opposite direction, passes other cars on blind curves that run uphill, drives at sixty miles an hour on narrow, curving roads when the road sign, a rusting, beat-up thing left over from colonial days, says 40 MPH. This might frighten you (you are on your holiday; you are a tourist); this might excite you (you are on your holiday; you are a tourist), though if you are from New York and take taxis you are used to this style of driving: most of the taxi drivers in New York are from places in the world like this. You are looking out the window (because you want to get your money's worth); you notice that all the cars you see are brand-new, or almost brand-new, and that they are all Japanese-made. There are no American cars in Antigua—no new ones, at any rate; none that were manufactured in the last ten years. You continue to look at the cars and you say to yourself, Why, they look brand-new, but they have an awful sound, like an old car—a very old, dilapidated car. How to account for that? Well, possibly it's because they use leaded gasoline in these brand-new cars whose engines were built to use non-leaded gasoline, but you musn't ask the person driving the car if this is so, because he or she has never heard of unleaded gasoline. You look closely at the car; you see that it's a model of a Japanese car that you might hesitate to buy; it's a model that's very expensive; it's a model that's quite impractical for a person who has to work as hard as you do and who watches every penny you earn so that you can afford this holiday you are on. How do they afford such a car? And do they live in a luxurious house to match such a car? Well, no. You will be surprised, then, to see that most likely the person driving this brand-new car filled with the wrong gas lives in a house that, in comparison, is far beneath the status of the car; and if you were to ask why you would be told that the banks are encouraged by the government to make loans available for cars, but loans for houses not so easily available; and if you ask again why, you will be told that the two main car dealerships in Antigua are owned in part or outright by ministers in government. Oh, but you are on holiday and the sight of these brand-new cars driven by people who may or may not have really passed their driving test (there was once a scandal about driving licences for sale) would not really stir up these thoughts in you. You pass a building sitting in a sea of dust and you think, It's some latrines for people just passing by, but when you look again you see the building has written on it PIGOTT'S SCHOOL. You pass the hospital, the Holberton Hospital, and how wrong you are not to think about this, for though you are a tourist on your holiday, what if your heart should miss a few beats? What if a blood vessel in your neck should break? What if one of those people driving those brand-new cars filled with the wrong gas fails to pass safely while going uphill on a curve and you are in the car going in the opposite direction? Will you be comforted to know that the hospital is staffed with doctors that no actual Antiguan trusts; that Antiguans always say about the doctors, "I don't want them near me"; that Antiguans refer to them not as doctors but as "the three men" (there are three of them); that when the Minister of Health himself doesn't feel well he takes the first plane to New York to see a real doctor; that if any one of the ministers in government needs medical care he flies to New York to get it?

It's a good thing that you brought your own books with you, for you couldn't just go to the library and borrow some. Antigua used to have a splendid library, but in The Earthquake (everyone talks about it that way—The Earthquake; we Antiguans, for I am one, have a great sense of things, and the more meaningful the thing, the more meaningless we make it) the library building was damaged. This was in 1974, and soon after that a sign was placed on the front of the building saying, THIS BUILDING WAS DAMAGED IN THE EARTHQUAKE OF 1974. REPAIRS ARE PENDING. The sign hangs there, and hangs there more than a decade later, with its unfulfilled promise of repair, and you might see this as a sort of quaintness on the part of these islanders, these people descended from slaves—what a strange, unusual perception of time they have. REPAIRS ARE PENDING, and here it is many years later, but perhaps in a world that is twelve miles long and nine miles wide (the size of Antigua) twelve years and twelve minutes and twelve days are all the same. The library is one of those splendid old buildings from colonial times, and the sign telling of the repairs is a splendid old sign from colonial times. Not very long after The Earthquake Antigua got its independence from Britain, making Antigua a state in its own right, and Antiguans are so proud of this that each year, to mark the day, they go to church and thank God, a British God, for this. But you should not think of the confusion that must lie in all that and you must not think of the damaged library. You have brought your own books with you, and among them is one of those new books about economic history, one of those books explaining how the West (meaning Europe and North America after its conquest and settlement by Europeans) got rich: the West got rich not from the free (free—in this case meaning got-for-nothing) and then undervalued labour, for generations, of the people like me you see walking around you in Antigua but from the ingenuity of small shopkeepers in Sheffield and Yorkshire and Lancashire,[1] or wherever; and what a great part the invention of the wristwatch played in it, for there was nothing noble-minded men could not do when they discovered they could slap time on their wrists just like that (isn't that the last straw; for not only did we have to suffer the unspeakableness of slavery, but the satisfaction to be had from "We made you bastards rich" is taken away, too), and so you needn't let that slightly funny feeling you have from time to time about exploitation, oppression, domination develop into full-fledged unease, discomfort; you could ruin your holiday. They are not responsible for what you have; you owe them nothing; in fact, you did them a big favour, and you can provide one hundred examples. For here you are now, passing by Government House. And here you are now, passing by the Prime Minister's Office and the Parliament Building, and overlooking these, with a splendid view of St. John's Harbour, the American Embassy. If it were not for you, they would not have Government House, and Prime Minister's Office, and Parliament Building and embassy of powerful country. Now you are passing a mansion, an extraordinary house painted the colour of old cow dung, with more aerials and antennas attached to it than you will see even at the American Embassy. The people who live in this house are a merchant family who came to Antigua from the Middle East less than twenty years ago. When this family first came to Antigua, they sold dry goods door to door from suitcases they carried on their backs. Now they own a lot of Antigua; they regularly lend money to the government, they build enormous (for Antigua), ugly (for Antigua), concrete buildings in Antigua's capital, St. John's, which the government then rents for huge sums of money; a member of their family is the Antiguan Ambassador to Syria; Antiguans hate them. Not far from this mansion is another mansion, the home of a drug smuggler. Everybody knows he's a drug smuggler, and if just as you were driving by he stepped out of his door your driver might point him out to you as the notorious person that he is, for this drug smuggler is so rich people say he buys cars in tens—ten of this one, ten of that one—and he bought a house (another mansion) near Five Islands,[2] contents included,

---

[1] Sheffield, city in England; Yorkshire and Lancashire, counties in England.

[2] Second largest city in Antigua.

with cash he carried in a suitcase: three hundred and fifty thousand American dollars, and, to the surprise of the seller of the house, lots of American dollars were left over. Overlooking the drug smuggler's mansion is yet another mansion, and leading up to it is the best paved road in all of Antigua—even better than the road that was paved for the Queen's visit in 1985 (when the Queen came, all the roads that she would travel on were paved anew, so that the Queen might have been left with the impression that riding in a car in Antigua was a pleasant experience). In this mansion lives a woman sophisticated people in Antigua call Evita. She is a notorious woman. She's young and beautiful and the girlfriend of somebody very high up in the government. Evita is notorious because her relationship with this high government official has made her the owner of boutiques and property and given her a say in cabinet meetings, and all sorts of other privileges such a relationship would bring a beautiful young woman.

Oh, but by now you are tired of all this looking, and you want to reach your destination—your hotel, your room. You long to refresh yourself; you long to eat some nice lobster, some nice local food. You take a bath, you brush your teeth. You get dressed again; as you get dressed, you look out the window. That water—have you ever seen anything like it? Far out, to the horizon, the colour of the water is navy-blue; nearer, the water is the colour of the North American sky. From there to the shore, the water is pale, silvery, clear, so clear that you can see its pinkish-white sand bottom. Oh, what beauty! Oh, what beauty! You have never seen anything like this. You are so excited. You breathe shallow. You breathe deep. You see a beautiful boy skimming the water, godlike, on a Windsurfer. You see an incredibly unattractive, fat, pastrylike-fleshed woman enjoying a walk on the beautiful sand, with a man, an incredibly unattractive, fat, pastrylike-fleshed man; you see the pleasure they're taking in their surroundings. Still standing, looking out the window, you see yourself lying on the beach, enjoying the amazing sun (a sun so powerful and yet so beautiful, the way it is always overhead as if on permanent guard, ready to stamp out any cloud that dares to darken and so empty rain on you and ruin your holiday; a sun that is your personal friend). You see yourself taking a walk on that beach, you see yourself meeting new people (only they are new in a very limited way, for they are people just like you). You see yourself eating some delicious, locally grown food. You see yourself, you see yourself . . . You must not wonder what exactly happened to the contents of your lavatory when you flushed it. You must not wonder where your bathwater went when you pulled out the stopper. You must not wonder what happened when you brushed your teeth. Oh, it might all end up in the water you are thinking of taking a swim in; the contents of your lavatory might, just might, graze gently against your ankle as you wade carefree in the water, for you see, in Antigua, there is no proper sewage-disposal system. But the

Caribbean Sea is very big and the Atlantic Ocean is even bigger; it would amaze even you to know the number of black slaves this ocean has swallowed up. When you sit down to eat your delicious meal, it's better that you don't know that most of what you are eating came off a plane from Miami. And before it got on a plane in Miami, who knows where it came from? A good guess is that it came from a place like Antigua first, where it was grown dirt-cheap, went to Miami, and came back. There is a world of something in this, but I can't go into it right now.

The thing you have always suspected about yourself the minute you become a tourist is true: A tourist is an ugly human being. You are not an ugly person all the time; you are not an ugly person ordinarily; you are not an ugly person day to day. From day to day, you are a nice person. From day to day, all the people who are supposed to love you on the whole do. From day to day, as you walk down a busy street in the large and modern and prosperous city in which you work and live, dismayed, puzzled (a cliché, but only a cliché can explain you) at how alone you feel in this crowd, how awful it is to go unnoticed, how awful it is to go unloved, even as you are surrounded by more people than you could possibly get to know in a lifetime that lasted for millennia, and then out of the corner of your eye you see someone looking at you and absolute pleasure is written all over that person's face, and then you realise that you are not as revolting a presence as you think you are (for that look just told you so). And so, ordinarily, you are a nice person, an attractive person, a person capable of drawing to yourself the affection of other people (people just like you), a person at home in your own skin (sort of; I mean, in a way; I mean, your dismay and puzzlement are natural to you, because people like you just seem to be like that, and so many of the things people like you find admirable about yourselves—the things you think about, the things you think really define you—seem rooted in these feelings): a person at home in your own house (and all its nice house things), with its nice back yard (and its nice back-yard things), at home on your street, your church, in community activities, your job, at home with your family, your relatives, your friends—you are a whole person. But one day, when you are sitting somewhere, alone in that crowd, and that awful feeling of displacedness comes over you, and really, as an ordinary person you are not well equipped to look too far inward and set yourself aright, because being ordinary is already so taxing, and being ordinary takes all you have out of you, and though the words "I must get away" do not actually pass across your lips, you make a leap from being that nice blob just sitting like a boob in your amniotic sac of the modern experience to being a person visiting heaps of death and ruin and feeling alive and inspired at the sight of it; to being a person lying on some faraway beach, your stilled body stinking and glistening in the sand, looking like something first forgotten, then remembered, then not important enough to go back for; to being a person marvelling at the harmony (ordinarily, what you would say is the backwardness) and the union these other people (and they are other people) have with nature. And you look at the things they can do with a piece of ordinary cloth, the things they fashion out of cheap, vulgarly colored (to you) twine, the way they squat down over a hole they have made in the ground, the hole itself is something to marvel at, and since you are being an ugly person this ugly but joyful thought will swell inside you: their ancestors were not clever in the way yours were and not ruthless in the way yours were, for then would it not be you who would be in harmony with nature and backwards in that charming way? An ugly thing, that is what you are when you become a tourist, an ugly, empty thing, a stupid thing, a piece of rubbish pausing here and there to gaze at this and taste that, and it will never occur to you that the people who inhabit the place in which you have just paused cannot stand you, that behind their closed doors they laugh at your strangeness (you do not look the way they look); the physical sight of you does not please them; you have bad manners (it is their custom to eat their food with their hands; you try eating their way, you look silly; you try eating the way you always eat, you look silly); they do not like the way you speak (you have an accent); they collapse helpless from laughter, mimicking the way they imagine you must look as you carry out some everyday bodily function. They do not like you. *They do not like me!* That thought never actually occurs to you. Still, you feel a little uneasy. Still, you feel a little foolish. Still, you feel a little out of place. But the banality of your own life is very real to you; it drove you to this extreme, spending your days and your nights in the company of people who despise you, people you do not like really, people you would not want to have as your actual neighbour. And so you must devote yourself to puzzling out how much of what you are told is really, really true (Is ground-up bottle glass in peanut sauce really a delicacy around here, or will it do just what you think ground-up bottle glass will do? Is this rare, multicoloured, snout-mouthed fish really an aphrodisiac, or will it cause you to fall asleep permanently?). Oh, the hard work all of this is, and is it any wonder, then, that on your return home you feel the need of a long rest, so that you can recover from your life as a tourist?

That the native does not like the tourist is not hard to explain. For every native of every place is a potential tourist, and every tourist is a native of somewhere. Every native everywhere lives a life of overwhelming and crushing banality and boredom and desperation and depression, and every deed, good and bad, is an attempt to forget this. Every native would like to find a way out, every native would like a rest, every native would like a tour. But some natives—most natives in the world—cannot go anywhere. They are too poor. They are too poor to go anywhere. They are too poor to escape the reality of their lives; and they are too poor to live properly in the place where they live, which is the very place you, the tourist, want to go—so when the natives see you, the tourist, they envy you, they envy your ability to leave your own banality and boredom, they envy your ability to turn their own banality and boredom into a source of pleasure for yourself.

STUDY AND DISCUSSION QUESTIONS

1. Why do you think Kincaid chooses to use the second person ("you") point of view? What does this choice of perspective allow the author to do? What effect does it have on the reader?

2. How are "you" characterized? What kind of person are "you"?

3. How would you describe the tone of this essay? Give examples.

4. Why is it almost a relief when Kincaid says, at the beginning of the second part of the essay, that "The thing you have always suspected about yourself the minute you became a tourist is true: a tourist is an ugly human being"?

5. According to Kincaid, specifically what is a tourist? What is a native?

6. How is the issue of relative poverty or wealth at the center of the argument Kincaid is making?

7. Discuss and give examples of Kincaid's use of detail.

8. What is the effect of Kincaid's repetition of "too poor" in the closing paragraph?

SUGGESTIONS FOR WRITING

1. Describe an experience of your own in which you were either a tourist or a native.

2. Compare and contrast the two sections of Kincaid's essay, examining both their style and content. How do these two sections work together?

MIKE LEFEVRE

Studs Terkel

Studs Terkel (born Louis Terkel, in 1912) grew up in New York but went to college in Chicago and settled there. He's best known for his books of interviews, mostly with ordinary people. Among them are Hard Times: An Oral History of the Great Depression *(1970)*, Working: People Talk about What They Do All Day and How They Feel about What They Do *(1974)*, from which the following is taken, The Great Divide: Second Thoughts on the American Dream *(1988)*, and Race: How Blacks and Whites Think and Feel about the American Obsession *(1992)*.

Who built the seven towers of Thebes?
The books are filled with the names of kings.
Was it kings, who hauled the craggy blocks of stone? . . .
In the evening when the Chinese wall was finished
Where did the masons go? . . .

—Bertolt Brecht

It is a two-flat dwelling, somewhere in Cicero, on the outskirts of Chicago. He is thirty-seven. He works in a steel mill. On occasion, his wife Carol works as a waitress in a neighborhood restaurant; otherwise, she is at home, caring for their two small children, a girl and a boy.

At the time of my first visit, a sculpted statuette of Mother and Child was on the floor, head severed from body. He laughed softly as he indicated his three-year-old daughter: "She Doctor Spock'd it."

I'm a dying breed. A laborer. Strictly muscle work . . . pick it up, put it down, pick it up, put it down. We handle between forty and fifty thousand pounds of steel a day. (Laughs) I know this is hard to believe—from four hundred pounds to three- and four-pound pieces. It's dying.

You can't take pride any more. You remember when a guy could point to a house he built, how many logs he stacked. He built it and he was proud of it. I don't really think I could be proud if a contractor built a home for me. I would be tempted to get in there and kick the carpenter in the ass (laughs), and take the saw away from him. 'Cause I would have to be part of it, you know.

It's hard to take pride in a bridge you're never gonna cross, in a door you're never gonna open. You're mass-producing things and you never see the end result of it. (Muses) I worked for a trucker one time. And I got this tiny satisfaction when I loaded a truck. At least I could see the truck depart loaded. In a steel mill, forget it. You don't see where nothing goes.

I got chewed out by my foreman once. He said, "Mike, you're a good worker but you have a bad attitude." My attitude is that I don't get excited about my job. I do my work but I don't say whoopee-doo. The day I get excited about my job is the day I go to a head shrinker. How are you gonna get excited about pullin' steel? How are you gonna get excited when you're tired and want to sit down?

It's not just the work. Somebody built the pyramids. Somebody's going to build something. Pyramids, Empire State Building—these things just don't happen. There's hard work behind it. I would like to see a building, say, the Empire State, I would like to see on one side of it a foot-wide strip from top to bottom with the name of every bricklayer, the name of every electrician, with all the names. So when a guy walked by, he could take his son and say, "See, that's me over there on the forty-fifth floor. I put the steel beam in." Picasso can point to a painting. What can I point to? A writer can point to a book. Everybody should have something to point to.

It's the not-recognition by other people. To say a woman is *just* a housewife is degrading, right? Okay. *Just* a housewife. It's also degrading to say *just* a laborer. The difference is that a man goes out and maybe gets smashed.

When I was single, I could quit, just split. I wandered all over the country. You worked just enough to get a poke, money in your pocket. Now I'm married and I got two kids . . . (trails off). I worked on a truck dock one time and I was single. The foreman came over and he grabbed my shoulder, kind of gave me a shove. I punched him and knocked him off the dock. I said, "Leave me alone. I'm doing my work, just stay away from me, just don't give me the with-the-hands business."

Hell, if you whip a damn mule he might kick you. Stay out of my way, that's all. Working is bad enough, don't bug me. I would rather work my ass off for eight hours a day with nobody watching me than five minutes with a guy watching me. Who you gonna sock? You can't sock General Motors, you can't sock anybody in Washington, you can't sock a system.

A mule, an old mule, that's the way I feel. Oh yeah. See. (Shows black and blue marks on arms and legs, burns.) You know what I heard from more than one guy at work? "If my kid wants to work in a factory, I am going to kick the hell out of him." I want my kid to be an effete snob. Yeah, mm-hmm. (Laughs.) I want him to be able to quote Walt Whitman, to be proud of it.

If you can't improve yourself, you improve your posterity. Otherwise life isn't worth nothing. You might as well go back to the cave and stay there. I'm sure the first caveman who went over the hill to see what was on the other side—I don't think he went there wholly out of curiosity. He went there because he wanted to get his son out of the cave. Just the same way I want to send my kid to college.

I work so damn hard and want to come home and sit down and lay around. *But I gotta get it out.* I want to be able to turn around to somebody and say, "Hey fuck you." You know? (Laughs.) The guy sitting next to me on the bus too. 'Cause all day I wanted to tell my foreman to go fuck himself, but I can't.

So I find a guy in a tavern. To tell him that. And he tells me too. I've been in brawls. He's punching me and I'm punching him, because we actually want to punch somebody else. The most that'll happen is the bartender will bar us from the tavern. But at work, you lose your job.

This one foreman I've got, he's a kid. He's a college graduate. He thinks he's better than everybody else. He was chewing me out and I was saying, "Yeah, yeah, yeah." He said, "What do you mean, yeah, yeah, yeah. Yes, *sir*." I told him, "Who the hell are you, Hitler? What is this *"Yes, sir"* bullshit? I came here to work, I didn't come here to crawl. There's a fuckin' difference." One word led to another and I lost.

I got broke down to a lower grade and lost twenty-five cents an hour, which is a hell of a lot. It amounts to about ten dollars a week. He came over—after breaking me down. The guy comes over and smiles at me. I blew up. He didn't know it, but he was about two seconds and two feet away from a hospital. I said, "Stay the fuck away from me." He was just about to say something and was pointing his finger. I just reached my hand up and just grabbed his finger and I just put it back in his pocket. He walked away. I grabbed his finger because I'm married. If I'd a been single, I'd a grabbed his head. That's the difference.

You're doing this manual labor and you know that technology can do it. (Laughs.) Let's face it, a machine can do the work of a man; otherwise they wouldn't have space probes. Why can we send a rocket ship that's unmanned and yet send a man in a steel mill to do a mule's work?

Automation? Depends how it's applied. It frightens me if it puts me out on the street. It doesn't frighten me if it shortens my work week. You read that little thing: what are you going to do when this computer replaces you? Blow up computers. (Laughs.) Really. Blow up computers. I'll be goddamned if a computer is gonna eat before I do! I want milk for my kids and beer for me. Machines can either liberate man or enslave 'im, because they're pretty neutral. It's man who has the bias to put the thing one place or another.

If I had a twenty-hour workweek, I'd get to know my kids better, my wife better. Some kid invited me to go on a college campus. On a Saturday.

It was summertime. Hell, if I have a choice of taking my wife and kids to a picnic or going to a college campus, it's gonna be the picnic. But if I worked a twenty-hour week, I could go do both. Don't you think with that extra twenty hours people could really expand? Who's to say? There are some people in factories just by force of circumstance. I'm just like the colored people. Potential Einsteins don't have to be white. They could be in cotton fields, they could be in factories.

The twenty-hour week is a possibility today. The intellectuals, they always say there are potential Lord Byrons, Walt Whitmans, Roosevelts, Picassos working in construction or steel mills or factories. But I don't think they believe it. I think what they're afraid of is the potential Hitlers and Stalins that are there too. The people in power fear the leisure man. Not just the United States. Russia's the same way.

What do you think would happen in this country if, for one year, they experimented and gave everybody a twenty-hour week? How do they know that the guy who digs Wallace[1] today doesn't try to resurrect Hitler tomorrow? Or the guy who is mildly disturbed at pollution doesn't decide to go to General Motors and shit on the guy's desk? You can become a fanatic if you had the time. The whole thing is time. That is, I think, one reason rich kids tend to be fanatic about politics: they have time. Time, that's the important thing.

It isn't that the average working guy is dumb. He's tired, that's all. I picked up a book on chess one time. That thing laid in the drawer for two or three weeks, you're too tired. During the weekends you want to take your kids out. You don't want to sit there and the kid comes up: "Daddy, can I go to the park?" You got your nose in a book? Forget it.

I know a guy fifty-seven years old. Know what he tells me? "Mike, I'm old and tired *all* the time." The first thing happens at work: when the arms start moving, the brain stops. I punch in about ten minutes to seven in the morning. I say hello to a couple of guys I like, I kid around with them. One guy says good morning to you and you say good morning. To another guy you say fuck you. The guy you say fuck you to is your friend.

I put on my hard hat, change into my safety shoes, put on my safety glasses, go to the bonderizer. It's the thing I work on. They rake the metal, they wash it, they dip it in a paint solution, and we take if off. Put it on, take it off, put it on, take it off, put it on, take it off . . .

I say hello to everybody but my boss. At seven it starts. My arms get tired about the first half-hour. After that, they don't get tired any more until maybe the last half-hour at the end of the day. I work from seven to three thirty. My arms are tired at seven thirty and they're tired at three o'clock. I hope to God I never get broke in, because I always want my arms to be tired

---

[1] George Wallace, militantly segregationist governor of Alabama.

at seven thirty and three o'clock. (Laughs.) 'Cause that's when I know that there's a beginning and there's an end. That I'm not brainwashed. In between, I don't even try to think.

If I were to put you in front of a dock and I pulled up a skid in front of you with fifty hundred-pound sacks of potatoes and there are fifty more skids just like it, and this is what you're gonna do all day, what would you think about—potatoes? Unless a guy's a nut, he never thinks about work or talks about it. Maybe about baseball or about getting drunk the other night or he got laid or he didn't get laid. I'd say one out of a hundred will actually get excited about work.

Why is it that the communists always say they're for the workingman, and as soon as they set up a country, you got guys singing to tractors? They're singing about how they love the factory. That's where I couldn't buy communism. It's the intellectuals' utopia, not mine. I cannot picture myself singing to a tractor, I just can't. (Laughs.) Or singing to steel. (Singsongs.) Oh whoop-dee-doo, I'm at the bonderizer, oh how I love this heavy steel. No thanks. Never happen.

Oh yeah, I daydeam. I fantasize about a sexy blonde in Miami who's got my union dues. (Laughs.) I think of the head of the union the way I think of the head of my company. Living it up. I think of February in Miami. Warm weather, a place to lay in. When I hear a college kid say, "I'm oppressed," I don't believe him. You know what I'd like to do for one year? Live like a college kid. Just for one year. I'd love to. Wow! (Whispers) Wow! Sports car! Marijuana! (Laughs.) Wild, sexy broads. I'd love that, hell yes, I would.

Somebody has to do this work. If my kid ever goes to college, I just want him to have a little respect, to realize that his dad is one of those somebodies. This is why even on—(muses) yeah, I guess, sure—on the black thing . . . (Sighs heavily.) I can't really hate the colored fella that's working with me all day. The black intellectual I got no respect for. The white intellectual I got no use for. I got no use for the black militant who's gonna scream three hundred years of slavery to me while I'm busting my ass. You know what I mean? (Laughs.) I have one answer for that guy: go see Rockefeller. See Harriman.[2] Don't bother me. We're in the same cotton field. So just don't bug me. (Laughs.)

After work I usually stop off at a tavern. Cold beer. Cold beer right away. When I was single, I used to go into hillbilly bars, get in a lot of brawls. Just to explode. I got a thing on my arm here (indicates scar). I got slapped with a bicycle chain. Oh, wow! (Softly) Mmm. I'm getting older. (Laughs.) I don't explode as much. You might say I'm broken in. (Quickly) No, I'll never be broken in. (Sighs.) When you get a little older, you exchange the words. When you're younger, you exchange the blows.

---

[2] Nelson Rockefeller, governor of New York and then vice president of the United States; Averill Harriman, diplomat and U.S. Undersecretary of State.

When I get home, I argue with my wife a little bit. Turn on TV, get mad at the news. (Laughs.) I don't even watch the news that much. I watch Jackie Gleason.[3] I look for any alternative to the ten o'clock news. I don't want to go to bed angry. Don't hit a man with anything heavy at five o'clock. He just can't be bothered. This is his time to relax. The heaviest thing he wants is what his wife has to tell him.

When I come home, know what I do for the first twenty minutes? Fake it. I put on a smile. I got a kid three years old. Sometimes she says, "Daddy, where've you been?" I say, "Work." I could have told her I'd been in Disneyland. What's work to a three-year-old kid? If I feel bad, I can't take it out on the kids. Kids are born innocent of everything but birth. You can't take it out on your wife either. This is why you go to a tavern. You want to release it there rather than do it at home. What does an actor do when he's got a bad movie? I got a bad movie every day.

I don't even need the alarm clock to get up in the morning. I can go out drinking all night, fall asleep at four, and bam! I'm up at six—no matter what I do. (Laughs.) It's a pseudo-death, more or less. Your whole system is paralyzed and you give all the appearance of death. It's an in-grown clock. It's a thing you just get used to. The hours differ. It depends. Sometimes my wife wants to do something crazy like play five hundred rummy or put a puzzle together. It could be midnight, could be ten o'clock, could be nine thirty.

What do you do weekends?

Drink beer, read a book. See that one? *Violence in America.* It's one of them studies from Washington. One of them committees they're always appointing. A thing like that I read on a weekend. But during the weekdays, gee . . . I just thought about it. I don't do that much reading from Monday through Friday. Unless it's a horny book. I'll read it at work and go home and do my homework. (Laughs.) That's what the guys at the plant call it—homework. (Laughs.) Sometimes my wife works on Saturday and I drink beer at the tavern.

I went out drinking with one guy, oh, a long time ago. A college boy. He was working where I work now. Always preaching to me about how you need violence to change the system and all that garbage. We went into a hillbilly joint. Some guy there, I didn't know him from Adam, he said, "You think you're smart." I said, "What's your pleasure?" (Laughs.) He said, "My pleasure's to kick your ass." I told him I really can't be bothered. He said, "What're you, chicken?" I said, "No, I just don't want to be bothered." He came over and said something to me again. I said, "I don't beat women, drunks, or fools. Now leave me alone."

---

[3] Comedian and actor.

The guy called his brother over. This college boy that was with me, he came nudging my arm, "Mike, let's get out of here." I said, "What are you worried about?" (Laughs.) This isn't unusual. People will bug you. You fend it off as much as you can with your mouth and when you can't, you punch the guy out.

It was close to closing time and we stayed. We could have left, but when you go into a place to have a beer and a guy challenges you—if you expect to go in that place again, you don't leave. If you have to fight the guy, you fight.

I got just outside the door and one of these guys jumped on me and grabbed me around the neck. I grabbed his arm and flung him against the wall. I grabbed him here (indicates throat), and jiggled his head against the wall quite a few times. He kind of slid down a little bit. This guy who said he was his brother took a swing at me with a garrison belt. He just missed and hit the wall. I'm looking around for my junior Stalin (laughs), who loves violence and everything. He's gone. Split. (Laughs.) Next day I see him at work. I couldn't get mad at him, he's a baby.

He saw a book in my back pocket one time and he was amazed. He walked up to me and he said, "You read?" I said, "What do you mean, I read?" He said, "All these dummies read the sports pages around here. What are you doing with a book?" I got pissed off at the kid right away. I said, "What do you mean, all these dummies? Don't knock a man who's paying somebody else's way through college." He was a nineteen-year-old effete snob.

Yet you want your kid to be an effete snob?

Yes. I want my kid to look at me and say, "Dad you're a nice guy, but you're a fuckin' dummy." Hell yes, I want my kid to tell me that he's not gonna be like me . . .

If I were hiring people to work, I'd try naturally to pay them a decent wage. I'd try to find out their first names, their last names, keep the company as small as possible, so I could personalize the whole thing. All I would ask a man is a handshake, see you in the morning. No applications, nothing. I wouldn't be interested in the guy's past. Nobody ever checks on the pedigree on a mule, do they? But they do on a man. Can you picture walking up to a mule and saying, "I'd like to know who his granddaddy was?"

I'd like to run a combination bookstore and tavern. (Laughs.) I would like to have a place where college kids came and a steelworker could sit down and talk. Where a workingman could not be ashamed of Walt Whitman and where a college professor could not be ashamed that he painted his house over the weekend.

If a carpenter built a cabin for poets, I think the least the poets owe the carpenter is just three or four one-liners on the wall. A little plaque: Though we labor with our minds, this place we can relax in was built by someone who can work with his hands. And his work is as noble as ours. I think the poet owes something to the guy who builds the cabin for him.

I don't think of Monday. You know what I'm thinking about on Sunday night? Next Sunday. If you work real hard, you think of a perpetual vacation. Not perpetual sleep . . . What do I think of on a Sunday night? Lord, I wish the fuck I could do something else for a living.

I don't know who the guy is who said there is nothing sweeter than an unfinished symphony. Like an unfinished painting and an unfinished poem. If he creates this thing one day—let's say, Michelangelo's Sistine Chapel. It took him a long time to do this, this beautiful work of art. But what if he had to create this Sistine Chapel a thousand times a year? Don't you think that would even dull Michelangelo's mind? Or if da Vinci had to draw his anatomical charts thirty, forty, fifty, sixty, eighty, ninety, a hundred times a day? Don't you think that would even bore da Vinci?

Way back, you spoke of the guys who built the pyramids, not the pharaohs, the unknowns. You put yourself in their category?

Yes. I want my signature on 'em, too. Sometimes, out of pure meanness, when I make something, I put a little dent in it. I like to do something to make it really unique. Hit it with a hammer. I deliberately fuck it up to see if it'll get by, just so I can say I did it. It could be anything. Let me put it this way: I think God invented the dodo bird so when we get up there we could tell Him, "Don't you ever make mistakes?" and He'd say, "Sure, look." (Laughs.) I'd like to make my imprint. My dodo bird. A mistake, *mine.* Let's say the whole building is nothing but red bricks. I'd like to have just the black one or the white one or the purple one. Deliberately fuck up.

This is gonna sound square, but my kid is my imprint. He's my freedom. There's a line in one of Hemingway's books. I think it's from *For Whom the Bell Tolls.* They're behind the enemy lines, somewhere in Spain, and she's pregnant. She wants to stay with him. He tells her no. He says, "if you die, I die," knowing he's gonna die. But if you go, I go. Know what I mean? The mystics call it the brass bowl. Continuum. You know what I mean? This is why I work. Every time I see a young guy walk by with a shirt and tie and dressed up real sharp, I'm lookin' at my kid, you know? That's it.

STUDY AND DISCUSSION QUESTIONS

1. What are some of LeFevre's main complaints about his job?
2. What is the impact of reading the words of the worker himself? Does it surprise you that LeFevre alludes to Whitman and Hemingway?

3. What are LeFevre's feelings about the value of education? What does he want for his children? (And, by the way, does he have the same educational goals in mind for his daughter and for his son?)

4. What's the difference between being a single worker and a married worker, according to LeFevre?

5. What's LeFevre's attitude toward race and social class?

6. Describe a typical work day for LeFevre, from the time he wakes up until the time he goes to bed that night.

7. What are some of LeFevre's hopes and fantasies: (1) about work and (2) about himself and his family?

8. What is the tone of LeFevre's piece? Point to specific words, phrases, images, incidents that support your assessment.

SUGGESTIONS FOR WRITING

1. "What's work to a three year old kid"? LeFevre asks this question half jokingly, but consider it seriously as the beginning of a definition of "work."

2. LeFevre has had the experience of being underestimated because of the work he does. Have you ever had this experience? Have you ever been on the other side and judged someone because of what they do for a living? Describe and discuss.

3. What would happen if there were a twenty-hour work week as LeFevre suggests? If they had the time, would people try to change society as LeFevre imagines, or would they just go to bars and start fights more often? What would you do with the time?

WHISTLE WHILE YOU WORK

Barbara Garson

Barbara Garson was born in Brooklyn, New York and studied at the University of California, Berkeley. Her Vietnam War-era satirical play MacBird! *made a big splash and was produced in over three hundred theaters. She has written* All the Livelong Day: The Meaning and Demeaning of Routine Work *(1975), the foreword to which appears below, and* The Electronic Sweatshop: How Computers are Transforming the Office of the Future into the Factory of the Past *(1989).*

At the Bumble Bee seafood plant in Oregon I talked to a tuna cleaner named Starlein. Her job was to pull the veins of dark meat (cat food) from the skinned white loins of tuna.

"The loins come past me on a moving belt," she explained. "I put the clean loins on the second belt and the cat food on the third belt and I save my bones." [The supervisor later checks her output by counting the bones.]

"Do you talk a lot to the other women?" I asked.

"Not really," she answered.

"What do you do all day?"

"I daydream."

"What do you daydream about?"

"About sex."

At this point her boyfriend apologized proudly. "I guess that's my fault," he grinned.

"No it's not you," she said. "It's the tuna fish."

I wondered what she meant.

"Well first it's the smell. You've got that certain smell in your nose all day. . . . It's not like out here. [Starlein and I and the boyfriend were talking in the smelly cannery yard.] Your own fish next to you is sweet. . . . But it's mostly *handling* the loins. Not the touch itself, because we wear gloves. But the soft colors. The reds, the whites, and the purples. The most exciting thing is the dark meat. It comes in streaks. It's red-brown and you have to pull it out with your knife. You pile it next to your loin and it's crumbly and dark red and moist like earth.

"You're supposed to put the cat food on the belt at you finish each loin. But I hold it out to make as big a pile of dark meat as I can."

Starlein was new at the cannery then. The next time I met her the tuna cleaning process had lost some of its sensual allure.

"I still try to see how much cat food I can collect but it's just for the size of the pile now."

At a Ping-Pong factory in Rhode Island I talked to a girl whose job was to stack Ping-Pong paddles into piles of fifty.

"Maybe it wouldn't have been so bad if I could have seen all the piles I stacked at the end of the day. But they were taking them down as fast as I was piling them up. That was the worst part of the job."

At the same Ping-Pong plant a Haitian box assembler amused himself by doing the job with his eyes closed. He was very proud of the fact that if the foreman passed behind him he could not tell the difference.

Many assembly-line workers deliberately slow their pace from time to time and watch the pieces pile up. Sometimes this is for revenge against the company that "treats us like machines," "uses us like tools." More often it's just for a break, a chance to talk, kid around, take a drink of water. But the most common motive is one that I hadn't expected.

Young workers like to let the work pile up just so they can race to catch up with the line. This creates a few minutes of seemingly purposeful exertion. It makes hills and troughs, minor goals and fulfillments while you're waiting for the day to end or the line to break down.

I have spent the last two years examining the way people cope with routine and monotonous work. I expected to find resentment, and I found it. I expected to find boredom, and I found it. I expected to find sabotage, and I found it in clever forms that I could never have imagined.

But the most dramatic thing I found was quite the opposite of noncooperation. *People passionately want to work.*

Whatever creativity goes into sabotage, a more amazing ingenuity goes into manufacturing goals and satisfactions on jobs where measurable achievement has been all but rationalized out. Somehow in an unending flow of parts or papers, with operations subdivided beyond any recognizable unit of accomplishment, people still find ways to define certain stacks of work as "theirs," certain piles as "today's" and "tomorrow's."

Almost everyone wants to feel she is getting something accomplished— to see that stack of paddles, the growing pile of dark meat, or to master the job blindfolded since there's not much to master the other way.

Which is not to say that workers don't also resent and resist the subdivision and trivialization of their jobs.

At the Fair Plan Insurance Company a young clerk named Ellen told me about a not quite so co-operative game.

"The other day when I was proofreading endorsements I noticed some guy had insured his store for $165,000 against vandalism and $5,000 against fire. Now that's bound to be a mistake. They probably got it backwards.

"I was just about to show it to Gloria [the supervisor] when I figured, 'Wait a minute! I'm not supposed to read these forms. I'm just supposed to check one column against another. And they do check. So it couldn't be counted as my error.'

"Then I thought about this poor guy when his store burns down and they tell him he's only covered for $5,000. But I figured the hell with it. It'll get straightened out one way or another."

I must have looked disapproving at that moment.

"Listen," she apologized, "for all I know he took out the insurance just to burn down the store himself." Then growing angry: "Goddamn it! They don't explain this stuff to me. I'm not supposed to understand it. I'm supposed to check one column against the other.

"If they're gonna give me a robot's job to do, I'm gonna do it like a robot."

I met a few more people who played that passive resistance game— "gonna be as dumb as they think I am." But not too many. And as matter of fact, when I questioned further it turned out that Ellen had reported the error after all. For most people it is hard and uncomfortable to do a bad job.

At Lordstown, Ohio, General Motors runs the fastest assembly line in the world, manned by a work force whose average age is twenty-four. At 101 cars an hour, each young worker has thirty-six seconds to perform his assigned snaps, knocks, twists, or squirts on each passing vehicle.

I visited Lordstown the week before a strike amid union charges of speed-up, company charges of sabotage, and a great deal of national publicity about "the new worker," "the changing work ethic."

While a young Vega[1] worker and his friends argued in the living room about the strike and disciplinary layoffs, I talked to his mother in the kitchen. Someone in the supermarket where she works had said that those young kids were "just lazy."

"One thing, Tony is not lazy. He'll take your car apart and put it together any day . . . the slightest knock and he takes care of it. And he never will leave it half done. He even cleans up after himself.

---

[1] Car model made by Chevrolet, a division of General Motors.

"And I'm not lazy either. I love to cook. But supposing they gave me a job just cracking eggs with bowls moving past on a line. Pretty soon I'd get to a point where I'd wish the next egg was rotten just to spoil their whole cake."

Occasionally Lordstown workers toss in a rotten egg of their own by dropping an ignition key down the gas tank, lighting a work glove, locking it in the trunk, and waiting to see how far down the line it will be stopped, or just scratching a car as it goes past because you can't keep up with the pace.

But sabotage, though much publicized, is really quite limited. Much of the ingenuity at Lordstown goes into creating escape devices and games that can be squeezed into the thirty-six-second cycle.

No ingenuity at all goes into building cars.

I wasn't particularly surprised by the negative things I saw in factories: speed, heat, humiliation, monotony. I'm sure the reader will have guessed that I began this research prepared to expose and denounce "the system."

It was the positive things I saw that touched me the most. Not that people are beaten down (which they are) but that they almost always pop up. Not that people are bored (which they are) but the ways they find to make it interesting. Not that people hate their work (which they do) but that even so, they try to make something out of it.

In factories and offices around this country work is systematically reduced to the most minute and repetitious tasks. Supervision ranges from counting bones, raising hands to use the bathroom, issuing "report cards" with number and letter grades for quantity, quality, co-operation, dependability, attendance, etc.

Through all this workers make a constant effort, sometimes creative, sometimes pathetic, sometimes violent, to put meaning and dignity back into their daily activity.

I realize now, much more deeply than ever, that work is a human need following right after the need for food and the need for love.

The crime of modern industry is not forcing us to work, but denying us real work. For no matter what tricks people play on themselves to make the day's work meaningful, management seems determined to remind them, "You are just tools for our use."

STUDY AND DISCUSSION QUESTIONS

1. List some complaints people interviewed by Garson have about their work.

2. List ways in which these people make their work interesting.

3. Why do you think much work in the modern world has been reduced to minute, repetitive, and closely supervised tasks?

4. Garson wrote this piece about twenty years ago. Do you think attitudes toward work have shifted at all since then, or is her assertion that work is a basic human need still true today? Give examples to support your opinion.

SUGGESTIONS FOR WRITING

1. *"People passionately want to work."* Argue for or against Garson's conclusion. Support your argument with examples from the text and/or from your own experience.

2. Using specific detail, describe a "routine and monotonous" work experience of your own. (It needn't be paid work.) How did you cope with the boredom?

ON THE DOCKS
IT WAS COLD

Jesus Colón

Jesus Colón (1901–1974) was born in Puerto Rico and moved to the United States at age seventeen. At various times he was employed as a dishwasher, dock worker, postal worker, and labor organizer. Colón wrote steadily for a variety of leftist newspapers in the United States and Puerto Rico and he ran for the New York State Senate on the American Labor Party ticket. Much of his life is described in A Puerto Rican in New York and Other Sketches (1961), from which the following is taken.

I open this old black tin box once every five or six years. There I keep things that have made a mark or change in my life. Here is the red membership card they gave me when I joined the Socialist Party of the United States at its Tompkins Park Branch in Brooklyn around the year 1923. Here is the first photograph Concha gave me from a Kodak box camera . . . thin and delicate like a soul with a skirt and a blouse on. And here is that old working badge from the yards of the Lackawanna Railroad. About forty years ago I swore I would never change it for the money that was owed me upon its presentation for payment. For this badge reminded me of my experiences as a dock and train-yard worker.

I started on what were in those days called the Hamburg American Line docks in Hoboken. They were the long streamlined docks taken over from the Germans by the United States government during the first World War. The dockworkers seemed to me to be all "six-footers." The ones who were visibly smaller were built like beer barrels to which legs of football players had been attached by nature.

When Mr. Clark, the big tall Negro foreman with the gangling walk, told me: "You're on," I did not believe it. As he kept on talking, it started to make sense. "You are young, small and light in weight. We need somebody like you. Somebody to go up on top of the piled-up sacks and release the 'knot' on top. There are many chores on the docks that could be handled better by light men. We will teach you the ropes." As time went on, I learned Mr. Clark's "ropes" and a few other tricks of the trade from the workers which proved to me in practice what my uncle Marcelo liked to say very often: "Mas vale mana que fuerza." "It is better to have skill than strength."

When the transport Batterland came in from France during the first World War, it carried back thousands of canned food boxes, camp tents and boxes of small tent pegs. Those boxes were piled up in stacks of twos and fours that extended high up toward the dock's ceiling. At the top of each stack, two or four boxes were placed in such positions as to "tie" the stack together. When we received the order to place boxes in one of the transport ships, somebody had to go up to the top of each of those piles using nimble feet and a fine sense of balance, sharp quick reflexes and sharp eyes. They had to untie these by seeing that the boxes on top came into the same position as the others. With a sure, but swift push with one foot, while balancing on the other side of the stack with the other foot, you could see from the top how boxes came down to the dock floor. It was similar to those circus acrobats who, after standing on each other's shoulders for a moment decide to come down together from their human tower into the circus arena . . . Mr. Clark took me into his gang and told me how to do these simple things. Simple, after you knew how. Simple if you were young, a little carefree and adventurous.

I liked Mr. Clark. We all liked him and respected him very much. This respect and liking were the result of the knowledge he had about wharves, docks and dockwork in general. A knowledge that he demonstrated time and again. I never knew Mr. Clark's name. I think very few people knew it. But we all knew that he was born in Panama of Jamaican parents. Perhaps his father was one of those workers from Jamaica and the other English-speaking West Indies islands, who went to Panama at the beginning of the century to give their youth and blood in the building of the Panama Canal. Mr. Clark spoke fluently in many languages—Spanish, French, English—just as the descendants of West Indians frequently do and so too do many of the inhabitants of the islands. He knew how to load a ship better than anybody else . . . What should be loaded first, and what should go after. And what is more important, how to secure and place everything in the ship's bottom, so that no matter what the whims of the waves and storms, the cargo would stay right where Mr. Clark told us to place it.

Mr. Clark taught me everything of the art and science of using the hook . . . that very valuable all-purpose instrument of the dockworker. After you knew what to do and how to do it, you felt at home on a dock. Then you sort of sensed that Mr. Clark was there somewhere watching every move you made. He told us how to watch and safeguard each other's life and limb. Our gang was like a well-integrated team in which everybody participated in every move and decision and by which you were benefiting every hour as a result of the long work experience of everybody else.

It was in a certain way very funny. Everybody was Joe and Jack and Pedro and Tony but we only had one mister . . . that was Mr. Clark.

The only thing that bothered me from the beginning was the coldness of the docks. It was so cold during the winter that, if you spat on the floor, the spit almost instantly converted itself into a round greyish spot of ice.

Besides the heavy working shoes that we all wore, we had gotten ourselves some burlap sacks that we used to tie around our heavy shoes and legs making us walk in a zig-zag fashion like old bears ready for their final icy resting place. Most of us wore heavy undergarments which covered us from the shoulders down to our ankles. Over them we wore a heavy woolen shirt, and an old vest, muffler, coat and overcoat with a rope around the waist. We used to hang the hook from there when we were not using it. With all this you had to be jumping constantly from one foot to the other, keeping in motion doing something or other in order to generate heat for your cold body. The intermittent run to the dock lavatories was mostly to hog a place in front of the plumber's pipes attached to the walls and used as steam heat radiators. After a moment there, you went back to the docks and believe it or not, you felt the cold more.

The war finished, our gang dispersed around the docks of the New York-New Jersey waterfronts. For a time, I could not find any work. Finally I found work . . . trucking . . . at what they called the fruit docks at the foot of Chambers Street on the Hudson River side. Times were very bad. It was what they called the period of readjustment. You had to take any kind of work to keep body and soul together. Some forty years ago I worked on those fruit docks

from 11:30 at night to eight o'clock in the morning at $2.75 for an 8-hour day
... that is night. And all the apples and pears that you could disentangle from
the fragile fruit boxes. We got half an hour for "lunch" at three-thirty in the
morning. The only trouble with the fruit docks was that they were colder than
the Hamburg American docks in Hoboken. It was real cold at the fruit docks.
It seemed to me that the owner kept them that way, with hardly any steam in
the men's lavatory so that you would not have the tendency to sit overlong in
the toilet and so that you would have to be moving and on the go during the
whole time you were working.

Another bad feature of the fruit docks during those years was that the
hand trucks were the old fashioned ones with the two big wheels on the outside, heavy and burdensome to manage. But the worst part of the fruit docks
was that after you came back from "lunch," at four in the morning, the light
fruit boxes of pears, apples and peaches converted themselves as if by magic
into the heavy little nail barrels that you see beside the counter of the old-
fashioned hardware stores and other similar "light" articles to tickle your
back as you trucked along during the night over the bumpy, cold pavement.
You were supposed to carry three of those stout little nail barrels in your
hand truck each time it was loaded for you.

One morning, as I was coming from work on the fruit dock, I met one of
the workers in Mr. Clark's old gang. He told me that they were looking for me
as our old gang was getting together to work for the Lackawanna Railroad next
day. He told me where they were to meet. I did not go back to work on the fruit
docks any more. I went with Mr. Clark to work on the Lackawanna Railroad.

Your work did not actually start until you were placed on one of the
numerous trunk trains, river barges or storage houses that Lackawanna had
on both sides of the river. Some days it took half an hour walking in the snow,
hail and cold weather before a call from the general office could tell us where
our gang was most needed. The last day I worked there we were assigned to
unload train wagons of coffee bags onto barges on the river below. The train
wagons and the barges were connected by heavy gangplanks on which you almost had to fly to get to the barge while handling your hand truck with two
heavy bags of coffee. While almost flying with the hand truck preceding you,
one man in front of you, one on your heels, there were about half-a-dozen
truckers on the barge trying to get away from where they figured you would
land with your truck and coffee bags, while others were already moving
themselves away in the train wagon on another less steep gangplank. As you
reached the floor of the barge you had to maneuver your hand truck in between the two men who were ready to take the coffee bags off your truck and
stack them up with others on the barge. You had about a minute to complete
the operation unless you wanted to get run over, hand truck and all, by the
men who were coming down the gangplank after you.

One of the times I was coming down the plank, it seemed that I gained too much speed with the result that the hand truck reeled down on just its left wheel. The two bags on my hand truck were perilously inclined to one side. It seemed as if any minute they were going to leave my truck to be gobbled up in the icy, cold waters of the river down below. I thought and acted fast. I moved the whole left part of my body to the right while pressing down the truck with my right hand and arm to the floor of the gangplank for a few seconds. While doing this it seemed that a counterforce inclined my body and truck handles way out into the left and off the gangplank floor. While I was trying to place myself into position to continue, I found myself in the air and entirely off the gangplank for a few seconds. My eyes kept contemplating the murky cold water of the river through the two handles of the hand truck. Those were the longest few seconds I had experienced in my life. As I reached the surface of the barge safely with my two precious bags of coffee intact, I waited until the two workers took them off my truck. I ran the empty truck up the other gangplank into the train wagon and instead of taking my turn on line to return to the barge I ran my truck into a corner. Without a word to anybody, I just left the Lackawanna yards without cashing in my badge.

And there is the badge looking at me from the bottom of my old tin box. After almost forty years its shining red and silver is fresh and brilliant as the very day Mr. Clark handed it to me that cold winter morning, saying: "You are on." There is the badge beside my old 1923 membership card in the Socialist Party, and the first picture of Concha—my wife—looking thin and delicate, like a soul with a skirt and blouse on. Anybody else who sees the badge will say: "Just another badge."

But to me it is not "Just another badge." To me it represents the millions of men and women on the seas and in the fields, in the mines and in the foundries, in the factories and on the docks who risk and lose their lives as their fathers' fathers have been doing for hundreds of years before them, every day doing thousands of dangerous tasks.

I would not say it will happen tomorrow. But one day in these United States the workers will ask themselves collectively: "For whom all this toil?" "For what?" And their collective answer will be heard around the world.

STUDY AND DISCUSSION QUESTIONS

1. The narrator begins and ends by referring to the collection of momentos in his old black tin box. What does the narrator keep in the box? Why and how do this box and its contents become a frame for the essay? Is this technique effective?

2. Discuss the relation between Mr. Clark and his workers. What makes Mr. Clark a good foreman?

3. What jobs does the narrator describe in this narrative? Which one does he like best? Which one least? Why does he leave the last job?

4. Colón titles his piece "On the Docks It Was Cold." Show how the cold is used in all three depictions of work.

5. The narrator's Lackawanna Railroad working badge becomes a symbol by the end of the essay. What does it symbolize for the narrator?

SUGGESTIONS FOR WRITING

1. Write a description of a day at work based on a job experience of your own. Assume your reader knows nothing about the type of work you are describing. You will need to use plenty of details and vivid, sense-based language so that your reader can see, hear, smell, taste, and touch the work and your relation to it.

2. Imagine that you are a foreman or supervisor at a workplace. What would your responsibilities be to the work, to your boss, and to your workers? What would you like your workers to say about you?

I WANT A WIFE

Judy Brady

Judy Brady was born in San Francisco in 1937 and after studying painting at the University of Iowa, she married and raised two children. Now divorced, she works as a political activist and writer. The following essay originally appeared in 1971, in the first issue of Ms. magazine.

I belong to that classification of people known as wives. I am A Wife. And, not altogether incidentally, I am a mother.

Not too long ago a male friend of mine appeared on the scene fresh from a recent divorce. He had one child, who is, of course, with his ex-wife. He is obviously looking for another wife. As I thought about him while I was ironing one evening, it suddenly occurred to me that I, too, would like to have a wife. Why do I want a wife?

I would like to go back to school so that I can become economically independent, support myself, and, if need be, support those dependent upon me. I want a wife who will work and send me to school. And while I am going to school I want a wife to take care of my children. I want a wife to keep track of the children's doctor and dentist appointments. And to keep track of mine, too. I want a wife to make sure my children eat properly and are kept clean. I want a wife who will wash the children's clothes and keep them mended. I want a wife who is a good nurturant attendant to my children, who arranges for their schooling, makes sure that they have an adequate social life with their peers, takes them to the park, the zoo, etc. I want a wife who takes care of the children when they are sick, a wife who arranges to be around when the children need special care, because, of course, I cannot miss classes at school. My wife must arrange to lose time at work and not lose the job. It may mean a small cut in my wife's income from time to time, but I guess I can tolerate that. Needless to say, my wife will arrange and pay for the care of the children while my wife is working.

I want a wife who will take care of *my* physical needs. I want a wife who will keep my house clean. A wife who will pick up after me. I want a wife who will keep my clothes clean, ironed, mended, replaced when need be, and who will see to it that my personal things are kept in their proper place so that I can find what I need the minute I need it. I want a wife who cooks the meals, a wife who is a *good* cook. I want a wife who will plan the menus, do the necessary grocery shopping, prepare the meals, serve them pleasantly, and then do the cleaning up while I do my studying. I want a wife who will care for me when I am sick and sympathize with my pain and loss of time from school. I want a wife to go along when our family takes a vacation so that someone can continue to care for me and my children when I need a rest and change of scene.

I want a wife who will not bother me with rambling complaints about a wife's duties. But I want a wife who will listen to me when I feel the need to explain a rather difficult point I have come across in my course of studies. And I want a wife who will type my papers for me when I have written them.

I want a wife who will take care of the details of my social life. When my wife and I are invited out by my friends, I want a wife who will take care of the babysitting arrangements. When I meet people at school that I like and want to entertain, I want a wife who will have the house clean, will prepare a special meal, serve it to me and my friends, and not interrupt when I talk about the things that interest me and my friends. I want a wife who will have arranged that the children are fed and ready for bed before my guests arrive so that the children do not bother us.

And I want a wife who knows that sometimes I need a night out by myself.

I want a wife who is sensitive to my sexual needs, a wife who makes love passionately and eagerly when I feel like it, a wife who makes sure that I am satisfied. And, of course, I want a wife who will not demand sexual attention when I am not in the mood for it. I want a wife who assumes the complete responsibility for birth control, because I do not want more children. I want a wife who will remain sexually faithful to me so that I do not have to clutter up my intellectual life with jealousies. And I want a wife who understands that *my* sexual needs may entail more than strict adherence to monogamy. I must, after all, be able to relate to people as fully as possible.

If, by chance, I find another person more suitable as a wife than the wife I already have, I want the liberty to replace my present wife with another one. Naturally, I will expect a fresh, new life; my wife will take the children and be solely responsible for them so that I am left free.

When I am through with school and have a job, I want my wife to quit working and remain at home so that my wife can more fully and completely take care of a wife's duties.

My god, who *wouldn't* want a wife?

STUDY AND DISCUSSION QUESTIONS

1. What is Brady doing in her short first paragraph?

2. Consider Brady's second paragraph. Why does she mention her divorced male friend? How is it significant that this essay begins as a meditation over an ironing board?

3. Discuss the use of repetition in this essay. What is the effect on the reader of beginning so many sentences with "I want . . ."?

4. How does Brady organize her "wants" in "I Want a Wife"? Categorize her paragraphs by subject. Is the order of the paragraphs in which she lists her wants significant?

5. Why do you think Brady uses the form of satire here instead of simply telling us directly how she feels about being a wife? What does this form allow her to do? What effect does it have on the reader?

6. What do you think Brady's purpose was in writing this essay?

SUGGESTIONS FOR WRITING

1. In the twenty-five years or so since this essay was written, to what extent has the definition of "wife" that Brady gives us changed? Go

through the essay paragraph by paragraph and consider each category of Brady's job description. Provide contemporary evidence to demonstrate how the job description has or has not changed.

2. Would a parallel essay called "I Want a Husband" have equal force? Explain. Or try to write one.

3. Does the job of being a wife in Brady's terms differ from paid work? If so, how? What other kinds of work is it like or not like? Discuss.

THE COMPANY MAN

Ellen Goodman

Ellen Goodman was born in Boston in 1941. She has worked as a journalist for Newsweek, The Detroit Free Press, *and* The Boston Globe *and has won a Pulitzer Prize for her commentary. Her newspaper columns have been collected in* Close to Home *(1979), where the selection below appeared,* Making Sense *(1989),* Value Judgments *(1993), and other volumes.*

He worked himself to death, finally and precisely, at 3:00 A.M. Sunday morning.

The obituary didn't say that, of course. It said that he died of a coronary thrombosis—I think that was it—but everyone among his friends and acquaintances knew it instantly. He was a perfect Type A, a workaholic, a classic, they said to each other and shook their heads—and thought for five or ten minutes about the way they lived.

This man who worked himself to death finally and precisely at 3:00 A.M. Sunday morning—on his day off—was fifty-one years old and a vice-president. He was, however, one of six vice-presidents, and one of three who might conceivably—if the president died or retired soon enough—have moved to the top spot. Phil knew that.

He worked six days a week, five of them until eight or nine at night, during a time when his own company had begun the four-day week for everyone but the executives. He worked like the Important People. He had no outside "extracurricular interests," unless, of course, you think about a monthly golf game that way. To Phil, it was work. He always ate egg salad sandwiches at his desk. He was, of course, overweight, by 20 or 25 pounds. He thought it was okay, though, because he didn't smoke.

On Saturdays, Phil wore a sports jacket to the office instead of a suit, because it was the weekend.

He had a lot of people working for him, maybe sixty, and most of them liked him most of the time. Three of them will be seriously considered for his job. The obituary didn't mention that.

But it did list his "survivors" quite accurately. He is survived by his wife, Helen, forty-eight years old, a good woman of no particular marketable skills, who worked in an office before marrying and mothering. She had, according to her daughter, given up trying to compete with his work years ago, when the children were small. A company friend said, "I know how much you will miss him." And she answered, "I already have."

"Missing him all these years," she must have given up part of herself which had cared too much for the man. She would be "well taken care of."

His "dearly beloved" eldest of the "dearly beloved" children is a hard-working executive in a manufacturing firm down South. In the day and a half before the funeral, he went around the neighborhood researching his father, asking the neighbors what he was like. They were embarrassed.

His second child is a girl, who is twenty-four and newly married. She lives near her mother and they are close, but whenever she was alone with her father, in a car driving somewhere, they had nothing to say to each other.

The youngest is twenty, a boy, a high-school graduate who has spent the last couple of years, like a lot of his friends, doing enough odd jobs to stay in grass and food. He was the one who tried to grab at his father, and tried to mean enough to him to keep the man at home. He was his father's favorite. Over the last two years, Phil stayed up nights worrying about the boy.

The boy once said, "My father and I only board here."

At the funeral, the sixty-year-old company president told the forty-eight-year-old widow that the fifty-one-year-old deceased had meant much to the company and would be missed and would be hard to replace. The widow didn't look him in the eye. She was afraid he would read her bitterness and, after all, she would need him to straighten out the finances—the stock options and all that.

Phil was overweight and nervous and worked too hard. If he wasn't at the office, he was worried about it. Phil was a Type A, a heart-attack natural. You could have picked him out in a minute from a lineup.

So when he finally worked himself to death, at precisely 3:00 A.M. Sunday morning, no one was really surprised.

By 5:00 P.M. the afternoon of the funeral, the company president had begun, discreetly of course, with care and taste, to make inquiries about his replacement. One of three men. He asked around: "Who's been working the hardest?"

STUDY AND DISCUSSION QUESTIONS

1. What words, phrases, and sentences does Goodman repeat in this editorial? What is the effect of the repetitions?
2. List the ways in which Phil was "precise."
3. Describe the company man's relationship to his family as a whole and to each family member.
4. Describe Phil's relation to his work. Why do you think Goodman chooses not to tell us anything specific about the actual work Phil does?
5. Look at some obituaries in the newspaper. What is Ellen Goodman doing with the obituary form in "The Company Man"?
6. Phil has a high status job, seems to make good money, and can provide for his family. What went wrong?

SUGGESTIONS FOR WRITING

1. "The Company Man" was written before corporations began "downsizing" enthusiastically. Because of downsizing in the 1980s and 1990s, corporate life has been more of a roller coaster ride than it used to be. Write an obituary for a contemporary man or woman whose work life has been characterized by this current situation.

CORPORATIONS AS MACHINES

Jerry Mander

*Jerry Mander (b. 1936) was the president of a commercial public re-
lations company and later of an advertising agency, but left in the
1970s to work in nonprofit organizations devoted to social change and
the environment. He has published* Four Arguments for the Elimination of Television *(1978),* In the Absence of the Sacred: The
Failure of Technology and the Survival of the Indian Nations *(1991), from which the following chapter is taken, and* The
Case Against the Global Economy *(1996), edited with Edward
Goldsmith.*

The great French philosopher and technology critic Jacques Ellul makes it
one of his central points that evaluations of technology must not be confined
to the machines themselves. Equally important, he says, is to grasp that in
technological society, the structure of all of human life and its systems of organization reflect the logic of the machine. All are encompassed by Ellul
within the single term *technique,* which suggests that in contemporary society, human behavior, human thought, and human political and economic
structures are part of a seamless fabric inseparable from machines. *Technique* is machine logic extended to all human endeavors.

This point is most easily understood when we think about our relationship to the assembly line, or to the automobile or the clock; how we tune
in to and reflect the characteristics of those machines. Those examples suggest a human-machine symbiosis that alters both sides of the connection, as
part of a long, back-and-forth process of merging, or coevolution.

But *technique* is also apparent in the modes of organization that tend to
gain favor in technological society. This will be dealt with more thoroughly
in Part III, when we compare technological and native societies. This chapter, however, will focus on one particular organizational mode, a very dominant mode in our society—the corporation. The corporation is not as
subject to human control as most people believe it is; rather, it is an autonomous technical structure that behaves by a system of logic uniquely well
suited to its primary function: to give birth and impetus to profitable new
technological forms, and to spread techno-logic around the globe.

* * *

Given the extent to which corporations affect both technical change and the forces of nature, it is surprising how little attention we give them. It's not that we are entirely unaware of them; we hear their names trumpeted and flashed at us whichever way we turn. But most of us accept their existence unquestioningly, unconsciously, like background noise. We don't focus on them as the primary players they are, and we have very little understanding of *why* they behave as they do.

We usually become aware of corporate behavior only when a flagrant transgression is reported in the news: the dumping of toxic wastes, the releasing of pollutants, the suppression of research regarding health effects of various products, the tragic mechanical breakdowns such as at Three Mile Island, in Bhopal, or in Prince William Sound, Alaska.[1] Sometimes we become concerned about a large corporation closing a factory, putting 5,000 people out of work, and moving to another country.

Even when we hear such news, our tendency is to respond as if the behaviors described stem from the *people* within the corporate structure—people who are irresponsible, dishonest, greedy, or overly ambitious. Or else we attribute the problem to the moral decline of the times we live in, or to the failure of the regulatory process.

Seeing corporate behavior as rooted in the people who work within them is like believing that the problems of television are attributable solely to its program content. With corporations, as with television, the basic problems are actually structural. They are problems inherent in the forms and rules by which these entities are compelled to operate. If the problems could be traced to the personnel involved, they could be solved by changing the personnel. Unfortunately, however, *all* employees are obliged to act in concert, to behave in accordance with corporate form and corporate law. If someone attempted to revolt against these tenets, it would only result in the corporation throwing the person out, and replacing that person with another who would act according to the rules. Form determines content. Corporations are machines.

* * *

The failure to grasp the nature and inevitabilities of corporate structure has left our society far too unconscious and passive to corporate desires, and has helped corporations increase their influence, power, and freedom from accountability. Corporations already influence our conceptions of how life should be lived more than any other institution, including government.

---

[1] Three Mile Island, in Pennsylvania, scene of major nuclear reactor accident in 1979; Bhopal, India, site of 1984 Union Carbide chemical plant explosion that killed 2,500; Prince William Sound, location of massive 1989 oil spill by an Exxon tanker.

Corporate ideology, corporate priorities, corporate styles of behavior, corporate value systems, and corporate modes of organization have become synonymous with "our way of life." Corporate "culture" has become the virtual definition of American life, to be defended at all costs, even militarily. When Secretary of State George Schultz said in 1985 that in Nicaragua and El Salvador "we are fighting for our way of life," it was the threat of collectivism to free enterprise and commodity culture that motivated his remarks. Conversely, when our leaders celebrate the new "freedom" of Eastern Europe, they are really celebrating free enterprise and the market economy.

Living in the United States today, there is scarcely a moment when you are not in contact with a corporation, or its manifestation.

It is very likely that you work for a corporation. If so, your daily schedule is determined by corporate needs. You dress and behave according to corporate concepts, you interact with the machines by which corporations accomplish their tasks—computers, typewriters, telephones, fax machines, copiers. You spend your day living within corporate rhythms.

The building you live in was probably created by a corporation, as were your furniture, appliances, the clothes in your closet, your perfume—all the result of corporate concepts and action.

Taken as a group, corporations are the largest landowners in the United States, with the exception of the federal government. Corporations are also the major financial backers of electoral campaigns, and the major lobbyists for laws that benefit corporate goals.

If you switch on your radio or television, or open your newspaper, corporations speak to you. They do it through public relations and through advertising. American corporations spend more then $100 billion yearly on advertising, which is far more than is spent on all secondary education in this country. In some ways corporate advertising is the dominant education institution in our country, surely in the realm of lifestyle.

As I mentioned in Chapter 5, the average American now views 21,000 commercials every year. Twenty-one thousand times, corporations place images in your brain to suggest something great about commodities. Some commercials advertise cars, other advertise drugs—but all commercials agree that you should buy *something,* and that human life is most satisfying when inundated with commodities. Between commercials there are programs, also created by corporations, that espouse values consistent with the ads.

Corporations are also the major providers of educational materials for American schools. Some of the largest corporations are now providing books, tapes, films, and computer programs free of charge to public and private schools, as a "public service" in these budget-conscious times. They get a lot of praise for these contributions. Oil and chemical companies have been particularly generous in providing materials to help explain nature to young people—materials that portray nature as a valuable resource for human use and that celebrate concepts such as "managing nature" through chemicals, pesticides, and large-scale agribusiness. Thus, a generation of youngsters is trained to regard nature in a way that coincides with corporate objectives. They are also trained to accept corporate interpretations and perspectives from a very early age, and are thereby prepared for what is to come.

CORPORATE SHAME

I keep awaiting the day when a corporate president expresses shame for a corporate transgression against the public or the environment. The statement would go something like this:

"On behalf of my company, its management, and its shareholders, I wish to express our grief concerning injuries suffered by people living downstream from our factory, along the Green River. We are ashamed to admit that over the years, our poisonous wastes have found their way into the river, putting the community in peril. We will do anything to relieve the suffering we have caused. We are also concerned that safe storage for such potent chemicals now seems impossible, and so henceforth we will only use our facilities for safer forms of manufacturing. Under no circumstances will we give thought to abandoning this community or its workers."

No such statement has ever been made, nor will ever be made, by a publicly held corporation in America, for several reasons.

No corporate manager could ever place community welfare above corporate interest. An individual executive might personally wish to do so, but to make this sort of admission would subject the company, and the individual, to legal action by local, state, and federal authorities, as well as to damage suits by victims.

It could also open management to lawsuits from its own shareholders. U.S. corporate law holds that management of publicly held companies must act primarily in the economic interests of shareholders. If not, management can be sued by shareholders and firings would surely occur. So managers are legally obliged to ignore community welfare (e.g., worker health and satisfaction, environmental concerns) if those needs interfere with profitability. And corporate managers must also deny that corporate acts have a negative impact of any kind, if that impact might translate into costly damage suits that hinder profits.

As a result, we have witnessed countless cases in which corporate acts caused death or injury or illness, while the company denied any responsibility. We have heard cigarette companies deny that cigarettes are harmful. We have heard the same from manufacturers of pesticides, chemicals, asbestos, and birth-control technologies.

Often, corporations are privately aware of the dangers of their products or processes, but withhold that information. Even as I write these words, a National Public Radio[2] news program is reporting on the efforts of certain plastic-wrapping manufacturers to conceal from the government and the public what their own research had told them twenty years before the government or public found out: The plastic wrapping on our supermarket meats, fish, and other items can leave carcinogenic residues on our food.

In instances such as these, withholding information means that people—perhaps tens of thousands of people—become sick. Some people die. In other contexts, murder charges would be in order.

CORPORATE SCHIZOPHRENIA

That murder charges are not levied against corporations, and that corporations do not express shame at their own actions, is a direct result of the peculiar nature of corporate form, its split personality. Though human beings work inside corporations, a corporation is not a person, and does not have feelings. In most senses a corporation is not even a "thing." It may have offices, and/or a factory or products, but a corporation does not have any physical existence or form—no corporality. So when conditions in a community or country become unfavorable—safety standards become too rigid, or workers are not submissive—a corporation can dematerialize and then rematerialize in another town or country.

If a corporation is not a person or a thing, what is it? It is basically a *concept* that is given a name, and a legal existence, on paper. Though there is no such actual creature, our laws recognize the corporation as an entity. So does the population. We think of corporations as having concrete form, but their true existence is only on paper and in our minds.

Even more curious than a corporation's ephemeral quality is that our laws give this nonexistent entity a great many rights similar to those given to human beings. The law calls corporations "fictitious persons," with the right to buy and sell property, or to sue in court for injuries or for slander and libel. And "corporate speech"—advertising, public relations—is protected under the First Amendment to the Constitution, governing freedom of speech. This latter right has been extended to corporations despite the fact that when the Bill of Rights was written in 1792, corporations as we now know them did not exist. (The First Amendment was originally intended to protect *personal* speech, in a century when the only media consisted of single news-sheets, handbills, and books. The net result of expanding First Amendment protection to *corporate* speech is that $100 billion worth of advertising from a relative handful of sources gets to dominate

---

[2] Radio network funded primarily by grants and listener contributions.

public perception, free from nearly all government attempts at regulation. Democracy is effectively thwarted, rather than aided.)

Though corporations enjoy many "human" rights, they have not been required to abide by human responsibilities. Even in cases of negligence causing death or injury, the state cannot jail or execute the corporation. In rare instances, individuals within a corporation can be prosecuted, if they perpetrate acts that they know can cause injury. And a corporation may be fined or ordered to alter practices, but its structure is never altered, its "life" is never threatened.

In fact, unlike human beings, corporations do not die a natural death. A corporation usually outlives the human beings who have been part of it, even those who "own" it. A corporation actually has the possibility of immortality. Of course, the owners of a corporation can put it to death under certain conditions, but society cannot exercise that kind of control.

Lacking the sort of physical, organic reality that characterizes human existence, this entity, this concept, this collection of paperwork called a "corporation" is not capable of feelings such as shame or remorse. Instead, corporations behave according to their own unique systems of standards, rules, forms, and objectives.

The most basic rule of corporate operation is that it must produce income, and (except for that special category of "nonprofit corporations") must show a profit over time. Among publicly held companies there is another basic rule: It must expand and grow, since growth is the standard by which the stock market judges a company. All other values are secondary: the welfare of the community, the happiness of workers, the health of the planet, and even the general prosperity.

So human beings within the corporate structure, whatever their personal morals and feelings, are prevented from operating on their own standards. Like the assembly-line workers who must operate at the speed of the machine, corporate employees are strapped onto the apparatus of the corporation, and operate by its rules.

In this sense a corporation is essentially a machine, a technological structure, an organization that follows its own principles and its own morality, and in which human morality is anomalous. Because of this double standard—one for human beings and another for "fictitious persons" like corporations—we sometimes see bizarre behavior from executives who, though knowing what is right and moral, behave in a contrary fashion.

THE CORPORATE/HUMAN DILEMMA: THREE CASES

In 1986, Union Carbide Corporation's chemical plant in Bhopal, India, accidentally released methyl isocynate into the air, injuring some 200,000 people and killing more than 2,000. Soon after the accident the chairman of the board of Union Carbide, Warren M. Anderson, was so upset at what happened that he informed the media that he would spend the rest of his life attempting to correct the problems his company had caused and to make amends. Only one year later, however, Mr. Anderson was quoted in *Business Week* as saying that he had "overreacted," and was now prepared to lead the company in its legal fight *against* paying damages and reparations. What happened? Very simply, Mr. Anderson at first reacted as a human being. Later, he realized (and perhaps was pressed to realize) that this reaction was inappropriate for a chairman of the board of a company whose primary obligations are not to the poor victims of Bhopal, but to shareholders; that is, to its profit picture. If Mr. Anderson had persisted in expressing his personal feelings or acknowledging the company's culpability, he certainly would have been fired.

When the *Exxon Valdez* crashed onto a reef in 1989, and spilled its oil into the sea and onto the beaches of Alaska—in part because of the intoxication of the ship's captain—the corporation at first reacted with apologies, and promised to make amends: clean the water, clean the beaches, save the animals, pay for damages. I was surprised at the company's stance. It ran counter to the normal manner in which corporations react. Perhaps in this case the cause and effect were simply indisputable, unlike cases of birth malformations from herbicide spraying or injury to workers in computer manufacturing, where causes and effects are separated by many years. On the other hand, maybe certain top executives at Exxon *were* truly horrified and felt moved to make things right. If so, like Union Carbide's Anderson, they soon came to their senses. The cleanup turned out to be very expensive. Within six months the company ceased all of its efforts to allay the effects of the spill. In a typical corporate cost-benefit approach, it was reasoned that fighting the lawsuits and making settlements that courts or negotiators might require would certainly be cheaper than cleaning the mess.

For me, the most disturbing example of corporate schizophrenia occurred in the personal context of a family event during the late 1960s. At the time, I was involved in efforts to retard the Manhattanization of San Francisco. I authored a series of ads attempting to halt the construction of high-rise office buildings that were increasing traffic and pollution, and destroying the vistas that are a big part of life in that city. Among our arguments was that high-rise development cost the city—in services such as police, fire, sewage, expanded electrical power generation, and road maintenance—far more than could be redeemed in property taxes. We had studies to prove this.

While working on these campaigns a friend of my family's—I will call her Genevieve—telephoned to say that her father was in town from Chicago for a few days. She wanted to drop by with him and the kids. At that moment we realized that Genevieve's father was president of one of the largest corporate developers of skyscrapers. Several of his buildings were ones we were opposing.

On a bright Sunday morning, Genevieve and her family came for brunch in our garden. Mr. Butterfield turned out to be most charming: friendly, personable, affectionate with his grandchildren and with our children.

Out of friendship for Genevieve, I did not raise any environmental issues on this occasion. But when Mr. Butterfield remarked on how wonderful it was that we enjoyed such a lush garden in the midst of the crowded city, and asked about the vacant lot adjoining our house, things changed. We informed him that only three days ago a bulldozer had been in the adjoining lot to level a lovely Victorian house and a wonderful formal Italian garden with tomatoes, beans, squash, roses, geraniums, and two small redwood trees. The garden had been tended by an elderly Italian couple who had lived in the house for forty years. When the couple died—the husband within three weeks of the wife—the bank sold the property to developers, who planned to build a twenty-six-unit apartment building. Soon, our views would be blocked and shadows would fall on our garden.

Mr. Butterfield was aghast. "How horrible," he said. "It is amazing they would permit huge apartments on such a lovely quiet street."

I could no longer restrain myself. Assuming that Mr. Butterfield would easily see the parallels between the destruction of our views and the far larger problems caused by his own thirty-story buildings less than a mile away, I told him of the campaigns to stop such development. He was attentive and concerned. He said he had no idea there was resistance in San Francisco to high-rise development.

This statement, in turn, shocked me. The movement against these new buildings had been going on for several years and included public protests and considerable media attention. I wondered if he was being truthful with me. I knew that among top corporate executives, who live in a world of spreadsheets and financial manipulations, there is sometimes little awareness of how their actions affect real people. Maybe the protests in San Francisco were not sufficiently threatening that the president of a Chicago corporation would even know about them. If so, it was a humbling reality for anyone seeking to influence corporate actions. I decided to take Mr. Butterfield at his word. In any event, it was the polite way of handling the situation.

The conversation went on. He asked me why people were opposed, and I told him about the studies showing the effects of this kind of development. He was fascinated. He handed me his business card and asked me to write to him directly, and to forward the studies and any other relevant information. He said he would personally assess the situation and get back to me. He thanked me warmly for the news I brought.

I came away from the exchange convinced the man was in earnest. And probably, while sitting in my garden, he was.

I gathered the material, wrote him a long explanatory letter, and sent it in a package marked "Personal," as he had suggested. I soon received a reply saying he would study the reports and be in touch very soon. He never wrote back. A subsequent letter that I sent to him was not acknowledged. Finally, I decided that his polite behavior at brunch was, like my own, out of concern for his daughter. Back at corporate headquarters, a different set of rules superseded all feelings.

ELEVEN INHERENT RULES OF CORPORATE BEHAVIOR

It is clear that human beings within a corporation are seriously constrained in their ability to influence corporate behavior. And yet, I have mentioned only two of the rules that serve to constrain this influence: the profit imperative and the need for growth. The following list is an attempt to articulate more of the obligatory rules by which corporations operate. Some of the rules overlap, but taken together they help reveal why corporations behave as they do, and how they have come to dominate their environment and the human beings within it.

1. The Profit Imperative

As noted earlier, profit is the ultimate measure of all corporate decisions. It takes precedence over community well-being, worker health, public health, peace, environmental preservation, or national security. Corporations will even find ways of trading with national "enemies"—Libya, Iran, the Soviet Union, Cuba—when public policy abhors it. The profit imperative and the growth imperative are the most fundamental corporate drives; together they represent the corporation's instinct to "live."

2. The Growth Imperative

Corporations live or die by whether they can sustain growth. On this depends relationships to investors, to the stock market, to banks, and to public perception. The growth imperative also fuels the corporate desire to find and develop scarce resources in obscure parts of the world.

This effect is now clearly visible, as the world's few remaining pristine places are sacrificed to corporate production. The peoples who inhabit these resource-rich regions are similarly pressured to give up their traditional ways and climb on the wheel of production-consumption. Corporate planners consciously attempt to bring "less developed societies into the modern world," in order to create infrastructures for development, as well as new workers and new consumers. Corporations claim they do this for altruistic reasons—to raise the living standard—but corporations have no altruism.

Theoretically, privately held corporations—those owned by individuals or families—do not have the imperative to expand. In practice, however, the behavior is the same. There are economies of scale, and usually increased profits from size. Such privately held giants as Bechtel Corporation[3] have shown no propensity to moderate growth; their behavior, in fact, shows quite the opposite.

3. Competition and Aggression

On the one hand, corporations require a high degree of cooperation within management. On the other hand, they place every person in management in fierce competition with each other. Anyone interested in a corporate career must hone his or her abilities to seize the moment. This applies to gaining an edge over another company, or over a colleague within the company. As an employee, you are expected to be part of the "team"—you must aggressively push to win over the other corporations—but you also must be ready to climb over your own colleagues.

The comparison with sports is clear. All members of a professional football team (itself a corporation) compete with each other, yet all players must cooperate to defeat an opposing team.

Corporate (or athletic) ideology holds that competition improves worker incentive and corporate performance, and therefore benefits society. Our society has accepted this premise utterly. Unfortunately, however, it also surfaces in personal relationships. Living by standards of competition and aggression on the job, human beings have few avenues to express softer, more personal feelings. We all know what happens to anyone who cries under stress in business or in politics. (In politics, nonaggressive behavior is interpreted as weakness.) And yet, in the intimacy of the home, such true expressions of real feelings are what tend to matter the most. Such contrary standards on the job and at home can lead to a kind of schizophrenia that often plays itself out in busted relationships.

4. Amorality

Not being human, not having feelings, corporations do not have morals or altruistic goals. So decisions that may be antithetical to community goals or environmental health are made without suffering misgivings. In fact, corporate executives praise "nonemotionality" as a basis for "objective" decisions.

---

[3] Construction company based in San Francisco.

Corporations, however, seek to hide their amorality, and attempt to act as if they were altruistic. Lately there has been a concerted effort by American industry to seem concerned with contemporary social issues, such as environmental cleanups, community arts, or drug programs. The effort to exhibit social responsibility by corporations comes precisely because they are innately *not* responsible to the public; they have no interest in community goals except the ones that serve their purposes. This false altruism should not be confused with the genuine altruism human beings exhibit for one another when, for example, one goes for help on behalf of a sick neighbor, or takes care of the kids, or loans money. Corporate efforts that seem altruistic are really public relations ploys, or else are directly self-serving projects, such as providing schools with educational materials about nature. In other cases, apparent altruism is only "damage control," to offset public criticism.

For example, there has recently been a spurt of corporate advertising about how corporations work to clean the environment. A company that installs offshore oil rigs will run ads about how fish are thriving under the rigs. Logging companies known for their clear-cutting practices will run millions of dollars' worth of ads about their "tree farms," as if they were interested in renewable resources, when they are not.

Other corporations will show ads of happy employees; usually these are companies with serious labor problems. Or companies will run ads about how they are assisting in community programs—day care, the arts, drug education, historic preservation—in communities where citizens have been outraged by corporate irresponsibility. In fact, it is a fair rule of thumb that corporations will tend to advertise the very qualities they do not have, in order to allay a negative public perception. When corporations say "we care," it is almost always in response to the widespread perception that they do not care. And they don't. How could they? Corporations do not have feelings or morals. All acts are in service to profit. All apparent altruism is measured against possible public relations benefit. If the benefits do not accrue, the altruistic pose is dropped. When Exxon realized that its cleanup of the Alaskan shores was not easing the public rage about the oil spill, it simply dropped all pretense of altruism and ceased working.

5. Hierarchy

Corporate law requires that corporations be structured into classes of superiors and subordinates within a centralized pyramidal structure: chairman, directors, CEO, vice presidents, division managers, and so on. The efficiency of this hierarchical form, which also characterizes the military, the government, and most institutions in our society, is rarely questioned.

The effect on society from all organizations adopting hierarchical form is to make it seem natural that we have all been placed within a national pecking order. Some jobs are better than others, some lifestyles are better than others, some neighborhoods, some races, some kinds of knowledge. Men over women. Westerners over non-Westerners. Humans over nature.

That effective, nonhierarchical modes of organization exist on the planet, and have been successful for millennia, is barely known by most Americans.

6. Quantification, Linearity, and Segmentation

Corporations require that subjective information be translated into objective form, i.e., numbers. This excludes from the decision-making process all values that do not so translate. The subjective or spiritual aspects of forests, for example, cannot be translated, and so do not enter corporate equations. Forests are evaluated only as "board feet." Production elements that pose danger to public health or welfare—pollution, toxic waste, carcinogens—are translated to value-free objective concepts, such as "cost-benefit ratio" or "trade-off." Auto manufacturers evaluating the safety level of certain production standards calculate the number of probable accidents and deaths at each level of the standard. This number is then compared with the cost of insurance payments and lawsuits from dead drivers' families. A number is also assigned to the public relations problem, and a balance is sought.

When corporations are asked to clean up their smokestack emissions, they lobby to relax the new standard, to contain costs. The result is that a predictable number of people are expected to become sick and die.

The operative corporate standard is not "as safe as humanly possible," but rather, "as safe as possible commensurate with maintaining acceptable profit."

The drive toward objectification enters every aspect of corporate activity. For example, on the production end, great effort is made, through time-and-motion studies, to measure each fragment of every process performed by a worker. The eventual goal is to sufficiently segment tasks so that they may be automated, eliminating workers altogether. Where the task is not eliminated, it is reduced to its simplest repetitive form. As a result, workers become subject to intense comparisons with other workers. If they survive on the jobs, doing the repetitive tasks leaves them horribly bored and without a sense of participating in corporate goals. They feel like they are part of a machine, and they are.

7. Dehumanization

If the environment and the community are objectified by corporations, with all decisions measured against public relations or profit standards, so is the employee objectified and dehumanized.

Corporations make a conscious effort to depersonalize. The recent introduction of computer surveillance technology into business operations, especially in measuring and supervising the performance of office workers, has made this dehumanization task simpler and more thorough. Now, every keystroke and every word of every worker can be counted by a central computer that compares each individual's performance against others and against corporate standards. Those people found to be too slow, or inconsistent, or who take too many breaks, are simpler to find and to discipline or dismiss.

In very small businesses, the tendency toward dehumanization is obviously mitigated, since some employer-employee personal contact can scarcely be avoided. But in the great majority of corporations, employees are viewed as ciphers, as cogs in the wheel, replaceable by others or by machines.

As for management employees, not subject to quite the same indignities, they nonetheless must practice a style of decision-making that "does not let feelings get in the way." This applies as much to firing employees as it does to dealing with the consequences of corporate behavior in the environment or the community. But, as has been described, the manager's behavior, objectifying all decisions and all people, also acts to objectify and dehumanize himself or herself.

8. Exploitation

All corporate profit is obtained by a simple formula: Profit equals the difference between the amount paid to an employee and the economic value of the employee's output, and/or the difference between the amount paid for raw materials used in production (including costs of processing) and the ultimate sales price of the processed raw materials. Karl Marx was right: A worker is not compensated for the full value of his or her labor; neither is the raw material supplier. The owners of capital skim off part of the value as profit. Profit is based on underpayment.

Capitalists argue that this is a fair deal, since both workers and the people who mine or farm the resources (usually in Third World environments) get paid. But this arrangement is inherently imbalanced. The owner of the capital—the corporation or the bank—always obtains additional benefit. While the worker makes a wage, the owner of the capital gets the benefit of the worker's labor, plus the surplus profit the worker produces, which is then reinvested to produce yet more surplus. This even applies to the rare cases where workers are very highly paid, as with professional athletes and entertainers. In those cases, the corporations pay high wages because the workers will produce more income for the corporation than they are paid. So the formula remains intact: Profit is based on paying less than actual value for workers and resources. This is called exploitation.

9. Ephemerality

Corporations exist beyond time and space. As we have seen, they are legal creations that only exist on paper. They do not die a natural death; they outlive their own creators. And they have no commitment to locale, employees, or neighbors. This makes the modern corporation entirely different from the baker or grocer of previous years who survived by cultivating intimacy with the neighbors. Having no morality, no commitment to place, and no physical nature (a factory someplace, while being a physical entity, is not the corporation), a corporation can relocate all of its operations to another place at the first sign of inconvenience: demanding employees, too high taxes, restrictive environmental laws. The traditional ideal of community engagement is antithetical to corporate behavior.

10. Opposition to Nature

Though individuals who work for corporations may personally love nature, corporations themselves, and corporate societies, are intrinsically committed to intervening in, altering, and transforming nature. For corporations engaged in commodity manufacturing, profit comes from transmogrifying raw materials into saleable forms. Metals from the ground are converted into cars. Trees are converted into boards and then into houses, furniture, and paper products. Oil is converted into energy. In all such activity, a piece of nature is taken from where it belongs and processed into a new form. In rare instances, elements of nature can be renewed, or trees can be replanted, but even in such cases they do not return to their original forms. So all manufacturing activity depends upon intervention and reorganization of nature. After natural resources are used up in one part of the globe, the corporation moves on to another part. With the transformation process well under way in Southeast Asia and the Pacific, Antarctica is the new target. Soon it will be the moon.

This transformation of nature occurs in all societies where community manufacturing takes place. But in capitalist, corporate societies, the process is accelerated because capitalist societies and corporations *must* grow. Extracting resources from nature and reprocessing them at an ever-quickening pace is intrinsic to their existence. Meanwhile, the consumption end of the cycle is also accelerated—corporations have an intrinsic interest in convincing people that commodities bring satisfaction. Modes of fulfillment that are based on self-sufficiency—inner satisfaction, contentment in nature or in relationships, a lack of desire to acquire wealth—are subversive to corporate goals. For production to be hyped, i.e., for natural materials to be transformed into commodities and then into profit, the consumption end of the cycle must similarly be hyped. The net effect is the ravaging of nature.

Corporate entities that do not directly engage in processing raw materials, such as banks or insurance companies, are nevertheless engaged in ravaging nature. Banks finance the conversion of nature; insurance companies help reduce the financial risks involved. The more nature is exploited the greater the profit for all corporations. Of course, on a finite planet, the process cannot continue indefinitely.

11. Homogenization

American rhetoric claims that commodity society delivers greater choice and diversity than other societies. "Choice" in this context means *product* choice, choice in the marketplace: many brands to choose from, and diverse features on otherwise identical products. Actually, however, corporations have a stake in all of us living our lives in a similar manner, achieving our pleasures from things that we buy. While it is true that different corporations seek different segments of the market—elderly people, let's say, or organic food buyers—*all* corporations share an identical economic, cultural, and social vision, and seek to accelerate society's (and individual) acceptance of that vision.

Lifestyles and economic systems that emphasize sharing commodities and work, that do not encourage commodity accumulation, or that celebrate nonmaterial values, are not good for business. People living collectively, for example, sharing such hard goods as washing machines, cars, and appliances—or worse, getting along without them—are outrageous to corporate commodity society. The nuclear family is a far better idea for maintaining corporate commodity society: Each family lives alone in a single-family home and has all the same machines as every other family on the block. Recently, the singles phenomenon has proved even more productive than the nuclear family, since each *person* duplicates the consumption patterns of every other person.

As for native societies, which celebrate an utterly nonmaterial relationship to life, the planet, and the spirit, and which are at opposite poles to corporate ideology, they are regarded as inferior and unenlightened. Backward.

We are told they envy the choices we have. To the degree these societies continue to exist, they represent a threat to the homogenization of worldwide markets and culture. Corporate society works hard to retrain such people in attitudes and values appropriate to corporate goals. But in the undeveloped parts of the world, where corporations are just arriving, the ideological retraining process is just getting under way. Satellite communications technology, which brings Western television and advertising, is combined with a technical infrastructure to speed up the pace of development. Most of this activity is funded by the World Bank and the International Monetary Fund, as well as agencies such as U.S. AID, the Inter-American Bank, and the Asian-American Bank, all of which serve multinational corporate enterprise.

As for the ultimate goal? In *Trilateralism,* editor Holly Sklar quotes the president of Nabisco Corporation: "One world of homogeneous consumption ... [I am] looking forward to the day when Arabs and Americans, Latins and Scandinavians will be munching Ritz crackers as enthusiastically as they already drink Coke or brush their teeth with Colgate."

Sklar goes on: "Corporations not only advertise products, they promote lifestyles rooted in consumption, patterned largely after the United States. ... [They] look forward to a postnational age in which [Western] social, economic, and political values are transformed into universal values ... a world economy in which all national economies beat to the rhythm of transnational corporate capitalism. ... The Western way is the good way, national culture is inferior."

FORM IS CONTENT

The most important aspect of these eleven rules is the degree to which they are inherent in corporate structure. Corporations are *inherently* bold, aggressive, and competitive. Though they exist in a society that claims to operate by moral principles, they are structurally amoral. It is inevitable that they will dehumanize people who work for them, and dehumanize the overall society as well. They are disloyal to workers, including their own managers. If community goals conflict with corporate goals, then corporations are similarly disloyal to the communities they may have been part of for many years. It is *inherent* in corporate activity that they seek to drive all consciousness into one-dimensional channels. They must attempt to dominate alternative cultures and to effectively clone the world population into a form more to their liking. Corporations do not care about nations; they live beyond boundaries. They are intrinsically committed to destroying nature. And they have an inexorable, unabatable, voracious need to grow and to expand. In dominating other cultures, in digging up the earth, corporations blindly follow the codes that have been built into them as if they were genes.

Would our society have been better off if we had been told, from the beginning, that corporations would behave as they do? As with every other new piece of machinery, large or small, we were only presented with the pros, never the cons, of this creature called the corporation. There was never a vote as to whether, on balance, corporations destroy more than they contribute. Nor was there ever any effort to articulate the principles by which they operate and the manner in which they would inevitably behave. Articulating these principles now gives us a picture we should have been given a long time ago.

Now that we see the inherent direction of corporate activity, we must abandon the idea that corporations can reform themselves, or that a new generation of executive managers can be re-educated. We must also abandon the assumption that the form of the structure is "neutral." To ask corporate executives to behave in a morally defensible manner is absurd. Corporations, and the people within them, are not subject to moral behavior. They are following a system of logic that leads inexorably toward dominant behaviors. To ask corporations to behave otherwise is like asking an army to adopt pacifism. Form is content.

STUDY AND DISCUSSION QUESTIONS

1. Define Jacques Ellul's term "technique."

2. What is a corporation, according to Mander? Why is it a mistake to attribute the behavior of corporations solely to the people who manage them?

3. In what ways do corporations affect our daily life, according to Mander?

4. In what ways do corporations influence education?

5. What is the nature of a corporation's "split personality"? How is the law's acceptance of this split personality beneficial to corporations and dangerous to human beings?

6. What is the "corporate/human dilemma" in the three cases Mander summarizes? How is this dilemma connected to the split personality of corporations?

7. List Mander's "eleven inherent rules of corporate behavior."

8. Define "profit."

9. "Modes of fulfillment that are based on self-sufficiency—inner satisfaction, contentment in nature or in relationships, a lack of desire to acquire wealth—are subversive to corporate goals," writes Mander. How and why?

10. How is the progressive breakup of the community and the family good for corporations?

11. How is form content when applied to corporations?

SUGGESTIONS FOR WRITING

1. Would you prefer to have small individual or family-owned stores and industries in your community—or branches of corporations? Make an argument either way, engaging Mander's essay as well as your own experience.

2. Imagine that corporations have run out of natural resources to exploit for their continued growth. Write a scenario that speculates on what will happen next.

3. Mander argues that many of the abuses and the exploitation of people and nature attributable to corporations are due not primarily to bad/greedy/dishonest people who work for or run corporations but are inherent in the very structure and definition of what a corporation is. If this is so, what can be done about the situation?

4. If you wanted to escape from corporations, what would you have to do and how would you go about doing it?

SCIENCE AND TECHNOLOGY

It is they [men of science] who hold the secret of the mysterious property of the mind by which error ministers to truth, and truth slowly but irrevocably prevails. Theirs is the logic of discovery, the demonstration of the advance of knowledge and the development of ideas, which, as the earthly wants and the passions of men remain almost unchanged, are the charter of progress, and the vital spark of history.

—Lord Acton, 1895

The unbounded optimism that characterized so much thinking about science and technology a century ago today competes with growing skepticism and unease. The old faith that science and technology would inevitably bring us ever greater understanding, material comfort, and happiness lives on, but uneasily, amid a degraded natural environment, a worldwide arsenal of weapons of mass destruction, and a growing sense that our technological society is somehow alienating us from others and from ourselves. That airplanes and microwave ovens and nuclear power plants (usually) work may prove that science is correct but not that it has necessarily been good for us.

Recent advances in computer technology have accelerated at a dazzling rate. Four decades ago, a computer filled a large room; today, a chip the size of a postage stamp can perform the same calculations, and faster. But, as Ellen Ullman suggests in "Out of Time: Reflections on the Programming Life," our gee-whiz response to such technological miracles may blind us to some serious problems, for example, that the people who design the software we spend more and more time with live and work in a bizarre subculture far removed from ordinary life.

Biological technology, too, has been advancing rapidly in recent years. "Test tube babies" are now commonplace (perhaps someone you know has had one), artificial and transplanted organs keep many of us going, and genetic engineering may soon even permit parents to predetermine the characteristics of their offspring. But what are we giving up? In "Three Generations of Native American Women's Birth Experience," Joy Harjo offers a serious critique of the cold impersonality of high tech medicine and its indifference to the wisdom and humanity of traditional ways.

What about science, apart from technology? Can we really blame science and scientists for the misapplication of what they discover? Aren't many scientists engaged in "pure research," the simple pursuit of truth? In "To Make Nature an Accomplice," William II. Tucker argues that this pursuit has not always been so pure or so simple, that in physical sciences, like biology, and in social sciences, like anthropology and psychology, researchers have often projected their own and society's prejudices onto the phenomena they claimed to be studying objectively. Tucker traces the long and shameful history of scientists' attempts to "prove" that black people—as well as women, immigrants, and the poor—are mentally inferior.

Scientists and others studying the animal world have also sometimes leaped to conclusions that lent ideological support to social inequality. Some have argued that humans are territorial and competitive by nature, just like our animal ancestors. In his somewhat whimsical essay "The Tucson Zoo," physician Lewis Thomas argues that the intense affection for beavers and otters he felt one day at the zoo might suggest the opposite, that human nature is essentially altruistic, even though "our kind of civilization" offers us little chance to demonstrate it.

To Susan Griffin, the problem is not misguided scientists but science itself, a fundamentally flawed male enterprise that wrongly seeks to quantify and control nature; science, not just technology, is a destructive force. Her poetic essay "His Certainty: How He Rules the Universe" dramatizes the deadened and dehumanizing ways of thinking that for her are the essence of science.

To Paul Goodman, on the other hand, science and technology are tools that hold great potential for improving the lives of us all. But a handful of powerful people, among them weapons manufacturers, control the decisions about what technology gets developed and even what scientific research gets done. "The wandering dialogue of science with the unknown," he writes, "is straitjacketed for petty military projects." His essay "A Causerie at the Military-Industrial" recounts an angry speech he delivered to a convention of the National Security Industrial Association. Goodman accuses these military industrialists of hijacking, for their own profit, what should be a vehicle for universal human liberation.

Science promises liberation of a different kind to an eighth-grade girl in Judith Ortiz Cofer's humorous autobiographical essay "Advanced Biology." Study sessions with Ira, a year older, offer young Judith a way to rebel against her strict religious upbringing. She and Ira even discuss sex, a subject "unmentionable" at home; science's straightforward descriptions of reproductive biology empty sex of sin, and Judith soon finds herself talking back to her mother.

Though evolutionary biologist Stephen Jay Gould believes that "there is nothing in science which is opposed to a belief in God and religion," he sees a serious threat in efforts to disguise religious beliefs as science and mandate their inclusion in high school biology courses. Evolution is a *"fact,"* he writes, well established by fossil evidence, and to bend to pressure and teach otherwise—as do the three textbook authors named in his essay's title, "Moon, Mann, and Otto"—is opportunistic, even cowardly. Scientists may be blinded by their biases, as Gould himself has frequently documented, but the scientific method does offer a means for approaching truth about the physical world and, as biologist Thomas Henry Huxley (much admired by Gould) wrote over a century ago, "Truth is better than much profit."

No matter where you yourself stand in all these debates (and if you're still deciding, these readings may help), it seems pretty clear that science and technology are here to stay, that they are tightly bound up with other social issues, and that a better society would mean better science and more humane technology.

OUT OF TIME: REFLECTIONS ON THE PROGRAMMING LIFE

Ellen Ullman

Ellen Ullman has worked as a software programmer and engineer and as a consulting editor for Byte *magazine. She is the author of* Close to the Machine: Technophilia and Its Discontents: A Memoir *(1997). The following essay originally appeared in* Resisting the Virtual Life: The Culture and Politics of Information *(1995), edited by James Brook and Iain A. Boal.*

I.

People imagine that programming is logical, a process like fixing a clock. Nothing could be further from the truth. Programming is more like an illness, a fever, an obsession. It's like those dreams in which you have an exam but you remember you haven't attended the course. It's like riding a train and never being able to get off.

The problem with programming is not that the computer isn't logical—the computer is terribly logical, relentlessly literal-minded. Computers are supposed to be like brains, but in fact they are idiots because they take everything you say completely at face value. You can say to a toddler, "Are yew okay tewday?" But it's not possible for a programmer to say anything like that to a computer. There will be a syntax error.

When you program, your mind is full of details, millions of bits of knowledge. This knowledge is in human form, which is to say rather chaotic, coming at you from one perspective then another, then a random thought, then something else important, then the same thing with a what-if attached. For example, try to think of everything you know about something as simple as an invoice. Now try to tell an idiot how to prepare one. That is programming.

A computer program is an algorithm that must be written down in order, in a specific syntax, in a strange language that is only partially readable by regular human beings. To program is to translate between the chaos of human life and the line-by-line world of computer language. It is an act of taking dictation from your own mind.

You must not lose your own attention. As the human-world knowledge tumbles about in your mind, you must keep typing, typing. You must not be interrupted. Any break in your listening causes you to lose a line here or there. Some bit comes then—oh no, it's leaving, please come back. It may not come back. You may lose it. You will create a bug and there's nothing you can do about it.

Every single computer program has a least one bug. If you are a programmer, it is guaranteed that your work has errors. These errors will be discovered over both short and long periods of time, most coming to light after you've moved to a new job. But your name is on the program. The code library software keeps a permanent record card of who did what and when. At the old job, they will say terrible things about you after you've gone. This is normal life for a programmer: problems trailing behind you through time, humiliation in absentia.

People imagine that programmers don't like to talk because they prefer machines to people. This is not completely true. Programmers don't talk because they must not be interrupted.

This inability to be interrupted leads to a life that is strangely asynchronous to the one lived by other human beings. It's better to send e-mail than to call a programmer on the phone. It's better to leave a note on the chair than to expect the programmer to come to a meeting. This is because the programmer must work in mind-time but the phone rings in real time. Similarly, meetings are supposed to take place in real time. It's not just ego that prevents programmers from working in groups—it's the synchrony problem. To synchronize with other people (or their representation in telephones, buzzers, and doorbells) can only mean interrupting the thought-train. Interruptions mean certain bugs. You must not get off the train.

I used to have dreams in which I was overhearing conversations I had to program. Once, I had to program two people making love. In my dream they sweated and tumbled while I sat with a cramped hand writing code. The couple went from gentle caresses to ever-widening passions, and I despaired as I tried desperately to find a way to express the act of love in the C computer language.

No matter what anyone tells you about the allure of computers, I can tell you for a fact that love cannot be programmed.

II.

I once had a job where I didn't talk to anyone for two years. Here was the arrangement: I was the first engineer hired by a start-up software company. In exchange for large quantities of stock that might be worth something someday, I was supposed to give up my life.

I sat in a large room with two other engineers and three Sun workstations. The fans of the machines whirred, the keys of the keyboards clicked. Occasionally one or the other of us would grunt or mutter. Otherwise, we did not speak. Now and then, I would have a temper outburst in which I pounded the keyboard with my fists, setting off a barrage of beeps. My colleagues might look up but never said anything about this.

Once a week, I had a five-minute meeting with my boss. He was a heavy-set bearded man with glasses who looked like everyone's stereotype of a nerd; as a matter of fact, he looked almost exactly like my previous boss, another heavy-set bearded man with glasses. At this meeting I would routinely tell him I was on schedule. Since being on schedule is a very rare thing in software engineering, my boss would say good, good, see you next week.

I remember watching my boss disappear down the row of cubby-hole partitions. He always wore exactly the same clothes: he had several outfits, each one exactly the same, khaki pants and a checked shirt of the same pattern. So, week to week, the image of his disappearing down the row of partitions remained unchanged. The same khaki pants, the same pattern in the checked shirt. Good, good, see you next week.

Real time was no longer compelling. Days, weeks, months, and years came and went without much physical change in my surroundings. Surely I was aging. My hair must have grown, I must have cut it, grown more gray hairs. Gravity must have been working on my late-thirties body, but I didn't notice. I only paid attention to my back and shoulders because they seized up on me from long sitting. Later, after I left the company, there was a masseuse on staff. That way, even the back and shoulders could be ignored.

What was compelling was the software. I was making something out of nothing, I thought, and I admit the software had more life for me than my brief love affair, my friends, my cat, my house, my neighbor who was stabbed and nearly killed by her husband. I was creating ("creating," that is the word we used) a device-independent interface library. One day, I sat in a room by myself surrounded by computer monitors from various manufacturers. I remember looking at the screens of my companions and saying, "Speak to me."

I completed the interface library in two years and left the company. Five years later, the company's stock went public. For the engineers who'd stayed the original arrangement was made good: in exchange for giving up seven years of their lives, they became very, very wealthy. As for me, I bought a car. A red one.

III.

Frank was thinking he had to get closer to the machine. Somehow, he'd floated up. Up from memory heaps and kernels. Up from file systems. Up through utilities. Up to where he was now: an end-user query tool. Next thing, he could find himself working on general ledgers, invoices—God— *financial reports.* Somehow he had to get closer to the machine.

Frank hated me. Not only was I closer to the machine, I had won the coin toss to get the desk near the window. Frank sat in full view of the hallway and he was further from the machine.

Frank was nearly forty. His wife was pregnant. Outside in the parking lot (which he couldn't see through my window), his new station wagon was heating up in the sun. Soon, he'd have a kid, a wife who had just quit her job, a wagon with a child-carrier, and an end-user query tool. Somehow he had to get closer to the machine.

Here are the reasons Frank wanted to be closer to the machine: The machine means midnight dinners of Diet Coke. It means unwashed clothes and bare feet on the desk. It means anxious rides through mind-time that have nothing to do with the clock. To work on things used only by machines or other programmers—that's the key. Programmers and machines don't care how you live. They don't care when you live. You can stay, come, go, sleep, or not. At the end of the project looms a deadline, the terrible place where you must get off the train. But, in between, for years at a stretch, you are free: free from the obligations of time.

To express the idea of being "closer to the machine," an engineer refers to "low-level code." In regular life, "low" usually signifies something bad. In programming, "low" is good. Low is better.

If the code creates programs that do useful work for regular human beings, it is called "higher." Higher-level programs are called "applications." Applications are things that people use. Although it would seem that usefulness by people would be a good thing, from a programmer's point of view, direct people-use is bad. If regular people, called "users," can understand the task accomplished by your program, you will be paid less and held in lower esteem. In the regular world, the term "higher" may be better, but, in programming, higher is worse. High is bad.

If you want money and prestige, you need to write code that only machines or other programmers understand. Such code is "low." It's best if you write microcode, a string of zeroes and ones that only a processor reads. The next best thing is assembler code, a list of instructions to the processor, but readable if you know what you're doing. If you can't write microcode or assembler, you might get away with writing in the C or C++ language. C and C++ are really sort of high, but they're considered "low." So you still get to be called a "software engineer." In the grand programmer-scheme of things, it's vastly better to be a "software engineer" than a "programmer." The difference is about thirty thousand dollars a year and a potential fortune in stock.

My office-mate Frank was a man vastly unhappy in his work. He looked over my shoulder, everyone's shoulder, trying to get away from the indignity of writing a program used by regular people. This affected his work. His program was not all it should have been, and for this he was punished. His punishment was to have to talk to regular people.

Frank became a sales-support engineer. Ironically, working in sales and having a share in bonuses, he made more money. But he got no more stock options. And in the eyes of other engineers, Frank was as "high" as one could get. When asked, we said, "Frank is now in sales." This was equivalent to saying he was dead.

IV.

Real techies don't worry about forced eugenics. I learned this from a real techie in the cafeteria of a software company.

The project team is having lunch and discussing how long it would take to wipe out a disease inherited recessively on the X chromosome. First come calculations of inheritance probabilities. Given some sized population, one of the engineers arrives at a wipeout date. Immediately, another suggests that the date could be moved forward by various manipulations of the inheritance patterns. For example, he says, there could be an education campaign.

The six team members then fall over one another with further suggestions. They start with rewards to discourage carriers from breeding. Immediately they move to fines for those who reproduce the disease. Then they go for what they call "more effective" measures: Jail for breeding. Induced abortion. Forced sterilization.

Now they're hot. The calculations are flying. Years and years fall from the final doom-date of the disease.

Finally, they get to the ultimate solution. "It's straightforward," someone says, "just kill every carrier." Everyone responds to this last suggestion with great enthusiasm. One generation and—bang!—the disease is gone.

Quietly I say, "You know, that's what the Nazis did."

They all look at me in disgust. It's the look boys give a girl who has interrupted a burping contest. One says, "This is something my wife would say."

When he says "wife," there is no love, warmth, or goodness in it. In this engineer's mouth, "wife" means wet diapers and dirty dishes. It means someone angry with you for losing track of time and missing dinner. Someone *sentimental*. In his mind (for the moment), "wife" signifies all programming-party-pooping, illogical things in the universe.

Still, I persist. "It started as just an idea for the Nazis, too, you know."

The engineer makes a reply that sounds like a retch. "This is how I know you're not a real techie," he says.

V.

A descendent of Italian princes directs research projects at a well-known manufacturer of UNIX workstations. I'm thrilled. In my then five years of being a consultant, the director is the first person to compliment me on what I am wearing to the interview.

It takes me a while, but I soon see I must forget all the usual associations with either Italians or princes. There will be no lovely long lunches that end with deftly peeled fruit. There will be no well-cut suits of beautiful fabrics. The next time I am wearing anything interesting, the director (I'll call him Paolo) tells me I look ridiculous.

Paolo's Italianism has been replaced, like a pod from outer space, with some California New Age, Silicon Valley engineering creature. He eats no fat. He spoons tofu-melange stuff out of a Tupperware container. Everything he does comes in response to beeps emitted from his UNIX workstation: he eats, goes to meetings, goes rollerblading in the parking lot, buys and sells stock, calls his wife solely in response to signals he has programmed into his calendar system. (The clock on his wall has only the number twelve on it.) Further, Paolo swears he has not had a cold since the day he decided that he would always wear two sweaters. Any day now, I expect to see him get out of his stock-option Porsche draped in garlic.

I know that Paolo has been replaced because I have met his wife. We are at a team beer-fest in the local programmer hangout on a Friday afternoon. It's full of men in T-shirts and jeans. Paolo's wife and I are the only people wearing makeup. She looks just the way I expect a no-longer-young Italian woman to look—she has children, she has taken time with her appearance, she is trying to talk to people. Across the swill of pitchers and chips glopped with cheesy drippings, she eyes me hopefully: another grown-up woman. At one point, she clucks at Paolo, who is loudly describing the effects of a certain burrito. "The only thing on earth that instantly turns a solid into a gas," he says.

The odder Paolo gets, the more he fits in with the research team. One engineer always eats his dessert first (he does this conscientiously; he wants you, dares you to say something; one simply doesn't). Another comes to work in something that looks suspiciously like his pajamas. To work on this project, he has left his wife and kids back East. He obviously views the absence of his family as a kind of license: he has stopped shaving and (one can't help noticing) he has stopped washing. Another research engineer comes to work in shorts in all weather; no one has ever seen his knees covered. Another routinely makes vast changes to his work the day before deadlines; he is completely unmoved by any complaints about this practice. And one team member screens all e-mail through a careful filter, meaning most mail is deposited in a dead-letter file. This last engineer, the only woman permanently on the project, has outdone everyone on oddness: she has an unlisted work phone. To reach her, you must leave a message with her manager. The officially sanctioned asynchrony of the unlisted phone amazes me. In my fifteen years in the software industry, I have never seen anything like it.

These research engineers can be as odd as they like because they are very, very close to the machine. At their level, it is an honor to be odd. Strange behavior is expected, it's respected, a sign that you are intelligent and as close to the machine as you can get. Any decent software engineer can have a private office, come and go at all hours, exist out of normal time. But to be permanently and sincerely eccentric—this is something only a senior research engineer can achieve.

In meetings, they behave like children. They tell each other to shut up. They call each other idiots. They throw balled-up paper. One day, a team member screams at his Korean colleague, "Speak English!" (A moment of silence follows this outburst, at least.) It's like dropping in at the day-care center by mistake.

They even behave like children when their Japanese sponsors come to visit. The research is being funded through a chain of agencies and bodies that culminates in the Japan Board of Trade. The head of the sponsoring department comes with his underlings. They all wear blue suits. They sit at the conference table with their hands folded neatly in front of them. When they speak, it is with the utmost discretion; their voices are so soft, we have to lean forward to hear. Meanwhile, the research team behaves badly, bickers, has the audacity to ask when they'll get paid.

The Japanese don't seem to mind. On the contrary, they appear delighted. They have received exactly what their money was intended to buy. They have purchased bizarre and brilliant Californians who can behave any way they like. The odd behavior reassures them: Ah! These must be real top-rate engineers!

VI.

We are attending conventions. Here is our itinerary: we will be traveling closer and closer to the machine. Our journey will be like crossing borders formed by mountain ranges. On the other side, people will be very, very different.

We begin "high," at a conference of computer trainers and technical writers. Women are everywhere. There is a great deal of nail polish, deep red, and briefcases of excellent leathers. In the cold, conditioned air of the conference hall drifts a faint, sweet cloud of perfume.

Next we travel to Washington, D.C., to an applications development conference, the Federal Systems Office Expo. It is a model of cultural diversity.

Men, women, whites, blacks, Asians—all qualified applicants are welcome. Applications development ("high-level," low-status, and relatively low-paying) is the civil service of computing.

Now we move west and lower. We are in California to attend a meeting of SIGGRAPH, the graphics special interest group of the Association of Computing Machinery (ACM). African Americans have virtually disappeared. Young white men predominate, with many Asians among them. There are still some women: graphics can be seen, after all. Though we have crossed the summit and have begun our descent, we are still not very "low."

On our map, we must now place this warning: "Below here be engineers."

We are about to descend rapidly into valleys of programming, to the low levels close to the machine. We go first to an operating-systems interest group of the ACM. Then, getting even closer to hardware, we attend a convention of chip designers. Not a female person in clear sight. If you look closely, however, you can see a few young Chinese women sitting alone, quiet, plainly dressed, succeeding at making themselves invisible. For these are gatherings of young men. This is the land of T-shirts and jeans, the country of perpetual graduate-studenthood.

Later, at a Borland[1] developers' conference, company engineers proudly call themselves "barbarians" (although they are not really as "low" as they think they are). In slides projected onto huge screens, they represent themselves in beards and animal skins, holding spears and clubs. Except for the public-relations women (their faint clouds of perfume drift among the hairy, exposed barbarian legs), there is only one woman (me).

A senior engineer once asked me why I left full-time engineering for consulting. At the time, I had never really addressed the question, and I was surprised by my own answer. I muttered something about being a middle-age woman. "Excuse me," I found myself saying, "but I'm afraid I find the engineering culture very teenage-boy puerile."

This engineer was a brilliant man, good-hearted, and unusually literate for a programmer. I had great respect for him and I really did not mean to offend him. "That's too bad," he answered as if he meant it, "because we obviously lose talent that way."

I felt immense gratitude at this unexpected opening. I opened my mouth to go on, to explore the reasons for the cult of the boy engineer.

But immediately we were interrupted. The company was about to have an interdivisional water-balloon fight. For weeks, the entire organization had been engaged in the design of intricate devices for the delivery of rubberized

---

[1] Borland International, producer of software for business.

inflatable containers filled with fluid. Work had all but stopped; all "spare brain cycles" were involved in preparations for war.

The engineer joined the planning with great enthusiasm, and I left the room where we had been having our conversation. The last I saw of him, he was covering a paper napkin with a sketch of a water-balloon catapult.

Here is a suggested letter home from our journey closer to the machine: Software engineering is a meritocracy. Anyone with the talents and abilities can join the club. However, if rollerblading, Frisbee playing, and water-balloon wars are not your idea of fun, you are not likely to stay long.

VII.

I once designed a graphical user interface with a man who wouldn't speak to me. My boss hired this man without letting anyone else sit in on the interview; my boss lived to regret it.

I was asked to brief my new colleague and, with a third member of the team, we went into a conference room. There, we filled two whiteboards with lines, boxes, circles, and arrows in four marker colors. After about half an hour, I noticed that the new hire had become very agitated.

"Are we going too fast?" I asked him.

"Too much for the first day?" said the third.

"No," said our new man, "I just can't do it like this."

"Do what?" I asked. "Like what?"

His hands were deep in his pockets. He gestured with his elbows. "Like this," he said.

"You mean design?" I asked.

"You mean in a meeting?" asked the third.

No answer from our new colleague. A shrug. Another elbow gesture.

Something terrible was beginning to occur to me. "You mean talking?" I asked.

"Yeah, talking," he said. "I can't do it by talking."

By this time in my career, I had met many strange engineers. But here was the first one who wouldn't talk at all. Besides, this incident took place before the existence of standard user interfaces like Windows and Motif, so we had a lot of design work to do. No talking was certainly going to make things difficult.

"So how *can* you do it?" I asked.

"Mail," he said immediately, "send me e-mail."

So, given no choice, we designed a graphical user interface by e-mail.

Corporations across North America and Europe are still using a system designed by three people who sent e-mail and one who barely spoke.

VIII.

Pretty graphical interfaces are commonly called "user-friendly." But they are not really your friends. Underlying every user-friendly interface is a terrific human contempt.

The basic idea of a graphical interface is that it does not allow anything alarming to happen. You can pound on the mouse button all you want, and the system will prevent you from doing anything stupid. A monkey can pound on the keyboard, your cat can run across it, your baby can fist it, but the system should not crash.

To build such a crash-proof system, the designer must be able to imagine—and disallow—the dumbest action. He or she cannot simply rely on the user's intelligence: who knows who will be on the other side of the program? Besides, the user's intelligence is not quantifiable; it's not programmable; it cannot protect the system. No, the real task is to forget about the intelligent person on the other side and think of every single stupid thing anyone might possibly do.

In the designer's mind, gradually, over months and years, there is created a vision of the user as imbecile. The imbecile vision is mandatory. No good, crash-proof system can be built except it be done for an idiot.

The designer's contempt for your intelligence is mostly hidden deep in the code. But, now and then, the disdain surfaces. Here's a small example: You're trying to do something simple like copy files onto a diskette on your Mac. The program proceeds for a while then encounters an error. Your disk is defective, says a message, and, below the message, is a single button. You absolutely must click this button. If you don't click it, the program hangs there indefinitely. So, your disk is defective, your files may be bollixed up, and the designer leaves you only one possible reply: You must say, "OK."

The prettier the user interface, and the fewer odd replies the system allows you to make, the dumber you once appeared in the mind of the designer.

IX.

The computer is about to enter our lives like blood in the capillaries. Soon, everywhere we look, we will see pretty, idiot-proof interfaces designed to make us say, "OK."

A vast delivery system for retail computing is about to come into being, and the system goes by the name "interactivity." Telephones, televisions, sales kiosks will all be wired for interactive, on-demand services. The very word—interactivity—implies something good and wonderful. Surely a response, a reply, an answer is a positive thing. Surely it signifies an advance over something else, something bad, something that doesn't respond, reply or answer. There is only one problem: what we will be interacting with is a machine.

Interactive services are supposed to be delivered "on demand." What an aura of power—demand! See a movie, order seats to a basketball game, make hotel reservations, send a card to mother—all services waiting for us on our television or computer whenever we want them. Midnight, dawn, or day. Sleep or order a pizza: it no longer matters exactly what we do when. We don't need to involve anyone else in the satisfactions of our needs. We don't even have to talk. We get our services when we want them, free from the obligations of regularly scheduled time. We can all live closer to the machine.

"Interactivity" is misnamed. It should be called "asynchrony": the engineering culture coming to everyday life.

In the workplace, home office, sales floor, service kiosk, home—we will be "talking" to programs that are beginning to look surprisingly alike: all full of animated little pictures we are supposed to pick, like push-buttons on a toddler's toy. The toy is supposed to please us. Somehow, it is supposed to replace the satisfactions of transacting meaning with a mature human being, in the confusion of a natural language, together, in a room, at a touching distance.

As the computer's pretty, helpfully waiting face (and contemptuous underlying code) penetrates deeply into daily life, the cult of the boy engineer comes with it. The engineer's assumptions and presumptions are in the code. That's the purpose of the program, after all: to sum up the intelligence and intentions of all the engineers who worked on the system over time—tens and hundreds of people who have learned an odd and highly specific way of doing things. The system contains them. It reproduces and reenacts life as engineers know it: alone, out-of-time, disdainful of anyone far from the machine.

Engineers seem to prefer the asynchronous life, or at least be used to it. But what about the rest of us? A taste of the out-of-time existence is about to become possible for everyone with a television. Soon, we may all be living the programming life. Should we?

STUDY AND DISCUSSION QUESTIONS

1. Ullman writes that a programmer lives a life "strangely asynchronous to the one lived by other human beings." What does she mean? Why does this happen? What are the consequences?

2. What does it mean to get "closer to the machine"? Why do programmers desire this?

3. According to Ullman, how do programmers relate to their own bodies? Why?

4. Ullman works as a woman in a very male world. How does this fact shape her perceptions of her fellow programmers and engineers? How do the male programmers view women?

5. Ullman writes that "asynchrony" is "coming to everyday life." What, in her view, is wrong with that?

SUGGESTIONS FOR WRITING

1. According to one engineer, Ullman's objection to the conclusion of the eugenics discussion proves that she's "not a real techie." What does this suggest about "real techies"? Are there any implications here for a society in which "techies" play an increasingly important role?

2. Do you think the world of programming would change significantly if many more women got "closer to the machine"?

3. Imagine you're one of the programmers or engineers described by Ullman and have just read her essay. Write a reply defending yourself.

4. What roles do computers play in your life? What would you change about this if you could?

THREE GENERATIONS OF NATIVE AMERICAN WOMEN'S BIRTH EXPERIENCE

Joy Harjo

Joy Harjo, a Creek (Muscogee) Indian, was born in Tulsa, Oklahoma in 1951, went to college in New Mexico and Iowa, and has taught creative writing and Native American literature at Arizona State University and elsewhere. She has published a number of volumes of poetry, including The Last Song *(1975),* She Had Some Horses *(1983),* In Mad Love and War *(1990), and* The Woman Who Fell from the Sky *(1996). The following essay appeared in* Ms. *magazine in 1991.*

It was still dark when I awakened in the stuffed back room of my mother-in-law's small rented house with what felt like hard cramps. At 17 years of age I had read everything I could from the Tahlequah Public Library about pregnancy and giving birth. But nothing prepared me for what was coming. I awakened my child's father and then ironed him a shirt before we walked the four blocks to the Indian hospital because we had no car and no money for a taxi. He had been working with another Cherokee artist silk-screening signs for specials at the supermarket and making $5 a day, and had to leave me alone at the hospital because he had to go to work. We didn't awaken his mother. She had to get up soon enough to fix breakfast for her daughter and granddaughter before leaving for her job at the nursing home. I knew my life was balanced at the edge of great, precarious change and I felt alone and cheated. Where was the circle of women to acknowledge and honor this birth?

It was still dark as we walked through the cold morning, under oaks that symbolized the stubbornness and endurance of the Cherokee people who had made Tahlequah their capital in the new lands. I looked for hand-holds in the misty gray sky, for a voice announcing this impending miracle. I wanted to change everything; I wanted to go back to a place before child-hood, before our tribe's removal to Oklahoma. What kind of life was I bringing this child into? I was a poor, mixed-blood woman heavy with a child who would suffer the struggle of poverty, the legacy of loss. For the second time in my life I felt the sharp tug of my own birth cord, still connected to my mother. I believe it never pulls away, until death, and even then it becomes a streak in the sky symbolizing that most important warrior road. In my teens I had fought my mother's weaknesses with all my might, and here I was at 17, becoming as my mother, who was in Tulsa, cooking breakfasts and preparing for the lunch shift at a factory cafeteria as I walked to the hospital to give birth. I should be with her; instead, I was far from her house, in the house of a mother-in-law who later would try to use witchcraft to destroy me.

After my son's father left me I was prepped for birth. This meant my pubic area was shaved completely and then I endured the humiliation of an enema, all at the hands of strangers. I was left alone in a room painted government green. An overwhelming antiseptic smell emphasized the sterility of the hospital, a hospital built because of the U.S. government's treaty and responsibility to provide health care to Indian people.

I intellectually understood the stages of labor, the place of transition, of birth—but it was difficult to bear the actuality of it, and to bear it alone. Yet in some ways I wasn't alone, for history surrounded me. It is with the birth of children that history is given form and voice. Birth is one of the most sacred acts we take part in and witness in our lives. But sacredness seemed to be far from my lonely labor room in the Indian hospital. I heard a woman screaming in the next room with her pain, and I wanted to comfort her. The nurse used her as a bad example to the rest of us who were struggling to keep our suffering silent.

The doctor was a military man who had signed on this watch not for the love of healing or out of awe at the miracle of birth, but to fulfill a contract for medical school payments. I was another statistic to him; he touched me as if he were moving equipment from one place to another. During my last visit I was given the option of being sterilized. He explained to me that the moment of birth was the best time to do it. I was handed the form but chose not to sign it, and am amazed now that I didn't think too much of it at the time. Later I would learn that many Indian women who weren't fluent in English signed, thinking it was a form giving consent for the doctor to deliver their babies. Others were sterilized without even the formality of signing. My light skin had probably saved me from such a fate. It wouldn't be the first time in my life.

When my son was finally born I had been deadened with a needle in my spine. He was shown to me—the incredible miracle nothing prepared me for—then taken from me in the name of medical progress. I fell asleep with the weight of chemicals and awoke yearning for the child I had suffered for, had anticipated in the months proceeding from his unexpected genesis when I was still 16 and a student at Indian school. I was not allowed to sit up or walk because of the possibility of paralysis (one of the drug's side effects), and when I finally got to hold him, the nurse stood guard as if I would hurt him. I felt enmeshed in a system in which the wisdom that had carried my people from generation to generation was ignored. In that place I felt ashamed I was an Indian woman. But I was also proud of what my body had accomplished despite the rape by the bureaucracy's machinery, and I got us out of there as soon as possible. My son would flourish on beans and fry bread, and on the dreams and stories we fed him.

My daughter was born four years later, while I was an art student at the University of New Mexico. Since my son's birth I had waitressed, cleaned hospital rooms, filled cars with gas (while wearing a miniskirt), worked as a nursing assistant, and led dance classes at a health spa. I knew I didn't want to cook and waitress all my life, as my mother had done. I had watched the varicose veins grow branches on her legs, and as they grew, her zest for dancing and sports dissolved into utter tiredness. She had been born with a caul over her face, the sign of a gifted visionary.

My earliest memories are of my mother writing songs on an ancient Underwood typewriter after she had washed and waxed the kitchen floor on her hands and knees. She too had wanted something different for her life. She had left an impoverished existence at age 17, bound for the big city of Tulsa. She was shamed in a time in which to be even part Indian was to be an outcast in the great U.S. system. Half her relatives were Cherokee full-bloods from near Jay, Oklahoma, who for the most part had nothing to do with white people. The other half were musically inclined "white trash" addicted to country-western music and Holy Roller fervor. She thought she could disappear in the city; no one would know her family, where she came from. She had dreams of singing and had once been offered a job singing on the radio but turned it down because she was shy. Later one of her songs would be stolen before she could copyright it and would make someone else rich. She would quit writing songs. She and my father would divorce and she would be forced to work for money to feed and clothe four children, all born within two years of each other.

As a child growing up in Oklahoma, I liked to be told the story of my birth. I would beg for it while my mother cleaned and ironed. "You almost killed me," she would say. "We almost died." That I could kill my mother filled me with remorse and shame. And I imagined the push-pull of my life, which is a legacy I deal with even now when I am twice as old as my mother was at my birth. I loved to hear the story of my warrior fight for my breath. The way it was told, it had been my decision to live. When I got older, I realized we were both nearly casualties of the system, the same system flourishing in the Indian hospital where later my son Phil would be born.

My parents felt lucky to have insurance, to be able to have their children in the hospital. My father came from a fairly prominent Muscogee Creek family. *His* mother was a full-blood who in the early 1920s got her degree in art. She was a painter. She gave birth to him in a private hospital in Oklahoma City; at least that's what I think he told me before he died at age 53. It was something of which they were proud.

This experience was much different from my mother's own birth. She and five of her six brothers were born at home, with no medical assistance. The only time a doctor was called was when someone was dying. When she was born her mother named her Wynema, a Cherokee name my mother says means beautiful woman, and Jewell, for a can of shortening stored in the room where she was born.

I wanted something different for my life, for my son, and for my daughter, who later was born in a university hospital in Albuquerque. It was a bright summer morning when she was ready to begin her journey. I still had no car, but I had enough money saved for a taxi for a ride to the hospital. She was born "naturally," without drugs. I could look out of the hospital window while I was in labor at the bluest sky in the world. I had support. Her father was present in the delivery room—though after her birth he disappeared on a drinking binge. I understood his despair, but did not agree with the painful means to describe it. A few days later Rainy Dawn was presented to the sun at her father's pueblo and given a name so that she will always be recognized as a part of the people, as a child of the sun.

That's not to say that my experience in the hospital reached perfection. The clang of metal against metal in the delivery room had the effect of a tuning fork reverberating fear in my pelvis. After giving birth I held my daughter, but they took her from me for "processing." I refused to lie down to be wheeled to my room after giving birth; I wanted to walk out of there to find my daughter. We reached a compromise and I rode in a wheelchair. When we reached the room I stood up and walked to the nursery and demanded my daughter. I knew she needed me. That began my war with the nursery staff, who deemed me unknowledgeable because I was Indian and poor. Once again I felt the brushfire of shame, but I'd learned to put it out much more quickly, and I demanded early release so I could take care of my baby without the judgment of strangers.

I wanted something different for Rainy, and as she grew up I worked hard to prove that I could make "something" of my life. I obtained two degrees as a single mother. I wrote poetry, screenplays, became a professor, and tried to live a life that would be a positive influence for both of my children. My work in this life has to do with reclaiming the memory stolen from our peoples when we were dispossessed from our lands east of the Mississippi; it has to do with restoring us. I am proud of our history, a history so powerful that it both destroyed my father and guarded him. It's a history that claims my mother as she lives not far from the place her mother was born, names her as she cooks in the cafeteria of a small college in Oklahoma.

When my daughter told me she was pregnant, I wasn't surprised. I had known it before she did, or at least before she would admit it to me. I felt despair, as if nothing had changed or ever would. She had run away from Indian school with her boyfriend and they had been living in the streets of Gallup, a border town notorious for the suicides and deaths of Indian peoples. I brought her and her boyfriend with me because it was the only way I could bring her home. At age 16, she was fighting me just as I had so fiercely fought my mother. She was making the same mistakes. I felt as if everything I had accomplished had been in vain. Yet I felt strangely empowered, too, at this repetition of history, this continuance, by a new possibility of life and love, and I steadfastly stood by my daughter.

I had a university job, so I had insurance that covered my daughter. She saw an obstetrician in town who was reputed to be one of the best. She had the choice of a birthing room. She had the finest care. Despite this, I once again battled with a system in which physicians are taught the art of healing by dissecting cadavers. My daughter went into labor a month early. We both knew intuitively the baby was ready, but how to explain that to a system in which numbers and statistics provide the base of understanding? My daughter would have her labor interrupted; her blood pressure would rise because of the drug given to her to stop the labor. She would be given an unneeded amniocentesis and would have her labor induced—after having it artificially stopped! I was warned that if I took her out of the hospital so her labor could occur naturally my insurance would cover nothing.

My daughter's induced labor was unnatural and difficult, monitored by machines, not by touch. I was shocked. I felt as if I'd come full circle, as if I were watching my mother's labor and the struggle of my own birth. But I was there in the hospital room with her, as neither my mother had been for me, nor her mother for her. My daughter and I went through the labor and birth together.

And when Krista Rae was born she was born to her family. Her father was there for her, as were both her grandmothers and my friend who had flown in to be with us. Her paternal great-grandparents and aunts and uncles had also arrived from the Navajo Reservation to honor her. Something *had* changed.

Four days later, I took my granddaughter to the Saguaro forest before dawn and gave her the name I had dreamed for her just before her birth. Her name looks like clouds of mist settling around a sacred mountain as it begins to speak. A female ancestor approaches on a horse. We are all together.

STUDY AND DISCUSSION QUESTIONS

1. The birth of Harjo's son was a miserable experience for her. List the things that made it so.

2. How was the birth of Harjo's daughter, four years later, different from the birth of her son? How was it similar?

3. "Something *had* changed," Harjo writes, comparing her daughter's experience giving birth to her own experiences. What had changed? What hadn't?

4. Harjo also discusses the birth of her mother and her own birth. What is her point in writing about each? Why does she describe them in the middle of her essay, not (since they came first) at the start?

5. Harjo criticizes "a system in which physicians are taught the art of healing by dissecting cadavers." What assumptions lie behind this criticism? Is it fair?

SUGGESTIONS FOR WRITING

1. Remembering how she was prepped at the hospital for the birth of her son, Harjo writes, "my pubic area was shaved completely and then I endured the humiliation of an enema"—and then adds, "all at the hands of strangers." Were you surprised by that last phrase? Is it better to have one's family and friends do such things? What do Harjo's response, and yours, suggest about the acceptance by most of us of the routine impersonality of medical care?

2. Describing the birth of her son, Harjo writes, "I felt enmeshed in a system in which the wisdom that had carried my people from generation to generation was ignored." Write as much as you can about what that wisdom might be.

3. Do you know any birth stories from your own family, perhaps the story of your own birth? What role did medical science and technology play? What were the attitudes of those involved towards that science and technology. Did their attitudes change?

4. If you hope some day to be involved in a birth experience (whether as mother, father, family, or close friend), what would you like it to be like? What role should medical science and medical technology play?

TO MAKE NATURE
AN ACCOMPLICE

William H. Tucker

William H. Tucker teaches psychology at Rutgers University and has been involved as a community activist in Camden, New Jersey. The following is the introduction to his book The Science and Politics of Racial Research *(1994).*

In 1947 Henry E. Garrett, full professor and chair of the Psychology Department at Columbia University, president at various times of the American Psychological Association, the Eastern Psychological Association, and the Psychometric Society, fellow of the American Association for the Advancement of Science, member of the National Research Council, and for ten years editor of the American Psychology Series, authored an article in the scholarly publication *Scientific Monthly* entitled "Negro-White Differences in Mental Ability in the United States." In support of his sharp disagreement with those who desired to explain away race differences as "somehow reprehensible and socially undesirable," Garrett cited a study of the comparative abilities of sixty-eight white and sixty black babies from two to eleven months old. Each baby had been given a series of mental tests constructed for use during the first two years of life from which a "developmental quotient"—essentially an infant IQ score—had been calculated. The average DQ for the white babies was 105, for the blacks, 92; the average DQ for the whites was higher than for the blacks at every age level, with the degree of superiority ranging from two to twenty-five points and averaging thirteen. From these results Garrett concluded that the blacks' consistently lower performance could not possibly be explained by a difference in environmental opportunities. In addition, he noted, the comparison of American whites with blacks, who frequently had some degree of mixed ancestry, did not represent "true racial differences." Garrett consequently expected an even greater disparity between the performance of African blacks and European whites.[1]

Perhaps mindful of the importance of finding these "true racial differences," some years later Hans J. Eysenck, world-renowned social scientist, founder and head of the Psychological Department and Laboratory at the Institute of Psychiatry of the University of London, and author of more than fifty books and hundreds of articles in professional journals, compared the performance of black African babies with white norms on measures of development. The African children showed a consistent precocity until age three, after which they fell behind white children. Like Garrett, Eysenck found it "implausible" that such an "astonishing difference" at the early ages could have been produced by "socio-economic differences or other extrinsic variables." The fact that these differences were opposite from those considered by Garrett did not prevent Eysenck from arriving at the same conclusion concerning blacks' innate inferiority. Eysenck found the superior performance of the black infants consistent with a little-known "general law in biology according to which the more prolonged the infancy, the greater in general are the cognitive or intellectual abilities of the species."[2]

In the United States we have come to take for granted the widespread manipulation that characterizes public media-centered culture. Every time we turn on television or look through a magazine, someone is trying to persuade us to buy a product, vote for a candidate, or adopt a point of view. But we also cherish the notion that there are safe, protected areas, oases of reason, effectively insulated from attempts to sell consumer goods or political ideologies. Here, where the atmosphere is less hysterical, calmer, more serious and reflective, scientific inquiries, disinterested in political agendas and influenced only by objective evidence, can transcend ideology in the pursuit of truth. Indeed, it is exactly on the basis of such disinterest that scientists stake their claim to public trust and respect.

---

[1] H. E. Garrett, "Negro-White Differences in Mental Ability in the United States," *Scientific Monthly* 65 (1947): 329–33. [Author's note]

[2] H. J. Eysenck, *The IQ Argument* (New York: Library Press, 1971), 79. [Author's note]

There are, however, critics within the scientific community who maintain that much social research is somewhat less than a model of objective inquiry. George Albee, a professor of psychology at the University of Vermont, offered the following opinion in his address to an American Psychological Association conference as a recipient of the Award for Distinguished Contribution to Community Psychology:

> I have come to believe that I have had the whole "scientific" process reversed. Instead of facts being useful as the objective building blocks of theories, rather it is more accurate to say that people, and especially social scientists, select theories that are consistent with their personal values, attitudes, and prejudices and then go out into the world or into the laboratory, to seek the facts that validate their beliefs about the world and about human nature, neglecting or denying observations that contradict their personal prejudices.[3]

These are strong words, but it is difficult to account in any other way for the identical conclusions of black inferiority Garrett and Eysenck derived from antithetical evidence.

Such consensus in the face of contradictory data is not an isolated occurrence in research on racial differences. When one scientist found at the turn of the century that blacks generally performed better than whites on tests of memory, he explained that their superior mnemonic ability was "naturally expected" since "in both races . . . the memory is in decadence from primitive conditions, but . . . the blacks are much nearer those conditions."[4] A decade later a famous English researcher found that on tests of memory the sons of the rich displayed "complete superiority" over the sons of the working class, a result that led him to the obvious conclusion that a disciplined memory was characteristic of greater intelligence.[5] Yet when a well-known contemporary psychologist found that poor and black children with low IQ scores had excellent memories, he concluded that memory should not properly be considered a component of "intelligence."[6]

Early demonstrations that blacks had a quicker reaction time than whites were also offered as proof that "the negro is, in the truest sense, a race inferior to that of the white" since faster reflexes were claimed to be a characteristic of lower intelligence. "Men, in proportion to their intellectuality,"

---

[3] G. W. Albee, "The Politics of Nature and Nurture," *American Journal of Community Psychology* 65 (1982): 5. [Author's note]

[4] G. R. Stetson, "Some Memory Tests of Whites and Blacks," *Psychological Review* 4 (1897): 288. [Author's note]

[5] C. Burt, "Experimental Texts of General Intelligence," *British Journal of Psychology* 3 (1909): 143–44. [Author's note]

[6] A. R. Jensen, "What Is the Question? What Is the Evidence?" in *The Psychologists*, vol. 2, ed. T. S. Krawiec (New York: Oxford University Press, 1974), 222–25. [Author's note]

wrote a scientist who had found whites to react slower than both Indians and blacks, "should tend less and less to quickness of response in the automatic sphere."[7] But when research many years later showed faster reaction times for whites, this too became evidence for white intellectual superiority. Speed of reaction was now offered as an indication of "brain activity," and a leading social scientist even claimed (incorrectly) that Muhammad Ali had "a very average" reaction time.[8]

Though blacks have almost always performed lower than whites on paper-and-pencil tests, even the rare occasion on which they have scored higher has somehow also confirmed their inferiority. When two researchers found that blacks did better than whites on simple arithmetic problems, they explained that "the more complicated a brain, the more numerous its 'association fibers,' the less satisfactorily it performs the simple numerical problems which a calculating machine does so quickly and accurately."[9]

Differing evolutionary theories have also been able to produce identical conclusions about black inferiority. Many scientists in the 1920s claimed that blacks were the evolutionary predecessors of whites and that "Negroid stock," having evolved long before whites, was thus not only older but closer to its anthropoid ancestors, both physically and mentally; blacks were intellectually inferior to whites because they had evolved earlier.[10] A few decades later a distinguished anthropologist proposed that blacks had crossed the evolutionary threshold into homo sapiens long after other races and thus had had less time to develop; blacks were intellectually inferior because they had evolved later.[11]

Some studies of group differences have not violated the rules of logic as much as they have strained the bounds of credibility. In 1913 the famous psychologist Henry H. Goddard administered mental tests to a sample of newly arrived immigrants at Ellis Island, which had been carefully selected to omit both the "obviously feeble-minded" and the very few of "obviously high grade intelligence." In the group thus remaining—what Goddard called "the great mass of 'average immigrants,'"—he reported that 83 percent of Jews,

[7] R. M. Bache, "Reaction Time with Reference to Race," *Psychological Review* 2 (1895): 479, 481. [Author's note]

[8] A. R. Jensen, "Techniques for Chronometric Study of Mental Abilities," in *Methodological and Statistical Advances in the Study of Individual Differences,* ed. C. R. Reynolds and V. L. Willson (New York: Plenum, 1985), 55. [Author's note]

[9] C. B. Davenport and M. Steggerda, *Race Crossing in Jamaica* (Washington, D.C.: Carnegie Institute, 1929), 469. [Author's note]

[10] See, for example, R. B. Bean, *The Races of Man* (New York: University Society, 1932), 30–37; and H. F. Osborn, "The Evolution of Human Races," *Natural History* 26 (January–February 1926): 5. [Author's note]

[11] C. S. Coon, *The Origin of Races* (New York: Alfred A. Knopf, 1962). [Author's note]

80 percent of Hungarians, 79 percent of Italians, and 87 percent of Russians were "feeble-minded." Probably anticipating the appropriate term for these results, Goddard informed his readers that "many a scientific discovery has seemed at first glance absurd." Nevertheless, he insisted, "it is never wise to discard a scientific result because of apparent absurdity," especially when it had come from a "fair and conscientious" analysis of the data.[12]

It appears Albee has not exaggerated. Although some of these examples might be dismissed as "cheap shots," egregious exceptions noteworthy by their contrast with more sober, restrained investigations that are the norm, many of them are not so much counterexamples to the mainstream as they are organic extensions of it. For over a century there have been scientists obsessed with proving that minorities, poor people, foreigners, and women are innately inferior to upper-class white males of northern European extraction.

Though some of these researchers have been overt racists, civil libertarians and social liberals have also been responsible for many foolish claims. Edward M. East, for example, a Harvard geneticist in the 1920s, "could see no reasonable excuse for oppression and discrimination on a colour-line basis . . . [and had] no sympathy with a regimen of repression on the part of the whites." He was positively outraged over someone "who is denied a seat in a Pullman car, a restaurant, a theatre, or a room in a college dormitory" due to the "gaucheries of a provincial people, on a par with the guffaws of a troop of yokels." Nevertheless, as a scientist, he concluded that blacks were physically as well as mentally inferior and had little of value to contribute to the higher white race. "Gene packets of African origin are not valuable supplements to the gene packets of European origin," wrote East; "it is the white germ plasm that counts."[13]

The scientific conflict over genetic differences between groups is now well into its second century. Unlike other, more traditional scientific controversies, in which the argument diminishes as new discoveries are made or as scientists with opposing views retire or die away,[14] the bitter dispute over race has arisen anew in each generation, to be debated all over again in almost exactly the same terms but with a fervor that seems more theological than scientific. Nor has the argument confined itself to academic journals and scientific conferences; the subject of racial differences has been debated in barrooms and cocktail parties and, for a scientific issue, has

---

[12] H. H. Goddard, "Mental Tests and the Immigrant," *Journal of Delinquency* 2 (1917): 244, 266; the percentages appear in a table on 252. [Author's note]

[13] E. M. East, *Heredity and Human Affairs* (New York: Charles Scribner's Sons, 1929), 181, 199, 200. [Author's note]

[14] T. S. Kuhn, *The Structure of Scientific Revolutions* (Chicago: University of Chicago Press, 1962). [Author's note]

received unprecedented coverage in the popular press. Despite the length and intensity of the debate, however, there has been no significant advance in scientific knowledge. Although the techniques of data analysis have become increasingly sophisticated, the arguments on both sides have changed very little. Contemporary scientists often sound indistinguishable from their predecessors of thirty, sixty, or ninety years ago. More than a century of research has produced a lot of heat but virtually no light.

"No Political, No Religious, and No Social Prejudices"

The truth is that though waged with scientific weapons, the goal in this controversy has always been political; indeed, the debate has no strictly scientific purpose or value. The question of genetic differences between races has arisen not out of purely scientific curiosity or the desire to find some important scientific truth or to solve some significant scientific problem but only because of the belief, explicit or unstated, that the answer has political consequences. The claim that one group is genetically less desirable or capable than another has invariably been part of what Marquis de Condorcet called an attempt "to make nature herself an accomplice of political inequality."[15] Rather than an injustice that needs to be rectified, social and political oppression thus becomes the rational—indeed, the unavoidable—reflection of natural differences.

The first suggestion that inequality should be based on nature occurred over two thousand years ago when Aristotle observed that "there are species in which a distinction is already marked, immediately at birth, between those of its members who are intended for being ruled and those who are intended to rule."[16] Applying an idiosyncratic technique for the measurement of individual differences—though one not all that different from the method used twenty-two hundred years later by the famous English scientist Sir Francis Galton—Aristotle distinguished those to be ruled as differing from others in power of reason "as the body differs from the soul, or an animal from a man," and he concluded that "it is thus clear that, just as some are by nature free, so others are by nature slaves, and for these latter the condition of slavery is both just and beneficial."[17]

Although Aristotle's reference to innate, empirically observable distinctions suggested a quasi-scientific justification for slavery—in Thomas Hobbes's

---

[15] A. N. de Condorcet, *Sketch for a Historical Picture of the Progress of the Human Mind,* trans. J. Barraclough (London: Weidenfeld and Nicolson, 1955 [1795]), 83. [Author's note]

[16] E. Barker, *The Politics of Aristotle* (London: Oxford University Press, 1950), 14. [Author's note]

[17] *Ibid.*, 16, 17. [Author's note]

words, "as if master and servant were not introduced by consent of men but by difference of wit"[18]—it was not until the nineteenth century that the linkage between science and politics was made explicit. At that time U.S. doctors and anthropologists began to assess intelligence through various anatomical and physiognomic characteristics in scientific attempts at a linear evaluation of racial and ethnic groups, and in England Galton began to study the dichotomization of nature and nurture that eventually led to the psychometric tradition. As these two lines of investigation merged at the turn of the century, a movement arose that attempted to derive moral and behavioral guidelines from what were claimed to be scientific-physicalist laws. Questions of human rights and freedoms—who should vote, who should be educated, who should have children, who should be allowed into the country—were transferred from their appropriate place in the domain of political discourse to the domain of science. In particular, an understanding of racial differences was claimed to be the key to social progress; public education, social harmony, national welfare, indeed the future of the species were all said to depend on it. What began as the study of hereditary characteristics thus quickly burgeoned into a presumptuous field marked by immodest pronouncements on the limits of democracy, the necessity of racial segregation, the futility of education, the biological inevitability of vast socioeconomic disparities, and the necessity for controlling the birthrate of certain groups.

The belief that the operation of science was synonymous with the termination of politics made appeals to scientific authority a powerful strategy for influencing public policy. Critics of the obsession with racial differences could easily be dismissed as emotional and unscientific, preferring sentimentality, idealism, and wishful thinking to the perhaps unpleasant but nonetheless undeniable truths that emerged from impartial data; the researchers had scientific objectivity and rigor on their side. As Karl Pearson, one of the greatest contributors to contemporary statistics, wrote in the introduction to a 1925 article on Jewish immigration to Great Britain, "We have no axes to grind, we have no governing body to propitiate by well advertised discoveries; we are paid by nobody to reach results of a given bias. We have no electors, no subscribers to encounter in the market place. We firmly believe that we have no political, no religious and no social prejudices. . . . We rejoice in numbers and figures for their own sake."[19] Thus unencumbered by bias of any kind or by political or economic pressure, Pearson was led, by the numbers and figures, to conclude that Jewish

---

[18] T. Hobbes, *Leviathan* (New York: Bobbs-Merrill, 1958 [1651]), 127. [Author's note]

[19] K. Pearson and M. Moul, "The Problem of Alien Immigration into Great Britain Illustrated by an Examination of Russian and Polish Jewish Children," *Annals of Eugenics* 1 (1925): 8. [Author's note]

immigrants were mentally and physically inferior to the native English population, that the newcomers would develop into a "parasitic race," and that there was "no evidence that a lessening of the aliens' poverty, an improvement in their food, or an advance in their cleanliness will substantially alter their average grade of intelligence, and with it their outlook on life." Naturally, Pearson concluded, "there should be no place" in society for such a demonstrably inferior group, an opinion that was soon to be shared by the leaders of another European country.[20]

As a consequence of this viewpoint, for more than a century nature has been played as a trump card in political arguments on the side of repression. Sometimes scientists have only hinted at significant, and ominous, implications. The psychologist Lewis Terman, an early developer of the IQ test, insisted, for example, that a "less naive definition of . . . democracy . . . will have to square with the demonstrable facts of biological and psychological science."[21] More often, specific proposals have been offered, most of which are intolerable in a free society. When a medical journal reported the latest scientific finding in 1907—that the brain of blacks was "more animal in type and incapable of producing those thoughts which have built up civilization"—the editors found it "dreadful that we did not know these anatomical facts when we placed a vote in the possession of this brain which cannot comprehend its use" and hoped that it was not too late to deprive blacks of the franchise.[22] A popular 1933 scientific textbook opposed efforts to eradicate discrimination against blacks because these efforts ignored "biological and social facts."[23] A group of scientists in the late 1950s and 1960s attempted to overturn the unanimous Supreme Court verdict that struck down school segregation on the grounds that blacks were intellectually inferior to whites. The logic underlying all these proposals viewed political inequality as the natural consequence of biological inferiority; science should demonstrate the latter so society might have appropriate justification to implement the former. As one writer who opposed equality for blacks early in the century frankly admitted, unless blacks were "racially inferior," the "denial of . . . equality appears as a colossal injustice, an immeasurable wrong."[24] The role of science was to confirm that no such injustice was taking place.

---

[20] *Ibid.*, 124, 125. [Author's note]

[21] L. M. Terman, "The Psychological Determinist; or Democracy and the IQ," *Journal of Educational Research* 6 (1922): 62. [Author's note]

[22] Unsigned editorial, *American Medicine* (April 1907): 197. [Author's note]

[23] P. Popenoe and R. H. Johnson, *Applied Eugenics* (New York: Macmillan, 1933), 302. [Author's note]

[24] W. B. Smith, *The Color Line* (New York: Negro Universities Press, 1969 [1905]), 71. [Author's note]

Since the mid-1960s, in a social atmosphere much less tolerant of blatant deprivations of civil rights, the science of racial differences has encouraged more subtle political implications. For example, poverty among blacks was explained by some scientists as the economic consequence of natural inequality. Blacks' claims of continuing racial prejudice could thus be dismissed as "social paranoia" since the real problem lay in their genes. As one well-known psychologist noted, "Failure to succeed is less apt to be perceived as personal failure if one identifies with a group which is claimed, justifiably or not, to be discriminated against. Having the status of an unprivileged caste, real or imagined, makes personal failure more tolerable."[25]

Some scientists also insisted that government programs of assistance to the poor, which had originated with Lyndon Johnson's War on Poverty, could be justified only if there were no genetic differences in ability between races. Thus, they argued, their "proof" that such differences did exist made these programs scientifically unsound.

Finally, even when the results of research have not been intended as justification for policies of repression and discrimination, they turn out to be made to order for the proponents of such policies. Whenever scientists have concluded some group to be genetically inferior, some of the investigators have wound up in either organizational or informal alliance with right-wing political groups, often fascists or racists who have been more than pleased to use scientific authority as a source of prestige for their own doctrines. The use of science for this purpose has generally been accomplished with the cooperation of, or at the very least without protest from, the scientists. That is, although it has usually been the ideologues in these coalitions who have fired the shots, the scientists have furnished the ammunition with no reservations over its use.

Though it might be argued that the political exploitation of scientific results is a *mis*use of science, the following chapters demonstrate that the effort to prove the innate intellectual inferiority of some groups has led *only* to oppressive and antisocial proposals; it has had no *other* use. Indeed, there is no "legitimate" application for such a finding. Even if there were convincing proof of genetic differences between races, as opposed to the flawed evidence that has been offered in the past, it would serve no purpose other than to satisfy curiosity about the matter. While the desire for knowledge, whether or not it has practical value, is not to be denigrated, a judicious use of our scientific resources would seem inconsistent with the pursuit of a goal that is probably scientifically chimerical and certainly lends itself to socially pernicious ends.

---

[25] A. R. Jensen, "The Price of Inequality," *Oxford Review of Education* 1 (1975): 61. [Author's note]

STUDY AND DISCUSSION QUESTIONS

1. Why does Tucker describe the credentials of Henry E. Garrett and Hans J. Eysenck at such great length in his first two paragraphs?

2. Why do you think Tucker uses the word "accomplice," a word we usually associate with crime, in his title?

3. "To Make Nature an Accomplice" focuses on work by scientists that "proves" the inferiority of blacks. Why, then, does Tucker also mention scientists' conclusions about Jews and other immigrants, about "the sons of the working class," and about women?

4. Why have biological theories of social inequality been so persistent?

5. IQ test developer Lewis Terman wrote that a "less naive definition of . . . democracy . . . will have to square with the demonstrable facts of biological and psychological science." What might Terman have meant? Why does Tucker quote him?

6. The essay discusses the case of Edward M. East, a scientist who was "positively outraged" over racist treatment of black people yet nonetheless concluded that they were inferior. How can we explain this? Does this disparity undermine Tucker's larger point, or does it somehow broaden that point?

SUGGESTIONS FOR WRITING

1. What opinions and "theories" have you been exposed to about inborn differences in intelligence (or other characteristics) between groups, for example, between men and women, between social classes, or between different racial or ethnic groups? Did Tucker's essay change your thinking in any way?

2. Imagine that scientists *have* conclusively proved that one group, say left-handed people, are on average less intelligent than others, given some reasonable definition of "intelligent." What social policies, if any, do you think should follow from this knowledge?

3. Tucker writes that we "cherish the notion" that the work of scientists is "effectively insulated from attempts to sell consumer goods or political ideologies." Can you think of any examples, besides the ones he discusses, of the misuse of the prestige and authority given to science in our society?

THE TUCSON ZOO

Lewis Thomas

Lewis Thomas (1913–1993) had a distinguished career in medicine but is more widely known for his essays, which are often poetic, personal, and philosophical. Among his books are The Lives of a Cell: Notes of a Biology Watcher *(1974), which won the National Book Award,* The Medusa and the Snail: More Notes of a Biology Watcher *(1979), where the following appeared, and* Late Night Thoughts on Listening to Mahler's Ninth Symphony *(1984).*

Science gets most of its information by the process of reductionism, exploring the details, then the details of the details, until all the smallest bits of the structure, or the smallest parts of the mechanism, are laid out for counting and scrutiny. Only when this is done can the investigation be extended to encompass the whole organism or the entire system. So we say.

Sometimes it seems that we take a loss, working this way. Much of today's public anxiety about science is the apprehension that we may forever be overlooking the whole by an endless, obsessive preoccupation with the parts. I had a brief, personal experience of this misgiving one afternoon in Tucson, where I had time on my hands and visited the zoo, just outside the city. The designers there have cut a deep pathway between two small artificial ponds, walled by clear glass, so when you stand in the center of the path you can look into the depths of each pool, and at the same time you can regard the surface. In one pool, on the right side of the path, is a family of otters; on the other side, a family of beavers. Within just a few feet from your face, on either side, beavers and otters are at play, underwater and on the surface, swimming toward your face and then away, more filled with life than any creatures I have ever seen before, in all my days. Except for the glass, you could reach across and touch them.

I was transfixed. As I now recall it, there was only one sensation in my head: pure elation mixed with amazement at such perfection. Swept off my feet, I floated from one side to the other, swiveling my brain, staring astounded at the beavers, then at the otters. I could hear shouts across my corpus callosum, from one hemisphere to the other. I remember thinking, with what was left in charge of my consciousness, that I wanted no part of the science of beavers and otters; I wanted never to know how they performed their marvels; I wished for no news about the physiology of their breathing, the co-ordination of their muscles, their vision, their endocrine systems, their digestive tracts. I hoped never to have to think of them as collections of cells. All I asked for was the full hairy complexity, then in front of my eyes, of whole, intact beavers and otters in motion.

It lasted, I regret to say, for only a few minutes, and then I was back in the late twentieth century, reductionist as ever, wondering about the details by force of habit, but not, this time, the details of otters and beavers. Instead, me. Something worth remembering had happened in my mind, I was certain of that; I would have put it somewhere in the brain stem; maybe this was my limbic system at work. I became a behavioral scientist, an experimental psychologist, an ethologist, and in the instant I lost all the wonder and the sense of being overwhelmed. I was flattened.

But I came away from the zoo with something, a piece of news about myself: I am coded, somehow, for otters and beavers. I exhibit instinctive behavior in their presence, when they are displayed close at hand behind glass, simultaneously below water and at the surface. I have receptors for this display. Beavers and otters possess a "releaser" for me, in the terminology of ethology, and the releasing was my experience. What was released? Behavior. What behavior? Standing, swiveling flabbergasted, feeling exultation and a rush of friendship. I could not, as the result of the transaction, tell you anything more about beavers and otters than you already know. I learned nothing new about them. Only about me, and I suspect also about you, maybe about human beings at large: we are endowed with genes which code out our reaction to beavers and otters, maybe our reaction to each other as well. We are stamped with stereo-typed, unalterable patterns of response, ready to be released. And the behavior released in us, by such confrontations, is, essentially, a surprised affection. It is compulsory behavior and we can avoid it only by straining with the full power of our conscious minds, making up conscious excuses all the way. Left to ourselves, mechanistic and autonomic, we hanker for friends.

Everyone says, stay away from ants. They have no lessons for us; they are crazy little instruments, inhuman, incapable of controlling themselves, lacking manners, lacking souls. When they are massed together, all touching, exchanging bits of information held in their jaws like memoranda, they become a single animal. Look out for that. It is a debasement, a loss of individuality, a violation of human nature, an unnatural act.

Sometimes people argue this point of view seriously and with deep thought. Be individuals, solitary and selfish, is the message. Altruism, a jargon word for what used to be called love, is worse than weakness, it is sin, a violation of nature. Be separate. Do not be a social animal. But this is a hard argument to make convincingly when you have to depend on language to make it. You have to print up leaflets or publish books and get them bought and sent around, you have to turn up on television and catch the attention of millions of other human beings all at once, and then you have to say to all of them, all at once, all collected and paying attention: be solitary; do not depend on each other. You can't do this and keep a straight face.

Maybe altruism is our most primitive attribute, out of reach, beyond our control. Or perhaps it is immediately at hand, waiting to be released, disguised now, in our kind of civilization, as affection or friendship or attachment. I don't see why it should be unreasonable for all human beings to have strands of DNA coiled up in chromosomes, coding out instincts for usefulness and helpfulness. Usefulness may turn out to be the hardest test of fitness for survival, more important than aggression, more effective, in the long run, than grabbiness. If this is the sort of information biological science holds for the future, applying to us as well as to ants, then I am all for science.

One thing I'd like to know most of all: when those ants have made the Hill, and are all there, touching and exchanging, and the whole mass begins to behave like a single huge creature, and *thinks,* what on earth is that thought? And while you're at it, I'd like to know a second thing: when it happens, does any single ant know about it? Does his hair stand on end?

STUDY AND DISCUSSION QUESTIONS

1. How does Thomas's experience at the zoo suggest the limitation of what, in his first sentence, he calls "reductionism"?

2. Exhilarated by the otters and beavers, Thomas "could hear shouts across [his] corpus callosum." What does he mean? (Look up "corpus callosum" if you need to.) How does this way of describing his experience relate to the larger points he is making?

3. Thomas writes: "I am coded, somehow, for otters and beavers." What exactly is he saying? What conclusions does he draw from this?

4. What point is Thomas trying to make in his discussion of ants and of the lessons usually drawn from observing them? Throughout the essay, Thomas seems to be engaged in a debate with other scientists. What can you infer about their views? What are Thomas's responses?

5. What is the meaning of the last paragraph of "The Tucson Zoo"?

SUGGESTIONS FOR WRITING

1. "Maybe altruism is our most primitive attribute," writes Thomas, more fundamental to human nature than selfishness or aggression. What relevance might this idea have to the world of politics and economics?

Why might altruism, a general feeling towards others, be "disguised now, in our kind of civilization, as affection or friendship or attachment"—that is, as a feeling toward a few particular individuals?

2. "The Tucson Zoo" takes a number of large steps from one individual's fleeting experience to grand (though tentative) generalizations about human beings. Trace these steps. To what extent are you persuaded?

HIS CERTAINTY: HOW HE RULES THE UNIVERSE

Susan Griffin

Susan Griffin was born in Los Angeles in 1943, attended San Francisco State University, and has worked as a waitress, a teacher, and a house painter. Her writings include the poetry collections Like the Iris of an Eye *(1976) and* Unremembered Country *(1987) as well as such works of nonfiction as* Woman and Nature: The Roaring Inside Her *(1978),* Rape: The Politics of Consciousness *(1979), and* The Eros of Everyday Life: Essays on Ecology, Gender, and Society *(1996). The following essay is from* Woman and Nature.

Quantity

Mathematics is thought moving in the sphere of complete abstraction from any particular instance of what it is talking about.

TOBIAS DANZIG, *Number, The Language of Science*

Granted, granted that there is no flaw in all that reasoning, that all I have concluded this last month is as clear as day, true as arithmetic. . . .

RASKOLNIKOV in Dostoyevsky, *Crime and Punishment*

He says that through numbers 1 2 3 4 5 6 7 we find the ultimate reality of things 8 9 10 11 He says 12 13 14 that quantities are the most rigorous test of things 12 13 He says God created numbers and our minds to understand numbers 14 15 16 He says the final proof 16 17 is always a sum 18 19 20 (Counting. She is counting. The number of seconds in a minute, the number of minutes in an hour, the number of hours) He measures the distance from his land to his neighbor's land. He measures his wealth. He numbers his wives. He numbers his children 21 22 23 24 25 26 He weighs what will be traded (1 Faning Mill[1] $17.25, 1 red-faced cow $13.25, 1 yearling calf $4.25) He calculates the worth of what he has (1 plow $1.60, 1 Wench and child $156.00, 8 fancy chairs $9.25) He assesses the value of what is his. (He measures the gallons of milk she produces. He measures the board feet they yield. He measures the hours she works, the value of her labor.)

He tells us how big he is. He measures his height. He demonstrates his strength. He measures what he can lift, what he can conquer. He calculates his feelings. He numbers his armies. *He measures our virtue. He counts the reasons why we fell.* (570 through poverty, he says, 647 through loss of their parents or their homes, 29 orphaned with elder brothers and sisters to care for.) *He counts the reasons why we fell from grace.* (23 widowed women with small children, 123 servant girls seduced and discharged by their masters.) *He tells us how strong he is.* He counts the sperm in his seminal fluid. He numbers his genes. . . . (She numbers the seconds. She numbers the hours. She numbers the days.) 27 28 29 30 31

Counting. They count. They count one billion suffering from hunger. 32 33 34 35 They count twelve thousand dying of starvation. 36 37 38 39 He counts the number of children being born. 40 41 42 He measures the growth of food. 43 44 45 He calculates the sum. 46 47 48 He says that through quantities we find ultimate reality. (She is counting the number of days in a week. The number of months in a year.)

He tells us how rich he is. He is counting his possessions and all he might possess. He measures his intelligence. He measures the coal in the ground. He calculates his life expectancy. He estimates the oil in the sea. He adds up the value of his life. He measures productive acres. He calculates the value of his existence. 49 50 51 52 53

He tells us how long he will live. He measures his neighbor's land. He numbers their children, the bellies of their cows, the spans of their horses, the numbers of their bridges, their cities, their hospitals, their armies. He counts their dead. He counts his dead. He calculates. He calculates the sum. *He gives us the final proof.*

54 55 56 57 58 59 60 (She has numbered each second of each hour of each day of each year. She has been counting.) 61 62 63 64 65 66 67 68 69 70 71 72 73 74 75 76 77 78 79 80 81

---

[1] Machine once used for separating grain from chaff and dirt.

He counts 82 83 necessity. He counts what he imagines to be necessary. He says six combat divisions are necessary; he counts thirteen training
divisions as necessary, four brigades, two maneuver area commands. 84 85
86 87 88 89 He says 1,700 ballistic missiles are needed and seven hundred
bombers. 90 91 92 93 94 He counts bombs, he counts 70,000 bombs.
95 96 He says when people. He counts the number of people. He says when
people have nothing they starve. He counts four hundred million on the edge
of starvation. He says when starving people are fed. He counts ten million
children risking death from starvation. When starving people are fed, he says,
they reproduce. He counts. 97 98 99 100 101 (She has numbered her children. She has counted the days of their lives. On this day, she can say, this
one learned to pronounce her name. In this month, she can say, this one
learned to walk. She has counted the moments.) 102 103

    104   105   106 He has counted. 107 He has counted the effects.
108 109 One roentgen, he says 110 111 shortens a life by 3.5 days. 112 113
114 One hundred roentgens will shorten a life 115 116 by one year 117 and
one thousand roentgens by ten years. 118 119 120 121 122123124125126127
Counting. They have counted the targets. Of 224 targets they count, 71 were
cities. They count the bombs. 128 129 130 They count 263 bombs and 1,446
megatons. 131 132 133 They count the dead to be 42 million. They imagine
42 million to be dead. They count the injured to be 17 million. They imagine
17 million injured.

    134 135 136 137 *He tells us how powerful he is.* 138 139 And they
count what they imagine will survive. They count 23 percent of electrical
machinery. They estimate 28 percent of fabricated metal products. They say
29 percent of rubber products. Thirty percent of apparel. Thirty-four percent of machinery. Forty percent of chemicals. Fifty-one percent of furniture. 138 139 140 141142143144145146

    (Counting. She has counted on this life continuing. She has counted
on continuing. Each day she has counted, each day she has done what she
must, done what she must to go on.)

    147148149 57 percent of food, 60 percent of construction, 89 percent
of mining, 94.6 percent of agriculture. Counting. He is counting how much.
He is counting how much tragedy is acceptable. He imagines ten roentgens
of radiation. 150 151 152 He imagines the birth of one million defective
children. Counting. He counts 153 154 155 156 157

    *Counting. We count each second. No moment do we forget. We live
through every hour. We are counting the number he has killed, the number he
has bound into servitude, the number he has maimed, stolen from, left to starve.
We measure his virtue. We count the value of our lives. We are counting the least
act of the smallest one, her slightest gesture, and we count the ultimate reality*

of her breath barely visible now in the just cold air, 1, 2, 3, we say, as it shows it-self in small clouds, 4, 5 and 6, and disappears from moment 7, 8, 9 to moment.

Probability

The theory of chance consists in reducing all the events of the same kind to a certain number of cases equally possible . . . and in deter-mining the number of cases favorable to the event whose possibility is sought.

> PIERRE SIMON DE LAPLACE, "Concerning Probability"

. . . within a mere ten to fifteen years a woman will be able to buy a tiny frozen embryo, take it to the doctor, have it implanted in her uterus, carry it for nine months, and then give birth to it as though it had been conceived in her own body. The embryo would, in effect, be sold with a guarantee that the resultant baby would be free of genetic defect. The purchaser would also be told in advance the color of the baby's eyes and hair, its sex, its probable size at maturity, and its probable I.Q.

> DR. E. S. E. HAFEZ

Where he begins. How he begins. Where he begins to doubt. Where he begins to doubt how he began. If this should happen. If he does this. Where he begins to think himself a prisoner (Supposing that a thin coin is thrown into the air with opposite faces, heads and tails. To figure the probability of throw-ing heads at least one time in two throws, it is shown that four equally possi-ble cases may arise, heads at first and at second, heads at first and tails at second, tails at first and heads at second, and tails at both throws.) of fate. How circumstance determines him. If he does this. Each step. If he moves this way. Each possibility. Where he arrives. All the dangers He has no assurance. Where he begins, he has no assurance, he does not know what will happen.

(And thus the first three cases being favorable to the event, the proba-bility is equal to three quarters and it is a bet of three to one that heads will be thrown at least once in two throws.)

And he considers that he may not have begun. That this may not have been his starting place. That he may never have seen this place. That he may have been born differently. That he may have been born blind. That he may have been born someone else and not himself. That he may not have been born.

(And discovering the numerical correspondence between the number of groups of hereditary qualities and the number of pairs of chromosomes and determining that there are twenty-three chromosomes, there are then over a million possible kinds of germ cells, and two such sets will give a possible number of combinations which is vastly greater.)

He sees her swelling. She is growing bigger. What is beginning in her he does not know. What will come out of her he does not know. (The doctor guides a four-inch needle through the abdominal wall, into the peritoneal cavity, through the uterine wall, and lastly, into the amniotic sac.) But what is inside her grows without his willing it. (This must be done without nicking a blood vessel, or any of the blood-filled sinuses laced around the uterus, without penetrating the fetus, or any portion of the umbilical cord, not trusting to luck, not blindly, but knowing exactly how the fetus lies and the location of the placenta.)

He says she is a mystery to him, that he does not know what is inside her, that he cannot penetrate her. (The amniotic fluid obtained in this way reveals if the fetus suffers a genetic defect, and if it is male or female.) He knows there is no mystery in him. What he does is always perfectly clear. And if he can learn what will happen next, he says, then what he will do will also be clear. (To carry out conception in vitro, oocytes, surgically freed from the ovary, are placed in a glass tube, in a carefully balanced fertilization medium into which spermatozoa are introduced. After fertilization, oocytes are then washed and transferred to a culture medium.) The movements of his life, he says, are determined by the predictable lines of logic. Each move he makes is an improvement, he declares. All his efforts lead to betterment. His body was made to struggle for this, he says. His mind was meant to find the way. He was determined at the beginning, he says, to determine what will happen. He fulfills necessity, he says. The history of his life (In order to alter genetic structure) may have been predicted (the plasmid DNA was snipped open with a restriction enzyme) from events in the past which in turn were determined (and into the broken ends of the ring, synthetic rings of DNA were attached) by the events in the past, so that what exists could not be otherwise, he points out, and what will be (with DNA complementary to plasmid DNA acting as glue) is inevitable.

Gravity

Sooner or later the uniformly moving body will collide with the wall of the elevator destroying the uniform motion. Sooner or later, the whole elevator will collide with the earth destroying the observers and their experiments.

ALBERT EINSTEIN and LEOPOLD INFELD,
The Evolution of Physics

... it is always possible to be "oriented" in a world that has a sacred history, a world in which every prominent feature is associated with a mythical event.

　　　　　　　　　MIRCEA ELIADE, "A Mythical Geography"

The scientists are in a box. There are no windows. Nothing tells them which is right side up. The walls are empty. The ceiling and the floor are the same. They are standing in a perfect cube. Every surface is a square. This they measure and prove with their rulers. The scientists prove by experiment what is the nature of this world. One drops his handkerchief into space. It does not fall to the ground. It rests where the scientist's hand left it. Over time the handkerchief still does not move. This experiment is repeated with another scientist's eyeglasses. The scientist's eyeglasses do not move from where he has placed them in space. This experiment is repeated with different objects. First they push the eyeglasses, lending them motion, then the handkerchief, a pen, a piece of paper, and then their ruler. Each object moves continuously across space until it collides with the opposite wall. The scientists are delighted. They discover they are living in a perfect inertial system. Every body continues in a state of rest or motion. They will continue resting infinitely. They are delighted with this perfection. But gradually one scientist allows a question to enter his mind. It occurs to him that they do not know if they are at rest in an inertial system or if they are moving at a continuous rate of acceleration. Perhaps in a vacuum. Perhaps, and now the scientist feels a sense of disquiet, perhaps they are in a field of gravity, and *are* therefore accelerating continuously. He realizes that they do not know for certain where they are, nor where they are going, if they are going. He decides to break through the cube. Suddenly air rushes in. (They were suffocating, he realizes.) Through the hole he has made he sees the face of the earth coming closer and closer.

"Do you suppose that what we thought was true is not true?" he says with alarm. "We are falling," he admits, "down." Headfirst, the scientists dive from their cube. "I know where we are now," the doubting scientist shouts. "We are in a field of gravity." "And we are no longer falling at the same rate," another observes, "because of the resistance of the air." "Air!" another scientist sighs. "We are certainly not at rest now," the scientists assent. "We *are* moving," they agree.

"We know where we are now relative to the earth," they pronounce.

"And we know where we are going," another adds quickly.

"To the earth," they whisper.

"Where we were born," one says.

"And we know what will happen next," all of the scientists choir back. "We will all of us die."

SOURCES

Quantity: The examples of quantification in this section were drawn from various sources, including Hermàn Kahn, *On Thermo-Nuclear Warfare;* Ralph E. Lapp, *Kill and Overkill;* "Mathematics, Population and Food," in Newman, *The World of Mathematics.*

Probability: See Amitai Etzioni, *The Genetic Fix.* See also U.C. Clip Sheet, December 2, 1975, April 6 and November 2, 1976. See also Pierre Simon de Laplace, "Concerning Probability," and Gregor Mendel, "Mathematics of Heredity," in Newman, *The World of Mathematics.*

STUDY AND DISCUSSION QUESTIONS

1. Who is "he"? Who is "she"? Who are "we"?

2. What are some of the things "he" quantifies? Why does he do so?

3. What are the consequences of all this quantifying?

4. "She," too, is counting. What is she counting? How is her counting different from his?

5. "His Certainty: How He Rules the Universe" devotes much attention to military and to reproductive technologies. Why these two?

6. What is the point of the third section, "Gravity"? What is its relation to the other two sections?

7. Griffin writes in the last paragraph of "Probability": "And if he can learn what will happen next, he says, then what he will do will also be clear." What's wrong with that?

SUGGESTIONS FOR WRITING

1. Griffin's essay seems to argue not only that science and technology can be put to destructive ends but that the ways of thinking that they involve are themselves destructive. Do you agree?

2. Griffin seems to be saying that science and technology are not just predominantly but *fundamentally* male enterprises. What do you think?

3. Does Griffin hint at any alternative to the approach to the world she criticizes in her essay? What alternatives are there? What approach should we take?

A Causerie at the Military-Industrial

Paul Goodman

An obituary for Paul Goodman (1911–1972) called him a "lecturer, psychotherapist, humanist, polemicist, essayist, poet, novelist, and social critic." Among his more influential books are Gestalt Therapy *(1951), written with Frederick S. Perls and Ralph Hefferline,* Growing Up Absurd: Problems of Youth in the Organized System *(1960),* Compulsory Mis-Education *(1964), and* New Reformation: Notes of a Neolithic Conservative *(1970).*

The National Security Industrial Association (NSIA) was founded in 1944 by James Forrestal, to maintain and enhance the beautiful wartime communication between the armament industries and the government. At present it comprises 400 members, including of course all the giant aircraft, electronics, motors, oil, and chemical corporations, but also many one would not expect: not only General Dynamics, General Motors, and General Telephone and Electronics, but General Foods and General Learning; not only Sperry Rand, RCA, and Lockheed, but Servco and Otis Elevators. It is a wealthy club. The military budget is $84 billion.

At the recent biennial symposium, held on October 18 and 19 in the State Department auditorium, the theme was "Research and Development in the 1970s." To my not unalloyed pleasure, I was invited to participate as one of the seventeen speakers and assigned the topic "Planning for the Socio-Economic Environment." Naturally I could make the usual speculations about why I was thus "co-opted." I doubt that they expected to pick my brains for any profitable ideas. But it is useful for feeders at the public trough to present an image of wide-ranging discussion. It is comfortable to be able to say, "You see? these far-outniks are impractical." And business meetings are dull and I am notoriously stimulating. But the letter of invitation from Henri Busignies of ITT, the chairman of the symposium committee, said only, "Your accomplishments throughout your distinguished career eminently qualify you to speak with authority on the subject."

What is an intellectual man to do in such a case? I agree with the Gandhian principle, always co-operate, within the limits of honor, truth, and justice. But how to co-operate with the military-industrial club! during the Vietnam war

1967! It was certainly not the time to reason about basic premises, as is my usual approach, so I decided simply to confront them and soberly tell them off.

Fortunately it was the week of the demonstration at the Pentagon, when there would be thousands of my friends in Washington. So I tipped them off and thirty students from Cornell and Harpur drove down early to picket the auditorium, with a good leaflet about the evil environment for youth produced by the military corporations. When they came, the white helmets sprang up, plus the cameras and reporters. In the face of this dangerous invasion, the State Department of the United States was put under security, the doors were bolted, and the industrialists [and I] were not allowed to exit—on the 23rd Street side. Inside, I spoke as follows:

R & D[1] for the Socio-Economic Environment of the 1970s

I am astonished that at a conference on planning for the future, you have not invited a single speaker under the age of thirty, the group that is going to live in that future. I am pleased that some of the young people have come to pound on the door anyway, but it is too bad that they aren't allowed to come in.

This is a bad forum for this topic. Your program mentions the "emerging national goals" of urban development, continuing education, and improving the quality of man's environment. I would add another essential goal, reviving American democracy; and at least two indispensable international goals, to rescue the majority of mankind from deepening poverty, and to insure the survival of mankind as a species. These goals indeed require research and experimentation of the highest sophistication, but not by you. You people are unfitted by your commitments, your experience, your customary methods, your recruitment, and your moral disposition. You are the military industrial of the United States, the most dangerous body of men at the present in the world, for you not only implement our disastrous policies but are an overwhelming lobby for them, and you expand and rigidify the wrong use of brains, resources, and labor so that change becomes difficult. Most likely the trends you represent will be interrupted by a shambles of riots, alienation, ecological catastrophes, wars, and revolutions, so that current long-range planning, including this conference, is irrelevant. But if we ask what *are* the technological needs and what ought to be researched in this coming period, in the six areas I have mentioned, the best service that you people could perform is rather rapidly to phase yourselves out, passing on your relevant knowledge to people better qualified, or reorganizing yourselves with entirely different sponsors and commitments, so that you learn to think and feel in a

---

[1] Research and development.

different way. Since you are most of the R&D that there is, we cannot do without you as people, but we cannot do with you as you are.

In aiding technically underdeveloped regions, the need in the foreseeable future is for an intermediate technology, scientifically sophisticated but tailored to their local skills, tribal or other local social organization, plentiful labor force, and available raw materials. The aim is to help them out of starvation, disease, and drudgery without involving them in an international cash nexus of an entirely different order of magnitude. Let them take off at their own pace and in their own style. For models of appropriate technological analyses, I recommend you to E. F. Schumacher, of the British Coal Board, and his associates. Instead, you people—and your counterparts in Europe and Russia—have been imposing your technology, seducing native elites mostly corrupted by Western education, arming them, indeed often using them as a dumping ground for obsolete weapons. As Dr. Busignies pointed out yesterday, your aim must be, while maintaining leadership, to allow very little technical gap, in order to do business. Thus, you have involved these people in a wildly inflationary economy, have driven them into instant urbanization, and increased the amount of disease and destitution. You have disrupted ancient social patterns, debauched their cultures, fomented tribal and other wars, and in Vietnam yourselves engaged in genocide. You have systematically entangled them in Great Power struggles. It is not in your interest, and you do not have the minds or the methods, to take these peoples seriously as people.

The survival of the human species, at least in a civilized State, demands radical disarmament, and there are several feasible political means to achieve this if we willed it. By the same token, we must drastically de-energize the archaic system of Nation-States, e.g. by internationalizing space exploration, expanding operations like the international Geophysical Year, de-nationalizing Peace Corps and aid programs, opening scientific information and travel. Instead, you—and your counterparts in Europe, Russia, and China—have rigidified and aggrandized the States with a Maginot-line kind of policy called Deterrence, which has continually escalated rather than stabilized. As Jerome Wiesner[2] has demonstrated, past a certain point your operations have increased insecurity rather than diminished it. But this has been to your interest. Even in the present condition of national rivalry, it has been estimated, by Marc Raskin who sat in on the National Security Council, that the real needs of our defence should cost less than a fourth of the budget you have pork-barrelled. You have tried, unsuccessfully, to saddle us with the scientifically ludicrous Civil Defense program. You have sabotaged the technology of

---

[2] Scientific adviser to President John F. Kennedy.

inspection for disarmament. Now you are saddling us with the anti-missile missiles and the multi-warhead missiles (MIRV). You have corrupted the human adventure of space with programs for armed platforms in orbit. Although we are the most heavily armed and the most naturally protected of the Great Powers, you have seen to it that we spend a vastly greater amount and perhaps a higher proportion of our wealth on armaments than any other nation.

This brings me to your effect on the climate of the economy. The wealth of a nation is to provide useful goods and services, with an emphasis first on necessities and broad-spread comforts, simply as a decent background for un-economic life and culture; and indefinitely expanding economy is a rat-race. There ought to be an even spread regionally, and no group must be allowed to fall outside of society. At present, thanks to the scientific ingenuity and hard work of previous generations, we could in America allow a modest livelihood to everyone as a constitutional right. And on the other hand, as the young have been saying by their style and actions, there is an imperative need to simplify the standard of living, since the affluent standard has become frivolous, tawdry, and distracting from life itself. But you people have distorted the structure of a rational economy. Since 1945, half of new investment has gone into your products, not subject to the market nor even to Congressional check. This year, 86 percent of money for research is for arms and rockets. You push through the colossally useless Super-Sonic Transport. At least 20 percent of the economy is directly dependent of your enterprises. The profits and salaries of these enterprises are not normally distributed but go heavily to certain groups while others are excluded to the point of being out-caste. Your system is a major factor in producing the riots in Newark.[3] *[At this remark there were indignant protests.]*

Some regions of the country are heavily favored—especially Pasadena and Dallas—and others disadvantaged. Public goods have been neglected. A disproportionate share of brains has been drained from more useful invention and development. And worst of all, you have enthusiastically supported an essentially mercantilist economics that measures economic health in terms of abstract Gross National Product and rate of growth, instead of concrete human well-being. Both domestically and internationally, you have been the bellwether of meaningless expansion, and this has sharpened poverty in our own slums and rural regions and for the majority of mankind. It has been argued that military expenditure, precisely because it is isolated and wasteful, is a stabilizer of an economy, providing employment and investment opportunities when necessary; but your unbridled expansion has been the chief factor of social instability.

---

[3] In 1967, riots broke out in impoverished black neighborhoods in a number of United States cities, including Newark, New Jersey.

Dramatically intervening in education, you have again disrupted the normal structure. Great universities have come to be financed largely for your programs. Faculties have become unbalanced; your kind of people do not fit into the community of scholars. The wandering dialogue of science with the unknown is straitjacketed for petty military projects. You speak increasingly of the need for personal creativity, but this is not to listen to the Creator Spirit for ideas, but to harness it to your ideas. This is blasphemous. There has been secrecy, which is intolerable to true academics and scientists. The political, and morally dubious co-opting of science, engineering, and social science has disgusted and alienated many of the best students. Further, you have warped the method of education, beginning with the primary grades. Your need for narrowly expert personnel has led to processing the young to be test-passers, with a gross exaggeration of credits and grading. You have used the wealth of the public and parents to train apprentices for yourselves. Your electronics companies have gone into the "education industries" and tried to palm off teaching machines, audio-visual aids, and programmed lessons in excess of the evidence for their utility. But the educational requirements of our society in the foreseeable future demand a very different spirit and method. Rather than processing the young, the problem is how to help the young grow up free and inventive in a highly scientific and socially complicated world. We do not need professional personnel so much as autonomous professionals who can criticize the programs handed to them and be ethically responsible. Do you encourage criticism of your programs by either the subsidized professors or the students? [At this, Mr. Charles Herzfeld, the chairman of the meeting, shouted, "Yes!" and there was loud applause for the interruption, yet I doubt that there is much such encouragement.] We need fewer lessons and tests, and there ought to be much less necessity and prestige attached to mandarin requirements.

Let us turn to urbanism. *Prima facie,* there are parts of urban planning—construction, depollution, the logistics of transportation—where your talents ought to be peculiarly useful. Unfortunately, it is your companies who have oversold the planes and the cars, polluted the air and water, and balked at even trivial remedies, so that I do not see how you can be morally trusted with the job. The chief present and future problems in this field, however, are of a different kind. They are two. The long-range problem is to diminish the urbanization and suburban sprawl altogether, for they are economically unviable and socially harmful. For this, the most direct means, and the one I favor, is to cut down rural emigration and encourage rural return, by means of rural reconstruction and regional cultural development. The aim should be a 20 percent rural ration instead of the present 5 percent. This is an aspect of using high technology for simplification, increasing real goods but probably diminishing the Gross National Product measured in cash. Such a program is not for you.

Your thinking is never to simplify and retrench, but always to devise new equipment to alleviate the mess that you have helped to make with your previous equipment.

Secondly, the immediately urgent urban problem is how to diminish powerlessness, anomie, alienation, and mental disease. For this the best strategy is to decentralize urban administration, in policing, schooling, social welfare, neighborhood renewal, and in real-estate and business ownership. Such community development often requires heightening conflict and risking technical inefficiency for intangible gains of initiative and solidarity. This also is obviously not your style. You want to concentrate capital and power. Your systems analyses of social problems always tend toward standardization, centralization, and bureaucratic control, although these are not necessary in the method. You do not like to feed your computers indefinite factors and unknown parameters where spirit, spite, enthusiasm, revenge, invention, etc., will make the difference. To be frank, your programs are usually grounded in puerile theories of social psychology, political science, and moral philosophy. There is a great need for research and trying out in this field, but the likely cast of characters might be small farmers, Negro matriarchs, political activists, long-haired students, and assorted sages. Not you. Let's face it. You are essentially producers of exquisite hardware and good at the logistics of moving objects around, but mostly with the crude aim of destroying things rather than reconstructing or creating anything, which is a harder task. Yet you boldly enter into fields like penology, pedagogy, hospital management, domestic architecture, and planning the next decade—wherever there is a likely budget.

I will use the last heading, improving the quality of man's environment, as a catch-all for some general remarks. In a society that is cluttered, over-centralized, and overadministered, we should aim at simplification, decentralization, and decontrol. These require highly sophisticated research to determine where, how, and how much. Further, for the first time in history, the scale of the artificial and technological has dwarfed the natural landscape. In prudence, we must begin to think of a principled limitation on artifice and to cut back on some of our present gigantic impositions, if only to insure that we do not commit some terrible ecological blunder. But as Dr. Smelt of Lockheed[4] explained to us yesterday, it is the genius of American technology to go very rapidly from R&D to application: in this context, he said, prudence is not a virtue. A particular case is automation: which human functions should be computerized or automated, which should not? This question—it is both an analytic and an empirical one—ought to be critical in the next decade, but I would not trust IBM salesmen to solve it. Another problem is how man can

---

[4] Aerospace corporation.

feel free and at home within the technological environment itself. For instance, comprehending a machine and being able to repair it is one thing; being a mere user and in bondage to service systems is another. Also, to feel free, a man must have a rather strong say in the close environment that he must deal with. But these requirements of a technology are not taken into account by you. Despite Dr. Smelt, technology *is* a branch of moral philosophy, subordinate to criteria like prudence, modesty, safety, amenity, flexibility, cheapness, easy comprehension, repairability, and so forth. If such moral criteria became paramount in the work of technologists, the quality of the environment would be more livable.

Still a further problem is how to raise the scientific and technical culture of the whole people, and here your imperialistic grab of the R&D money and of the system of education has done immeasurable damage. You have seen to it that the lion's share has gone to your few giant firms and a few giant universities, although in fact very many, perhaps more than half of, important innovations still come from independents and tiny firms. I was pleased that Dr. Dessauer of Xerox pointed this out this morning. If the money were distributed more widely, there would probably be more discovery and invention, and what is more important, there would be a larger pool of scientific and competent people. You make a fanfare about the spin-off of a few socially useful items, but your whole enterprise is notoriously wasteful—for instance, five billions go down the drain when after a couple of years you change the design of a submarine, sorry about that. When you talk about spin-off, you people remind me of the TV networks who, after twenty years of nothing, boast that they did broadcast the McCarthy hearings and the Kennedy funeral. *[This remark led to free and friendly laughter; I do not know whether at the other industry or at their own hoax.]* Finally, concentrating the grants, you narrow the field of discovery and innovation, creating an illusion of technological determinism, as if we *had* to develop in a certain style. But if we had put our brains and money into electric cars, we would now have electric cars; if we had concentrated on intensive agriculture, we would now find that this is the most efficient, and so forth. And in grabbing the funds, you are not even honest; 90 percent of the R&D money goes in fact to shaping up for production, which as entrepreneurs you should pay out of your own pockets.

No doubt some of these remarks have been unfair and ignorant. *[Frantic applause.]* By and large they are undeniable, and I have not been picking nits.

These remarks have certainly been harsh and moralistic. We are none of us saints, and ordinarily I would be ashamed to use such a tone. But you are the manufacturers of napalm, fragmentation bombs, the planes that destroy rice. Your weapons have killed hundreds of thousands in Vietnam and you will kill other hundreds of thousands in other Vietnams. I am sure that most of you would concede that much of what you do is ugly and harmful, at home and abroad. But you would say that it is necessary for the American way of life, at home and abroad, and therefore you cannot do otherwise. Since we believe, however, that that way of life itself is unnecessary, ugly, and un-American [*Shouts of "Who are we?"*]—we are I and those people outside—we cannot condone your present operations; they should be wiped off the slate.

Most of the 300 in the audience did not applaud these remarks, but there was quite strong applause from a couple of dozen. Afterward these sought me out singly and explained, "Thanks for having the courage" or more significantly, "Those kids outside are right. My son is doing the same thing in Boston—Ohio State—etc."

The chairman of the session, Charles Herzfeld of ITT, felt obliged to exclaim, "The remark about our committing genocide in Vietnam is obscene. He does not say what is really intolerable there, the Viet Cong single out college graduates for extermination."!!

More poignantly, the director of the symposium, a courteous and intelligent man, apologized to the gathering for having exposed them to me, which must have been a wrench for him to say. He had of course seen my text beforehand.

We went out by the exit onto the other avenue, and I was able to rejoin the more amiable company of the young people, who were now sitting with their backs pressed against the auditorium doors, still among the white helmets. I answered their questions about the proceedings and we dispersed.

STUDY AND DISCUSSION QUESTIONS

1. What is a "causerie"? Why does Goodman use that word?

2. According to Goodman, how do the needs of poor nations differ from what the United States "military industrial" offers them? What are the consequences of this difference?

3. How have military industrialists "increased insecurity rather than diminished it"?

4. What effect has the power of military industrialists had on education?

5. Goodman agrees with the conference organizers about the importance of solving urban problems, but tells his audience, "I do not see how you can be morally trusted with the job." Why not?

6. Goodman says: "At present, thanks to the scientific ingenuity and hard work of previous generations, we could in America allow a modest livelihood to everyone as a constitutional right." What stands in the way of this goal?

7. Why did the National Security Industrial Association invite Goodman to speak? Do you think he succeeded in undermining their purpose, or was he successfully *"co-opted"*?

8. Why is it so important to Goodman that young people are picketing outside?

SUGGESTIONS FOR WRITING

1. Goodman delivered this speech in 1967. How might he view the present technological, military, and corporate landscape? Write a brief speech that he might deliver to today's military industrialists.

2. Goodman calls technology "a branch of moral philosophy." What does he mean? Do you agree?

3. Goodman believes that "we should aim at simplification, decentralization, and decontrol." How do his views differ from those of today's conservatives, many of whom say similar things?

4. "No doubt some of these remarks have been unfair and ignorant. *[Frantic applause.]*" What do you think?

ADVANCED BIOLOGY

Judith Ortiz Cofer

Judith Ortiz Cofer was born in Puerto Rico in 1952 and moved to the United States as a small girl. She studied at Augusta College, at Florida Atlantic University, and at Oxford and she now teaches at the University of Georgia at Athens. Cofer has published several books of poetry, including Terms of Survival *(1987), as well as the essay collection* Silent Dancing *(1990). Her novel* The Line of the Sun *(1989) was nominated for a Pulitzer Prize. The following essay appeared in* The Latin Deli: Prose and Poetry *(1993).*

As I lay out my clothes for the trip to Miami to do a reading from my recently published novel, then on to Puerto Rico to see my mother, I take a close look at my travel wardrobe—the tailored skirts in basic colors easily coordinate with my silk blouses—I have to smile to myself, remembering what my mother had said about my conservative outfits when I visited her the last time—that I looked like the Jehovah's Witnesses who went from door to door in her pueblo trying to sell tickets to heaven to the die-hard Catholics. I would scare people, she said. They would bolt their doors if they saw me approaching with my briefcase. As for her, she dresses in tropical colors—a red skirt and parakeet yellow blouse look good on her tan skin, and she still has a good enough figure that she can wear a tight black cocktail dress to go dancing at her favorite club, El Palacio, on Saturday nights. And, she emphasizes, still make it to the ten o'clock mass on Sunday. Catholics can have fun and still be saved, she has often pointed out to me, but only if you pay your respects to God and all his court with the necessary rituals. She knows that over the years I have gradually slipped away from the faith in which I was so strictly brought up.

As I pack my clothes into the suitcase, I recall our early days in Paterson, New Jersey, where we lived for most of my adolescence while my father was alive and stationed in Brooklyn Yard[1] in New York. At that time, our Catholic faith determined our family's views on most things, from clothing to the unmentioned subject of sex. Religion was the shield we had developed against the cold foreign city. These days we have traded places in a couple of areas since she has gone home to make a new life for herself after my father's death. I chose to attend college in the United States and make a living as an English teacher and, lately, on the lecture circuit as a novelist and poet. But though our lives are on the surface radically different, my mother and I have affected each other reciprocally over the past twenty years; she has managed to liberate herself from the rituals, mores, and traditions that "cramp" her style while retaining her femininity and "Puertoricanness," while I struggle daily to consolidate my opposing cultural identities. In my adolescence, divided into my New Jersey years and my Georgia years, I received an education in the art of cultural compromise.

In Paterson in the 1960s I attended a public school in our neighborhood. Still predominantly white and Jewish, it was rated very well academically in a city where the educational system was in chaos, deteriorating rapidly as the best teachers moved on to suburban schools following the black and Puerto Rican migration into, and the white exodus from, the city proper. The Jewish community had too much at stake to make a fast retreat; many of the small businesses and apartment buildings in the city's core were owned by Jewish families of the World War II generation. They had seen worse things happen than the influx of black and brown people that was scaring away the Italians and the Irish. But they too would gradually move their

---

[1] United States Navy base.

families out of the best apartments in their buildings and into houses in East Paterson, Fairlawn, and other places with *lawns*. It was how I saw the world then; either you lived without your square of grass, or you bought a house to go with it. But for most of my adolescence, I lived among the Jewish people of Paterson. We rented an apartment owned by the Milsteins, proprietors also of the deli on the bottom floor. I went to school with their children. My father took his business to the Jewish establishments, perhaps because these men symbolized "dignified survival" to him. He was obsessed with privacy and could not stand the personal turns conversations almost always took when two or more Puerto Ricans met casually over a store counter. The Jewish men talked too, but they concentrated on externals. They asked my father about his job, politics, his opinion on Vietnam, Lyndon Johnson. And my father, in his quiet voice, answered their questions knowledgeably. Sometimes before we entered a store, the cleaners, or a shoe repair shop, he would tell me to look for the blue-inked numbers on the owner's left forearm. I would stare at these numbers, now usually faded enough to look like veins in the wrong place. I would try to make them out. They were a telegram from the past, I later decided, informing the future of the deaths of millions. My father discussed the Holocaust with me in the same hushed tones my mother used to talk about God's Mysterious Ways. I could not reconcile both in my mind. This conflict eventually led to my first serious clash with my mother over irreconcilable differences between the "real world" and religious doctrine.

It had to do with the Virgin Birth.

And it had to do with my best friend and study partner, Ira Nathan, the acknowledged scientific genius at school. In junior high school it was almost a requirement to be "in love" with an older boy. I was an eighth grader and Ira was in the ninth grade that year and preparing to be sent away to some prep school in New England. I chose him as my boyfriend (in the eyes of my classmates, if a girl spent time with a boy, that meant they were "going together") because I needed tutoring in biology—one of his best subjects. I ended up having a crush on him after our first Saturday morning meeting at the library. Ira was my first exposure to the wonders of an analytical mind.

The problem was the subject. Biology is a dangerous topic for young teenagers, who are themselves walking laboratories, experimenting with interesting combinations of chemicals every time they make a choice. In my basic biology class, we were looking at single-cell organisms under the microscope, and watching them reproduce in slow-motion films in a darkened classroom. Though the process was as unexciting as watching a little kid blow bubbles, we were aroused by the concept itself. Ira's advanced class was dissecting fetal pigs. He brought me a photograph of his project, inner organs labeled neatly on the paper the picture had been glued to. My eyes refused to budge from the line drawn from "genitals" to a part of the pig to which it pertained. I felt a wave of heat rising from my chest to my scalp. Ira must have seen my discomfort, though I tried to keep my face behind the black curtain of my hair, but as the boy scientist, he was relentless. He actually traced the line from label to pig with his pencil.

"All mammals reproduce sexually," he said in a teacherly monotone.

The librarian, far off on the other side of the room, looked up at us and frowned. Logically, it was not possible that she could have heard Ira's pronouncement, but I was convinced that the mention of sex enhanced the hearing capabilities of parents, teachers, and librarians by 100 percent. I blushed more intensely, and peeked through my hair at Ira.

He was holding the eraser of his pencil on the pig's blurry sexual parts and smiling at me. His features were distinctly Eastern European. I had recently seen the young singer Barbra Streisand on the Red Skelton show and had been amazed at how much similarity there was in their appearances. She could have been his sister. I was particularly attracted to the wide mouth and strong nose. No one that I knew in school thought that Ira was attractive, but his brains had long ago overshadowed his looks as his most impressive attribute. Like Ira, I was a straight A student and also considered odd because I was one of the few Puerto Ricans on the honor roll. So it didn't surprise anyone that Ira and I had drifted toward each other. Though I could not have articulated it then, Ira was seducing me with his No. 2 pencil and the laboratory photograph of his fetal pig. The following Saturday, Ira brought in his advanced biology book and showed me the transparencies of the human anatomy in full color that I was not meant to see for a couple more years. I was shocked. The cosmic jump between paramecium and the human body was almost too much for me to take in. These were the first grown people I had ever seen naked, and they revealed too much.

"Human sexual reproduction can only take place when the male's sperm is introduced into the female womb and fertilization of the egg takes place," Ira stated flatly.

The book was open to the page labeled "The Human Reproductive System." Feeling that my maturity was being tested, as well as my intelligence, I found my voice long enough to contradict Ira.

"There has been one exception to this, Ira." I was feeling a little smug about knowing something that Ira obviously did not.

"Judith, there are no exceptions in biology, only mutations, and adaptations through evolution." He was smiling in a superior way.

"The Virgin Mary had a baby without . . ." I couldn't say *having sex* in the same breath as the name of the Mother of God. I was totally unprepared for the explosion of laughter that followed my timid statement. Ira had crumpled in his chair and was laughing so hard that his thin shoulders shook. I could hear the librarian approaching. Feeling humiliated, I started to put my books together. Ira grabbed my arm.

"Wait, don't go," he was still giggling uncontrollably. "I'm sorry. Let's talk a little more. Wait, give me a chance to explain."

Reluctantly, I sat down again, mainly because the librarian was already at our table, hands on hips, whispering angrily: "If you *children* cannot behave in this *study area,* I will have to ask you to leave." Ira and I both apologized, though she gave him a nasty look because his mouth was still stretched from ear to ear in a hysterical grin.

"Listen, listen. I'm sorry that I laughed like that. I know you're Catholic and you believe in the Virgin Birth" (he bit his lower lip trying to regain his composure), "but it's just not biologically possible to have a baby without" (he struggled for control) "losing your virginity."

I sank down on my hard chair. "Virginity." He had said another of the forbidden words. I glanced back at the librarian who was keeping her eye on us. I was both offended and excited by Ira's blasphemy. How could he deny a doctrine that people had believed in for two thousand years? It was part of my prayers every night. Our family talked about *La Virgen* as if she were our most important relative.

Recovering from his fit of laughter, Ira kept his hand discreetly on my elbow as he explained in the seductive language of the scientific laboratory how babies were made and how it was impossible to violate certain natural laws.

"Unless God wills it," I argued feebly.

"There is no God," said Ira, and the last shred of my innocence fell away as I listened to his arguments backed up by irrefutable scientific evidence.

Our meetings continued all that year, becoming more exciting with every chapter in his biology book. My grades improved dramatically, since one-celled organisms were no mystery to a student of advanced biology. Ira's warm, moist hand often brushed against mine under the table at the library, and walking home one bitter cold day, he asked me if I would wear his Beta Club pin. I nodded, and when we stepped inside the hallway of my building, where he removed his thick mittens which his mother had knitted, he pinned the blue enamel B to my collar. And to the hissing of the steam heaters, I received a serious kiss from Ira. We separated abruptly when we heard Mrs. Milstein's door open.

"Hello, Ira."

"Hello, Mrs. Milstein."

"And how is your mother? I haven't seen Fritzie all week. She's not sick, is she?

"She's had a mild cold, Mrs. Milstein. But she is steadily improving." Ira's diction became extremely precise and formal when he was in the presence of adults. As an only child and a prodigy, he had to live up to very high standards.

"I'll call her today," Mrs. Milstein said, finally looking over at me. Her eyes fixed on the collar of my blouse which was, I later saw in our hall mirror, sticking straight up with Ira's pin attached crookedly to the edge.

"Good-bye, Mrs. Milstein."

"Nice to see you, Ira."

Ira waved awkwardly to me as he left. Mrs. Milstein stood in the humid hallway of her building, watching me run up the stairs.

Our "romance" lasted only a week; long enough for Mrs. Milstein to call Ira's mother and for Mrs. Nathan to call my mother. I was subjected to a lecture on moral behavior by my mother, who, carried away by her anger and embarrassed that I had been seen kissing a boy (understood: a boy who was not even Catholic), had begun reciting a litany of metaphors for the loss of virtue.

"A cheap item," she said trembling before me as I sat on the edge of my bed, facing her accusations, "a girl begins to look like one when she allows herself to be *handled* by men."

"Mother . . ." I wanted her to lower her voice so that my father, sitting at the kitchen table, reading, would not hear. I had already promised her that I would confess my sin that Saturday and take communion with a sparkling clean soul. I had not been successful at keeping the sarcasm out of my voice. Her fury was fueled by her own bitter catalogue.

"A burden to her family . . ." She was rolling with her Spanish now. Soon the Holy Mother would enter into the picture for good measure. "It's not as if I had not taught you better. Don't you know that those people do not have the example of the Holy Virgin Mary and her Son to follow, and that is why they do things for the wrong reasons? Mrs. Nathan said she did not want her son messing around with you—not because of the wrongness of it—but because it would interfere with his studies!" She was yelling now. "She's afraid that he will" (she crossed herself at the horror of the thought) "make you pregnant!"

"We could say an angel came down and put a baby in my stomach, Mother." She had succeeded in dragging me into her field of hysteria.

"I do not want you associating any more than necessary with people who do not have God, do you hear me?"

"They have a god!" I was screaming now too, trying to get away from her: "They have an intelligent god who doesn't ask you to believe that a woman can get pregnant without having sex!"

"Nazi," I hissed, "I bet you'd like to send Ira and his family to a con-centration camp!" At that time I thought that was the harshest thing I could have said to anyone. I was certain that I had sentenced my soul to eternal damnation the minute the words came out of my mouth: but I was so angry I wanted to hurt her.

Father walked into my room at that moment, looking shocked at the sight of the two of us entangled in mortal combat.

"Please, please," his voice sounded agonized. I ran to him, and he held me in his arms while I cried my heart out on his starched white shirt. My mother, also weeping quietly, tried to walk past us, but he pulled her into the circle. After a few moments, she put her trembling hand on my head.

"We are a family," my father said, "there is just us against the world. Please, please . . ." But he did not follow the "please" with any suggestions as to what we could do to make things right in a world that was as confusing to my mother as it was to me.

I finished the eighth grade in Paterson, but Ira and I never got together to study again. I sent his Beta Club pin back to him via a mutual friend. Once in a while I saw him in the hall or the playground. But he seemed to be in the clouds, where he belonged. In the fall, I was enrolled at the Catholic high school where everyone believed in the Virgin Birth, and I never had to take a test on the human reproductive system. It was a chapter that was not emphasized.

In 1968, my father retired from the navy and began looking for a bet-ter place for us to live. He decided to move us to Augusta, Georgia, where he had relatives who had settled after retiring from the army at Fort Gordon. They had convinced him that it was a healthier place to rear teenagers. For me it was a shock to the senses, like moving from one planet to another: where Paterson had concrete to walk on and gray skies, bitter winters, and a smorgasbord of an ethnic population, Georgia was red like Mars, and Au-gusta was green—exploding in colors in more gardens of azaleas and dog-wood and magnolia trees—more vegetation than I imagined was possible anywhere not tropical like Puerto Rico. People seemed to come in two basic colors: black and blond. And I could barely understand my teachers when they talked in a slowed-down version of English like one of those old 78-speed recordings played at 33. But I was placed in all advanced classes, and one of them was biology. This is where I got to see my first real fetal pig, which my assigned lab partner had chosen. She picked it up gingerly by the ends of the plastic bag in which it was stored: "Ain't he cute?" she asked. I nodded, nearly fainting from the overwhelming combination of the smell of formaldehyde and my sudden flashback to my brief but intense romance with Ira Nathan.

"What you want to call him?"

My partner unwrapped our specimen on the table, and I surprised myself by my instant recall of Ira's chart. I knew all the parts. In my mind's eye I saw the pencil lines, the labeled photograph. I had had an excellent teacher.

"Let's call him Ira."

"That's a funny name, but OK." My lab partner, a smart girl destined to become my mentor in things southern, then gave me a conspiratorial wink and pulled out a little perfume atomizer from her purse. She sprayed Ira from snout to tail with it. I noticed this operation was taking place at other tables too. The teacher had conveniently left the room a few minutes before. I was once again stunned—almost literally knocked out by a fist of smell:

"What is it?"

"*Intimate*," my advanced biology partner replied, smiling.

And by the time our instructor came back to the room, we were ready to delve into this mystery of muscle and bone; eager to discover the secrets that lie just beyond fear and a little past loathing; acknowledging the corruptibility of the flesh and our own fascination with the subject.

As I finish packing, the telephone rings and it's my mother. She is reminding me to be ready to visit relatives, to go to a dance with her, and of course, to attend a couple of the services at the church. It is the feast of the Black Virgin, revered patron saint of our home town in Puerto Rico. I agree to everything and find myself anticipating the eclectic itinerary. Why not allow Evolution and Eve, Biology and the Virgin Birth? Why not take a vacation from logic? I will not be away for too long, I will not let myself be tempted to remain in the sealed garden of blind faith; I'll stay just long enough to rest myself from the exhausting enterprise of leading the examined life.

STUDY AND DISCUSSION QUESTIONS

1. What does science mean to Ira? Why it might appeal to him?

2. What does science mean to the young Judith? Why might it appeal to her?

3. What are the sources of Judith's attraction to Ira and of Ira's to Judith?

4. "Advanced Biology" sets up a number of contrasts between science and religion, as seen by the young Judith, by her mother, by Ira, and by the adult Judith. List as many as you can.

5. What might explain the difference between Judith's mother's attitude towards Jews and her father's?

6. Why does Judith name the fetal pig "Ira"? What attitudes towards her earlier experience with Ira does this act suggest?

7. Why does Judith have an easier relationship with her mother's religious beliefs as an adult than as a teenager?

8. Discuss the last paragraph. What's happened to the conflict between science and religion that Judith's experience with Ira dramatized? Where does Judith stand now?

SUGGESTIONS FOR WRITING

1. Imagine that Ira, now an adult, has come across "Advanced Biology" and has decided to write Cofer a letter. How might the letter go?

2. If you are a religious believer, describe a time when your faith was challenged. If you are not, describe a time when your unwillingness to believe was challenged.

MOON, MANN, AND OTTO

Stephen Jay Gould

Stephen Jay Gould (b. 1941) teaches geology, zoology, and paleontology at Harvard University. Aside from his technical work in evolutionary theory, Gould is known for his popular science writing, much of it collected in such volumes as Ever Since Darwin *(1977),* The Panda's Thumb *(1980),* Hen's Teeth and Horse's Toes *(1983), where the following appeared,* Bully for Brontosaurus *(1991), and* Dinosaur in a Haystack *(1996).*

Little Rock, Arkansas
December 10, 1981

This morning's *Arkansas Gazette* features a cartoon with searchlights focused on a state map. The map displays neither topography nor political boundaries, but merely contains the words, etched in black from Oklahoma to the Mississippi: "Scopes Trial[1] II. Notoriety." I spent most of yesterday—with

---

[1] John Scopes, a high school teacher, violated Tennessee state law by teaching evolution. His 1925 trial—argued by two famous lawyers of the time, Clarence Darrow for the defense and William Jennings Bryan for the prosecution—touched off a national debate about science and religion. Scopes lost, but the conviction was later overturned on a technicality.

varying degrees of pleasure, righteousness, discomfort, and disbelief—in the witness box, trying to convince Federal Judge William R. Overton that all the geological strata on earth did not form as a result of a single Noachian deluge. We are engaged in the first legal test upon the new wave of creationist bills that mandate equal time or "balanced treatment" for evolution and a thinly disguised version of the Book of Genesis read literally, but masquerading under the nonsense phrase "creation science." The judge, to say the least, seems receptive to my message and as bemused as I am by the fact that such a trial can be held just a few months before the hundredth anniversary of Darwin's death.

The trial of John Scopes in 1925 has cast such a long shadow into our own times that the proceedings in Little Rock inevitably invite comparison. I appreciate the historical continuity but am more impressed by the differences. I sit in a massive alabaster building, a combined courthouse and post office, a no-nonsense, no-frills edifice, surrounded by the traffic noises of downtown Little Rock. The Rhea County Courthouse of Dayton, Tennessee—the building that hosted Scopes, Darrow, and Bryan in 1925—is a gracious, shaded, and decorated Renaissance Revival structure that dominates the cross-roads of its two-street town. The Scopes trial was directly initiated by Dayton's boosters to put their little town on the map; many, probably most, citizens of Arkansas are embarrassed by the anachronism on their doorstep. John Scopes was convicted for even mentioning that humans had descended from "a lower order of animals"; we have made some progress in half a century, and modern creationists clamor for the official recognition of their pseudoscience, not (at least yet) for the exclusion of our well-documented conclusions.

I decided to be a paleontologist when I was five, after an awe-struck encounter with *Tyrannosaurus* at the Museum of Natural History in New York. The phenomenology of big beasts might have been enough to sustain my interest, but I confirmed my career six years later when I read, far too early and with dim understanding, G. G. Simpson's *Meaning of Evolution* and discovered that a body of exciting ideas made sense of all those bodies of bone. Three years later, I therefore approached my first high school science course with keen anticipation. In a year of biology, I would surely learn all about evolution. Imagine my disappointment when the teacher granted Mr. Darwin and his entire legacy only an apologetic two days at the very end of a trying year. I always wondered why, but was too shy to ask. Then I just forgot my question and continued to study on my own.

Six months ago, in a secondhand bookstore, I found a copy of my old high school text, *Modern Biology,* by T. J. Moon, P. B. Mann, and J. H. Otto. We all appreciate how powerful an unexpected sight or odor can be in triggering a distant "remembrance of things past." I knew what I had the minute I saw the familiar red binding with its embossed microscope in silver and its frontispiece in garish color, showing a busy beaver at work. The book, previously the property of a certain "Lefty," was soon mine for ninety-five cents.

Now, more than half a life later (I studied high school biology in 1954), I finally understand why Mrs. Blenderman had neglected the subject that so passionately interested me. I had been a victim of Scopes's ghost (or rather, of his adversary, Bryan's). Most people view the Scopes trial as a victory for evolution, if only because Paul Muni and Spencer Tracy served Clarence Darrow so well in theatrical and film versions of *Inherit the Wind*,[2] and because the trial triggered an outpouring of popular literature by aggrieved and outraged evolutionists. Scopes's conviction (later quashed on a technicality) had been a mere formality; the battle for evolution had been won in the court of public opinion. Would it were so. As several historians have shown, the Scopes trial was a rousing defeat. It abetted a growing fundamentalist movement and led directly to the dilution or elimination of evolution from all popular high school texts in the United States. No arm of the industry is as cowardly and conservative as the publishers of public school texts—markets of millions are not easily ignored. The situation did not change until 1957, a year too late for me, when the Russian Sputnik provoked a searching inquiry into the shameful state of science education in America's high schools.

Moon, Mann, and Otto commanded the lion's share of the market in the mid-1950s; readers of my generation will probably experience that exhilarating sense of *déjà vu* with me. Like many popular books, it was the altered descendant of several earlier editions. The first, *Biology for Beginners*, by Truman J. Moon, was published in 1921, before the Scopes trial. Its frontispiece substituted Mr. Darwin for the industrious beaver, and its text reflected a thorough immersion in evolution as the focal subject of the life sciences. Its preface proclaimed: "The course emphasizes the fact that biology is a unit science, based on the fundamental idea of evolution rather than a forced combination of portions of botany, zoology and hygiene." Its text contains several chapters on evolution and continually emphasizes Darwin's central contention that the *fact* of evolution is established beyond reasonable doubt, although scientists have much to learn about the *mechanism* of evolutionary change. Chapter 35, on "The Method of Evolution," begins: "Proof of the *fact* of similarity between the various forms of living things and of their very evident relationship, still leaves a more difficult question to be answered. *How* did this descent and modification take place, by what means has nature developed one form from another? [Moon's italics]"

I then examined my new purchase with a growing sense of amusement mixed with disgust. The index contained such important entries as "fly

---

[2] 1955 play by Jerome Lawrence and Robert Edwin Lee, and 1960 film directed by Stanley Kramer.

specks, disease germs in," but nothing about evolution. Indeed, the word evolution does not occur anywhere in the book. The subject is not, however, entirely absent. It receives a scant eighteen pages in a 662-page book, as chapter 58 of 60 (pp. 618–36). In this bowdlerized jiffy, it is called "The hypothesis of racial development." Moon, Mann, and Otto had gone the post-Scopes way of all profitable texts: eliminate and risk no offense. (Those who recall the reality of high school courses will also remember that many teachers never got to those last few chapters at all.)

This one pussyfooting chapter is as disgraceful in content as in brevity. Its opening two paragraphs are a giveaway and an intellectual sham compared with Moon's forthright words of 1921. The first paragraph provides a fine statement of historical continuity and change in the *physical* features of our planet:

> This is a changing world. It changes from day to day, year to year, and from age to age. Rivers deepen their gorges as they carry more land to the sea. Mountains rise, only to be leveled gradually by winds and rain. Continents rise and sink into the sea. Such are the gradual changes of the physical earth as days add into years and years combine to become ages.

Now what could be more natural and logical than to extend this same mode of reasoning and style of language to life? The paragraph seems to be set up for such a transition. But note how the tone of the second paragraph subtly shifts to avoid any commitment to historical continuity for organic change:

> During these ages, species of plants and animals have appeared, have flourished for a time, and then have perished as new species took their places. . . . When one race lost in the struggle for survival, another race appeared to take its place.

Four pages later, we finally get an inkling that genealogy may be behind organic transitions through time: "This geological story of the rocks, showing fossil gradations from simple to complex organisms, is what we should expect to find if there had been racial development throughout the past." Later on the page, Moon, Mann, and Otto ask the dreaded question and even venture the closest word they dare to "evolution": "Are these prehistoric creatures the ancestors of modern animals?" If you read carefully through all the qualifications, they answer their question with a guarded "yes"—but you have to read awfully hard.

Thus were millions of children deprived of their chance to study one of the most exciting and influential ideas in science, the central theme of all biology. A few hundred, myself included, possessed the internal motivation to transcend this mockery of education, but citing us seems as foolish and cruel as the old racist argument, "what about George Washington Carver or Willie Mays," used to refute the claim that poor achievement might be linked to economic disadvantage and social prejudice.

Now I can mouth all the grandiloquent arguments against such a dilution of education: we will train a generation unable to think for themselves, we will weaken the economic and social fabric of the nation if we raise a generation illiterate in science, and so on. I even believe all these arguments. But this is not what troubled me most as I read chapter 58 in Moon, Mann, and Otto. I wasn't even much angered, but merely amused, by the tortured pussyfooting and glaring omissions. Small items with big implications are my bread and butter. I do not react strongly to generalities. I can ignore a displeasing general tenor, but I cannot bear falsification and debasement of something small and noble. I was not really shaken until I read the last paragraph of chapter 58, but then an interior voice rose up and began to compose this essay. For to make a valid point in the context of their cowardice, Moon, Mann, and Otto had perverted (perhaps unknowingly) one of my favorite quotations. If cowardice can inspire such debasement, then it must be rooted out.

The last paragraph is titled: Science and Religion. I agree entirely with the first two sentences: "There is nothing in science which is opposed to a belief in God and religion. Those who think so are mistaken in their science or their theology or both." They then quote (with some minor errors, here corrected) a famous statement of T. H. Huxley, using it to argue that a man may be both a Darwinian and a devout Christian:

> Science seems to me to teach in the highest and strongest manner the great truth which is embodied in the Christian conception of entire surrender to the will of God. Sit down before fact as a little child, be prepared to give up every preconceived notion, follow humbly wherever and to whatever abysses nature leads, or you shall learn nothing. I have only begun to learn content and peace of mind since I have resolved at all risks to do this.

Now a man may be both an evolutionist and a devout Christian. Millions successfully juxtapose these two independent viewpoints, but Thomas Henry Huxley did not. This quote, in its proper context, actually speaks of Huxley's courageous agnosticism. It also occurs in what I regard as the most beautiful and moving letter ever written by a scientist.

The tragic setting of this long letter explains why Huxley cited, only in analogy as Moon, Mann, and Otto did not understand, "the Christian conception of entire surrender to the will of God." Huxley's young and favorite son had just died. His friend, the Reverend Charles Kingsley (best remembered today as author of *The Water-Babies* and *Westward Ho!*) had written a long and kind letter of condolence with a good Anglican bottom line: see here Huxley, if you could only abandon your blasted agnosticism and accept the Christian concept of an immortal soul, you would be comforted.

Huxley responded in tones that recall the chief of police in Gilbert and Sullivan's *Pirates of Penzance* who, when praised by General Stanley's daughters for expected bravery in a coming battle that would probably lead to his bloody death, remarked:

> Still, perhaps it would be wise
> Not to carp or criticise,
> For it's very evident
> These attentions are well meant.

Huxley thanks Kingsley for his sincerely proffered comfort, but then explains in several pages of passionate prose why he cannot alter a set of principles, established after so much thought and deliberation, merely to assuage his current grief.

He has, he maintains, committed himself to science as the only sure guide to truth about matters of fact. Since matters of God and soul do not lie in this realm, he cannot know the answers to specific claims and must remain agnostic. "I neither deny nor affirm the immortality of man," he writes. "I see no reason for believing in it, but, on the other hand, I have no means of disproving it." Thus, he continues, "I cannot assert the certainty of immortality to placate my loss." Uncomfortable convictions, if well founded, are those that require the most assiduous affirmation, as he states just before the passage quoted by Moon, Mann, and Otto: "My business is to teach my aspirations to conform themselves to fact, not to try and make facts harmonize with my aspirations."

Later, in the most moving statement of the letter, he speaks of the larger comfort that a commitment to science has provided him—a comfort more profound and lasting than the grief that his uncertainty about immortality now inspires. Among three agencies that shaped his deepest beliefs, he notes, "Science and her methods gave me a resting-place independent of authority and tradition." (For his two other agencies, Huxley cites "love" that "opened up to me a view of the sanctity of human nature," and his recognition that "a deep sense of religion was compatible with the entire absence of theology.") He then writes:

> If at this moment I am not a worn-out, debauched, useless carcass of a man, if it has been or will be my fate to advance the cause of science, if I feel that I have a shadow of a claim on the love of those about me, if in the supreme moment when I looked down into my boy's grave my sorrow was full of submission and without bitterness, it is because these agencies have

worked upon me, and not because I have ever cared whether my poor personality shall remain distinct forever from the All from whence it came and whither it goes.

And thus, my dear Kingsley, you will understand what my position is. I may be quite wrong, and in that case I know I shall have to pay the penalty for being wrong. But I can only say with Luther, "Gott helfe mir, ich kann nichts anders [God help me, I cannot do otherwise]."

Thus we understand what Huxley meant when he spoke of "the Christian conception of entire surrender to the will of God" in the passage cited by Moon, Mann, and Otto. It is obviously not, as they imply, his profession of Christian faith, but a burning analogy: as the Christian has made his commitment, so have I made mine to science. I cannot do otherwise, despite the immediate comfort that conventional Christianity would supply in my current distress.

Today I sat in the court of Little Rock, listening to the testimony of four splendid men and women who teach science in primary and secondary schools of Arkansas. Their testimony contained moments of humor, as when one teacher described an exercise he uses in the second grade. He stretches a string across the classroom to represent the age of the earth. He then asks students to stand in various positions marking such events as the origin of life, the extinction of dinosaurs, and the evolution of humans. What would you do, asked the assistant attorney general in cross-examination, to provide balanced treatment for the 10,000-year-old earth advocated by creation scientists. "I guess I'd have to get a short string," replied the teacher. The thought of twenty earnest second graders, all scrunched up along a millimeter of string, created a visual image that set the court rocking with laughter.

But the teachers' testimony also contained moments of inspiration. As I listened to their reasons for opposing "creation science," I thought of T. H. Huxley and the courage required by dedicated people who will not, to paraphrase Lillian Hellman, tailor their convictions to fit current fashions. As Huxley would not simplify and debase in order to find immediate comfort, these teachers told the court that mechanical compliance with the "balanced treatment" act, although easy enough to perform, would destroy their integrity as teachers and violate their responsibility to students.

One witness pointed to a passage in his chemistry text that attributed great age to fossil fuels. Since the Arkansas act specifically includes "a relatively recent age of the earth" among the definitions of creation science requiring "balanced treatment," this passage would have to be changed. The witness claimed that he did not know how to make such an alteration. Why not? retorted the assistant attorney general in his cross-examination. You only need to insert a simple sentence: "Some scientists, however, believe that fossil fuels are relatively young." Then, in the most impressive statement of the entire trail, the teacher responded. I could, he argued, insert such a sentence in mechanical compliance with the act. But I cannot, as a conscientious teacher, do so. For "balanced treatment" must mean "equal dignity" and I would therefore have to justify the insertion. And this I cannot do, for I have heard no valid arguments that would support such a position.

Another teacher spoke of similar dilemmas in providing balanced treatment in a conscientious rather than a mechanical way. What then, he was asked, would he do if the law were upheld. He looked up and said, in his calm and dignified voice: It would be my tendency not to comply. I am not a revolutionary or a martyr, but I have responsibilities to my students, and I cannot forgo them.

God bless the dedicated teachers of this world. We who work in unthreatened private colleges and universities often do not adequately appreciate the plight of our colleagues—or their courage in upholding what should be our common goals. What Moon, Mann, and Otto did to Huxley epitomizes the greatest danger of imposed antirationalism in classrooms—that one must simplify by distortion, and remove both depth and beauty, in order to comply.

In appreciation for the teachers of Arkansas, then, and for all of us, one more statement in conclusion from Huxley's letter to Kingsley:

> Had I lived a couple of centuries earlier I could have fancied a devil scoffing at me . . . and asking me what profit it was to have stripped myself of the hopes and consolations of the mass of mankind? To which my only reply was and is—Oh devil! truth is better than much profit. I have searched over the grounds of my belief, and if wife and child and name and fame were all to be lost to me one after the other as the penalty, still I will not lie.

Postscript

On January 5, 1982, Federal District Judge William R. Overton declared the Arkansas act unconstitutional because it forces biology teachers to purvey religion in science classrooms.

STUDY AND DISCUSSION QUESTIONS

1. The first edition of *Modern Biology*, Gould writes, "emphasizes . . . that the *fact* of evolution is established beyond a reasonable doubt, although scientists have much to learn about the *mechanism* of evolutionary change." Explain the distinction Gould is making here and why it is important.

2. Gould says that he agrees with the assertion in the revised edition of *Modern Biology* that "there is nothing in science which is opposed to a belief in God and religion." Why, then, does he so strenuously oppose the teaching of "creation" alongside evolution in biology classes?

3. What motivated Moon, Mann, and Otto, and their publisher, to eliminate the discussion of evolution in the later edition of their text? How does Gould contrast them to Huxley and the teachers who testified in court?

4. What else was lost, besides scientific accuracy and thoroughness, as a result of the revisions Gould discusses?

5. Huxley writes: "My business is to teach my aspirations to conform themselves to fact, not to try and make facts harmonize with my aspirations." What does he mean by this statement? What is its relevance to Gould's arguments?

6. Why was it Moon, Mann, and Otto's misuse of Huxley's statement that finally drove Gould to write his essay? Was it only that this was one of Gould's favorite quotations?

SUGGESTIONS FOR WRITING

1. Gould writes that "no arm of the industry is as cowardly and conservative as the publishers of public school texts." Examine a school textbook, perhaps one you yourself have used. How does it handle politically sensitive topics, say abortion or the Vietnam War?

2. Imagine that a parents' committee, a religious organization, a school board, or some other group has insisted that a textbook you are using in a high school class be removed. (Choose your own particulars: the subject, the reason the text was found objectionable, etc.) Write a letter to the local newspaper supporting or opposing this action.

3. Do you agree that "there is nothing in science which is opposed to a belief in God and religion"?

Nature / The Environment

"Continue to contaminate your bed and you will one day lay in your
own waste."

—Chief Seattle, 1854

Contemporary environmental issues include air and water pollution;
solid, industrial, and nuclear waste management; energy conservation in
homes and industries; noise pollution; acid rain; holes in the ozone layer;
global warming. Questions about the environment often intersect with social policy, as when toxic disposal sites are placed primarily in low income
neighborhoods. Consider some epidemiological consequences of pollution:
How many people are sick or have died directly from pollution? How many
children's immune systems have been knocked askew by high levels of contamination in the environment? As technological progress and the human
population growth accelerate, many of us are concerned about the extinction of species, the quality of life on our planet, and the ethical and spiritual consequences of our treatment of the environment. We have called this
section "Nature/The Environment" because while scientists, politicians,
and journalists tend to talk about "the environment," creative writers like
Susan Griffin, Alice Walker, and Joyce Carol Oates more often conceptualize the world around us as "Nature," a word of longer tradition and richer
connotation. "Environment," more recent and carrying more scientific

associations, is a good word too, though Joy Williams in her essay in this section calls it a "bloodless . . . flatfooted word with a shrunken heart." We think that those who write about the "environment" and those who write about "Nature" address many of the same concerns.

The essays in this section share a recurring theme: that human beings have increasingly moved into an oppositional relation to nature in the wake of the Industrial Revolution, the rise of monopoly capitalism, and the explosion of population growth. At least three factors contribute to the opposition between humans and the environment: first, an ever increasing human population that encroaches on the natural world; second, advances in technology and the increased human reliance on that technology alone in preference to working with nature; and, third, something that can only be called attitude—a philosophy of human eminence and a psychology of human dominance or control. The two components of this attitude lead human beings to see themselves as separate from nature rather than as an interlocking part of a global ecology. Humans often see their role as one of mastering and exploiting the natural world to serve their purposes, however short-sighted such an approach might prove.

How important is ecological responsibility in comparison to technological advancement and economic profit? How serious is the ethical dilemma posed by the conflict between these forces? Environmental ethicists such as Ruth Richardson note, on the one hand, that environmental extremists see any kind of technology as a threat to the balance of nature. On the other hand, pure technologists view the natural world as something to be manipulated in the interest of economic and technological progress. Somewhere in between are those who feel technology should be checked by ecological responsibility. Most of the writers included in this section fall into this middle group, which comprises a wide range of opinion about where to draw the lines between actions that are ecologically healthy and those that are harmful.

Joy Williams's essay "Save the Whales, Screw the Shrimp" embodies in its form the opposition between the "consumer" and the environment in its form. She characterizes a "me," who believes we are all part of nature, and a "you," who sees himself as separate from nature. Both are busily involved in "editing" the environment, or at least in sitting back and enjoying the consumer items that others' editing has produced. Rich with examples of the exploitation of nature—from planned communities to new age zoos—Williams's lively and engaging essay challenges us to wake up before we have edited the planet beyond recognition.

In a more sober and expository mode, Barry Commoner educates his readers about some basic ecological realities, explaining why we currently have a hole in the ozone layer, how changes in the earth's vegetation affect the earth's climate, how human population growth affects the earth's vegetation, and how and why everything in the ecosphere is inevitably connected to everything else. We are familiar with the concept that nature functions in cycles; that technology is inevitably linear in function may be a newer concept for most of us. "At War with the Planet" demonstrates with terrifying clarity the disastrous and accelerating separation between ecosphere and "technosphere." The matter-of-fact style in which Commoner writes only makes this separation seem all the more alarming.

The environment is an area in which ethics and practice meet daily on personal, municipal, federal, and global levels and in which one's own behavior may ultimately affect people on the other side of the planet. Where does individual pursuit of happiness fit into the scheme of environmental ethics and practices? Unlike Williams's and Commoner's essays, which were published in the 1990s, Wendell Berry's "Mayhem in the Industrial Paradise" was written in the early 1970s. The countryside spoiled by strip mining about which he writes can still be seen in many parts of eastern Kentucky and West Virginia, however, and will remain ruined for many thousands of years. Berry contends that corporate pursuit of happiness— e.g., profit—in complete disregard of the balance of nature and the lives of working people, has been the cause of this devastation of almost Old Testament proportions. Berry thus comments on the same contrasts between individual and corporate volition as Jerry Mander does in the section on Money, Work, and Social Class.

In "When People of Color Are an Endangered Species," Elizabeth Martinez reports on the work of the SouthWest Organizing Project, an activist group that educates communities, corporations, the military, and environmental groups about the realities of environmental racism and classism. Martinez reports sobering statistics on the percentage of toxic waste sites located near low income, African American, Latino, and Native American communities. The irony of Martinez's title becomes clear when she writes about educating environmental groups such as the Sierra Club, which have tended to focus more on saving spotted owls and blunt-nosed leopard lizards than on saving low income factory workers and children in communities adjacent to factories. Predictably, Martinez is able to report more productive communication with environmental groups than with corporations. In one story she tells, a corporation, in response to protests about toxic pollution of a poor United States neighborhood, simply moved its dangerous chemicals across the border to Juarez, Mexico.

The next pair of pieces in this section, Susan Griffin's philosophical prose poem "Matter: How We Know" and Alice Walker's narrative essay "Am I Blue?", use lyrical forms to express their authors' sense of the deep connection between human beings and the natural world. Griffin's "Matter: How We Know" is a section from her book length meditation *Woman and Nature*. Densely textured in language and image, "Matter: How We Know" gains resonance, as does any poem, when read aloud. Griffin's thesis, "because we know ourselves to be made from this earth," is as much about the process and the necessity of *knowing* as it is about the fact of our connection with all that lives. Alice Walker's double meaning title, "Am I Blue?", is answered in the affirmative by the essay's end after she has taken us with her on a narrative and philosophical exploration of her relationship with her neighbor in the meadow next to her summer house, a large white horse named Blue.

Taking a more humorous tone, Michael Pollan's "Why Mow? The Case Against Lawns" elegantly and wittily argues against our continued bondage to that ubiquitous feature of the American suburban landscape. For many of us, the experience of summer in America is the sound of a million lawnmowers, the mingled smells of newly cut grass and gasoline, and the sight of a green altar of smooth vegetation before which people on their knees uproot the heresy of dandelions. Pollan gives us a lesson in landscape, civic, and personal history. Tracing the development of his own evolving revolutionary consciousness, he makes an eloquent argument for growing gardens instead of lawns.

We end this section on Nature/The Environment with a dissenting voice, that of Joyce Carol Oates in "Against Nature." Here Oates takes on the tradition of what she considers sentimental paeans to nature. (She would probably place Alice Walker's and Susan Griffin's essays in that category.) In an essay stuffed with literary allusion, Oates enlists many famous writers, from Henry David Thoreau to Oscar Wilde, to argue on her side. Her opening list of nature's characteristics, "the writer's resistance to nature," leans heavily on nature's very lack of human qualities and on the inability of human beings to make any kind of meaningful contact with something as alien as "nature-in-itself." Oates sees "Nature-as-experience," on the other hand, as "the self's (flattering) mirror"; she contends that, whatever meaning nature has, humans have bestowed upon it.

Each one of us inevitably is attached to the world around us, whether we think of that world as merely what we see on the way from the apartment to the car and again from the car to our workplace or whether we picture stands of old growth forest in the Pacific Northwest, the dense and colorful rain forests of the Amazon Basin, or the salt marsh ecology of the ocean's border with the land. What increasingly has happened is that, as the world conceptually and informationally shrinks, the complexity of our interdependency with the physical world expands. Ultimately our lives and the lives of our children will depend on how deeply we understand our relation to that physical world, to nature, to the environment.

SAVE THE WHALES,
SCREW THE SHRIMP

Joy Williams

*Joy Williams was born in Chelmsford, Massachusetts in 1944, stud-
ied at Marietta College and the University of Iowa, and worked for
two years at a marine laboratory in Florida. Her writing includes the
novels* State of Grace *(1973) and* Breaking and Entering *(1988)
and the story collections* Taking Care *(1982) and* Escapes *(1990).
The following appeared in* Esquire *magazine and was repeated in* The
Best American Essays 1990.

I don't want to talk about *me*, of course, but it seems as though far too much
attention has been lavished on *you* lately—that your greed and vanities and
quest for self-fulfillment have been catered to far too much. You just want
and want and want. You haven't had a mandala dream since the eighties
began. To have a mandala dream you'd have to instinctively know that it was
an attempt at self-healing on the part of Nature, and you don't believe in Nature anymore. It's too isolated from you. You've abstracted it. It's so messy
and damaged and sad. Your eyes glaze as you travel life's highway past all the
crushed animals and the Big Gulp cups. You don't even take pleasure in looking at nature photographs these days. Oh, they can be just as pretty, as always, but don't they make you feel increasingly . . . anxious? Filled with more
trepidation than peace? So what's the point? You see the picture of the baby
condor or the panda munching on a bamboo shoot, and your heart just sinks,
doesn't it? A picture of a poor old sea turtle with barnacles on her back, all
ancient and exhausted, depositing her five gallons of doomed eggs in the
sand hardly fills you with joy, because you realize, quite rightly, that just outside the frame falls the shadow of the condo. What's cropped from the shot
of ocean waves crashing on a pristine shore is the plastics plant, and just
beyond the dunes lies a parking lot. Hidden from immediate view in the
butterfly-bright meadow, in the dusky thicket, in the oak and holly wood, are
the surveyors' stakes, for someone wants to build a mall exactly there—some
gas stations and supermarkets, some pizza and video shops, a health club,
maybe a bulimia treatment center. Those lovely pictures of leopards and
herons and wild rivers, well, you just know they're going to be accompanied

by a text that will serve only to bring you down. You don't want to think about it! It's all so uncool. And you don't want to feel guilty either. Guilt is uncool. Regret maybe you'll consider. *Maybe.* Regret is a possibility, but don't push me, you say. Nature photographs have become something of a problem, along with almost everything else. Even though they leave the bad stuff out—maybe because you *know* they're leaving all the bad stuff out—such pictures are making you increasingly aware that you're a little too late for Nature. Do you feel that? Twenty years too late, maybe only ten? Not *way* too late, just a little too late? Well, it appears that you are. And since you are, you've decided you're just not going to attend this particular party.

Pascal said that it is easier to endure death without thinking about it than to endure the thought of death without dying. This is how you manage to dance the strange dance with that grim partner, nuclear annihilation. When the U.S. Army notified Winston Churchill that the first atom bomb had been detonated in New Mexico, it chose the code phrase BABIES SATIS- FACTORILY BORN. So you entered the age of irony, and the strange double life you've been leading with the world ever since. Joyce Carol Oates suggests that the reason writers—*real* writers, one assumes—don't write about Nature is that it lacks a sense of humor and registers no irony. It just doesn't seem to be of the times—these slick, sleek, knowing, objective, indulgent times. And the word *Environment.* Such a bloodless word. A flat-footed word with a shrunken heart. A word increasingly disengaged from its association with the natural world. Urban planners, industrialists, economists, and developers use it. It's a lost word, really. A cold word, mechanistic, suited strangely to the coldness generally felt toward Nature. It's their word now. You don't mind giving it up. As for *Environmentalist,* that's one that can really bring on the yawns, for you've tamed and tidied it, neutered it quite nicely. An environmentalist must be calm, rational, reasonable, and willing to compromise, otherwise you won't listen to him. Still, his beliefs are *opinions* only, for this is the age of radical subjectivism. Not long ago, Barry Commoner[1] spoke to the Environmental Protection Agency. He scolded them. They loved it. The way they protect the environment these days is apparently to find an "acceptable level of harm from a pollutant and then issue rules allowing industry to pollute to that level." Commoner suggested that this was inappropriate. An EPA employee suggested that any other approach would place limits on economic growth and implied that Commoner was advocating this. Limits on economic growth! Commoner vigorously denied this. Oh, it was a healthy exchange of ideas, healthier certainly than our air and water. We needed that little spanking, the EPA felt. It was refreshing. The agency has

---

[1] Environmentalist—see headnote to his essay in this section.

recently lumbered into action in its campaign to ban dinoseb. You seem to have liked your dinoseb. It's been a popular weed killer, even though it has been directly linked with birth defects. You must hate weeds a lot. Although the EPA appears successful in banning the poison, it will still have to pay the disposal costs and compensate the manufacturers for the market value of the chemicals they still have in stock.

That's ironic, you say, but farmers will suffer losses, too, oh dreadful financial losses, if herbicide and pesticide use is restricted.

Farmers grow way too much stuff anyway. They grow surplus crops with subsidized water created by turning rivers great and small into a plumbing system of dams and canals. Rivers have become *systems*. Wetlands are increasingly being referred to as *filtering systems*—things deigned *useful* because of their ability to absorb urban run-off, oil from roads, et cetera.

We know that. We've known that for years about farmers. We know a lot these days. We're very well informed. If farmers aren't allowed to make a profit by growing surplus crops, they'll have to sell their land to developers, who'll turn all that *arable land* into office parks. Arable land isn't Nature anyway, and besides, we like those office parks and shopping plazas, with their monster supermarkets open twenty-four hours a day with aisle after aisle after aisle of *products*. It's fun. Products are fun.

Farmers like their poisons, but ranchers like them even more. There are well-funded predominantly federal and cooperative programs like the Agriculture Department's Animal Damage Control Unit that poison, shoot, and trap several thousand animals each year. This unit loves to kill things. It was created to kill things—bobcats, foxes, black bears, mountain lions, rabbits, badgers, countless birds—all to make this great land safe for the string bean and the corn, the sheep and the cow, even though you're not consuming as much cow these days. A burger now and then, but burgers are hardly cows at all, you feel. They're not all *our* cows in any case, for some burger matter is imported. There's a bit of Central American burger matter in your bun. Which is contributing to the conversion of tropical rain forest into cow pasture. Even so, you're getting away from meat these days. You're eschewing cow. It's seafood you love, shrimp most of all. And when you love something, it had better watch out, because you have a tendency to love it to death. Shrimp, shrimp, shrimp. It's more common on menus than chicken. In the wilds of Ohio, far, far from watery shores, four out of the six entrées on a menu will be shrimp, for some modest sum. Everywhere, it's all the shrimp you can eat or all you *care* to eat, for sometimes you just don't feel like eating all you *can*. You are intensively *harvesting* shrimp. Soon there won't be any left and then you can stop. It takes that, often, to make you stop. Shrimpers shrimp, of course. That's their *business*. They put out these big nets and in these nets, for each pound of shrimp, they catch more than ten times that amount of fish, turtles, and dolphins. These, quite the worse for wear, they dump back in. There is an object called TED (Turtle Excluder Device), which would save thousands of turtles and some dolphins from dying in the nets, but the shrimpers are loath to use TEDs, as they say it would cut the size of their shrimp catch.

We've heard about TED, you say.

They want you, all of you, to have all the shrimp you can eat and more. At Kiawah Island, off the coast of South Carolina, visitors go out on Jeep "safaris" through the part of the island that hasn't been developed yet. ("Wherever you see trees," the guide says, "really, that's a lot.") The safari comprises six Jeeps, and these days they go out at least four times a day, with more trips promised soon. The tourists drive their own Jeeps and the guide talks to them by radio. Kiawah has nice beaches, and the guide talks about turtles. When he mentions the shrimpers' role in the decline of the turtle, the shrimpers, who share the same frequency, scream at him. Shrimpers and most commercial fishermen (many of them working with drift and gill nets anywhere from six to thirty miles long) think of themselves as an *endangered species*. A recent newspaper headline said, "Shrimpers Spared Anti-Turtle Devices." Even so, with the continuing wanton depletion of shrimp beds, they will undoubtedly have to find some other means of employment soon. They might, for instance, become part of that vast throng laboring in the *tourist industry*.

Tourism has become an industry as destructive as any other. You are no longer benign in your traveling somewhere to look at the scenery. You never thought there was much gain in just looking anyway, you've always preferred to *use* the scenery in some manner. In your desire to get away from what you've got, you've caused there to be no place to get away *to*. You're just all bumpered up out there. Sewage and dumps have become prime indicators of America's lifestyle. In resort towns in New England and the Adirondacks, measuring the flow into the sewage plant serves as a business barometer. Tourism is a growth industry. You believe in growth. *Controlled* growth, of course. Controlled exponential growth is what you'd really like to see. You certainly don't want to put a moratorium or a cap on anything. That's illegal, isn't it? Retro you're not. You don't want to go back or anything. Forward. Maybe ask directions later. Growth is *desirable* as well as being *inevitable*. Growth is the one thing you seem to be powerless before, so you try to be realistic about it. Growth is—it's weird—it's like cancer or something.

Recently you, as tourist, have discovered your national parks and are quickly *overburdening* them. Spare land and it belongs to you! It's exotic land too, not looking like all the stuff around it that looks like everything else. You want to take advantage of this land, of course, and use it in every way you can. Thus the managers—or *stewards,* as they like to be called—have developed *wise* and *multiple-use* plans, keeping in mind exploiters' interests (for they have their needs, too) as well as the desires of the backpackers. Thus mining, timbering, and ranching activities take place in the national forests, where the Forest Service maintains a system of logging roads eight times larger than the interstate highway system. The national parks are more of a public playground and are becoming increasingly Europeanized in their look and management. Lots of concessions and motels. You deserve a clean bed and a hot meal when you go into the wilderness. At least your stewards think that you do. You keep your stewards busy. Not only must they cater to your multiple and conflicting desires, they have to manage your wildlife *resources.* They have managed wildfowl to such an extent that the reasoning has become, If it weren't for hunters, ducks would disappear. Duck stamps and licensing fees support the whole rickety duck-management system. Yes! If it weren't for the people who killed them, wild ducks wouldn't exist! Managers are managing all wild creatures, not just those that fly. They track and tape and tag and band. They relocate, restock, and reintroduce. They cull and control. It's hard to keep it all straight. Protect or poison? Extirpate or just mostly eliminate? Sometimes even the stewards get mixed up.

This is the time of machines and models, hands-on management and master plans. Don't you ever wonder as you pass that billboard advertising another MASTER-PLANNED COMMUNITY just what master they are actually talking about? Not the Big Master, certainly. Something brought to you by one of the tiny masters, of which there are many. But you like these tiny masters and have even come to expect and require them. In Florida they've just started a ten-thousand-acre city in the Everglades. It's a *megaproject,* one of the largest ever in the state. Yes, they must have thought you wanted it. No, what you thought of as the Everglades, the Park, is only a little bitty part of the Everglades. Developers have been gnawing at this irreplaceable, strange land for years. It's like they just *hate* this ancient sea of grass. Maybe you could ask them about this sometime. Roy Rogers is the senior vice president of strategic planning, and the old cowboy says that every tree and bush and inch of sidewalk in the project has been planned. Nevertheless, because the whole thing will take twenty-five years to complete, the plan is going to be constantly changed. You can understand this. The important thing is that there be a blueprint. You trust a blueprint. The tiny masters know what you like. You like *a secure landscape* and *access to services.* You like grass—that is, lawns. The ultimate lawn is the golf course, which you've been told has "some ecological value." You believe this! Not that it really matters, you just like to play golf. These golf courses require a lot of watering. So much that the more inspired of the masters have taken to watering them with effluent, *treated* effluent, but yours, from all the condos and villas built around the stocked artificial lakes you fancy.

I really don't want to think about sewage, you say, but it sounds like progress.

It is true that the masters are struggling with the problems of your incessant flushing. Cuisine is also one of their concerns. Advances in sorbets—sorbet intermezzos—in their clubs and fine restaurants. They know what you want. You want A HAVEN FROM THE ORDINARY WORLD. If you're A NATURE LOVER in the West you want to live in a $200,000 home in A WILD ANIMAL HABITAT. If you're eastern and consider yourself more hip, you want to live in new towns—brand-new reconstructed-from-scratch towns—in a house of NINETEENTH-CENTURY DESIGN. But in these new towns the masters are building, getting around can be confusing. There is an abundance of curves and an infrequency of through streets. It's the new wilderness without any trees. You can get lost, even with all the "mental bread crumbs" the masters scatter about as visual landmarks—the windmill, the water views, the various groupings of landscape "material." You *are* lost, you know. But you trust a Realtor will show you the way. There are many more Realtors than tiny masters, and many of them have to make do with less than a loaf—that is, trying to sell stuff that's already been built in an environment already "enhanced" rather than something being planned—but they're everywhere, willing to show you the path. If Dante returned to Hell today, he'd probably be escorted down by a Realtor, talking all the while about how it was just another level of Paradise.

> *When have you last watched a sunset? Do you remember where you were? With whom? At Loews Ventana Canyon Resort, the Grand Foyer will provide you with that opportunity through lighting which is computerized to diminish with the approaching sunset!*

The tiny masters are willing to arrange Nature for you. They will compose it into a picture that you can look at at your leisure, when you're not doing work or something like that. Nature becomes scenery, a prop. At some golf courses in the Southwest, the saguaro cacti are reported to be repaired with green paste when balls blast into their skin. The saguaro can attempt to heal themselves by growing over the balls, but this takes time, and the effect can be somewhat . . . baroque. It's better to get out the pastepot. Nature has become simply a visual form of entertainment, and it had better look snappy.

Listen, you say, we've been at Ventana Canyon. It's in the desert, right? It's very, very nice, a world-class resort. A totally self-contained environment with everything that a person could possibly want, on more than a thousand acres in the middle of zip. It sprawls but nestles, like. And they've maintained the integrity of as much of the desert ecosystem as possible. Give them credit for that. *Great* restaurant, too. We had baby bay scallops there. Coming into the lobby there are these two big hand-carved coyotes, mutely howling. And that's the way we like them, *mute*. God, why do those things howl like that?

Wildlife is a personal matter, you think. The attitude is up to you. You can prefer to see it dead or not dead. You might want to let it mosey about its business or blow it away. Wild things exist only if you have the graciousness to allow them to. Just outside Tucson, Arizona, there is a brand-new structure modeled after a French foreign legion outpost. It's the *International Wildlife Museum*, and it's full of dead animals. Three hundred species are there, at least a third of them—the rarest ones—killed and collected by one C. J. McElroy, who enjoyed doing it and now shares what's left with you. The museum claims to be educational because you can watch a taxidermist at work or touch a lion's tooth. You can get real close to these dead animals, closer than you can in a zoo. Some of you prefer zoos, however, which are becoming bigger, better, and bioclimatic. New-age zoo designers want the animals to *flow right out into your space.* In Dallas there will soon be a Wilds of Africa exhibit; in San Diego there's a simulated rain forest, where you can thread your way "down the side of a lush canyon, the air filled with a fine mist from 300 high-pressure nozzles"; in New Orleans you've constructed a swamp, the real swamp not far away on the verge of disappearing. Animals in these places are abstractions—wandering relics of their true selves, but that doesn't matter. Animal behavior in a zoo is nothing like natural behavior, but that doesn't really matter, either. Zoos are pretty, contained, and accessible. These new habitats can contain one hundred different species—not more than one or two of each thing, of course—on seven acres, three, one. You don't want to see *too much* of anything, certainly. An *example* will suffice. Sort of like a biological Crabtree & Evelyn[2] basket selected with *you* in mind. You like things reduced, simplified. It's easier to take it all in, park it in your mind. You like things inside better than outside anyway. You are increasingly looking at and living in proxy environments created by substitution and simulation. *Resource economists* are a wee branch in the tree of tiny masters, and one, Martin Krieger, wrote, "Artificial prairies and wildernesses have been created, and there is no reason to believe that these artificial environments need be unsatisfactory for those who experience them. . . . We will have to realize that the way in which we experience nature is conditioned by our society—which more and more is seen to be receptive to responsible intervention."

Nature has become a world of appearances, a mere source of materials. You've been editing it for quite some time; now you're in the process of deleting it. Earth is beginning to look like not much more than a launching pad. Back near Tucson, on the opposite side of the mountain from the dead-animal

---

[2] Manufacturer of fancy preserved foods and bath products, often packaged in variety gift baskets.

habitat, you're building Biosphere II (as compared with or opposed to Biosphere I, more commonly known as Earth)—a 2½-acre terrarium, an artificial ecosystem that will include a rain forest, a desert, a thirty-five-foot ocean, and several thousand species of life (lots of microbes), including eight human beings, who will cultivate a bit of farmland. You think it would be nice to colonize other worlds after you've made it necessary to leave this one.

Hey, that's pretty good, you say, all that stuff packed into just 2½ acres. That's only about three times bigger than my entire *house*.

It's small all right, but still not small enough to be, apparently, useful. For the purposes of NASA, say, it would have to be smaller, oh much smaller, and energy-efficient too. Fiddle, fiddle, fiddle. You support fiddling, as well as meddling. This is how you learn. Though it's quite apparent the environment has been grossly polluted and the natural world abused and defiled, you seem to prefer to continue pondering effects rather than preventing causes. You want proof, you insist on proof. A Dr. Lave from Carnegie-Mellon[3]—and he's an expert, an economist, and an environmental *expert*—says that scientists will have to prove to you that you will suffer if you don't become less of a "throw-away society." *If you really want me to give up my car or my air conditioner, you'd better prove to me first that the earth would otherwise be uninhabitable,* Dr. Lave says. *Me* is *you*, I presume, whereas *you* refers to them. You as in me—that is, *me, me, me*—certainly strike a hard bargain. Uninhabitable the world has to get before you rein in your requirements. You're a consumer after all, *the* consumer upon whom so much attention is lavished, the ultimate user of a commodity that has become, these days, everything. To try to appease your appetite for proof, for example, scientists have been leasing for experimentation forty-six pristine lakes in Canada.

They don't want to *keep* them, they just want to *borrow* them.

They've been intentionally contaminating many of the lakes with a variety of pollutants dribbled into the propeller wash of research boats. *It's one of the boldest experiments in lake ecology ever conducted.* They've turned these remote lakes into huge *real-world test tubes.* They've been doing this since 1976! And what they've found so far in these *preliminary* studies is that pollutants are really destructive. The lakes get gross. Life in them ceases. It took about eight years to make this happen in one of them, everything carefully measured and controlled all the while. Now the scientists are slowly reversing the process. But it will take hundreds of years for the lakes to recover. They think.

Remember when you used to like rain, the sound of it, the feel of it, the way it made the plants and trees all glisten. We needed that rain, you would

---

[3] Private university in Pittsburgh.

say. It looked pretty too, you thought, particularly in the movies. Now it rains and you go, Oh-oh. A nice walloping rain these days means *overtaxing our sewage treatment plants.* It means *untreated waste discharged directly into our waterways.* It means . . .

Okay. Okay.

Acid rain! And we all know what this is. Or most of us do. People of power in government and industry still don't seem to know what it is. Whatever it is, they say, they don't want to curb it, but they're willing to study it some more. Economists call air and water pollution "externalities" anyway. Oh, acid rain. You do get so sick of hearing about it. The words have already become a white-noise kind of thing. But you think in terms of *mitigating* it maybe. As for *the greenhouse effect,* you think in terms of *countering* that. One way that's been discussed recently is the planting of new forests, not for the sake of the forests alone, oh my heavens, no. Not for the sake of majesty and mystery or of Thumper and Bambi,[4] are you kidding me, but because, as every school child knows, trees absorb carbon dioxide. They just soak it up and store it. They just love it. So this is the plan: you plant millions of acres of trees, and you can go on doing pretty much whatever you're doing—driving around, using staggering amounts of energy, keeping those power plants fired to the max. Isn't Nature remarkable? So willing to serve? You wouldn't think it had anything more to offer, but it seems it does. Of course these "forests" wouldn't exactly be forests. They would be more like trees. *Managed* trees. The Forest Service, which now manages our forests by cutting them down, might be called upon to evolve in their thinking and allow these trees to grow. They would probably be patented trees after a time. Fast-growing, uniform, genetically-created-to-be-toxin-eating *machines.* They would be *new-age* trees, because the problem with planting the old-fashioned variety to *combat* the greenhouse effect, which is caused by pollution, is that they're already dying from it. All along the crest of the Appalachians from Maine to Georgia, forests struggle to survive in a toxic soup of poisons. They can't *help* us if we've killed them, now can they?

All right, you say, wow, lighten up will you? Relax. Tell about yourself.

Well, I say, I live in Florida . . .

Oh my God, you say. Florida! Florida is a joke! How do you expect us to take you seriously if you still live there! Florida is crazy, it's pink concrete. It's paved, it's over. And a little girl just got eaten by an alligator down there. It came out of some swamp next to a subdivision and just carried her off. That set your Endangered Species Act back fifty years, you can bet.

I . . .

---

[4] Rabbit and deer in *Bambi,* children's story by Felix Salten.

Listen, we don't want to hear any more about Florida. We don't want to hear about Phoenix or Hilton Head or California's Central Valley. If our wetlands—our *vanishing* wetlands—are mentioned one more time, we'll scream. And the talk about condors and grizzlies and wolves is becoming too de trop. We had just managed to get whales out of our minds when those three showed up under the ice in Alaska. They even had *names*. Bone is the dead one, right? It's almost the twenty-first century! Those last condors are *pathetic*. Can't we just get this over with?

Aristotle said that all living things are ensouled and striving to participate in eternity.

Oh, I just bet he said that, you say. That doesn't sound like Aristotle. He was a humanist. We're all humanists here. This is the age of humanism. And it has been for a long time.

You are driving with a stranger in the car, and it is the stranger behind the wheel. In the back seat are your pals for many years now—DO WHAT YOU LIKE and his swilling sidekick, WHY NOT. A deer, or some emblematic animal, something from that myriad natural world you've come from that you now treat with such indifference and scorn—steps from the dimming woods and tentatively upon the highway. The stranger does not decelerate or brake, not yet, maybe not at all. The feeling is that whatever it is *will get out of the way*. Oh, it's a fine car you've got, a fine machine, and oddly you don't mind the stranger driving it, because in a way, everything has gotten too complicated, way, way out of your control. You've given the wheel to the masters, the managers, the comptrollers. Something is wrong, *maybe,* you feel a little sick, *actually,* but the car is luxurious and fast and you're *moving,* which is the most important thing by far.

Why make a fuss when you're so comfortable? Don't make a fuss, make a baby. Go out and get something to eat, build something. Make *another* baby. Babies are cute. Babies show you have faith in the future. Although faith is perhaps too strong a word. They're everywhere these days, in all the crowds and traffic jams, there are the babies too. You don't seem to associate them with the problems of population increase. They're just babies! And you've come to believe in them again. They're a lot more tangible than the afterlife, which, of course, you haven't believed in in ages. At least not for yourself. The afterlife now belongs to plastics and poisons. Yes, plastics and poisons will have a far more extensive afterlife than you, that's known. A disposable diaper, for example, which is all plastic and wood pulp—you like them for all those babies, so easy to use and toss—will take around four centuries to degrade. Almost all plastics do, centuries and centuries. In the sea, many marine animals die from ingesting or being entangled in discarded plastic. In the dumps, plastic squats on more than 25 percent of dump space. But your heart is disposed toward plastic. Someone, no doubt the plastics industry, told you it was convenient. This same industry is now looking into recycling in an attempt to get the critics of their nefarious, multifarious products off their backs. That should make you feel better, because *recycling* has become an honorable word, no longer merely the hobby of Volvo owners. The fact is that people in plastics are born obscurants. Recycling (practically impossible) won't solve the plastic glut, only reduction of production will, and the plastics industry isn't looking into that, you can be sure. Waste is not just the stuff you throw away, of course, it's the stuff you use to excess. With the exception of *hazardous waste,* which you do worry about from time to time, it's even thought you have a declining sense of emergency about the problem. Builders are building bigger houses because you want bigger. You're trading up. Utility companies are beginning to worry about your constantly rising consumption. Utility companies! You haven't entered a new age at all but one of upscale nihilism, deluxe nihilism.

In the summer, particularly in *the industrial Northeast,* you did get a little excited. The filth cut into your fun time. Dead stuff floating around. Sludge and bloody vials. Hygienic devices—appearing not quite so hygienic out of context—all coming in on the tide. The air smelled funny, too. You tolerate a great deal, but the summer of '88 was truly creepy. It was even thought for a moment that the environment would become a political issue. But it didn't. You didn't want it to be, preferring instead to continue in your politics of subsidizing and advancing avarice. The issues were the same as always—jobs, defense, the economy, maintaining and improving the standard of living in this greedy, selfish, expansionistic, industrialized society.

You're getting a little shrill here, you say.

You're pretty well off. You expect to be better off soon. You do. What does this mean? More software, more scampi, more square footage? You have created an ecological crisis. The earth is infinitely variable and alive, and you are killing it. It seems safer this way. But you are not safe. You want to find wholeness and happiness in a land increasingly damaged and betrayed, and you never will. More than material matters. You must change your ways.

What is this? *Sinners in the Hands of an Angry God?*

The ecological crisis cannot be resolved by politics. It cannot be solved by science or technology. It is a crisis caused by culture and character, and a deep change in personal consciousness is needed. Your fundamental attitudes toward the earth have become twisted. You have made only brutal contact with nature, you cannot comprehend its grace. You must change. Have few desires and simple pleasures. Honor nonhuman life. Control yourself, become more authentic. Live lightly upon the earth and treat it with respect. Redefine the word *progress* and dismiss the managers and masters. Grow inwardly and with knowledge become truly wiser. Make connections. Think differently, behave differently. For this is essentially a moral issue we face and moral decisions must be made.

A *moral issue!* Okay, this discussion is now toast. A *moral* issue . . . And who's this *we* now? Who are *you* is what I'd like to know. You're not me, anyway. I admit, someone's to blame and something should be done. But I've got to go. It's getting late. That's dusk out there. That is dusk, isn't it? It certainly doesn't look like any dawn I've ever seen. Well, take care.

STUDY AND DISCUSSION QUESTIONS

1. What effect does the title of this essay have on you? What does it lead you to expect the essay to be about?

2. How is this the "age of irony"? Note three examples of irony that Williams cites.

3. What is TED and why is it not used more?

4. How has tourism become a destructive industry?

5. Pick five or six of the words Williams italicizes and define them. What do they have in common?

6. Who are the "tiny masters" and what do they do?

7. What follows from defining people as "consumers"? Look up the word "consumer" and discuss its literal definition, including the root word it comes from, along with what the word has come to mean.

8. What are "managed trees"?

9. Look up "nihilism." What does Williams mean when she accuses us of "upscale nihilism"?

10. Characterize "me" and "you," as Williams presents them. What are the qualities and the politics of each?

11. Discuss Williams's change of approach, and perhaps of tone, in her last few paragraphs. How does she want her reader to feel by the end of the essay?

SUGGESTIONS FOR WRITING

1. Increasingly, what is people's relation to nature and the environment, according to Joy Williams? Do you agree or disagree with her thesis in this essay? Use examples from the essay in your discussion.

2. Why do you think Williams chooses to characterize environmental issues in a "you"/"me" fashion? That is, why does she suggest that you're either with nature or against it? Why not see people's positions as existing on a scale? Does Williams present the absolute distinction between these positions simply for the sake of rhetoric or does she see the

antagonism between them as central to the situation? Discuss, with specific reference to the essay.

3. Think about an environmental issue in your own experience—anything from whether or not to use air conditioners or disposable diapers to where and how to spend your vacation—and argue the issue, perhaps as a dialogue or debate.

AT WAR WITH THE PLANET

Barry Commoner

Barry Commoner was born in New York City in 1917 and educated at Columbia and Harvard Universities. He taught for many years at Washington University in St. Louis and now directs the Center for Biology of Natural Systems at Queens College in New York. A longtime critic of environmental policies, he ran for United States president on the Citizens Party ticket in 1980. Among his books are Science and Survival *(1966),* The Closing Circle *(1971),* The Poverty of Power *(1976), and* The Politics of Energy *(1979). The following is the first chapter of his 1990 book,* Making Peace with the Planet.

People live in two worlds. Like all living things, we inhabit the natural world, created over the Earth's 5-billion-year history by physical, chemical, and biological processes. The other world is our own creation: homes, cars, farms, factories, laboratories, food, clothing, books, paintings, music, poetry. We accept responsibility for events in our own world, but not for what occurs in the natural one. Its storms, droughts, and floods are "acts of God," free of human control and exempt from our responsibility.

Now, on a planetary scale, this division has been breached. With the appearance of a continent-sized hole in the Earth's protective ozone layer and the threat of global warming, even droughts, floods, and heat waves may become unwitting acts of man.

Like the Creation, the portending global events are cosmic: they change the relationship between the planet Earth and its star, the sun. The sun's powerful influence on the Earth is exerted by two forces: gravity and solar radiation. Gravity is a nearly steady force that fixes the planet's path around the sun. Solar radiation—largely visible and ultraviolet light—is a vast stream of energy that bathes the Earth's surface, fluctuating from day to night and season to season. Solar energy fuels the energy-requiring processes of life; it creates the planet's climate and governs the gradual evolution and the current behavior of its huge and varied population of living things. We have been tampering with this powerful force, unaware, like the Sorcerer's Apprentice, of the potentially disastrous consequences of our actions.

We have become accustomed to the now mundane image of the Earth as seen from the first expedition to the moon—a beautiful blue sphere decorated by swirls of fleecy clouds. It is a spectacularly natural object; at that distance, no overt signs of human activity are visible. But this image, now repeatedly thrust before us in photographs, posters, and advertisements, is misleading. Even if the global warming catastrophe never materializes, and the ozone hole remains an esoteric, polar phenomenon, already human activity has profoundly altered global conditions in ways that may not register on the camera. Everywhere in the world, there is now radioactivity that was not there before, the dangerous residue of nuclear explosions and the nuclear power industry; noxious fumes of smog blanket every major city; carcinogenic synthetic pesticides have been detected in mother's milk all over the world; great forests have been cut down, destroying ecological niches and their resident species.

As it reaches the Earth's surface, solar radiation is absorbed and sooner or later converted to heat. The amount of solar radiation that falls on the Earth and of the heat that escapes it depends not only on the daily turning of the Earth and the yearly change of the seasons, but also on the status of the thin gaseous envelope that surrounds the planet. One of the natural constituents of the outer layer of Earth's gaseous skin—the stratosphere—is ozone, a gas made of three oxygen atoms (ordinary oxygen is made of two atoms). Ozone absorbs much of the ultraviolet light radiated from the sun and thereby shields the Earth's surface from its destructive effects. Carbon dioxide and several other atmospheric components act like a valve: they are transparent to visible light but hold back invisible infrared radiation. The light that reaches the Earth's surface during the day is converted to heat that radiates outward in the form of infrared energy. Carbon dioxide, along with several other less prominent gases in the air, governs the Earth's temperature by holding back this outward radiation of heat energy. The greater the carbon dioxide content of the atmosphere, the higher the Earth's temperature. Glass has a similar effect, which causes the winter sun to warm a greenhouse; hence, the "greenhouse effect," the term commonly applied to global warming.

These global effects are not new; they have massively altered the condition of the Earth's surface over its long history. For example, because the early Earth lacked oxygen and therefore the ozone shield, it was once so heavily bathed in solar ultraviolet light as to limit living things to dark places;

intense ultraviolet radiation can kill living cells and induce cancer. Similarly, analyses of ice (and the entrapped air bubbles) deposited in the Antarctic over the last 150,000 years indicate that the Earth's temperature fluctuated considerably, closely paralleled by changes in the carbon dioxide level.[1]

Changes in the Earth's vegetation can be expected to influence the carbon dioxide content of the atmosphere. Thus, the massive growth of forests some 200 million to 300 million years ago took carbon dioxide out of the air, eventually converting its carbon into the deposits of coal, oil, and natural gas produced by geological transformation of the dying trees and plants. The huge deposits of fossil fuel, the product of millions of years of photosynthesis, remained untouched until coal, and later petroleum and natural gas, were mined and burned, releasing carbon dioxide into the atmosphere. The amounts of these fuels burned to provide human society with energy represent the carbon captured by photosynthesis over millions of years. So, by burning them, in the last 750 years we have returned carbon dioxide to the atmosphere thousands of times faster than the rate at which it was removed by the early tropical forests. The atmosphere's carbon dioxide content has increased by 20 percent since 1850, and there is good evidence that the Earth's average temperature has increased about 1 degree Fahrenheit since then. If nothing is done to change this trend, temperatures may rise by about 2.5 to 10 degrees more in the next fifty years. This is about the same change in temperature that marked the end of the last ice age about 15,000 years ago—an event that drastically altered the global habitat.[2] If the new, man-made warming occurs, there will be equally drastic changes, this time endangering a good deal of the world that people have fashioned for themselves. Polar ice will melt and the warmer oceans will expand, raising the sea level and flooding many cities; productive agricultural areas, such as the U.S. Midwest, may become deserts; the weather is likely to become more violent.

Regardless of how serious the resultant warming of the Earth turns out to be, and what, if anything, can be done to avoid its cataclysmic effects, it demonstrates a basic fact: that in the short span of its history, human society has exerted an effect on its planetary habitat that matches the size and impact of the natural processes that until now solely governed the global condition.

The ozone effect leads to the same conclusion. This problem arises not from the rapid man-made reversal of a natural process, but from the intrusion of an unnatural one on global chemistry. The chief culprits are the

---

[1] See article on global climate change by R. A. Haughton and G. M. Woodwell in *Scientific American*, April 1989. Numerous articles and reports on this subject have appeared recently; this one is particularly comprehensive. [Author's note]

[2] These data are summarized in the article cited above.[Author's note]

synthetic chemicals known as CFCs or chlorofluorocarbons. Like most of the petrochemical industry's products, CFCs do not occur in nature; they are synthesized for use in air conditioners, refrigerators, and spray cans, as solvents, and as a means of producing foam plastics. CFCs readily evaporate and are extraordinarily stable; escaping from confinement in a junked air conditioner or a discarded plastic cup, they migrate upward into the stratosphere. There they encounter ozone molecules, generated by the impact of solar radiation on ordinary oxygen molecules. A complex catalytic reaction ensues, in which each CFC molecule causes the destruction of numerous ozone molecules. This chemical process has already eaten a huge hole in the protective ozone layer over Antarctica, evidence that here, too, a process recently created by human society matches in scope a natural, protective component of the Earth's global envelope. Serious damage to people, wildlife, and crops is likely if the process continues: a large increase in skin cancer; eye problems; suppression of photosynthesis. Moreover, the CFCs act like carbon dioxide toward heat radiation and, along with methane and several minor gases, contribute to global warming.

Clearly, we need to understand the interaction between our two worlds: the natural ecosphere, the thin global skin of air, water, and soil and the plants and animals that live in it, and the man-made technosphere—powerful enough to deserve so grandiose a term. The technosphere has become sufficiently large and intense to alter the natural processes that govern the ecosphere. And in turn, the altered ecosphere threatens to flood our great cities, dry up our bountiful farms, contaminate our food and water, and poison our bodies—catastrophically diminishing our ability to provide for basic human needs. The human attack on the ecosphere has instigated an ecological counterattack. The two worlds are at war.

The two spheres in which we live are governed by very different laws. One of the basic laws of the ecosphere can be summed up as "Everything is connected to everything else." This expresses the fact that the ecosphere is an elaborate network, in which each component part is linked to many others. Thus, in an aquatic ecosystem a fish is not only a fish, the parent of other fish. It is also the producer of organic waste that nourishes microorganisms and ultimately aquatic plants; the consumer of oxygen produced photosynthetically by the plants; the habitat of parasites; the fish hawk's prey. The fish is not only, existentially, a fish, but also an element of this network, which defines its functions. Indeed, in the evolutionary sense, a good part of the network—the microorganisms and plants, for example—preceded the fish, which could establish itself only because it fitted properly into the preexisting system.[3]

[3] The informal "laws" that describe the behavior of ecosystems are elucidated in some detail in my earlier book *The Closing Circle* (New York: Knopf, 1971). [Author's note]

In the technosphere, the component parts—the thousands of different man-made objects—have a very different relation to their surroundings. A car, for example, imposes itself on the neighborhood rather than being defined by it; the same car is sold for use on the densely packed Los Angeles freeways or in a quiet country village. It is produced solely as a salable object—a commodity—with little regard for how well it fits into either sphere: the system of transportation or the environment. It is true, of course, that all cars must have a width that is accommodated by the traffic lanes, and must have proper brakes, lights, and horn, and so on. But as every resident of Los Angeles or New York knows, in recent years their crowded streets and highways have been afflicted with longer and longer limousines, designed to please the buyer and profit the producer, but hardly suitable to their habitat.

Defined so narrowly, it is no surprise that cars have properties that are hostile to their environment. After World War II, the American car was arbitrarily redefined as a larger, heavier object than its predecessors. That narrow decision dictated a more powerful engine; in turn, this required a higher engine compression ratio; in keeping with physical laws, the new engines ran hotter; at the elevated temperature, oxygen and nitrogen molecules in the cylinder air reacted chemically, producing nitrogen oxides; leaving the engine exhaust pipe, nitrogen oxides trigger the formation of the noxious smog that now envelops every major city. The new cars were successfully designed to carry people more comfortably at higher speed; but no attention was paid to an essential component in their habitat—the people themselves, and their requirement for clean, smog-free air.[4]

Even a part of the technosphere as close to nature as the farm suffers from the same sort of clash with the environment. As a man-made object, the farm is designed for the sole purpose of producing crops. Guided by that purpose, after World War II agronomists urged the increasingly heavy application of chemical nitrogen fertilizer. Yields rose, but not in proportion to the rate of fertilizer application; year by year, less and less of the applied fertilizer was taken up by the crop and progressively more drained through the soil into groundwater, in the form of nitrate that contaminated rivers, lakes, and water supplies. Nitrogen fertilizer is a commodity sold with the narrow purpose of raising yields and manufactured with the even narrower purpose of increasing the chemical industry's profits. When inorganic nitrogen fertilizer was introduced in the 1950s, little or no attention was paid to its ecological behavior in the soil/water system or to the harmful effects of elevated nitrate levels in drinking water.[5]

---

[4] Chap. 4 in *The Closing Circle* (cited above) is a detailed account of this issue. [Author's note]

[5] Chap. 5 in *The Closing Circle* is a detailed account of this issue. [Author's note]

The second law of ecology—"Everything has to go somewhere"—together with the first, expresses the fundamental importance of cycles in the ecosphere. In the aquatic ecosystem, for example, the participating chemical elements move through closed cyclical processes. As they respire, fish produce carbon dioxide, which in turn is absorbed by aquatic plants and is used, photosynthetically, to produce oxygen—which the fish respire. The fish excrete nitrogen-containing organic compounds in their waste; when the waste is metabolized by aquatic bacteria and molds, the organic nitrogen is converted to nitrate; this, in turn, is an essential nutrient for the aquatic algae; these, ingested by the fish, contribute to their organic waste, and the cycle is complete. The same sort of cycle operates in the soil: plants grow, nourished by carbon dioxide from the air and nitrate from the soil; eaten by animals, the crop sustains their metabolism; the animals excrete carbon dioxide to the air and organic compounds to the soil—where microorganisms convert them into compounds such as nitrate, which nourish the crop. In such a closed, circular system, there is no such thing as "waste"; everything that is produced in one part of the cycle "goes somewhere" and is used in a later step.

The technosphere, in contrast, is dominated by *linear* processes. Crops and the animals to which they are fed are eaten by people; their waste is flushed into the sewer system, altered in composition but not in amount at a treatment plant, and the residue is dumped into rivers or the ocean as waste—which upsets the natural aquatic ecosystem. Uranium is mined, processed into nuclear fuel which, in generating power, becomes highly radioactive waste that must be carefully guarded—ineffectually thus far—from contaminating the environment for thousands of years. The petrochemical industry converts ethylene prepared from petroleum and chlorine prepared from brine into vinyl chloride, a synthetic, carcinogenic chemical. This is manufactured into the plastic, polyvinyl chloride, which is made into tile, boots, and food wrapping; sooner or later discarded, these become trash that must be disposed of. When burned in an incinerator, the polyvinyl chloride produces carbon dioxide and dioxin; both are injected, as waste, into the ecosphere where the one contributes to global warming and the other to the risk of cancer. The energy sources that now power the technosphere are mostly fossil fuels, stores that, once depleted, will never be renewed. The end result of this linear process is air pollution and the threat of global warming. Thus, in the technosphere goods are converted, linearly, into waste: crops into sewage; uranium into radioactive residues; petroleum and chlorine into dioxin; fossil fuels into carbon dioxide. In the technosphere, the end of the line is always waste, an assault on the cyclical processes that sustain the ecosphere.

The third informal law of ecology is "Nature knows best." The ecosystem is consistent with itself; its numerous components are compatible with each other and with the whole. Such a harmonious structure is the outcome of a very long period of trial and error—the 5 billion years of biological evolution. The biological sector of the ecosphere—the biosphere—is composed of living things that have survived this test because of their finely tuned adaptation to the particular ecological niche that they occupy. Left to their own devices, ecosystems are conservative; the rate of evolution is very slow, and temporary changes, such as an overpopulation of rabbits, for example, are quickly readjusted by the wolves.

The same sort of conservative self-consistency governs the chemical process that occur in living cells. For example, there are severe constraints imposed on the variety of organic (carbon-containing) compounds that are the basic components of biochemical processes. As the physicist Walter Elsasser has pointed out, the weight of one molecule of each of the proteins that *could* be formed from the twenty different amino acids that comprise them would be greater than the weight of the known universe.[6] Obviously, living things are constrained to produce only a very small number of the *possible* proteins. Constraints are also exercised by the enzymes, present in all living things, that catalyze the degradation of organic compounds. It is an unbroken rule that for every organic compound produced by a living thing, there is somewhere in the ecosystem an enzyme capable of breaking it down. Organic compounds incapable of enzymatic degradation are not produced by living things. This arrangement is essential to the harmony of the ecosystem. If, for example, there were no enzymes that degrade cellulose, an otherwise very stable major constituent of plant cell walls, the Earth's surface would eventually become buried in it.

Similarly, certain molecular arrangements are shunned in the chemistry of life. Thus, very few chlorinated organic compounds, in which chlorine atoms are attached to carbons, occur in living things.[7] This suggests that the vast number of chlorinated organic compounds that are possible chemically (many of them now produced by the petrochemical industry), have been rejected in the long course of evolution as *biochemical* components. The absence of a particular substance from nature is often a sign that it is incompatible with the chemistry of life. For example, the fact that mercury plays no biochemical role and does not normally occur in living cells—and is lethal when it does—is readily explained by the fact that it poisons a number of essential enzymes. In the same way, many man-made chlorinated

---

[6] See his interesting work *Atom and Organism: A New Approach to Theoretical Biology* (Princeton, N.J.: Princeton University Press, 1966). [Author's note]

[7] See article by D. John Faulkner in *Tetrahedron Report* no. 28 (Elmsford, N.Y.: Pergamon Press, 1977). [Author's note]

organic compounds that do not occur in nature, such as DDT or dioxin, are very toxic.

In sum, the living things that comprise the biosphere, and their chemical composition, reflect constraints that severely limit their range of variation. The mermaid and the centaur are, after all, mythical animals; even the vaunted exploits of genetic engineering will never produce an elephant-sized mouse or a flying giraffe. In the same way, no natural biochemical system includes DDT, PCB, or dioxin. Unfortunately, these highly toxic substances are not mythical—a fact that sharply illuminates the difference between the ecosphere and the technosphere.

In contrast to the ecosphere, the technosphere is composed of objects and materials that reflect a rapid and relentless process of change and variation. In less than a century, transport has progressed from the horse-drawn carriage, through the Model T Ford, to the present array of annually modified cars and aircraft. In a not much longer period, writing instruments have evolved from the quill pen to the typewriter and now the word processor. Synthetic organic chemistry began innocuously enough about 150 years ago with the laboratory production of a common natural substance—urea—but soon departed from this imitative approach to produce a huge array of organic compounds never found in nature and, for that reason, often incompatible with the chemistry of life. Nylon, for example, unlike a natural polymer such as cellulose, is not biodegradable—that is, there is no enzyme in any known living organism that can break it down. As a result, when it is discarded into the ecosphere, nylon, like plastics generally, persists. Thus, oceanographers now find in their collecting nets bits of orange, blue, and white nylon and larger pieces jammed in the digestive tracts of dead turtles—the residue of nylon marine cordage. In the technosphere, nylon is a useful new commodity; in the ecosphere, nylon, untested by evolution, is a harmful intruder.

"Nature knows best" is shorthand for the view that during the several billion years in which they have evolved, living things have created a limited but self-consistent array of substances and reactions that are essential to life. The petrochemical industry has departed from these restrictions, producing thousands of new man-made substances. Since they are based on the same fundamental patterns of carbon chemistry as the natural compounds, the new ones are often readily accepted into biochemical processes. They therefore can play an insidious, destructive role in living things. For example, synthetic organic compounds may easily fit into the same reactive enzyme niches as natural molecules or may be accepted into the structure of DNA. However, they are sufficiently different from the natural compounds to then disrupt normal biochemistry, leading to mutations, cancer, and in many different ways to death. In effect, the petrochemical industry produces substances that—like the fantasies of human society invaded by look-alike but danger-ous aliens—cunningly enter the chemistry of life, and attack it.

Finally, it is useful to compare the ecosphere and the technosphere with respect to the consequences of failure. In the ecosphere, this is expressed by the idea that "there is no such thing as a free lunch," meaning that any distor-tion of an ecological cycle, or the intrusion of an incompatible component (such as a toxic chemical), leads unavoidably to harmful effects. At first glance, the technosphere appears to be extraordinarily free of mistakes—that is, a tech-nological process or product that failed not because of some unanticipated ac-cident but because it was unable to do what it was designed to do. Yet nearly every modern technology has grave faults, which appear not as a failure to ac-complish its designed purpose but as a serious impact on the environment. Cars usually run very well, but produce smog; power plants efficiently gener-ate electricity, but also emit dangerous pollutants; modern chemical farming is very productive but contaminates groundwater with nitrate and wildlife and people with pesticides. Even the spectacular nuclear disasters at Three Mile Is-land and Chernobyl were far less serious as technical failures than they were in their ecological effects. Regarded only as a failure in the plant's function, the accident at Chernobyl amounts to a serious but local fire that destroyed the plant. But the resultant release of radioactivity threatens many thousands of people all over Europe with cancer. In sum, there are numerous failures in the modern technosphere; but their effects are visited upon the ecosphere.

A free lunch is really a debt. In the technosphere, a debt is an acknowl-edged but unmet cost—the mortgage on a factory building, for example. Such a debt is tolerable because the technosphere is a system of production, which—if it functions properly—generates goods that represent wealth po-tentially capable of repaying the debt. In the technosphere, debts are repaid from within and, at least in theory, are always capable of being paid off, or, in some cases, canceled. In contrast, when the debts represented by environ-mental pollution are created by the technosphere and transferred to the eco-sphere, they are never canceled; damage is unavoidable. The debts represented by the radioactivity disseminated from the nuclear accident at Chernobyl, and by the toxic chemicals that enveloped Bhopal, have not been canceled. These debts were merely transferred to the victims, and are paid as they sicken and die.

Since they inhabit both worlds, people are caught in the clash between the ecosphere and the technosphere. What we call the "environmental cri-sis"—the array of critical unsolved problems ranging from local toxic dumps to the disruption of global climate—is a product of the drastic mismatch be-tween the cyclical, conservative, and self-consistent processes of the ecosphere and the linear, innovative, but ecologically disharmonious processes of the technosphere.

Since the environmental crisis has been generated by the war between the two worlds that human society occupies, it can be properly understood only in terms of their interplay. Of course, as in a conventional war, the issues can be simplified by taking sides: ignoring the interests of one combatant or the other. But this is done only at the cost of understanding. If the ecosphere is ignored, it is possible to define the environmental crisis solely in terms of the factors that govern the technosphere: production, prices, and profits, and the economic processes that mediate their interaction. Then, for example, one can concoct a scheme, as recently proposed by President Bush, in which factories are allotted the right to emit pollutants up to some acceptable level and, in a parody of the "free market," to buy and sell these rights.[8] But unlike the conventional marketplace, which deals in goods—things that serve a useful purpose—this scheme creates a marketplace in "bads"—things that are not only useless but often deadly. Apart from the issue of morality, it should be noted that such a scheme cannot operate unless the right to produce pollutants is exercised—hardly an inducement to eliminating them.

If the technosphere is ignored, the environmental crisis can be defined in purely ecological terms. Human beings are then seen as a peculiar species, unique among living things, that is doomed to destroy its own habitat. Thus simplified, the issue attracts simplistic solutions: reduce the number of people; limit their share of nature's resources; protect all other species from the human marauder by endowing them with "rights."

This approach raises a profound, unavoidable moral question: Is the ecosphere to be protected from destruction for its own sake, or to enhance the welfare of the human beings who depend on it? This leads to a further question regarding the term "welfare." Some environmental advocates believe that human welfare would be improved if people were less dependent on the artifacts of the technosphere and lived in closer harmony with their regional ecosystem—baking bread instead of buying it; walking or pedaling a bike instead of driving a car; living in small towns instead of cities. The thrust of this approach is to deny the value to society of, let us say, a woman who uses time saved by buying bread instead of baking it in order to work as a curator in an urban museum. Nor does it allow for the possibility that time- and labor-saving technologies can be compatible with the integrity of the environment. It assumes that the technosphere, no matter how designed, is necessarily an environmentally unacceptable means of giving people access to resources that are not part of their ecological niche. But as we shall see, this assumption is wrong; although nearly every aspect of the *current* technosphere is counter-ecological, technologies exist that—although little used thus far—*are* compatible with the ecosphere.

---

[8] This is contained in his new Clean Air Bill, as announced in June 1989. [Author's note]

The view that people are to be regarded *solely* as components of the ecosystem can lead to extreme and often inhumane proposals. Consider the global warming issue, for example. The humanist approach dictates a vigorous effort to halt the process because it is a massive threat to human society: flooded cities, drought-ridden agriculture, and prolonged heat waves. However, judged only in ecological terms, global warming can be regarded merely as a change in the structure of the global ecosystem similar to the warming that accompanied the last postglacial period, albeit more rapid. Viewed in this way, there is no more reason to oppose global warming than to be unhappy about the last ice age and the rise in global temperature that ended it. At its farthest reach, this nonhumanist position becomes antihumanist, as exemplified in an article in the publication of a group called Earth First!, which favored the spread of AIDS as a means of reducing the human population without threatening other animal species.[9] Of course, at the other extreme is the potentially suicidal view that the enormous value of modern production technology to human society justifies whatever damage to the ecosphere it entails.

The ambiguity created by the dual habitat in which we live has led to a very wide range of responses. The extreme interpretations of the relationship between the two spheres that human society occupies—and a sometimes bewildering array of intermediate positions—is compelling evidence that we have not yet understood how the two systems have come into conflict and, as a result, are unable as yet to resolve that conflict.

This book is an effort to analyze the war between the ecosphere and the technosphere, written with the conviction that understanding it—as distinct from reacting to it—is the only path to peace. It is less a lament over the war's numerous casualties than an inquiry into how future casualties can be prevented. It is not so much a battle cry for one side or the other, as a design for negotiating an end to this suicidal war—for making peace with the planet.

STUDY AND DISCUSSION QUESTIONS

1. What are the two worlds people live in and how has their relationship changed in the twentieth century?

2. Discuss Commoner's allusion to the Sorcerer's Apprentice. What point is he trying to make with this allusion?

3. Summarize Commoner's discussion of the nature and function of ozone. What keeps the ozone layer functioning? What two main

---

[9] See *Utne Reader,* Dec. 1987. [Author's note]

changes have occurred in the ozone layer since 1850? How have these changes affected it and what will the consequences be?

4. Find the thesis paragraph of "At War with the Planet." What is Commoner's thesis in this essay? Why does he place his thesis paragraph where he does, instead of at the beginning of the essay where one might expect it to be?

5. What are the four basic laws of the ecosphere?

6. Give two examples of the technosphere in operation.

7. Define "waste" in the ecosphere and in the technosphere.

8. Compare the process and rate of change and variation in the ecosphere and in the technosphere.

9. How is a free lunch "really a debt"?

10. What does Commoner say has produced the environmental crisis?

11. Give some examples of the extreme effects of simplistic solutions to environmental problems.

SUGGESTIONS FOR WRITING

1. Commoner suggests that, though "current technology is counterecological, technologies exist that—although little used thus far—are compatible with the ecosphere." Speculate on what some of those technologies might be.

2. Compare/contrast the very different approaches to writing taken by Commoner and by Joy Williams in "Save the Whales, Screw the Shrimp." How would you describe each mode of writing? What do the two writers have in common? How do they differ? Do you find one or the other approach more amenable? Why?

3. Imagine that you desire intensely to do your part to destroy the ecosphere. Describe in detail a day in which you would work very hard to do so. Step by step, take us through such a day with you.

MAYHEM IN THE INDUSTRIAL PARADISE

Wendell Berry

Wendell Berry was born in Kentucky in 1934 and has spent most of his life there, teaching at the University of Kentucky, writing, and farming. He has published numerous novels, short story collections, books of essays, and volumes of poetry. The following is from A Continuous Harmony: Essays Cultural and Agricultural *(1972).*

. . . they have made my pleasant field a desolate wilderness . . .

Jeremiah 12:10

I have just spent two days flying over the coal fields of both eastern and western Kentucky, looking at the works of the strip miners. Several times before, I had driven and walked to look at strip mines, mainly in the eastern part of the state, but those earlier, ground-level experiences did not prepare me at all for what I saw from the air. In scale and desolation—and, I am afraid, in duration—this industrial vandalism can be compared only with the desert badlands of the West. The damage has no human scale. It is a geologic upheaval. In some eastern Kentucky counties, for mile after mile after mile, the land has been literally hacked to pieces. Whole mountain tops have been torn off and cast into the valleys. And the ruin of human life and possibility is commensurate with the ruin of the land. It is a scene from the Book of Revelation.[1] It is a domestic Vietnam.

So far as I know, there are only two philosophies of land use. One holds that the earth is the Lord's, or it holds that the earth belongs to those yet to be born as well as to those now living. The present owners, according to this view, only have the land in trust, both for all the living who are dependent on it now, and for the unborn who will be dependent on it in time to come. The model of this sort of use is a good farm—a farm that, by the return of wastes and by other safeguards, preserves the land in production without diminishing its ability to produce. The standard of this sort of land use is fertility, which preserves the interest of the future.

---

[1] Last book of the New Testament.

The other philosophy is that of exploitation, which holds that the interest of the present owner is the only interest to be considered. The standard, according to this view, is profit, and it is assumed that whatever is profitable is good. The most fanatical believers in the rule of profit are the strip miners. The earth, these people would have us believe, is not the Lord's, nor do the unborn have any share in it. It belongs, instead, to rich organizations with names like Peabody, Kentucky River Coal, Elkhorn Coal, National Steel, Bethlehem Steel, Occidental Petroleum, The Berwind Corporation, Tennessee Valley Authority, Chesapeake & Ohio, Ford Motor Company, and many others. And the earth, they would say, is theirs not just for a time, but forever, and in proof of their claim they do not hesitate to destroy it forever—that is, if it is profitable to do so, and earth-destruction has so far been exceedingly profitable to these organizations.

The gospel of the strip miners is the "broad form deed," under which vast acreages of coal rights were bought up for as little as twenty-five and fifty cents an acre before modern strip-mine technology ever had been conceived. The broad form deed holds that the coal may be taken out "in any and every manner that may be deemed necessary or convenient for mining. . . . " Kentucky is one of the few coal states that still honor the broad form deed. In Kentucky, under the sanction of this deed, the strip miners continue to ravage other people's private property. They have overturned or covered up thousands of acres of farm and forest land; they have destroyed the homes and the burial grounds of the people; they have polluted thousands of miles of streams with silt and mine acid; they have cast the overburden of the mines into the water courses and into the public roads. Their limits are technological, not moral. They have made it plain that they will stop at nothing to secure the profit, which is their only motive. And in Kentucky they have been aided and abetted at every turn by lawmakers, judges, and other public officials who are too cowardly or too greedy to act in the interest of those they are sworn to protect. Though the violations of the inadequate strip-mine regulations passed by the legislature have been numerous and well publicized, the regulations have been weakly enforced.

If the model of good land use is to be found in a good farm, then it is a strange sort of farming indeed that is practiced by these strip miners, whose herds are not cattle eating grass, but machines devouring the earth. That sounds fantastical, but then strip mining is an industry *based* upon fantasy. It proceeds upon the assumption that there is no law of gravity, that no heavy rains will fall, that water and mud and rock will not move downhill, that money is as fertile as topsoil, that the wealthy do not ultimately share the same dependences and the same fate as the poor, that the oppressed do not turn against their oppressors—that, in other words, there are no natural or moral or social consequences. Such are the luxuries that our society affords to the warlords of the exploitive industries.

People who live nearer to the results of strip mining know better. Those whose homes and belongings have been destroyed, or who live beneath the spoil banks, or who inhabit the flood plains of mutilated streams and rivers, or who have been driven into ruin and exile—and there are now many thousands of them—they know that the costs are inconceivably greater than any shown on coal-company ledgers, and they are keeping their own accounts. They know that the figment of legality that sanctions strip mining is contrary to the laws of nature and of morality and of history. And they know that in such a contradiction is the seed of social catastrophe.

The most vicious fantasy of all is the endlessly publicized notion that the net profit of the coal companies somehow represents the net profit of the whole society. Historically, however, the enrichment of the coal interests in Kentucky has always involved the impoverishment of the people of the mining regions. And of all methods of mining, strip mining is the most enriching to the rich and the most impoverishing to the poor; it has fewer employees and more victims. The net profit is net only to the coal companies, only on the basis of an annual accounting. The corporate profit is reckoned on so short a term. But the public expenditure that supports this private profit is long-term; the end of it is not now foreseeable. By the time all the reclaimable mined lands are reclaimed, and all the social and environmental damages accounted for, strip mining will be found to have been the most extravagantly subsidized adventure ever undertaken.

An estimate of the public meaning of strip-mine profits may be made from the following sentences by James Branscome in the New York *Times* of December 12, 1971: "The Corps of Engineers has estimated . . . that it would cost the public $26-million to restore the extensively strip-mined Coal River watershed in West Virginia. This is an amount approximately equal to the private profit taken by the mining companies from the watershed." But even this may be too limited an accounting. It does not consider the environmental damage, or the property damage, that may have occurred outside the boundaries of the immediate watershed between the opening of the coal seam and the completion of reclamation. It does not attempt to compute the cost of what may have been the permanent degradation of the appearance and the fertility of the land. Nor does it consider the economic consequences of the social upheaval that must always accompany an upheaval of the environment. There is, then, every reason to believe that the large net profit of a strip-mine company will prove to be a large net loss to society.

This, as all Kentuckians should be aware, is largely the responsibility of absentee owners. Of the thirty-three largest owners of mineral rights in the Kentucky coal fields, as recently listed by the *Courier-Journal*, only two are based in the state. But even those owners who live in the state are absentee owners in the strict sense of the term: they do not live with the consequences of what they do. As exploitive industrialists have done from the beginning, they live apart, in enclaves of the well-to-do, where they are neither offended nor immediately threatened by the ugliness and the dangers that they so willingly impose upon others. It is safe, I think, to say that not many coal-company executives and stockholders are living on the slopes beneath the spoil banks of their mines; not many of them have had their timber uprooted and their farms buried by avalanches of overburden; not many of them have had their water supply polluted by mine acid, or had their houses torn from the foundations by man-made landslides; not many of them see from their doorsteps the death of the land of their forefathers and the wreckage of their own birthright; not many of them see in the faces of their wives and children the want and the grief and the despair with which the local people subsidize the profits of strip mining. On the contrary, the worries of the coal companies are limited strictly to coal. When the coal is gone they do not care what is left. The inescapable conclusion is that Kentucky has been made a colony of the coal companies, who practice here a mercantilism as heartless and greedy as any in history.

In this new year[2] the state's lawmakers have once again assembled in Frankfort. Again they have the opportunity to put a stop to this awful destruction, and to assure to the state the benefits of its own wealth, and to give to the people of the coal fields the same protections of the law that are enjoyed by people everywhere else. If the men in power will do these things that are so clearly right and just, they will earn the gratitude of the living and of the unborn. If they will not do them, they will be infamous, and will be unworthy of the respect of any honest citizen.[3]

Remembering the new deserts of this once bountiful and beautiful land, my mind has gone back repeatedly to those Bible passages that are haunted by the memory of good land laid waste, and by fear of the human suffering that such destruction has always caused. Our own time has come to be haunted by the same thoughts, the same sense of a fertile homeland held in the contempt of greed, sold out, and destroyed. Jeremiah[4] would find this evil of ours bitterly familiar:

> I brought you into a fruitful land
> to enjoy its fruit and the goodness of it;
> but when you entered upon it you defiled it
> and made the home I gave you loathsome.

---

[2] 1972. [Author's note]

[3] They did not do them, and they are as unworthy of respect as I said they would be. [Author's note]

[4] Old Testament prophet.

The damages of strip mining are justified in the name of electrical power. We need electrical power, the argument goes, to run our factories, to heat and light and air-condition our homes, to run our household appliances, our TV sets, our children's toys, and our mechanical toothbrushes. And we must have more and more electricity because we are going to have more and more gadgets that will make us more and more comfortable. This, of course, is the reasoning of a man eating himself to death. We have to begin to distinguish between the uses that are necessary and those that are frivolous. Though it is the last remedy that would occur to a glutton or a coal company, we must cut down on our consumption—that is, our destruction—of the essential energies of our planet. We must use these energies less and with much greater care. We must see the difference between the necessity of warmth in winter and the luxury of air conditioning in the summer, between light to read or work by and those "security lights" with which we are attempting to light the whole outdoors, between an electric sewing machine and an electric toothbrush. Immediate comfort, we must say to the glutton, is no guarantee of a long life; too much now is, rather, a guarantee of too little later on. Our comfort will be paid for by someone else's distress. "We dig coal to light your tree," said a recent advertisement of the coal industry. That, we must realize, is not a Christmas greeting, but a warning of our implication in an immitigable evil.

In the name of Paradise, Kentucky, and in its desecrations by the strip miners, there is no shallow irony. It was named Paradise because, like all of Kentucky in the early days, it was recognized as a garden, fertile and abounding and lovely; some pioneer saw that it was good. ("Heaven," said one of the frontier preachers, "is a Kentucky of a place.") But the strip miners have harrowed Paradise, as they would harrow heaven itself were they to find coal there. Where the little town once stood in the shade of its trees by the riverbank, there is now a blackened desert. We have despised our greatest gift, the inheritance of a fruitful land. And for such despite—for the destruction of Paradise—there will be hell to pay.

STUDY AND DISCUSSION QUESTIONS

1. Why do you think Wendell Berry begins with a biblical quote? Look up Jeremiah 12:10 and discuss the context of the verse Berry quotes.

2. What are the two philosophies of land use Berry mentions?

3. What is the "broad form deed"?

4. Mention some fantasies that support the continued practice of strip mining.

5. What does Berry say about social class and social responsibility?

6. "The damages of strip mining are justified in the name of electrical power," writes Berry. Why do we need so much electric power? How, specifically, could we use less?

SUGGESTIONS FOR WRITING

1. Find some paintings or photographs of strip mined countryside and describe in your own words what you see.
2. Note all the biblical references in "Mayhem in the Industrial Paradise." Discuss how Berry uses the biblical story from Jeremiah as an extended metaphor in his argument about the destructive consequences of strip mining.

WHEN PEOPLE OF COLOR ARE AN ENDANGERED SPECIES

Elizabeth Martinez

Elizabeth Martinez (b. 1925) has worked as a United Nations researcher, an editor at Simon & Schuster, a book review editor for the Nation magazine, and the director of the New York City office of the Student Nonviolent Coordinating Committee. She founded El Grito del Norte, a Chicano newspaper, as well as the Chicano Communications Center, both in New Mexico. Among her books are Letters from Mississippi (1965), under the name Elizabeth Sutherland, and Four Hundred Fifty Years of Chicano History (1976). She teaches ethnic studies at California State University at San Francisco. The following essay appeared in Z magazine in 1991.

The San Jose parish church in Albuquerque, New Mexico, was full last November 20 as neighborhood people sat waiting to hear what the city councilors, county commissioners, and other officials would say.

The residents of Mountainview, a low-income, mostly Chicano neighborhood, were tired of having poisonous chemicals, bad smells, and pollution dumped on them. The Gulf War[1] hadn't started yet, but they were already angry at the military for being the most likely source of poisons in their drinking water for the past 25 years. Also, the city had put a smelly sewage plant within a mile of their homes; now it was proposing to put a garbage transfer station (under a nicer name) in their midst. Tonight they would speak out.

Facing the people, city officials in jackets and ties sat next to a table covered by a white cloth. The mayor of Albuquerque had been invited but did not come, with no regrets or reason given. A hand-lettered sign on the table said "Mayor Louis Saavedra" and behind it, in the mayor's absence, sat a large, neatly trussed turkey. The turkey was very bare, very white, very visible.

As he rose to speak, the director of Albuquerque's Solid Waste Management Department looked unhappy. "It's too bad this kind of disrespect . . ." he told the crowd. But nobody moved the turkey; it just sat there through the entire meeting.

Mountainview's people had seen their very lives treated with disrespect—by the military, industry, and government—for years. One resident watched her six-month-old son almost die in her arms after drinking formula made with tap water. The day I arrived last winter, the area had to be evacuated because of a chlorine leak. But here and elsewhere in the United States, Chicanos alongside African Americans and Native Americans have been mounting strong campaigns to challenge all those enemy forces—the military, industry, and government. Sometimes they have also confronted ignorance, indifference, and opposition from self-declared environmentalists.

Exposing Environmental Racism

It's a contemporary struggle with very old roots. For decades radioactive uranium tailings, lead and chlorine poisoning, asbestos, and pesticides have sickened and killed untold numbers of Latinos, African Americans, Native Americans, and other people of color. Yet the concept of environmental racism went unrecognized. Then, in 1982, North Carolina decided to put a PCB disposal site only 15 feet above the water table (instead of the 50 feet generally required) in Warren County—whose residents were 60 percent black and 4 percent Native American. A series of protests, with over 500 people arrested, failed to stop the PCB dump. They did arouse widespread concern.

---

[1] 1991 war against Iraq by United States-led coalition, following the Iraqi invasion of Kuwait.

Soon after, a U.S. General Accounting Office survey confirmed the co-incidence of hazardous-waste landfills and poor black communities in the southeastern U.S. In 1987 a much broader study, "Toxic Wastes and Race in the United States," was prepared by the United Church of Christ's Commission on Racial Justice under Dr. Ben Chavis, Jr. After examining 25 cities the report found "a striking relationship" between where commercial hazardous wastes were dumped and race. Class also played an important role, but "race still proved to be more significant." Hair-raising examples abounded:

- The nation's biggest hazardous-waste landfill, which serves 45 states plus several foreign countries, is located in Emelle, Alabama (Sumter County)—78.9 percent black.
- The predominantly African American and Latino South Side of Chicago has the greatest concentration of hazardous waste sites in the nation.
- Los Angeles County, about 30 percent Latino, is home to 14 (or 34 percent) of all of California's commercial hazardous waste facilities and 233 (or 25 percent) of the state's uncontrolled waste sites.
- In Houston, Texas, six of the eight municipal incinerators and all five municipal landfills are located in predominantly African American neighborhoods.

And that is not to mention the poisoning of Navajo Indians by uranium mining, or the 300,000 cases of pesticide-related illness among Latinos or the widespread pollution of Puerto Rico or the massive amount of radiation illness in numerous Pacific islands. Or the fact that women are the most frequent victims of all contamination.

How to explain these findings? The realities of racism and class oppression are one clear reason. People of color have historically been drawn into the worst jobs in agribusiness and heavy industry; they often end up living in areas of heavy pollution. Further, as Rev. Leon White, a prime organizer of the Warren County protests, said: "As long as there are poor and minority areas to dump on, corporate America won't be serious about finding alternatives to the way toxic materials are produced and managed." Another reason: areas where residents do not appear to have a high degree of political clout are often preferred for hazardous or uncontrolled waste facilities.

Then we have economic blackmail. As Mike Guerrero and Louis Head of the SouthWest Organizing Project have written, "Depressed communities are sold the notion that hazardous waste landfills and deadly industries offer hope of employment and economic development. . . . When industry is challenged on its polluting practices, the community is threatened with plant shutdowns and job cutbacks to pay for pollution control and clean-up."

As for government regulators such as the Environmental Protection Agency (EPA), the agency "has never acknowledged that many environmental problems adversely affect minority groups to a much greater extent than the population at large," according to EPA staff attorneys Alex Varela and Arthur Ray. The two lawyers went on to point out in a Howard University student newspaper article that endangered species such as the blunt-nose leopard lizard are provided more pesticide protection under federal law than farmworkers, 95 percent of whom are Latino and black.

The deadly effects of environmental racism were further exposed at the "Inter-Denominational Hearings on Toxics in Minority Communities," held September 29–30, 1989, in Albuquerque, New Mexico. Co-sponsored by the SouthWest Organizing Project and the National Council of Churches' Eco-Justice Task Force, the high point of the hearings came when a dozen New Mexicans and borderland Mexicans presented testimony to a panel of religious leaders. One after the other, they told personal stories of how government and industry had poisoned their workplaces and communities.

The most unforgettable testimony came from Virginia Candelaria, one of many workers exposed to poisonous solvents and wastes in Albuquerque's General Telephone and Electronics (GTE) plant. Candelaria suffered severe damage to her central nervous system after nine years of cleaning circuit boards. Other women had children with birth defects, and eventually 465 workers filed suit. When asked if GTE had changed the process, Candelaria had difficulty speaking: her attorney replied for her, "Most of the dangerous processes, most of the dangerous chemicals, have been moved to Juarez, Mexico. There is a plant across the border now."

Observers at the hearings were taken on tours of areas around Albuquerque where toxins have turned up, including neighborhoods with paint factories, gas refineries, sewage treatment centers, and a dog food factory where unused animal parts were heaped outdoors to rot. It became nauseously evident that communities inhabited by people of color are targeted for toxin-producing industries and facilities which wouldn't be allowed in other neighborhoods. For people of color, then, environmental issues are issues of social, economic, and racial justice. It's time to dump the myth that people of color never care about the environment because they are too concerned with mere survival. If anything, their survival is an environmental issue.

Fighting Back

Such is the perspective of the SouthWest Organizing Project (SWOP) in Albuquerque, which has won some precedent-setting victories against environmental racism as practiced by industry and the military. SWOP's home state, New Mexico, presents a unique combination of circumstances and offers some key lessons for environmental as well as community organizers. This is a state where the cycle of nuclear energy runs its full course, from uranium mining to radioactive waste. It is a state whose economy remains overwhelmingly dependent on the federal government, especially the military. It is a state with a history of Chicano-Indian resistance to Anglo incursion that goes back to 1847. A state where people know how to call a turkey a turkey.

SWOP became nationally known when it took on ten major U.S. environmentalist organizations in March 1990. It sent them a sharply critical letter signed by over 100 community activists charging "a clear lack of accountability . . . toward Third World communities." The criticisms ranged from the Sierra Club and the Wilderness Society supporting the creation of a tourist-attracting national monument on sacred Native American land, to the almost total lack of people of color in the "Big Ten's" decision-making positions.

Since then nine of the Big Ten environmental organizations have committed themselves to participating in dialogue. A "National Minority Environmental Leadership Summit" meeting has been convened by the United Church of Christ's Commission for Racial Justice for October 1991 in Washington, D.C. This historic gathering, which the SWOP letter helped stimulate, will aim to create a national agenda focused on race, poverty, and the environment, with a view to diversifying the policies of mainline environmental organizations.

Also in 1990 SWOP organized the Southwest Network for Environmental and Economic Justice to link up people—primarily of color—active in struggles for environmental and economic rights. Two months after the letter to the Big Ten, the Network wrote to ten not-so-big environmental organizations such as Greenpeace and the National Toxics Campaign. This missive generated a lot of what SWOP staffer Louis Head has called "positive consternation."

The letter expressed gratitude to the groups for past support to communities of color, and informed them about SWOP's views and activities. It then called on them to "set an example and take responsibility to assure that the environmental movement is multi-racial, and that it work side by side with other movements for civil and human rights." For example, within a year, people of color should compose 50 percent of the staff and board of directors of these groups.

Some of those addressed have since made efforts to multi-nationalize; one group put its first African-American on its board. Others have moved away from the concept of "advocacy for" to "advocacy with" communities of color. Even where a group reacted negatively to the strong but not unfriendly letter, controversy itself seems useful. In general, the letter stimulated dialogue *within* the groups, and that will prove healthy.

Meanwhile, the Network has been growing steadily and meeting regularly. Today it includes representatives of over 50 organizations in eight states and Indian Nations. Its goals include compensation for victims of toxic poisoning; no transfer of polluting industry to the Mexican border region; and a ban on the export of hazardous wastes to the Third World.

The First Victory

How has all this been done, and what tactics have proved useful? The basic answer is SWOP's persistent grassroots organizing and creative strategy. Born in 1981, it is a multiracial, multi-issue community organization working "to empower the disenfranchised in the Southwest to realize social, racial, and economic justice." Its founders had worked together previously on racism and police abuse, and include Richard Moore—a community activist of Puerto Rican background who goes back to the Chicano movement and the Black Berets[2] of the 1960s. Today he and Jean Gauna co-direct SWOP, which is funded primarily by church groups and has a mostly Latino staff.

SWOP became involved with fighting pollution when it began organizing in the Sawmill barrio of Albuquerque in 1984 and heard families complain of health problems they attributed to a particle-board company in the area. Ponderosa Products Inc. was generating polluted groundwater, sawdust flying through the air constantly, and intolerable noise. In the struggle that followed, and the victory it produced, we can see key aspects of SWOP's general strategy.

A first, basic goal was to demystify policymaking. "Have you ever wondered how decisions are made as to which streets get paved, how our community is zoned, or who receives loans to purchase homes? Who plans the way our neighborhood is developed? Everyone, It Seems, Makes Plans For Our Community Except Sawmill Area Residents!" Those were the headlines—in both English and Spanish—on just one of many SWOP leaflets. They set the tone for a process that included door-to-door surveys of residents' complaints; community meetings to inform residents about the technical and legal aspects of a struggle; setting up a neighborhood organization (in this case, the Sawmill Advisory Council); and voter registration so that residents could hold elected officials accountable.

Ponderosa Products finally agreed to clean up the groundwater. But then the new Republican governor, Garrey Carruthers, took office and two weeks

---

[2] Perhaps the Black Panthers, a militant activist group whose members wore black berets.

later the agreements were rescinded. Another long round of struggle began, in which SWOP fought to prevent the Ponderosa clean-up from being negotiated behind closed doors—one of its key principles.

Along with more community organizing and petitions as well as winning support from some Chicano legislators, SWOP worked to educate news reporters by taking them on tours through the barrio—a tactic that helped generate favorable treatment by the mass media. These tours have been given not only to the press but also visiting church people, academics, government officials, community activists, and political figures.

In 1987 Ponderosa finally signed the Groundwater Reclamation Plan to pump out bad water and reduce noise emission (the sawdust problem is not totally resolved). The company has spent $3 million thus far on cleanup. That plan stands as the first urban cleanup agreement between industry, government, and the community in New Mexico—and probably in the whole Southwest.

Taking On The Generals

Like Sawmill, the Mountainview-San Jose area of Albuquerque has also been a major focus of SWOP activism. For years its problem of bad well water remained a mystery. Slowly but surely the finger pointed increasingly at Kirtland Air Force Base as the source of nitrate/nitroglycerin contamination. Again SWOP helped set up a local body, the Mountainview Advisory Council, in 1987; again it surveyed, educated, conducted tours. Above all, SWOP helped combat the military's efforts to exclude affected residents from the investigation of Kirtland. As usual the generals preferred to investigate themselves.

Every time one Commanding Officer seemed to agree to let residents participate, he was replaced by a new face; at least five COs have come and gone. Finally Kirtland signed a contract to allow community participation in the investigation, as did the federal EPA, the state Environment Improvement Division (EID), and the Mountainview Advisory Council. SWOP refrained from signing until February 22, 1991, in order to assure Kirtland's agreement on a large public ceremony to formalize the agreement. Again, the principle: no closed doors, maximum information.

"Keep Your Stinking Jobs!"

Last June, the struggle against environmental racism was linked with a labor struggle when 70 workers went on strike at the Montana de Fibra fiberboard plant in Las Vegas, N.M. The workers, routinely exposed to dangerous levels of formaldehyde and other poisonous chemicals, demanded better wages and working conditions. Father Bill Sanchez, a courageous local priest, called SWOP for help and it came with information, experience, and bodies. But it stayed to learn.

Given an ultimatum by the company to return to work, the Las Vegas strikers refused: "We don't want the damn jobs back." In one of the poorest areas of a very poor state, where few jobs pay the Montana de Fibra top salary of $6 an hour, this refusal was extraordinary. Richard Moore of SWOP explains the workers' response by the fact that they had become too hip about the deadly chemicals which they saw being dumped behind the factory and contaminating the water. "They were not the same people as when they went on strike," he said. Under the most difficult conditions, they stood up to economic blackmail.

At this writing, many have continued struggling: 23 workers and their relatives have become SWOP members. One unusual victory has been won. When the striking workers were refused unemployment benefits, they sued with SWOP's help—and finally won their benefits.

SWOP is fully aware that "we cannot just tell people to forget about jobs, when New Mexico needs jobs more than anything else," Moore affirmed. "That's why we have to be pro-active, not just reactive. We can't just be denouncing industry." One of the current targets in this struggle is a federal Urban Development Action Grant (UDAG) agreement, the largest made in the U.S. to date. It gave $10 million plus millions in parking, catering, and other "incentives" to Albuquerque to build a luxury hotel and office tower. In return, 1,582 jobs were to be created—50 percent going to minorities, 51 percent to people from "pockets of poverty" and 75 percent to people of low-to-moderate income. The developer, BetaWest Properties, isn't fully complying with those conditions and SWOP now has a full-time staff person on BetaWest. "A climate has been created in this city where people will call industry on its shit," Richard Moore commented in a recent interview.

"The only reason we've had success, *when* we've had it, is our multi-issue approach," he added. "This may not be traditional environmentalism, but it's the kind that has concerned people of color for centuries. Some say there is more awareness now among people of color about environmental problems. But there was plenty before. In 1968, 1970, we marched—Brown Berets[3] and Black Berets, with Mexican flags flying—against that sewage plant in Mountain View. In Kansas City, in the 1960s and 1970s, Brown Berets marched against a slaughterhouse. So it is not new for Latinos to be concerned about the environment."

---

[3] Chicano activist organization.

Two Different Views of Environmental Issues

"Environmentalists didn't oppose those things because they didn't see them as environmental issues. We have always known them to be race and class issues. The siting of toxic wastes is a race issue, period. The problem is that we perceive environmental issues as one thing and they perceive them as another. Those people may not perceive that sewage plant as an environmental problem, but they don't live there . . . Most environmentalists have no contact with the workers in a plant that's polluting, or in a community where people live with the problem. We do."

"The organizing principle of SWOP is to demystify what 'environment' means," Moore said. "At any community meeting, just ask, 'How many people here have lived near a chemical plant?—please stand up.' Then ask, 'How many have lived near a slaughterhouse?' Then, 'How many have lived near a sewage plant?' And pretty soon everybody in the room will be standing. We are getting past the perception of environmentalism as a middle-class, white movement that excludes the human factor."

Jean Gauna pointed out, "They perceive environmentalism as conservation, but for us it's the survival of our communities. In New Mexico, environmentalists are like new colonizers. They love the culture and hate the people. They will patronize Don Benito[4] to death but they'll never give control to the Don Benitos."

Paternalistic exclusion by advocacy organizations of the people for whom they supposedly advocate has plagued other parts of America, too. In Lima, Peru, the Indigenous Peoples' Organizations helps coordinate the activities of groups representing a total of 1.2 million Indians across South America. This body released a pointed statement to environmentalists in 1989. It said, first, that the environmental community has typically been concerned about the preservation of tropical forests, their plant and animal inhabitants, while showing little interest in their human inhabitants as also being part of that biosphere. Second, environmentalists have failed to recognize that recognition of indigenous land claims and "models for living" is the best way to defend the Amazonian biosphere. Third, that the indigenous people want to represent themselves directly in all negotiations.

In its work SWOP has recognized the primacy of Native American land rights, which have often been overlooked by Chicano activists pressing the land claims of their own people. This is a whole arena of discussion in itself; here, we will note that SWOP has worked closely with the Isleta Pueblo near

---

[4] Fictitious character who represents the indigenous people of New Mexico.

Albuquerque on toxic waste problems and has supported numerous Indian demands on other issues. Relations with African Americans have been positive, although limited by the fact that in Albuquerque this community tends to be geographically dispersed and middle-class rather than low-income. SWOP has an international program formulated over the years in ways ranging from adoption of a Nicaraguan child-development center to activism against U.S. policy in the Persian Gulf.

Opposing The War

Opposing the Gulf War was a SWOP priority. This work includes working in coalitions to organize or support demonstrations, rallies, teach-ins, TV panel discussions, high school student walkouts, and other general anti-war activities. In its outreach SWOP has focused on Chicanos, African Americans, and other people of color. For such outreach to be successful—for the anti-war movement in general to grow—SWOP believes it is critical to show the links between the war and the staggering domestic problems facing those groups and other low-income people.

In this connection, SWOP brings a perspective to bear from its work against environmental racism. People of color (often women) now working in high-tech industry face the possibility of being poisoned by chemicals they use in producing equipment for the military. Because such equipment is manufactured in parts for future assembly, workers often do not know what they are actually making. This and other problems make it difficult to establish the links. But SWOP knows of at least one worker at Motorola in Albuquerque who was exposed during the last few years to fumes from solvents used in producing weapons components. In another case, a woman worker at Honeywell in Albuquerque was given a poisonous fluid to clean computer chip boards for the instrument panels of fighter planes. That kind of environmentalism could rock some big boats.

In early December 1990, the Mountainview Advisory Council met to screen a video of that November 20 community meeting with city officials and evaluate what happened. Seven people—four of them women—and SWOP organizer Mike Guerrero sat in a Mountainview home watching the tape, stopping it to analyze some incident, then watching more. When the turkey came on the screen they stopped the video. One woman criticized Guerrero for having publically disagreed with the turkey tactic, which the group had carried out on its own. Mike said he had been wrong. "Well," the woman smiled, "of course, maybe it should have been a chicken."

And that, I thought, is how "empowerment" begins. Sophistication, initiative, enough trust to criticize openly—after only three years of working together. Watch out, all you turkeys.

STUDY AND DISCUSSION QUESTIONS

1. Define "environmental racism." Were you aware of any of the statistics and stories Martinez cites? Why do you suppose these haven't been widely reported?

2. Give four reasons that race and class might be factors in the location of toxic pollution sites.

3. Are pro-environment activists and workers free of environmental racism, according to Martinez?

4. List and briefly describe four different moderate successes of the SouthWest Organizing Project.

5. Why are women "the most frequent victims of all contamination"?

6. Who do you think is the intended audience of "When People of Color Are an Endangered Species"?

SUGGESTIONS FOR WRITING

1. Discuss the ways in which environmentalists need to be educated about the realities of race and class issues, according to Martinez.

2. Write a dialogue between Elizabeth Martinez and either Joy Williams, Barry Commoner, or Wendell Berry.

MATTER: HOW WE KNOW

Susan Griffin

*Susan Griffin was born in Los Angeles in 1943, attended San Fran-
cisco State University, and has worked as a waitress, a teacher, and a
house painter. Her writings include the poetry collections* Like the
Iris of an Eye *(1976) and* Unremembered Country *(1987) as well
as such works of nonfiction as* Woman and Nature: The Roaring
Inside Her *(1978),* Rape: The Politics of Consciousness *(1979),
and* The Eros of Everyday Life: Essays on Ecology, Gender, and
Society *(1996). The following is from* Woman and Nature.

*Because we know ourselves to be made from this earth. See this grass. The patches
of silver and brown. Worn by the wind. The grass reflecting all that lives in the
soil. The light. The grass needing the soil. With roots deep in the earth. And
patches of silver. Like the patches of silver in our hair. Worn by time. This bird
flying low over the grass. Over the tules. The cattails, sedges, rushes, reeds, over
the marsh. Because we know ourselves to be made from this earth. Temporary
as this grass. Wet as this mud. Our cells filled with water. Like the mud of this
swamp. Heather growing here because of the damp. Sphagnum moss floating on
the surface, on the water standing in these pools. Places where the river washes
out. Where the earth was shaped by the flow of lava. Or by the slow movements
of glaciers. Because we know ourselves to be made from this earth, and shaped
like the earth, by what has gone before. The lives of our mothers.* What she told
me was her life. And what I saw in her hands. The calcium in the joints, the
aching as she hemmed my dress. These clothes she made for me. *The pools
overgrown by grass, reed, sedge, the marsh over time, becoming dry, over centuries, plankton disappearing, crustaceans gone, clams, worms, sponges, what we
see now floating in these pools, fish, birds flying close to the waters. This bird
with the scarlet shoulders. This bird with the yellow throat. And the beautiful
song. The song like flutes. Like violoncellos in an orchestra. The orchestra in our
mind. The symphony which we imagine. The music which was our idea. What
we wanted to be. The lives of our grandmothers. What we imagined them to be.*
She told me what she had wanted to be. What she had wanted to do. That she
wanted to act on the stage. To write. She showed me the stories she wrote before she was married. Before I was born. *Why we were born when we were, as
we were, we imagined. We imagined what she imagined then, what lay under the*

surface, this still water, the water not running over rocks, lacking air, the bacteria, fungi, dwelling at the bottom, without light, no green bodies, freeing no air, the scent of marsh gas, this bog we might lose ourselves in, sink in, the treachery here, our voices calling for help and no one listening, the silence, we made from this earth, returning to earth, the mud covering us, we giving ourselves up to this place, the fungi, bacteria, fish, everything struggling for air in this place, beetles capturing air bubbles on the surface of the pond, mosquitoes reaching with tubes to the surface of the water, fish with gills on the outsides of their bodies, fish gulping air at the surface, air captured in small hairs on the bodies of insects, stored in spaces in the stems of plants, in pockets in the tissue of leaves, everything in this place struggling for light, stems and leaves with thin skins, leaves divided into greater surfaces, numerous pores, tall plants in shallow water, open to the light; a jungle of growth in the shallow water at the edge, interwoven stems, matted leaves, places for wrens to hide, for rails, bitterns, for.red-winged blackbirds to protect their nests. Fish hiding in plants underwater, insects' and snails' eggs, pupa cases, larvae and nymphs and crayfish. Sunlight pouring into plants, ingested into the bodies of fish, into the red-winged blackbird, into the bacteria, into the fungi, into the earth itself, because we know ourselves to be made of this earth, because we know sunlight moves through us, water moves through us, everything moves, everything changes, and the daughters are returned to their mothers. She always comes back. Back from the darkness. And the earth grows green again. So we were moved to feel these things. The body of the animal buried in the ground rotting feeds the seed. The sheaf of grain held up to us silently. Her dreams, I know, she said, live on in my body as I write these words. *This proof. This testimony. This shape of possibility. What we dreamed to be. What we labored for. What we had burned desiring. What always returns. What she is to me. What she is to me, we said, and do not turn your head away, we told them, those who had tried to name us, those who had tried to keep us apart, do not turn your head away when we tell you this, we said,* how she was smaller than I then, *we try to tell you,* what tenderness I then felt for her, *we said,* as if she were my daughter, as if some part of myself I had thought lost forever were returned to me, *we said,* and then held her fiercely, *and we then made you listen, you turning your head away, you who tried to make us be still, you dividing yourself from this night we were turning through, but we made you listen, we said, do not pretend you do not hear what we say to each other, we say,* when she was returned to me and I to her that I became small to her, that my face became soft against her flesh, that through that night she held me, as if part of herself had returned, like mother to daughter *because we know we are made of this earth, and we know these meanings reach you, we said, the least comment of the stare, we said, the barely perceptible moment of despair,* I told her, *the eloquence of arms, those threaded daily causes, the fundaments of sound, cradling the infant's head,* these cries, the crying I heard in her body, *the years we had known together,* I know these meanings reach you, *we said, and the stars and their light we hold in our hands, this light telling the birds where they are, the same light which guides these birds to this place, and the light through which we imagine ourselves in the bodies of these birds, flying with them, low over the grass, weaving our nests like hammocks from blade to blade, from reed to reed. We standing at the edge of the marsh. Not daring to move closer. Keeping our distance. Watching these birds through the glass. Careful not to frighten them off. As they arrive. First the males, jet black, with a flash of red at their shoulders, a startling red which darts out of their blackness as they spread their wings. First the males and then the females flying together in the winter, now joining the males. The females with yellow throats, their wings brown and black, and light around their eyes. Now all of them calling. Calling or singing. Liquid and pleasant. Like the violoncello. We imagine like the violoncello, the cello we have made in our minds, the violin we have imagined, as we have imagined the prison, as we have made up boundaries, or decided what the fate of these birds should be, as we have invented poison, as we have invented the cage, now we stand at the edge of this marsh and do not go closer, allow them their distance, penetrate them only with our minds, only with our hearts, because though we can advance upon the blackbird, though we may cage her, though we may torture her with our will, with the boundaries we imagine, this bird will never be ours, he may die, this minute heart stop beating, the body go cold and hard, we may tear the wings apart and cut open the body and remove what we want to see, but still this blackbird will not be ours and we will have nothing. And even if we keep her alive. Train her to stay indoors. Clip her wings. Train her to sit on our fingers, though we feed her, and give her water, still this is not the blackbird we have captured, for the blackbird, which flies now over our heads, whose song reminds us of a flute, who migrates with the stars, who lives among reeds and rushes, threading a nest like a hammock, who lives in flocks, chattering in the grasses, this creature is free of our hands, we cannot control her, and for the creature we have tamed, the creature we keep in our house, we must make a new word. For we did not invent the blackbird, we say, we only invented her name. And we never invented ourselves, we admit.* And my grandmother's body is now part of the soil, she said. *Only now, we name ourselves. Only now, as we think of ourselves as passing, do we utter the syllables. Do we list all that we are. That we know in ourselves. We know ourselves to be made from this earth. We know this earth is made from our bodies. For we see ourselves. And we are nature. We are nature seeing nature. We are nature with a concept of nature. Nature weeping. Nature speaking of nature to nature. The red-winged blackbird flies in us, in our inner sight. We see the arc of her flight. We measure the ellipse. We predict its climax. We are amazed. We are moved. We fly. We watch her wings negotiate the wind, the substance of the air, its elements and the elements of those elements, and count those elements found in other beings, the sea urchin's sting, ink, this paper, our bones, the flesh of our tongues with which we make the sound "blackbird," the ears with which we hear, the eye which travels the arc of her flight. And yet the blackbird does not fly in us but is somewhere else free of our minds, and now even free of our sight, flying in the path of her own will,* she wrote, the ink from her pen flowing on this paper, her words, she thought, having nothing to do with this bird, except, she thought, as she breathes in the air this bird flies through, except, she thought, as the grass needs the body of the bird to pass its seeds, as the earth needs the grass, as we are made from this earth, she said, and the sunlight in the grass enters the body of the bird, *enters us,* she wrote on this paper, and the sunlight is pouring into my eyes from your eyes. Your eyes. Your eyes. The sun is in your eyes. I have made you smile. Your lips part. The sunlight in your mouth. Have I made the sun come into your mouth? I put my mouth on yours. To cover that light. To breathe it in. My tongue inside your mouth, your lips on my tongue, my body filled with light, filled with light, with light, shuddering, you make me shudder, you make the movement of the earth come into me, you fill me, you fill me with sound, is that my voice crying out? The sunlight in you is making my breath sing, sing your name, your name to you, beautiful one, I could kiss your bones, put my teeth in you, white gleam, whiteness, I chew, beautiful one, I am in you, I am filled with light inside you, I have no boundary, the light has extinguished my skin, I am perished in light, light filling you, shining through you, carrying you out, through the roofs of our mouths, the sky, the clouds, bursting, raining, raining free, falling piece by piece, dispersed over this earth, into the soil, deep, deeper into you, into the least hair on the deepest root in this earth, into the green heart flowing, into the green leaves and they grow, they grow into a profusion, moss, fern, and they bloom, cosmos, and they bloom, cyclamen, in your ears, in your ears, calling their names, this sound from my throat echoing, my breath in your ears, your eyes, your eyes continuing to see, continuing, your eyes telling, telling the light, the light. And she wrote, when I let this bird fly to her own purpose, when this bird flies in the path of his own will, the light from this bird enters my body, and when I see the beautiful arc of her flight, I love this bird, when I see, the arc of her flight, I fly with her, enter her with my mind, leave myself, die for an instant, live in the body of this bird whom I cannot live without, as part of the body of the bird will enter my daughter's body, because I know I am made from this earth, as my mother's hands were made from this earth, as her dreams came from this earth and all that I know, I know in this earth, the body of the bird, this pen, this paper, these hands, this tongue speaking, all that I know speaks to me through this earth and I long to tell you, you who are earth too, and listen *as we speak to each other of what we know: the light is in us.*

STUDY AND DISCUSSION QUESTIONS

1. What is the physical setting of Griffin's essay/prose poem?

2. List several ways Griffin tells us we are "made from this earth."

3. Why do you think Griffin includes her mother, her grandmothers, and her daughter in the essay?

4. Find two or three recurring images and trace each through the essay.

5. Read "Matter: How We Know" out loud (or if not the whole essay, a substantial section of it). What do you notice about the language and the rhythm? How is hearing this piece of writing a different experience from reading it silently?

SUGGESTIONS FOR WRITING

1. Griffin offers at least three possible relations to the blackbirds in the long central passage that begins, "the stars and their light we hold in our hands." Discuss these options, their benefits and consequences.

2. Contrast Susan Griffin's vision of the connectedness of all life in "Matter: How We Know" with Joyce Carol Oates's sense of our separation from nature in "Against Nature." Cite specific examples from each piece to support your analysis.

3. How do we *know*, according to Griffin? Is this a different kind of knowing than we are accustomed to? Give examples from the text and trace the progress of the speaker's coming to know.

AM I BLUE?

Alice Walker

Alice Walker was born in 1944 in Eatonton, Georgia, where her parents were sharecroppers. She attended Spelman and Sarah Lawrence Colleges and was active in the civil rights movement. Among her many books are the novels Meridian *(1976),* The Color Purple *(1982), which won the Pulitzer Prize, and* Possessing the Secret of Joy *(1992); the poetry volume* Once *(1968); and the essay collections* In Search of Our Mothers' Gardens: Womanist Prose *(1983) and* Living by the Word *(1988), where the following essay appeared.*

> *"Ain't these tears in these*
> *eyes tellin' you?"**

For about three years my companion and I rented a small house in the country that stood on the edge of a large meadow that appeared to run from the end of our deck straight into the mountains. The mountains, however, were quite far away, and between us and them there was, in fact, a town. It was one of the many pleasant aspects of the house that you never really were aware of this.

It was a house of many windows, low, wide, nearly floor to ceiling in the living room, which faced the meadow, and it was from one of these that I first saw our closest neighbor, a large white horse, cropping grass, flipping its mane, and ambling about—not over the entire meadow, which stretched well out of sight of the house, but over the five or so fenced-in acres that were next to the twenty-odd that we had rented. I soon learned that the horse, whose name was Blue, belonged to a man who lived in another town, but was boarded by our neighbors next door. Occasionally, one of the children, usually a stocky teen-ager, but sometimes a much younger girl or boy, could be seen riding Blue. They would appear in the meadow, climb up on his back, ride furiously for ten or fifteen minutes, then get off, slap Blue on the flanks, and not be seen again for a month or more.

There were many apple trees in our yard, and one by the fence that Blue could almost reach. We were soon in the habit of feeding him apples, which

---

*©1929 Warner Bros., Inc. (renewed). By Grant Clarke and Harry Akst. All rights reserved. Used by permission.

he relished, especially because by the middle of summer the meadow grasses—so green and succulent since January—had dried out from lack of rain, and Blue stumbled about munching the dried stalks half-heartedly. Sometimes he would stand very still just by the apple tree, and when one of us came out he would whinny, snort loudly, or stamp the ground. This meant, of course: I want an apple.

It was quite wonderful to pick a few apples, or collect those that had fallen to the ground overnight, and patiently hold them, one by one, up to his large, toothy mouth. I remained as thrilled as a child by his flexible dark lips, huge, cubelike teeth that crunched the apples, core and all, with such finality, and his high, broad-breasted *enormity;* beside which, I felt small indeed. When I was a child, I used to ride horses, and was especially friendly with one named Nan until the day I was riding and my brother deliberately spooked her and I was thrown, head first, against the trunk of a tree. When I came to, I was in bed and my mother was bending worriedly over me; we silently agreed that perhaps horseback riding was not the safest sport for me. Since then I have walked, and prefer walking to horseback riding—but I had forgotten the depth of feeling one could see in horses' eyes.

I was therefore unprepared for the expression in Blue's. Blue was lonely. Blue was horribly lonely and bored. I was not shocked that this should be the case; five acres to tramp by yourself, endlessly, even in the most beautiful of meadows—and his was—cannot provide many interesting events, and once rainy season turned to dry that was about it. No, I was shocked that I had forgotten that human animals and nonhuman animals can communicate quite well; if we are brought up around animals as children we take this for granted. By the time we are adults we no longer remember. However, the animals have not changed. They are in fact *completed* creations (at least they seem to be, so much more than we) who are not likely *to* change; it is their nature to express themselves. What else are they going to express? And they do. And, generally speaking, they are ignored.

After giving Blue the apples, I would wander back to the house, aware that he was observing me. Were more apples not forthcoming then? Was that to be his sole entertainment for the day? My partner's small son had decided he wanted to learn how to piece a quilt; we worked in silence on our respective squares as I thought . . .

Well, about slavery: about white children, who were raised by black people, who knew their first all-accepting love from black women, and then, when they were twelve or so, were told they must "forget" the deep levels of communication between themselves and "mammy" that they knew. Later they would be able to relate quite calmly, "My old mammy was sold to another good family." "My old mammy was _____ _____ ." Fill in the blank. Many more years later a white woman would say: "I can't understand these Negroes, these blacks. What do they want? They're so different from us."

And about the Indians, considered to be "like animals" by the "settlers" (a very benign euphemism for what they actually were), who did not understand their description as a compliment.

And about the thousands of American men who marry Japanese, Korean, Filipina, and other non-English-speaking women and of how happy they report they are, *"blissfully,"* until their brides learn to speak English, at which point the marriages tend to fall apart. What then did the men see, when they looked into the eyes of the women they married, before they could speak English? Apparently only their own reflections.

I thought of society's impatience with the young. "Why are they playing the music so loud?" Perhaps the children have listened to much of the music of oppressed people their parents danced to before they were born, with its passionate but soft cries for acceptance and love, and they have wondered why their parents failed to hear.

I do not know how long Blue had inhabited his five beautiful, boring acres before we moved into our house; a year after we had arrived—and had also traveled to other valleys, other cities, other worlds—he was still there.

But then, in our second year at the house, something happened in Blue's life. One morning, looking out the window at the fog that lay like a ribbon over the meadow, I saw another horse, a brown one, at the other end of Blue's field. Blue appeared to be afraid of it, and for several days made no attempt to go near. We went away for a week. When we returned, Blue had decided to make friends and the two horses ambled or galloped along together, and Blue did not come nearly as often to the fence underneath the apple tree.

When he did, bringing his new friend with him, there was a different look in his eyes. A look of independence, of self-possession, of inalienable *horse*ness. His friend eventually became pregnant. For months and months there was, it seemed to me, a mutual feeling between me and the horses of justice, of peace. I fed apples to them both. The look in Blue's eyes was one of unabashed "this is *it*ness."

It did not, however, last forever. One day, after a visit to the city, I went out to give Blue some apples. He stood waiting, or so I thought, though not beneath the tree. When I shook the tree and jumped back from the shower of apples, he made no move. I carried some over to him. He managed to half-crunch one. The rest he let fall to the ground. I dreaded looking into his eyes—because I had of course noticed that Brown, his partner, had gone—but I did look. If I had been born into slavery, and my partner had been sold or killed, my eyes would have looked like that. The children next door explained that Blue's partner had been "put with him" (the same expression that old people used, I had noticed, when speaking of an ancestor during slavery who had been impregnated by her owner) so that they could mate and she conceive. Since that was accomplished, she had been taken back by her owner, who lived somewhere else.

Will she be back? I asked.

They didn't know.

Blue was like a crazed person. Blue *was,* to me, a crazed person. He galloped furiously, as if he were being ridden, around and around his five beautiful acres. He whinnied until he couldn't. He tore at the ground with his hooves. He butted himself against his single shade tree. He looked always and always toward the road down which his partner had gone. And then, occasionally, when he came up for apples, or I took apples to him, he looked at me. It was a look so piercing, so full of grief, a look so *human,* I almost laughed (I felt too sad to cry) to think there are people who do not know that animals suffer. People like me who have forgotten, and daily forget, all that animals try to tell us. "Everything you do to us will happen to you; we are your teachers, as you are ours. We are one lesson" is essentially it, I think. There are those who never once have even considered animals' rights: those who have been taught that animals actually want to be used and abused by us, as small children "love" to be frightened, or women "love" to be mutilated and raped. . . . They are the great-grandchildren of those who honestly thought, because someone taught them this: "Women can't think," and "niggers can't faint." But most disturbing of all, in Blue's large brown eyes was a new look, more painful than the look of despair: the look of disgust with human beings, with life; the look of hatred. And it was odd what the look of hatred did. It gave him, for the first time, the look of a beast. And what that meant was that he had put up a barrier within to protect himself from further violence; all the apples in the world wouldn't change that fact.

And so Blue remained, a beautiful part of our landscape, very peaceful to look at from the window, white against the grass. Once a friend came to visit and said, looking out on the soothing view: "And it *would* have to be a *white* horse; the very image of freedom." And I thought, yes, the animals are forced to become for us merely "images" of what they once so beautifully expressed. And we are used to drinking milk from containers showing "contented" cows, whose real lives we want to hear nothing about, eating eggs and drumsticks from "happy" hens, and munching hamburgers advertised by bulls of integrity who seem to command their fate.

As we talked of freedom and justice one day for all, we sat down to steaks. I am eating misery, I thought, as I took the first bite. And spit it out.

STUDY AND DISCUSSION QUESTIONS

1. List the different meanings of the title "Am I Blue?"

2. Why do you think Walker includes lyrics from a blues song as an epigraph?

3. Discuss the contrast and tension between the setting, on the one hand, and the human and equine characters, on the other.

4. List four groups whose condition Walker's narrator is reminded of.

5. What correspondences does the narrator find between the experiences of slaves and the experiences of domesticated animals?

6. What point does the narrator make about the American men (often soldiers stationed overseas) who married non-English-speaking women? How does this example advance her argument about Blue?

7. Discuss some of the ironies that Walker mentions at the end of her essay.

SUGGESTIONS FOR WRITING

1. Is Walker projecting human emotions onto Blue or do you believe that animals (mammals, say) experience feelings we might recognize, even if they are not exactly the same as our own? Make a case either way, using examples from your own experience as well as from "Am I Blue?"

2. How does the experience of knowing Blue change the narrator? Note how she views animals at the beginning and at the end of her essay. Trace the evolution of her attitude through the essay. What are the turning points outside her? Which happen internally?

3. According to Walker, animals try to tell us that, "Everything you do to us will happen to you; we are your teachers, as you are ours. We are one lesson." If we believe this, then what kind of behavior, on an individual and social level, should we practice? Contrariwise, if we don't agree with Walker's statement about the interconnectedness of life, then what kind of behavior would appropriately follow? Give specific examples either way.

WHY MOW? THE CASE AGAINST LAWNS

Michael Pollan

Michael Pollan has worked as an editor at Harper's *magazine and as an architecture columnist for* House and Garden. *He has written widely on gardening and nature for a variety of publications and has published* Second Nature: A Gardener's Education *(1991), where the following essay appeared, and* A Place of My Own: The Education of an Amateur Builder *(1997).*

Anyone new to the experience of owning a lawn, as I am, soon figures out that there is more at stake here than a patch of grass. A lawn immediately establishes a certain relationship with one's neighbors and, by extension, the larger American landscape. Mowing the lawn, I realized the first time I gazed into my neighbor's yard and imagined him gazing back into mine, is a civic responsibility.

For no lawn is an island, at least in America. Starting at my front stoop, this scruffy green carpet tumbles down a hill and leaps across a one-lane road into my neighbor's yard. From there it skips over some wooded patches and stone walls before finding its way across a dozen other unfenced properties that lead down into the Housatonic Valley, there to begin its march south to the metropolitan area. Once below Danbury, the lawn—now purged of weeds and meticulously coiffed—races up and down the suburban lanes, heedless of property lines. It then heads west, crossing the New York border; moving now at a more stately pace, it strolls beneath the maples of Scarsdale, unfurls across a dozen golf courses, and wraps itself around the pale blue pools of Bronxville before pressing on toward the Hudson. New Jersey next is covered, an emerald postage stamp laid down front and back of ten thousand split levels, before the broadening green river divides in two.

One tributary pushes south, and does not pause until it has colonized the thin, sandy soils of Florida. The other dilates and spreads west, easily overtaking the Midwest's vast grid before running up against the inhospitable western states. But neither flinty soil nor obdurate climate will impede the lawn's march to the Pacific: it vaults the Rockies and, abetted by a monumental irrigation network, proceeds to green great stretches of western desert.

Nowhere in the world are lawns as prized as in America. In little more than a century, we've rolled a green mantle of grass across the continent, with scarcely a thought to the local conditions or expense. America has more than fifty thousand square *miles* of lawn under cultivation, on which we spend an estimated $30 billion a year—this according to the Lawn Institute, a Pleasant Hill, Tennessee, outfit devoted to publicizing the benefits of turf to Americans (surely a case of preaching to the converted).

Like the interstate highway system, like fast-food chains, like television, the lawn has served to unify the American landscape; it is what makes the suburbs of Cleveland and Tucson, the streets of Eugene and Tampa, look more alike than not. According to Ann Leighton, the late historian of gardens, America has made essentially one important contribution to world garden design: the custom of "uniting the front lawns of however many houses there may be on both sides of a street to present an untroubled aspect of expansive green to the passer by." France has its formal, geometric gardens, England its picturesque parks, and America this unbounded democratic river of manicured lawn along which we array our houses.

It is not easy to stand in the way of such a powerful current. Since we have traditionally eschewed fences and hedges in America (looking on these as Old World vestiges), the suburban vista can be marred by the negligence—or dissent—of a single property owner. This is why lawn care is regarded as such an important civic responsibility in the suburbs, and why the majority will not tolerate the laggard. I learned this at an early age, growing up in a cookie-cutter subdivision in Farmingdale, Long Island.

My father, you see, was a lawn dissident. Whether owing to laziness or contempt for his neighbors I was never sure, but he could not see much point in cranking up the Toro more than once a month or so. The grass on our quarter-acre plot towered over the crew-cut lawns on either side of us and soon disturbed the peace of the entire neighborhood.

That subtle yet unmistakable frontier, where the closely shaved lawn rubs up against a shaggy one, is a scar on the face of suburbia, an intolerable hint of trouble in paradise. The scar shows up in *The Great Gatsby*,[1] when Nick Carraway rents the house next to Gatsby's and fails to maintain his lawn according to West Egg standards. The rift between the two lawns so troubles Gatsby that he dispatches his gardener to mow Nick's grass and thereby erase it.

Our neighbors in Farmingdale displayed somewhat less class. "Lawn mower on the fritz?" they'd ask. "Want to borrow mine?" But the more heavily they leaned on my father, the more recalcitrant he became, until one summer—probably 1959, or 1960—he let the lawn go altogether. The grass plants grew tall enough to flower and set seed; the lawn rippled in the breeze like a

---

[1] Novel by F. Scott Fitzgerald.

flag. There was beauty here, I'm sure, but it was not visible in this context. Stuck in the middle of a row of tract houses on Long Island, our lawn said *turpitude* rather than *meadow,* even though strictly speaking that is what it had become.

That summer I felt the hot breath of the majority's tyranny for the first time. No one said anything now, but you could hear it all the same: *Mow your lawn or get out.* Certain neighbors let it be known to my parents that I was not to play with their children. Cars would slow down as they drove by. Probably some of the drivers were merely curious: they saw the unmowed lawn and wondered if someone had left in a hurry, or perhaps died. But others drove by in a manner that was unmistakably expressive, slowing down as they drew near and then hitting the gas angrily as they passed—pithy driving, the sort of move that is second nature to a Klansman.

We got the message by other media, too. Our next-door neighbor, a mild engineer who was my father's last remaining friend in the development, was charged with the unpleasant task of conveying the sense of the community to my father. It was early on a summer evening that he came to deliver his message. I don't remember it all (I was only four or five at the time), but I can imagine him taking a highball glass from my mother, squeaking out what he had been told to say about the threat to property values, and then waiting for my father—who next to him was a bear—to respond.

My father's reply could not have been more eloquent. Without a word he strode out to the garage and cranked up the rusty old Toro for the first time since fall; it's a miracle the thing started. He pushed it out to the curb and then started back across the lawn to the house, but not in a straight line: he swerved right, then left, then right again. He had cut an *S* in the high grass. Then he made an *M,* and finally a *P.* These are his initials, and as soon as he finished writing them he wheeled the lawn mower back to the garage, never to start it up again.

I wasn't prepared to take such a hard line on my new lawn, at least not right off. So I bought a lawn mower, a Toro, and started mowing. Four hours every Saturday. At first I tried for a kind of Zen approach, clearing my mind of everything but the task at hand, immersing myself in the lawn-mowing here-and-now. I liked the idea that my weekly sessions with the grass would acquaint me with the minutest details of my yard. I soon knew by heart the exact location of every stump and stone, the tunnel route of each resident mole, the address of every anthill. I noticed that where rain collected white clover flourished, that it was on the drier rises that crabgrass thrived. After a few weekends I had a map of the lawn in my head as precise and comprehensive as the mental map one has of the back of one's hand.

The finished product pleased me too, the fine scent and the sense of order restored that a new-cut lawn exhales. My house abuts woods on two sides, and mowing the lawn is, in both a real and metaphorical sense, how I keep the forest at bay and preserve my place in this landscape. Much as we've come to distrust it, the urge to dominate nature is a deeply human one, and lawn mowing answers to it. I thought of the lawn mower as civilization's knife and my lawn as the hospitable plane it carved out of the wilderness. My lawn was a part of nature made fit for human habitation.

So perhaps the allure of lawns is in the genes. The sociobiologists think so: they've gone so far as to propose a "Savanna Syndrome" to explain our fondness for grass. Encoded in our DNA is a preference for an open grassy landscape resembling the short-grass savannas of Africa on which we evolved and spent our first few million years. This is said to explain why we have re-made the wooded landscapes of Europe and North America in the image of East Africa.

Such theories go some way toward explaining the widespread appeal of grass, but they don't really account for the American Lawn. They don't, for instance, account for the keen interest Jay Gatsby takes in Nick Carraway's lawn, or the scandal my father's lawn sparked in Farmingdale. Or the fact that, in America, we have taken down our fences and hedges in order to combine our lawns. And they don't even begin to account for the unmistakable odor of virtue that hovers in this country over a scrupulously maintained lawn.

If any individual can be said to have invented the American lawn, it is Frederick Law Olmsted. In 1868, he received a commission to design Riverside, outside Chicago, one of the first planned suburban communities in America. Olmsted's design stipulated that each house be set back thirty feet from the road and it proscribed walls. He was reacting against the "high dead-walls" of England, which he felt made a row of homes there seem "as of a series of private madhouses." In Riverside, each owner would maintain one or two trees and a lawn that would flow seamlessly into his neighbors', creating the impression that all lived together in a single park.

Olmsted was part of a generation of American landscape designer-reformers who set out at midcentury to beautify the American landscape. That it needed beautification may seem surprising to us today, assuming as we do that the history of the landscape is a story of decline, but few at the time thought otherwise. William Cobbett, visiting from England, was struck at the "out-of-door slovenliness" of American homesteads. Each farmer, he wrote, was content with his "shell of boards, while all around him is as barren as the sea beach . . . though there is no English shrub, or flower, which will not grow and flourish here."

The land looked as if it had been shaped and cleared in a great hurry—as indeed it had: the landscape largely denuded of trees, makeshift fences outlining badly plowed fields, tree stumps everywhere one looked. As Cobbett and many other nineteenth-century visitors noted, hardly anyone practiced ornamental gardening; the typical yard was "landscaped" in the style southerners would come to call "white trash"—a few chickens, some busted farm equipment, mud and weeds, an unkempt patch of vegetables.

This might do for farmers, but for the growing number of middle-class city people moving to the "borderland" in the years following the Civil War, something more respectable was called for. In 1870, Frank J. Scott, seeking to make Olmsted's ideas accessible to the middle class, published the first volume ever devoted to "suburban home embellishment": *The Art of Beautifying Suburban Home Grounds,* a book that probably did more than any other to determine the look of the suburban landscape in America. Like so many reformers of his time, Scott was nothing if not sure of himself: "A smooth, closely shaven surface of grass is by far the most essential element of beauty on the grounds of a suburban house."

Americans like Olmsted and Scott did not invent the lawn; lawns had been popular in England since Tudor times. But in England, lawns were usually found only on estates; the Americans democratized them, cutting the vast manorial greenswards into quarter-acre slices everyone could afford. Also, the English never considered the lawn an end in itself: it served as a setting for lawn games and as a backdrop for flower beds and trees. Scott subordinated all other elements of the landscape to the lawn; flowers were permissible, but only on the periphery of the grass: "Let your lawn be your home's velvet robe, and your flowers its not too promiscuous decoration."

But Scott's most radical departure from Old World practice was to dwell on the individual's responsibility to his neighbors. "It is unchristian," he declared, "to hedge from the sight of others the beauties of nature which it has been our good fortune to create or secure." One's lawn, Scott held, should contribute to the collective landscape. "The beauty obtained by throwing front grounds open together, is of that excellent quality which enriches all who take part in the exchange, and makes no man poorer." Like Olmsted before him, Scott sought to elevate an unassuming patch of turfgrass into an institution of democracy.

With our open-faced front lawns we declare our like-mindedness to our neighbors—and our distance from the English, who surround their yards with "inhospitable brick wall, topped with broken bottles," to thwart the envious gaze of the lower orders. The American lawn is an egalitarian conceit, implying that there is no reason to hide behind fence or hedge since we all occupy the same middle class. We are all property owners here, the lawn announces, and that suggests its other purpose: to provide a suitably grand stage for the proud display of one's own house. Noting that our yards were organized "to capture the admiration of the street," one garden writer in 1921 attributed the popularity of open lawns to our "infantile instinct to cry 'hello!' to the passer-by, to lift up our possessions to his gaze."

Of course the democratic front yard has its darker, more coercive side, as my family learned in Farmingdale. In specifying the "plain style" of an unembellished lawn for American front yards, the mid-century designer-reformers were, like Puritan ministers, laying down rigid conventions governing our relationship to the land, our observance of which would henceforth be taken as an index of our character. And just as the Puritans would not tolerate any individual who sought to establish his or her own back-channel relationship with the divinity, the members of the suburban utopia do not tolerate the homeowner who establishes a relationship with the land that is not mediated by the group's conventions.

The parallel is not as farfetched as it might sound, when you recall that nature in America has often been regarded as divine. Think of nature as Spirit, the collective suburban lawn as the Church, and lawn mowing as a kind of sacrament. You begin to see why ornamental gardening would take so long to catch on in America, and why my father might seem an antinomian in the eyes of his neighbors. Like Hester Prynne,[2] he claimed not to need their consecration for his actions; perhaps his initials in the front lawn were a kind of Emerald Letter.

Possibly because it is this common land, rather than race or tribe, that makes us all Americans, we have developed a deep distrust of individualistic approaches to the landscape. The land is too important to our identity as Americans to simply allow everyone to have his own way with it. And once we decide that the land should serve as a vehicle of consensus, rather than an arena of self-expression, the American lawn—collective, national, ritualized, and plain—begins to look inevitable.

After my first season of lawn mowing, the Zen approach began to wear thin. I had taken up flower and vegetable gardening, and soon came to resent the four hours that my lawn demanded of me each week. I tired of the endless circuit, pushing the howling mower back and forth across the vast page of my yard, recopying the same green sentences over and over: "I am a conscientious homeowner. I share your middle-class values." Lawn care was gardening aimed at capturing "the admiration of the street," a ritual of consensus I did not have my heart in. I began to entertain idle fantasies of rebellion:

---

[2] Main character of Nathaniel Hawthorne's novel *The Scarlet Letter,* who is forced to wear a scarlet "A" on her dress for having committed adultery.

Why couldn't I plant a hedge along the road, remove my property from the national stream of greensward and do something else with it?

The third spring I planted fruit trees in the front lawn, apple, peach, cherry, and plum, hoping these would relieve the monotony and begin to make the lawn productive. Behind the house, I put in a perennial border. I built three raised beds out of old chestnut barnboards and planted two dozen different vegetable varieties. Hard work though it was, removing the grass from the site of my new beds proved a keen pleasure. First I outlined the beds with string. Then I made an incision in the lawn with the sharp edge of a spade. Starting at one end, I pried the sod from the soil and slowly rolled it up like a carpet. The grass made a tearing sound as I broke its grip on the earth. I felt a little like a pioneer subduing the forest with his ax; I daydreamed of scalping the entire yard. But I didn't do it—I continued to observe front-yard conventions, mowing assiduously and locating all my new garden beds in the back yard.

The more serious about gardening I became, the more dubious lawns seemed. The problem for me was not, as it was for my father, the relation to my neighbors that a lawn implied; it was the lawn's relationship to nature. For however democratic a lawn may be with respect to one's neighbors, with respect to nature it is authoritarian. Under the mower's brutal indiscriminate rotor, the landscape is subdued, homogenized, dominated utterly. I became convinced that lawn care had about as much to do with gardening as floor waxing or road paving. Gardening was a subtle process of give and take with the landscape, a search for some middle ground between culture and nature. A lawn was nature under culture's boot.

Mowing the lawn, I felt that I was battling the earth rather than working it; each week it sent forth a green army and each week I beat it back with my infernal machine. Unlike every other plant in my garden, the grasses were anonymous, massified, deprived of any change or development whatsoever, not to mention any semblance of self-determination. I ruled a totalitarian landscape.

Hot, monotonous hours behind the mower gave rise to existential speculations. I spent part of one afternoon trying to decide who, in the absurdist drama of lawn mowing, was Sisyphus. Me? A case could certainly be made. Or was it the grass, pushing up through the soil every week, one layer of cells at a time, only to be cut down and then, perversely, encouraged (with fertilizer, lime, etc.) to start the whole doomed process over again? Another day it occurred to me that time as we know it doesn't exist in the lawn, since grass never dies or is allowed to flower and set seed. Lawns are nature purged of sex and death. No wonder Americans like them so much.

And just where *was* my lawn, anyway? The answer's not as obvious as it seems. Gardening, I had come to appreciate, is a painstaking exploration of place; everything that happens in my garden—the thriving and dying of particular plants, the maraudings of various insects and other pests—teaches me to know this patch of land intimately, its geology and microclimate, the particular ecology of its local weeds and animals and insects. My garden prospers to the extent I grasp these particularities and adapt to them.

Lawns work on the opposite principle. They depend for their success on the *overcoming* of local conditions. Like Jefferson superimposing one great grid over the infinitely various topography of the Northwest Territory, we superimpose our lawns on the land. And since the geography and climate of much of this country is poorly suited to turfgrasses (none of which are native), this can't be accomplished without the tools of twentieth-century industrial civilization—its chemical fertilizers, pesticides, herbicides, and machinery. For we won't settle for the lawn that will grow here; we want the one that grows *there,* that dense springy supergreen and weed-free carpet, that Platonic ideal of a lawn we glimpse in the ChemLawn commercials, the magazine spreads, the kitschy sit-com yards, the sublime links and pristine diamonds. Our lawns exist less here than there; they drink from the national stream of images, lift our gaze from the real places we live and fix it on unreal places elsewhere. Lawns are a form of television.

Need I point out that such an approach to "nature" is not likely to be environmentally sound? Lately we have begun to recognize that we are poisoning ourselves with our lawns, which receive, on average, more pesticide and herbicide per acre than just about any crop grown in this country. Suits fly against the national lawn-care companies, and interest is kindled in "organic" methods of lawn care. But the problem is larger than this. Lawns, I am convinced, are a symptom of, and a metaphor for, our skewed relationship to the land. They teach us that, with the help of petrochemicals and technology, we can bend nature to our will. Lawns stoke our hubris with regard to the land.

What is the alternative? To turn them into gardens. I'm not suggesting that there is no place for lawns *in* these gardens or that gardens by themselves will right our relationship to the land, but the habits of thought they foster can take us some way in that direction.

Gardening, as compared to lawn care, tutors us in nature's ways, fostering an ethic of give and take with respect to the land. Gardens instruct us in the particularities of place. They lessen our dependence on distant sources of energy, technology, food, and, for that matter, interest.

For if lawn mowing feels like copying the same sentence over and over, gardening is like writing out new ones, an infinitely variable process of invention and discovery. Gardens also teach the necessary if rather un-American lesson that nature and culture can be compromised, that there might be some middle ground between the lawn and the forest—between those who would complete the conquest of the planet in the name of progress and those who believe it's time we abdicated our rule and left the earth in the care of its more innocent species. The garden suggests there might be a place where we can meet nature halfway.

Probably you will want to know if I have begun to practice what I'm preaching. Well, I have not ripped out my lawn entirely. But each spring larger and larger tracts of it give way to garden. Last year I took a half acre and planted a meadow of black-eyed Susans and oxeye daisies. In return for a single annual scything, I am rewarded with a field of flowers from May until frost.

The lawn is shrinking, and I've hired a neighborhood kid to mow what's left of it. Any Saturday that Bon Jovi, Twisted Sister, or Van Halen[3] isn't playing the Hartford Civic Center, this large blond teenaged being is apt to show up with a forty-eight-inch John Deere mower that shears the lawn in less than an hour. It's $30 a week, but he's freed me from my dark musings about the lawn and so given me more time in the garden.

Out in front, along the road where my lawn overlooks my neighbors', and in turn the rest of the country's, I have made my most radical move. I built a split rail fence and have begun to plant a hedge along it—a rough one made up of forsythia, lilac, bittersweet, and bridal wreath. As soon as this hedge grows tall and thick, my secession from the national lawn will be complete.

Anything then is possible. I *could* let it all revert to meadow, or even forest, except that I don't go in for that sort of self-effacement. I could put in a pumpkin patch, a lily pond, or maybe an apple orchard. And I could even leave an area of grass. But even if I did, this would be a very different lawn from the one I have now. For one thing, it would have a frame, which means it could accommodate plants more subtle and various than the screaming marigolds, fierce red salvias, and musclebound rhododendrons that people usually throw into the ring against a big unfenced lawn. Walled off from the neighbors, no longer a tributary of the national stream, my lawn would now form a distinct and private space—become part of a garden rather than a substitute for one.

Yes, there might well be a place for a small lawn in my new garden. But I think I'll wait until the hedge fills in before I make a decision. It's a private matter, and I'm trying to keep politics out of it.

STUDY AND DISCUSSION QUESTIONS

1. How is mowing the lawn a civic responsibility in America, according to Pollan?

---

[2] Heavy metal rock groups.

2. Pollan tells the story of his father's last stand as a "lawn dissident." Though he says his father's behavior might have been due either to laziness or contempt, how does he actually present his father in this anecdote?

3. How is no lawn an island in America? Why might Pollan have chosen to adapt and allude to John Donne's "no man is an island"?

4. Who was Frederick Law Olmsted? What was the state of the landscape around the American homestead when he started his work? What did Frank J. Scott add to Olmsted's landscape philosophy?

5. Trace the progress, according to Pollan, of how our lawns have become a character issue, an index to our morality. According to the philosophy that accepts our lawns as an index to our morality, what happens to the American right to individual expression of identity?

6. How is the narrator like Sisyphus?

7. Is Pollan, finally, carrying on his family's tradition with respect to lawns? How does he modify his father's philosophy and tactics?

8. Define a garden, a forest, and a lawn in Pollan's terms.

SUGGESTIONS FOR WRITING

1. How does Pollan use the notion that lawns in the United States are an expression of democracy to structure his essay and develop his argument? Note references to citizenship, government, and political philosophies throughout the essay.

2. How do gardens differ from lawns and how does gardening differ from taking care of a lawn, according to Pollan? How would *you* characterize these differences?

3. How is Pollan's argument about the relative merits of gardens and lawns a practical expression of Barry Commoner's thesis in "At War with the Planet"?

4. Make the case *for* lawns.

AGAINST NATURE

Joyce Carol Oates

Novelist, poet, playwright, and essayist Joyce Carol Oates (b. 1938) has written so many books that she's had to publish some of them under a pseudonym (Rosamond Smith) in order to avoid flooding the market. Her work includes the novels Expensive People *(1967),* Bellefleur *(1980), and* We Were the Mulvaneys *(1996); the poetry collection* The Time Traveler *(1989); the nonfiction* On Boxing *(1987); and* Twelve Plays *(1991). The following appeared in her essay collection* The Profane Art *(1983).*

We soon get through with Nature. She excites an expectation which she cannot satisfy.

THOREAU, *Journal*, 1854

Sir, if a man has experienced the inexpressible, he is under no obligation to attempt to express it.

SAMUEL JOHNSON

The writer's resistance to Nature.

It has no sense of humor: in its beauty, as in its ugliness, or its neutrality, there is no laughter.

It lacks a moral purpose.

It lacks a satiric dimension, registers no irony.

Its pleasures lack resonance, being accidental; its horrors, even when premeditated, are equally perfunctory, "red in tooth and claw,"[1] et cetera.

It lacks a symbolic subtext—excepting that provided by man.

It has no (verbal) language.

It has no interest in ours.

It inspires a painfully limited set of responses in "nature writers"—REVERENCE, AWE, PIETY, MYSTICAL ONENESS.

It eludes us even as it prepares to swallow us up, books and all.

---

[1] "Nature, red in tooth and claw" is a line from Alfred, Lord Tennyson's poem "In Memoriam."

I was lying on my back in the dirt gravel of the towpath beside the Delaware and Raritan Canal, Titusville, New Jersey, staring up at the sky and trying, with no success, to overcome a sudden attack of tachycardia that had come upon me out of nowhere—such attacks are always "out of nowhere," that's their charm—and all around me Nature thrummed with life, the air smelling of moisture and sunlight, the canal reflecting the sky, red-winged blackbirds testing their spring calls; the usual. I'd become the jar in Tennessee,[2] a fictitious center, or parenthesis, aware beyond my erratic heartbeat of the numberless heartbeats of the earth, its pulsing, pumping life, sheer life, incalculable. Struck down in the midst of motion—I'd been jogging a minute before—I was "out of time" like a fallen, stunned boxer, privileged (in an abstract manner of speaking) to be an involuntary witness to the random, wayward, nameless motion on all sides of me.

Paroxysmal tachycardia can be fatal, but rarely; if the heartbeat accelerates to 250–270 beats a minute you're in trouble, but the average attack is about 100–150 beats and mine seemed about average; the trick now was to prevent it from getting worse. Brainy people try brainy strategies, such as thinking calming thoughts, pseudo-mystic thoughts, *If I die now it's a good death,* that sort of thing, *if I die this is a good place and good time;* the idea is to deceive the frenzied heartbeat that, really, you don't care: you hadn't any other plans for the afternoon. The important thing with tachycardia is to prevent panic! you must prevent panic! otherwise you'll have to be taken by ambulance to the closest emergency room, which is not so very nice a way to spend the afternoon, really. So I contemplated the blue sky overhead. The earth beneath my head. Nature surrounding me on all sides; I couldn't quite see it but I could hear it, smell it, sense it, there is something *there,* no mistake about it. Completely oblivious to the predicament of the individual but that's only "natural," after all, one hardly expects otherwise.

When you discover yourself lying on the ground, limp and unresisting, head in the dirt, and, let's face it, helpless, the earth seems to shift forward as a presence; hard, emphatic, not mere surface but a genuine force—there is no other word for it but *presence.* To keep in motion is to keep in time, and to be stopped, stilled, is to be abruptly out of time, in another time dimension perhaps, an alien one, where human language has no resonance. Nothing to be said about it expresses it, nothing touches it, it's an absolute against which nothing human can be measured. . . . Moving through space and time by way of your own volition you inhabit an interior consciousness, a hallucinatory consciousness, it might be said, so long as breath, heartbeat, the body's autonomy hold; when motion is stopped you are jarred out of it. The interior

---

[2] See Wallace Stevens's poem, "Anecdote of the Jar."

is invaded by the exterior. The outside wants to come in, and only the self's fragile membrane prevents it.

The fly buzzing at Emily's death.[3]

Still, the earth *is* your place. A tidy grave site measured to your size. Or, from another angle of vision, one vast democratic grave.

Let's contemplate the sky. Forget the crazy hammering heartbeat, don't listen to it, don't start counting, remember that there is a clever way of breathing that conserves oxygen as if you're lying below the surface of a body of water breathing through a very thin straw but you *can* breathe through it if you're careful, if you don't panic; one breath and then another and then another, isn't that the story of all lives? careers? Just a matter of breathing. Of course it is. But contemplate the sky, it's there to be contemplated. A mild shock to see it so blank, blue, a thin airy ghostly blue, no clouds to disguise its emptiness. You are beginning to feel not only weightless but near-bodiless, lying on the earth like a scrap of paper about to be blown off. Two dimensions and you'd imagined you were three! And there's the sky rolling away forever, into infinity—if "infinity" can be "rolled into"—and the forlorn truth is, that's where you're going too. And the lovely blue isn't even blue, is it? isn't even there, is it? a mere optical illusion, isn't it? no matter what art has urged you to believe.

Early Nature memories. Which it's best not to suppress.

. . . Wading, as a small child, in Tonawanda Creek near our house, and afterward trying to tear off, in a frenzy of terror and revulsion, the sticky fat black bloodsuckers that had attached themselves to my feet, particularly between my toes.

. . . Coming upon a friend's dog in a drainage ditch, dead for several days, evidently the poor creature had been shot by a hunter and left to die, bleeding to death, and we're stupefied with grief and horror but can't resist sliding down to where he's lying on his belly, and we can't resist squatting over him, turning the body over.

. . . The raccoon, mad with rabies, frothing at the mouth and tearing at his own belly with his teeth, so that his intestines spill out onto the ground . . . a sight I seem to remember though in fact I did not see. I've been told I did not see.

Consequently, my chronic uneasiness with Nature mysticism; Nature adoration; Nature-as-(moral)-instruction-for-mankind. My doubt that one can, with philosophical validity, address "Nature" as a single coherent noun,

---

[3] See Emily Dickinson's poem, "I heard a Fly buzz—when I died—."

anything other than a Platonic, hence discredited, is-ness. My resistance to "Nature writing" as a genre, except when it is brilliantly fictionalized in the service of a writer's individual vision—Thoreau's books and *Journal*, of course, but also, less known in this country, the miniaturist prose poems of Colette *(Flowers and Fruit)* and Ponge *(Taking the Side of Things)*—in which case it becomes yet another, and ingenious, form of storytelling. The subject is *there* only by the grace of the author's language.

Nature has no instructions for mankind except that our poor beleaguered humanist-democratic way of life, our fantasies of the individual's high worth, our sense that the weak, no less than the strong, have a right to survive, are absurd. When Edmund of *King Lear* said excitedly, "Nature, be thou my goddess!" he knew whereof he spoke.

In any case, where *is* Nature, one might (skeptically) inquire. Who has looked upon her/its face and survived?

But isn't this all exaggeration, in the spirit of rhetorical contentiousness? Surely Nature is, for you, as for most reasonably intelligent people, a "perennial" source of beauty, comfort, peace, escape from the delirium of civilized life; a respite from the ego's ever-frantic strategies of self-promotion, as a way of ensuring (at least in fantasy) some small measure of immortality? Surely Nature, as it is understood in the usual slapdash way, as human, if not dilettante, *experience* (hiking in a national park, jogging on the beach at dawn, even tending, with the usual comical frustrations, a suburban garden), is wonderfully consoling; a place where, when you go there, it has to take you in?—a palimpsest of sorts you choose to read, layer by layer, always with care, always cautiously, in proportion to your psychological strength?

Nature: as in Thoreau's upbeat Transcendentalist mode ("The indescribable innocence and beneficence of Nature,—such health, such cheer, they afford forever! and such sympathy have they ever with our race, that all Nature would be affected . . . if any man should ever for a just cause grieve"), and not in Thoreau's grim mode ("Nature is hard to be overcome but she must be overcome").

Another way of saying, not *Nature-in-itself* but *Nature-as-experience.*

The former, Nature-in-itself, is, to allude slantwise to Melville,[4] a blankness ten times blank; the latter is what we commonly, or perhaps always, mean, when we speak of Nature as a noun, a single entity—something of *ours.* Most of the time it's just an activity, a sort of hobby, a weekend, a few days, perhaps a few hours, staring out the window at the mind-dazzling autumn foliage of, say, northern Michigan, being rendered

---

[4] Herman Melville, nineteenth century American novelist and author of *Moby Dick.*

speechless—temporarily—at the sight of Mt. Shasta, the Grand Canyon, Ansel Adams's West. Or Nature writ small, contained in the back yard. Nature filtered through our optical nerves, our "senses," our fiercely romantic expectations. Nature that pleases us because it mirrors our souls, or gives the comforting illusion of doing so.

Nature as the self's (flattering) mirror, but not ever, no, never, Nature-in-itself.

Nature is mouths, or maybe a single mouth. Why glamorize it, romanticize it?—well, yes, but we must, we're writers, poets, mystics (of a sort) aren't we, precisely what else are we to do but glamorize and romanticize and generally exaggerate the significance of anything we focus the white heat of our "creativity" upon? And why not Nature, since it's there, common property, mute, can't talk back, allows us the possibility of transcending the human condition for a while, writing prettily of mountain ranges, white-tailed deer, the purple crocuses outside this very window, the thrumming dazzling "life force" we imagine we all support. Why not?

Nature *is* more than a mouth—it's a dazzling variety of mouths. And it pleases the senses, in any case, as the physicists' chill universe of numbers certainly does not.

Oscar Wilde, on our subject:

Nature is no great mother who has borne us. She is our creation. It is in our brain that she quickens to life. Things are because we see them, and what we see, and how we see it, depends on the Arts that have influenced us. To look at a thing is very different from seeing a thing. . . . At present, people see fogs, not because there are fogs, but because poets and painters have taught them the mysterious loveliness of such effects. There may have been fogs for centuries in London. I dare say there were. But no one saw them. They did not exist until Art had invented them. . . . Yesterday evening Mrs. Arundel insisted on my going to the window and looking at the glorious sky, as she called it. And so I had to look at it. . . . And what was it? It was simply a very second-rate Turner, a Turner of a bad period, with all the painter's worst faults exaggerated and over-emphasized.

"The Decay of Lying," 1889

(If we were to put it to Oscar Wilde that he exaggerates, his reply might well be, "Exaggeration? I don't know the meaning of the word.")

Walden, that most artfully composed of prose fictions, concludes, in the rhapsodic chapter "Spring," with Henry David Thoreau's contemplation of death, decay, and regeneration as it is suggested to him, or to his protagonist, by the spectacle of vultures feeding off carrion. There is a dead horse close by his cabin, and the stench of its decomposition, in certain winds, is daunting. Yet "the assurance it gave me of the strong appetite and inviolable health of Nature was my compensation for this. I love to see that Nature is so rife with life that myriads can be afforded to be sacrificed and suffered to prey upon one another; that tender organizations can be so serenely squashed out of existence like pulp,—tadpoles which herons gobble up, and tortoises and toads run over in the road; and that sometimes it has rained flesh and blood! . . . The impression made on a wise man is that of universal innocence."

Come off it, Henry David. You've grieved these many years for your elder brother, John, who died a ghastly death of lockjaw; you've never wholly recovered from the experience of watching him die. And you know, or must know, that you're fated too to die young of consumption. . . . But this doctrinaire Transcendentalist passage ends *Walden* on just the right note. It's as impersonal, as coolly detached, as the Oversoul itself: a "wise man" filters his emotions through his brain.

Or through his prose.

Nietzsche: "We all pretend to ourselves that we are more simple-minded than we are: that is how we get a rest from our fellow men."

> Once out of nature I shall never take
> My bodily form from any natural thing,
> But such a form as Grecian goldsmiths make
> Of hammered gold and gold enamelling
> To keep a drowsy Emperor awake;
> Or set upon a golden bough to sing
> To lords and ladies of Byzantium
> Of what is past, or passing, or to come.
>
> William Butler Yeats, "Sailing to Byzantium"

Yet even the golden bird is a "bodily form [taken from a] natural thing." No, it's impossible to escape!

The writer's resistance to Nature.

Wallace Stevens: "In the presence of extraordinary actuality, consciousness takes the place of imagination."

Once, years ago, in 1972 to be precise, when I seemed to have been another person, related to the person I am now as one is related, tangentially, sometimes embarrassingly, to cousins not seen for decades—once, when we were living in London, and I was very sick, I had a mystical vision. That is, I "had" a "mystical vision"—the heart sinks: such pretension—or something resembling one. A fever dream, let's call it. It impressed me enormously and impresses me still, though I've long since lost the capacity to see it with my mind's eye, or even, I suppose, to believe in it. There is a statute of limitations on "mystical visions," as on romantic love.

I was very sick, and I imagined my life as a thread, a thread of breath, or heartbeat, or pulse, or light—yes, it was light, radiant light; I was burning with fever and I ascended to that plane of serenity that might be mistaken for (or *is*, in fact) Nirvana, where I had a waking dream of uncanny lucidity:

> My body is a tall column of light and heat.
> My body is not "I" but "it."
> My body is not one but many.

My body, which "I" inhabit, is inhabited as well by other creatures, unknown to me, imperceptible—the smallest of them mere sparks of light.

My body, which I perceive as substance, is in fact an organization of infinitely complex, overlapping, imbricated structures, radiant light their manifestation, the "body" a tall column of light and blood heat, a temporary agreement among atoms, like a high-rise building with numberless rooms, corridors, corners, elevator shafts, windows. . . . In this fantastical structure the "I" is deluded as to its sovereignty, let alone its autonomy in the (outside) world; the most astonishing secret is that the "I" doesn't exist!—but it behaves as if it does, as if it were one and not many.

In any case, without the "I" the tall column of light and heat would die, and the microscopic life particles would die with it . . . will die with it. The "I," which doesn't exist, is everything.

> But Dr. Johnson is right, the inexpressible need not be expressed.
> And what resistance, finally? There is none.

This morning, an invasion of tiny black ants. One by one they appear, out of nowhere—that's their charm too!—moving single file across the white Parsons table where I am sitting, trying without much success to write a poem. A poem of only three or four lines is what I want, something short, tight, mean; I want it to hurt like a white-hot wire up the nostrils, small and compact and turned in upon itself with the density of a hunk of rock from the planet Jupiter. . . .

But here come the black ants: harbingers, you might say, of spring. One by one by one they appear on the dazzling white table and one by one I kill them with a forefinger, my deft right forefinger, mashing each against the surface of the table and then dropping it into a wastebasket at my side. Idle labor, mesmerizing, effortless, and I'm curious as to how long I can do it—sit here in the brilliant March sunshine killing ants with my right forefinger—how long I, and the ants, can keep it up.

After a while I realize that I can do it a long time. And that I've written my poem.

STUDY AND DISCUSSION QUESTIONS

1. Note the various layers of Oates's writing style, particularly at the beginning of the essay.

2. Discuss the opening *scene*. Why do you think Oates chooses to begin in this way? What does she accomplish by doing so?

3. Why are Oates's "early nature memories" all so grim and loathsome?

4. What is nature-in-itself, according to Oates?

5. How is nature-as-experience a mirror, according to Oates?

6. List as many literary allusions as you can find in this essay. Some are more hidden than others.

7. Consider the closing scene of "Against Nature." How is it an appropriate conclusion, given Oates's argument? What effect does it have on you?

8. Discuss the passage from Oscar Wilde. Do you think it is a good capsule summary of Oates's position in "Against Nature"? What is the relation between nature and art that Wilde proposes? Do you agree?

SUGGESTIONS FOR WRITING

1. Joyce Carol Oates focuses on the writer's relation to nature in this essay, though her comments are certainly applicable to people who don't write for a living. What are the components of her essay that particularly deal with writers and the way in which language and art influence our perception?

2. Compare/contrast Oates's "Against Nature" and Alice Walker's "Am I Blue?" in 1) the conclusions they come to; 2) the images they use and how they use them (for example, what is a mirror for Oates and for Walker, respectively?); and 3) their respective writing styles. How is each woman's writing style in her essay appropriate for her subject and her stance?

3. Write down one or two of your own early memories of nature.

WAR

Compared to later American wars, particularly the war in Vietnam, World War II was "the good war"; our cause was undeniably just, our enemies incomparably evil, and our victory clear and decisive. Yet for at least one participant, Paul Fussell, there was little good about it. Whatever the war's larger historical significance, whatever heroic and redemptive narrative we may construct for it, World War II, for that U.S foot-soldier, meant "corpses, maddened dogs, deserters and looters, pain, Auschwitz, weeping, scandal, cowardice, mistakes and defeats, sadism, hangings, horrible wounds, fear and panic." As Fussell describes it in "My War," he entered the war an eager, optimistic, naive young man and left fully convinced that he "was not and never would be in a world that was reasonable and just." His physical injuries were serious, but the greater casualty was his belief in human possibility.

Of course, civilians also suffered in various ways during World War II. Jeanne Wakatsuki Houston learned what it meant to be Japanese American in the wake of the attack on Pearl Harbor. The excerpt included here from her memoir *Farewell to Manzanar*, written with James D. Houston, recaptures the experience of a young girl watching her father being taken away by FBI agents as a "potential saboteur." Eventually, over one hundred thousand Japanese Americans were deprived of their property and forcibly relocated to internment camps for the duration of the war. The FBI interrogation of her father that Houston recreates suggests the suspicious and repressive mentality that war can foster; the fact that people of Japanese but not of German descent were rounded up reminds us that war can also fuel racism.

Perhaps the most intense and dramatic example of the impact of World War II on civilians is the atomic bombing of Hiroshima, which, as Jonathan

Schell writes, "transform[ed] a city of some three hundred and forty thousand people into hell in the space of a few seconds." One hundred thousand people were killed instantaneously; thirty thousand more died over the next three months; numerous others were seriously damaged, some genetically, thus carrying the blight into the next generation. Numbers like one hundred thousand are too large for us to take in emotionally and too abstract to convey the quality of suffering and loss. As Schell writes, "Part of the horror of thinking about a holocaust lies in the fact that it leads us to supplant the human world with a statistical world; we seek a human truth and come up with a handful of figures." So, in the selection here from his aptly titled book *The Fate of the Earth*, Schell quotes the testimony of Hiroshima survivors, whose memories offer fragments of the larger picture on a scale we may begin to comprehend: an image of "a stark naked man standing in the rain with his eyeball in his palm" or of a parade of lost people so badly injured "you couldn't tell whether you were looking at them from in front or in back."

The bombing of Hiroshima was significant not only for what it put an end to but for what it began. A new era of military technology had arrived: a single bomb had destroyed a city. Seven years later, the United States developed the far more potent hydrogen bomb, and by 1982, when Schell wrote, the world's nuclear arsenal had the power to destroy a million Hiroshimas. The Cold War and the nuclear arms race that followed World War II threatened to destroy all life on earth. Barbara Kingsolver borrows an analogy from astronomer Carl Sagan: "we are all locked together in a room filled with gasoline vapors, insisting that because *they* have two hundred matches, *we* won't be safe until we have *three* hundred." Her essay "In the Belly of the Beast" uses the occasion of a visit to a nuclear missile museum to discuss the cost of the Cold War, in social programs underfunded and in a certain regimentation of thinking under the relentless propaganda that sustained American public support for continued militarization.

The Vietnam War too had its costs, quantifiable, perhaps, but still immeasurable. The numbers are striking—fifty-eight thousand Americans killed and over two million Vietnamese—but, again, it is essential to put individual faces on the suffering. In Gloria Emerson's *Winners and Losers*, excerpted here, we meet the Humbers of Westborough, Massachusetts and see in painful detail the repercussions (including the eventual dissolution of a thirty-year marriage) after Teddy Humber returns home from the war terribly injured, condemned to unending pain. Teddy and his parents may never have understood what the war was about, but they come to understand quite well what it meant for the families, more often than not working-class families, whose sons (and sometimes daughters) were its casualties.

Why, then, would someone ever go to war? As Tim O'Brien sees it, shame, embarrassment, fear of "patriotic ridicule" play no small part. Governments work hard to mobilize their citizens psychologically and ideologically for a war, and the pressures on a young person to enlist and believe can be immense. But O'Brien, in his autobiographical story "On the Rainy River," reminds us that it may be possible to resist such pressures. "I was drafted to fight a war I hated," his narrator explains and, despite the jingoism of the small town he grew up in, he considers escaping to Canada. Inverting traditional values, he argues that this would be the truly heroic act, while succumbing to the demand to fight in a war he considers immoral would simply be cowardice.

In "On War and War and War and . . . ," written in the midst of the Gulf War of 1991, June Jordan responds with fury to the United States attack on Iraq. The war is costing a billion dollars a day, she tells us, money desperately needed by poor communities of color like Oakland, California, where she has spoken at an antiwar rally. Behind protest against a war lies the assumption that things *can* change; the intensity of Jordan's anger may reflect the depth of her hope. Unlike Paul Fussell, permanently disillusioned by his combat experiences, Jordan still seems to believe the world can be made "reasonable and just." Her essay, like the others in this section, has nothing good to say about war. But then, perhaps hope lies not in believing that the next war will be a "good war," but that it can be stopped.

MY WAR

Paul Fussell

Paul Fussell was born in 1924 and is an English professor at the University of Pennsylvania. He has written a number of scholarly books on literature, but is probably better known for his writing on war. The Great War and Modern Memory won the National Book Award as well as the National Book Critics Circle Award in 1976. Among his other works are The Boy Scout Handbook and Other Observations (1982), in which the following essay appeared, Thank God for the Atom Bomb and Other Essays (1988), and Doing Battle: The Making of a Skeptic (1996).

Over the past few years I find I've written a great deal about war, which is odd because I'm supposed to be a professor of English literature. And I find I've given the Second World War a uniformly bad press, rejecting all attempts to depict it as a sensible proceeding or to mitigate its cruelty and swinishness. I have rubbed readers' noses in some very noisome materials—corpses, maddened dogs, deserters and looters, pain, Auschwitz, weeping, scandal, cowardice, mistakes and defeats, sadism, hangings, horrible wounds, fear and panic. Whenever I deliver this unhappy view of the war, especially when I try to pass it through a protective screen of irony, I hear from outraged readers. Speaking of some ironic aesthetic observations I once made on a photograph of a mangled sailor on his ruined gunmount, for example, a woman from Brooklyn found me "callous," and accused me of an "overwhelming deficiency in human compassion." Another reader, who I suspect has had as little empirical contact with the actualities of war face to face as the correspondent from Brooklyn, found the same essay "black and monstrous" and concluded that the magazine publishing it (*Harper's*, actually) "disgraced itself."

How did I pick up this dark, ironical, flip view of the war? Why do I enjoy exhibiting it? The answer is that I contracted it in the infantry. Even when I write professionally about Walt Whitman or Samuel Johnson, about the theory of comparative literature or the problems facing the literary biographer, the voice that's audible is that of the pissed-off infantryman, disguised as a literary and cultural commentator. He is embittered that the Air Corps had beds to sleep in, that Patton's Third Army got all the credit, that noncombatants of the Medical Administrative and Quartermaster Corps wore the same battle stars as he, that soon after the war the "enemy" he had labored to destroy had been rearmed by his own government and positioned to oppose one of his old allies. "We broke our ass for nothin'," says Sergeant Croft in *The Naked and the Dead.* These are this speaker's residual complaints while he is affecting to be annoyed primarily by someone's bad writing or slipshod logic or lazy editing or pretentious ideas. As Louis Simpson says, "The war made me a foot-soldier for the rest of my life," and after any war foot soldiers are touchy.

My war is virtually synonymous with my life. I entered the war when I was nineteen, and I have been in it ever since. Melville's Ishmael[1] says that a whale ship was his Yale College and his Harvard. An infantry division was mine, the 103rd, whose dispirited personnel wore a colorful green-and-yellow cactus on their left shoulders. These hillbillies and Okies, drop-outs and used-car salesmen and petty criminals were my teachers and friends.

How did an upper-middle-class young gentleman find himself in so unseemly a place? Why wasn't he in the Navy, at least, or in the OSS or Air Corps administration or editing *Stars and Stripes*[2] or being a general's aide? The answer is comic: at the age of twenty I found myself leading forty riflemen over the Vosges Mountains and watching them being torn apart by German artillery and machine guns because when I was sixteen, in junior college, I was fat and flabby, with feminine tits and a big behind. For years the thing I'd hated most about school was gym, for there I was obliged to strip and shower communally. Thus I chose to join the ROTC (infantry, as it happened) because that was a way to get out of gym, which meant you never had to take off your clothes and invite—indeed, compel—ridicule. You rationalized by noting that this was 1939 and that a little "military training" might not, in the long run, be wasted. Besides, if you worked up to be a cadet officer, you got to wear a Sam Browne belt, from which depended a nifty saber.

When I went on to college, it was natural to continue my technique for not exposing my naked person, and luckily my college had an infantry ROTC unit, where I was welcomed as something of an experienced hand. This was in 1941. When the war began for the United States, college students were solicited by various "programs" of the Navy and Marine Corps and Coast Guard with plans for transforming them into officers. But people enrolled in the ROTC unit were felt to have committed themselves already. They had opted for the infantry, most of them all unaware, and that's where they were going to stay. Thus, while shrewder friends were enrolling in Navy V-1 or signing up for the pacific exercises of the Naval Japanese Language Program or the

---

[1] Narrator of Herman Melville's novel *Moby Dick.*

[2] Newspaper published by the United States armed forces.

Air Corps Meteorological Program, I signed up for the Infantry Enlisted Reserve Corps, an act guaranteeing me one extra semester in college before I was called. After basic training, advancement to officer training was promised, and that seemed a desirable thing, even if the crossed rifles on the collar did seem to betoken some hard physical exertion and discomfort—marching, sleeping outdoors, that sort of thing. But it would help "build you up," and besides, officers, even in the infantry, got to wear those wonderful pink trousers and receive constant salutes.

It was such imagery of future grandeur that, in spring 1943, sustained me through eighteen weeks of basic training in hundred-degree heat at dreary Camp Roberts, California, where, to toughen us—it was said—water was forbidden from 8:00 A.M. to 5:00 P.M. ("water discipline," this was called). Within a few weeks I'd lost all my flab and with it the whole ironic "reason" I found myself there at all. It was abundantly clear already that "infantry" had been a big mistake: it was not just stupid and boring and bloody, it was athletic, and thus not at all for me. But supported by vanity and pride I somehow managed to march thirty-five miles and tumble through the obstacle course, and a few months later I found myself at the Infantry School, Fort Benning, Georgia, where, training to become an officer, I went through virtually the same thing over again.

As a second lieutenant of infantry I "graduated" in the spring of 1944 and was assigned to the 103rd Division at Camp Howze, Texas, the local equivalent of Camp Roberts, only worse: Roberts had white-painted two-story clapboard barracks, Howze, one-story tarpaper shacks. But the heat was the same, and the boredom, and the local whore culture, and the hillbilly songs:

> Who's that gal with the red dress on?
> Some folks call her Dinah.
> She stole my heart away,
> Down in Carolina.

The 103rd Division had never been overseas, and all the time I was putting my rifle platoon through its futile exercises we were being prepared for the invasion of southern France, which followed the landings in Normandy. Of course we didn't know this, and assumed from the training ("water discipline" again) that we were destined for the South Pacific. There were some exercises involving towed gliders that seemed to portend nothing but self-immolation, we were so inept with these devices. In October 1944, we were all conveyed by troop transports to Marseilles.

It was my first experience of abroad, and my lifelong affair with France dates from the moment I first experienced such un-American phenomena as: formal manners and a respect for the language; a well-founded skepticism; the pollarded plane trees on the Avenue R. Schumann; the red wine and real bread; the *pissoirs*[3] in the streets; the international traffic signs and the visual public language hinting at a special French understanding of things—*Hôtel de Ville, Défense d'afficher;*[4] the smell of Turkish tobacco when one has been brought up on Virginia and burley. An intimation of what we might be opposing was supplied by the aluminum Vichy coinage. On one side, a fasces and *État Français.*[5] No more Republic. On the other, *Liberté, Égalité, Fraternité* replaced by *Travail* (as in *Arbeit Macht Frei*), *Famille,* and *Patrie* (as in *Vaterland*).[6] But before we had time to contemplate all this, we were moving rapidly northeast. After a truck ride up the Rhône valley, still pleasant with girls and flowers and wine, our civilized period came to an abrupt end. On the night of November 11 (nice irony there) we were introduced into the line at St. Dié, in Alsace.

We were in "combat." I find the word embarrassing, carrying as it does false chivalric overtones (as in "single combat"). But synonyms are worse: "fighting" is not accurate, because much of the time you are being shelled, which is not fighting but suffering; "battle" is too high and remote; "in action" is a euphemism suited more to dire telegrams than description. "Combat" will have to do, and my first hours of it I recall daily, even now. They fueled, and they still fuel, my view of things.

Everyone knows that a night relief is among the most difficult of infantry maneuvers. But we didn't know it, and in our innocence we expected it to go according to plan. We and the company we were replacing were cleverly and severely shelled; it was as if the Germans a few hundred feet away could see us in the dark and through the thick pine growth. When the shelling finally stopped, at about midnight, we realized that although near the place we were supposed to be, until daylight we were hopelessly lost. The order came down to stop where we were, lie down among the trees, and get some sleep. We would finish the relief at first light. Scattered over several hundred yards, the 250 of us in F Company lay down in a darkness so thick we could see nothing at all. Despite the terror of our first shelling (and several people had been hit), we slept as soundly as babes. At dawn I awoke, and what I saw all around were numerous objects I'd miraculously not tripped over in the

[3] Urinals (French).

[4] Town hall; post no bills (both French).

[5] The French State (French).

[6] *"Liberté, Égalité, Fraternité"* (French for "liberty, equality, brotherhood") was the motto of the French Republic; *"Travail, Famille, Patrie"* (French for "work, family, country") was the motto of Nazi-occupied France; *"Arbeit Macht Frei"* (German for "Work makes you free") was the slogan over the entrance to the Nazi concentration camp Auschwitz; "Vaterland" is German for "fatherland."

dark. These objects were dozens of dead German boys in greenish-gray uniforms, killed a day or two before by the company we were relieving. If darkness had hidden them from us, dawn disclosed them with open eyes and
greenish-white faces like marble, still clutching their rifles and machine pis-
tols in their seventeen-year-old hands, fixed where they had fallen. (For the
first time I understood the German phase for the war dead: *die Gefallenen*.)
Michelangelo could have made something beautiful out of these forms, in
the Dying Gaul[7] tradition, and I was startled to find that at first, in a way I
couldn't understand, they struck me as beautiful. But after a moment, no
feeling but shock and horror. My adolescent illusions, largely intact to that
moment, fell away all at once, and I suddenly knew I was not and never would
be in a world that was reasonable or just. The scene was less apocalyptic than
shabbily ironic: it sorted so ill with modern popular assumptions about the
idea of progress and attendant improvements in public health, social welfare, and social justice. To transform guiltless boys into cold marble after
passing them through unbearable fear and humiliation and pain and contempt seemed to do them an interesting injustice. I decided to ponder these
things. In 1917, shocked by the Battle of the Somme and recovering from
neurasthenia, Wilfred Owen was reading a life of Tennyson. He wrote his
mother: "Tennyson, it seems, was always a great child. So should I have been,
but for Baumont Hamel." So should I have been, but for St. Dié.

After that, one day was much like another: attack at dawn, run and fall
and crawl and sweat and worry and shoot and be shot at and cower from
mortar shells, always keeping up a jaunty carriage in front of one's platoon;
and at night, "consolidate" the objective, usually another hill, sometimes a
small town, and plan the attack for the next morning. Before we knew it we'd
lost half the company, and we all realized then that for us there would be no
way out until the war ended but sickness, wounds, or oblivion. And the war
would end only as we pressed our painful daily advance. Getting it over was
our sole motive. Yes, we knew about the Jews. But our skins seemed to us
more valuable at the time.

The word for the German defense all along was "clever," a word that never
could have been applied to our procedures. It was my first experience, to be
repeated many times in later years, of the cunning ways of Europe versus the
blunter ways of the New World. Although manned largely by tired thirty-
year-old veterans (but sharp enough to have gotten out of Normandy alive),
old men, and crazy youths, the German infantry was officered superbly, and
their defense, which we experienced for many months, was disciplined and

---

[7] Greek sculpture of a solider dying with great dignity.

orderly. My people would have run, or at least "snaked off." But the Germans didn't, until the very end. Their uniforms were a scandal—rags and beat-up boots and unauthorized articles—but somehow they held together. Nazis or not, they did themselves credit. Lacking our lavish means, they compensated by patience and shrewdness. It was not until well after the war that I discovered that many times when they unaccountably located us hidden in deep woods and shelled us accurately, they had done so by inferring electronically the precise positions of the radios over which we innocently conversed.

As the war went on, the destruction of people became its sole means. I felt sorry for the Germans I saw killed in quantity everywhere—along the roads, in cellars, on rooftops—for many reasons. They were losing, for one thing, and their deaths meant nothing, though they had been persuaded that resistance might "win the war." And they were so pitifully dressed and accoutered: that was touching. Boys with raggedy ad hoc uniforms and Panzerfausts[8] and too few comrades. What were they doing? They were killing themselves; and for me, who couldn't imagine being killed, for people my age voluntarily to get themselves killed caused my mouth to drop open.

Irony describes the emotion, whatever it is, occasioned by perceiving some great gulf, half-comic, half-tragic, between what one expects and what one finds. It's not quite "disillusion," but it's adjacent to it. My experience in the war was ironic because my previous innocence had prepared me to encounter in it something like the same reasonableness that governed prewar life. This, after all, was the tone dominating the American relation to the war: talk of "the future," allotments and bond purchases carefully sent home, hopeful fantasies of the "postwar world." I assumed, in short, that everyone would behave according to the clear advantages offered by reason. I had assumed that in war, like chess, when you were beaten you "resigned"; that when outnumbered and outgunned you retreated; that when you were surrounded you surrendered. I found out differently, and with a vengeance. What I found was people obeying fatuous and murderous "orders" for no reason I could understand, killing themselves because someone "told them to," prolonging the war when it was hopelessly lost because—because it was unreasonable to do so. It was my introduction to the shakiness of civilization. It was my first experience of the profoundly irrational element, and it made ridiculous all talk of plans and preparations for the future and goodwill and intelligent arrangements. Why did the red-haired young German machine-gunner firing at us in the woods not go on living—marrying, going to university, going to the beach, laughing, smiling—but keep firing long after he had made his point, and so require us to kill him with a grenade?

---

[8] German bazookas.

Before we knew it it was winter, and the winter of 1944–1945 was the coldest in Europe for twenty-five years. For the ground troops conditions were unspeakable, and even the official history admits the disaster, imputing the failure to provide adequate winter clothing—analogous to the similar German oversight when the Russian winter of 1941–1942 surprised the planners—to optimism, innocence, and "confidence":

> Confidence born of the rapid sweep across Europe in the summer of 1944 and the conviction on the part of many that the successes of Allied arms would be rewarded by victory before the onset of winter contributed to the unpreparedness for winter combat.

The result was 64,008 casualties from "cold injury"—not wounds but pneumonia and trench foot. The official history sums up: "This constitutes more than four 15,000-man divisions. Approximately 90 percent of cold casualties involved riflemen and there were about 4,000 riflemen per infantry division. Thus closer to thirteen divisions were critically disabled for combat." We can appreciate those figures by recalling that the invasion of Normandy was initially accomplished by only six divisions (nine if we add the airborne). Thus crucial were little things like decent mittens and gloves, fur-lined parkas, thermal underwear—all of which any normal peacetime hiker or skier would demand as protection against prolonged exposure. But "the winter campaign in Europe was fought by most combat personnel in a uniform that did not give proper protection": we wore silly long overcoats, right out of the nineteenth century; thin field jackets, designed to convey an image of manliness at Fort Bragg; and wool dress trousers. We wore the same shirts and huddled under the same blankets as Pershing's troops in the expedition against Pancho Villa in 1916. Of the 64,008 who suffered "cold injury" I was one. During February 1945, I was back in various hospitals for a month with pneumonia. I told my parents it was flu.

That month away from the line helped me survive for four weeks more but it broke the rhythm and, never badly scared before, when I returned to the line early in March I found for the first time that I was terrified, unwilling to take the chances that before had seemed rather sporting. My month of safety had renewed my interest in survival, and I was psychologically and morally ill prepared to lead my platoon in the great Seventh Army attack of March 15, 1945. But lead it I did, or rather push it, staying as far in the rear as was barely decent. And before the day was over I had been severely rebuked by a sharp-eyed lieutenant-colonel who threatened court martial if I didn't pull myself together. Before that day was over I was sprayed with the contents of a soldier's torso when I was lying behind him and he knelt to fire at a machine gun holding us up: he was struck in the heart, and out of the holes in the back of his field jacket flew little clouds of tissue, blood, and powdered cloth. Near him another man raised himself to fire, but the machine gun caught him in the mouth, and as he fell he looked back at me with surprise, blood and teeth dribbling out onto the leaves. He was one to whom early on I had given the Silver Star for heroism, and he didn't want to let me down.

As if in retribution for my cowardice, in the late afternoon, near Ingwiller, Alsace, clearing a woods full of Germans cleverly dug in, my platoon was raked by shells from an .88, and I was hit in the back and leg by shell fragments. They felt like red-hot knives going in, but I was as interested in the few quiet moans, like those of a hurt child drifting off to sleep, of my thirty-seven-year-old platoon sergeant—we'd been together since Camp Howze—killed instantly by the same shell. We were lying together, and his immediate neighbor on the other side, a lieutenant in charge of a section of heavy machine guns, was killed instantly too. My platoon was virtually wiped away. I was in disgrace, I was hurt, I was clearly expendable—while I lay there the supply sergeant removed my issue wristwatch to pass on to my replacement—and I was twenty years old.

I bore up all right while being removed from "the field" and passed back through the first-aid stations where I was known. I was deeply on morphine, and managed brave smiles as called for. But when I got to the evacuation hospital thirty miles behind the lines and was coming out of the anesthetic from my first operation, all my affectations of control collapsed, and I did what I'd wanted to do for months. I cried, noisily and publicly, and for hours. I was the scandal of the war. There were lots of tears back there: in the operating room I saw a nurse dissolve in shoulder-shaking sobs when a boy died with great stertorous gasps on the operating table she was attending. That was the first time I'd seen anyone cry in the whole European theater of operations, and I must have cried because I felt that there, out of "combat," tears were licensed. I was crying because I was ashamed and because I'd let my men be killed and because my sergeant had been killed and because I recognized as never before that he might have been me and that statistically if in no other way he was me, and that I had been killed too. But ironically I had saved my life by almost losing it, for my leg wound providentially become infected, and by the time it was healed and I was ready for duty again, the European war was over, and I journeyed back up through a silent Germany to rejoin my reconstituted platoon "occupying" a lovely Tyrolean valley near Innsbruck. For the infantry there was still the Japanese war to sweat out, and I was destined for it, despite the dramatic gash in my leg. But, thank God, the Bomb was dropped while I was on my way there, with the result that I can write this.

That day in mid-March that ended me was the worst of all for F Company. We knew it was going to be bad when it began at dawn, just like an episode from the First World War, with an hour-long artillery preparation and a smokescreen for us to attack through. What got us going and carried us through was the conviction that, suffer as we might, we were at least "making history." But we didn't even do that. Liddell-Hart's 766-page *History of the Second World War* never heard of us. It mentions neither March 15 nor the 103rd Infantry Division. The only satisfaction history has offered is the evidence that we caused Joseph Goebbels some extra anxiety. The day after our attack he entered in his log under "Military Situation":

> In the West the enemy has now gone over to the attack in the sector between Saarbrücken and Hagenau in addition to the previous flashpoints. . . . His objective is undoubtedly to drive in our front on the Saar and capture the entire region south of the Moselle and west of the Rhine.

And he goes on satisfyingly: "Mail received testifies to a deep-seated lethargy throughout the German people degenerating almost into hopelessness. There is very sharp criticism of the . . . entire national leadership." One reason: "The Moselle front is giving way." But a person my age whom I met thirty years later couldn't believe that there was still any infantry fighting in France in the spring of 1945, and, puzzled by my dedicating a book of mine to my dead platoon sergeant with the date March 15, 1945, confessed that he couldn't figure out what had happened to him.

To become disillusioned you must earlier have been illusioned. Evidence of the illusions suffered by the youth I was is sadly available in the letters he sent, in unbelievable profusion, to his parents. They radiate a terrible naïveté, together with a pathetic disposition to be pleased in the face of boredom and, finally, horror. The young man had heard a lot about the importance of "morale" and ceaselessly labored to sustain his own by sustaining his addressees'. Thus: "We spent all of Saturday on motor maintenance," he writes from Fort Benning; "a very interesting subject." At Benning he believes all he's told and fails to perceive that he's being prepared for one thing only, and that a nasty, hazardous job, whose performers on the line have a life expectancy of six weeks. He assures his parents: "I can get all sorts of assignments from here: . . . battalion staff officer, mess officer, rifle-platoon leader, weapons-platoon leader, company executive officer, communications officer, motor officer, etc." (Was it an instinct for protecting himself from a truth half-sensed that made him bury *rifle-platoon leader* in the middle of this list?) Like a bright schoolboy, he is pleased when grown-ups tell him he's done well. "I got a compliment on my clean rifle tonight. The lieutenant said, 'Very good.' I said, 'Thank you, sir.'" His satisfaction in making Expert Rifleman is touching; it is "the highest possible rating," he announces. And although he is constantly jokey, always on the lookout for what he terms "laffs," he seems to have no sense of humor:

> We're having a very interesting week . . . taking up the carbine, auto-
> matic rifle, rifle grenade, and the famous "bazooka." We had the bazooka
> today, and it was very enjoyable, although we could not fire it because of lack
> of ammunition.

He has the most impossible standards of military excellence, and he enlists
his critical impulse in the service of optimistic self-deception. Appalled by
the ineptitude of the 103rd Division in training, he writes: "As I told you last
time, this is a very messed up division. It will never go overseas as a unit, and
is now serving mainly as a replacement training center, disguised as a combat division."

Because the image of himself actually leading troops through bullets
and shellfire is secretly unthinkable, fatuous hope easily comes to his assistance. In August 1944, with his division preparing to ship abroad, he asserts
that the Germans seem to be "on their last legs." Indeed, he reports, "bets are
being made . . . that the European war will be over in six weeks." But October finds him on the transport heading for the incredible, and now he "expects," he says, that "this war will end some time in November or December,"
adding, "I feel very confident and safe." After the epiphanies of the line in
November and December, he still entertains hopes for an early end, for the
Germans are rational people, and what rational people would persist in im-
molating themselves once it's clear that they've lost the war? "This *can't* last
much longer," he finds.

The letters written during combat are full of requests for food packages
from home, and interpretation of this obsession is not quite as simple as it
seems. The C and K rations were tedious, to be sure, and as readers of *All Quiet
on the Western Front* and *The Middle Parts of Fortune* know, soldiers of all times
and places are fixated on food. But how explain this young man's requests for
"fantastic items" like gherkins, olives, candy-coated peanuts (the kind "we used
to get out of slot-machines at the beach"), cans of chili and tamales, cashew
nuts, deviled ham, and fig pudding? The lust for a little swank is the explanation, I think, the need for some exotic counterweight to the uniformity, the
dullness, the lack of point and distinction he sensed everywhere. These items
also asserted an unbroken contact with home, and a home defined as the sort
of place fertile not in corned-beef hash and meat-and-vegetable stew but gum
drops and canned chicken. In short, an upper-middle-class venue.

Upper middle class too, I suspect, is the unimaginative cruelty of some
of these letters, clear evidence of arrested emotional development. "Period"
anti-Semitic remarks are not infrequent, and they remain unrebuked by any
of his addressees. His understanding of the American South (he's writing
from Georgia) can be gauged from his remark "Everybody down here is illiterate." In combat some of his bravado is a device necessary to his emotional
survival, but some bespeaks a genuine insensitivity:

Feb. 1, 1945

Dear Mother and Dad:

Today is the division's 84th consecutive day on line. The average is 90–100 days, although one division went 136 without being relieved. . . .

This house we're staying in used to be the headquarters of a local German Motor Corps unit, and it's full of printed matter, uniforms, propaganda, and pictures of Der Führer. I am not collecting any souveniers [sic], although I have had ample opportunity to pick up helmets, flags, weapons, etc. The only thing I have kept is a Belgian pistol, which one German was carrying who was unfortunate enough to walk right into my platoon. This is the first one I had the job of shooting. I have kept the pistol as a souvenier of my first Kraut.

It is odd how hard one becomes after a little bit of this stuff, but it gets to be more like killing mad dogs than people. . . .

Love to all,
Paul

The only comfort I can take today in contemplating these letters is the ease with which their author can be rationalized as a stranger. Even the handwriting is not now my own. There are constant shows of dutifulness to parents, and even grandparents, and mentions of churchgoing, surely anomalous in a leader of assault troops. Parental approval is indispensable: "This week I was 'Class A Agent Officer' for Co. F, paying a $6000 payroll without losing a cent! I felt very proud of myself!" And the complacency! The twittiness! From the hospital, where for a time he's been in an enlisted men's ward: "Sometimes I enjoy being with the men just as much as associating with the officers." (*Associating* is good.) The letter-writer is more pretentious than literate ("Alright," "thank's," "curiousity"), and his taste is terrible. He is thrilled to read Bruce Barton's *The Man Nobody Knows* ("It presents Christ in a very human light"), Maugham's *The Summing Up,* and the short stories of Erskine Caldwell. Even his often-sketched fantasies of the postwar heaven are grimly conventional: he will get married (to whom?); he will buy a thirty-five-foot sloop and live on it; he will take a year of nonserious literary graduate study at Columbia; he will edit a magazine for yachtsmen. He seems unable to perceive what is happening, constantly telling his addressee what will please rather than what he feels. He was never more mistaken than when he assured his parents while recovering from his wounds, "Please try not to worry, as no permanent damage has been done."

But the shock of these wounds and the long period recovering from them seem to have matured him a tiny bit, and some of his last letters from the hospital suggest that one or two scales are beginning to fall from his eyes:

One of the most amazing things about this war is the way the bizarre and unnatural become the normal after a short time. Take this hospital and its atmosphere: after a long talk with him, an eighteen-year-old boy without legs seems like the *normal* eighteen-year-old. You might even be surprised if a boy of the same age should walk in on both his legs. He would seem the freak and the object of pity. It is easy to imagine, after seeing some of these men, that *all* young men are arriving on this planet with stumps instead of limbs.

The same holds true with life at the front. The same horrible unrealness that is so hard to describe. . . . I think I'll have to write a book about all this sometime.

But even here, he can't conclude without reverting to cliché and twerpy optimism:

Enough for this morning. I'm feeling well and I'm very comfortable, and the food is improving. We had chicken and ice cream yesterday!

He has not read Swift yet, but in the vision of the young men with their stumps there's perhaps a hint that he's going to. And indeed, when he enrolled in graduate school later, the first course he was attracted to was on Swift and Pope. And ever since he's been trying to understand satire, and even to experiment with it himself.

It was in the army that I discovered my calling. I hadn't known that I was a teacher, but I found I could explain things: the operation of flamethrowers, map-reading, small-arms firing, "field sanitation." I found I could "lecture" and organize and make things clear. I could start at the beginning of a topic and lead an audience to the end. When the war was over, being trained for nothing useful, I naturally fell into the course that would require largely a mere continuation of this act. In becoming a college teacher of literature I was aware of lots of company: thousands of veterans swarmed to graduate school to study literature, persuaded that poetry and prose could save the world, or at least help wash away some of the intellectual shame of the years we'd been through. From this generation came John Berryman and Randall Jarrell and Delmore Schwartz and Saul Bellow and Louis Simpson and Richard Wilbur and William Meredith and all the others who, afire with the precepts of the New Criticism, embraced literature, and the teaching of it, as quasi-religious obligation.

To this day I tend to think of all hierarchies, especially the academic one, as military. The undergraduate students, at the "bottom," are the recruits and draftees, privates all. Teaching assistants and graduate students are the noncoms, with grades (only officers have "ranks") varying according to seniority: a G-4 is more important than a G-1, etc. Instructors, where they still exist, are the second and first lieutenants, and together with the assistant professors (captains) make up the company-grade officers. When we move up to the tenured ranks, associate professors answer to field-grade officers, majors and colonels. Professors are generals, beginning with brigadier—that's a newly promoted one. Most are major-generals, and upon retirement they will be advanced to lieutenant-general ("professor emeritus"). The main academic administration is less like a higher authority in the same structure than an adjacent echelon, like a group of powerful congressmen, for example, or people from the judge advocate's or inspector general's departments. The board of trustees, empowered to make professorial appointments and thus confer academic ranks and privileges, is the equivalent of the president of the United States, who signs commissions very like letters of academic appointment: "Reposing special trust and confidence in the . . . abilities of _____ , I do appoint him," etc. It is not hard to see also that the military principle crudely registered in the axiom "rank has its privileges" operates in academic life, where there are such plums to be plucked as frequent leaves of absence, single-occupant offices, light teaching loads, and convenient, all-weather parking spaces.

I think this generally unconscious way of conceiving of the academic hierarchy is common among people who went to graduate school immediately after the war, and who went on the G.I. Bill.[9] Perhaps many were attracted to university teaching as a postwar profession because in part they felt they understood its mechanisms already. Hence their ambitiousness, their sense that if to be a first lieutenant is fine, to work up to lieutenant-general is wonderful. And I suspect that their conception of instruction is still, like mine, tinged with Army. I think all of us of that vintage feel uneasy with forms of teaching that don't recognize a clear hierarchy—team-teaching, for example, or even the seminar, which assumes the fiction that leader and participants possess roughly equal knowledge and authority. For students (that is, enlisted men) to prosecute a rebellion, as in the Sixties and early Seventies, is tantamount to mutiny, an offense, as the Articles of War[10] indicate, "to be punished by death, or such other punishment as a court-martial shall direct." I have never been an enthusiast for the Movement.

In addition to remaining rank-conscious, I persist in the army habit of exact personnel classification. For me, everyone still has an invisible "spec number" indicating what his job is or what he's supposed to be doing. Thus a certain impatience with people of ambiguous identity or, worse, people who don't seem to do anything, like self-proclaimed novelists and poets who generate no apprehensible product. These seem to me the T-5s of the postwar world, mere technicians fifth grade, parasites, drones, noncombatants.

Twenty years after the First World War Siegfried Sassoon reports that he is still having dreams about it, dreams less of terror than of obligation. He dreams that

---

[9] Package of economic and educational benefits for World War II veterans.

[10] The laws that governed United States Army and Air Force personnel (now replaced by the Uniform Code of Military Justice).

the War is still going on and I have got to return to the Front. I complain bitterly to myself because it hasn't stopped yet. I am worried because I can't find my active-service kit. I am worried because I have forgotten how to be an officer. I feel that I can't face it again, and sometimes I burst into tears and say, "It's no good, I can't do it." But I know that I can't escape going back, and search frantically for my lost equipment.

That's uniquely the dream of a junior officer. I had such dreams too, and mine persisted until about 1960, when I was thirty-six, past recall age.

Those who actually fought on the line in the war, especially if they were wounded, constitute an in-group forever separate from those who did not. Praise or blame does not attach: rather, there is the accidental possession of a special empirical knowledge, a feeling of a mysterious shared ironic awareness manifesting itself in an instinctive skepticism about pretension, publicly enunciated truths, the vanities of learning, and the pomp of authority. Those who fought know a secret about themselves, and it's not very nice. As Frederic Manning said in 1929, remembering 1914–1918: "War is waged by men; not by beasts, or by gods. It is a peculiarly human activity. To call it a crime against mankind is to miss at least half its significance; it is also the punishment of a crime."

And now that those who fought have grown much older, we must wonder at the frantic avidity with which we struggled then to avoid death, digging our foxholes like madmen, running from danger with burning lungs and pounding hearts. What, really, were we so frightened of? Sometimes now the feeling comes over us that Housman's lines, which in our boyhood we thought attractively cynical, are really just:

> Life, to be sure, is nothing much to lose;
> But young men think it is, and we were young.

STUDY AND DISCUSSION QUESTIONS

1. Why is Fussell so concerned with finding the right word to use for "combat"?

2. What does Fussell mean by irony? Why is it central to his perspective on his war experiences? What are some of the major ironies in Fussell's life?

3. What is Fussell's view of heroism in war?

4. How does Fussell's being "an upper-middle-class young gentleman" shape his response to his experiences during the war? And after?

5. "To become disillusioned you must earlier have been illusioned," Fussell writes by way of introducing his youthful letters. What were his "illusions" and where might they have come from?

6. Why do you think Fussell refers to himself as "he"—not "I"—when discussing his letters to his parents?

7. How do the lines from Housman at the end of "My War" change or deepen the essay's meaning?

SUGGESTIONS FOR WRITING

1. "I felt sorry for the Germans I saw killed in quantity everywhere," Fussell writes. How common do you think such feeling is among those in battle? Why is it not more common?

2. "Why did the red-haired young German machine-gunner firing at us in the woods not go on living—marrying, going to university, going to the beach, laughing, smiling—but keep firing long after he had made his point, and so require us to kill him with a grenade?" Can you offer one or two explanations that are plausible, if not satisfying?

3. Do you know someone who has experienced combat? (Perhaps you yourself have.) Were the consequences like those faced by Fussell?

FROM *FAREWELL*
TO *MANZANAR*

Jeanne Wakatsuki Houston and James D. Houston

Jeanne Wakatsuki Houston was born in 1934 in Inglewood, California, the daughter of Japanese immigrants. During World War II, she and her family were imprisoned in Manzanar, one of several internment camps for Japanese Americans. She eventually studied journalism and sociology at San Jose State University and, together with her husband James D. Houston, wrote Farewell to Manzanar: A True Story of Japanese American Experience During and After the World War II Internment *(1973), the first and seventh chapters of which are excerpted here. She later published* Beyond Manzanar and Other Views of Asian-American Womanhood *(1985). James D. Houston (b. 1933) has written a number of novels, including* Gig *(1969),* A Native Son of the Golden West *(1971), and* Love Life *(1985), as well as nonfiction.*

"What Is Pearl Harbor?"

On that first weekend in December there must have been twenty or twenty-five boats getting ready to leave. I had just turned seven. I remember it was Sunday because I was out of school, which meant I could go down to the wharf and watch. In those days—1941—there was no smog around Long Beach. The water was clean, the sky a sharp Sunday blue, with all the engines of that white sardine fleet puttering up into it, and a lot of yelling, especially around Papa's boat. Papa loved to give orders. He had attended military school in Japan until the age of seventeen, and part of him never got over that. My oldest brothers, Bill and Woody, were his crew. They would have to check the nets again, and check the fuel tanks again, and run back to the grocery store for some more cigarettes, and then somehow everything had been done, and they were easing away from the wharf, joining the line of boats heading out past the lighthouse, into the harbor.

Papa's boat was called *The Nereid*—long, white, low-slung, with a fore-deck wheel cabin. He had another smaller boat, called *The Waka* (a short version of our name), which he kept in Santa Monica, where we lived. But *The Nereid* was his pride. It was worth about $25,000 before the war, and the way he stood in the cabin steering toward open water you would think the whole fleet was under his command. Papa had a mustache then. He wore knee-high rubber boots, a rust-colored turtleneck Mama had knitted him, and a black skipper's hat. He liked to hear himself called "Skipper."

Through one of the big canneries he had made a deal to pay for *The Nereid* with percentages of each catch, and he was anxious to get it paid off. He didn't much like working for someone else if he could help it. A lot of fishermen around San Pedro Harbor had similar contracts with the canneries. In typical Japanese fashion, they all wanted to be independent commercial fishermen, yet they almost always fished together. They would take off from Terminal Island, help each other find the schools of sardine, share nets and radio equipment—competing and cooperating at the same time.

You never knew how long they'd be gone, a couple of days, sometimes a week, sometimes a month, depending on the fish. From the wharf we waved goodbye—my mother, Bill's wife, Woody's wife Chizu, and me. We yelled at them to have a good trip, and after they were out of earshot and the sea had swallowed their engine noises, we kept waving. Then we just stood there with the other women, watching. It was a kind of duty, perhaps a way of adding a little good luck to the voyage, or warding off the bad. It was also marvelously warm, almost summery, the way December days can be sometimes in southern California. When the boats came back, the women who lived on Terminal Island would be rushing to the canneries. But for the moment there wasn't much else to do. We watched until the boats became a row of tiny white gulls on the horizon. Our vigil would end when they slipped over the edge and disappeared. You had to squint against the glare to keep them sighted, and with every blink you expected the last white speck to be gone.

But this time they didn't disappear. They kept floating out there, suspended, as if the horizon had finally become what it always seemed to be from shore: the sea's limit, beyond which no man could sail. They floated a while, then they began to grow, tiny gulls becoming boats again, a white armada cruising toward us.

"They're coming back," my mother said.

"Why would they be coming back?" Chizu said.

"Something with the engine."

"Maybe somebody got hurt."

"But they wouldn't *all* come back," Mama said, bewildered.

Another woman said, "Maybe there's a storm coming."

They all glanced at the sky, scanning the unmarred horizon. Mama shook her head. There was no explanation. No one had ever seen anything like this before. We watched and waited, and when the boats were still about half a mile off the lighthouse, a fellow from the cannery came running down to the wharf shouting that the Japanese had just bombed Pearl Harbor.

Chizu said to Mama, "What does he mean? What is Pearl Harbor?"
Mama yelled at him, "What is Pearl Harbor?"

But he was running along the docks, like Paul Revere, bringing the news, and didn't have time to explain.

That night Papa burned the flag he had brought with him from Hiroshima thirty-five years earlier. It was such a beautiful piece of material, I couldn't believe he was doing that. He burned a lot of papers too, documents, anything that might suggest he still had some connection with Japan. These precautions didn't do him much good. He was not only an alien; he held a commercial fishing license, and in the early days of the war the FBI was picking up all such men, for fear they were somehow making contact with enemy ships off the coast. Papa himself knew it would only be a matter of time.

They got him two weeks later, when we were staying overnight at Woody's place, on Terminal Island. Five hundred Japanese families lived there then, and FBI deputies had been questioning everyone, ransacking houses for anything that could conceivably be used for signaling planes or ships or that indicated loyalty to the Emperor. Most of the houses had radios with a short-wave band and a high aerial on the roof so that wives could make contact with the fishing boats during these long cruises. To the FBI every radio owner was a potential saboteur. The confiscators were often deputies sworn in hastily during the turbulent days right after Pearl Harbor, and these men seemed to be acting out the general panic, seeing sinister possibilities in the most ordinary household items: flashlights, kitchen knives, cameras, lanterns, toy swords.

If Papa were trying to avoid arrest, he wouldn't have gone near that island. But I think he knew it was futile to hide out or resist. The next morning two FBI men in fedora hats and trench coats—like out of a thirties movie—knocked on Woody's door, and when they left, Papa was between them. He didn't struggle. There was no point to it. He had become a man without a country. The land of his birth was at war with America; yet after thirty-five years here he was still prevented by law from becoming an American citizen. He was suddenly a man with no rights who looked exactly like the enemy.

About all he had left at this point was his tremendous dignity. He was tall for a Japanese man, nearly six feet, lean and hard and healthy-skinned from the sea. He was over fifty. Ten children and a lot of hard luck had worn him down, had worn away most of the arrogance he came to this country with. But he still had dignity, and he would not let those deputies push him out the door. He led them.

Mama knew they were taking all the alien men first to an interrogation center right there on the island. Some were simply being questioned and released. In the beginning she wasn't too worried; at least she wouldn't let herself be. But it grew dark and he wasn't back. Another day went by and we still had heard nothing. Then word came that he had been taken into custody and shipped out. Where to, or for how long? No one knew. All my brothers' attempts to find out were fruitless.

What had they charged him with? We didn't know that either, until an article appeared the next day in the Santa Monica paper, saying he had been arrested for delivering oil to Japanese submarines offshore.

My mother began to weep. It seems now that she wept for days. She was a small, plump woman who laughed easily and cried easily, but I had never seen her cry like this. I couldn't understand it. I remember clinging to her legs, wondering why everyone was crying. This was the beginning of a terrible, frantic time for all my family. But I myself didn't cry about Papa, or have any inkling of what was wrenching Mama's heart, until the next time I saw him, almost a year later.

Fort Lincoln:[1] An Interview

"What is your full name?"

"Wakatsuki Ko."

"Your place of birth?"

"Ka-ke, a small town in Hiroshima-ken, on the island of Honshu."

"What schools did you attend in Japan?"

"Four years in Chuo Gakko, a school for training military officers."

"Why did you leave?"

"The marching. I got tired of the marching. That was not what I wanted to do."

"Have you any relatives serving in the military, now or in the past?"

"My uncle was a general, a rather famous general. He led the regiment which defeated the Russians at Port Arthur[2] in nineteen five."

"Have you ever been in contact with him since coming to the United States?"

"No. I have contacted no one in Japan."

"Why not?"

"I am what you call the black sheep in the family."

"So you have never returned to your homeland?"

"No."

---

[1] Military installation in Bismarck, North Dakota, where Papa has been imprisoned in a camp for "enemy aliens."

[2] Site of decisive battle in the Russo-Japanese War of 1904–05.

"*Because you are the black sheep.*"

"*And because I have never been able to afford the trip. I have ten children.*"

"*What are their names?*"

"*How can I remember that many names?*"

"*Try.*"

"*William is the oldest. Then Eleanor, Woodrow, Frances, Lillian, Reijiro, Martha, Kiyo, and let's see, yes, May.*"

"*That is only nine.*"

"*Nine?*"

"*You said there were ten.*"

"*I told you, it is too many to remember.*"

"*It says here that you are charged with delivering oil to Japanese submarines off the coast of California.*"

"*That is not true.*"

"*Several submarines have been sighted there.*"

"*If I had seen one, I would have laughed.*"

"*Why?*"

"*Only a very foolish commander would take such a vessel that far from his home fleet.*"

"*How can you explain this photograph?*"

"*Let me see it.*"

"*Aren't those two fifty-gallon drums on the deck of your boat?*"

"*Yes.*"

"*What were you carrying in fifty-gallon drums ten miles from shore?*"

"*Chum.*"

"*Chum?*"

"*Bait. Fish guts. Ground-up fish heads. You dump it overboard and it draws the mackerel, and you pull in your nets, and they are full of fresh fish. Who took this photograph anyway? I haven't gone after mackerel in over a year.*"

"*What do you think of the attack on Pearl Harbor?*"

"*I am sad for both countries. It is the kind of thing that always happens when military men are in control.*"

"*What do you think of the American military? Would you object to your sons serving?*"

"*Yes. I would protest it. The American military is just like the Japanese.*"

"*What do you mean?*"

"*They also want to make war when it is not necessary. As long as military men control the country you are always going to have a war.*"

"*Who do you think will win this one?*"

"*America, of course. It is richer, has more resources, more weapons, more people. The Japanese are courageous fighters, and they will fight well. But their leaders are stupid. I weep every night for my country.*"

"*You say Japan is still your country?*"

"*I was born there. I have relatives living there. In many ways, yes, it is still my country.*"

"*Do you feel any loyalty to Japan or to its Emperor?*"

Silence.

"*I said, do you feel any loyalty . . .*"

"*How old are you?*"

"*Twenty-nine.*"

"*When were you born?*"

"*I am the interrogator here, Mr. Wakatsuki, not you.*"

"*I am interested to know when you were born.*"

"*Nineteen thirteen.*"

"*I have been living in this country nine years longer than you have. Do you realize that? Yet I am prevented by law from becoming a citizen. I am prevented by law from owning land. I am now separated from my family without cause . . .*"

"*Those matters are out of my hands, Mr. Wakatsuki.*"

"*Whose hands are they in?*"

"*I do not like North Dakota any more than you do. The sooner we finish these questions, the sooner we'll both be out of here.*"

"*And where will you go when you leave?*"

"*Who do you want to win this war?*"

"*I am interested to know where you will be going when you leave.*"

"*Mr. Wakatsuki, if I have to repeat each one of these questions we will be here forever. Who do you want . . . ?*"

"*When your mother and your father are having a fight, do you want them to kill each other? Or do you just want them to stop fighting?*"

STUDY AND DISCUSSION QUESTIONS

1. Why is watching the boats disappear described at such length?

2. What, besides security concerns, might explain the FBI's treatment of Papa and the others?

3. What is revealed during Papa's exchange with the interrogator about the names of his ten children?

4. Why does Papa ask where his interrogator will go when he leaves North Dakota?

5. What kind of person does Papa seem to be in the first chapter? How does this characterization of him affect our reaction to the interrogation?

6. What do we learn about Papa from his response to his interrogation?

SUGGESTIONS FOR WRITING

1. Write a letter from Papa to his seven-year-old daughter explaining why he's in North Dakota.

2. Write a sketch of Papa's interrogator. Infer what you can and imagine the rest.

FROM *THE FATE* *OF THE EARTH*

Jonathan Schell

Jonathan Schell (b. 1941) has worked as a staff writer for the New Yorker *magazine, where much of his work originally appeared, and as a columnist for* Newsday. *Among his books are* The Village of Ben Suc *(1967),* The Time of Illusion *(1976),* The Fate of the Earth *(1982), from which the following is taken,* Observing the Nixon Years *(1989), and* World Enough and Time: A Political Chronicle *(1997).*

The yardsticks by which one can measure the destruction that will be caused by weapons of different sizes are provided by the bombings of Hiroshima and Nagasaki and American nuclear tests in which the effects of hydrogen bombs with up to sixteen hundred times the explosive yield of the Hiroshima bomb were determined. The data gathered from these experiences make it a straightforward matter to work out the distances from the explosion at which different intensities of the various effects of a bomb are likely to occur. In the back of the Glasstone book,[1] the reader will find a small dial computer that places all this information at his fingertips. Thus, if one would like to know how deep a crater a twenty-megaton ground burst will leave in wet soil one has only to set a pointer at twenty megatons and look in a small window showing crater size to find that the depth would be six hundred feet—a hole deep enough to bury a fair-sized skyscraper. Yet

---

[1] *The Effects of Nuclear Weapons,* edited by Samuel Glasstone and Philip J. Dolan.

this small circular computer, on which the downfall of every city on earth is distilled into a few lines and figures, can, of course, tell us nothing of the human reality of nuclear destruction. Part of the horror of thinking about a holocaust lies in the fact that it leads us to supplant the human world with a statistical world; we seek a human truth and come up with a handful of figures. The only source that gives us a glimpse of that human truth is the testimony of the survivors of the Hiroshima and Nagasaki bombings. Because the bombing of Hiroshima has been more thoroughly investigated than the bombing of Nagasaki, and therefore more information about it is available, I shall restrict myself to a brief description of that catastrophe.

On August 6, 1945, at 8:16 A.M., a fission bomb with a yield of twelve and a half kilotons was detonated about nineteen hundred feet above the central section of Hiroshima. By present-day standards, the bomb was a small one, and in today's arsenals it would be classed among the merely tactical weapons. Nevertheless, it was large enough to transform a city of some three hundred and forty thousand people into hell in the space of a few seconds. "It is no exaggeration," the authors of "Hiroshima and Nagasaki" tell us, "to say that the whole city was ruined instantaneously." In that instant, tens of thousands of people were burned, blasted, and crushed to death. Other tens of thousands suffered injuries of every description or were doomed to die of radiation sickness. The center of the city was flattened, and every part of the city was damaged. The trunks of bamboo trees as far away as five miles from ground zero—the point on the ground directly under the center of the explosion—were charred. Almost half the trees within a mile and a quarter were knocked down. Windows nearly seventeen miles away were broken. Half an hour after the blast, fires set by the thermal pulse and by the collapse of the buildings began to coalesce into a firestorm, which lasted for six hours. Starting about 9 A.M. and lasting until late afternoon, a "black rain" generated by the bomb (otherwise, the day was fair) fell on the western portions of the city, carrying radioactive fallout from the blast to the ground. For four hours at midday, a violent whirlwind, born of the strange meteorological conditions produced by the explosion, further devastated the city. The number of people who were killed outright or who died of their injuries over the next three months is estimated to be a hundred and thirty thousand. Sixty-eight per cent of the buildings in the city were either completely destroyed or damaged beyond repair, and the center of the city was turned into a flat, rubble-strewn plain dotted with the ruins of a few of the sturdier buildings.

In the minutes after the detonation, the day grew dark, as heavy clouds of dust and smoke filled the air. A whole city had fallen in a moment, and in and under its ruins were its people. Among those still living, most were injured, and of these most were burned or had in some way been battered or had suffered both kinds of injury. Those within a mile and a quarter of ground zero had also been subjected to intense nuclear radiation, often in lethal doses. When people revived enough from their unconsciousness or shock to see what was happening around them, they found that where a second before there had been a city getting ready to go about its daily business on a peaceful, warm August morning, now there was a heap of debris and corpses and a stunned mass of injured humanity. But at first, as they awakened and tried to find their bearings in the gathering darkness, many felt cut off and alone. In a recent volume of recollections by survivors called "Unforgettable Fire," in which the effects of the bombing are rendered in drawings as well as in words, Mrs. Haruko Ogasawara, a young girl on that August morning, recalls that she was at first knocked unconscious. She goes on to write:

> How many seconds or minutes had passed I could not tell, but, regaining consciousness, I found myself lying on the ground covered with pieces of wood. When I stood up in a frantic effort to look around, there was darkness. Terribly frightened, I thought I was alone in a world of death, and groped for any light. My fear was so great I did not think anyone would truly understand. When I came to my senses, I found my clothes in shreds, and I was without my wooden sandals.

Soon cries of pain and cries for help from the wounded filled the air. Survivors heard the voices of their families and their friends calling out in the gloom. Mrs. Ogasawara writes:

> Suddenly, I wondered what had happened to my mother and sister. My mother was then forty-five, and my sister five years old. When the darkness began to fade, I found that there was nothing around me. My house, the next door neighbor's house, and the next had all vanished. I was standing amid the ruins of my house. No one was around. It was quiet, very quiet—an eerie moment. I discovered my mother in a water tank. She had fainted. Crying out, "Mama, Mama," I shook her to bring her back to her senses. After coming to, my mother began to shout madly for my sister: "Eiko! Eiko!"
>
> I wondered how much time had passed when there were cries of searchers. Children were calling their parents' names, and parents were calling the names of their children. We were calling desperately for my sister and listening for her voice and looking to see her. Suddenly, Mother cried "Oh Eiko!" Four or five meters away, my sister's head was sticking out and was calling my mother. . . . Mother and I worked desperately to remove the plaster and pillars and pulled her out with great effort. Her body had turned purple from the bruises, and her arm was so badly wounded that we could have placed two fingers in the wound.

Others were less fortunate in their searches and rescue attempts. In "Unforgettable Fire," a housewife describes a scene she saw:

A mother, driven half-mad while looking for her child, was calling his name. At last she found him. His head looked like a boiled octopus. His eyes were half-closed, and his mouth was white, pursed, and swollen.

Throughout the city, parents were discovering their wounded or dead children, and children were discovering their wounded or dead parents. Kikuno Segawa recalls seeing a little girl with her dead mother:

A woman who looked like an expectant mother was dead. At her side, a girl of about three years of age brought some water in an empty can she had found. She was trying to let her mother drink from it.

The sight of people in extremities of suffering was ubiquitous. Kinzo Nishida recalls:

While taking my severely wounded wife out to the riverbank by the side of the hill of Nakahiro-machi, I was horrified, indeed, at the sight of a stark naked man standing in the rain with his eyeball in his palm. He looked to be in great pain, but there was nothing that I could do for him.

Many people were astonished by the sheer sudden absence of the known world. The writer Yoko Ota later wrote:

I just could not understand why our surroundings had changed so greatly in one instant. . . . I thought it might have been something which had nothing to do with the war—the collapse of the earth, which it was said would take place at the end of the world, and which I had read about as a child.

And a history professor who looked back at the city after the explosion remarked later, "I saw that Hiroshima had disappeared."

As the fires sprang up in the ruins, many people, having found injured family members and friends, were now forced to abandon them to the flames or to lose their own lives in the firestorm. Those who left children, husbands, wives, friends, and strangers to burn often found these experiences the most awful of the entire ordeal. Mikio Inoue describes how one man, a professor, came to abandon his wife:

It was when I crossed Miyuki Bridge that I saw Professor Takenaka, standing at the foot of the bridge. He was almost naked, wearing nothing but shorts, and he had a ball of rice in his right hand. Beyond the streetcar line, the northern area was covered by red fire burning against the sky. Far away from the line, Ote-machi was also a sea of fire.

That day, Professor Takenaka had not gone to Hiroshima University, and the A-bomb exploded when he was at home. He tried to rescue his wife, who was trapped under a roofbeam, but all his efforts were in vain. The fire was threatening him also. His wife pleaded, "Run away, dear!" He was forced to desert his wife and escape from the fire. He was now at the foot of Miyuki Bridge.

But I wonder how he came to hold that ball of rice in his hand. His naked figure, standing there before the flames with that ball of rice, looked to me as a symbol of the modest hopes of human beings.

In "Hiroshima," John Hersey describes the flight of a group of German priests and their Japanese colleagues through a burning section of the city:

> The street was cluttered with parts of houses that had slid into it, and with fallen telephone poles and wires. From every second or third house came the voices of people buried and abandoned, who invariably screamed, with formal politeness, "*Tasukete kure!* Help, if you please!" The priests recognized several ruins from which these cries came as the homes of friends, but because of the fire it was too late to help.

And thus it happened that throughout Hiroshima all the ties of affection and respect that join human beings to one another were being pulled and rent by the spreading firestorm. Soon processions of the injured—processions of a kind that had never been seen before in history—began to file away from the center of the city toward its outskirts. Most of the people suffered from burns, which had often blackened their skin or caused it to sag off them. A grocer who joined one of these processions has described them in an interview with Robert Jay Lifton which appears in his book "Death in Life":

> They held their arms bent [forward] . . . and their skin—not only on their hands but on their faces and bodies, too—hung down. . . . If there had been only one or two such people . . . perhaps I would not have had such a strong impression. But wherever I walked, I met these people. . . . Many of them died along the road. I can still picture them in my mind—like walking ghosts. They didn't look like people of this world.

The grocer also recalls that because of people's injuries "you couldn't tell whether you were looking at them from in front or in back." People found it impossible to recognize one another. A woman who at the time was a girl of thirteen, and suffered disfiguring burns on her face, has recalled, "My face was so distorted and changed that people couldn't tell who I was. After a while I could call others' names but they couldn't recognize me." In addition to being injured, many people were vomiting—an early symptom of radiation sickness. For many, horrifying and unreal events occurred in a chaotic jumble. In "Unforgettable Fire," Torako Hironaka enumerates some of the things that she remembers:

1. Some burned work-clothes.
2. People crying for help with their heads, shoulders, or the soles of their feet injured by fragments of broken window glass. Glass fragments were scattered everywhere.
3. [A woman] crying, saying "Aigo! Aigo!" (a Korean expression of sorrow).

4. A burning pine tree.
5. A naked woman.
6. Naked girls crying, "Stupid America!"
7. I was crouching in a puddle, for fear of being shot by a machine gun. My breasts were torn.
8. Burned down electric power lines.
9. A telephone pole had burned and fallen down.
10. A field of watermelons.
11. A dead horse.
12. What with dead cats, pigs, and people, it was just a hell on earth.

Physical collapse brought emotional and spiritual collapse with it. The survivors were, on the whole, listless and stupefied. After the escapes, and the failures to escape, from the firestorm, a silence fell over the city and its remaining population. People suffered and died without speaking or otherwise making a sound. The processions of the injured, too, were soundless. Dr. Michihiko Hachiya has written in his book "Hiroshima Diary":

> Those who were able walked silently toward the suburbs in the distant hills, their spirits broken, their initiative gone. When asked whence they had come, they pointed to the city and said, "That way," and when asked where they were going, pointed away from the city and said, "This way." They were so broken and confused that they moved and behaved like automatons.
>
> Their reactions had astonished outsiders, who reported with amazement the spectacle of long files of people holding stolidly to a narrow, rough path when close by was a smooth, easy road going in the same direction. The outsiders could not grasp the fact that they were witnessing the exodus of a people who walked in the realm of dreams.

Those who were still capable of action often acted in an absurd or an insane way. Some of them energetically pursued tasks that had made sense in the intact Hiroshima of a few minutes before but were now utterly inappropriate. Hersey relates that the German priests were bent on bringing to safety a suitcase, containing diocesan accounts and a sum of money, that they had rescued from the fire and were carrying around with them through the burning city. And Dr. Lifton describes a young soldier's punctilious efforts to find and preserve the ashes of a burned military code book while people around him were screaming for help. Other people simply lost their minds. For example, when the German priests were escaping from the firestorm, one of them, Father Wilhelm Kleinsorge, carried on his back a Mr. Fukai, who kept saying that he wanted to remain where he was. When Father Kleinsorge finally put Mr. Fukai down, he started running. Hersey writes:

> Father Kleinsorge shouted to a dozen soldiers, who were standing by the bridge, to stop him. As Father Kleinsorge started back to get Mr. Fukai,

Father LaSalle called out, "Hurry! Don't waste time!" So Father Kleinsorge just requested the soldiers to take care of Mr. Fukai. They said they would, but the little, broken man got away from them, and the last the priests could see of him, he was running back toward the fire.

In the weeks after the bombing, many survivors began to notice the appearance of petechiae—small spots caused by hemorrhages—on their skin. These usually signalled the onset of the critical stage of radiation sickness. In the first stage, the victims characteristically vomited repeatedly, ran a fever, and developed an abnormal thirst. (The cry "Water! Water!" was one of the few sounds often heard in Hiroshima on the day of the bombing.) Then, after a few hours or days, there was a deceptively hopeful period of remission of symptoms, called the latency period, which lasted from about a week to about four weeks. Radiation attacks the reproductive function of cells, and those that reproduce most frequently are therefore the most vulnerable. Among these are the bone-marrow cells, which are responsible for the production of blood cells. During the latency period, the count of white blood cells, which are instrumental in fighting infections, and the count of platelets, which are instrumental in clotting, drop precipitously, so the body is poorly defended against infection and is liable to hemorrhaging. In the third, and final, stage, which may last for several weeks, the victim's hair may fall out and he may suffer from diarrhea and may bleed from the intestines, the mouth, or other parts of the body, and in the end he will either recover or die. Because the fireball of the Hiroshima bomb did not touch the ground, very little ground material was mixed with the fission products of the bomb, and therefore very little local fallout was generated. (What fallout there was descended in the black rain.) Therefore, the fatalities from radiation sickness were probably all caused by the initial nuclear radiation, and since this affected only people within a radius of a mile and a quarter of ground zero, most of the people who received lethal doses were killed more quickly by the thermal pulse and the blast wave. Thus, Hiroshima did not experience the mass radiation sickness that can be expected if a weapon is ground-burst. Since the Nagasaki bomb was also burst in the air, the effect of widespread lethal fallout on large areas, causing the death by radiation sickness of whole populations in the hours, days, and weeks after the blast, is a form of nuclear horror that the world has not experienced.

In the months and years following the bombing of Hiroshima, after radiation sickness had run its course and most of the injured had either died of their wounds or recovered from them, the inhabitants of the city began to learn that the exposure to radiation they had experienced would bring about a wide variety of illnesses, many of them lethal, throughout the lifetimes of those who had been exposed. An early sign that the harm from

radiation was not restricted to radiation sickness came in the months immediately following the bombing, when people found that their reproductive organs had been temporarily harmed, with men experiencing sterility and
women experiencing abnormalities in their menstrual cycles. Then, over the
years, other illnesses, including cataracts of the eye and leukemia and other
forms of cancer, began to appear in larger than normally expected numbers
among the exposed population. In all these illnesses, correlations have been
found between nearness to the explosion and incidence of the disease. Also, fetuses exposed to the bomb's radiation in utero exhibited abnormalities and developmental retardation. Those exposed within the mile-and-a-quarter radius
were seven times as likely as unexposed fetuses to die in utero, and were also
seven times as likely to die at birth or in infancy. Surviving children who were
exposed in utero tended to be shorter and lighter than other children, and were
more often mentally retarded. One of the most serious abnormalities caused
by exposure to the bomb's radiation was microcephaly—abnormal smallness
of the head, which is often accompanied by mental retardation. In one study,
thirty-three cases of microcephaly were found among a hundred and sixty-
nine children exposed in utero.

STUDY AND DISCUSSION QUESTIONS

1. Why does Schell tell us at the start about the "dial computer" that cal-
    culates crater size?

2. Why does Schell quote rather than paraphrase the stories the sur-
    vivors tell?

3. One survivor describes an almost naked man holding a ball of rice, and
    adds: "His naked figure, standing there before the flames with that ball
    of rice, looked to me as a symbol of the modest hopes of human be-
    ings." Explain.

4. Why do you think Schell ends with a discussion of the effects of radi-
    ation on children "exposed in utero"?

SUGGESTIONS FOR WRITING

1. Historians today debate the "military necessity" of dropping the atomic
    bomb on Hiroshima (and Nagasaki); they ask whether doing so saved
    a significant number of American lives by ending the war sooner. Why
    might this matter? In what ways might it not matter?

2. Of the many images of suffering and destruction in Schell's essay, pick
    the one that most moved you and explain why.

IN THE BELLY OF THE BEAST

Barbara Kingsolver

Barbara Kingsolver was born in Annapolis, Maryland in 1955 and studied at DePauw University and the University of Arizona. She has written poetry, Another America *(1991); fiction, including* The Bean Trees *(1988),* Animal Dreams *(1990), and* Pigs in Heaven *(1993); and nonfiction,* Holding the Line: Women in the Great Arizona Mine Strike of 1983 *(1989) and* High Tide in Tucson: Essays from Now or Never *(1996), from which the following is taken.*

The Titans, in the stories of the ancient Greeks, were unearthly giants with heroic strength who ruled the universe from the dawn of time. Their parents were heaven and earth, and their children were the gods. These children squabbled and started a horrific, fiery war to take over ruling the universe.

A more modern legend goes this way: The Titans were giant missiles with atomic warheads. The Pentagon set them in neat circles around chosen American cities, and there they kept us safe and free for twenty-two years.

In the 1980s they were decommissioned. But one of the mummified giants, at least, was enshrined for public inspection. A Titan silo—a hole in the ground where an atomic bomb waited all its life to be launched—is now a missle museum just south of Tucson. When I first heard of it I was dismayed, then curious. What could a person possibly learn from driving down the interstate on a sunny afternoon and descending into the ground to peruse the technology of nuclear warfare?

Eventually I went. And now I know.

The Titan who sleeps in his sleek, deep burrow is surrounded with ugliness. The museum compound, enclosed by an unkind-looking fence, is set against a lifeless backdrop of mine tailings. The grounds are gravel flatlands. The front office is blank except for a glass display case of souvenirs: plastic hard hats, model missile kits for the kids, a Titan-missile golf shirt. I bought my ticket and was ushered with a few dozen others into a carpeted auditorium. The walls bore mementoes of this silo's years of active duty, including a missile-shaped silver trophy for special achievement at a Strategic Air Command combat competition. The lights dimmed and a gargly voice rose up against high-drama music as the film projector stuttered, then found its stride and began our orientation. A ring of Titan II missiles, we were told, encircled Tucson from 1962 until 1984. The Titan II was "conceived" in 1960 and hammered together in very short order with the help of General Motors, General Electric, Martin Marietta, and other contractors. The launch sites are below ground—"safely protected from a nuclear blast." The missile stands 103 feet tall, 10 feet in diameter, and weighs 150 tons. A fatherly-sounding narrator informed us, "Titan II can be up and out of its silo in less than a minute, hurling its payload at speeds of over 15,000 miles per hour nearly halfway around the world. This ICBM waits quietly underground, its retaliatory potential available on a moment's notice."

The film went on to describe the typical day of a missile crew, and the many tasks required to keep a Titan in a state of constant readiness. Finally we were told sternly, "Little remains to remind people that for 22 years a select group of men stood guard 24 hours a day, seven days a week, protecting the rights and freedom we enjoy in these United States." Day and night the vigilant crew monitored calls from their command post, "Waiting . . ." (a theatrical pause) "for a message that never came."

We filed out of the auditorium and stood in the hostile light of the gravel compound. Dave, our volunteer guide, explained about reinforced antennas that could go on transmitting during an attack (nuclear war disturbs radio transmissions, among other things). One small, cone-shaped antenna sat out in the open where anyone could trip over it. Dave told us a joke: they used to tell the rookies to watch out, this was the warhead. My mind roamed. What sort of person would volunteer to be a bomb-museum docent? The answer: he used to be a commander here. Now, semiretired, he trains cruise-missile operators.

It was still inconceivable that a missile stood erect under our feet, but there was its lid, an enormous concrete door on sliding tracks. Grate-covered holes in the ground bore a stenciled warning: TOXIC VAPORS. During accidents or miscalculations, deadly fuel would escape through these vents. I wondered if the folks living in the retirement community just downhill, with the excruciatingly ironic name of Green Valley, ever knew about this. Dave pointed to a government-issue weathervane, explaining that it would predict which way the poisonous gases would blow. What a relief.

We waited by the silo entry port while a Boy Scout troop emerged. I scanned the little boys' faces for signs of what I might be in for. Astonishment? Boredom? Our group then descended the cool stairwell into the silo. Just like a real missile crew, we put on hard hats to protect ourselves from low-hanging conduits and sharp edges. Signs warned us to watch for rattlesnakes. The hazards of snakes and bumped heads struck me as nearly comic against the steel-reinforced backdrop of potential holocaust. Or, put another way, being protected against these lesser hazards made the large one seem improbable.

A series of blast doors, each thicker than my body, were all propped open to let us pass. In the old days, you would have had to wait for security clearance at every door in turn before it would admit you and then heave shut, locking behind you. If you turned out to be an unauthorized intruder, Dave explained, you'd get a quick tour of the complex with your face very near the gravel.

Some forty steps down in the silo's bowels, we entered the "No Lone Zone," where at least two people stood guard at all times. This was the control room. Compared with my expectations, undoubtedly influenced by Hollywood, it seemed unsophisticated. The Titan control room was run on cathode-ray tubes and transistor technology. For all the world, it had the look of those fifties spaceship movies, where men in crewcuts and skinny ties dash around trying to figure out what went wrong. No modern computers here, no special effects. The Titan system was built, Dave said, with "we-need-it-now technology." I tried to get my mind around the notion of slapping together some little old thing that could blow up a city.

Dave was already moving on, showing us the chair where the missile commander sat. It looks exactly like a La-z-boy recliner. The commander and one designated enlisted man would have the responsibility of simultaneously turning two keys and engaging the missile, if that call came through. All of us stared mutely at the little holes where those keys would go in.

A changeable wooden sign—similar to the ones the Forest Service uses to warn that the fire danger today is MEDIUM—hung above the controls to announce the day's STRATEGIC FORCES READINESS CONDITION. You might suppose it went to ultimate-red-alert (or whatever it's called) only a few times in history. Not since the Cuban missile crisis, maybe. You would be wrong. Our guide explained that red-alerts come up all the time, sometimes triggered by a false blip on a radar, and sometimes (unbeknownst to crew members) as a test, checking their mental steadiness. Are they truly sane enough to turn that key and strike up nuclear holocaust? For twenty-two years, every activity and every dollar spent here was aimed toward that exact end, and no other.

"But only the President can issue that order," Dave said. I believe he meant this to be reassuring.

We walked deeper into the artificially lit cave of the silo, down a long green catwalk suspended from above. The entire control chamber hangs on springs like huge shock absorbers. No matter what rocked and raged above, the men here would not be jostled.

On the catwalk we passed an eyewash facility, an outfit resembling a space suit, and a shower in case of mishaps involving toxic missile-fuel vapors. At its terminus the catwalk circled the immense cylindrical hole where the missile stood. We peered through a window into the shaft. Sure enough it was in there, hulking like a huge, dumb killer dog waiting for orders.

This particular missile, of course, is impotent. It has been relieved of its nuclear warhead. Now that the Titans have been decommissioned, they're being used as launch missiles for satellites. A man in our group piped up, "Wasn't it a Titan that blew up a few weeks ago, when they were trying to launch a weather satellite?"

Dave said yes, it was, and he made an interesting face. No one pursued this line of thought, although questions certainly hammered against the roof of my mouth. "What if it'd been headed out of here carrying a payload of death and destruction, Dave, for keeping Tucson safe and free? What then?"

Like compliant children on a field trip, all of us silently examined a metal hatch opening into the missile shaft, through which service mechanics would gain access to the missile itself. A sign on the hatch reminds mechanics not to use their walkie-talkies while inside. I asked what would happen if they did, and Dave said it would totally screw up the missile's guidance system. Again, I felt strangely inhibited from asking very obvious questions: What does this mean, to "totally screw up the missile's guidance system"? That the bomb might then land, for example, on Seattle?

The Pentagon has never discussed it, but the Titan missiles surrounding Tucson were decommissioned, ostensibly, because of technical obsolescence. This announcement came in 1980, almost a decade before the fall of the Berlin Wall; it had nothing to do with letting down the nation's nuclear guard. Make no mistake about this: in 1994 the U.S. sank $11.9 billion into the production and maintenance of nuclear missiles, submarines, and warheads. A separately allocated $2.8 billion was spent on the so-called Star Wars[1] weapons research system. The U.S. government document providing budget authority for fiscal year 1996 states, "Although nuclear forces no longer play as prominent a role in our defense capability as they once did, they remain an important part of our overall defense posture." It's hard to see exactly how these forces are on the wane, as the same document goes on to project outlays of roughly $10 billion for the nuclear war enterprise again the following year, and more than $9 billion every year after that, right on through the end of the century. In Nevada, New Mexico, Utah, Texas, the Great Plains, and many places we aren't allowed to know about, real live atomic bombs stand ready. Our leaders are hard-pressed to pretend some foreign power might invade us, but we are investing furiously in the tools of invasion.

The Pentagon was forced to decommission the Titans because, in plain English, the Titans may have presented one of the most stupendous hazards to the U.S. public we've ever had visited upon us. In the 1960s a group of civilian physicists at the University of Arizona worked out that an explosion at any one of the silos surrounding Tucson would set up a chain reaction among the other Titans that would instantly cremate the city. I learned about

---

[1] Mocking popular name for President Ronald Reagan's "Strategic Defense Initiative," a program for developing a weapons system for outer space.

this in the late seventies, through one of the scientists who authored the extremely unpopular Titan report. I had months of bad dreams. It was not the first or last time I was floored by our great American capacity for denying objective reality in favor of defense mythology. When I was a child in grade school we had "duck and cover" drills, fully trusting that leaping into a ditch and throwing an Orlon sweater over our heads would save us from nuclear fallout. The Extension Service[2] produced cheerful illustrated pamphlets for our mothers, showing exactly how to stash away in the basement enough canned goods to see the family through the inhospitable aftermath of nuclear war. Now we can pass these pamphlets around at parties, or see the quaint documentary *Atomic Café,* and laugh at the antique charm of such naïveté. And still we go on living in towns surrounded by nuclear choke chains. It is our persistent willingness to believe in ludicrous safety measures that is probably going to kill us.

I tried to exorcise my nightmares in a poem about the Titans, which began:

> When God was a child
> and the vampire fled from the sign of the cross,
> belief was possible.
> Survival was this simple.
> But the savior clutched in the pocket
> encouraged vampires to prosper
> in the forest.
>
> The mistake
> was to carry the cross,
> the rabbit's foot,
> the spare tire,
> St. Christopher[3] who presides
> over the wrecks:
> steel cauliflowers
> proliferating in junkyard gardens.
> And finally
> to believe in the fallout shelter.
>
> Now we are left in cities ringed with giants.

Our tour finished, we clattered up the metal stairs and stood once again in the reassuring Arizona sun. Mine tailings on one side of the valley, the

---

[2] Part of the Department of Agriculture that helps with natural disasters.

[3] Patron saint of travelers.

pine-crowned Santa Rita mountains on the other side, all still there; beneath us, the specter of hell.

Dave opened the floor for questions. Someone asked about the accident at a Titan silo in Little Rock, Arkansas, where some guy dropped a wrench on the missile and it blew up. Dave wished to point out several things. First, it wasn't a wrench, it was a ratchet. Second, it was a crew of rookies who had been sent in to service the missile. But yes, the unfortunate rookie did drop a tool. It bounced and hit the missile's sheet-metal skin, which is only a quarter of an inch thick. And which doesn't *house* the fuel tank—it *is* the fuel tank. The Titan silo's "blast-proof" concrete lid weighs 740 tons. It was blown 300 yards through the air into a Little Rock cornfield.

Dave wanted us to know something else about this accident: the guys in the shock-absorber-suspended control room had been evacuated prior to the ill-fated servicing. One of them had been drinking a Coke. When they returned they were amazed to see how well the suspension system had worked. The Coke didn't spill.

We crossed the compound to a window where we could look straight down on the missile's nose from above. A woman near me gasped a little. A man asked where this particular missile had been headed for, back in the days when it was loaded, and Dave explained that it varied, and would depend on how much fuel it contained at any given time. Somewhere in the Soviet Union is all he could say for sure. The sight of these two people calmly discussing the specifics of fuel load and destination suddenly scared the living daylights out of me. Discussing that event like something that could really happen. They almost seemed disappointed that it never had.

For years I have wondered how anyone could willingly compete in a hundred-yard dash toward oblivion, and I believe I caught sight of an answer in the Titan museum—in faces that lit up when they discussed targets and suspension systems and megatons. I saw it in eyes and minds so enraptured with technology that they saw before them an engineering spectacle, not a machine designed for the sole purpose of reducing civilizations to rubble.

Throughout the tour I kept looking, foolishly I suppose, for what was missing in this picture: some evidence that the people who ran this outfit were aware of the potential effects of their 150-ton cause. A hint of reluctance, a suggestion of death. In the absence of this, it's easy to get caught up in the internal logic of fuel capacities, circuitry, and chemical reactions. One could even develop an itch to see if this amazing equipment really works, and to measure success in purely technical terms.

The Coke didn't spill.

Outside the silo after the tour, I sat and listened to a young man regaling his girlfriend with further details about the Little Rock disaster. She asked him, "But that guy who dropped the, whatever it was. Did he die?"

The man laughed. "Are you kidding? That door on top was built to withstand a nuclear attack, and it got blown sky-high. Seven hundred and forty tons. That should tell you what happened to the guys inside."

She was quiet for a while, and then asked him, "You really get into that, don't you?"

"Well, sure," he said. "I love machines. It fascinates me what man is capable of designing."

Since that day, I've had the chance to visit another bomb museum of a different kind: the one that stands in Hiroshima. A serene building set in a garden, it is strangely quiet inside, with hushed viewers and hushed exhibits. Neither ideological nor histrionic, the displays stand entirely without editorial comment. They are simply artifacts, labeled: china saki cups melted together in a stack. A brass Buddha with his hands relaxed into molten pools and a hole where his face used to be. Dozens of melted watches, all stopped at exactly eight-fifteen. A white eyelet petticoat with great, brown-rimmed holes burned in the left side, stained with black rain, worn by a schoolgirl named Oshita-chan. She was half a mile from the hypocenter of the nuclear blast, wearing also a blue short-sleeved blouse, which was incinerated except for its collar, and a blue metal pin with a small white heart, which melted. Oshita-chan lived for approximately twelve hours after the bomb.

On that August morning, more than six thousand school-children were working or playing in the immediate vicinity of the blast. Of most of them not even shreds of clothing remain. Everyone within a kilometer of the hypocenter received more than 1,000 rads and died quickly—though for most of them it was surely not quick enough. Hundreds of thousands of others died slower deaths; many would not know they were dying until two years later, when keloid scars would begin to creep across their bodies.

Every wooden building within two kilometers was annihilated, along with most of the earthquake-proof concrete ones, and within sixteen kilometers every window was smashed. Only concrete chimneys and other cylindrical things were left standing. Fire storms burned all day, creating howling winds and unmeasurable heat. Black rain fell, bringing down radioactive ash, staining walls with long black streaks, poisoning the water, killing fish. I can recite this story but I didn't, somehow, believe it until I looked at things a human being can understand: great handfuls of hair that fell from the head of Hiroko Yamashita, while she sat in her house eight hundred meters from the hypocenter. The pink dress of a girl named Egi-chan, whose blackened pocket held a train ticket out of the city. The charred apron of Mrs. Sato, who was nursing her baby.

The one bizarre, incongruous thing in the museum at Hiroshima, it seemed to me, was a replica of the bomb itself. Dark green, longer than a man, strangely knobbed and finned—it looks like some invention that has nothing to do with people. Nothing at all.

What they left out of the Titan Missile Museum was in plain sight in Hiroshima. Not a sound track with a politically balanced point of view. Just the rest of the facts, those that lie beyond suspension systems and fuel capacity. A missile museum, it seems to me, ought to be horrifying. It had better shake us, if only for a day, out of the illusion of predictability and control that cradles the whole of our quotidian lives. Most of us—nearly all, I would say—live by this illusion. We walk through our days with our minds on schedule—work, kids, getting the roof patched before the rainy season. We do not live as though literally everything we have, including a history and a future, could be erased by two keys turning simultaneously in a lock.

How could we? How even to pay our monthly bills, if we held in mind the fact that we are camped on top of a technological powder keg? Or to use Carl Sagan's more eloquent analogy: we are all locked together in a room filled with gasoline vapors, insisting that because *they* have two hundred matches, *we* won't be safe until we have *three* hundred.

The Cold War is widely supposed to have ended. But preparations for nuclear war have not ended. The Titan museum's orientation film is still telling the story we have heard so many times that it sounds, like all ultra-familiar stories, true. The story is that *they* would gladly drop bombs on us, if they weren't scared by the sheer toughness of our big missiles. *They* are the aggressors. *We* are practicing "a commitment to deterrence."

Imagine you have never heard that story before. Look it in the eye and see what it is. How do strategic-games trophies and Titan-missile golf shirts stack up against a charred eyelet petticoat and handfuls of hair? The United States is the only nation that has ever used an atomic bomb. Dropped it, on men and women and schoolchildren and gardens and pets and museums, two whole cities of quotidian life. We did it, the story goes, to hasten the end of the war and bring our soldiers home. Not such an obvious choice for Oshita-chan. "To protect the rights and freedoms we enjoy" is a grotesque euphemism. Every nuclear weapon ever constructed was built for the purpose of ending life, in a manner so horrific it is nearly impossible to contemplate. And U.S. nuclear science has moved steadily and firmly, from the moment of its birth, toward first-strike capacity.

If the Titan in Green Valley had ever been allowed to do the job for which it was designed, the fire storm wouldn't have ended a world away. Surely all of us, even missile docent Dave, understand that. Why, then, were we all so polite about avoiding the obvious questions? How is it that a waving flag can create an electromagnetic no-back-talk zone? In 1994, half a century after the bombing of Hiroshima, we spent $150 billion on the business and technology of war—nearly a tenth of it specifically on nuclear-weapons systems. Any talk of closing down a military base raises defensive and reverent ire, no matter how wasteful an installment it might be. And yet, public debate dickers and rages over our obligation to fund the welfare system—a contribution of about $25 a year from each taxpayer on average, for keeping the poorest among us alive. How can we haggle over the size of this meager life preserver, while shiploads of money for death sail by unchallenged? What religion of humankind could bless the travesty that is the U.S. federal budget?

Why did I not scream at the top of my lungs down in that hole?

I didn't, so I'll have to do it now, to anyone with the power to legislate or listen: one match in a gasoline-filled room is too many. I don't care a fig who is holding it.

I donned the hard hat and entered the belly of the beast, and I came away with the feeling of something poisonous on my skin. The specter of that beast could paralyze a person with despair. But only if you accept it as inevitable. And it's only inevitable if you are too paralyzed with despair to talk back. If a missile museum can do no more than stop up our mouths, with either patriotic silence or desperation, it's a monument the living can't afford. I say slam its doors for good. Tip a cement truck to the silo's gullet and seal in the evil pharaoh. If humanity survives long enough to understand what he really was, they can dig him up and put on display the grandiose depravity of the twentieth century.

I left, drove down into the innocent palm-shaded condominiums of Green Valley, and then, unexpectedly, headed up the other side of the valley into the mountains. When I reached the plateau of junipers and oaks I pulled off the road, hiked into the woods, and sat for a long time on a boulder in the middle of a creek. Water flowed away from me on either side. A canopy of sycamore leaves whispered above my head, while they waited for night, the close of one more day in which the world did not end.

In a poem called "Trinity," Sr. Margaret Baldwin explained why she would never go down to the site of the first atomic-bomb explosion, which is opened to the public every year:

> . . . I would come face to face with my sorrow, I
> would feel hope slipping from me and be afraid
> the changed earth would turn over and speak
> the truth to the thin black ribbons of my ribs.

STUDY AND DISCUSSION QUESTIONS

1. What lessons is the Titan missile museum intended to teach?

2. In the missile silo, Kingsolver "felt strangely inhibited from asking very obvious questions." Why do you think that was?

3. What is Kingsolver saying in the section of her poem that she quotes?

4. Analyze Dave's response to the question about the Titan silo accident in Little Rock, Arkansas. What is he trying to do, and how?

5. In the Hiroshima museum, "the displays stand entirely without editorial comment." Why do you think that is?

6. What is Kingsolver's response to the claim that United States nuclear missiles exist only to deter nuclear attack?

7. Why does Kingsolver feel there should be no Titan missile museum of any kind?

SUGGESTIONS FOR WRITING

1. Describing the reactions of other visitors to the Titan museum, Kingsolver writes of "eyes and minds so enraptured with technology" that they were oblivious to its destructive potential. Have you ever seen such a response to technology? Where might you look?

2. Why do you think "public debate dickers and rages" over welfare spending while far greater military spending is rarely challenged?

FROM *WINNERS AND LOSERS*

Gloria Emerson

Gloria Emerson covered the Vietnam War for the New York Times *in the early 1970s and in 1971 she won the George Polk Award for her reporting. Her first book,* Winners and Losers: Battles, Retreats, Gains, Losses, and Ruins from a Long War *(1977), won the National Book Award. Emerson has also written* Some American Men *(1985) and* Gaza: A Year in the Intifada: A Personal Account from an Occupied Land *(1992).*

This is how Mrs. Joseph Humber of Westborough, Massachusetts, found out what had happened to her oldest son, called Teddy.

THE SECRETARY OF THE ARMY HAS ASKED ME TO EXPRESS HIS DEEP REGRET THAT YOUR SON, SERGEANT JOSEPH E HUMBER, JR. WAS WOUNDED IN ACTION IN VIETNAM ON 19 OCTOBER 1969 BY FRAGMENTS FROM A BOOBY TRAP WHILE AT AN OBSERVATION POST. HE RECEIVED WOUNDS TO BOTH LEGS, BOTH ARMS, THE CHEST, FACE, ABDOMEN, AND GROIN AREA WITH TRAUMATIC AMPUTATION OF THE RIGHT LEG BELOW THE KNEE AND TRAUMATIC AMPUTATION OF THE LEFT LEG ABOVE THE KNEE. HE HAS BEEN PLACED ON THE VERY SERIOUSLY ILL LIST AND IN THE JUDGMENT OF THE ATTENDING PHYSICIAN HIS CONDITION IS OF SUCH SEVERITY THAT THERE IS CAUSE FOR CONCERN. PLEASE BE ASSURED THAT THE BEST MEDICAL FACILITIES AND DOCTORS HAVE BEEN MADE AVAILABLE AND EVERY MEASURE IS BEING TAKEN TO AID HIM. HE IS HOSPITALIZED IN VIETNAM. ADDRESS MAIL TO HIM AT THE HOSPITAL MAIL SECTION, APO SAN FRANCISCO 96381. YOU WILL BE PROVIDED PROGRESS REPORTS AND KEPT INFORMED OF ANY SIGNIFICANT CHANGES IN HIS CONDITION.

KENNETH G WICKHAM, MAJOR GENERAL, USA, C-2179, THE ADJUTANT GENERAL, DEPARTMENT OF THE ARMY, WASHINGTON, D.C.

Then she found out more, and still more.

ADDITIONAL INFORMATION RECEIVED STATES THAT YOUR SON, SERGEANT JOSEPH E HUMBER, JR. CONDITION REMAINS THE SAME. HE IS STILL VERY SERIOUSLY ILL. PERIOD FURTHER HOSPITALIZATION IS UNDETERMINED AT THIS TIME. EVACUATION IS NOT CURRENTLY CONTEMPLATED. YOU WILL BE PROMPTLY ADVISED AS ADDITIONAL INFORMATION IS RECEIVED.

ADDITIONAL INFORMATION RECEIVED STATES THAT YOUR SON, SERGEANT JOSEPH E HUMBER, JR. HAS ARRIVED AT THE 249TH GENERAL HOSPITAL, CAMP DRAKE, JAPAN. UPON ARRIVAL HE WAS REMOVED FROM THE VERY SERIOUSLY ILL LIST AND PLACED ON THE SERIOUSLY ILL LIST. IN THE JUDGMENT OF THE ATTENDING PHYSICIAN HIS CONDITION IS OF SUCH SEVERITY THAT THERE IS CAUSE FOR CONCERN BUT NO IMMINENT DANGER TO LIFE. PROGNOSIS IS FAIR. HIS MORALE IS GOOD AND HE CAN COMMUNICATE. EVACUATION TO THE UNITED STATES IS CONTEMPLATED IN APPROXIMATELY TEN DAYS. YOU WILL BE PROMPTLY ADVISED AS ADDITIONAL INFORMATION IS RECEIVED.

ADDITIONAL INFORMATION RECEIVED STATES THAT YOUR SON, SERGEANT JOSEPH E HUMBER, JR. HAS BEEN EVACUATED FROM VIETNAM TO CAMP DRAKE, JAPAN. ADDRESS MAIL TO HIM AT THE MEDICAL HOLDING COMPANY, 249TH GENERAL HOSPITAL APO SAN FRANCISCO 96267. YOU WILL BE PROMPTLY ADVISED AS ADDITIONAL INFORMATION IS RECEIVED.

REFERENCE MY TELEGRAM OF 27 OCTOBER 1969 STATING THAT YOUR SON, SERGEANT JOSEPH E HUMBER, JR. ARRIVED AT CAMP DRAKE, JAPAN. HE WAS NOT REPEAT NOT EVACUATED TO CAMP DRAKE. HE WAS EVACUATED TO CAMP ZAMA, JAPAN. ADDRESS MAIL TO HIM AT THE UNITED STATES ARMY HOSPITAL, CAMP ZAMA APO SAN FRANCISCO 96343. PLEASE ACCEPT MY SINCERE

APOLOGY FOR THIS INACCURATE INFORMATION. YOU WILL BE PROMPTLY AD-
VISED AS ADDITIONAL INFORMATION IS RECEIVED.

YOUR SON, SERGEANT JOSEPH E HUMBER, JR. HAS BEEN EVACUATED TO VAL-
LEY FORGE GENERAL HOSPITAL, PHOENIXVILLE, PENNSYLVANIA. YOU WILL BE
NOTIFIED OF HIS ARRIVAL BY THE COMMANDING OFFICER OF THAT HOSPITAL.

Many such telegrams were composed, all with instructions to Western
Union not to telephone the messages. All of them used the same clear, correct and faintly solicitous language developed and refined by the Department of the Army for such purposes.

In Westborough, Massachusetts—a town of fifteen thousand in eastern Massachusetts—a notice to call Western Union for delivery of a telegram
was left at the Humber house on October 30, 1969, at 8 A.M. No one was
home. It was a small two-story frame house on South Street which the Humbers had been renting for five years. Stacia Humber was already at work that
day; for fifteen years she had been employed as an assistant launderer at the
Westborough State Hospital. Her husband, Joseph, had worked there as a
handyman, but when I visited the family in late April 1973 he had been retired for some years—and it did not seem to suit him. His expression was
suspicious and abused; when he spoke it was in short claps of thunder. His
very bright eyes looked watery and accusing.

On that Tuesday when the notice of a telegram came, Mr. Humber was
in Essex Falls, Vermont, visiting the couple's oldest daughter, Rosemary, who
was married to a medical student named William Notis. It was Billy, one of
the Humbers' three sons, who took the notice to his mother in the hospital
and went with her to a telephone booth. Mrs. Humber had a lot of trouble.
The Western Union office in Worcester told her they had no telegram for her.
When she called Westborough no one in the Western Union office there
could locate the telegram. Billy was a great help in keeping her calm and providing dimes. Finally she spoke to one man who seemed to have a more helpful spirit.

"I got real upset," Mrs. Humber said. "I said 'Look I have a son in Vietnam and this telegram is worrying me.' I demanded that something be done.
He was gone for several minutes and came back and finally said 'Oh yes, I
located the telegram.' I asked him to read it to me. He said 'Ma'am, I'd rather
not.' 'What do you mean you'd rather not?' I said. He said 'I think it would be
better if you read it yourself.' I said 'In other words, it's bad.' He said yes."

Teddy, who is Joseph Humber, Jr., had enlisted in the Army before he finished high school, after eleven years of education. He did well and was promoted to sergeant. He was an expert marksman and a parachutist. He was in
Vietnam with the 173d Airborne Brigade for four months when that October
he stepped on a mine near Bong Son and lost most of both his legs. At that

time he was twenty years old. In November 1972, at Thanksgiving, he came back to Westborough to live at home, after surgery and prolonged hospitalization at the Valley Forge General Hospital in Phoenixville, Pennsylvania, and additional surgery and hospitalization at the Veterans Administration Hospital in West Roxbury; he also went to the V.A. Hospital in Jamaica Plains. Teddy said he was on his third pair of artificial legs.

All the children—except Jeffrey, a twenty-year-old college student—were at home that Saturday night when we talked. Billy, twenty-three, said he had wanted to be a conscientious objector but after Teddy was wounded he enlisted in the Army. Rosemary, who had two children, was there with her youngest child, a plump and docile baby. Kathleen, the youngest Humber child, was eighteen and also a student. We sat at the dining-room table, stitched together by Mrs. Humber's cheerfulness and calm, her desire to make the occasion seem normal to the caller. Anyone looking in at us might not have guessed that all the questions and all the answers, all the memories and all the opinions, had to do with Teddy's legs. They did not mind talking about it. Only Mr. Humber, who seemed the smallest and most frail-looking member of the family, glowered for no particular reason. The others did not look at him when from time to time he spoke.

The walls and floors of the house were not very thick. It was easy to hear Teddy moving about upstairs and taking a long time to come down the staircase, making slow, uneven thumps as he walked. His wheelchair was in the narrow hallway. Once seated, the ruined part of him hidden below the table, he was a pleasant-looking man, with dark-brown hair and deep eyes, big shoulders and strong arms. That night he wore a checked shirt with the sleeves buttoned. He rolled up the left sleeve to show the arm which still had dozens of tiny black marks made by shrapnel that had not yet worked its way out of the skin. Before the Army he had wanted to be a forest ranger, and now it was not certain what he could do. He said he had liked the Army.

"No, I would never have discouraged him from enlisting," Mrs. Humber said. "I never discouraged any of my children from enlisting. Just hope for the best." In World War II she had joined the Women's Army Corps and liked it. This may explain why Mrs. Humber is a neat and well-organized woman, why she kept the telegrams about Teddy, his papers and records filed in order in a Christmas box.

"I feel bitter about it, but not that bitter," Teddy said. "I mean, after all, we did save a lot of lives over there and we did save the country."

After he was wounded, Mrs. Humber said very brightly, everyone in Westborough was wonderful, wanting to console her but not quite knowing what to do or how to do it. She is an attractive white-haired woman, with a nice smile, who suggests that she has spent years learning how to keep propped up and cheerful. People in Westborough had started a collection to send her to Japan so she could visit Teddy in the hospital at Camp Zama, but then the telegram came that he was being sent to Valley Forge.

Kathleen, who liked being interviewed more than the others because she had never seen a reporter, was a lively, long-haired girl who held nothing back. She remembered, could not forget, how she had told her aunt when Teddy went to Vietnam that she was sure she would never see him again as he had been. "In the same condition" is how she put it, wanting to be tactful. Even so, Kathleen was not prepared for the news of Teddy when it came. "I think a lot of people were afraid. They didn't know what to say. You'd be on the street and they would face you, they didn't break down or anything, but they were afraid to come into our house."

Teddy did not seem to always know what the others were saying. He seemed busy with something else; perhaps it was pain. He sat at the table without moving, often without hearing. Once when the baby started whimpering, Teddy lifted his arms to take it, but the child was passed by him and quickly handed to someone else to cuddle and soothe.

"I think I can be very truthful," Mrs. Humber said. "I think most people will tell you the same. We realized there was a war on, we thought it was horrible, but actually you don't realize how horrible it is until it involves one of your own. I think any mother will tell you the same thing. Even the people in Westborough didn't realize the horrors of the war until Teddy was killed."

No one noticed that she said Teddy was killed. This is what I heard.

Rosemary said her brother was the first casualty in Westborough, which she described as "a middle-class, an upper-class bedroom town" where ninety-five percent of the students in Westborough High School go on to higher education. The people who were training for jobs, who were headed toward a profession, did not go into the war, she said.

Mr. Humber suddenly came to life, and erupted. "Money talks," he said. "I'll go back to the old saying: the rich man gets richer and the poor man gets poorer."

"Money talks," Teddy said. "People with money, people going to college on an athletic scholarship or something, they went into the reserves."

He knew nothing of the long history of Bong Son, a coastal city in Binh Dinh province, or what Americans had been there before him and the 173d. Few soldiers ever did. They did not care. The war was cut into pieces that never came together for them; all that soldiers knew was what they saw and felt in the months they were there. But in 1966, when Teddy Humber was in high school, the 1st Air Cavalry Division fought its longest and largest operation around Bong Son. The campaign, known as MASHER/WHITE WING, lasted for forty-one consecutive days.

There is a big black volume, a congratulatory record, of the history of the 1st Air Cavalry Division in Vietnam—*Memoirs of the First Team,* it says—

that calls the Bong Son campaign a success. "The statistics of the operation were impressive: 1,342 enemy killed by the Cav, with an additional 808 killed by Free World Forces. Five of the nine enemy battalions engaged were rendered ineffective and three field hospitals were taken," the Cav "yearbook" says. No American casualties during MASHER/WHITE WING were given. It was always that way. The names of the different operations are in big black type, those foolish names the generals so loved: SHINY BAYONET, MATADOR, MASHER/WHITE WING, CLEAN HOUSE, CRAZY HORSE, WHEELER/WALLOWA ("the NVA[1] never knew what hit them"). Even President Lyndon Johnson found some of the names grating. In talking to senior American and South Vietnamese officials after the issuance of a joint communiqué at their Honolulu Conference, February 9, 1966, President Johnson spoke his mind. "I don't know who names your operations," he said. "But 'Masher.' I get kind of mashed myself."[2] The name WHITE WING was added as a precaution against an unpleasant, or squeamish, public reaction.

It was Binh Dinh province, with its long history of resistance against the French, which became the focus of American hope early in 1966 for their pacification program. But year after year, despite the American occupation of it, Binh Dinh never became a place they could overwhelm and change to be what they wanted. The number of dead Vietnamese and the refugees grew: Binh Dinh was never pacified.

Teddy Humber knew nothing of this, or even which side had almost killed him. It was not so strange for a soldier to be unsure. "It could have been a dead round," he said matter-of-factly. "It could have been planted by an American."

"I think people over there began to live a much better life as a result of the war going on and our boys being there," Mrs. Humber said. Teddy did not contradict her. No one in the family called them Vietnamese, only "those people" or "people over there."

There was still shrapnel in his eyes. He had headaches, Teddy said. But all agreed that the Army had given him marvelous medical care; all praised the Army for keeping him alive.

"Yes, the Army—but the V.A. is very bad," Teddy said. "The people think they are doing you a favor. Even now you go into a V.A. hospital and they will give more attention to a World War I, World War II or Korean veteran than to a Vietnam veteran." Then he told a few stories about the V.A. hospitals he knew, how in the ward the most helpless depended on the other men to assist them, how sad a place it had been, how uncaring the staff was.

---

[1] North Vietnamese Army.

[2] President Johnson's criticism of the name MASHER is in the Pentagon papers as published by *The New York Times*, Quadrangle Books. [Author's note]

Teddy said he was against war, that he thought everybody was against war, and if they were not, they should be locked up. "But those people, they came to the United States for help. If somebody came to you to ask for help and if you thought it was worth it, you'd help them. That's what Kennedy did. Then the United States got more involved—in my estimation the politicians and everybody started to prolong it because the country was making money. America was making money on it."

Mr. Humber brightened. "Money talks," he said. Billy wanted to explain why he had been a member of the Baha'i faith, which he described as a religion of Persian origin that believes in all the prophets and is against violence. His allegiance to the Baha'i had diminished when he was at a community college and had so much work. Mrs. Humber smiled sweetly as Billy went on; she said she tried to be open-minded when it came to the younger children. Mr. Humber looked furious.

"I was against the war and I was for the war. I had a personal grudge against the war because it hit the home front, it hit my brother, okay?" Billy said. "If I had really done what I wanted to do, I would have probably gone over there and shot every one of those people over there myself. But, then, obviously, I was still against it, so there was a conflict. I didn't know which way to swing."

Rosemary said we certainly had no business telling another country how to run their country, but that the antiwar movement had not helped or even made a difference. This reminded Mrs. Humber of something unpleasant that had happened when Rosemary's husband graduated from medical school at the University of Vermont in May 1972. She could not get over the sight of some of the demonstrators, although they were few in number. "They were dressed as Chinese, with grey faces, no, white faces, whitish grey," she said. "With hunched backs and old dirty bandages. Dressed as Chinese, apparently the Communist Chinese people."

Rosemary corrected her mother: the demonstrators were supposed to be North Vietnamese "who were being tortured by the Americans." The demonstrators played a death roll on drums, she said. They shrieked and groaned. They carried fake guns. They fell down.

"I had a camera so, oh my, without thinking, I took a picture," Mrs. Humber said. "There were eight, maybe ten, of them. I think they were young people but they appeared to be very old people. It was eerie, it was frightening, they looked so horrible."

"We were appalled," Rosemary said. "I think there was no reason to demonstrate at this particular graduation. They only chose it because they knew there would be news media there and they could get attention."

Mrs. Humber said it certainly wasn't called for, especially during such a happy occasion. "I was upset because it was something I wouldn't do, and

I wouldn't want any member of my family to do anything that violent," she said. "We all have our beliefs but we don't express them in a way that would hurt people. It was very, very wrong."

Teddy said people should be able to express themselves freely but without violence. Mr. Humber said there were a lot of Communists in the United States making trouble. He said it twice.

"Outside of the family we try not to express our feelings," Mrs. Humber said. There was silence. Then she said it was nice to have a family in troubled times. "Together but not together. It keeps you going."

On the porch, as I said goodbye, Mrs. Humber suddenly looked less cheerful and serene. She had her head down. A few months later I went back to leave her a plant. Mr. Humber came darting out of the house as if he expected savage intruders and then disappeared again. Teddy leaned out of his bedroom window. His face looked strange and excited. "I'm busy," he called out. I said that was fine and went away.

You kept on seeing Bong Son in the wire service stories from Vietnam, the stories that no one ever read. In January 1975 North Vietnamese forces attacked three hilltop positions west of Bong Son. The military command in Saigon said the enemy fired six hundred shells at government positions, then followed up with an infantry attack. Reinforcements moved in and drove back the attack, the command said. Bong Son fell on a Friday; there was no fighting.

It was ten years after MASHER/WHITE WING.

A medic with the 173d Airborne, whose headquarters was at Bong Son, wrote a little piece about the end of the war. "It was there in the blue-black floors of the jungle that I learned to root for the Viet Cong," he said. But soldiers who felt as he did, the veteran wrote, did not stop pursuing and killing the Vietnamese on the other side, who, after all, were trying to kill them too.

"The Viet Cong were capable of butchery, they committed their My Lais too, but they never sold their sisters, never licensed greed and there was no cowardice in them," the veteran wrote. "You had to admit they were the better men . . . Finally I realized I was angry because they were burying part of my history on Landing Zone English, and in the rest of those green hills. I had spent my nineteenth birthday there and I resented the idea that Americans probably won't be welcome there until I am no longer young. The melancholy lingers in the part of me that wants to go back to see how far I've come."[3]

---

[3] The fighting in Bong Son was described in an AP story, January 14, 1975. The former medic with the 173rd Airborne who wrote about the end of the war was John Hamill, in *The Village Voice*, April 7, 1975. [Author's note]

Stacia Humber had many things to say when I saw her two years later. The family was no longer in the house on South Street. She and her husband lived in an apartment, but they were moving out because she and Mr. Humber, after thirty years of marriage, were separating. Mrs. Humber had retired from the laundry and at the age of fifty-six wanted to start over. The marriage had not been a tranquil one, she said.

"I think it was worse for the children," she said. Teddy and the other children approved of her decision. Billy had finished college and married a nurse. Rosemary's husband was a doctor on the staff of a good hospital and they now had three children. Jeffrey had married and gone into the Army. "That's my third boy; he's been in for a year," Mrs. Humber said. She regretted that he was not pleased with military life. It had something to do with some training he wanted but was not getting. Kathleen had quit college, gone to work for the telephone company in Boston and then joined the Air Force. Rosemary and her husband were heartbroken, Mrs. Humber said, but Kathleen wanted to "advance."

Her most cheerful news was that Teddy had been married on May 26, 1975, to an eighteen-year-old girl named Bonnie Ryan, whom he had been seeing for a year and a half. "You wouldn't know him now," Mrs. Humber said. "Bonnie gets him up and out every single day. So far, so good."

Only Billy had attended the wedding ceremony, for Teddy had not wanted the entire family to come. At the reception for twenty-five people, all the Humbers had been there. She showed me the color photographs: Teddy with a mustache, standing up, a white rose in his lapel, his hair cut, in maroon trousers and a striped jacket. He looked tall next to his wife, a tiny, dark-haired girl whom she described as ambitious.

"The state took her away from her mother when she was twelve," Mrs. Humber said, "and placed her with foster parents. Bonnie met Teddy through a priest who was counseling her. We had such problems with Teddy. I used to rush home at times and never know what I would find. If she sticks by him, we'll have no more problems. He had nothing to live for, you see; a child needs more than the love of a mother and father . . . He'll always be in pain. The stumps still bother him. He has headaches. But when his stumps blister he treats himself. He hates the hospital. He's scared to death in them. They're not very nice to him—well, a little nicer in West Roxbury than Jamaica Plains, but they have no compassion at all for these Vietnam boys."

The collapse of South Vietnam, the television films of a ruined army and of refugees were depressing. She thought that Teddy was resentful, but of course, his wife Bonnie didn't realize what it was all about. "Teddy is the type of boy that shows no emotions, he was always very quiet," Mrs. Humber said. "But there was so much sadness, the bombed people fleeing their homes, totally poverty-stricken. All those people coming here. America's a lucky place for them. They could never stand on their own."

The Watergate conspiracies, the jail sentences of important men in the government, the resignation of a President had been more shocking than Vietnam, Mrs. Humber said. Her husband came in as she was saying once again how much Teddy had liked the Army. "He wanted to reenlist, he enjoyed it and was doing so well," she said wistfully.

There was nothing wistful about Mr. Humber, who said no son of his would ever go off to war again. He glared. "I went through it once with one boy. I don't care what the President says, they'll stay right here in the United States," he said. "If it costs me the last red penny I got."

Then he began to cry. He kept looking at us as the tears went down his face. He did not wipe them away, blow his nose or cover his face. He did not seem to know he was crying. It was not over for Teddy either, he said. "The doctors told me they don't know where they're going to stop cutting," Mr. Humber said.

His wife protested that she had never heard the doctors say any such thing, but it was no use. Her husband gave her a dreadful look. Mrs. Humber said she didn't quite know what she'd do if another war like Vietnam meant her other sons would be called up. "I wouldn't demonstrate," she said. "I'd go along with it and hope for the best."

Mr. Humber had not stopped crying when I left. He seemed to be talking to himself.

STUDY AND DISCUSSION QUESTIONS

1. Why do you think Emerson includes the text of all those telegrams?

2. In what ways does the Humbers' social class shape their experience?

3. "... until Teddy was killed," says Mrs. Humber. How might you account for this slip?

4. Why do you think the military gives "foolish names" like SHINY BAYONET and MATADOR to their operations?

5. Why does Emerson recount the history of Bong Son before and after Teddy's injury?

6. What's revealed about Mrs. Humber, about Rosemary, and about Teddy in their discussion of the antiwar demonstration at Rosemary's husband's graduation?

7. At the end of the excerpt, Mr. and Mrs. Humber talk of what they'd do if their sons were called to fight in another war. How might you explain the different places to which their experience has brought them?

8. Are there things Emerson wants the reader to understand about the Humbers and their experience that they themselves do not understand?

SUGGESTIONS FOR WRITING

1. "Billy, twenty-three, said he had wanted to be a conscientious objector but after Teddy was wounded he enlisted in the Army." If you were in Billy's place, would this have been your reaction? Explain why or why not.

2. We learn, near the end, that Mr. and Mrs. Humber are separating. If you were a marriage counselor, what might you say to them?

3. Pick one of the Humbers and write a letter to her or him expressing your feelings after reading the excerpt from Emerson's book.

ON THE RAINY RIVER

Tim O'Brien

Tim O'Brien was born in 1946 in Austin, Minnesota and lived a life not unlike that of the Tim O'Brien who narrates the allegedly fictional memoir The Things They Carried: A Work of Fiction *(1990), from which the following chapter is excerpted. Among his other books are* If I Die in a Combat Zone, Box Me Up and Ship Me Home *(1973),* Going After Cacciato *(1978), which won the National Book Award,* The Nuclear Age *(1981), and* In the Lake of the Woods *(1994).*

This is one story I've never told before. Not to anyone. Not to my parents, not to my brother or sister, not even to my wife. To go into it, I've always thought, would only cause embarrassment for all of us, a sudden need to be elsewhere, which is the natural response to a confession. Even now, I'll admit, the story makes me squirm. For more than twenty years I've had to live with it, feeling the shame, trying to push it away, and so by this act of remembrance, by putting the facts down on paper, I'm hoping to relieve at least some of the pressure on my dreams. Still, it's a hard story to tell. All of us, I suppose, like to believe that in a moral emergency we will behave like the heroes of our youth, bravely and forthrightly, without thought of personal loss or discredit. Certainly that was my conviction back in the summer of 1968. Tim O'Brien: a secret hero. The Lone Ranger.[1] If the stakes ever became high enough—if the evil were evil enough, if the good were good enough—I would simply tap a secret reservoir of courage that had been accumulating inside me over the years. Courage, I seemed to think, comes to us in finite quantities, like an inheritance, and by being frugal and stashing it away and letting it earn interest, we steadily increase our moral capital in preparation for that day when the account must be drawn down. It was a comforting theory. It dispensed with all those bothersome little acts of daily courage; it offered hope and grace to the repetitive coward; it justified the past while amortizing the future.

In June of 1968, a month after graduating from Macalester College, I was drafted to fight a war I hated. I was twenty-one years old. Young, yes, and politically naive, but even so the American war in Vietnam seemed to me wrong. Certain blood was being shed for uncertain reasons. I saw no unity of purpose, no consensus on matters of philosophy or history or law. The very facts were shrouded in uncertainty: Was it a civil war? A war of national liberation or simple aggression? Who started it, and when, and why? What really happened to the USS *Maddox*[2] on that dark night in the Gulf of Tonkin? Was Ho Chi Minh a Communist stooge, or a nationalist savior, or both, or neither? What about the Geneva Accords[3]? What about SEATO and the Cold War? What about dominoes? America was divided on these and a thousand other issues, and the debate had spilled out across the floor of the United States Senate and into the streets, and smart men in pinstripes could not agree on even the most fundamental matters of public policy. The only certainty that summer was moral confusion. It was my view then, and still is, that you don't make war without knowing why. Knowledge, of course, is always imperfect, but it seemed to me that when a nation goes to war it must have reasonable confidence in the justice and imperative of its cause. You can't fix your mistakes. Once people are dead, you can't make them undead.

In any case those were my convictions, and back in college I had taken a modest stand against the war. Nothing radical, no hothead stuff, just ringing a few doorbells for Gene McCarthy,[4] composing a few tedious, uninspired

---

[1] Hero of radio, film, and television Westerns.

[2] One of two United States naval vessels that the United States government claimed (probably inaccurately) were attacked off the coast of North Vietnam in August 1964; the attack helped President Lyndon Johnson get congressional approval for a major escalation of the Vietnam War.

[3] Agreements made in Geneva, Switzerland in 1954 that ended the war between the French colonial authorities and the Vietnamese independence movement, temporarily dividing Vietnam into northern and southern zones; elections for a unified Vietnam scheduled for 1956 were blocked by the United States and its allies in the southern zone.

[4] Eugene McCarthy, Minnesota senator who sought the Democratic nomination for president in 1968 and opposed the war.

editorials for the campus newspaper. Oddly, though, it was almost entirely an intellectual activity. I brought some energy to it, of course, but it was the energy that accompanies almost any abstract endeavor; I felt no personal danger; I felt no sense of an impending crisis in my life. Stupidly, with a kind of smug removal that I can't begin to fathom, I assumed that the problems of killing and dying did not fall within my special province.

The draft notice arrived on June 17, 1968. It was a humid afternoon, I remember, cloudy and very quiet, and I'd just come in from a round of golf. My mother and father were having lunch out in the kitchen. I remember opening up the letter, scanning the first few lines, feeling the blood go thick behind my eyes. I remember a sound in my head. It wasn't thinking, it was just a silent howl. A million things all at once—I was too *good* for this war. Too smart, too compassionate, too everything. It couldn't happen. I was above it. I had the world dicked—Phi Beta Kappa and summa cum laude and president of the student body and a full-ride scholarship for grad studies at Harvard. A mistake, maybe—a foul-up in the paperwork. I was no soldier. I hated Boy Scouts. I hated camping out. I hated dirt and tents and mosquitoes. The sight of blood made me queasy, and I couldn't tolerate authority, and I didn't know a rifle from a slingshot. I was a *liberal,* for Christ sake: If they needed fresh bodies, why not draft some back-to-the-stone-age hawk? Or some dumb jingo in his hard hat and Bomb Hanoi button? Or one of LBJ's pretty daughters? Or Westmoreland's whole family—nephews and nieces and baby grandson? There should be a law, I thought. If you support a war, if you think it's worth the price, that's fine, but you have to put your own life on the line. You have to head for the front and hook up with an infantry unit and help spill the blood. And you have to bring along your wife, or your kids, or your lover. A *law,* I thought.

I remember the rage in my stomach. Later it burned down to a smoldering self-pity, then to numbness. At dinner that night my father asked what my plans were.

"Nothing," I said. "Wait."

I spent the summer of 1968 working in an Armour meatpacking plant in my hometown of Worthington, Minnesota. The plant specialized in pork products, and for eight hours a day I stood on a quarter-mile assembly line—more properly, a disassembly line—removing blood clots from the necks of dead pigs. My job title, I believe, was Declotter. After slaughter, the hogs were decapitated, split down the length of the belly, pried open, eviscerated, and strung up by the hind hocks on a high conveyer belt. Then gravity took over. By the time a carcass reached my spot on the line, the fluids had mostly drained out, everything except for thick clots of blood in the neck and upper chest cavity. To remove the stuff, I used a kind of water gun. The machine was heavy, maybe eighty pounds, and was suspended from the ceiling by a heavy rubber cord. There was some bounce to it, an elastic up-and-down give, and the trick was to maneuver the gun with your whole body, not lifting with the arms, just letting the rubber cord do the work for you. At one end was a trigger; at the muzzle end was a small nozzle and a steel roller brush. As a carcass passed by, you'd lean forward and swing the gun up against the clots and squeeze the trigger, all in one motion, and the brush would whirl and water would come shooting out and you'd hear a quick splattering sound as the clots dissolved into a fine red mist. It was not pleasant work. Goggles were a necessity, and a rubber apron, but even so it was like standing for eight hours a day under a lukewarm blood-shower. At night I'd go home smelling of pig. I couldn't wash it out. Even after a hot bath, scrubbing hard, the stink was always there—like old bacon, or sausage, a dense greasy pig-stink that soaked deep into my skin and hair. Among other things, I remember, it was tough getting dates that summer. I felt isolated; I spent a lot of time alone. And there was also that draft notice tucked away in my wallet.

In the evenings I'd sometimes borrow my father's car and drive aimlessly around town, feeling sorry for myself, thinking about the war and the pig factory and how my life seemed to be collapsing toward slaughter. I felt paralyzed. All around me the options seemed to be narrowing, as if I were hurtling down a huge black funnel, the whole world squeezing in tight. There was no happy way out. The government had ended most graduate school deferments; the waiting lists for the National Guard and Reserves were impossibly long; my health was solid; I didn't qualify for CO status—no religious grounds, no history as a pacifist. Moreover, I could not claim to be opposed to war as a matter of general principle. There were occasions, I believed, when a nation was justified in using military force to achieve its ends, to stop a Hitler or some comparable evil, and I told myself that in such circumstances I would've willingly marched off to the battle. The problem, though, was that a draft board did not let you choose your war.

Beyond all this, or at the very center, was the raw fact of terror. I did not want to die. Not ever. But certainly not then, not there, not in a wrong war. Driving up Main Street, past the courthouse and the Ben Franklin store, I sometimes felt the fear spreading inside me like weeds. I imagined myself dead. I imagined myself doing things I could not do—charging an enemy position, taking aim at another human being.

At some point in mid-July I began thinking seriously about Canada. The border lay a few hundred miles north, an eight-hour drive. Both my conscience and my instincts were telling me to make a break for it, just take off and run like hell and never stop. In the beginning the idea seemed purely abstract, the word Canada printing itself out in my head; but after a time I could see particular shapes and images, the sorry details of my own future—a hotel room in Winnipeg, a battered old suitcase, my father's eyes as I tried to explain myself over the telephone. I could almost hear his voice, and my mother's. Run, I'd think. Then I'd think, Impossible. Then a second later I'd think, *Run.*

It was a kind of schizophrenia. A moral split. I couldn't make up my mind. I feared the war, yes, but I also feared exile. I was afraid of walking away from my own life, my friends and my family, my whole history, everything that mattered to me. I feared losing the respect of my parents. I feared the law. I feared ridicule and censure. My hometown was a conservative little spot on the prairie, a place where tradition counted, and it was easy to imagine people sitting around a table down at the old Gobbler Café on Main Street, coffee cups poised, the conversation slowly zeroing in on the young O'Brien kid, how the damned sissy had taken off for Canada. At night, when I couldn't sleep, I'd sometimes carry on fierce arguments with those people. I'd be screaming at them, telling them how much I detested their blind, thoughtless, automatic acquiescence to it all, their simple-minded patriotism, their prideful ignorance, their love-it-or-leave-it platitudes, how they were sending me off to fight a war they didn't understand and didn't want to understand. I held them responsible. By God, yes, I *did.* All of them—I held them personally and individually responsible—the polyestered Kiwanis boys, the merchants and farmers, the pious churchgoers, the chatty housewives, the PTA and the Lions club[5] and the Veterans of Foreign Wars and the fine upstanding gentry out at the country club. They didn't know Bao Dai[6] from the man in the moon. They didn't know history. They didn't know the first thing about Diem's tyranny, or the nature of Vietnamese nationalism, or the long colonialism of the French—this was all too damned complicated, it required some reading—but no matter, it was a war to stop the Communists, plain and simple, which was how they liked things, and you were a treasonous pussy if you had second thoughts about killing or dying for plain and simple reasons.

I was bitter, sure. But it was so much more than that. The emotions went from outrage to terror to bewilderment to guilt to sorrow and then back again to outrage. I felt a sickness inside me. Real disease.

Most of this I've told before, or at least hinted at, but what I have never told is the full truth. How I cracked. How at work one morning, standing on the pig line, I felt something break open in my chest. I don't know what it was. I'll never know. But it was real, I know that much, it was a physical rupture—a cracking-leaking-popping feeling. I remember dropping my water gun. Quickly, almost without thought, I took off my apron and walked out of the plant and drove home. It was midmorning, I remember, and the house

---

[5] Kiwanis and Lions clubs, community service organizations of business and professional people; Veterans of Foreign Wars, an organization of military personnel who have seen active duty abroad.

[6] Emperor of Vietnam 1949–1955, under French colonial rule.

was empty. Down in my chest there was still that leaking sensation, something very warm and precious spilling out, and I was covered with blood and hog-stink, and for a long while I just concentrated on holding myself together. I remember taking a hot shower. I remember packing a suitcase and carrying it out to the kitchen, standing very still for a few minutes, looking carefully at the familiar objects all around me. The old chrome toaster, the telephone, the pink and white Formica on the kitchen counters. The room was full of bright sunshine. Everything sparkled. My house, I thought. My life. I'm not sure how long I stood there, but later I scribbled out a short note to my parents.

What it said, exactly, I don't recall now. Something vague. Taking off, will call, love Tim.

I drove north.

It's a blur now, as it was then, and all I remember is a sense of high velocity and the feel of the steering wheel in my hands. I was riding on adrenaline. A giddy feeling, in a way, except there was the dreamy edge of impossibility to it—like running a dead-end maze—no way out—it couldn't come to a happy conclusion and yet I was doing it anyway because it was all I could think of to do. It was pure flight, fast and mindless. I had no plan. Just hit the border at high speed and crash through and keep on running. Near dusk I passed through Bemidji, then turned northeast toward International Falls. I spent the night in the car behind a closed-down gas station a half mile from the border. In the morning, after gassing up, I headed straight west along the Rainy River, which separates Minnesota from Canada, and which for me separated one life from another. The land was mostly wilderness. Here and there I passed a motel or bait shop, but otherwise the country unfolded in great sweeps of pine and birch and sumac. Though it was still August, the air already had the smell of October, football season, piles of yellow-red leaves, everything crisp and clean. I remember a huge blue sky. Off to my right was the Rainy River, wide as a lake in places, and beyond the Rainy River was Canada.

For a while I just drove, not aiming at anything, then in the late morning I began looking for a place to lie low for a day or two. I was exhausted, and scared sick, and around noon I pulled into an old fishing resort called the Tip Top Lodge. Actually it was not a lodge at all, just eight or nine tiny yellow cabins clustered on a peninsula that jutted northward into the Rainy River. The place was in sorry shape. There was a dangerous wooden dock, an old minnow tank, a flimsy tar paper boathouse along the shore. The main building, which stood in a cluster of pines on high ground, seemed to lean heavily to one side, like a cripple, the roof sagging toward Canada. Briefly, I thought about turning around, just giving up, but then I got out of the car and walked up to the front porch.

The man who opened the door that day is the hero of my life. How do I say this without sounding sappy? Blurt it out—the man saved me. He offered exactly what I needed, without questions, without any words at all. He took me in. He was there at the critical time—a silent, watchful presence. Six days later, when it ended, I was unable to find a proper way to thank him, and I never have, and so, if nothing else, this story represents a small gesture of gratitude twenty years overdue.

Even after two decades I can close my eyes and return to that porch at the Tip Top Lodge. I can see the old guy staring at me. Elroy Berdahl: eighty-one years old, skinny and shrunken and mostly bald. He wore a flannel shirt and brown work pants. In one hand, I remember, he carried a green apple, a small paring knife in the other. His eyes had the bluish gray color of a razor blade, the same polished shine, and as he peered up at me I felt a strange sharpness, almost painful, a cutting sensation, as if his gaze were somehow slicing me open. In part, no doubt, it was my own sense of guilt, but even so I'm absolutely certain that the old man took one look and went right to the heart of things—a kid in trouble. When I asked for a room, Elroy made a little clicking sound with his tongue. He nodded, led me out to one of the cabins, and dropped a key in my hand. I remember smiling at him. I also remember wishing I hadn't. The old man shook his head as if to tell me it wasn't worth the bother.

"Dinner at five-thirty," he said. "You eat fish?"

"Anything," I said.

Elroy grunted and said, "I'll bet."

We spent six days together at the Tip Top Lodge. Just the two of us. Tourist season was over, and there were no boats on the river, and the wilderness seemed to withdraw into a great permanent stillness. Over those six days Elroy Berdahl and I took most of our meals together. In the mornings we sometimes went out on long hikes into the woods, and at night we played Scrabble or listened to records or sat reading in front of his big stone fireplace. At times I felt the awkwardness of an intruder, but Elroy accepted me into his quiet routine without fuss or ceremony. He took my presence for granted, the same way he might've sheltered a stray cat—no wasted sighs or pity—and there was never any talk about it. Just the opposite. What I remember more than anything is the man's willful, almost ferocious silence. In all that time together, all those hours, he never asked the obvious questions: Why was I there? Why alone? Why so preoccupied? If Elroy was curious about any of this, he was careful never to put it into words.

My hunch, though, is that he already knew. At least the basics. After all, it was 1968, and guys were burning draft cards, and Canada was just a boat ride away. Elroy Berdahl was no hick. His bedroom, I remember, was cluttered with books and newspapers. He killed me at the Scrabble board, barely concentrating, and on those occasions when speech was necessary he had a way of compressing large thoughts into small, cryptic packets of language. One evening, just at sunset, he pointed up at an owl circling over the violet-lighted forest to the west.

"Hey, O'Brien," he said. "There's Jesus."

The man was sharp—he didn't miss much. Those razor eyes. Now and then he'd catch me staring out at the river, at the far shore, and I could almost hear the tumblers clicking in his head. Maybe I'm wrong, but I doubt it.

One thing for certain, he knew I was in desperate trouble. And he knew I couldn't talk about it. The wrong word—or even the right word—and I would've disappeared. I was wired and jittery. My skin felt too tight. After supper one evening I vomited and went back to my cabin and lay down for a few moments and then vomited again; another time, in the middle of the afternoon, I began sweating and couldn't shut it off. I went through whole days feeling dizzy with sorrow. I couldn't sleep; I couldn't lie still. At night I'd toss around in bed, half awake, half dreaming, imagining how I'd sneak down to the beach and quietly push one of the old man's boats out into the river and start paddling my way toward Canada. There were times when I thought I'd gone off the psychic edge. I couldn't tell up from down, I was just falling, and late in the night I'd lie there watching weird pictures spin through my head. Getting chased by the Border Patrol—helicopters and searchlights and barking dogs— I'd be crashing through the woods, I'd be down on my hands and knees—people shouting my name—the law closing in on all sides—my hometown draft board and the FBI and the Royal Canadian Mounted Police. It all seemed crazy and impossible. Twenty-one years old, an ordinary kid with all the ordinary dreams and ambitions, and all I wanted was to live the life I was born to—a mainstream life—I loved baseball and hamburgers and cherry Cokes—and now I was off on the margins of exile, leaving my country forever, and it seemed so impossible and terrible and sad.

I'm not sure how I made it through those six days. Most of it I can't remember. On two or three afternoons, to pass some time, I helped Elroy get the place ready for winter, sweeping down the cabins and hauling in the boats, little chores that kept my body moving. The days were cool and bright. The nights were very dark. One morning the old man showed me how to split and stack firewood, and for several hours we just worked in silence out behind his house. At one point, I remember, Elroy put down his maul and looked at me for a long time, his lips drawn as if framing a difficult question, but then he shook his head and went back to work. The man's self-control was amazing.

He never pried. He never put me in a position that required lies or denials. To an extent, I suppose, his reticence was typical of that part of Minnesota, where privacy still held value, and even if I'd been walking around with some horrible deformity—four arms and three heads—I'm sure the old man would've talked about everything except those extra arms and heads. Simple politeness was part of it. But even more than that, I think, the man understood that words were insufficient. The problem had gone beyond discussion. During that long summer I'd been over and over the various arguments, all the pros and cons, and it was no longer a question that could be decided by an act of pure reason. Intellect had come up against emotion. My conscience told me to run, but some irrational and powerful force was resisting, like a weight pushing me toward the war. What it came down to, stupidly, was a sense of shame. Hot, stupid shame. I did not want people to think badly of me. Not my parents, not my brother and sister, not even the folks down at the Gobbler Café. I was ashamed to be there at the Tip Top Lodge. I was ashamed of my conscience, ashamed to be doing the right thing.

Some of this Elroy must've understood. Not the details, of course, but the plain fact of crisis.

Although the old man never confronted me about it, there was one occasion when he came close to forcing the whole thing out into the open. It was early evening, and we'd just finished supper, and over coffee and dessert I asked him about my bill, how much I owed so far. For a long while the old man squinted down at the tablecloth.

"Well, the basic rate," he said, "is fifty bucks a night. Not counting meals. This makes four nights, right?"

I nodded. I had three hundred and twelve dollars in my wallet.

Elroy kept his eyes on the tablecloth. "Now that's an on-season price. To be fair, I suppose we should knock it down a peg or two." He leaned back in his chair. "What's a reasonable number, you figure?"

"I don't know," I said. "Forty?"

"Forty's good. Forty a night. Then we tack on food—say another hundred? Two hundred sixty total?"

"I guess."

He raised his eyebrows. "Too much?"

"No, that's fair. It's fine. Tomorrow, though . . . I think I'd better take off tomorrow."

Elroy shrugged and began clearing the table. For a time he fussed with the dishes, whistling to himself as if the subject had been settled. After a second he slapped his hands together.

"You know what we forgot?" he said. "We forgot wages. Those odd jobs you done. What we have to do, we have to figure out what your time's worth. Your last job—how much did you pull in an hour?"

"Not enough," I said.

"A bad one?"

"Yes. Pretty bad."

Slowly then, without intending any long sermon, I told him about my days at the pig plant. It began as a straight recitation of the facts, but before I could stop myself I was talking about the blood clots and the water gun and how the smell had soaked into my skin and how I couldn't wash it away. I went on for a long time. I told him about wild hogs squealing in my dreams, the sounds of butchery, slaughter-house sounds, and how I'd sometimes wake up with that greasy pig-stink in my throat.

When I was finished, Elroy nodded at me.

"Well, to be honest," he said, "when you first showed up here, I wondered about all that. The aroma, I mean. Smelled like you was awful damned fond of pork chops." The old man almost smiled. He made a snuffling sound, then sat down with a pencil and a piece of paper. "So what'd this crud job pay? Ten bucks an hour? Fifteen?"

"Less."

Elroy shook his head. "Let's make it fifteen. You put in twenty-five hours here, easy. That's three hundred seventy-five bucks total wages. We subtract the two hundred sixty for food and lodging, I still owe you a hundred and fifteen."

He took four fifties out of his shirt pocket and laid them on the table.

"Call it even," he said.

"No."

"Pick it up. Get yourself a haircut."

The money lay on the table for the rest of the evening. It was still there when I went back to my cabin. In the morning, though, I found an envelope tacked to my door. Inside were the four fifties and a two-word note that said EMERGENCY FUND.

The man knew.

Looking back after twenty years, I sometimes wonder if the events of that summer didn't happen in some other dimension, a place where your life exists before you've lived it, and where it goes afterward. None of it ever seemed real. During my time at the Tip Top Lodge I had the feeling that I'd slipped out of my own skin, hovering a few feet away while some poor yo-yo with my name and face tried to make his way toward a future he didn't understand and didn't want. Even now I can see myself as I was then. It's like watching an old home movie: I'm young and tan and fit. I've got hair—lots of it. I don't smoke or drink. I'm wearing faded blue jeans and a white polo shirt. I can see myself sitting on Elroy Berdahl's dock near dusk one evening, the sky a bright shimmering pink, and I'm finishing up a letter to my parents that tells what

I'm about to do and why I'm doing it and how sorry I am that I'd never found the courage to talk to them about it. I ask them not to be angry. I try to explain some of my feelings, but there aren't enough words, and so I just say that it's a thing that has to be done. At the end of the letter I talk about the vacations we used to take up in this north country, at a place called Whitefish Lake, and how the scenery here reminds me of those good times. I tell them I'm fine. I tell them I'll write again from Winnipeg or Montreal or wherever I end up.

On my last full day, the sixth day, the old man took me out fishing on the Rainy River. The afternoon was sunny and cold. A stiff breeze came in from the north, and I remember how the little fourteen-foot boat made sharp rocking motions as we pushed off from the dock. The current was fast. All around us, I remember, there was a vastness to the world, an unpeopled rawness, just the trees and the sky and the water reaching out toward nowhere. The air had the brittle scent of October.

For ten or fifteen minutes Elroy held a course upstream, the river choppy and silver-gray, then he turned straight north and put the engine on full throttle. I felt the bow lift beneath me. I remember the wind in my ears, the sound of the old outboard Evinrude. For a time I didn't pay attention to anything, just feeling the cold spray against my face, but then it occurred to me that at some point we must've passed into Canadian waters, across that dotted line between two different worlds, and I remember a sudden tightness in my chest as I looked up and watched the far shore come at me. This wasn't a daydream. It was tangible and real. As we came in toward land, Elroy cut the engine, letting the boat fishtail lightly about twenty yards off shore. The old man didn't look at me or speak. Bending down, he opened up his tackle box and busied himself with a bobber and a piece of wire leader, humming to himself, his eyes down.

It struck me then that he must've planned it. I'll never be certain, of course, but I think he meant to bring me up against the realities, to guide me across the river and to take me to the edge and to stand a kind of vigil as I chose a life for myself.

I remember staring at the old man, then at my hands, then at Canada. The shoreline was dense with brush and timber. I could see tiny red berries on the bushes. I could see a squirrel up in one of the birch trees, a big crow looking at me from a boulder along the river. That close—twenty yards—and I could see the delicate latticework of the leaves, the texture of the soil, the browned needles beneath the pines, the configurations of geology and human history. Twenty yards. I could've done it. I could've jumped and started swimming for my life. Inside me, in my chest, I felt a terrible squeezing pressure. Even now, as I write this, I can still feel that tightness. And I want you to feel it—the wind coming off the river, the waves, the silence, the wooded frontier. You're at the bow of a boat on the Rainy River. You're twenty-one years old, you're scared, and there's a hard squeezing pressure in your chest.

What would you do?

Would you jump? Would you feel pity for yourself? Would you think about your family and your childhood and your dreams and all you're leaving behind? Would it hurt? Would it feel like dying? Would you cry, as I did?

I tried to swallow it back. I tried to smile, except I was crying.

Now, perhaps, you can understand why I've never told this story before. It's not just the embarrassment of tears. That's part of it, no doubt, but what embarrasses me much more, and always will, is the paralysis that took my heart. A moral freeze: I couldn't decide, I couldn't act, I couldn't comport myself with even a pretense of modest human dignity.

All I could do was cry. Quietly, not bawling, just the chest-chokes.

At the rear of the boat Elroy Berdahl pretended not to notice. He held a fishing rod in his hands, his head bowed to hide his eyes. He kept humming a soft, monotonous little tune. Everywhere, it seemed, in the trees and water and sky, a great worldwide sadness came pressing down on me, a crushing sorrow, sorrow like I had never known it before. And what was so sad, I realized, was that Canada had become a pitiful fantasy. Silly and hopeless. It was no longer a possibility. Right then, with the shore so close, I understood that I would not do what I should do. I would not swim away from my hometown and my country and my life. I would not be brave. That old image of myself as a hero, as a man of conscience and courage, all that was just a threadbare pipe dream. Bobbing there on the Rainy River, looking back at the Minnesota shore, I felt a sudden swell of helplessness come over me, a drowning sensation, as if I had toppled overboard and was being swept away by the silver waves. Chunks of my own history flashed by. I saw a seven-year-old boy in a white cowboy hat and a Lone Ranger mask and a pair of holstered six-shooters; I saw a twelve-year-old Little League shortstop pivoting to turn a double play; I saw a sixteen-year-old kid decked out for his first prom, looking spiffy in a white tux and a black bow tie, his hair cut short and flat, his shoes freshly polished. My whole life seemed to spill out into the river, swirling away from me, everything I had ever been or ever wanted to be. I couldn't get my breath; I couldn't stay afloat; I couldn't tell which way to swim. A hallucination, I suppose, but it was as real as anything I would ever feel. I saw my parents calling to me from the far shoreline. I saw my brother and sister, all the townsfolk, the mayor and the entire Chamber of Commerce and all my old teachers and girlfriends and high school buddies. Like some weird sporting event: everybody screaming from the sidelines, rooting me on—a loud stadium roar. Hotdogs and popcorn—stadium smells, stadium heat. A squad of cheerleaders did cartwheels along the banks of the Rainy River; they had megaphones and pompoms and smooth brown thighs. The crowd swayed left and right. A marching band played fight songs. All my aunts and uncles were there, and Abraham Lincoln, and Saint George, and a nine-year-old girl named Linda who had died of a brain tumor back in fifth grade, and several members of the United States Senate, and a blind poet scribbling notes, and LBJ, and Huck Finn, and Abbie Hoffman,[7] and all the dead soldiers back from the grave, and the many thousands who were later to die—villagers with terrible burns, little kids without arms or legs—yes, and the Joint Chiefs of Staff were there, and a couple of popes, and a first lieutenant named Jimmy Cross, and the last surviving veteran of the American Civil War, and Jane Fonda dressed up as Barbarella,[8] and an old man sprawled beside a pigpen, and my grandfather, and Gary Cooper, and a kind-faced woman carrying an umbrella and a copy of Plato's *Republic,* and a million ferocious citizens waving flags of all shapes and colors—people in hard hats, people in headbands—they were all whooping and chanting and urging me toward one shore or the other. I saw faces from my distant past and distant future. My wife was there. My unborn daughter waved at me, and my two sons hopped up and down, and a drill sergeant named Blyton sneered and shot up a finger and shook his head. There was a choir in bright purple robes. There was a cabbie from the Bronx. There was a slim young man I would one day kill with a hand grenade along a red clay trail outside the village of My Khe.

The little aluminum boat rocked softly beneath me. There was the wind and the sky.

I tried to will myself overboard.

I gripped the edge of the boat and leaned forward and thought, *Now.*

I did try. It just wasn't possible.

All those eyes on me—the town, the whole universe—and I couldn't risk the embarrassment. It was as if there were an audience to my life, that swirl of faces along the river, and in my head I could hear people screaming at me. Traitor! they yelled. Turncoat! Pussy! I felt myself blush. I couldn't tolerate it. I couldn't endure the mockery, or the disgrace, or the patriotic ridicule. Even in my imagination, the shore just twenty yards away, I couldn't make myself be brave. It had nothing to do with morality. Embarrassment, that's all it was.

And right then I submitted.

---

[7] LBJ, President Lyndon Baines Johnson; Huck Finn, hero of Mark Twain's novel *The Adventures of Huckleberry Finn;* Abbie Hoffman, radical political activist.

[8] Actor Jane Fonda starred in the film *Barbarella* and was an outspoken critic of the war.

I would go to the war—I would kill and maybe die—because I was embarrassed not to.

That was the sad thing. And so I sat in the bow of the boat and cried.

It was loud now. Loud, hard crying.

Elroy Berdahl remained quiet. He kept fishing. He worked his line with the tips of his fingers, patiently, squinting out at his red and white bobber on the Rainy River. His eyes were flat and impassive. He didn't speak. He was simply there, like the river and the late-summer sun. And yet by his presence, his mute watchfulness, he made it real. He was the true audience. He was a witness, like God, or like the gods, who look on in absolute silence as we live our lives, as we make our choices or fail to make them.

"Ain't biting," he said.

Then after a time the old man pulled in his line and turned the boat back toward Minnesota.

I don't remember saying goodbye. That last night we had dinner together, and I went to bed early, and in the morning Elroy fixed breakfast for me. When I told him I'd be leaving, the old man nodded as if he already knew. He looked down at the table and smiled.

At some point later in the morning it's possible that we shook hands—I just don't remember—but I do know that by the time I'd finished packing the old man had disappeared. Around noon, when I took my suitcase out to the car, I noticed that his old black pickup truck was no longer parked in front of the house. I went inside and waited for a while, but I felt a bone certainty that he wouldn't be back. In a way, I thought, it was appropriate. I washed up the breakfast dishes, left his two hundred dollars on the kitchen counter, got into the car, and drove south toward home.

The day was cloudy. I passed through towns with familiar names, through the pine forests and down to the prairie, and then to Vietnam, where I was a soldier, and then home again. I survived, but it's not a happy ending. I was a coward. I went to the war.

STUDY AND DISCUSSION QUESTIONS

1. Why is O'Brien opposed to the war?

2. Why does O'Brien describe his work in the meat-packing plant in such detail?

3. O'Brien holds the people in his town who support the war "responsible" for his predicament. Why?

4. Why doesn't Elroy Berdahl ever ask O'Brien any questions?

5. Of his decision not to go to Canada, O'Brien writes, "Embarrassment, that's all it was." Is this accurate?

6. *The Things They Carried,* in which this piece appeared, calls itself "A Work of Fiction," even though the narrator of "On the Rainy River" refers to himself as "Tim O'Brien" right at the start. How might you explain this?

SUGGESTIONS FOR WRITING

1. Did O'Brien make the right decision?

2. Write the letter O'Brien might have written to his parents if he had decided to go to Canada.

3. When O'Brien gets his draft notice, he thinks, "There should be a law . . . . If you support a war . . . you have to put your own life on the line." How *should* those who fight in a war be chosen?

ON WAR AND WAR AND WAR AND . . .

June Jordan

June Jordan was born in Harlem in 1936 and studied at Barnard College and the University of Chicago. She has worked at a number of colleges and now teaches African American studies at the University of California at Berkeley. Her poetry includes Some Changes *(1971),* Passion *(1980),* Naming Our Destiny *(1989), and* Haruko/Love Poems *(1994). Her essays have been collected in* Civil Wars *(1981),* Moving Towards Home *(1989),* Technical Difficulties: African-American Notes on the State of the Union *(1994), and other volumes. The following was written during the Gulf War of 1991.*

On a recent, cold Sunday morning in Kennebunkport, Maine, George Bush and his wife, Barbara, apparently seated themselves inside a small country church of God. (To think about what?)

Alma Powell, wife of the Joint Chief Commander of U.S. Armed Forces, reports that she likes to keep "comforting foods," like vegetable soup, ready on top of the stove for Colin, her certainly hardworking husband. Alma adds that, these days, she just "knows" that her Colin doesn't want to hear "little stories" about the children.

(Just the soup, ma'am.)

Secretary of Defense Dick Cheney, second only to his boss in blood-thirst for arm's-length/armchair warfare, has never served half an hour, even, in the army, the navy, the air force, or the marines.

(I know; it's not right to pick on him just for that.)

Last Saturday, at a local antiwar rally organized by the Middle East Children's Alliance, I noted, aloud, that the war, to date, was costing us fifty-six billion dollars. Every twenty-four hours, the cost is one billion, at least. I, therefore, proposed the following to the crowd scattered on the grass and under the trees:

One billion dollars a day for seven days for Oakland!

Can you imagine that?

One billion dollars a day!

But to hell with imagination!

This is our city!

This is our money!

These are our lives!

One billion dollars a day for seven days for Oakland!

(Or) do we accept that there is only "the will and the wallet" when it's about kill or be killed?

Do we need this money or not?

Do we need it here?

Do we need it now? (And so on.)

When I left the stage a reporter came up to me: "You meant one *million* dollars, didn't you?"

"No!" I answered him, amazed: "One billion: one billion dollars a day for seven days for Oakland! That's the bill, that's our bill for housing and drug rehabilitation and books in the public schools and hospital care and all of that good stuff. One billion dollars a day! It's a modest proposal. In less than three months, those maniacs in the White House and the Pentagon have spent fifty-six billion dollars in my name and with my taxes, trying to obliterate Iraq and its people and their leader. I'm saying, call home the troops and the bucks! We need these big bucks to make this a homeland, not a desert, right here, for the troops and for you and for me. What's the problem? It's a bargain! Seven billion dollars on the serious improvement of American life in Oakland versus fifty-six billion dollars for death and destruction inside Iraq! What's the problem?"

But the reporter was giving me a weak smile of farewell that let me understand he found my proposal preposterous. One *million* dollars for life, okay. Billions for kill or be killed, okay. But really big bucks on us, the people of these United States? One billion dollars a day to promote, for example, the safety and educational attainment and communal happiness of 339,000 Americans? I must be kidding!

As I walked away from the park, I felt a heavy depression overtaking me; the reporter, a tall white man with clear eyes, could not contemplate the transfer of his and my aggregate resources from death to life as a reasonable idea. Worse, he could not suppose his and my life to be worth anything close to the value of organized, high-tech, and boastful murder.

But then, other people stopped me to ask, "How can we do that? Do we write letters or what?" And so, as I write this column tonight, I am reassured because not everybody American has lost her mind or his soul. Not every one of my compatriots has become a flag-wrapped lunatic lusting after oil/power/the perversions of "kicking ass," preferably via TV.

A huge number of Americans has joined with enormous numbers of Arab peoples and European communities in Germany, England, France, Italy, Spain, and Muslim communities throughout India and Pakistan to cry out, "Stop!"

And when I say "huge," I mean it: If 1,000 Americans contacted by some pollster can be said to represent 250 million people, then how many multi-multi-millions do we, antiwar movement gatherings of more than 100,000, coast to coast and on every continent, how many do we represent?!

And how come nobody ever does that kind of political math?

And tonight, February 2, 1991, when, yet again, the ruling white men of America despise peace and sneer at negotiations and intensify their arm's-length/armchair prosecution of this evil war, this display of a racist value system that will never allow for any nationalism that is not their own and that will never allow Third World countries to control their own natural resources and that will never ever express, let alone feel, regret or remorse or shame or horror at the loss of any human life that is not white, tonight I am particularly proud to be an African-American.

By launching the heaviest air assault in history against Iraq on January 15, George Bush dared to desecrate the birthday of Martin Luther King, Jr. Tonight (and 83,000 bombing missions later) is the twenty-sixth anniversary of the assassination of Malcolm X. On this sorry evening the world has seen the pathological real deal behind the sanctimonious rhetoric of Bush and Company: The Persian Gulf War is not about Iraqi withdrawal from Kuwait. The war is not about Kuwait at all. Clearly it's not about international law or respect of United Nations' resolutions since, by comparison to Washington, Tel Aviv, and Pretoria, "the Butcher of Baghdad"[1] is a minor league Johnny-Come-Lately to the realm of outlaw conduct and contempt for world opinion!

What has happened tonight is that the Soviet leader, Mikhail Gorbachev, and the government of Iraq have reached an agreement whereby Iraq would withdraw from Kuwait and that is a fact—regardless of anything else included or omitted by the proposal. This agreement should provide for immediate cease-fire, a cessation of the slaughter of Iraqi men and women and a halt to the demolition, nationwide, of their water supply, their access to food, their securement of shelter.

So what is the response of the Number One White Man in America? He's gone off "to the theater." I guess that means that the nearest church was closed. Or that Colin Powell was busy dipping his spoon into the comfort of a pot of soup somebody else cooked for him. And that Dick Cheney was fit to be tied into any kind of uniform so long as it meant nobody would take away his Patriot missiles and Apache helicopters and B-52 cluster-bomb bombers and Black and Brown and poor White soldiers and sailors and all the rest of these toys for a truly big-time coward.

Confronted with the "nightmare" prospect of peace, Bush goes off to the theater because he'll be damned if he will acknowledge that Saddam Hussein is a man, is the head of a sovereign state, is an enemy to be reckoned with, an opponent with whom one must negotiate: Saddam Hussein is not a white man! He and his Arab peoples must be destroyed! No peace! No cease-fire! No negotiations!

And I am proud tonight to remember Dr. King and Malcolm X, and to mourn their absence, even as I pursue the difficult challenge of their legacy. Both of these men became the targets of white wrath when they, in their different ways, developed into global visionaries persisting against racism in Alabama, in Harlem, in South Africa, in Vietnam. Neither of these men could have failed to condemn this current attack against the Arab world. Neither of these men ever condoned anything less than equal justice and equal rights. Hence, the undeniably racist double standards now levied against Saddam Hussein would have appalled and alienated both of them, completely.

I am proud to shake hands with the increasing number of African-American conscientious objectors. I am proud to remark the steadfast moral certainty of U.S. Congressman Ronald Dellums's opposition to this war. I am proud to hear about the conscientious objections of congressmen Gus Savage and John Conyers and Mervyn Dymally. I am proud to observe that, even while African-Americans remain disproportionately represented in the U.S. armed forces, we, as a national community, stand distinct, despite and apart

---

[1] What President George Bush and others called Saddam Hussein, leader of Iraq.

from all vagaries of popular opinion; we maintain a proportionately higher-than-white level of opposition to this horrible war, this horrendous evasion of domestic degeneration and decay.

And I want to say something else, specific to you, Mr. President: It's true you can humiliate and you can hound and you can smash and burn and terrify and smirk and boast and defame and demonize and dismiss and incinerate and starve and, yes, you can force somebody, force a people, to surrender what remains of their bloody bowels into your grasping, bony, dry hands.

But all of us who are weak, we watch you. And we learn from your hatred. And we do not forget.

And we are many, Mr. President. We are most of the people of this godforsaken planet.

STUDY AND DISCUSSION QUESTIONS

1. Why does Jordan begin her essay with George and Barbara Bush in church and Alma Powell making soup for Colin?

2. The reporter, Jordan writes, "could not suppose his life and my life to be worth anything close to the value of organized, high-tech, and boastful murder." Why not, do you think?

3. Jordan calls the war a "display of a racist value system." What does she mean?

4. Colin Powell is African American. How might Jordan reply to the argument that this fact undermines her interpretation of the war in racial terms?

5. What is the significance of Jordan's last sentence?

6. Describe the audience Jordan seems to be writing for.

SUGGESTIONS FOR WRITING

1. Read about the Gulf War of 1991 and then reread Jordan's essay. Is your response the same as it was after your first reading?

2. How might Jordan's essay have been different if written after, rather than during, the war?

PROTEST AND CHANGE

Why do people engage in protest? Is their own situation so intolerable that they have no choice? Is their moral outrage at injustice suffered by others so great that they can no longer just watch? Do they feel that not to protest is to be complicit in inequity? Do they feel the need to be part of something larger than themselves, something that will give greater meaning to their lives? Do they simply wish to leave a better world for those who come after them? The readings in this section involve all these reasons, and behind most of them lies a belief that change is indeed possible and that protest can bring it about, a belief fortunately borne out by the history of this country.

"The personal is political" was an important slogan in the women's liberation movement of the late 1960s and early 1970s. It meant, for example, that the struggle for equality in relationships between men and women was politically important in the same way as the struggle to end racism or the war in Vietnam. Patricia Mainardi's satirical essay "The Politics of Housework" describes her efforts to get her husband to take seriously what he sees as a "trivial" issue and to do his share. In this battle for justice in one household, we can see some of the elements of larger, more public conflicts: her righteous protest, his resistance, even the creation of an ideology to defend the status quo. "I don't mind sharing the housework," he insists, "but I don't do it very well. We should do the things we are best at."

The very public protest Paul Monette describes in "Mustering" is no less personal. In April 1993, an estimated one million gay men, lesbians, and bisexuals (along with heterosexual supporters) marched on Washington, D.C.

to demand equal rights and increased AIDS funding. For many, the act of marching was a transformative experience, an act of self-definition, a bold step out of the closet, from fear and shame to defiance and pride; and the sheer size of the march represented an attack against enforced invisibility. Though a well-known writer who was already quite public about his sexual orientation, Monette felt such a fierce need to be part of this event that he dragged himself to Washington despite the debilitation and intense pain caused by his continuing battle with AIDS.

"I had found something outside myself that gave meaning to my life" writes Anne Moody of the civil rights movement. The movement may have been "something outside" Moody, but as her autobiography *Coming of Age in Mississippi* makes clear, the racist oppression it challenged was as central to her own experience as heterosexism was to Monette's. The excerpt included here describes a sit-in staged by an integrated group at a whites-only Woolworth's lunch counter. In light of the violent intensity of white resistance to integration, the actions of Moody and her fellow "sit-inners" were quite simply heroic, and the movement of which they were a part amazingly successful, a model and an inspiration for later protest movements.

The person whose name is most closely associated with the civil rights movement—though he was one of many leaders and many thousands of activists—is, of course, the Reverend Martin Luther King, Jr. His "Letter from Birmingham Jail" offers moral and religious justification for the practice of nonviolent civil disobedience, which was the heart of the movement. As King sees it, "one has a moral responsibility to disobey unjust laws"; his profound moral vision informed a determined militancy. King is particularly critical of moderates, advocates of gradual change; the world, in his view, needs "creative extremists."

The thoroughly secular Noam Chomsky is no less passionate a moral thinker than Martin Luther King, Jr. His participation in a protest against the Vietnam War, detailed in "On Resistance," did not derive from any personal stake in ending the war (he was well past draft age) but from a profound sense that American involvement in Vietnam was evil and that as a moral person he had no choice but to work to end it. Chomsky finds especially appalling the amoral cost-benefit analyses of technocratic policy planners as well as defense (and even criticism) of the war in terms of "national interest." He insists on asking a "fundamental" question: "Suppose that it were in the American 'national interest' to pound into rubble a small nation that refuses to submit to our will. Would it then be legitimate and proper for us to act 'in this national interest'?"

Brian Willson, whom we meet in Alice Walker's "Journal," answers this question as Chomsky would. Willson, Walker, and others met to plan to blockade a train leaving the Concord Naval Weapons Station carrying arms bound for Central America. Willson spoke of the necessity to take risks on behalf of those the weapons would eventually maim and kill: "We are not more than they, he said; they are not less than we." Protest of this sort is rooted in a willingness to sacrifice, a sense of moral obligation, and an ability to identify with others, people often far away and living very different kinds of lives. At the end of Walker's journal entries, we learn that the weapons train sped up as it approached the demonstrators and that Willson lost both his legs.

Wendell Berry, author of "Think Little," argues that the environmental protest movement must also involve sacrifice, or at least change in how we live. If the personal is political for feminists like Patricia Mainardi, for Berry, the political is personal; that is, we must live the ideas we espouse. It is not enough to protest against corporate polluters; "the environmental crisis has its roots in our *lives.*" Driving less, turning down the thermostat, and living without air conditioning will not only make our protests more authentic, Berry insists, but will also make our lives "richer in meaning and more abundant in real pleasure."

The political is personal in another way for Joe and Jean Gump: protesting brings them genuine happiness. First Jean and later Joe gladly went to jail for hammering and pouring blood on nuclear missiles as a protest against the continued stockpiling of these malignant weapons. What might seem like a great sacrifice—her sentence is six years, his thirty months—represents a sort of fulfillment for them, the only right, indeed the only possible thing to do. The cheerful optimism of these two grandparents is a reminder that protest can be empowering, their age proof that it is not just the province of the young. Jean tells Studs Terkel, who interviews them in jail, "I'm very much at peace here"; Joe says, "I feel great."

THE POLITICS OF HOUSEWORK

Patricia Mainardi

Patricia Mainardi was a founder of the feminist group Redstockings in the 1960s and now teaches art history at the City University of New York. She has written Quilts: The Great American Art *(1978),* Art and Politics of the Second Empire *(1987), and* The End of the Salon *(1993). A slightly longer version of the essay below appeared in 1970 in* Sisterhood is Powerful, *edited by Robin Morgan.*

> Though women do not complain of the power of husbands, each complains of her own husband, or of the husbands of her friends. It is the same in all other cases of servitude; at least in the commencement of the emancipatory movement. The serfs did not at first complain of the power of the lords, but only of their tyranny.
>
> —John Stuart Mill, *On the Subjection of Women*

Liberated women—very different from women's liberation! The first signals all kinds of goodies, to warm the hearts (not to mention other parts) of the most radical men. The other signals—*housework*. The first brings sex without marriage, sex before marriage, cozy housekeeping arrangements ("You see, I'm living with this chick") and the self-content of knowing that you're not the kind of man who wants a doormat instead of a woman. That will come later. After all, who wants that old commodity anymore, the Standard American Housewife, all husband, home and kids. The New Commodity, the Liberated Woman, has sex a lot and has a Career, preferably something that can be fitted in with the household chores—like dancing, pottery, or painting.

On the other hand is women's liberation—and housework. What? You say this is all trivial? Wonderful! That's what I thought. It seemed perfectly reasonable. We both had careers, both had to work a couple of days a week to earn enough to live on, so why shouldn't we share the housework? So I suggested it to my mate and he agreed—most men are too hip to turn you down flat. "You're right," he said, "It's only fair."

Then an interesting thing happened. I can only explain it by stating that we women have been brainwashed more than even we can imagine. Probably too many years of seeing television women in ecstasy over their shiny waxed floors or breaking down over their dirty shirt collars. Men have no such conditioning. They recognize the essential fact of housework right from the very beginning. Which is that it stinks. Here's my list of dirty chores: buying groceries, carting them home and putting them away; cooking meals and washing dishes and pots; doing the laundry; digging out the place when things get out of control; washing floors. The list could go on but the sheer necessities are bad enough. All of us have to do these things, or get some one else to do them for us. The longer my husband contemplated these chores, the more repulsed he became, and so proceeded the change from the normally sweet considerate Dr. Jekyll into the crafty Mr. Hyde who would stop at nothing to avoid the horrors of—*housework*. As he felt himself backed into a corner laden with dirty dishes, brooms, mops, and reeking garbage, his front teeth grew longer and pointier, his fingernails haggled and his eyes grew wild. Housework trivial? Not on your life! Just try to share the burden.

So ensued a dialogue that's been going on for several years. Here are some of the high points:

"I don't mind sharing the housework, but I don't do it very well. We should each do the things we're best at."

Meaning: Unfortunately I'm no good at things like washing dishes or cooking. What I do best is a little light carpentry, changing light bulbs, moving furniture *(how often do you move furniture?).*

Also Meaning: Historically the lower classes (black men and us) have had hundreds of years experience doing menial jobs. It would be a waste of manpower to train someone else to do them now.

Also Meaning: I don't like the dull stupid boring jobs, so you should do them.

"I don't mind sharing the work, but you'll have to show me how to do it."

Meaning: I ask a lot of questions and you'll have to show me everything everytime I do it because I don't remember so good. Also don't try to sit down and read while I'm doing my jobs because I'm going to annoy the hell out of you until it's easier to do them yourself.

"We used to be so happy!" (Said whenever it was his turn to do something.)

Meaning: I used to be so happy.

Meaning: Life without housework is bliss. *(No quarrel here. Perfect agreement.)*

"We have different standards, and why should I have to work to your standards. That's unfair."

Meaning: If I begin to get bugged by the dirt and crap I will say "This place sure is a sty" or "How can anyone live like this?" and wait for your reaction. I know that all women have a sore called "Guilt over a messy house" or "Household work is ultimately my responsibility." I know that men have caused that sore—if anyone visits and the place *is* a sty, they're not going to leave and say, "He sure is a lousy housekeeper." You'll take the rap in any case. I can outwait you.

Also Meaning: I can provoke innumerable scenes over the housework issue. Eventually doing all the housework yourself will be less painful to you than trying to get me to do half. Or I'll suggest we get a maid. She will do my share of the work. You will do yours. It's women's work.

"I've got nothing against sharing the housework, but you can't make me do it on your schedule."

Meaning: Passive resistance. I'll do it when I damned well please, if at all. If my job is doing dishes, it's easier to do them once a week. If taking out laundry, once a month. If washing the floors, once a year. If you don't like it, do it yourself oftener, and then I won't do it at all.

"I *hate* it more than you. You don't mind it so much."

Meaning: Housework is garbage work. It's the worst crap I've ever done. It's degrading and humiliating for someone of *my* intelligence to do it. But for someone of *your* intelligence . . .

"Housework is too trivial to even talk about."

Meaning: It's even more trivial to do. Housework is beneath my status. My purpose in life is to deal with matters of significance. Yours is to deal with matters of insignificance. You should do the housework.

"This problem of housework is not a man-woman problem! In any relationship between two people one is going to have a stronger personality and dominate."

Meaning: That stronger personality had better be *me*.

"In animal societies, wolves, for example, the top animal is usually a male even where he is not chosen for brute strength but on the basis of cunning and intelligence. Isn't that interesting?"

Meaning: I have historical, psychological, anthropological, and biological justification for keeping you down. How can you ask the top wolf to be equal?

"Women's liberation isn't really a political movement."

Meaning: The Revolution is coming too close to home.

Also Meaning: I am only interested in how *I* am oppressed, not how I oppress others. Therefore the war, the draft, and the university are political. Women's liberation is not.

"Man's accomplishments have always depended on getting help from other people, mostly women. What great man would have accomplished what he did if he had to do his own housework?"

Meaning: Oppression is built into the System and I, as the white American male receive the benefits of this System. I don't want to give them up.

Postscript

Participatory democracy begins at home. If you are planning to implement your politics, there are certain things to remember.

1. He *is* feeling it more than you. He's losing some leisure and you're gaining it. The measure of your oppression is his resistance.

2. A great many American men are not accustomed to doing monotonous repetitive work which never ushers in any lasting let alone important achievement. This is why they would rather repair a cabinet than wash dishes. If human endeavors are like a pyramid with man's highest achievements at the top, then keeping oneself alive is at the bottom. Men have always had servants (us) to take care of this bottom strata of life while they have confined their efforts to the rarefied upper regions. It is thus ironic when they ask of women—where are your great painters, statesmen, etc? Mme. Matisse ran a millinery shop so he could paint. Mrs. Martin Luther King kept his house and raised his babies.

3. It is a traumatizing experience for someone who has always thought of himself as being against any oppression or exploitation of one human being by another to realize that in his daily life he has been accepting and implementing (and benefiting from) this exploitation; that his rationalization is little different from that of the racist who says "Black people don't feel pain" (women don't mind doing the shitwork); and that the oldest form of oppression in history has been the oppression of 50 percent of the population by the other 50 percent.

4. Arm yourself with some knowledge of the psychology of oppressed peoples everywhere, and a few facts about the animal kingdom. I admit playing top wolf or who runs the gorillas is silly but as a last resort men bring it up all the time. Talk about bees. If you feel really hostile bring up the sex life of spiders. They have sex. She bites off his head.

The psychology of oppressed people is not silly. Jews, immigrants, black men, and all women have employed the same psychological mechanisms to survive: admiring the oppressor, glorifying the oppressor, wanting to be like the oppressor, wanting the oppressor to like them, mostly because the oppressor held all the power.

5. In a sense, all men everywhere are slightly schizoid—divorced from the reality of maintaining life. This makes it easier for them to play games with it. It is almost a cliché that women feel greater grief at sending a son off to war or losing him to that war because they bore him, suckled him, and raised him. The men who foment those wars did none of those things and have a more superficial estimate of the worth of human life. One hour a day is a low estimate of the amount of time one has to spend "keeping" oneself. By foisting this off on others, man gains seven hours a week—one working day more to play with his mind and not his human needs. Over the course of generations it is easy to see whence evolved the horrifying abstractions of modern life.

6. With the death of each form of oppression, life changes and new forms evolve. English aristocrats at the turn of the century were horrified at the idea of enfranchising working men—were sure that it signaled the death of civilization and a return to barbarism. Some working men were even deceived by this line. Similarly with the minimum wage, abolition of slavery, and female suffrage. Life changes but it goes on. Don't fall for any line about the death of everything if men take a turn at the dishes. They will imply that you are holding back the Revolution (their Revolution). But you are advancing it (your Revolution).

7. Keep checking up. Periodically consider who's actually *doing* the jobs. These things have a way of backsliding so that a year later once again the woman is doing everything. After a year make a list of jobs the man has rarely if ever done. You will find cleaning pots, toilets, refrigerators and ovens high on the list. Use time sheets if necessary. He will accuse you of being petty. He is above that sort of thing—(housework). Bear in mind what the worst jobs are, namely the ones that have to be done every day or several times a day. Also the ones that are dirty—it's more pleasant to pick up books, newspapers etc. than to wash dishes. Alternate the bad jobs. It's the daily grind that gets you down. Also make sure that you don't have the responsibility for the housework with occasional help from him. "I'll cook dinner for you tonight" implies it's really your job and isn't he a nice guy to do some of it for you.

8. Most men had a rich and rewarding bachelor life during which they did not starve or become encrusted with crud or buried under the litter. There is a taboo that says that women mustn't strain themselves in the presence of men: we haul around 50 pounds of groceries if we have to but aren't allowed

to open a jar if there is someone around to do it for us. The reverse side of the coin is that men aren't supposed to be able to take care of themselves without a woman. Both are excuses for making women do the housework.

9. Beware of the double whammy. He won't do the little things he always did because you're now a "Liberated Woman," right? Of course he won't do anything else either . . .

I was just finishing this when my husband came in and asked what I was doing. Writing a paper on housework. Housework? he said, *Housework?* Oh my god how trivial can you get. A paper on housework.

STUDY AND DISCUSSION QUESTIONS

1. In what sense is Mainardi calling her husband a hypocrite?

2. "The measure of your oppression," Mainardi tells women, "is his resistance." What does she mean?

3. Explain the significance of a statement like, "I'll cook dinner for you tonight." What might Mainardi rather hear her husband say?

4. What indications are there of the social class of this couple? How would the situation be different if they were significantly poorer? Richer?

5. Is this essay only aimed at women? What might a male reader get out of it?

SUGGESTIONS FOR WRITING

1. Imagine that this couple had a young child. Using Mainardi's form (what her husband says, followed by what it really means), write several additions to their "dialogue."

2. What do you think of Mainardi's characterization of some housework as "shitwork"?

3. "The Politics of Housework" was published in 1970. What's different today?

MUSTERING

Paul Monette

*Much of the poetry, fiction, and autobiographical writing of Paul Mon-
ette (1945–1995) focuses on his identity as a gay man and on the
struggles those he knew and he himself fought with AIDS. Among his
books are the poetry collection* Love Alone: Eighteen Elegies for Rog
(1988), the novels Afterlife *(1990) and* Halfway Home *(1991), and
the memoirs* Borrowed Time *(1988) and* Becoming a Man: Half a
Life Story *(1992), a National Book Award winner. The essay below
is from the collection* Last Watch of the Night *(1994).*

We didn't know till the last minute whether we'd make it to Washington for
the March. I couldn't pack; I couldn't even think. In those last days I was on
a scavenger hunt for medicine, a doctor who would somehow halt the downward slide. I was just coming off four weeks of radiation—my second course
of it in three months, only this time it hadn't worked. My radiation team had
triumphed in the first go-round, excising a cluster of KS lesions[1] on my penis,
more horrible to contemplate than causing any pain or problems making
water. Radiation hadn't even hurt. That is, until the radiation burn came on
at the end of treatment. Two weeks of walking bow-legged as a cowboy, wearing boxer shorts sized XXL so as not to rub myself the wrong way.

But this second course was a trickier business. The area to be zapped was
my left thigh, which had been swelling with edema for some months now, returning to "normal" size only after a night spent prone in bed. No pain. You
couldn't *see* anything—no purple spots, I mean—and for months my oncolo-
gist's advice was to leave it alone. The thigh hadn't really "bloomed" yet, and
Dr. Thommes wanted to keep me off chemo as long as possible. This is called
buying time in the cancer business. Besides, I had a slot in a protocol at UCLA[2]
for a new drug that showed promise in treating KS, and I'd have to drop out
of the study if I was taking chemo. The problem was, the UCLA drug still
wasn't available—a monthly broken promise by the pharmaceutical company,
which kept finding reasons to postpone the study. My swollen leg did not factor into their decisions.

---

[1] Kaposi's sarcoma, a cancer characterized by purple tumors on the skin, which is often a com-
plication of AIDS.

[2] University of California at Los Angeles.

All my oncology team agreed I'd better go ahead with more radiation, for the area along my inner thigh had begun to harden—turning "woody," to use their grisly euphemism. Clearly the KS had spread to my lymph system. Still, I plunged ahead confidently, stoked at having been given back my penis minus the purple nasties, convinced my thigh would respond as quickly.

But two weeks into treatment the leg was swelling more, not less. Blips of lesions began to bloom on the surface of the radiated skin. The most difficult aspect of all of this—getting over to the hospital every day, finding a parking space without resorting to my Uzi[3]—had finally become a physical challenge. I'd developed the beginnings of a gimp as I struggled to get out of the car and made the trek to Radiology.

They finally gave up on my thigh, muttering in frustration about this "leg thing." It was cropping up more and more these days, it seemed, and dodging the zap of their x-rays. I could've told them that my very first case of AIDS—César in 1983—had started with a leg like mine, swelling over the next two years till it was truly the size of a tree trunk, woody indeed. Then it began to suppurate and developed gangrene, not perhaps the thing that took him in the end but the major assault of his illness. I *knew* about this thing. But since it was time to move on to chemo, I blocked all memories of the sufferings of the past. Surely treatment had advanced in the ten years since César had been experimented on.

What it all had to do with Washington was that my first dose of chemo was scheduled for Tuesday, the 20th of April, the day before we were leaving for the March. *Don't worry,* the chemo team reassured me, *we can take care of this.* Sounding ominously like the radiation team a month before, though it seemed bad faith to bring that up now. Perversely, now, I missed the radiation staff—missed even the daily trips to Century City Hospital. As if to leave behind the brute technology of zapping were to wave goodbye to a simpler world, Arcadian compared to the exigencies of chemo.

Still, they all agreed I could go to Washington as planned, though warning me I wouldn't be at my best for a few days after. Meanwhile they would withhold the *really* toxic drug in the chemo arsenal, the one that takes your hair and makes you want to throw up all the time. For that they would wait till we got home. Despite these assurances, Winston and I were gun-shy. The previous June, just hours before we were to leave on a book tour, the bags packed, my doctor called and ordered me into the hospital. My brain scan had revealed that I was abloom with toxoplasmosis (I was turning into a veritable garden of exotic flowers), thus explaining my peculiar site-specific headaches, as if I'd

---

[3] Israeli-made submachine gun.

been beaned by a golf ball. There followed the arduous hit-and-miss of trying to find a treatment I wasn't allergic to. We stopped the infection with 566C80, a last-ditch protocol. My brain had been stable for seven months, but the memory of unpacking lingered, a curse on flying away.

And now the headaches had returned. The doctors deemed it prudent that I submit to another brain scan. Which I did on the Monday before the Wednesday departure. I was scarcely able to keep the two emergencies separate in my head, the brain infection and the cancer—it was like careening down a mountain road and having to steer two cars at once.

Why were we going to Washington? Our friend Victor put it most succinctly: "I guess because we're still here."

On Tuesday evening when I came home from a string of doctors' appointments, Winston had everything out, ready to go in the suitcase. My barber kindly paid a house call, hacking at my unruly mop so I would be presentable in the nation's capital, instead of looking like the fourth Stooge.[4] I dripped my daily IV infusion to keep from going blind. By midnight the phone hadn't rung, so Winston went ahead and packed the cases. We hardly slept at all, expecting a six-thirty cab to the airport. I slipped a volume of Sappho's poems into my carry-on bag, and we headed out.

Late at night, never asleep before three, I'd taken to reading the fragments of her poems to settle myself—a respite from the brain-and-cancer obstacle course. It was Winston who'd come across one of the lyrics in his reading:

> Without warning
>
> As a whirlwind
> swoops on an oak
> Love shakes my heart.

I dug out my Mary Barnard translation so he could see the full range, finding myself captivated all over again. One night I looked Sappho up in the *Oxford Companion*, reading aloud the citation, Winston beside me in bed. I read the part about her being "the leading personality among a circle of women and girls who must have comprised her audience." The great poet of Lesbos, who made the island synonymous with women loving women. The entry ends with a judgment, almost casual in its certainty:

---

[4] The Three Stooges were a slapstick comedy team.

Sappho created a form of subjective lyric never equaled in the ancient world in its immediacy and intensity.[5]

Dazzling, that. I turned to Winston and said, *Do you know how good you have to be to be called unequaled after twenty-six hundred years?* I felt just then an enormous pride of ancestry, and a vivid sense of linkage with the language of the heart.

> Some say a cavalry corps
> some infantry, some, again,
> will maintain that the swift oars
>
> of our fleet are the finest
> sight on dark earth; but I say
> that whatever one loves, is.

On the plane to D.C., fully half the passengers queer, I leafed through *Vanity Fair* and *The Advocate* and the L.A. *Times,* but turned again to Sappho. Caught up in her unequaled feeling, I was overcome with a great relief. Even if all the books are burned, I thought, somehow the emotions survive. Twenty-six hundred years from now, someone will still be struggling to set it all down—perhaps without any sense of ancestry, but that won't really matter. The grope for immediacy and intensity continues.

I understand that this is a somewhat discredited view of the classics, too romantic by half, the appropriation of classical sources and the certainty that we moderns feel just like they did, or they like us. A distinctly nineteenth-century notion, akin to the sloppy idea that we experience Democracy on a sort of continuum with Athens in the Golden Age, ignoring their slaves and the general powerlessness of women. Add to this the headache-making rift in gay and lesbian studies, where the "social constructionists" (also called "new-inventionists") argue that there was no such thing as a gay or lesbian person until late in the nineteenth century, when "homosexual" was coined. Plato would never have thought of himself as gay, nor would Sappho or anyone else, because the world was perceived entirely differently. The post-structural theorists define what "knowing" is, and it doesn't include self-knowledge about sexual orientation.

Doesn't make any sense to me, but then my own limited expertise is the history of the heart, and there are no breaks in its utterance through all written time. What else do you do with a lyric like this:

---

[5] M. C. Howatson, ed., *The Oxford Companion to Classical Literature* (Oxford, 1990), pages 506–507. [Author's note]

Afraid of losing you

I ran fluttering
like a little girl
after her mother.[6]

Self-awareness so deep it takes the breath away, whether or not the poet would ever have said she was a lesbian. (As opposed to Lesbian, which she surely was, as a resident of that deep-harbored island off the coast of Asia Minor.) I guess I have to accept that I read with a nineteenth-century eye, while secretly hoping for the passing of new-inventionism.

In addition to which, there had just been published in the previous week a study which averred that gay people are only one percent of the population, thus starting a new firestorm of marginalization among the Christian right. A study that turned out to be checkered from beginning to end. Only men were interviewed, for one thing, and some of us were beginning to feel that queer didn't parse that way, separating by gender. We were gender-*variant* if anything. And if not yet a fully unified tribe, then at least groping toward it. In addition, as Dr. Betty Berzon remarked, all the questions in the study were about sexual activity. "If you never had sex again for the next forty years," she told me, "you'd still be gay." But perhaps most tellingly, thirty percent of the men contacted by the researchers refused to take part in a sexual survey. The interviews were face to face, the interviewer always a woman, and there was no perception that closeted men would lie despite the assurance of "confidentiality."

Yet no red flags were raised in the mainstream press, which reported the study as gospel only a week before the March on Washington, with no follow-up questioning of any sort. It was left to the gay press to query the study's methods, especially the reach for geographical balance, when clearly it was the cities that had drawn gay men and women of the postwar generations. And the coincidence of the study's release on the eve of the high-water event of the gay and lesbian struggle was surely something short of innocent.

Winston and I had already been in Washington in late January, 1993, when I delivered the National Book Award speech at the Library of Congress. Then, only a week after the inauguration of the new administration, there was a quickness of spirit and an optimism that were palpable in the winter air, a sense that the nation had somehow survived the tyranny and arrogance of Reagan/Bush. Twelve years in the wilderness, and a legacy so bankrupt, so

---

[6] All quotations from Sappho are from Mary Barnard's *Sappho: A New Translation* (Univ. of California Press, 1966). [Author's note]

indifferent to human suffering, that one wondered if anyone could jigsaw the country back together.

The lifting of the ban on gay and lesbian personnel in the military had thrown us off-base a little. Most of our leaders in the community would never have called it the top priority. We all thought the President was going to announce an AIDS czar first thing. How could he not? We'd been waiting twelve years for some leadership in the epidemic—*any* leadership. What no one could have predicted was the tidal wave of homophobia unleashed by the military proposal: the pathological obtuseness of top brass, drunk on their misogynist prerogatives, coupled with the din of the Christian right.

One shrugged the usual shrug. Better that all their sewage and paranoia were aired in public, and not kept festering in churches and locker rooms and paramilitary boys' clubs. Decent people would surely see how crazy was the phobes' agenda. The head of the Texas Republican Party said that homosexuality should be a capital crime, punishable by death. And yet the country as a whole remained singularly ignorant when it came to fundamentalism. No one seemed to want to draw the circle that connected the World Trade Center bombing, the killing of a doctor at an abortion clinic in Florida, the standoff in Waco.[7] No one in America was interested in the rise of worldwide fundamentalism, the politics of retreat from the modern world. Meanwhile, the Constitutional protection offered by freedom of religion had been used to obliterate the line between Church and State. The Christian supremacists wanted a Christian nation, thank you. Freedom of religion only if the free religion was *their* religion.

What was needed more than anything just then was leadership at the top: the President simply had to address the hatred. Using the bully pulpit, he could plead for tolerance and unity. Instead he held a news conference in which he seemed to suggest that gay and lesbian soldiers might be segregated, thus starting his own bonfire. He pushed the wrong button on civil rights. And though I didn't feel personally betrayed by the printed transcript of his remarks, the silence of the White House over the next several days was deafening. No clarifications, no bully pulpit. Little did the White House staff know that in our world silence had come to equal death.

I had been balking for several weeks about my own participation in the March, because there seemed a conscious wish among the organizers that AIDS be relegated to the background. It became increasingly clear that people with AIDS would not be on the rostrum—"because that's not what this

---

[7] Three 1993 events: a bomb was set off in the World Trade Center in New York City, killing six and injuring hundreds; a doctor who performed abortions was murdered by an abortion opponent; and a fifty-one day federal siege of the Branch Davidian religious cult's compound in Waco, Texas ended with the death of seventy-four inhabitants.

March is about," as an organizer put it bluntly to a high-placed official with AIDS who wanted to speak. I couldn't get over my own sense of disjunction. I kept envisioning a joyous parade of celebration, a giddy triumphal love-in where I did not belong. I bore no animus toward the organizers for wanting their March to be an arrival—no apologies for "lifestyle" anymore, but full participation in our rights as free citizens. I would doubtless applaud that kind of March but didn't especially want to be there, relegated to the status of "a downer."

But the call went out with greater and greater urgency that all of us had to *be* there, if for nothing else than to prove we could rally the whole "one per-cent" of us to petition for equal rights. Besides, the mood had changed since the hearings had begun on the lifting of the military ban, under the chair-manship of Sister Nunn,[8] a puffed-up Chicken Little who thought the world would collapse if we let queers in. When we heard that the President planned *not* to attend, not to address the March at all, the simmering impatience made it plain that we weren't gathering for a love-in for President Clinton.

Not to put too fine a point on it, one began to realize that the question being raised—beyond equal rights, beyond a cure—was, what did it mean to be gay and lesbian *now?* We couldn't leave it to the scholars and the pollsters, that was for damn sure. All those fights over the very name of the March, which had flared up during the National Gay and Lesbian Task Force conference in November. Bisexuals were clamoring for inclusion. By the end of the confer-ence it was being called The March on Washington for Gay and Lesbian, Bi-sexual, Transgender and Transsexual Rights, or some such agglomeration. Perhaps one had to go to Washington simply to discover if one still existed.

I weathered the flight pretty well. By mid-evening on Wednesday we were in our rooms at the Park Hyatt, rooms we'd booked in November. The message light was flashing as we entered. My doctor had called from L.A. to say that the results of the MRI on my brain seemed to indicate further activ-ity in the cerebellum. Unhappily the hospital appeared to have lost the x-rays from the previous scan six weeks ago, so there was nothing to compare the current pictures with. As if on cue, my head began to throb again. Tylenol barely made a dent.

We decided not to get up next morning for the dedication of the Holo-caust Memorial, though that was why we'd come early. In January we'd toured the exhibit models prior to installation, and the staff had invited us to be pre-sent for the public unveiling. I was rattled by what I saw, even in miniature, and impressed by its defiant challenge of historical truth. The drumbeat of the Memorial was the constant question why: *Why was this allowed to happen?*

---

[8] Senator Sam Nunn from Georgia, who opposed President Clinton's efforts in 1993 to allow gays and lesbians to serve openly in the military.

We gave our tickets to Jehan and Dwora, our lesbian friends from L.A. who were staying just down the hall. Dwora's mother had been in the camps and still bore the tattoo on her forearm. A couple of months before, in fact, she'd been hospitalized in Florida with heart problems. The doctor who examined her blanched when he saw the blurred numbers. "That's not what I think it is, is it?" he said, pointing at her arm. "No, I'm a fashion model," Dwora's mother replied with fine Viennese hauteur. "Didn't you know, this is the latest thing."

I woke up Thursday very slowly, glad we'd decided to skip the ceremony because it was cold and rainy out. Winston returned invigorated from an ACT UP action at the White House—three hundred people strong, a third of them women, demanding increased funding for AIDS. They had gathered in Lafayette Park, but the D.C. police wouldn't let them cross the street to the sidewalk in front of the Executive Mansion. As the cops grew more truculent and confrontive, Winston had shaken a finger at one of them. "You better behave," he warned, "'cause there's going to be a million of us here this weekend!"

Already there was TV coverage of the ceremony at the Holocaust Memorial. Outdoors in the blustery chill, Elie Wiesel stood at the podium, hair so askew he appeared to have been tearing at it for days. Which he had been, actually, because another poll had been released that week, indicating that one in five Americans was ready to believe the Holocaust never happened. Wiesel had gone speechless in an accompanying interview, as if this knowledge was too much even for him, mocking as it did a half century of "witnessing."

But today he had reinvigorated his moral fire, gesticulating from the podium as he listed all the departments in Washington that *knew.* The decision not to bomb the rail lines to the camps in Poland, just miles from the military targets we did hit—all this he placed at Roosevelt's door. And he turned like an Old Testament prophet and pointed a quivering finger at the President. *Now what are you going to do about Bosnia?* he trumpeted, the connection clear to any child. He'd been there himself, seen all the madness and slaughter, seen it *again.* The question hung in the air that blasted him about like Lear on the heath. The President cast his eyes down, waiting his turn to speak.

A not bad speech, as it turned out, but fireless. One wondered what the world would be like if leaders had the passion of Elie Wiesel. Personally I'd rather have a leader tearing his hair out, than all the dulcet tones of a briefing with the National Security Council. Meanwhile there was little doubt, in my mind anyway, that the one in five who disbelieved the Holocaust was a real good Christian. Larry Kramer[9] had remarked about the polls supporting

---

[9] Gay activist, writer, and founder of ACT UP (AIDS Coalition to Unleash Power).

the military ban, that no one would ever ask *Should Jews be allowed in the military?* But if such a poll were conducted, added Larry with laser precision, the Jews would probably lose.

We conferred with the doctor again by phone. In consultation with the infectious disease specialist, he was prescribing two more drugs for me to take along with the 566C80. We were to arrange with the pharmacist in L.A. to send them on to Washington by overnight mail. I was still feeling pretty rocky from Tuesday's chemo dose, and the throb in my head hadn't abated. But I had the wherewithal to tell him I'd proven allergic to one of those drugs last summer. He told me to go ahead anyway, starting with a quarter capsule, working up to dosage. The missing x-rays had finally been located, but it wasn't clear if they'd been looked at yet. Dr. Aronow, my neurologist, was on his way to Washington for the March.

Thursday afternoon we took a cab with Jehan and Dwora and made our way to the Jefferson Memorial. The wind chill off the Tidal Basin was daunting, so that we had to walk with our heads bent. Very few tourists had come this far today, but we waved to several queers we knew from Los Angeles. The city was filling up with us. Yet we had the domed interior practically to ourselves as we made our shivering circuit, reading Jefferson's words on the walls. The ringing condemnation of slavery, from a man who kept house slaves himself:

> Commerce between master and slave is despotism. Nothing is more certainly written in the Book of Fate than that these people are to be free.

The groping toward the future, setting the course for Enlightenment:

> . . . laws and institutions must go hand in hand with the progress of the human mind. As that becomes more developed, more enlightened, as new discoveries are made, new truths discovered and manners and opinions change, with the change of circumstances, institutions must advance also to keep pace with the times.

One wondered if gay and lesbian freedom was part of the change he foresaw—a man who probably hadn't the shred of a clue about the love that dare not speak its name. Did this faith in the constant betterment of the citizenry, the certainty that slavery would collapse of its own guilty weight, did its reach extend to peoples he couldn't conceive? His friend John Adams used to say that he studied politics and war so his son could study philosophy and his grandson poetry. Did Jefferson trust the poets to conceive a world he wouldn't even recognize, as long as it held to the first commandment, that *All men are created equal?*

What would the mood of the March be? Celebration or dissent—or both in concert? Would we leave no doubt that we were assembling here for patriotism's sake? Demanding that America honor its own vision of a place for everyone. No more invisibility. "I hold it," Jefferson wrote to Madison in

1787, "that a little rebellion, now and then, is a good thing, and as necessary in the political world as storms in the physical." Let us have a little rebellion then. Let the mood be so diverse that not even the most rabid phobes could say we were all the same—not godless deviants, nor a threat to their white-bread kids, but a people newly free, of every kind and stripe imaginable, with earrings to match.

We left the Jeff and had the taxi let us out at Dupont Circle, the heart of gay and lesbian D.C. Strolling up Connecticut Avenue, we could feel the gathering force-field of people arriving from everywhere. At Lambda Rising, the line to get into a *bookstore* stretched all the way to the corner. Storefront spaces had been leased up and down the avenue to sell buttons and tee-shirts and programs of the weekend's events. It was our first encounter with the tee-shirt that read STRAIGHT BUT NOT NARROW, proudly sported by a hetero couple holding hands and beaming at us, their brothers and sisters.

We ducked into a basement coffee shop to rest because my leg was gimping up. The queer behind the counter promised us the best hot chocolate we'd ever had, a recipe specially made for the March. As we sat with our mugs at the counter, a gaunt man with a knapsack came in, dressed in combat fatigues and sporting a chestful of lift-the-ban buttons over his combat ribbons. He told us he had just driven in from San Diego with a carful of gay vets. He was weak and tired but ready to march. He and his group were camping out in a campground in Maryland, where they froze their nuts off the night before. He'd decided to bunk in a friend's apartment for the rest of the weekend, because "I don't want to go home sick."

That night we were meant to attend the National Minority AIDS Council dinner in the Great Hall at the Library of Congress. But by six o'clock I was being hammered by a migraine and a general air of malaise, like being seasick in calm waters, and the boat wasn't even moving. So we made our apologies and only heard later that night, in a flurry of telephone bulletins, that Larry Kramer and a group of ACT UP-pers had disrupted the evening, preventing Donna Shalala from speaking. Our source, a member of the upper-echelon leadership, fretted and clucked that we mustn't be seen as disrupting free speech and assembly. I bit my tongue, glad that Larry was out there making noise. I was no fan of the Secretary of Health and Human Services, who had not so much as mentioned the A word since taking office three months before.

I finally connected with Larry by phone on Friday morning. No, he said, they hadn't prevented Madame Secretary from speaking. They'd simply passed around a bunch of leaflets, and then Larry and a woman of color had stood behind the Secretary at the podium, holding up signs that said DONNA DO-NOTHING. It was painful to think of the clash between the organizers of the dinner—some of whom I knew had fought long and hard to make this event happen—and the more aggressive tactics of the street activists. It was billed as a Congressional Dinner and titled "Our Place at the Table." But there probably wasn't a more appropriate place to showcase the tactical poles of the movement, our variety and our political diversity. And if push came to shove in the Great Hall, there was no question which side I was on: "ACT UP, fight back, fight AIDS!"

There was a documentary crew that had been following Winston and me around for months. To us they seemed to have shot enough footage to remake *Birth of a Nation*,[10] but they wanted a clip of us marching on Sunday. At this point I was scheduled to ride up front on a trolley bus, provided through the good graces of Marvin Liebman, the conservative movement's former darling and now *bête noire*. So the hobbled and the ancient of days were to lead the throng onto the Mall.

Already, though, I was starting to question the wisdom of my staying out all day Sunday, and to wonder if I'd come this far in order to miss the parade. We told the documentarians that they could accompany us to the Lincoln Memorial on Friday afternoon, in case I had to disappoint them Sunday. The Lincoln was a touchstone where we'd been planning to pay our respects for months. The weather had grown mild during the night, and with the last puffs of the passing storm pillowing the bright blue sky, Washington had recovered its gaudy airs of spring.

We piled all four into a cab driven by an Indian, who was so friendly and eager to please that he could have been Aziz in *A Passage to India*,[11] oversolicitous but not without charm. When we got to the Lincoln, I gave him twenty dollars and told him to wait for us, ten minutes at most. My cabmates gave me a look, as if I were throwing money away, at which Aziz drew himself up with dignity and said, "You think I going to steal your twenty dollars? Don't worry, I be right here."

Monte and Lesli hoisted the equipment and followed me and Winston up the steps. I'd been there before, but probably not in twenty-five years. It had never struck me till now that Lincoln's memorial temple was the size and shape of the Parthenon; not by scientific measure probably, but feelingly at least, a most moving evocation of the daddy of public buildings, and thus of the democratic Age of Pericles that built it. And having made that connection, I further realized as I climbed the steps that the Jefferson echoed in its own way the sanctuary of Athena Pronaia at Delphi. There the most heartstopping ruin is the Tholos, a circular temple with only three columns still in place and a lintel above, but enough to reconstruct a

---

[10] Silent film by D. W. Griffith.

[11] Novel by E. M. Forster.

classical heaven on earth—for us nineteenth-century types anyway. It seemed nicely fortuitous that the Parthenon and the Tholos both were temples to Pallas Athena, goddess of war but also wisdom.

There is nothing to match the Lincoln, in America anyway, for noble proportion and spiritual lift. You pass inside the Doric colonnade, and the columns in the entryway change to Ionic, with the ram's-horn capitals, a subtle shift to a more sophisticated style. Still, nothing quite prepares you for the power of the seated Lincoln—not the hundred cherry-blossom postcards that have passed through your hands over the years, not even the patriotic swoop shots from helicopters that crop up in every civic documentary across the political spectrum.

You approach this massive marble pedestal, with the figure by Daniel Chester French looming above you. The toe of Lincoln's boot is off the pedestal, just above your head—a human touch that suggests a tall and rangy man who's too restless to sit in one place for long. And it's true, the eyes are haunted—staring out over the nation's city with a prophet's unshifting gaze, melancholy but also rock-solid sure that the nation's wounds would heal. No wonder it draws so many whose hope is faltering.

On the wall to the left is the Gettysburg Address; on the right the Second Inaugural. *With malice toward none, with charity for all.* I suddenly needed to stand on the spot where Marian Anderson sang her Easter concert, barred from Independence Hall by the D.A.R. I needed to honor Eleanor Roosevelt, who resigned from the organization and pestered Franklin to approve the Lincoln Memorial site. In the end Eleanor herself didn't attend, fearing to politicize the event even further. But there's a lovely detail in Joseph Lash's *Eleanor and Franklin:* Eleanor sitting quietly in the White House, the balcony doors thrown open, hearing the great contralto's voice as it floated over Washington.

All under the eyes of Lincoln, eighty years after the Emancipation Proclamation. Another quarter century later, and the tempered gaze of Lincoln—warrior and wise man—bore witness to the passion of Dr. King. I didn't think the Lincoln of my understanding would have had any trouble equating the Civil Rights struggle of people of color with the latter-day dreams of the gay and lesbian movement. There's too much compelling evidence in his own life—the bed he shared for four years with Joshua Speed above the general store in Springfield; the breakdown he suffered when family duties sent them apart—of the "dear love of comrades."[12]

---

[12] Whitman's phrase. A most suggestive reading about Lincoln's relations with Joshua Speed is in Charley Shively's *Drum Beats* (Gay Sunshine Press, 1989). And note Shively's caveat: "The romantic cult of male friendship may have sometimes been completely non-sexual, but it provided a convenient form in which homosexual men could conceptualize their feelings for other men." (*Drum Beats,* page 88). [Author's note]

In any case, I was choked with tears and in awe to be there, blubbering into my clip-on mike as the visit was recorded, a sort of super-video souvenir of a family trip to Washington. Standing in the shadow of the man who saved his country, it wasn't hard to see the religious right as a sort of Confederate belligerence. Only now they were hiding behind fundamentalist morality instead of States' Rights. And oh, how we needed a Lincoln to stand for equal justice and bind us all together again.

It was time to move on, because we'd promised Lesli and Monte a photo op in front of the White House. We trundled into the parking lot looking for Aziz, but he'd taken off with my twenty after all. I craned my neck to try and spot him, sure he was just circling the monument and would be back momentarily. Winston and Lesli and Monte rolled their eyes at my naivete, biting their tongues to keep from saying *I told you so.*

As we were coming up the street toward Pennsylvania Avenue, passing the Old Executive Office Building, we suddenly saw Larry Kramer, about to duck into a taxi directly in front of us. We raised a cry to stop him, and I clambered over to embrace him. Lesli and Monte, delirious at their luck, were already shooting. Larry introduced himself to Winston, and then we were off like a band of rebels, strolling past the Executive Mansion, Larry and I arm in arm. Though we talked by phone with a certain regularity, this was the first time I'd seen my friend in over two years.

We gossiped first, of course. The private Larry is a total *mensch,* warm and loving, the definition of decency. Those who were only familiar with his heroic public stance in the fight against AIDS, his Jeremiah role, often missed the heart's core of him. More than once during the weekend just beginning, I would hear his name taken in vain: *Larry goes too far. That's not the image we want to project.* And I'd reply what I always said: *What would things be like if we didn't have at least one like this?* More than a witness, more than a leader, in his own way like the Elie Wiesel who stood on the heath tearing his hair. With a constitutional inability to abide fools, was it any wonder that he shrieked and raged in this Swiftian Capitol of Fools?

It was a wonder to me that Larry could still fight like a full-blooded warrior. Perhaps it was my own diminished capacity, fighting a pitched battle against the predations of the virus, that made me value Larry so. A stand-in for thousands of us teetering on the brink, someone who knew in his gut that a quarter of a million of us were going to die on Clinton's watch, even if the President proved to be a visionary leader in the epidemic.

Hearing us jabber and laugh, Winston was immediately reminded of Lincoln and Whitman. In the evening light the poet would be returning this way from the hospital, from his work as a wound-dresser. An aide would alert the President, and Lincoln would rush to the window to watch the passage of the country's premier bard. A poet who'd freed his own soul in the process of extolling the incalculable beauty of his country and its workers. No one has ever recorded an actual meeting of the two, though Whitman was as much in awe of Lincoln as the President was of the poet. But the well-thumbed copy of *Leaves of Grass* in the White House stood in moving counterpoint to the great funeral ode the poet would write on the death of his hero.

We stopped in front of the iron fence; beyond it was the great lawn sweeping up to the mansion. Larry pointed across Lafayette Park, where he used to stand as a boy in his father's office, watching the inaugurals. We became aware of a couple of corn-fed college kids, drawn by the documentary crew and unabashedly gaping at us. One of them got up the courage to approach Larry. "I think I recognize you," he said haltingly.

"Well, of course you do," I declared with a kind of avuncular pride. "This is Larry Kramer."

Larry squeezed my arm, adding, "And this is Paul Monette. You've struck gold."

The boys were from Lacrosse, Wisconsin—this was their first march, indeed their first trip to Washington. We asked them if they were the sum of the out queers of Lacrosse, and they shrugged their agreement. "There's another one," hazarded the taller of the boys. "But we're not sure if she made it."

It was the story of a thousand towns across the nation. Some of us making the trek to swell our ranks, ambassadors for the ones who could not come, who perhaps weren't out of the closet yet, even to themselves. Many among us coming out to family and friends by way of announcing they were on their way to the March, using this historic moment as a goad, as a diving board if you will. And so many others blowing their savings to get here, convinced that this watershed event would serve as a measure of their own freedom and self-regard, perhaps for the rest of their lives. Something to take home to Lacrosse, Wisconsin.

By the time we got back to the hotel I was reeling from exhaustion, the woodpecker still knocking at my head, my bum leg swollen to bursting. The overnight package had arrived from the pharmacy in L.A. I took out the three new medicines—Zithromax, Daraprim, Leucovorin, sounding like a trio of intergalactic villains out of *Star Trek*. I lined them up on the dresser across from the bed, staring at them. I was meant to start popping them right away, but I needed to somehow get used to them first. I was already taking thirty pills a day, not including the IV drip for CMV retinitis. How much medication could the body tolerate before the liver collapsed, or the kidneys? Not that I had any intention of rebelling, as I'd watched so many friends do—stopping all their medications cold, enough was enough, they'd rather be dead. And for a while at least they'd feel quite well, freed of the toxins and side effects of this sewer of drugs. And then they'd die.

I rested for two or three hours, husbanding my energy, readying myself for the evening ahead. A dinner party in Georgetown had been arranged to honor me, by straight friends who were tireless allies in the gay and lesbian cause. Ties and jackets in place, Winston and Victor and I made our way to a flouncing Victorian row house off N Street. Our hosts, Bob Shrum and Marylouise Oates, greeted us with a fanfare of enthusiasm. The guest list was still in flux, but the Speaker of the House was definitely coming. Michael Kinsley would be right over as soon as he finished shooting *Crossfire.* And Tom Stoddard, head of the campaign to lift the military ban, would be a little later still because he was doing *Larry King Live.*

A rich mix of power politics, and to us outlanders a rare taste of being "off the record." It was implicit in the rough-and-tumble conversation over cocktails, this quick and brainy gathering of the savviest men and women, that the house off N Street was a journalistic safe house, no Mont Blancs[13] and notebooks allowed. The talk was dizzyingly frank, about the filibuster and campaign reform and "how the President's doing." As a news junkie I could just keep up, and Winston murmured to Victor how refreshing it was that no one talked about movies. I thought of the Abolitionists, their heated meetings in parlors just like this one. (Lincoln, on being introduced to Harriet Beecher Stowe: "So you're the little woman who wrote the book that started this great war!") Or the Transcendental gatherings at Mr. Emerson's house in Concord. Philosophical politics.

At dinner I was seated across from Tom Foley, a witty and forthright man, appealingly modest and human, who came across altogether differently than he did on the Capitol steps, speaking *ex cathedra* into a thicket of network mikes. I couldn't bring myself to call him Tom, mostly because I preferred the rolling cadence of "Mr. Speaker." There was considerable conversation about the upcoming March and its potential effect on the hearings to lift the ban. (The consensus: no effect at all.) I shifted the ground of inquiry to AIDS, and the best and brightest of the journalists, on my left, reacted with genuine puzzlement.

"But you're going to get an AIDS czar eventually," he said, "and the funding's going to be there." The underlying question being, why were some of our people still protesting, and especially why so hard against the first President ever to be our sympathetic partisan? A very trenchant point; and how to explain what it meant that we'd been waiting not four months but twelve *years* and four months? We feared the epidemic, which had taken back-burner status after the military ban, would suffer from White House caution that the President not be perceived as giving "too much to the gays." (After all our railing that AIDS was not a gay disease but a global catastrophe.) Not that we doubted the President's personal commitment, but the polls apparently

---

[13] Expensive brand of pens.

showed a nosedive whenever he reached out a hand to us. I withheld my personal trump card for hospitality's sake—that nothing could save me now, and yet I would still be out there railing for my brothers, unto my last breath.

There was talk among the straight folk at the table who worried that the March would hurt our cause. The argument went that Mid-America would be frightened off by our numbers and our rhetoric, and the inevitable press attention on the drag queens and the faeries. What they didn't seem to understand was that our March was for us first and not for anyone else's sake. Besides, we could scarcely have more enemies than we already had. And as one sequined man sporting a ball gown and a full beard opined to a minicam crew: "My wearing a dress doesn't infringe on anyone else's rights. And besides, it's after six. Time for evening clothes."

I found myself trying to explain to my end of the table my perceptions about the inadequacy of social-constructionist theory, which had reduced our ranks historically with sweeping abandon. And then this jerkwater poll that had pegged us at one percent. I told them about reading Sappho and the survival of feeling. They listened politely till one of the women, a superbrain in overdrive who'd managed the funding of the '92 campaign in California, inquired with a nice candor: "Who's Sappho?"

I blinked like an aging professor long since put out to pasture. How could a sharp, well-educated woman not know the name of the supreme ancestor of *our* sort of women? I tried not to react like a stuffy prig, contemptuous of the spotty education of the young. I gave the poet her proper footnote, reciting some verses to back it up, then gave the floor back to political passions. I felt more nineteenth century than ever.

Back at the hotel I shook out a red capsule from the prescription bottle: Zithromax, ruler of the planet Toxo. I opened the capsule, dumped three quarters of the drug and swallowed the remnant. For the next twenty-four hours I'd be dashing in and out of the bathroom, lifting my shirt to examine my belly for rashy spots. I lay down exhausted, but not enough to sleep, reading my thriller till four A.M. One of the minor irritations of AIDS—*minor* as in not life-threatening, but even more *minor* on somebody else's skin—was an itching so intense that you wanted to flay yourself. No scratching seemed to quell it, though that didn't stop you tearing at it. Variously it had been diagnosed as eczema, as a side effect of one of my meds (but who could say which), and most comprehensively as "somehow connected with the virus." Meaning nobody had a clue. One of the doctors prescribed an unguent that seemed to help a little, only it left me feeling like a greased pig.

On Saturday morning I woke up shaky, realizing I hadn't been eating enough all week. 566C80, the drug that had held the toxo in check, had to be taken by mouth four times a day. But because it absorbed so badly, it needed to be taken with fats. So for months I'd been eating groggily in the dark—

doughnuts and cheese and whole milk—helping along the five A.M. dose. I mostly ate ice cream for the waking doses, but that left my appetite stubbornly curbed. And even at that, the 566C80 wasn't doing the job anymore, so I had the feeling of losing ground with every doughnut.

I ordered a big room service breakfast, popped a full capsule of Zithromax, and encouraged Winston not to miss the ACT UP action at the Capitol. For the first time really all week, I started to feel trapped by AIDS. Mournfully I considered that this trip could be my last. I never doubted that I needed to be here; but what about Italy and Jerusalem? The world had shrunk quite suddenly in the last couple of weeks, as I began to understand the intractability of the nexus of tumors in my leg, and grew terrified that my brain was clouding up. I had yet to get through to my neurologist, thought we'd both left clusters of messages at one another's hotel. I sat down to my melancholy coffee and croissants, feeling acutely left out.

I had a call from Richard Isay—the doctor who had rethought the psychoanalytic development of gay men, rescuing us from stereotypes and defining our health in terms of self-esteem. We had never met but had promised to be in touch in Washington, hoping to find a free hour for a cup of tea. I begged off by reason of general tottering and queasiness, and Richard asked if there was anything he could do. I tumbled out the tale of my leg and my brain, trying to be matter-of-fact and not awash with self-pity. But that was exactly what his ear was tuned to, and over the next two days he checked in regularly. Not imposing himself but serving as an anchor, especially in the absence of my medical team. A wound-dresser indeed, like a Whitman of the psyche.

I read the *Washington Post* all the way through, checking out the queer coverage. We were definitely the main news this weekend, with coming-out profiles that let us speak for ourselves about the witch hunts that characterized the military ban. Meanwhile the Navy had released its appalling report on the Tailhook scandal,[14] all the woman-hating details, hoping that it might get buried in the hoop-la surrounding the March. These were the Navy geniuses who had tried to pin the U.S.S. *Iowa* explosion[15] on the broken heart of one gay sailor, only to have to take it all back a year later. The same Navy that had lied to Allen Schindler's[16] mother, saying her son had been killed in a fight, just an unfortunate accident. And one of his murderers went free, and the other showed no remorse at his arraignment. The truth would never have come out at all if Allen's gay brothers in Japan hadn't blown the cover-up.

---

[14] Revelations that United States Navy and Marine aviators had sexually assaulted numerous women at the Tailhook Society convention in 1991.

[15] 1989 explosion that killed forty-seven.

[16] United States Navy sailor who, in 1992, was beaten and killed by fellow sailors because he was gay.

The same Navy that had turned whole villages in the Philippines into brothels, keeping all the girls clean for the delectation of the drunken slobs who came ashore. And this was the Navy in which gay and lesbian people were not allowed to serve because we might hurt morale.

I had a visit that afternoon from the writer Harlan Greene and his lover, Olin. They had just been through a nightmare battle over Olin's health insurance—a battle they'd won in the end, but indicative of the Simon Legree tactics of the insurance cabal that was always scheming to throw people with AIDS out on their ear on the merest technicality. All of us lucky enough to *be* insured lived in constant dread of a cancellation letter. I'd had a case manager assigned to me some months ago, and she kept me posted on how much slack I had. Just the week before she'd left the information on my machine that I'd used up $156,722 toward my million-dollar cap. I was safe so far, but if the drug to save my eyes began to fail I'd have to move on to a three-hour drip that cost twenty-six thousand a month, just for the medication. Enough of those platinum Band-Aids, and you could blow your cap in a year.

We were talking about Baptists, Harlan and Olin and I—how the local parish tradition in the South had not always been a breeding-ground for homophobia. It was very recent, the assigning of diabolic status to queers. As usual, the hate-mongering had paralleled the growth of our movement, a pipe-bomb response to our coming out in droves. If only we wouldn't talk about it, they said, they wouldn't have to mount such a campaign against us. It was all our own fault. Meanwhile we'd just begun to hear rumors of the Nunn "compromise" that would come to be called "Don't ask. Don't tell." Why couldn't we see they could live with us—Baptists and generals and pundits all—if we'd just stay in the closet? We can live with you if you'll just play dead.

Winston came back from "Hands Around the Capitol," ACT UP's exorcism of Congress. Fifteen or twenty thousand people had shown up, ringing the Capitol dome and grounds in a chain of protest, demanding increased funding for AIDS research and care. The event was a neat combination of witches' sabbath and shamanic levitation, culminating in a round of angry speeches by the likes of Michael Petrellis and Larry Kramer, whose coining of "Bill the Welsher" had thrown a new gauntlet down. "He's beginning to sound like Roosevelt and the Jews," said Larry. "Talks a good line and then does nothing." Bringing it round in a circle to Elie Wiesel, shouting his bitter *J'accuse*[17] in the wind and rain. A circle of witness made tangible by the linking of all those hands.

On the Duty of Civil Disobedience, as the sage of Walden Pond called it. "Let your life be a counter-friction to stop the machine." And why? "I

---

[17] Elie Wiesel, Holocaust survivor and writer; *J'accuse* (French for "I accuse"), title of an 1898 open letter by French novelist Émil Zola denouncing the unfounded conviction of Jewish army officer Alfred Dreyfus for treason.

please myself with imagining a State at last which can afford to be just to all men. . . . "

When Olin and Harlan departed, I took to my bed again, beginning to feel positively neurasthenic. We'd been invited to several Eve-of-the-March receptions, including one which would preview the media spots for the lifting of the ban. A counter-friction, as it were, to the grotesque tissue of lies and hysteria which passed for the "family values" video making the rounds of Congress. But I couldn't pull it together, missing one gathering after another. Winston took care of me, soothing my imprisoned spirit. At nine o'clock I felt strong enough to get dressed, and we finally ventured out into the teeming throng of celebration, queers on every corner shivering with expectation of the day ahead.

I felt like their grandfather. Not unwelcome and not passed by, exactly—but bittersweet all the same, to find myself an elder before my time. Were it not for the virus I didn't doubt but that I would be capering in the streets myself. It was strange to be playing the reveler with Death so hot in pursuit, but somehow I rose to it. Probably because I was walking hand in hand with the man I loved. For here was the truly revolutionary act, to me the heart's core of what the enemy called the "militant homosexual agenda." Such a quiet gesture, really, no banners or slogans in evidence. Not proclaiming anything but a tenderness that had managed to endure the assaults of grief and sickness.

Jefferson made a great leap forward when he wrote the Declaration, amending the common-law notion of *life, liberty, and property* to the more felicitous *life, liberty, and the pursuit of happiness.* That was Winston and me. A careerist had asked us across a dinner table a couple of years before, "What are you working on now?" "Being happy," retorted Winston. A full-time job when you're living on a tightrope. Hard to choose a moment to represent all that, but perhaps that winter day, driving over the Continental Divide while I read him aloud the whole of Whitman's "I Sing the Body Electric." And finishing that, we suddenly saw on the blinding slope below the road a pair of wolves cavorting in the snow. We stopped to watch, silent a minute, till one of us remarked, "They mate for life, you know."

How to explain to a bigot so much resonance? The clasp of a hand on an evening's walk, the body electric, the mating of wolves. It's not written down in the militant agenda, and it isn't a "special right," as the current coinage had it when they passed the law against us in Colorado.[18] It was simply what Jefferson promised, *pursuit of happiness.* As useless to pass a law against as to pass one against the wolves.

---

[18] Colorado's Amendment 2 passed in 1993, making gay rights legislation, which had already passed in several Colorado cities, illegal.

Later we joined a group of friends for dinner, straight and queer together around a table, trading stories about the weekend's exuberant parade. Toasting our health with a clink of ten glasses, but really toasting the fact that we were still here. Herb told us about the powerful appearance Allen Schindler's mother had made earlier that evening at the March on Washington Gala. With her plainspoken heart she thanked the gay and lesbian community for helping her to expose the Navy coverup. But more than that, she wanted to tell us all that people were wrong who thought we were weird. Such goodness and so much support in her grief had shown her what a loving tribe we were. "Thank you for my son," she said.

In the cab back to the hotel, Winston and I finally faced the obvious: I wouldn't be able to march tomorrow. Insistently I urged that he must go for both of us, with Victor and Jehan and Dwora; that I would be fine watching it all on C-Span,[19] my leg propped up on pillows. He was just as insistent shaking his head no. He preferred to experience it all with me, however second-hand.

At midnight I finally connected by phone with my neurologist. Indeed he had seen the x-rays, and indeed there was new activity. Some swelling and edema of the lesion at the far edge of the cerebellum—a pain I felt about two inches behind my right ear—and indication of a new lesion, but this one just beginning, still very small. Had the 566C80 stopped working, I asked in trepidation, or had I developed resistance to it? No, it was just the absorption problem, nothing to panic over. I had a surreal vision of doubling my doughnut intake, liquefying whole boxes of Winchell's and feeding them through my IV line.

Dr. Aronow concurred with the rest of the team, that I should be adding the *Star Trek* trio to my regimen. As to allergic reaction, he thought the Hismanal I was taking to facilitate 566C80 would cover the new drugs as well. From the first he showed a fine capacity to calm my fears, and always with a jaunty assurance that he still had "other tricks up my sleeve." People with advanced toxo, he reminded me, were not giving lectures at the Library of Congress.

A reprieve then, though four weeks later I still make hourly forays to check my belly for allergy rash in the mirror above the sink. Part of the AIDS version of touching wood, a constant reminder that *now* is a temporary thing, all the more reason to seize it.

I got up at noon on Sunday, and Winston was already tuned to C-Span. The afternoon rally on the mall was just beginning, and we sat glued to it for six hours. The Woodstock energy was infectious and many of the speeches

---

[19] Television channel offering live coverage of congressional hearings and other public affairs.

very moving, though we wished they'd pan the crowd more as it surged along the March route, past the White House and down Pennsylvania Avenue. It took seven hours to bring the whole sea of us onto the Mall, evening already before the last groups arrived. Later we heard a chorus of complaints from people who hadn't heard a single speech. That the marshals were unprepared for these kinds of numbers. That the ACT UP die-in—thousands of protesters falling to the pavement and playing dead for the seven minutes that passed between one actual death and the next, the plague's clock—had slowed everything down.

And the numbers themselves. A lesbian friend, veteran of the '87 march,[20] was backstage when the Park Service arrived to make its estimate. They were notorious for undercounting, especially the likes of us. It was as if they'd learned their arithmetic from the pollsters who'd reduced us to one percent. My friend approached one of the youthful organizers and asked her where her negotiating team was. For this was the crucial bargaining moment with the Park Service, playing the poker of estimating crowds. A shrug from the organizers, who had no team in readiness. Giving the Park Service free rein to ball-park the lot of us at three hundred thousand, and this in the mid-afternoon as hundreds of thousands of us still flowed down Pennsylvania Avenue, nowhere near the Mall yet.

The D.C. police, no special friends of ours, put the figure at 1.2 million. The transit authority announced that four hundred fifty thousand extra riders had ridden the subway that day. But the media picked up the Park Service figure alone as being the only "official" figure.

With so many people to speak at the rally, the participants were sternly limited to just a few minutes apiece, the entertainers to a single song. One of the early appearances was made by our friend Judith Light—who made the point that we were all here to teach our fellow citizens as well as every tarpit dinosaur in Congress. For years she'd been one of the movement's tireless allies, serving as the token straight on so many boards and dinner committees, emceeing so many events; she'd eaten enough hotel ballroom chicken to qualify her for combat pay. A big ovation before and after she spoke, Winston and I joining in all the whistling applause from our room-serviced exile.

Cybill Shepherd, the other ambassador from Hollywood, roused the crowd by recounting the story of calling her father to tell him she'd be here. "But wait—they'll think you're one of them," he declared with some concern. "Who cares?" she retorted breezily, to roars of approval all along the Mall. *Who cares?* became a battle cheer that day, perhaps because so many of us had had to confront the same anxiety from family and friends who fretted

---

[20] Major lesbian, gay, and bisexual rights march in Washington, D.C.

about our going public. *Who cares?* undercut the drama just the way Queer Nation[21] did: *We're here, we're queer, get used to it.*

Urvashi Vaid, former head of the National Gay and Lesbian Task Force, gave a stirring rebuke to our enemies. Eyes flashing fire, she berated the "Christian Supremacists" whose own agenda was a determination to replace democracy with theocracy. She put them on notice in no uncertain terms that we'd be there to block them every step of the way.

Torie Osborne, who'd taken over the helm at NGLTF,[22] was just as impassioned in her reaching out to embrace us as a united people. Halfway through she had a coughing jag, pounding the podium in frustration, gasping that she'd been working on this speech for four months. She didn't realize how human she sounded then, how much she embodied the halting declarations of so many of us, groping to find the words to set us free. Undaunted, fierce Amazon warrior that she is, Torie called for lemon, chomped on a wedge and finished to cheers.

Then she turned around and drew Larry Kramer to the podium. We heard later that she had done so under threat of arrest from the March organizers, still stubbornly asserting that AIDS wasn't what this March was for. But Larry gave his stump speech uninterrupted, a welcome gust of ferocity. Followed not long after by David Mixner, who spoke with a thrilling quaver about the outrage of the military ban, swearing a blood oath that there would be no going back.

There were too many lesbian comics, or too many not-ready-for-prime-time yet. Afterwards we would hear a lot of clucking about the woman who'd made an extended joke about doing it with Hillary. Didn't bother me, but then I was all for *nothing sacred* as a general rule for all such gatherings. When Congresswoman Nancy Pelosi stepped up to read Bill Clinton's letter of support— such small potatoes and scraps from the table—she was greeted by a din of catcalls from the crowd. Bravely she went on reading into the whirlwind, the words drowned out by a groundswell of withering disdain. Words by proxy were not enough.

It only made more telling the startling show of support we got from the NAACP. They told us they were with us and didn't duck the parallel with their own struggle. This was news, for they knew even better than we what an uphill fight they faced with the chorus of black preachers for whom homophobia was Gospel, who had spent a decade turning away from people of color with AIDS, to them the wages of sin. The writer Henry Louis Gates, Jr., would

---

[21] Lesbian, gay, and bisexual activist organization.

[22] The National Gay and Lesbian Task Force, an advocacy organization.

later make the telling point that Bayard Rustin, organizer and godfather to the '63 March on Washington, had demoted himself in the leadership ranks to avoid media scrutiny. All because he was gay. He stood off to the side, an invisible shadow, sacrificed to the greater good of freedom for his black people. Now at last the shame of one hero's silence could begin to be rectified by his *other* people, gays and lesbians.

If we didn't have Marian Anderson to trumpet us *Free at last,* we did have Michael Callen and Holly Near. Michael had been battling KS in his lungs for months now, and had actually been told by a medical professional that he'd be dead by March 1st. But somehow he'd made it to Washington, thin as a stick and on chemo himself. In a crystalline tenor he sang the song that had become a kind of anthem for a generation of lovers challenged by HIV. *Love is all we have for now,* goes the haunting refrain. *What we don't have is time.*

Holly Near—veteran activist, fighter for all women and the disappeared—gave forth with her own thrilling echo of "We Shall Overcome," harking back to the protest songs of the Weavers and Woody Guthrie. *We are a gentle loving people/And we are singing, singing for our lives.* You could hear waves of people in the crowd joining the chorus, swaying with solidarity, survivors of the age of silence giving voice to their pride and dignity at last.

Perhaps my favorite of the speakers was Sir Ian McKellen, who offered a speech of Shakespeare's—from a play called *Sir Thomas More,* the collaborative effort of several playwrights that was never in the end performed. But Shakespeare's three pages, in which More confronts the mob of the King's men, constitute the only known example of the Bard's handwritten composition. In the play the King's men have passed a law forbidding "strangers" from settling in England—a slur against immigrants and a call for racial purity. Sir Ian stepped forward and trumpeted More's outrage. So they were going to forbid strangers, were they? And where would they go when the tables of history turned, when *they* would find themselves the strangers? It was an oratorical tour de force, giving historical weight to the discrimination suffered by those who were different.

All in all, a remarkable pageant of diversity. And from where I sat, the flow of force was most tellingly toward the young. Theirs was the first generation to grow up with the promise of acceptance, at least from one another, and a measure of self-respect that constituted our hard-won legacy to them. None of them had to be alone anymore, except by closeted choice. As for passing the baton to a fleeter team, I felt a measure of satisfaction—a family feeling, really—that was scarcely quantifiable. But it wasn't one percent of me, and was encoded in my genes for thousands of years, no matter if it had no name. Or as Sappho put it, in love's terms:

You may forget but

Let me tell you
this: someone in
some future time
will think of us.

For my own part, the invalid on the sofa, the phrase that kept repeating itself as a kind of mantra was the title of Coleridge's poem, "This Lime-Tree Bower My Prison." The poet had been waiting for months for a visit from his friend Charles Lamb, beside himself with anticipation of showing Lamb the glories of the Lake District. Alas, on the morning of his friend's arrival, Coleridge "met with an accident, which disabled him from walking during the whole time of their stay."[23] So he mapped a route and sent the others out to experience the earthly sublime. And all the while they're gone Coleridge sits in his garden-bower, which he ruefully compares to a prison cell, imagining his hiking friends as they follow his trail from mountain crag to sunset over the sea. Then the epiphany:

A delight
Comes sudden on my heart, and I am glad
As I myself were there!

Unexpectedly, the loving contemplation of his friend's adventure restores to him the beauty of his garden. The sublime is in every leaf, the dappled light on the walnut-tree: *No plot so narrow, be but Nature there.* Nothing so exalted in Room 404 of the Park Hyatt, but I felt the same heartened connection to the gathering of the tribe along the Mall—as if I myself were there. AIDS was my prison. Not very leafy, but sufficient to free the sympathetic imagination. Even in the throes of the viral assault, losing my body electric organ by organ, I could still make contact—no yielding yet to the isolation of dying.

And as the evening deepened and the rally stage was dismantled, I wondered how many had watched it all from the closet—that black garden where nothing grows, death-in-life. Would it spur them to a quicker recognition of who they were, watching us march a million strong? What would they muster of courage to free themselves? Torie Osborne had said that the real reverberations of this freedom march would be felt at the grass roots,

---

[23] From Coleridge's prefatory note to the poem. See I. A. Richards, ed., *The Portable Coleridge* (New York: Penguin, 1977), page 76. [Author's note]

when the million of us had returned home, there to confront the intolerance of neighbors and friends and family. Shaking the politics of Main Street.

Yet we all felt a certain reluctance to leave this crossroads moment of celebration, a recognition of the letdown that would inevitably follow in its wake. Myself, I would have to face my rage and sorrow that AIDS had been consigned to the back of the bus. The feel of second-class citizenship, even here at the top of the mountain. A fight that still had to be fought among us, over and over, so the sick would not be quarantined by a kind of AIDS apartheid. Noise would have to be made to ensure our full inclusion in the dream of a unified people.

But one thing was sure. Nobody left that marble city without a fuller grasp of what it meant to be gay and lesbian *now*. All the stereotypes lay in ruins. We didn't need our absent friend Bill Clinton to prove we had grown in political power. The torch had passed to the young, in the process lighting a million dark corners. The lonely frightened kids, trapped in fundamentalist families and all the lies of "Morning in America,"[24] would have at least a glimpse of what had gone on here, the counter-friction and the dear love of comrades.

In her peroration to the crowd, Urvashi Vaid had expressed it best in her charge to the heterosexual majority:

> I challenge and invite you to open your eyes and embrace us without fear. The gay rights movement is not a party. It is not a lifestyle. It is not a hairstyle. It is not a fad or a fringe or a sickness. It is not about sin or salvation. The gay rights movement is an integral part of the American promise of freedom.

Of course, what we would take away with us from Washington was also something much more personal. For me it began in a small town in Massachusetts forty years ago—a sickness of the soul about being different. And nothing more important, not breath itself, than the need to keep it secret. The stillborn journey of my life took off at last, the moment I opened the closet door. To know how dark a place you come from into the light of self-acceptance—it is to enact a sort of survivorship that leaves a trail for those who come after. But you carry that kid with you the rest of your life— wounded as he is by hate and lies—a shadow companion who needs you to free him.

And whatever is left of the hurt is washed away the longer you march, arm in arm with a comrade, rallying to the mustering of the tribe. Until there's no dislocation anymore between the broken shadow of your past and the fully human presence you've become. You have incorporated his pain and

---

[24] Slogan from television advertisement for President Ronald Reagan's 1984 reelection campaign.

come to understand that it is the very fuel that makes the torch burn. No matter if they tell you you are only one percent, or that two thousand years of your people have just been revised and thrown to the winds. Nothing can dim the burning light. You are home free, citizen and elder, one in a million. And there is no America without you.

STUDY AND DISCUSSION QUESTIONS

1. Why is the poet Sappho so important to Monette?
2. Monette describes many of the marchers as "convinced that this watershed event would serve as a measure of their own freedom and self-regard." Explain.
3. Why do you think Monette spends so much time discussing Jefferson and Lincoln?
4. Why are "straight" friends and march supporters important to Monette?
5. Why might the Park Service want to underestimate the number of people marching? Why does it matter so much to the marchers?
6. Why is Monette so pleased by NAACP support for the march?
7. Monette calls publicly holding hands with his lover, Winston, "the truly revolutionary act." Why?
8. Why do you think Monette keeps using the word "queer," usually an insult, to describe gay men and lesbians?

SUGGESTIONS FOR WRITING

1. Why do march organizers want to keep the issue of AIDS in the background? Do you think they are right?
2. Explain the meaning of the last two paragraphs of "Mustering."
3. Monette clearly has money and connections. Describe what his life with AIDS might be like if he had neither.

FROM COMING OF AGE IN MISSISSIPPI

Anne Moody

Anne Moody (b. 1940) grew up in rural Mississippi and threw her-self into the civil rights movement while at Natchez and Tougaloo Col-leges, in Mississippi. She worked as an organizer for the Congress of Racial Equality and later as counsel for a New York City poverty pro-gram. Coming of Age in Mississippi (1969), excerpted below, re-counts the first twenty-four years of her life. Moody has also published Mr. Death (1975), a short story collection.

I had counted on graduating in the spring of 1963, but as it turned out, I couldn't because some of my credits still had to be cleared with Natchez Col-lege. A year before, this would have seemed like a terrible disaster, but now I hardly even felt disappointed. I had a good excuse to stay on campus for the summer and work with the Movement, and this was what I really wanted to do. I couldn't go home again anyway, and I couldn't go to New Orleans—I didn't have money enough for bus fare.

During my senior year at Tougaloo, my family hadn't sent me one penny. I had only the small amount of money I had earned at Maple Hill. I couldn't afford to eat at school or live in the dorms, so I had gotten permission to move off campus. I had to prove that I could finish school, even if I had to go hun-gry every day. I knew Raymond and Miss Pearl[1] were just waiting to see me drop out. But something happened to me as I got more and more involved in the Movement. It no longer seemed important to prove anything. I had found something outside myself that gave meaning to my life.

I had become very friendly with my social science professor, John Salter, who was in charge of NAACP activities on campus. All during the year, while the NAACP conducted a boycott of the downtown stores in Jackson, I had been one of Salter's most faithful canvassers and church speakers. During the last week of school, he told me that sit-in demonstrations were about to start in Jackson and that he wanted me to be the spokesman for a team that would sit-in at Woolworth's lunch counter. The two other demonstrators would be

---

[1] Moody's mother's husband and mother-in-law.

classmates of mine, Memphis and Pearlena. Pearlena was a dedicated NAACP worker, but Memphis had not been very involved in the Movement on campus. It seemed that the organization had had a rough time finding students who were in a position to go to jail. I had nothing to lose one way or the other. Around ten o'clock the morning of the demonstrations, NAACP headquarters alerted the news services. As a result, the police department was also informed, but neither the policemen nor the newsmen knew exactly where or when the demonstrations would start. They stationed themselves along Capitol Street and waited.

To divert attention from the sit-in at Woolworth's, the picketing started at J. C. Penney's a good fifteen minutes before. The pickets were allowed to walk up and down in front of the store three or four times before they were arrested. At exactly 11 A.M., Pearlena, Memphis, and I entered Woolworth's from the rear entrance. We separated as soon as we stepped into the store, and made small purchases from various counters. Pearlena had given Memphis her watch. He was to let us know when it was 11:14. At 11:14 we were to join him near the lunch counter and at exactly 11:15 we were to take seats at it.

Seconds before 11:15 we were occupying three seats at the previously segregated Woolworth's lunch counter. In the beginning the waitresses seemed to ignore us, as if they really didn't know what was going on. Our waitress walked past us a couple of times before she noticed we had started to write our own orders down and realized we wanted service. She asked us what we wanted. We began to read to her from our order slips. She told us that we would be served at the back counter, which was for Negroes.

"We would like to be served here," I said.

The waitress started to repeat what she had said, then stopped in the middle of the sentence. She turned the lights out behind the counter, and she and the other waitresses almost ran to the back of the store, deserting all their white customers. I guess they thought that violence would start immediately after the whites at the counter realized what was going on. There were five or six other people at the counter. A couple of them just got up and walked away. A girl sitting next to me finished her banana split before leaving. A middle-aged white woman who had not yet been served rose from her seat and came over to us. "I'd like to stay here with you," she said, "but my husband is waiting."

The newsmen came in just as she was leaving. They must have discovered what was going on shortly after some of the people began to leave the store. One of the newsmen ran behind the woman who spoke to us and asked her to identify herself. She refused to give her name, but said she was a native of Vicksburg and a former resident of California. When asked why she had said what she had said to us, she replied, "I am in sympathy with the Negro movement." By this time a crowd of cameramen and reporters had gathered around us taking pictures and asking questions, such as Where were we from? Why did we sit-in? What organization sponsored it? Were we students? From what school? How were we classified?

I told them that we were all students at Tougaloo College, that we were represented by no particular organization, and that we planned to stay there even after the store closed. "All we want is service," was my reply to one of them. After they had finished probing for about twenty minutes, they were almost ready to leave.

At noon, students from a nearby white high school started pouring in to Woolworth's. When they first saw us they were sort of surprised. They didn't know how to react. A few started to heckle and the newsmen became interested again. Then the white students started chanting all kinds of anti-Negro slogans. We were called a little bit of everything. The rest of the seats except the three we were occupying had been roped off to prevent others from sitting down. A couple of the boys took one end of the rope and made it into a hangman's noose. Several attempts were made to put it around our necks. The crowds grew as more students and adults came in for lunch.

We kept our eyes straight forward and did not look at the crowd except for occasional glances to see what was going on. All of a sudden I saw a face I remembered—the drunkard from the bus station sit-in. My eyes lingered on him just long enough for us to recognize each other. Today he was drunk too, so I don't think he remembered where he had seen me before. He took out a knife, opened it, put it in his pocket, and then began to pace the floor. At this point, I told Memphis and Pearlena what was going on. Memphis suggested that we pray. We bowed our heads, and all hell broke loose. A man rushed forward, threw Memphis from his seat, and slapped my face. Then another man who worked in the store threw me against an adjoining counter.

Down on my knees on the floor, I saw Memphis lying near the lunch counter with blood running out of the corners of his mouth. As he tried to protect his face, the man who'd thrown him down kept kicking him against the head. If he had worn hard-soled shoes instead of sneakers, the first kick probably would have killed Memphis. Finally a man dressed in plain clothes identified himself as a police officer and arrested Memphis and his attacker.

Pearlena had been thrown to the floor. She and I got back on our stools after Memphis was arrested. There were some white Tougaloo teachers in the crowd. They asked Pearlena and me if we wanted to leave. They said that things were getting too rough. We didn't know what to do. While we were trying to make up our minds, we were joined by Joan Trumpauer. Now there were three of us and we were integrated. The crowd began to chant, "Communists, Communists, Communists." Some old man in the crowd ordered the students to take us off the stools.

"Which one should I get first?" a big husky boy said.

"That white nigger," the old man said.

The boy lifted Joan from the counter by her waist and carried her out of the store. Simultaneously, I was snatched from my stool by two high school students. I was dragged about thirty feet toward the door by my hair when someone made them turn me loose. As I was getting up off the floor, I saw Joan coming back inside. We started back to the center of the counter to join Pearlena. Lois Chaffee, a white Tougaloo faculty member, was now sitting next to her. So Joan and I just climbed across the rope at the front end of the counter and sat down. There were now four of us, two whites and two Negroes, all women. The mob started smearing us with ketchup, mustard, sugar, pies, and everything on the counter. Soon Joan and I were joined by John Salter, but the moment he sat down he was hit on the jaw with what appeared to be brass knuckles. Blood gushed from his face and someone threw salt into the open wound. Ed King, Tougaloo's chaplain, rushed to him.

At the other end of the counter, Lois and Pearlena were joined by George Raymond, a CORE field worker and a student from Jackson State College. Then a Negro high school boy sat down next to me. The mob took spray paint from the counter and sprayed it on the new demonstrators. The high school student had on a white shirt; the word "nigger" was written on his back with red spray paint.

We sat there for three hours taking a beating when the manager decided to close the store because the mob had begun to go wild with stuff from other counters. He begged and begged everyone to leave. But even after fifteen minutes of begging, no one budged. They would not leave until we did. Then Dr. Beittel, the president of Tougaloo College, came running in. He said he had just heard what was happening.

About ninety policemen were standing outside the store; they had been watching the whole thing through the windows, but had not come in to stop the mob or do anything. President Beittel went outside and asked Captain Ray to come and escort us out. The captain refused, stating the manager had to invite him in before he could enter the premises, so Dr. Beittel himself brought us out. He had told the police that they had better protect us after we were outside the store. When we got outside, the policemen formed a single line that blocked the mob from us. However, they were allowed to throw at us everything they had collected. Within ten minutes, we were picked up by Reverend King in his station wagon and taken to the NAACP headquarters on Lynch Street.

After the sit-in, all I could think of was how sick Mississippi whites were. They believed so much in the segregated Southern way of life, they would kill to preserve it. I sat there in the NAACP office and thought of how many times they had killed when this way of life was threatened. I knew that the killing had just begun. "Many more will die before it is over with," I thought. Before the sit-in, I had always hated the whites in Mississippi. Now

I knew it was impossible for me to hate sickness. The whites had a disease, an incurable disease in its final stage. What were our chances against such a disease? I thought of the students, the young Negroes who had just begun to protest, as young interns. When these young interns got older, I thought, they would be the best doctors in the world for social problems.

Before we were taken back to campus, I wanted to get my hair washed. It was stiff with dried mustard, ketchup and sugar. I stopped in at a beauty shop across the street from the NAACP office. I didn't have on any shoes because I had lost them when I was dragged across the floor at Woolworth's. My stockings were sticking to my legs from the mustard that had dried on them. The hairdresser took one look at me and said, "My land, you were in the sit-in, huh?"

"Yes," I answered. "Do you have time to wash my hair and style it?"

"Right away," she said, and she meant right away. There were three other ladies already waiting, but they seemed glad to let me go ahead of them. The hairdresser was real nice. She even took my stockings off and washed my legs while my hair was drying.

There was a mass rally that night at the Pearl Street Church in Jackson, and the place was packed. People were standing two abreast in the aisles. Before the speakers began, all the sit-inners walked out on the stage and were introduced by Medgar Evers. People stood and applauded for what seemed like thirty minutes or more. Medgar told the audience that this was just the beginning of such demonstrations. He asked them to pledge themselves to unite in a massive offensive against segregation in Jackson, and throughout the state. The rally ended with "We Shall Overcome" and sent home hundreds of determined people. It seemed as though Mississippi Negroes were about to get together at last.

Before I demonstrated, I had written Mama. She wrote me back a letter, begging me not to take part in the sit-in. She even sent ten dollars for bus fare to New Orleans. I didn't have one penny, so I kept the money. Mama's letter made me mad. I had to live my life as I saw fit. I had made that decision when I left home. But it hurt to have my family prove to me how scared they were. It hurt me more than anything else—I knew the whites had already started the threats and intimidations. I was the first Negro from my hometown who had openly demonstrated, worked with the NAACP, or anything. When Negroes threatened to do anything in Centreville, they were either shot like Samuel O'Quinn or run out of town, like Reverend Dupree.

I didn't answer Mama's letter. Even if I had written one, she wouldn't have received it before she saw the news on TV or heard it on the radio. I waited to hear from her again. And I waited to hear in the news that someone in Centreville had been murdered. If so, I knew it would be a member of my family.

STUDY AND DISCUSSION QUESTIONS

1. Why are Moody and her companions so eager to integrate the lunch counter?

2. Why are the sit-ins so carefully orchestrated?

3. Moody writes: "Then the white students started chanting all kinds of anti-Negro slogans. We were called a little bit of everything." What is her tone here? What might it reflect?

4. Why is white resistance to integrating the lunch counter so great? Why is there particular hostility towards Joan Trumpauer?

5. When the sit-inners began to pray, "all hell broke loose." Why does prayer especially anger the white crowd?

6. Is the sit-in a success or a failure?

SUGGESTIONS FOR WRITING

1. What can you infer from this brief narrative about life for African Americans in the segregated South?

2. Read Moody's narrative alongside Martin Luther King, Jr.'s "Letter from Birmingham Jail." What correspondences do you see?

3. Moody's mother wrote to her, "begging" her not to participate in the sit-in. Write the reply Moody might have written.

LETTER FROM
BIRMINGHAM JAIL

Martin Luther King, Jr.

*Martin Luther King, Jr. was born in Atlanta in 1929, attended seg-
regated schools, and began Morehouse College at age fifteen. He received a PhD in theology at Boston University and took a job
preaching at a Montgomery, Alabama church. In 1955 he led a boycott of segregated buses in Montgomery and in 1957 became president of the Southern Christian Leadership Conference. King led
numerous voter registration drives and helped organize the 1963 civil
rights march on Washington. In 1968, while in Memphis, Tennessee
to speak in support of striking sanitation workers, he was assassinated.
Among his books are* Why We Can't Wait *(1964), where the following appeared, and* Trumpet of Conscience *(1968).*

April 16, 1963

My Dear Fellow Clergymen:[1]

While confined here in the Birmingham city jail, I came across your recent
statement calling my present activities "unwise and untimely." Seldom do I
pause to answer criticism of my work and ideas. If I sought to answer all the
criticisms that cross my desk, my secretaries would have little time for anything other than such correspondence in the course of the day, and I would
have no time for constructive work. But since I feel that you are men of genuine good will and that your criticisms are sincerely set forth, I want to try
to answer your statement in what I hope will be patient and reasonable terms.

I think I should indicate why I am here in Birmingham, since you have
been influenced by the view which argues against "outsiders coming in." I
have the honor of serving as president of the Southern Christian Leadership

---

[1] This response to a published statement by eight fellow clergymen from Alabama (Bishop C.C.J.
Carpenter, Bishop Joseph A. Durick, Rabbi Hilton L. Grafman, Bishop Paul Hardin, Bishop Holan
B. Harmon, the Reverend George M. Murray, the Reverend Edward V. Ramage and the Reverend
Early Stallings) was composed under somewhat constricting circumstances. Begun on the margins of the newspaper in which the statement appeared while I was in jail, the letter was continued on scraps of writing paper supplied by a friendly Negro trusty, and concluded on a pad my
attorneys were eventually permitted to leave me. Although the text remains in substance unaltered, I have indulged in the author's prerogative of polishing it for publication. [Author's note]

Conference, an organization operating in every southern state, with headquarters in Atlanta, Georgia. We have some eighty-five affiliated organizations across the South, and one of them is the Alabama Christian Movement for Human Rights. Frequently we share staff, educational and financial resources with our affiliates. Several months ago the affiliate here in Birmingham asked us to be on call to engage in a nonviolent direct-action program if such were deemed necessary. We readily consented, and when the hour came we lived up to our promise. So I, along with several members of my staff, am here because I was invited here. I am here because I have organizational ties here.

But more basically, I am in Birmingham because injustice is here. Just as the prophets of the eighth century B.C. left their villages and carried their "thus saith the Lord" far beyond the boundaries of their home towns, and just as the Apostle Paul left his village of Tarsus and carried the gospel of Jesus Christ to the far corners of the Greco-Roman world, so am I compelled to carry the gospel of freedom beyond my own home town. Like Paul, I must constantly respond to the Macedonian call for aid.[2]

Moreover, I am cognizant of the interrelatedness of all communities and states. I cannot sit idly by in Atlanta and not be concerned about what happens in Birmingham. Injustice anywhere is a threat to justice everywhere. We are caught in an inescapable network of mutuality, tied in a single garment of destiny. Whatever affects one directly, affects all indirectly. Never again can we afford to live with the narrow, provincial "outside agitator" idea. Anyone who lives inside the United States can never be considered an outsider anywhere within its bounds.

You deplore the demonstrations taking place in Birmingham. But your statement, I am sorry to say, fails to express a similar concern for the conditions that brought about the demonstrations. I am sure that none of you would want to rest content with the superficial kind of social analysis that deals merely with effects and does not grapple with underlying causes. It is unfortunate that demonstrations are taking place in Birmingham, but it is even more unfortunate that the city's white power structure left the Negro community with no alternative.

In any nonviolent campaign there are four basic steps: collection of the facts to determine whether injustices exist; negotiation; self-purification; and direct action. We have gone through all these steps in Birmingham. There can be no gainsaying the fact that racial injustice engulfs this community. Birmingham is probably the most thoroughly segregated city in the United States. Its ugly record of brutality is widely known. Negroes have experienced

---

[2] Refers to the Apostle Paul, who, according to the New Testament, journeyed to Macedonia and other parts of Greece as a missionary.

grossly unjust treatment in the courts. There have been more unsolved bomb-ings of Negro homes and churches in Birmingham than in any other city in the nation. These are the hard, brutal facts of the case. On the basis of these conditions, Negro leaders sought to negotiate with the city fathers. But the latter consistently refused to engage in good-faith negotiation.

Then, last September, came the opportunity to talk with leaders of Birmingham's economic community. In the course of the negotiations, cer-tain promises were made by the merchants—for example, to remove the stores' humiliating racial signs. On the basis of these promises, the Reverend Fred Shuttlesworth and the leaders of the Alabama Christian Movement for Human Rights agreed to a moratorium on all demonstrations. As the weeks and months went by, we realized that we were the victims of a broken promise. A few signs, briefly removed, returned; the others remained.

As in so many past experiences, our hopes had been blasted, and the shadow of deep disappointment settled upon us. We had no alternative except to prepare for direct action, whereby we would present our very bodies as a means of laying our case before the conscience of the local and the national community. Mindful of the difficulties involved, we decided to undertake a process of self-purification. We began a series of workshops on nonviolence, and we repeatedly asked ourselves: "Are you able to accept blows without re-taliating?" "Are you able to endure the ordeal of jail?" We decided to sched-ule our direct-action program for the Easter season, realizing that except for Christmas, this is the main shopping period of the year. Knowing that a strong economic-withdrawal program would be the by-product of direct ac-tion, we felt that this would be the best time to bring pressure to bear on the merchants for the needed change.

Then it occurred to us that Birmingham's mayoralty election was com-ing up in March, and we speedily decided to postpone action until after elec-tion day. When we discovered that the Commissioner of Public Safety, Eugene "Bull" Connor, had piled up enough votes to be in the run-off, we decided again to postpone action until the day after the run-off so that the demon-strations could not be used to cloud the issues. Like many others, we waited to see Mr. Connor defeated, and to this end we endured postponement after postponement. Having aided in this community need, we felt that our direct-action program could be delayed no longer.

You may well ask: "Why direct action? Why sit-ins, marches and so forth? Isn't negotiation a better path?" You are quite right in calling for ne-gotiation. Indeed, this is the very purpose of direct action. Nonviolent direct action seeks to create such a crisis and foster such a tension that a commu-nity which has constantly refused to negotiate is forced to confront the issue. It seeks so to dramatize the issue that it can no longer be ignored. My citing the creation of tension as part of the work of the nonviolent-resister may sound rather shocking. But I must confess that I am not afraid of the word "tension." I have earnestly opposed violent tension, but there is a type of constructive, nonviolent tension which is necessary for growth. Just as Socrates felt that it was necessary to create a tension in the mind so that individuals could rise from the bondage of myths and half-truths to the unfettered realm of creative analysis and objective appraisal, so must we see the need for nonviolent gadflies to create the kind of tension in society that will help men rise from the dark depths of prejudice and racism to the majestic heights of understanding and brotherhood.

The purpose of our direct-action program is to create a situation so crisis-packed that it will inevitably open the door to negotiation. I therefore concur with you in your call for negotiation. Too long has our beloved Southland been bogged down in a tragic effort to live in monologue rather than dialogue.

One of the basic points in your statement is that the action that I and my associates have taken in Birmingham is untimely. Some have asked: "Why didn't you give the new city administration time to act?" The only answer that I can give to this query is that the new Birmingham administration must be prodded about as much as the outgoing one, before it will act. We are sadly mistaken if we feel that the election of Albert Boutwell as mayor will bring the millennium to Birmingham. While Mr. Boutwell is a much more gentle person than Mr. Connor, they are both segregationists, dedicated to maintenance of the status quo. I have hope that Mr. Boutwell will be reasonable enough to see the futility of massive resistance to desegregation. But he will not see this without pressure from devotees of civil rights. My friends, I must say to you that we have not made a single gain in civil rights without determined legal and nonviolent pressure. Lamentably, it is an historical fact that privileged groups seldom give up their privileges voluntarily. Individuals may see the moral light and voluntarily give up their unjust posture; but, as Reinhold Neibuhr has reminded us, groups tend to be more immoral than individuals.

We know through painful experience that freedom is never voluntarily given by the oppressor; it must be demanded by the oppressed. Frankly, I have yet to engage in a direct-action campaign that was "well timed" in the view of those who have not suffered unduly from the disease of segregation. For years now I have heard the word "Wait!" It rings in the ear of every Negro with piercing familiarity. This "Wait" has almost always meant "Never." We must come to see, with one of our distinguished jurists, that "justice too long delayed is justice denied."

We have waited for more than 340 years for our constitutional and God-given rights. The nations of Asia and Africa are moving with jet-like speed toward gaining political independence, but we still creep at horse-and-buggy pace toward gaining a cup of coffee at a lunch counter. Perhaps it is easy for those who have never felt the stinging darts of segregation to say, "Wait." But when you have seen vicious mobs lynch your mothers and fathers at will and drown your sisters and brothers at whim; when you have seen hate-filled policemen curse, kick and even kill your black brothers and sisters; when you see the vast majority of your twenty million Negro brothers smothering in an airtight cage of poverty in the midst of an affluent society; when you suddenly find your tongue twisted and your speech stammering as you seek to explain to your six-year-old daughter why she can't go to the public amusement park that has just been advertised on television, and see tears welling up in her eyes when she is told that Funtown is closed to colored children, and see ominous clouds of inferiority beginning to form in her little mental sky, and see her beginning to distort her personality by developing an unconscious bitterness toward white people; when you have to concoct an answer for a five-year-old son who is asking: "Daddy, why do white people treat colored people so mean?"; when you take a cross-country drive and find it necessary to sleep night after night in the uncomfortable corners of your automobile because no motel will accept you; when you are humiliated day in and day out by nagging signs reading "white" and "colored"; when your first name becomes "nigger," your middle name becomes "boy" (however old you are) and your last name becomes "John," and your wife and mother are never given the respected title "Mrs."; when you are harried by day and haunted by night by the fact that you are a Negro, living constantly at tiptoe stance, never quite knowing what to expect next, and are plagued with inner fears and outer resentments; when you are forever fighting a degenerating sense of "nobodiness"—then you will understand why we find it difficult to wait. There comes a time when the cup of endurance runs over, and men are no longer willing to be plunged into the abyss of despair. I hope, sirs, you can understand our legitimate and unavoidable impatience.

You express a great deal of anxiety over our willingness to break laws. This is certainly a legitimate concern. Since we so diligently urge people to obey the Supreme Court's decision of 1954 outlawing segregation in the public schools, at first glance it may seem rather paradoxical for us consciously to break laws. One may well ask: "How can you advocate breaking some laws and obeying others?" The answer lies in the fact that there are two types of laws: just and unjust. I would be the first to advocate obeying just laws. One has not only a legal but a moral responsibility to obey just laws. Conversely, one has a moral responsibility to disobey unjust laws. I would agree with St. Augustine that "an unjust law is no law at all."

Now, what is the difference between the two? How does one determine whether a law is just or unjust? A just law is a man-made code that squares with the moral law or the law of God. An unjust law is a code that is out of harmony with the moral law. To put it in the terms of St. Thomas Aquinas: An unjust law is a human law that is not rooted in eternal law and natural law. Any law that uplifts human personality is just. Any law that degrades human personality is unjust. All segregation statutes are unjust because segregation distorts the soul and damages the personality. It gives the segregator a false sense of superiority and the segregated a false sense of inferiority. Segregation, to use the terminology of the Jewish philosopher Martin Buber, substitutes an "I—it" relationship for an "I—thou" relationship and ends up relegating persons to the status of things. Hence segregation is not only politically, economically and sociologically unsound, it is morally wrong and sinful. Paul Tillich has said that sin is separation. Is not segregation an existential expression of man's tragic separation, his awful estrangement, his terrible sinfulness? Thus it is that I can urge men to obey the 1954 decision of the Supreme Court, for it is morally right; and I can urge them to disobey segregation ordinances, for they are morally wrong.

Let us consider a more concrete example of just and unjust laws. An unjust law is a code that a numerical or power majority group compels a minority group to obey but does not make binding on itself. This is *difference* made legal. By the same token, a just law is a code that a majority compels a minority to follow and that it is willing to follow itself. This is *sameness* made legal.

Let me give another explanation. A law is unjust if it is inflicted on a minority that, as a result of being denied the right to vote, had no part in enacting or devising the law. Who can say that the legislature of Alabama which set up that state's segregation laws was democratically elected? Throughout Alabama all sorts of devious methods are used to prevent Negroes from becoming registered voters, and there are some counties in which, even though Negroes constitute a majority of the population, not a single Negro is registered. Can any law enacted under such circumstances be considered democratically structured?

Sometimes a law is just on its face and unjust in its application. For instance, I have been arrested on a charge of parading without a permit. Now, there is nothing wrong in having an ordinance which requires a permit for a parade. But such an ordinance becomes unjust when it is used to maintain segregation and to deny citizens the First-Amendment privilege of peaceful assembly and protest.

I hope you are able to see the distinction I am trying to point out. In no sense do I advocate evading or defying the law, as would the rabid segregationist. That would lead to anarchy. One who breaks an unjust law must do so openly, lovingly, and with a willingness to accept the penalty. I submit that an individual who breaks a law that conscience tells him is unjust, and who willingly accepts the penalty of imprisonment in order to arouse the conscience of the community over its injustice, is in reality expressing the highest respect for law.

Of course, there is nothing new about this kind of civil disobedience. It was evidenced sublimely in the refusal of Shadrach, Meshach and Abednego to obey the laws of Nebuchadnezzar, on the ground that a higher moral law was at stake. It was practiced superbly by the early Christians, who were willing to face hungry lions and the excruciating pain of chopping blocks rather than submit to certain unjust laws of the Roman Empire. To a degree, academic freedom is a reality today because Socrates practiced civil disobedience. In our own nation, the Boston Tea Party[3] represented a massive act of civil disobedience.

We should never forget that everything Adolf Hitler did in Germany was "legal" and everything the Hungarian freedom fighters did in Hungary was "illegal." It was "illegal" to aid and comfort a Jew in Hitler's Germany. Even so, I am sure that, had I lived in Germany at the time, I would have aided and comforted my Jewish brothers. If today I lived in a Communist country where certain principles dear to the Christian faith are suppressed, I would openly advocate disobeying that country's antireligious laws.

I must make two honest confessions to you, my Christian and Jewish brothers. First, I must confess that over the past few years I have been gravely disappointed with the white moderate. I have almost reached the regrettable conclusion that the Negro's great stumbling block in his stride toward freedom is not the White Citizen's Counciler[4] or the Ku Klux Klanner, but the white moderate, who is more devoted to "order" than to justice; who prefers a negative peace which is the absence of tension to a positive peace which is the presence of justice; who constantly says: "I agree with you in the goal you seek, but I cannot agree with your methods of direct action"; who paternalistically believes he can set the timetable for another man's freedom; who lives by a mythical concept of time and who constantly advises the Negro to wait for a "more convenient season." Shallow understanding from people of good will is more frustrating than absolute misunderstanding from people of ill will. Lukewarm acceptance is much more bewildering than outright rejection.

I had hoped that the white moderate would understand that law and order exist for the purpose of establishing justice and that when they fail in this purpose they become the dangerously structured dams that block the flow of social progress. I had hoped that the white moderate would understand that the present tension in the South is a necessary phase of the transition from an obnoxious negative peace, in which the Negro passively accepted his unjust plight, to a substantive and positive peace, in which all men will respect the

---

[3] 1773 act of rebellion against a British tax on tea by American colonists, who dressed as Indians, boarded a British ship in Boston Harbor, and threw its tea cargo overboard.

[4] The White Citizens Councils were organized to retaliate economically against blacks who fought segregation.

dignity and worth of human personality. Actually, we who engage in nonviolent direct action are not the creators of tension. We merely bring to the surface the hidden tension that is already alive. We bring it out in the open, where it can be seen and dealt with. Like a boil that can never be cured so long as it is covered up but must be opened with all its ugliness to the natural medicines of air and light, injustice must be exposed, with all the tension its exposure creates, to the light of human conscience and the air of national opinion before it can be cured.

In your statement you assert that our actions, even though peaceful, must be condemned because they precipitate violence. But is this a logical assertion? Isn't this like condemning a robbed man because his possession of money precipitated the evil act of robbery? Isn't this like condemning Socrates because his unswerving commitment to truth and his philosophical inquiries precipitated the act by the misguided populace in which they made him drink hemlock? Isn't this like condemning Jesus because his unique God-consciousness and never-ceasing devotion to God's will precipitated the evil act of crucifixion? We must come to see that, as the federal courts have consistently affirmed, it is wrong to urge an individual to cease his efforts to gain his basic constitutional rights because the quest may precipitate violence. Society must protect the robbed and punish the robber.

I had also hoped that the white moderate would reject the myth concerning time in relation to the struggle for freedom. I have just received a letter from a white brother in Texas. He writes: "All Christians know that the colored people will receive equal rights eventually, but it is possible that you are in too great a religious hurry. It has taken Christianity almost two thousand years to accomplish what it has. The teachings of Christ take time to come to earth." Such an attitude stems from a tragic misconception of time, from the strangely irrational notion that there is something in the very flow of time that will inevitably cure all ills. Actually, time itself is neutral; it can be used either destructively or constructively. More and more I feel that the people of ill will have used time much more effectively than have the people of good will. We will have to repent in this generation not merely for the hateful words and actions of the bad people but for the appalling silence of the good people. Human progress never rolls in on wheels of inevitability; it comes through the tireless efforts of men willing to be co-workers with God, and without this hard work, time itself becomes an ally of the forces of social stagnation. We must use time creatively, in the knowledge that the time is always ripe to do right. Now is the time to make real the promise of democracy and transform our pending national elegy into a creative psalm of brotherhood. Now is the time to lift our national policy from the quicksand of racial injustice to the solid rock of human dignity.

You speak of our activity in Birmingham as extreme. At first I was rather disappointed that fellow clergymen would see my nonviolent efforts as those of an extremist. I began thinking about the fact that I stand in the middle of two opposing forces in the Negro community. One is a force of complacency, made up in part of Negroes who, as a result of long years of oppression, are so drained of self-respect and a sense of "somebodiness" that they have adjusted to segregation; and in part of a few middleclass Negroes who, because of a degree of academic and economic security and because in some ways they profit by segregation, have become insensitive to the problems of the masses. The other force is one of bitterness and hatred, and it comes perilously close to advocating violence. It is expressed in the various black nationalist groups that are springing up across the nation, the largest and best-known being Elijah Muhammad's Muslim movement. Nourished by the Negro's frustration over the continued existence of racial discrimination, this movement is made up of people who have lost faith in America, who have absolutely repudiated Christianity, and who have concluded that the white man is an incorrigible "devil."

I have tried to stand between these two forces, saying that we need emulate neither the "do-nothingism" of the complacent nor the hatred and despair of the black nationalist. For there is the more excellent way of love and nonviolent protest. I am grateful to God that, through the influence of the Negro church, the way of nonviolence became an integral part of our struggle.

If this philosophy had not emerged, by now many streets of the South would, I am convinced, be flowing with blood. And I am further convinced that if our white brothers dismiss as "rabble-rousers" and "outside agitators" those of us who employ nonviolent direct action, and if they refuse to support our nonviolent efforts, millions of Negroes will, out of frustration and despair, seek solace and security in black-nationalist ideologies—a development that would inevitably lead to a frightening racial nightmare.

Oppressed people cannot remain oppressed forever. The yearning for freedom eventually manifests itself, and that is what has happened to the American Negro. Something within has reminded him of his birthright of freedom, and something without has reminded him that it can be gained. Consciously or unconsciously, he has been caught up by the *Zeitgeist*, and with his black brothers of Africa and his brown and yellow brothers of Asia, South America and the Caribbean, the United States Negro is moving with a sense of great urgency toward the promised land of racial justice. If one recognizes this vital urge that has engulfed the Negro community, one should readily understand why public demonstrations are taking place. The Negro has many pent-up resentments and latent frustrations, and he must release them. So let him march; let him make prayer pilgrimages to the city hall; let him go on freedom rides— and try to understand why he must do so. If his repressed emotions are not released in nonviolent ways, they will seek expression through violence; this is not a threat but a fact of history. So I have not said to my people: "Get rid of your discontent." Rather, I have tried to say that this normal and healthy discontent can be channeled into the creative outlet of nonviolent direct action. And now this approach is being termed extremist.

But though I was initially disappointed at being categorized as an extremist, as I continued to think about the matter I gradually gained a measure of satisfaction from the label. Was not Jesus an extremist for love: "Love your enemies, bless them that curse you, do good to them that hate you, and pray for them which despitefully use you, and persecute you." Was not Amos an extremist for justice: "Let justice roll down like waters and righteousness like an ever-flowing stream." Was not Paul an extremist for the Christian gospel: "I bear in my body the marks of the Lord Jesus." Was not Martin Luther an extremist: "Here I stand; I cannot do otherwise, so help me God." And John Bunyan: "I will stay in jail to the end of my days before I make a butchery of my conscience." And Abraham Lincoln: "This nation cannot survive half slave and half free." And Thomas Jefferson: "We hold these truths to be self-evident, that all men are created equal . . ." So the question is not whether we will be extremists, but what kind of extremists we will be. Will we be extremists for hate or for love? Will we be extremists for the preservation of injustice or for the extension of justice? In that dramatic scene on Calvary's hill three men were crucified. We must never forget that all three were crucified for the same crime—the crime of extremism. Two were extremists for immorality, and thus fell below their environment. The other, Jesus Christ, was an extremist for love, truth and goodness, and thereby rose above his environment. Perhaps the South, the nation and the world are in dire need of creative extremists.

I had hoped that the white moderate would see this need. Perhaps I was too optimistic; perhaps I expected too much. I suppose I should have realized that few members of the oppressor race can understand the deep groans and passionate yearnings of the oppressed race, and still fewer have the vision to see that injustice must be rooted out by strong, persistent and determined action. I am thankful, however, that some of our white brothers in the South have grasped the meaning of this social revolution and committed themselves to it. They are still all too few in quantity, but they are big in quality. Some—such as Ralph McGill, Lillian Smith, Harry Golden, James McBride Dabbs, Ann Braden and Sarah Patton Boyle—have written about our struggle in eloquent and prophetic terms. Others have marched with us down nameless streets of the South. They have languished in filthy, roach-infested jails, suffering the abuse and brutality of policemen who view them as "dirty niggerlovers." Unlike so many of their moderate brothers and sisters, they have recognized the urgency of the moment and sensed the need for powerful "action" antidotes to combat the disease of segregation.

Let me take note of my other major disappointment. I have been so greatly disappointed with the white church and its leadership. Of course, there are some notable exceptions. I am not unmindful of the fact that each of you has taken some significant stands on this issue. I commend you. Reverend Stallings, for your Christian stand on this past Sunday, in welcoming Negroes to your worship service on a nonsegregated basis. I commend the Catholic leaders of this state for integrating Spring Hill College several years ago.

But despite these notable exceptions, I must honestly reiterate that I have been disappointed with the church. I do not say this as one of those negative critics who can always find something wrong with the church. I say this as a minister of the gospel, who loves the church; who was nurtured in its bosom; who has been sustained by its spiritual blessings and who will remain true to it as long as the cord of life shall lengthen.

When I was suddenly catapulted into the leadership of the bus protest in Montgomery, Alabama, a few years ago, I felt we would be supported by the white church. I felt that the white ministers, priests and rabbis of the South would be among our strongest allies. Instead, some have been outright opponents, refusing to understand the freedom movement and misrepresenting its leaders; all too many others have been more cautious than courageous and have remained silent behind the anesthetizing security of stained-glass windows.

In spite of my shattered dreams, I came to Birmingham with the hope that the white religious leadership of this community would see the justice of our cause and, with deep moral concern, would serve as the channel through which our just grievances could reach the power structure. I had hoped that each of you would understand. But again I have been disappointed.

I have heard numerous southern religious leaders admonish their worshipers to comply with a desegregation decision because it is the law, but I have longed to hear white ministers declare: "Follow this decree because integration is morally right and because the Negro is your brother." In the midst of blatant injustices inflicted upon the Negro, I have watched white churchmen stand on the sideline and mouth pious irrelevancies and sanctimonious trivialities. In the midst of a mighty struggle to rid our nation of racial and economic injustice, I have heard many ministers say: "Those are social issues, with which the gospel has no real concern." And I have watched many churches commit themselves to a completely other-worldly religion which makes a strange, un-Biblical distinction between body and soul, between the sacred and the secular.

I have traveled the length and breadth of Alabama, Mississippi and all the other southern states. On sweltering summer days and crisp autumn mornings I have looked at the South's beautiful churches with their lofty spires pointing heavenward. I have beheld the impressive outlines of her massive religious-education buildings. Over and over I have found myself asking: "What kind of people worship here? Who is their God? Where were their voices when the lips of Governor Barnett[5] dripped with words of interposition and nullification? Where were they when Governor Wallace gave a clarion call for defiance and hatred? Where were their voices of support when bruised and weary Negro men and women decided to rise from the dark dungeons of complacency to the bright hills of creative protest?"

Yes, these questions are still in my mind. In deep disappointment I have wept over the laxity of the church. But be assured that my tears have been tears of love. There can be no deep disappointment where there is not deep love. Yes, I love the church. How could I do otherwise? I am in the rather unique position of being the son, the grandson and the great-grandson of preachers. Yes, I see the church as the body of Christ. But, oh! How we have blemished and scarred that body through social neglect and through fear of being nonconformists.

There was a time when the church was very powerful—in the time when the early Christians rejoiced at being deemed worthy to suffer for what they believed. In those days the church was not merely a thermometer that recorded the ideas and principles of popular opinion; it was a thermostat that transformed the mores of society. Whenever the early Christians entered a town, the people in power became disturbed and immediately sought to convict the Christians for being "disturbers of the peace" and "outside agitators." But the Christians pressed on, in the conviction that they were "a colony of heaven," called to obey God rather than man. Small in number, they were big in commitment. They were too God-intoxicated to be "astronomically intimidated." By their effort and example they brought an end to such ancient evils as infanticide and gladiatorial contests.

Things are different now. So often the contemporary church is a weak, ineffectual voice with an uncertain sound. So often it is an archdefender of the status quo. Far from being disturbed by the presence of the church, the power structure of the average community is consoled by the church's silent—and often even vocal—sanction of things as they are.

But the judgment of God is upon the church as never before. If today's church does not recapture the sacrificial spirit of the early church, it will lose its authenticity, forfeit the loyalty of millions, and be dismissed as an irrelevant social club with no meaning for the twentieth century. Every day I meet young people whose disappointment with the church has turned into outright disgust.

Perhaps I have once again been too optimistic. Is organized religion too inextricably bound to the status quo to save our nation and the world? Perhaps I must turn my faith to the inner spiritual church, the church within

---

[5] Ross Barnett, governor of Mississippi, who opposed a court order to desegregate the University of Mississippi.

the church, as the true *ekklesia*[6] and the hope of the world. But again I am thankful to God that some noble souls from the ranks of organized religion have broken loose from the paralyzing chains of conformity and joined us as active partners in the struggle for freedom. They have left their secure congregations and walked the streets of Albany, Georgia, with us. They have gone down the highways of the South on tortuous rides for freedom. Yes, they have gone to jail with us. Some have been dismissed from their churches, have lost the support of their bishops and fellow ministers. But they have acted in the faith that right defeated is stronger than evil triumphant. Their witness has been the spiritual salt that has preserved the true meaning of the gospel in these troubled times. They have carved a tunnel of hope through the dark mountains of disappointment.

I hope the church as a whole will meet the challenge of this decisive hour. But even if the church does not come to the aid of justice, I have no despair about the future. I have no fear about the outcome of our struggle in Birmingham, even if our motives are at present misunderstood. We will reach the goal of freedom in Birmingham and all over the nation, because the goal of America is freedom. Abused and scorned though we may be, our destiny is tied up with America's destiny. Before the pilgrims landed at Plymouth, we were here. Before the pen of Jefferson etched the majestic words of the Declaration of Independence across the pages of history, we were here. For more than two centuries our forebears labored in this country without wages; they made cotton king; they built the homes of their masters while suffering gross injustice and shameful humiliation—and yet out of a bottomless vitality they continued to thrive and develop. If the inexpressible cruelties of slavery could not stop us, the opposition we now face will surely fail. We will win our freedom because the sacred heritage of our nation and the eternal will of God are embodied in our echoing demands.

Before closing I feel impelled to mention one other point in your statement that has troubled me profoundly. You warmly commended the Birmingham police force for keeping "order" and "preventing violence." I doubt that you would have so warmly commended the police force if you had seen its dogs sinking their teeth into unarmed, nonviolent Negroes. I doubt that you would so quickly commend the policemen if you were to observe their ugly and inhumane treatment of Negroes here in the city jail; if you were to watch them push and curse old Negro women and young Negro girls; if you were to see them slap and kick old Negro men and young boys; if you were to observe them, as they did on two occasions, refuse to give us food because we wanted to sing our grace together. I cannot join you in your praise of the Birmingham police department.

---

[6] Church (Greek).

It is true that the police have exercised a degree of discipline in handling the demonstrators. In this sense they have conducted themselves rather "nonviolently" in public. But for what purpose? To preserve the evil system of segregation. Over the past few years I have consistently preached that nonviolence demands that the means we use must be as pure as the ends we seek. I have tried to make clear that it is wrong to use immoral means to attain moral ends. But now I must affirm that it is just as wrong, or perhaps even more so, to use moral means to preserve immoral ends. Perhaps Mr. Connor and his policemen have been rather nonviolent in public, as was Chief Pritchett[7] in Albany, Georgia, but they have used the moral means of nonviolence to maintain the immoral end of racial injustice. As T. S. Eliot has said: "The last temptation is the greatest treason: To do the right deed for the wrong reason."

I wish you had commended the Negro sit-inners and demonstrators of Birmingham for their sublime courage, their willingness to suffer and their amazing discipline in the midst of great provocation. One day the South will recognize its real heroes. They will be the James Merediths,[8] with the noble sense of purpose that enables them to face jeering and hostile mobs, and with the agonizing loneliness that characterizes the life of the pioneer. They will be old, oppressed, battered Negro women, symbolized in a seventy-two-year-old woman in Montgomery, Alabama, who rose up with a sense of dignity and with her people decided not to ride segregated buses, and who responded with ungrammatical profundity to one who inquired about her weariness: "My feets is tired, but my soul is at rest." They will be the young high school and college students, the young ministers of the gospel and a host of their elders, courageously and nonviolently sitting in at lunch counters and willingly going to jail for conscience' sake. One day the South will know that when these disinherited children of God sat down at lunch counters, they were in reality standing up for what is best in the American dream and for the most sacred values in our Judaeo-Christian heritage, thereby bringing our nation back to those great wells of democracy which were dug deep by the founding fathers in their formulation of the Constitution and the Declaration of Independence.

Never before have I written so long a letter. I'm afraid it is much too long to take your precious time. I can assure you that it would have been much shorter if I had been writing from a comfortable desk, but what else can one do when he is alone in a narrow jail cell, other than write long letters, think long thoughts and pray long prayers?

---

[7] Eugene "Bull" Connor, police commissioner of Birmingham, Alabama; Laurie Pritchett, police chief of Albany, Georgia.

[8] In 1962, in the face of white rioting and with the assistance of federal marshals, James Meredith became the first black student to register at the University of Mississippi.

If I have said anything in this letter that overstates the truth and indicates an unreasonable impatience, I beg you to forgive me. If I have said anything that understates the truth and indicates my having a patience that allows me to settle for anything less than brotherhood, I beg God to forgive me.

I hope this letter finds you strong in the faith. I also hope that circumstances will soon make it possible for me to meet each of you, not as an integrationist or a civil rights leader but as a fellow clergyman and a Christian brother. Let us all hope that the dark clouds of racial prejudice will soon pass away and the deep fog of misunderstanding will be lifted from our fear-drenched communities, and in some not too distant tomorrow the radiant stars of love and brotherhood will shine over our great nation with all their scintillating beauty.

Yours for the cause of Peace and Brotherhood,

Martin Luther King, Jr.

STUDY AND DISCUSSION QUESTIONS

1. Why is King disappointed in "the white moderate"?
2. What is the relation, in King's view, between negotiation and direct action?
3. How does King reply to the charge that he is an "extremist"?
4. What distinction does King make between just and unjust laws? What is the purpose of breaking an unjust law, and how should it be done?
5. What view of human nature is implicit in King's strategy?
6. King writes: "Injustice anywhere is a threat to justice everywhere." How might that be?
7. Why do you think King refers so frequently to famous historical and biblical figures?

SUGGESTIONS FOR WRITING

1. What's the best reply to a five-year-old son who asks, "Daddy, why do white people treat colored people so mean?"
2. King writes that "it is an historical fact that privileged groups seldom give up their privileges voluntarily." In light of this assertion, outline a plan for addressing a contemporary social problem rooted in privilege.
3. King writes that "the means we use must be as pure as the ends we seek." Do you agree?

ON RESISTANCE

Noam Chomsky

Born in Philadelphia in 1928, Noam Chomsky studied at the University of Pennsylvania and then joined the faculty of the Massachusetts Institute of Technology, where he remains today. His theoretical work in linguistics in the 1950s and 1960s revolutionized the field and his social criticism, particularly of United States foreign policy, made him an important figure in the movement against the Vietnam War. Among his dozens of books are Syntactic Structures (1957), Aspects of the Theory of Syntax (1965), *and, with Edward Herman,* Manufacturing Consent (1988). *The following essay is from* American Power and the New Mandarins (1969).

Several weeks after the demonstrations in Washington,[1] I am still trying to sort out my impressions of a week whose quality is difficult to capture or express. Perhaps some personal reflections may be useful to others who share my instinctive distaste for activism, but who find themselves edging towards an unwanted but almost inevitable crisis.

For many of the participants, the Washington demonstrations symbolized the transition "from dissent to resistance." I will return to this slogan and its meaning, but I want to make clear at the outset that I do feel it to be not only accurate with respect to the mood of the demonstrations but, properly interpreted, appropriate to the present state of protest against the war. There is an irresistible dynamics to such protest. One may begin by writing articles and giving speeches about the war, by helping in many ways to create an atmosphere of concern and outrage. A courageous few will turn to direct action, refusing to take their place alongside the "good Germans" we

---

[1] This article first appeared in the *New York Review of Books,* December 7, 1967. It is reprinted with a few revisions. The demonstrations referred to took place at the Justice Department and the Pentagon, on the weekend of October 19–21, 1967. The draft card turn-in at the Justice Department was one of the events that led to the sentencing of Dr. Benjamin Spock, Rev. William Sloane Coffin, Mitchell Goodman, and Michael Ferber to two-year prison sentences for "conspiracy." For details, see Noam Chomsky, Paul Lauter, and Florence Howe, "Reflections on a Political Trial," *New York Review of Books,* August 22, 1968, pp. 23–30. The Pentagon demonstration, which by some estimates involved several hundred thousand people, was a remarkable, unforgettable manifestation of opposition to the war. The spirit and character of the demonstrations are captured, with marvelous accuracy and perception, in Norman Mailer's *The Armies of the Night* (New York, New American Library, 1968). [Author's note]

have all learned to despise. Some will be forced to this decision when they are called up for military service. The dissenting senators, writers, and professors will watch as young men refuse to serve in the armed forces, in a war that they detest. What then? Can those who write and speak against the war take refuge in the fact that they have not urged or encouraged draft resistance, but have merely helped to develop a climate of opinion in which any decent person will want to refuse to take part in a miserable war? It is a very thin line. Nor is it very easy to watch from a position of safety while others are forced to take a grim and painful step. The fact is that most of the one thousand draft cards and other documents turned in to the Justice Department on October 20 came from men who can escape military service but who insisted on sharing the fate of those who are less privileged. In such ways the circle of resistance widens. Quite apart from this, no one can fail to see that to the extent that he restricts his protest, to the extent that he rejects actions that are open to him, he accepts complicity in what the government does. Some will act on this realization, posing sharply a moral issue that no person of conscience can evade.

On Monday, October 16, on the Boston Common I listened as Howard Zinn[2] explained why he felt ashamed to be an American. I watched as several hundred young men, some of them my students, made a terrible decision which no young person should have to face: to sever their connection with the Selective Service System. The week ended, the following Monday, with a quiet discussion in Cambridge in which I heard estimates, by an academic consultant to the Department of Defense, of the nuclear megatonnage that would be necessary to "take out" North Vietnam ("Some will find this shocking, but . . ."; "No civilian in the government is suggesting this, to my knowledge . . ."; "Let's not use emotional words like 'destruction'"; etc.), and listened to a leading expert on Soviet affairs who explained how the men in the Kremlin are watching very carefully to determine whether wars of national liberation can succeed—if so, they will support them all over the world. (Try pointing out to such an expert that on these assumptions, if the men in the Kremlin are rational, they will surely support dozens of such wars right now, since at a small cost they can confound the American military and tear our society to shreds—you will be told that you don't understand the Russian soul.)

The weekend of the peace demonstrations in Washington left impressions that are vivid and intense, but unclear to me in their implications. The dominant memory is of the scene itself, of tens of thousands of young people surrounding what they believe to be—I must add that I agree—the most hideous institution on this earth and demanding that it stop imposing misery

---

[2] Historian and political activist.

and destruction. Tens of thousands of *young* people. This I find hard to comprehend. It is pitiful but true that by an overwhelming margin it is the young who are crying out in horror at what we all see happening, the young who are being beaten when they stand their ground, and the young who have to decide whether to accept jail or exile, or to fight in a hideous war. They have to face this decision alone, or almost alone. We should ask ourselves why this is so.

Why, for example, does Senator Mansfield[3] feel "ashamed for the image they have portrayed of this country," and not feel ashamed for the image of this country portrayed by the institution these young people were confronting, an institution directed by a sane and mild and eminently reasonable man who can testify calmly before Congress that the amount of ordnance expended in Vietnam has surpassed the total expended in Germany and Italy in World War II? Why is it that Senator Mansfield can speak in ringing phrases about those who are not living up to our commitment to "a government of laws"—referring to a small group of demonstrators, not to the ninety-odd responsible men on the Senate floor who are watching, with full knowledge, as the state they serve clearly, flagrantly violates the explicit provisions of the United Nations Charter, the supreme law of the land? He knows quite well that prior to our invasion of Vietnam there was no armed attack against any state. It was Senator Mansfield, after all, who informed us that "when the sharp increase in the American military effort began in early 1965, it was estimated that only about 400 North Vietnamese soldiers were among the enemy forces in the South which totaled 140,000 at that time"; and it is the Mansfield Report from which we learn that at that time there were 34,000 American soldiers already in South Vietnam, in violation of our "solemn commitment" at Geneva in 1954.[4]

The point should be pursued. After the first International Days of Protest in October 1965, Senator Mansfield criticized the "sense of utter irresponsibility" shown by the demonstrators. He had nothing to say then, nor has he since, about the "sense of utter irresponsibility" shown by Senator Mansfield and others who stand by quietly and vote appropriations as the cities and villages of North Vietnam are demolished, as millions of refugees in the South are driven from their homes by American bombardment. He has nothing to say about the moral standards or the respect for law of those who have permitted this tragedy.

---

[3] Mike Mansfield, Senate majority leader.

[4] The Geneva Accords, which ended the war between the French colonial authorities and the Vietnamese independence movement, temporarily dividing Vietnam into northern and southern zones pending elections for a unified Vietnam; the elections, scheduled for 1956, were blocked by the United States and its allies in the southern zone.

I speak of Senator Mansfield precisely because he is not a breast-beating superpatriot who wants America to rule the world, but is rather an American intellectual in the best sense, a scholarly and reasonable man—the kind of man who is the terror of our age. Perhaps this is merely a personal reaction, but when I look at what is happening to our country, what I find most terrifying is not Curtis LeMay,[5] with his cheerful suggestion that we bomb our "enemies" back into the Stone Age, but rather the calm disquisitions of the political scientists on just how much force will be necessary to achieve our ends, or just what form of government will be acceptable to us in Vietnam. What I find terrifying is the detachment and equanimity with which we view and discuss an unbearable tragedy. We all know that if Russia or China were guilty of what we have done in Vietnam, we would be exploding with moral indignation at these monstrous crimes.

There was, I think, a serious miscalculation in the planning of the Washington demonstrations. It was expected that the march to the Pentagon would be followed by a number of speeches, and that those who were committed to civil disobedience would then separate themselves from the crowd and go to the Pentagon, a few hundred yards away across an open field. I had decided not to take part in civil disobedience, and I do not know in detail what had been planned. As everyone must realize, it is very hard to distinguish rationalization from rationality in such matters. I felt, however, that the first large-scale acts of civil disobedience should be more specifically defined, more clearly in support of those who are refusing to serve in Vietnam, on whom the real burden of dissent must inevitably fall. While appreciating the point of view of those who wished to express their hatred of the war in a more explicit way, I was not convinced that civil disobedience at the Pentagon would be either meaningful or effective.

In any event, what actually happened was rather different from what anyone had anticipated. A few thousand people gathered for the speeches, but the mass of marchers went straight on to the Pentagon, some because they were committed to direct action, many because they were simply swept along. From the speakers' platform where I stood it was difficult to determine just what was taking place at the Pentagon. All we could see was the surging of the crowd. From secondhand reports, I understand that the marchers passed through and around the front line of troops and took up a position, which they maintained, on the steps of the Pentagon. It soon became obvious that it was wrong for the few organizers of the march and the mostly middle-aged group that had gathered near them to remain at the speakers' platform while the demonstrators themselves, most of them quite young, were at the Pentagon. (I recall seeing

---

[5] Air Force general.

near the platform Robert Lowell, Dwight Macdonald, Monsignor Rice, Sidney Lens, Benjamin Spock and his wife, Dagmar Wilson, Donald Kalish.) Dave Dellinger suggested that we try to approach the Pentagon. We found a place not yet blocked by the demonstrators, and walked up to the line of troops standing a few feet from the building. Dellinger suggested that those of us who had not yet spoken at the rally talk directly to the soldiers through a small portable sound system. From this point on, my impressions are rather fragmentary. Monsignor Rice spoke, and I followed. As I was speaking, the line of soldiers advanced, moving past me—a rather odd experience. I don't recall just what I was saying. The gist was, I suppose, that we were there because we didn't want the soldiers to kill and be killed, but I do remember feeling that the way I was putting it seemed silly and irrelevant.

The advancing line of soldiers had partially scattered the small group that had come with Dellinger. Those of us who had been left behind the line of soldiers regrouped, and Dr. Spock began to speak. Almost at once, another line of soldiers emerged from somewhere, this time in a tightly massed formation, rifles in hand, and moved slowly forward. We sat down. As I mentioned earlier, I had no intention of taking part in any act of civil disobedience, until that moment. But when that grotesque organism began slowly advancing— more grotesque because its cells were recognizable human beings—it became obvious that one could not permit that thing to dictate what one was going to do. I was arrested at that point by a federal marshal, presumably for obstructing the soldiers (the technical term for this behavior is "disorderly conduct"). I should add that the soldiers, so far as I could see (which was not very far), seemed rather unhappy about the whole matter, and were being about as gentle as one can be when ordered (I presume this was the order) to kick and club passive, quiet people who refuse to move. The federal marshals, predictably, were very different. They reminded me of the police officers I had seen in a Jackson, Mississippi, jail several summers ago, who had laughed when an old man showed us a bloody homemade bandage on his leg and tried to describe to us how he had been beaten by the police. In Washington, the ones who got the worst of it at the hands of the marshals were the young boys and girls, particularly boys with long hair. Nothing seemed to bring out the marshals' sadism more than the sight of a boy with long hair. Yet, although I witnessed some acts of violence by the marshals, their behavior largely seemed to range from indifference to petty nastiness. For example, we were kept in a police van for an hour or two with the doors closed and only a few air holes for ventilation— one can't be too careful with such ferocious criminal types.

In the prison dormitory and after my release I heard many stories, which I feel sure are authentic, of the courage of the young people, many of whom were quite frightened by the terrorism that began late at night after the TV cameramen and most of the press had left. They sat quietly hour after hour through the cold night; many were kicked and beaten and dragged across police lines (more "disorderly conduct"). I also heard stories, distressing ones, of provocation of the troops by the demonstrators—usually, it seems, those who were not in the front rows. Surely this was indefensible. Soldiers are unwitting instruments of terror; one does not blame or attack the club that is used to bludgeon someone to death. They are also human beings, with sensibilities to which one can perhaps appeal. There is in fact strong evidence that one soldier, perhaps three or four, refused to obey orders and was placed under arrest. The soldiers, after all, are in much the same position as the draft resisters. If they obey orders, they become brutalized by what they do; if they do not, the personal consequences are severe. It is a situation that deserves compassion, not abuse. But we should retain a sense of proportion in the matter. Everything that I saw or heard indicates that the demonstrators played only a small role in initiating the considerable violence that occurred.

The argument that resistance to the war should remain strictly nonviolent seems to me overwhelming. As a tactic, violence is absurd. No one can compete with the government in this arena, and the resort to violence, which will surely fail, will simply frighten and alienate some who can be reached, and will further encourage the ideologists and administrators of forceful repression. What is more, one hopes that participants in nonviolent resistance will themselves become human beings of a more admirable sort. No one can fail to be impressed by the personal qualities of those who have grown to maturity in the civil rights movement. Whatever else it may have accomplished, the civil rights movement has made an inestimable contribution to American society in transforming the lives and characters of those who took part in it. Perhaps a program of principled, nonviolent resistance can do the same for many others, in the particular circumstances that we face today. It is not impossible that this may save the country from a terrible future, from yet another generation of men who think it clever to discuss the bombing of North Vietnam as a question of tactics and cost-effectiveness, or who support our attempt to conquer South Vietnam, with the human cost that they well know, blandly asserting that "our primary motivation is self-interest—the self-interest of our own country in this shrinking world" (Citizens Committee for Peace with Freedom, *New York Times*, October 26, 1967).

Returning to the demonstrations, I must admit that I was relieved to find people whom I had respected for years in the prison dormitory—Norman Mailer, Jim Peck, Dave Dellinger,[6] and a number of others. I think it was reassuring to many of the kids who were there to be able to feel that they were not

---

[6] Norman Mailer, American novelist; Jim Peck, pacifist and civil rights activist; Dave Dellinger, antiwar activist.

totally disconnected from a world that they knew and from people whom they admired. It was moving to see that defenseless young people who had a great deal to lose were willing to be jailed for what they believed—young instructors from state universities, college kids who have a very bright future if they are willing to toe the line, many others whom I could not identify.

What comes next? Obviously, that is the question on everyone's mind. The slogan "From Dissent to Resistance" makes sense, I think, but I hope it is not taken to imply that dissent should cease. Dissent and resistance are not alternatives but activities that should reinforce each other. There is no reason why those who take part in tax refusal, draft resistance, and other forms of resistance should not also speak to church groups or town forums, or become involved in electoral politics to support peace candidates or referenda on the war. In my experience, it has often been those committed to resistance who have been most deeply involved in such attempts at persuasion. Putting aside the matter of resistance for a moment, I think it should be emphasized that the days of "patiently explain" are far from over. As the coffins come home and the taxes go up, many people who were previously willing to accept government propaganda will become increasingly concerned to try to think for themselves. The reasons for their change are unfortunate; the opportunities for educational activity are nevertheless very good.

Furthermore, the recent shift in the government's propaganda line offers important opportunities for critical analysis of the war. There is a note of shrill desperation in the recent defense of the American war in Vietnam. We hear less about "bringing freedom and democracy" to the South Vietnamese and more about the "national interest." Secretary Rusk[7] broods about the dangers posed to us by a billion Chinese; the Vice-President tells us that we are fighting "militant Asian Communism" with "its headquarters in Peking" and adds that a Vietcong victory would directly threaten the United States; Eugene Rostow argues that "it is no good building model cities if they are to be bombed in twenty years time," and so on (all of this "a frivolous insult to the United States Navy," as Walter Lippmann rightly commented).

This shift in propaganda makes it much easier for critical analysis to attack the problem of Vietnam at its core, which is in Washington and Boston, not in Saigon and Hanoi. There is something ludicrous, after all, in the close attention that opponents of the war give to the political and social problems of Vietnam. Those who were opposed to the Japanese conquest of Manchuria a generation ago did not place emphasis on the political and social and economic problems of Manchuria, but on those of Japan. They did not engage in farcical debate over the exact degree of support for the puppet emperor, but

---

[7] Secretary of State Dean Rusk.

looked to the sources of Japanese imperialism. Now opponents of the war can much more easily shift attention to the source of the aggression, to our own country, its ideology and institutions. We can ask whose "interest" is served by 100,000 casualties and 100 billion dollars expended in the attempt to subjugate a small country halfway around the world. We can point to the absurdity of the idea that we are "containing China" by destroying popular and independent forces on its borders, and to the cynicism of the claim that we are in Vietnam because "to Americans, peace and freedom are inseparable" and because "suppression of freedom" must not "go unchallenged" (the Citizens Committee again). We can ask why it is that those who make this claim do not suggest that an American expeditionary force be sent to Taiwan, to Rhodesia, to Greece, or to Mississippi, but only to Vietnam, where, they want us to believe, the master aggressor Mao Tse-tung is following a Hitlerian course in his cunning way, committing aggression without troops and announcing world conquest by insisting, through the medium of Lin Piao, that indigenous wars of national liberation can expect little from China beyond applause. We can ask why Secretary McNamara reads such statements as a new *Mein Kampf*[8]—or why those who admit that "a Vietnamese communist regime would probably be . . . anti-Chinese" (Ithiel de Sola Pool, *Asian Survey,* August 1967) nevertheless sign statements which pretend that in Vietnam we are facing the expansionist aggressors from Peking. We can ask what factors in American ideology make it so easy for intelligent and well-informed men to say that we "insist upon nothing for South Vietnam except that it be free to chart its own future" (Citizens Committee) although they know quite well that the regime we imposed excluded all those who took part in the struggle against French colonialism, "and properly so" (Secretary Rusk, 1963); that we have since been attempting to suppress a "civil insurrection" (General Stillwell) led by the only "truly mass-based political party in South Vietnam" (Douglas Pike); that we supervised the destruction of the Buddhist opposition; that we offered the peasants a "free choice" between the Saigon government and the National Liberation Front[9] by herding them into strategic hamlets from which NLF cadres and sympathizers were eliminated by the police (Roger Hilsman); and so on. The story is familiar. And we can emphasize what must be obvious to a person with a grain of political intelligence: that the present world problem is not "containing China" but containing the United States.

---

[8] Robert McNamara, Secretary of Defense; *Mein Kampf,* Adolf Hitler's autobiography and statement of political beliefs.

[9] Saigon, the corrupt and politically unstable capital of South Vietnam; the National Liberation Front (NLF), also known as the Viet Cong, a South Vietnamese organization that, together with its North Vietnamese allies, sought to overthrow the government of South Vietnam.

More important, we can ask the really fundamental question. Suppose that it were in the American "national interest" to pound into rubble a small nation that refuses to submit to our will. Would it then be legitimate and proper for us to act "in this national interest"? The Rusks and the Humphreys[10] and the Citizens Committee say yes. Nothing could show more clearly how we are taking the road of the fascist aggressors of a generation ago.

We are, of course, in a domestic political environment very different from that of the citizens of Germany or Japan. Here, it takes no heroism to protest. We have many avenues open to us to drive home the lesson that there is not one law for the United States and one for the rest of mankind, that no one has appointed us judge and executioner for Vietnam or anywhere else. Many avenues of political education, on and off the campus, have been explored in the past two years. There can be no question that this effort should continue and grow to whatever limit the degree of commitment permits.

Some seem to feel that resistance will "blacken" the peace movement and make it difficult to reach potential sympathizers through more familiar channels. I don't agree with this objection, but I feel that it should not be lightly disregarded. Resisters who hope to save the people of Vietnam from destruction must select the issues they confront and the means they employ in such a way as to attract as much popular support as possible for their efforts. There is no lack of clear issues and honorable means, surely, hence no reason why one should be impelled to ugly actions on ambiguous issues. In particular, it seems to me that draft resistance, properly conducted (as it has been so far), is not only a highly principled and courageous act, but one that might receive broad support and become politically effective. It might, furthermore, succeed in raising the issues of passive complicity in the war which are now much too easily evaded. Those who face these issues may even go on to free themselves from the mind-destroying ideological pressures of American life, and to ask some serious questions about America's role in the world, and the sources, in American society, for this criminal behavior.

Moreover, I feel that this objection to resistance is not properly formulated. The "peace movement" exists only in the fantasies of the paranoid right. Those who find some of the means employed or ends pursued objectionable can oppose the war in other ways. They will not be read out of a movement that does not exist; they have only themselves to blame if they do not make use of the other forms of protest that are available.

I have left to the end the most important question, the one about which I have least to say. This is the question of the forms resistance should take. We all take part in the war to a greater or lesser extent, if only by paying taxes and

---

[10] Hubert Humphrey, vice president under Lyndon Johnson.

permitting domestic society to function smoothly. A person has to choose for himself the point at which he will simply refuse to take part any longer. Reaching that point, he will be drawn into resistance. I believe that the reasons for resistance I have already mentioned are cogent ones: they have an irreducible moral element that admits of little discussion. The issue is posed in its starkest form for the boy who faces induction, and in a form that is somewhat more complex for the boy who must decide whether to participate in a system of selective service that may pass the burden from him to others less fortunate and less privileged. It is difficult for me to see how anyone can refuse to engage himself, in some way, in the plight of these young men. There are many ways to do so: legal aid and financial support; participation in support demonstrations; draft counseling, organization of draft-resistance unions or community-based resistance organizations; assisting those who wish to escape the country; the steps proposed by the clergymen who recently announced that they are ready to share the fate of those who will be sent to prison. About this aspect of the program of resistance I have nothing to say that will not be obvious to anyone who is willing to think the matter through.

Considered as a political tactic, resistance requires careful thought, and I do not pretend to have very clear ideas about it. Much depends on how events unfold in the coming months. Westmoreland's[11] war of attrition may simply continue with no foreseeable end, but the domestic political situation makes this unlikely. If the Republicans do not decide to throw the election again, they could have a winning strategy: they can claim that they will end the war, and remain vague about the means. Under such circumstances, it is unlikely that Johnson will permit the present military stalemate to persist. There are, then, several options. The first is American withdrawal, in whatever terms it would be couched. It might be disguised as a retreat to "enclaves," from which the troops could then be removed. It might be arranged by an international conference, or by permitting a government in Saigon that would seek peace among contending South Vietnamese and then ask us to leave. This policy might be politically feasible; the same public relations firm that invented terms like "revolutionary development" can depict withdrawal as victory. Whether there is anyone in the executive branch with the courage or imagination to urge this course, I do not know. A number of senators are proposing, in essence, that this is the course we should pursue, as are such critics of the war as Walter Lippmann and Hans Morgenthau, if I understand them correctly. A detailed and quite sensible plan for arranging withdrawal along with new, more meaningful elections in the South is outlined by Philippe Devillers in *Le Monde hebdomadaire* of October 26, 1967. Variants

---

[11] General William Westmoreland, commander of United States armed forces in Vietnam.

can easily be imagined. What is central is the decision to accept the principle of Geneva that the problems of Vietnam be settled by the Vietnamese.

A second possibility would be annihilation. No one doubts that we have the technological capacity for this, and only the sentimental doubt that we have the moral capacity as well. Bernard Fall predicted this outcome in an interview shortly before his death. "The Americans can destroy," he said, "but they cannot pacify. They may win the war, but it will be the victory of the graveyard. Vietnam will be destroyed."

A third option would be an invasion of North Vietnam. This would saddle us with two unwinnable guerrilla wars instead of one, but if the timing is right, it might be used as a device to rally the citizenry around the flag.

A fourth possibility is an attack on China. We could then abandon Vietnam and turn to a winnable war directed against Chinese industrial capacity. Such a move should win the election. No doubt this prospect also appeals to that insane rationality called "strategic thinking." If we intend to keep armies of occupation or even strong military bases on the Asian mainland, we would do well to make sure that the Chinese do not have the means to threaten them. Of course, there is the danger of a nuclear holocaust, but it is difficult to see why this should trouble those whom John McDermott calls the "crisis managers," the same men who were willing, in 1962, to accept a high probability of nuclear war to establish the principle that we, and we alone, have the right to keep missiles on the borders of a potential enemy.

There are many who regard "negotiations" as a realistic alternative, but I do not understand the logic or even the content of this proposal. If we stop bombing North Vietnam we might well enter into negotiations with Hanoi, but there would then be very little to discuss. As to South Vietnam, the only negotiable issue is the withdrawal of foreign troops; other matters can only be settled among whatever Vietnamese groups have survived the American onslaught. The call for "negotiations" seems to me not only empty, but actually a trap for those who oppose the war. If we do not agree to withdraw our troops, the negotiations will be deadlocked, the fighting will continue, American troops will be fired on and killed, the military will have a persuasive argument to escalate, to save American lives. In short, the Symington[12] solution: we offer them peace on our terms, and if they refuse—the victory of the graveyard.

Of the realistic options, only withdrawal (however disguised) seems to me at all tolerable, and resistance, as a tactic of protest, must be designed so as to increase the likelihood that this option will be selected. Furthermore, the time in which to take such action may be very short. The logic of

---

[12] Senator Stuart Symington of Missouri.

resorting to resistance as a tactic for ending the war is fairly clear. There is no basis for supposing that those who will make the major policy decisions are open to reason on the fundamental issues, in particular the issue of whether we, alone among the nations of the world, have the authority and the competence to determine the social and political institutions of Vietnam. What is more, there is little likelihood that the electoral process will bear on the major decisions. As I have pointed out, the issue may be settled before the next election. Even if it is not, it is hardly likely that a serious choice will be offered at the polls. And if by a miracle such a choice is offered, how seriously can we take the campaign promises of a "peace candidate" after the experience of 1964? Given the enormous dangers of escalation and its hateful character, it makes sense, in such a situation, to search for ways to raise the domestic cost of American aggression, to raise it to a point where it cannot be overlooked by those who have to calculate such costs. One must then consider in what ways it is possible to pose a serious threat. Many possibilities come to mind: a general strike, university strikes, attempts to hamper war production and supply, and so on.

Personally, I feel that disruptive acts of this sort would be justified were they likely to be effective in averting an imminent tragedy. I am skeptical, however, about their possible effectiveness. At the moment, I cannot imagine a broad base for such action, in the white community at least, outside the universities. Forcible repression would not, therefore, prove very difficult. My guess is that such actions would, furthermore, primarily involve students and younger faculty from the humanities and the theological schools, with a scattering of scientists. The professional schools, engineers, specialists in the technology of manipulation and control (much of the social sciences), would probably remain relatively uninvolved. Therefore the long-range threat, such as it is, would be to American humanistic and scientific culture. I doubt that this would seem important to those in decision-making positions. Rusk and Rostow[13] and their accomplices in the academic world seem unaware of the serious threat that their policies already pose in these spheres. I doubt that they appreciate the extent, or the importance, of the dissipation of creative energies and the growing disaffection among young people who are sickened by the violence and deceit that they see in the exercise of American power. Further disruption in these areas might, then, seem to them a negligible cost.

Resistance is in part a moral responsibility, in part a tactic to affect government policy. In particular, with respect to support for draft resistance, I feel that it is a moral responsibility that cannot be shirked. On the other hand,

---

[13] Walt W. Rostow, national security advisor to President Lyndon Johnson.

as a tactic, it seems to me of doubtful effectiveness, as matters now stand. I say this with diffidence and considerable uncertainty.

Whatever happens in Vietnam, there are bound to be significant domestic repercussions. It is axiomatic that no army ever loses a war; its brave soldiers and all-knowing generals are stabbed in the back by treacherous civilians. American withdrawal is likely, then, to bring to the surface the worst features of American culture, and perhaps to lead to a serious internal repression. On the other hand, an American "victory" might well have dangerous consequences both at home and abroad. It might give added prestige to an already far too powerful executive. There is, moreover, the problem emphasized by A. J. Muste: ". . . the problem after a war is with the victor. He thinks he has just proved that war and violence pay. Who will now teach him a lesson?" For the most powerful and most aggressive nation in the world, this is indeed a danger. If we can rid ourselves of the naive belief that we are somehow different and more pure—a belief held by the British, the French, the Japanese, in their moments of imperial glory—then we will be able honestly to face the truth in this observation. One can only hope that we will face this truth before too many innocents, on all sides, suffer and die.

Finally, there are certain principles that I think must be stressed as we try to build effective opposition to this and future wars. We must not, I believe, thoughtlessly urge others to commit civil disobedience, and we must be careful not to construct situations in which young people will find themselves induced, perhaps in violation of their basic convictions, to commit civil disobedience. Resistance must be freely undertaken. I also hope, more sincerely than I know how to say, that it will create bonds of friendship and mutual trust that will support and strengthen those who are sure to suffer.

STUDY AND DISCUSSION QUESTIONS

1. Why, in Chomsky's view, is the Vietnam War wrong?

2. Why does Chomsky mention his "instinctive distaste for activism" in his first paragraph?

3. What does Chomsky mean by resistance? How is it different from dissent? Why does he feel both are necessary?

4. Chomsky describes the formation of soldiers advancing on him and others as a "grotesque organism . . . more grotesque because its cells were recognizable human beings." What does he mean?

5. "Nothing seemed to bring out the [federal] marshals' sadism more than the sight of a boy with long hair." Why do you think that is?

6. Why is Chomsky so horrified by "men who think it clever to discuss the bombing of North Vietnam as a question of tactics and cost-effectiveness"?

7. Why does Chomsky consider "draft resistance" so important?

8. Why does Chomsky oppose the "call for 'negotiations'"? Why does he feel withdrawal of American troops is the only "tolerable" option?

SUGGESTIONS FOR WRITING

1. "What I find terrifying is the detachment and equanimity with which we view and discuss an unbearable tragedy." Chomsky is referring to the Vietnam War. What in our world today might such a statement apply to? How do you relate to such "tragedy"?

2. What would you do if drafted to fight in a war you considered immoral?

JOURNAL

Alice Walker

Alice Walker was born in 1944 in Eatonton, Georgia, where her parents worked as sharecroppers. She attended Spelman and Sarah Lawrence Colleges and was active in the civil rights movement. Among her many books are the novels Meridian *(1976),* The Color Purple *(1982), which won the Pulitzer Prize, and* Possessing the Secret of Joy *(1992); the poetry volume* Once *(1968); and the essay collections* In Search of Our Mothers' Gardens: Womanist Prose *(1983) and* Living by the Word *(1988), where the following appeared.*

June 17, 1987

Early this morning, as I was putting the finishing touches on this book, I received an urgent call from "Liz" of Neighbor to Neighbor, an activist group that successfully gets out news about the wars in Central America, using U.S. media, primarily television. Two days from now there will be a program it has organized called "The Peace Oscars"—named for Archbishop Oscar Romero, who was a defender of poor people's rights in El Salvador until his assassination, by an agent of the Salvadoran government, while he administered mass in his church. At the ceremony, which will be held in the beautiful Conservatory of Flowers in Golden Gate Park in San Francisco, six of the bravest and most compassionate of human beings will be honored: people who have risked their lives to take medicine, food, clothing, and technical skills to the poor and suffering people of Central America; men and women who have been arrested many times as they exercised their opposition to the often genocidal policies of the U.S. government; people who founded the Sanctuary Movement[1] in this country; one refugee woman from El Salvador, whose personal story of oppression, terror, escape, and commitment, told at hundreds of gatherings in the United States, radicalized the people who heard her and deepened their commitment to the struggle to end war. I am to cohost this program, and, in fact, give the Peace Oscar (a small blue ceramic bird) to the sister from El Salvador.

The urgent message from Liz, however, is that a bomb threat against the ceremony has been telephoned by a mechanical-sounding male voice that said our crime is that we do not want to fight communism. Because several of the participants and invited guests are federally appointed officials of the state of California, she tells me, there will be federal agents about, cordons of police and various SWAT[2] teams, whose job it will be to sweep the place clean of any bombs. This often happens to movements like ours, she sighs. She tells me everyone involved will be called, in order for each to decide whether to come or stay home.

Of course I remember bomb threats, and bombs, from the sixties. I think of the children, Angela Davis's young acquaintances, blown up while in Sunday school.[3] I think of Ralph Featherstone, a SNCC worker, blown up in his car. I think of the NAACP official, who, along with his wife, was blown up while in bed. When I lived in Mississippi, bombings occurred; when my husband and I moved there, the bombing/lynching of NAACP leader Vernon Dehmer was in the news. I remember the bombing of Dr. Martin Luther King's house. There is a long history of bombings in North America. This is not the first time "communism" has been used as an excuse.

I send along the message of the threat to the people I've invited. But I know I will not be deterred. I spend a few hours with my lawyer and finally draw up my overdue will and assign a durable power of attorney that will be

---

[1] Grassroots organization of religious and lay people formed in the early 1980s to oppose United States policy in Central America and to aid refugees.

[2] Special Weapons and Tactics teams, specially trained and equipped to handle extreme situations.

[3] Four young African American girls were killed in 1963 when a Baptist church in Birmingham, Alabama was bombed; Angela Davis is a political activist and writer.

effective through the weekend (the affair is to take place on a Friday night). It isn't fatalism, or courage; I simply can't imagine not being there to honor these amazing, but also ordinary, people. I can't imagine not being there to hug my sister from the south.

A writer, apparently, to the core (though I frequently kid myself that if I never write again it's fine with me; there's so much else to do—sitting in a rocking chair watching the ocean, for instance), I find my thoughts going to my unfinished manuscripts. If anything happened to me, I wonder what my editor, John the meticulous, could make of my unfinished novel, a third typed and in a drawer, a third typed and in the computer, a third in my notebook and head.

What of this book? I realize that, as it stands, it has the rounded neatness of contemplation, and I would like to leave the reader with the uneven (I almost said ragged) edge of activity. I returned to my notes for the past week, and this is what I found:

I am Nicaraguan; I am Salvadoran; I am Grenadian; I am Caribbean; and I am Central American.

For the past several days I have been thinking about this sentence, and wondering what I mean by it. I am also Norte Americana, an African-American, even an African-Indian-Gringo American, if I add up all the known elements of my racial composition (and include the white rapist grandfather). Perhaps this is one way that I am Nicaraguan, or Salvadoran, or Grenadian. For the people in those countries, too, are racially mixed; in their country, too, there are the reds, the blacks, the whites—and the browns.

But I think the primary reason that I feel so Central American/Caribbean is that when I look at those people—and even though I study but do not yet speak their language—I see myself. I see my family, I see my parents, I see the ancestors. When I look at Nicaraguans, at, for instance, the humble peasant woman being "interrogated" by a Contra[4] carrying several guns and knives and three times her size, when I see and identify with her terror, when I look at the vulnerable faces of the nearly naked and barefoot children, when I see the suffering and pain on the faces of the men, then I am seeing a great deal of my own life.

I, too, was born poor, in an impoverished part of the world. I was born on what had been a plantation in the South, in Georgia. My parents and grandparents worked hard all their lives for barely enough food and shelter to sustain them. They were sharecroppers—landless peasants—the product of whose labor was routinely stolen from them. Their parents and

---

[4] When the United States-supported Somoza dictatorship in Nicaragua was overthrown in 1979 by the Sandinistas, the United States trained, armed, and directed the anti-Sandinista Contras.

Protest and Change

grandparents were enslaved. To me, Central America is one large plantation; and I see the people's struggle to be free as a slave revolt.

I can remember in my own life the days of *injusticia*[5] that continue in
so much of the world today. The days when children withered in sickness
and disease (as I have withered) because there was no money to pay for their
care and no concern for their health anyway, by the larger society. I myself
have suffered the deprivations of poverty, so that when I look into the face of
a Central American peasant, a Caribbean peasant, I see myself.

And I remember the years of fighting the white bosses of Georgia, Alabama, and Mississippi, especially, and of occasionally winning our battles for
dignity and bread against them—though at a cost (so many of the people we
loved were brutalized or assassinated) that still bruises the heart. When I see
the proud though weary faces of the Sandinistas, I see our own young faces.
The faces that went south in the sixties to teach black people to read and
write, to go out to vote, to stand up and be counted. And to keep the eyes on
the prize.

It is the same spirit. The spirit of poor people who have been ground
down nearly to a fine powder of humanity and yet who stand like rocks and
refuse to be blown away.

I am Nicaraguan. I am Salvadoran. I am Grenadian, Honduran, I chant
to myself. It has almost become a mantra.

And yet, this year I paid more in taxes than my parents and grandparents
together earned all the years they worked the land of the gringos of the South.
And over half of that money will go to buy weapons that will be shipped from
the Concord Naval Weapons Station at Port Chicago, California, thirty miles
from my home, and used against these people that I think of as myself.

These were my thoughts a few days before I was arrested for blocking
one of the gates to the Concord Naval Weapons Station.

It was a hot, dusty day, June 12, 1987, and I woke up thinking of all the things
I needed to bring to the demonstration: a hat, sunblock, drinking water, food,
spare clothing (in case we were in jail for longer than a day), whatever medical supplies I might need. I drove to the weapons station with the three other
members of my affinity group: Robert, Belvie, and Paul. Belvie and I had designed beautiful turquoise-and-coral T-shirts with the name of our group
(Wild Trees), a large mushroom cloud, and the words "Remember Port
Chicago."

For the past ten years I have shared my life with the writer and sometimes political activist (primarily in the Civil Rights movement and against

---

[5] Injustice (Spanish).

the Vietnam War) Robert Allen, who all that time has been writing a book about the so-called accident at Port Chicago on July 17, 1944. What happened was that 320 men whose job it was to load the bombs being sent to use on Japan and other places in the Pacific were blown to bits (literally), along with the ships they were loading and much of the base and nearby town. Two hundred of those killed were black. Because theirs had been the job of loading the weapons onto the ships, theirs was also the job of picking up the pieces—of men and debris—left by the explosion. When asked to continue loading the bombs after this horrendous experience, most of the men said no. They were threatened, imprisoned, tried for mutiny. Sentenced. Sent to jail. Released years later with dishonorable discharges.

My friend Robert has tracked down many of the surviving "mutineers" and, over the years, continued to wrestle with the implications of this event for America.

Port Chicago is now Concord. The name has been changed and the old town of Port Chicago completely destroyed, razed, in fact, by the government. But the weapons remain. Rather, they remain long enough to be shipped out—to Japan (the bomb dropped on Hiroshima was shipped from here), Vietnam, Nicaragua, and now El Salvador.

A few days before the demonstration we—the organizers (The Pledge of Resistance), the news media, demonstrators-to-be, and I—stood on a hill overlooking the base. We could see the white trains—white to reflect the heat—going into bunkers built into the hillside. Inside those bunkers are some of the deadliest weapons ever devised. There is, for instance, something that sounds even worse than napalm: the white phosphorous rocket. The sparks from it burn through the skin and flesh and into the bone. It can take a week for the burning to be put out. I have seen photographs of children who have lost limbs to the sparks from this rocket. I have found unbearable the suffering and questions in their eyes.

The morning of the demonstration I dress in jeans, sneakers, sunglasses, and an old felt hat, and I carry with me a sweetfaced black doll with crisp, shiny hair. I've named her Windela after a newborn niece of the same name I have not yet seen, and because I want to symbolize the connection I feel to Winnie and Nelson Mandela and the common awareness that it is up to those of us who are adults to leave to all children a habitable planet.

During the previous week I have felt afraid. I have hardly been able to smile at anyone. Though I have risked arrest many times, while a student demonstrator at Spelman College, in Liberty County, Georgia, and in Mississippi as a civil rights worker, I have been arrested only once before, during a demonstration against apartheid at UC, Berkeley. I felt a lighthearted joy throughout that action; as I sat with other demonstrators I could not suppress smiles *and* song. I concluded that what was different this time was that I would be placing myself in such vulnerable proximity to an enormous pile of evil and death blandly passed off to motorists, who can actually see the trains and bunkers from the highway, as bucolic countryside: cows graze placidly in the grass about the bunkers, giving them the aspect of odd kinds of barns.

Still, as I filled my backpack with a toothbrush, aspirin, and fruit, I began to take heart, the image of the children, the trees, and the animals of the planet always before me. On arrival, we went immediately to the gate to be blocked. There were a few protesters, about a hundred, already there. Across a broad yellow line, soldiers dressed in helmets and camouflage fatigues stood spread-legged holding long riot sticks. Behind them stood a row of officers in khaki from the local sheriff's department. Behind them another row of officers, presumably a SWAT team, in navy blue. The four of us walked up to face the soldiers, who were staring straight ahead. Between their row and that of the officers from the sheriff's department stood a Catholic priest, a woman in her fifties, and two old people, a man and a woman. They were all white. It was then that I made an interesting observation: Aside from myself and two members of our affinity group, there were no other people of color there. The Army, represented by the soldiers standing in front of us, was much more integrated. *Merde!*[6] I thought. What does it mean, that the forces of destruction are more integrated than the forces of peace?

Almost at once a white car carrying an official of the base arrived at the gate. We turned to face it, not permitting it to go through. The driver consulted with an Army officer, and the car slowly pulled away. Another and another vehicle appeared. They were not admitted. Soon a woman drove up and said she needed to fill a prescription at the base; it was spontaneously agreed that she should be let through. Many of us walked behind her car to close the space behind her. Soon a man who said he had gout and was coming to see his doctor appeared. He was also let through. A woman next to me said that in anticipation of our blockade the weapons trains and trucks had been busy all night long.

We were arrested because we went through the line of soldiers—all of them mere children and obviously poor (bad skin, crooked teeth, a certain ghetto street-corner patina)—and stood with the priest and the woman in her fifties, and the two old people. The old woman, Teresa, with a wondrously wrinkled face and bright white hair (a true crone), clasped me to her thin chest. The old man, Abraham (yes), half Jewish and half American Indian, looked fixedly into the crowd behind us and sang a frail but steady version of "Amen." I felt very proud of our affinity group. Of Robert, who had joined this inner

---

[6] Shit! (French).

group first, of Paul, who had promptly followed, and of Belvie, who was now smiling and talking to Teresa as if they were old friends.

A lot of things went through my mind as I was being handcuffed. Would they take my doll, whom I'd managed to stuff under one arm? No, they did not. Had my statements to the press truly reflected my feelings about weapons and war? I had been asked why I was risking arrest and I had said because I can't stand knowing that the money I pay in taxes and that my own family needs—not to mention all the other poor and sick people in this country and world—pays for weapons and the policy that mains, kills, frightens, and horribly abuses babies, children, women, men, and the old. I don't want to be a murderer, I had said.

And once, as I was being lifted into the jail van, someone yelled, "What do you have to say now, as you go off to jail?" and I made a joke that was the truth: "I'm following my tax dollars," I said.

My tax dollars. Really the crux of the matter. When will I have the courage not to pay them? I remember being audited by the IRS when my husband and I were in the Civil Rights movement in Mississippi. I remember being audited here in California two years ago. It isn't so much courage that I would need, as the patience to endure the grinding malice of bureaucratic harassment. (Meanwhile, my letter to my congressman about implementation of a peace tax—a peace tax would go to build hospitals, schools, houses, and to provide food for people—has not been answered.)

My thoughts, while I was being frisked, fingerprinted, and photographed (I liked my mug shot) by very cordial men and women, some of whom admired my doll, turned to food. Of which, because I'd left my well-provisioned backpack in the car, I had none. As a vegetarian, which I've now been for a good three months, I get hungry frequently. I think about oranges, almonds, apples—and, yes, a well-cooked piece of chicken. As soon as I'm seated fairly comfortably in the holding area—a large gray "cattle car" from the Port Chicago explosion days—Sallie, the woman in her fifties, breaks out her stash of oranges, Swiss cheese, and Triscuits, and offers me some. I think about how hard it would be for me to engage in any kind of action now for justice and peace with the remains of murdered flesh in my body. I'm tempted to wonder about the cows who "gave" the "Swiss" cheese, but don't. I eat it with gratitude.

Apparently it is lunchtime for everyone. I look out the window of our cattle car and I see that the guards, the nurse, the people who checked us in (even the one black woman in a light-blue uniform, who asked for my autograph and said, "Oh, I'm *so* glad you're here!"), all are eating. Since this is California, they are eating thick whole-grain sandwiches fluffy with fillings, trailing juicy tomato slices, lettuce leaves, and sprouts. As we all munch, they outside and "free," me inside and "captive," I can't help a feeling of tenderness for them: the need to eat connects us. Perhaps that is why they have taken these jobs.

Though some of our demonstrators were brutalized by the police, we were not. In an effort to minimize the import of our action, the meaning of it, and to keep public anxiety about the close proximity of the nuclear weapons on the base as low as possible, they treated us, for the most part, courteously. In truth, many of them seemed bored, barely present in what they were doing. There are some demonstrators who feel it is best, as far as gaining publicity is concerned, to have at least some police brutality, but I am not one of those. The pictures of demonstrations that I like show the creativity as well as the determination of the crowd. I like costumes, slogans, effigies. I think if these things are true enough, the police can affirm them, too. The most encouraging demonstration picture I've seen recently is of a young Korean policeman, visor raised and shield lowered, smiling impishly at protesting students and giving them the victory sign. Of course, many policemen are brutal and take their position as guardians of the status quo seriously. Many of them are angry, because they feel they are poor and have to work while the demonstrators appear to be playing. I feel absolutely no anger toward the police just because they are police or toward the young men in the Army. The protection of evil must be the most self-destructive job of all.

The next day, freed, my doll Windela and I address a crowd of a thousand demonstrators, two hundred of whom will later be arrested. Among other things, I read a poem about a poor Salvadoran woman whose father, husband, and sons have been killed and whose remaining small children are starving; nevertheless she is paying her taxes. Later, I stand holding Windela beside the knee-high, coiled line of razor-blade wire, on the other side of which are the same young black, white, brown, and yellow recruits. They are, at the moment, receiving much shouted information from several huge Vietnam vets, so loud and intense they frighten me—"Why do you want to go fight their stupid war for them, huh?" "Here's a body bag"—*plop*—"do you want to come back in one of those?" "I swore when I was in Nam that if I ever got out alive I'd never sit back and let kids like you go!" As I stand there, I suddenly feel a small stroking along my thigh. I look down into the large brown eyes of a small, gentle-faced olive-brown girl. She is playing shyly with Windela's foot. I hand the doll to her, and she embraces it with joy. Beside her is her mother, holding an infant. She speaks to the little girl in Spanish. I ask the mother, who appears to be in her early twenties, where she is from. She tells me she is a refugee from El Salvador, that she lives in a refugee house in San Francisco. At some point in our halting conversation in her "leetle beet" of English and my truly tongue-tied smidgen of Spanish, I ask to hold the baby, a plump, six-month-old girl, who promptly yanks off one of my earrings and then, fortunately, has trouble finding her mouth. Her mother says she is look-ing for a job. Can I help her? I tell her I will try. But who will hire a young mother of two small children who speaks Spanish?

I leave the doll with her daughter, Sandra, last seen sitting on the ground, oblivious to the demonstrators, the arrests, the police, and the Army all around her, "being a mother." And yes, that is what motherhood more and more is like in this world. I am glad I have acted. Glad I am here, if only for her. She is the future. I want some of the best of me, of us, of this day, to go there with her.

September 1, 1987
Today Belvie called to tell me the news about Brian Willson. He was block-ing the tracks at the Concord Naval Weapons Station, along with several oth-ers, and the train ran over him, injuring his head and left ankle, and severing his right leg below the knee. He had been in a peace circle earlier in the morn-ing with our friend Dan, whom I called immediately. Dan told me that in fact, in addition to the head injuries, which he thought very grave, and the severed right leg, Brian's left foot and ankle had been crushed, so that leg, too, below the knee, was amputated. As he talks, I feel a flush of futility that this could happen, although we've all realized it could, and, already thinking of what Brian's life will be like without the use of his legs, I can barely absorb the information Dan is giving me. Apparently the train speeded up when the demonstrators were spotted. Moments before the attack, Brian, who was preparing for a forty-day fast and sit-in on the tracks, and who had been married eight days before, had said he was willing to give his life to the strug-gle for peace.

Brian. White, middle-aged, wonderfully warm and expressive brown eyes (lots of light), brown hair, with some gray, a mottled beard. A really lovely and intelligent smile (how would he smile now?)—and great legs.

We met at the planning of the original blockade of the weapons station, and I had liked him right away. A week later we were together, with hundreds of others, blockading the gates. Only later did I learn he'd been an Air Force officer during the Vietnam War, in intelligence, no less. I could see how sick he was of war, and of the lies that protect war. He spoke very quietly but with a knowledge of what we were up against, so often missing in those who wage peace. He had the aura of someone who had seen and had enough.

I remember him telling us that if the death trains got through our blockade and over our bodies, killing or maiming us, we should realize that when their weapons reached their destinations, in Nicaragua or El Salvador, this would also be the fate of the people there. We are not more than they, he said; they are not less than we. The weapons on the trains would maim and kill children, women, and men, he said. To which I mentally added animals, trees, rivers, families, communities, cultures, friendship, love—and our own self-respect.

> Whoever you are
> whatever you are
> start with that,
> whether salt
> of the earth
> or only
> white sugar.

STUDY AND DISCUSSION QUESTIONS

1. Why does Walker identify with the people of Central America? What limits her identification with them?

2. Why, in the third paragraph, does Walker call the United States "North America" rather than just "America"?

3. Why does it matter so much to Walker that *her* taxes are paying for weapons?

4. Why do you think the group of soldiers at the weapons station is more racially integrated than the band of protestors they face? Why does this fact bother Walker so much?

5. Why does Walker point out that these soldiers are "obviously poor"?

6. "Journal" consists of a long entry followed by a short one. Why does Walker put them together? Why doesn't she just conclude with the image of Sandra and the doll?

7. How does the poem at the end relate to the rest of "Journal"?

SUGGESTIONS FOR WRITING

1. What does Walker gain by telling her story in the loose form of journal entries rather than in a polished essay? What does she lose?

2. Read about the history of United States involvement in Central America, especially in Nicaragua and El Salvador. What does this history help you understand about "Journal"?

3. Write a journal entry describing your experience, real or imagined, attending an organized protest for a cause you support.

THINK LITTLE

Wendell Berry

Wendell Berry was born in Kentucky in 1934 and has spent most of his life there, teaching at the University of Kentucky, writing, and farming. He has published numerous novels, short story collections, books of essays, and volumes of poetry. The following is from A Continuous Harmony: Essays Cultural and Agricultural *(1972).*

First there was Civil Rights, and then there was the War, and now it is the Environment. The first two of this sequence of causes have already risen to the top of the nation's consciousness and declined somewhat in a remarkably short time. I mention this in order to begin with what I believe to be a justifiable skepticism. For it seems to me that the Civil Rights Movement and the Peace Movement, as popular causes in the electronic age, have partaken far too much of the nature of fads. Not for all, certainly, but for too many they have been the fashionable politics of the moment. As causes they have been undertaken too much in ignorance; they have been too much simplified; they have been powered too much by impatience and guilt of conscience and short-term enthusiasm, and too little by an authentic social vision and long-term conviction and deliberation. For most people those causes have remained almost entirely abstract; there has been too little personal involvement, and too much involvement in organizations that were insisting that *other* organizations should do what was right.

There is considerable danger that the Environment Movement will have the same nature: that it will be a public cause, served by organizations that will self-righteously criticize and condemn other organizations, inflated for a while by a lot of public talk in the media, only to be replaced in its turn by another fashionable crisis. I hope that will not happen, and I believe that there are ways to keep it from happening, but I know that if this effort is carried on solely as a public cause, if millions of people cannot or will not undertake it as a *private* cause as well, then it is *sure* to happen. In five years the energy of our present concern will have petered out in a series of public gestures—and no doubt in a series of empty laws—and a great, and perhaps the last, human opportunity will have been lost.

It need not be that way. A better possibility is that the movement to preserve the environment will be seen to be, as I think it has to be, not a digression from the civil rights and peace movements, but the logical culmination of those movements. For I believe that the separation of these three problems is artificial. They have the same cause, and that is the mentality of greed and exploitation. The mentality that exploits and destroys the natural environment is the same that abuses racial and economic minorities, that imposes on young men the tyranny of the military draft, that makes war against peasants and women and children with the indifference of technology. The mentality that destroys a watershed and then panics at the threat of flood is the same mentality that gives institutionalized insult to black people and then panics at the prospect of race riots. It is the same mentality that can mount deliberate warfare against a civilian population and then express moral shock at the logical consequence of such warfare at My Lai.[1] We would be fools to believe that we could solve any one of these problems without solving the others.

To me, one of the most important aspects of the environmental movement is that it brings us not just to another public crisis, but to a crisis of the protest movement itself. For the environmental crisis should make it dramatically clear, as perhaps it has not always been before, that there is no public crisis that is not also private. To most advocates of civil rights, racism has seemed mostly the fault of someone else. For most advocates of peace the war has been a remote reality, and the burden of the blame has seemed to rest mostly on the government. I am certain that these crises have been more private, and that we have each suffered more from them and been more responsible for them, than has been readily apparent, but the connections have been difficult to see. Racism and militarism have been institutionalized among us for too long for our personal involvement in those evils to be easily apparent to us. Think, for example, of all the Northerners who assumed—until black people attempted to move into *their* neighborhoods—that racism was a Southern phenomenon. And think how quickly—one might almost say how naturally—among some of its members the peace movement has spawned policies of deliberate provocation and violence.

But the environmental crisis rises closer to home. Every time we draw a breath, every time we drink a glass of water, every time we eat a bite of food we are suffering from it. And more important, every time we indulge in, or depend on, the wastefulness of our economy—and our economy's first principle is waste—we are *causing* the crisis. Nearly every one of us, nearly every day of his life, is contributing *directly* to the ruin of this planet. A protest meeting on the issue of environmental abuse is not a convocation of accusers, it is a convocation of the guilty. That realization ought to clear the smog of

---

[1] Vietnamese village where American soldiers massacred hundreds of unarmed civilians in March 1968.

self-righteousness that has almost conventionally hovered over these occasions, and let us see the work that is to be done.

In this crisis it is certain that every one of us has a public responsibility. We must not cease to bother the government and the other institutions to see that they never become comfortable with easy promises. For myself, I want to say that I hope never again to go to Frankfort to present a petition to the governor on an issue so vital as that of strip mining, only to be dealt with by some ignorant functionary—as several of us were not so long ago, the governor himself being "too busy" to receive us. Next time I will go prepared to wait as long as necessary to see that the petitioners' complaints and their arguments are heard *fully*—and by the governor. And then I will hope to find ways to keep those complaints and arguments from being forgotten until something is done to relieve them. The time is past when it was enough merely to elect our officials. We will have to elect them and then go and *watch* them and keep our hands on them, the way the coal companies do. We have made a tradition in Kentucky of putting self-servers, and worse, in charge of our vital interests. I am sick of it. And I think that one way to change it is to make Frankfort a less comfortable place. I believe in American political principles, and I will not sit idly by and see those principles destroyed by sorry practice. I am ashamed and deeply distressed that American government should have become the chief cause of disillusionment with American principles.

And so when the government in Frankfort again proves too stupid or too blind or too corrupt to see the plain truth and to act with simple decency, I intend to be there, and I trust that I won't be alone. I hope, moreover, to be there, not with a sign or a slogan or a button, but with the facts and the arguments. A crowd whose discontent has risen no higher than the level of slogans is *only* a crowd. But a crowd that understands the reasons for its discontent and knows the remedies is a vital community, and it will have to be reckoned with. I would rather go before the government with two men who have a competent understanding of an issue, and who therefore deserve a hearing, than with two thousand who are vaguely dissatisfied.

But even the most articulate public protest is not enough. We don't live in the government or in institutions or in our public utterances and acts, and the environmental crisis has its roots in our *lives*. By the same token, environmental health will also be rooted in our lives. That is, I take it, simply a fact, and in the light of it we can see how superficial and foolish we would be to think that we could correct what is wrong merely by tinkering with the institutional machinery. The changes that are required are fundamental changes in the way we are living.

What we are up against in this country, in any attempt to invoke private responsibility, is that we have nearly destroyed private life. Our people have given up their independence in return for the cheap seductions and the shoddy merchandise of so-called "affluence." We have delegated all our vital functions and responsibilities to salesmen and agents and bureaus and experts of all sorts. We cannot feed or clothe ourselves, or entertain ourselves, or communicate with each other, or be charitable or neighborly or loving, or even respect ourselves, without recourse to a merchant or a corporation or a public-service organization or an agency of the government or a style-setter or an expert. Most of us cannot think of dissenting from the opinions or the actions of one organization without first forming a new organization. Individualism is going around these days in uniform, handing out the party line on individualism. Dissenters want to publish their personal opinions over a thousand signatures.

The Confucian *Great Digest*[2] says that the "chief way for the production of wealth" (and he is talking about real goods, not money) is "that the producers be many and that the mere consumers be few. . . ." But even in the much-publicized rebellion of the young against the materialism of the affluent society, the consumer mentality is too often still intact: the standards of behavior are still those of kind and quantity, the security sought is still the security of numbers, and the chief motive is still the consumer's anxiety that he is missing out on what is "in." In this state of total consumerism—which is to say a state of helpless dependence on things and services and ideas and motives that we have forgotten how to provide ourselves—all meaningful contact between ourselves and the earth is broken. We do not understand the earth in terms either of what it offers us or of what it requires of us, and I think it is the rule that people inevitably destroy what they do not understand. Most of us are not directly responsible for strip mining and extractive agriculture and other forms of environmental abuse. But we are guilty nevertheless, for we connive in them by our ignorance. We are ignorantly dependent on them. We do not know enough about them; we do not have a particular enough sense of their danger. Most of us, for example, not only do not know how to produce the best food in the best way—we don't know how to produce any kind in any way. Our model citizen is a sophisticate who before puberty understands how to produce a baby, but who at the age of thirty will not know how to produce a potato. And for this condition we have elaborate rationalizations, instructing us that dependence for everything on somebody else is efficient and economical and a scientific miracle. I say, instead, that it is madness, mass produced. A man who understands the weather only in terms of golf is participating in a chronic public insanity that either he or his descendants will be bound to realize as suffering. I believe that the death of the

---

[2] Collected teachings of the Chinese philosopher Confucius.

world is breeding in such minds much more certainly and much faster than in any political capital or atomic arsenal.

For an index of our loss of contact with the earth we need only look at the condition of the American farmer—who must in our society, as in every society, enact man's dependence on the land, and his responsibility to it. In an age of unparalleled affluence and leisure, the American farmer is harder pressed and harder worked than ever before; his margin of profit is small, his hours are long; his outlays for land and equipment and the expenses of maintenance and operation are growing rapidly greater; he cannot compete with industry for labor; he is being forced more and more to depend on the use of destructive chemicals and on the wasteful methods of haste and anxiety. As a class, farmers are one of the despised minorities. So far as I can see, farming is considered marginal or incidental to the economy of the country, and farmers, when they are thought of at all, are thought of as hicks and yokels, whose lives do not fit into the modern scene. The average American farmer is now an old man whose sons have moved away to the cities. His knowledge, and his intimate connection with the land, are about to be lost. The small independent farmer is going the way of the small independent craftsmen and storekeepers. He is being forced off the land into the cities, his place taken by absentee owners, corporations, and machines. Some would justify all this in the name of efficiency. As I see it, it is an enormous social and economic and cultural blunder. For the small farmers who lived on their farms *cared* about their land. And given their established connection to their land—which was often hereditary and traditional as well as economic—they could have been encouraged to care for it more competently than they have so far. The corporations and machines that replace them will never be bound to the land by the sense of birthright and continuity, or by the love that enforces care. They will be bound by the rule of efficiency, which takes thought only of the volume of the year's produce, and takes no thought of the slow increment of the life of the land, not measurable in pounds or dollars, which will assure the livelihood and the health of the coming generations.

If we are to hope to correct our abuses of each other and of other races and of our land, and if our effort to correct these abuses is to be more than a political fad that will in the long run be only another form of abuse, then we are going to have to go far beyond public protest and political action. We are going to have to rebuild the substance and the integrity of private life in this country. We are going to have to gather up the fragments of knowledge and responsibility that we have parceled out to the bureaus and the corporations and the specialists, and we are going to have to put those fragments back together again in our own minds and in our families and households and neighborhoods. We need better government, no doubt about it. But we also need better minds, better friendships, better marriages, better communities. We need persons and households that do not have to wait upon organizations, but can make necessary changes in themselves, on their own.

For most of the history of this country our motto, implied or spoken, has been Think Big. I have come to believe that a better motto, and an essential one now, is Think Little. That implies the necessary change of thinking and feeling, and suggests the necessary work. Thinking Big has led us to the two biggest and cheapest political dodges of our time: plan-making and law-making. The lotus-eaters[3] of this era are in Washington, D.C., Thinking Big. Somebody comes up with a problem, and somebody in the government comes up with a plan or a law. The result, mostly, has been the persistence of the problem, and the enlargement and enrichment of the government.

But the discipline of thought is not generalization; it is detail, and it is personal behavior. While the government is "studying" and funding and organizing its Big Thought, nothing is being done. But the citizen who is willing to Think Little, and, accepting the discipline of that, to go ahead on his own, is already solving the problem. A man who is trying to live as a neighbor to his neighbors will have a lively and practical understanding of the work of peace and brotherhood, and let there be no mistake about it—he is *doing* that work. A couple who make a good marriage, and raise healthy, morally competent children, are serving the world's future more directly and surely than any political leader, though they never utter a public word. A good farmer who is dealing with the problem of soil erosion on an acre of ground has a sounder grasp of that problem and *cares* more about it and is probably doing more to solve it than any bureaucrat who is talking about it in general. A man who is willing to undertake the discipline and the difficulty of mending his own ways is worth more to the conservation movement than a hundred who are insisting merely that the government and the industries mend *their* ways.

If you are concerned about the proliferation of trash, then by all means start an organization in your community to do something about it. But before—*and while*—you organize, pick up some cans and bottles yourself. That way, at least, you will assure yourself and others that you mean what you say. If you are concerned about air pollution, help push for government controls, but drive your car less, use less fuel in your home. If you are worried about the damming of wilderness rivers, join the Sierra Club,[4] write to the government, but turn off the lights you're not using, don't install an air conditioner, don't be a sucker for electrical gadgets, don't waste water. In other words, if you are fearful of the destruction of the environment, then learn to quit being

---

[3] In Homer's *Odyssey,* people who ate the lotus and lived in a dream-like state.

[4] American and Canadian environmental organization.

an environmental parasite. We all are, in one way or another, and the remedies are not always obvious, though they certainly will always be difficult. They require a new kind of life—harder, more laborious, poorer in luxuries and gadgets, but also, I am certain, richer in meaning and more abundant in real pleasure. To have a healthy environment we will all have to give up things we like; we may even have to give up things we have come to think of as necessities. But to be fearful of the disease and yet unwilling to pay for the cure is not just to be hypocritical; it is to be doomed. If you talk a good line without being changed by what you say, then you are not just hypocritical and doomed; you have become an agent of the disease. Consider, for example, President Nixon, who advertises his grave concern about the destruction of the environment, and who turns up the air conditioner to make it cool enough to build a fire.

Odd as I am sure it will appear to some, I can think of no better form of personal involvement in the cure of the environment than that of gardening. A person who is growing a garden, if he is growing it organically, is improving a piece of the world. He is producing something to eat, which makes him somewhat independent of the grocery business, but he is also enlarging, for himself, the meaning of food and the pleasure of eating. The food he grows will be fresher, more nutritious, less contaminated by poisons and preservatives and dyes than what he can buy at a store. He is reducing the trash problem; a garden is not a disposable container, and it will digest and re-use its own wastes. If he enjoys working in his garden, then he is less dependent on an automobile or a merchant for his pleasure. He is involving himself directly in the work of feeding people.

If you think I'm wandering off the subject, let me remind you that most of the vegetables necessary for a family of four can be grown on a plot of forty by sixty feet. I think we might see in this an economic potential of considerable importance, since we now appear to be facing the possibility of widespread famine. How much food could be grown in the dooryards of cities and suburbs? How much could be grown along the extravagant right-of-ways of the interstate system? Or how much could be grown, by the intensive practices and economics of the small farm, on so-called marginal lands? Louis Bromfield[5] liked to point out that the people of France survived crisis after crisis because they were a nation of gardeners, who in times of want turned with great skill to their own small plots of ground. And F. H. King, an agriculture professor who traveled extensively in the Orient in 1907, talked to a Chinese farmer who supported a family of twelve, "one donkey, one cow . . . and two pigs on 2.5 acres of cultivated land"—and who did this, moreover, by agricultural methods that were sound enough organically to have maintained his land in prime

---

[5] American writer and scientific farmer.

fertility through several thousand years of such use. These are possibilities that are readily apparent and attractive to minds that are prepared to Think Little. To Big Thinkers—the bureaucrats and businessmen of agriculture—they are quite simply invisible. But intensive, organic agriculture kept the farms of the Orient thriving for thousands of years, whereas extensive—which is to say, exploitive or extractive—agriculture has critically reduced the fertility of American farmlands in a few centuries or even a few decades.

A person who undertakes to grow a garden at home, by practices that will preserve rather than exploit the economy of the soil, has set his mind decisively against what is wrong with us. He is helping himself in a way that dignifies him and that is rich in meaning and pleasure. But he is doing something else that is more important: he is making vital contact with the soil and the weather on which his life depends. He will no longer look upon rain as an impediment of traffic, or upon the sun as a holiday decoration. And his sense of man's dependence on the world will have grown precise enough, one would hope, to be politically clarifying and useful.

What I am saying is that if we apply our minds directly and competently to the needs of the earth, then we will have begun to make fundamental and necessary changes in our minds. We will begin to understand and to mistrust *and to change* our wasteful economy, which markets not just the produce of the earth, but also the earth's ability to produce. We will see that beauty and utility are alike dependent upon the health of the world. But we will also see through the fads and the fashions of protest. We will see that war and oppression and pollution are not separate issues, but are aspects of the same issue. Amid the outcries for the liberation of this group or that, we will know that no person is free except in the freedom of other persons, and that man's only real freedom is to know and faithfully occupy his place—a much humbler place than we have been taught to think—in the order of creation.

But the change of mind I am talking about involves not just a change of knowledge, but also a change of attitude toward our essential ignorance, a change in our bearing in the face of mystery. The principle of ecology, if we will take it to heart, should keep us aware that our lives depend upon other lives and upon processes and energies in an interlocking system that, though we can destroy it, we can neither fully understand nor fully control. And our great dangerousness is that, locked in our selfish and myopic economics, we have been willing to change or destroy far beyond our power to understand. We are not humble enough or reverent enough.

Some time ago, I heard a representative of a paper company refer to conservation as a "no-return investment." This man's thinking was exclusively oriented to the annual profit of his industry. Circumscribed by the demand that the profit be great, he simply could not be answerable to any other demand—not even to the obvious needs of his own children.

Consider, in contrast, the profound ecological intelligence of Black Elk, "a holy man of the Oglala Sioux," who in telling his story said that it was not his own life that was important to him, but what he had shared with all life: "It is the story of all life that is holy and it is good to tell, and of us two-leggeds sharing in it with the four-leggeds and the wings of the air and all green things. . . ." And of the great vision that came to him when he was a child he said: "I saw that the sacred hoop of my people was one of many hoops that made one circle, wide as daylight and as starlight, and in the center grew one mighty flowering tree to shelter all the children of one mother and father. And I saw that it was holy."

STUDY AND DISCUSSION QUESTIONS

1. Berry sees the environmental movement as "the logical culmination" of the civil rights and peace movements. How so?

2. What does Berry have against organizations?

3. According to Berry, living in a more environmentally sound way would mean a life "richer in meaning and more abundant in real pleasure." How might that be?

4. Why does Berry bemoan the decline of the small independent farmer?

5. Why does Berry attach such importance to gardening? What assumptions about his reader is he making in recommending it?

6. What is the point of the comparison, at the end of the essay, between Black Elk and the paper company representative?

7. Berry writes that "no person is free except in the freedom of other persons." What might this mean?

SUGGESTIONS FOR WRITING

1. Writing in 1972, Berry feared that environmentalism might become something of an empty fad. Do you see any evidence today that Berry's fears might have been realized?

2. "A couple who make a good marriage, and raise healthy, morally competent children, are serving the world's future more directly and surely than any political leader, though they never utter a public word." How would Berry justify this statement? Do you agree?

3. How aware are you of the effects of your own actions on the environment? How might you change?

"JOE GUMP, JEAN GUMP'S HUSBAND" AND "#03789-045, A.K.A. JEAN GUMP"

Studs Terkel

Studs Terkel (born Louis Terkel, in 1912) grew up in New York but went to college in Chicago and settled there. He's best known for his books of interviews, mostly with ordinary people. Among them are Hard Times: An Oral History of the Great Depression *(1970),* Working: People Talk about What They Do All Day and How They Feel about What They Do *(1974),* The Great Divide: Second Thoughts on the American Dream *(1988), from which the following is taken, and* Race: How Blacks and Whites Think and Feel about the American Obsession *(1992).*

It is August 18, 1987. It is thirteen days after his arrest. His voice, long-distance, sounds high-spirited, buoyant. "It is now my turn to do a little hammering," he had written in a letter received after his arrest.

He, together with a young Catholic pacifist, Jerry Ebner, is at the Wyandotte County Jail, Kansas City, Kansas. "The charge against us is destruction of government property. Helen Woodson was, in spirit, part of this action. She's doing twelve years up in Shakopee, Minnesota, at the state prison."

In the letter, Joe said: "There is no group more suited to work toward the total elimination of these weapons than my generation. We went to school, spent time in military service, married, had families, and worked toward achieving the American dream. We were either silent or cheered when the Bomb was dropped, paid taxes to develop more and better bombs. . . . I am not prepared to leave this legacy to my children or yours. With Jean, I am saying NO, no longer in my name.

"Please forgive me for not sharing my plans with you, dear friends. My silence in this regard was essential for your protection. . . . It also saved us from saying good-bye in a less casual way when we were last together."

On August 5, 1987, at approximately 5:15 P.M., Jerry and I entered the silo. They call them missile launch facilities. It's near Butler, Missouri, about fifty miles south of Kansas City. The time corresponds to 8:15, August 6, in Hiroshima, when the bomb exploded.

August 6 also happens to celebrate the Feast of Transfiguration. Christ and His apostles Peter, James, and John went to the mountain to pray. He became transfigured and His divinity was revealed. So we took the name Transfiguration Plowshares.

Jean chose silo M-10. About a year and a half alter, I chose silo K-9. We had a lot of choices (laughs). There are eleven groups of silos, and 150 warheads in this field. We carried our tools and banners in socks. This was recovered property that Jean and her friends had used on Good Friday. We were recycling (laughs).

We added a banner that had pictures of our two grandsons, who were born since Jean's action. It said: DISARMAMENT INSURES A FUTURE FOR THE CHILDREN. We hung them on the cyclone fence that surrounded the silo. Very ordinary. When you drive past these places, they're hardly noticeable.

We had all sorts of hammers: sledge, ball peen, pick. We chiseled a cross. On top of the cover, I poured three baby bottles of blood, Jerry's and mine, and made a cross out of it. We had brought our Bibles along, and after we had finished what we planned to do we sat on top of the silo, prayed, and sang songs. We drank a lot of ice water. It was about 100 degrees out there.

About forty-two minutes later, an air force station wagon came up the road. We were covered by three guys with automatic rifles. They had us raise our hands. We called out to them that we were unarmed and nonviolent and walked to the gate.

We lay face down on the ground, spread-eagled. They didn't even attempt to frisk us. They were real young kids and seemed rather nervous. They weren't quite sure they knew what they were doing, and a guy on the hill was giving them instructions. We were turned over to the county sheriff and handcuffed. By the time we left, there were about eight cars around.

So we were in a cell. About one-thirty in the morning, a guy from the air force special investigations came in. We refused to answer any of his questions. He was the one from whom we recovered the banners used in the previous Plowshare actions.

The grand jury reconvened yesterday. The charge, destruction of government property, carries a ten years' jail sentence, maximum, and a fine of $250,000. They'll most likely add a conspiracy charge. And possibly, sabotage.

Dan Stewart, the assistant to the U.S. Attorney, who handled Jean's case, will probably do the major trial work. We keep running into familiar faces. It's unlikely Jean's judge, Elmo Hunter, will handle this one. He recently made some statements in the paper that Jean's sentence wasn't severe enough, because it apparently didn't deter me.

We're going *pro se*. We will be our own attorneys. We will have a lawyer advising us, but he won't represent us in court.

Our defense is that we haven't committed a crime; that the crime really is the existence of these weapons of indiscriminate destruction that are violations of the Nuremburg principles, United Nations principles—that the crime would be for us to sit idly by. It's the necessity defense: the imminent danger posed by these weapons justifies what the law considers an illegal act.

I'm a chemical engineer, with an M.B.A. degree from the University of Chicago. For the past few years, I've worked as a salesman of food process equipment. You become a questionable commodity in the market at my age. The company I worked for had gone out of business, so I took up a new career: a resister to the military buildup. It's a real career change (laughs).

The first thing I did was to go to Alderson and visit Jean for five days. It will be the last time that we will be able to see each other for quite some time now. Actually, Jean will probably visit me in prison the next time.

I didn't tell the kids what I had in mind. They all suspected something, because they observed the way I was behaving over the past year or so. This is not something you just decide to do.

I feel great. This is a happy time right now. It was something I felt increasingly strongly about since Jean was in jail. We've made our statement and I feel good.

I'm sure her example had a lot to do with getting me interested. It's a time of real adjustment: reorientation of things you considered to be important from your earliest days. I guess you'd call it resetting your priorities.

Because our family was raised, I had no strong obligations that prevented me from doing something that would separate me from normal society for a number of years. We're at the point now where we can enjoy some of the free time, enjoy our grandchildren. But it's at this time that we have the freedom to make a statement like this. Ultimately it's going to benefit our grandchildren far more than anything we could do in a more normal course of events. If we're silent, there may be no planet for them to enjoy.

I'm not saying that people should go out and bang on a silo. There are so many other ways to resist. Once you cut through the obfuscation they throw at you, you realize our fate is being determined by pseudo-experts.

I'm going to be someone who questions. I will satisfy my own sense of understanding before I believe anything that is told to me. If I hear something said by the government that is blatantly false, I will speak out against it, I will resist it and I will suffer the consequences.

This feeling of happiness is something that has been acquired. It gives you such delight to be able to just feel this way, it's hard to describe.

Postscript: On December 11, 1987, Joe Gump and Jerry Ebner were sentenced to prison terms of thirty and forty months, respectively, and were ordered to make restitution for damages they caused August 5 (Chicago Sun-Times, *December 12, 1987*).

#03789-045, a.k.a. Jean Gump

August 15, 1987. It is a long-distance call from the Correctional Institution for Women, Alderson, West Virginia.

She is chuckling: "They don't do much correcting here. Heaven knows, they try, but it doesn't seem to be effective." She appears amused during much of the conversation.

Our conversation is being taped.

Yes, I've got the machine working—

I mean, by others. It's good. I've always believed in education. Of course all my letters are read. I like that. I usually put something in there that I would like the staff to see. If some of the staff are lazy and choose not to read the mail, I usually write on the envelope "Legal Mail." This way it will surely be read. It's important that we educate everybody as we go along.

It's exactly eleven months to this day that I've been here. I think this is the place for me at this time in my life. The feds probably think it's a good place for me for the rest of my life.

There are things here called contraband. Eighty percent of the inmates are here on drug-related charges. Drugs are of course contraband. But another real no-no is a brown paper bag. I'm not sure why. It might be a fire hazard, you think? A real awful thing is bubble gum. A person can go in the hole for that—solitary confinement. It's a funny thing, I haven't been there yet. I'm a kind of law-and-order freak. I follow rules extremely well.

I enjoy the compound and especially enjoy my sister inmates. As for the staff, the system is geared for them to do things they probably wouldn't do on the outside. Most of us would find reading other people's mail detestable. But that's part of the job. Lying is part of the job, too.

I have to think of my guards as individuals. We have to have strip searches. I find it so vulgar, so demeaning, so intrusive, it makes me cringe. But that guard is trying to feed her family—we have male guards here, too. Maybe if there were no other jobs, I'd be doing that, too.

As inmates, we're property. We belong to Mr. Meese,[1] we belong to the Bureau of Prisons. A month ago, a young woman had come here from another federal institution. She had been locked up for fourteen months without seeing the light of day. On arriving here, she was so happy to be out in the

---

[1] Edwin Meese, United States Attorney General.

sunlight, she lay down and got herself a sunburn. They wrote a shot—that's an incident report. The shot read: Destruction of government property. Her skin, okay?

What did she destroy?

Her skin. She got a sunburn.

You're putting me on.

I wouldn't tease you about a thing like that. That is a fact, okay? Her sunburn deterred her from working. Her skin, her being, is the property of the United States government.

How do the other inmates feel about me? I feel I'm respected, though they may think I'm kind of a ding-a-ling. But nice. I like them, too, though our backgrounds are very different. After eight and a half months, I'm finally in a double room. I'm on the bottom bunk. Unfortunately, my roommate was just put in the hole.

I wake up quite early in the morning and I meditate and read Scripture for an hour. I have to be at work at 7:45. I work in the greenhouse and it's delightful. We're with living plants and we have National Public Radio[2] on all day long. We listen to symphony music and the news. It's a peaceful place.

I get home about 3:45.

Home?

This is home, kid. Every inmate has to be in her room at 4:00. We have a count. They don't like to lose people. By 4:30, they've been able to count the 62 women in this cottage. There's something like 15 cottages, housing from 62 to 70 each. The facility was built to accommodate 300.

So many women here have experienced long separation from families. It hasn't been so with me. I think we're closer now, although I'm not present. When my son, Joey, graduated from law school, they had a big party at the house. They sent me a videotape. It was wonderful.

I'd like to have been there. I said to the warden, "Hey, listen, my son is gonna graduate. I think it would be nice if you gave me a furlough, so I could be there." He said I have to be eligible for release in two years and in community custody. That means the government trusts you enough to go home and say hello. I have what they call out-custody.

Let's say there was a death in the family. I would have to go home with federal marshals. They would take me to the wake in handcuffs to view the body. Then they'd put me in jail for overnight. They'd be staying at a hotel, which I would pay for. I'd pay for their meals as well. The next morning,

---

[2] Radio network funded primarily by grants and listener contributions.

they'd pick me up for the funeral, which I would attend in handcuffs. They play hard ball here, kid.

In addition to her six-year sentence, there is a five-year probation period, following release.

I owe the government $424.28 for the repair of the damage done to the nuclear missile. Plus $100 assessment. I chose not to pay this. I don't think nuclear weapons should be repaired. They should be abolished. The government will have to pay it itself, I'm sorry.

I've wondered what would happen, if after I've served my six years and I'm on probation, will I still owe the government the five hundred bucks? The fact of the matter is, I will.[3] I've written to my judge and told him I won't pay the money. If after I go back for five more years and have served eleven years, will I still owe them the $524.28? I think I will.

You could be in forever.[4]

I suggested an alternative in a letter to the U.S. Probation Office. I'm always interested in saving money for American taxpayers. It costs taxpayers $28,000 per year per inmate. If my arithmetic is correct, my confinement for eleven years will cost around $308,000. If the government should pay the $524.28, it will save the taxpayers $307,457.52. Not a bad deal, eh?

Did Joe surprise you doing what he did?

Oh, no. I don't know how to explain it. All the things we had most of our lives thought important were no longer that important. He asked me one time, "What would you think if I sat on a missile?" I said, "Joe, I wouldn't advise you on something like that. It's so very personal. It's your entire life we're talking about." I don't think anyone can make that kind of a decision for anyone else.

Each individual brings a certain difference to it. None of us is the same. There was a funny reaction here. I had called my sister at the time of Joe's arrest. I'd been fasting. With the news, it was a time of celebration. My sister inmates couldn't understand why one should celebrate a husband's imprisonment.

We were celebrating because someone whom I love very much had decided to take this stand. Oh, it's a hard spot to be in, but it's not an impossible

---

[3] In an exchange of letters with the supervising probation officer, it was determined that her refusal of restitution would constitute violation of parole and she would be subject to further imprisonment. [Author's note]

[4] A remembrance of a Willie and Eugene Howard sketch is evoked. They were two celebrated vaudeville comics whose most memorable routine dealt with a two-dollar fine and a refusal to pay and years and years in prison. [Author's note]

one. It is saying to the people of the world that we have to give up a little of our comfort now, in a critical time, to point up the horrendous errors of a government. I always thought Joe and I had a lovely love affair when we were young. It's only gotten better. We're not going to see each other for a while—that's hard.

My health? Funny you should ask that. I had a little problem with blood pressure prior to coming here. The other day I had it taken and it was 110 over 80. This is what a stressless life will bring you. I'm very much at peace here.

I never viewed myself as a troublemaker. I like things nice and easy, I really do. But I don't want the goodies that the government has to offer at the expense of my grandchildren's future here. Oh, God, I have a tremendous hope. I figure if somebody like me can put aside her selfish interests and do something, anybody in the United States can. When Eisenhower was leaving office, he said, Someday people are going to want peace so bad, the government had better step aside and let them have it. I think that's coming to pass.

(Suddenly) Can you remember your number?

Certainly. It's like my toothbrush. (Rattles it off) 03789-045 (laughs).

STUDY AND DISCUSSION QUESTIONS

1. In his letter to friends, Joe claims that his is the generation most suited to work to eliminate nuclear weapons. Why?

2. According to Joe, "our fate is being determined by pseudo-experts." What does he mean?

3. Thirteen days after his arrest, why does Joe feel "great"?

4. Why does Terkel title his second interview "#03789-045, aka Jean Gump"?

5. How is Jean able to be so forgiving of her guards?

6. Jean's determination not to pay $524.28 for damages to the missile will mean five more years of imprisonment at a cost to the government of $28,000 per year. Why is the government unlikely just to let her go? Why is she not going to pay?

SUGGESTIONS FOR WRITING

1. Joe and Jerry want to represent themselves in court. Write their opening statement.

2. "[W]e haven't committed a crime . . . the crime really is the existence of these weapons . . . the crime would be for us to sit idly by." Do you agree?

ELEVEN

ART AND
THE ARTIST

How do artists position themselves in relation to their subject, their materials, their audience, their social context? The essays and memoirs included in this section on art and the artist explore questions of art and politics, reality and representation, memory and identity. What is creativity? From whence does the artist gather his or her materials? What factors produce and shape a work of art? Barbara Kingsolver points out in her essay "Jabberwocky" that Americans often think of art and politics as existing in two separate spheres, and that the label "political" usually is attached only to the work of writers and artists who challenge the status quo. Yet it is impossible to get through a day without interacting with the society you live in and to do so is, inevitably, to be political. Poet Imamu Amiri Baraka (LeRoi Jones) has recounted the history of the explicitly political Black Arts Movement of the 1960s; its aims were to produce an art that was identifiably Afro-American, an art that would draw from the strength of the people and would go back into the community. He spoke of one project (Operation Bootstrap) which brought art to Harlem in the early 1960s. Four "wagons"—a poetry wagon, a theater wagon, a music wagon, and a painting wagon—moved around to different locations bringing art into a community that had been labeled as not ready for avant-garde art, but which in fact instantly embraced and understood it. Americans have been increasingly "dumbed down" culturally—television (see the section on "Mass Culture") has had a role in this trend, though it is not the only culprit—and therefore poets and other cultural workers have had a hard time supporting themselves so that they can do their work. Further, we seem to live in a society which values (literally, through cash payment) football players and movie stars far more than it does poets and painters.

The section opens with Adrienne Rich's "How does a poet put bread on the table?" which asks how writers support themselves in a culture that doesn't value creative work. It is a question particularly pertinent to poets, since Americans have had a longerstanding aversion to poetry than to fiction or to drama. To tell your parents you've decided to be a poet when you grow up is almost sure to elicit groans and late night discussions about how they (or you) have failed. Rich discusses how poets have to cobble together a living in a variety of ways: by doing part-time work, from teaching to cleaning houses, while also being part-time poets; by working full-time and giving their writing the crumbs of their attention; by possessing the luxury of independent wealth or wealthy friends to support them; or by winning one of the exceedingly rare grants available to poets that allow them to devote full time to their poetry for a few months. We like to imagine a different sort of society, one in which poetry would be valued. In such a society, corporations and governments would compete to support the best poets and to discover new talent—because the work of poets would be seen as essential to the growth and renewal of that society's soul.

The next two pieces, an excerpt from John Edgar Wideman's *Brothers and Keepers* and Chang-Rae Lee's "The Faintest Echo of Our Language," address similar concerns: each writer tries to reach some truth about humanity and art by writing repeatedly about one or two defining moments in his past. Wideman reacts to two events, which for him remain entangled. His brother Robby was involved in an armed robbery and murder in their hometown of Pittsburgh. Wideman writes of the night Bobby arrives, on the run, at Wideman's new home in Laramie, Wyoming, two thousand miles from Pittsburgh. Wideman's memory is also filled with the difficult birth of his daughter Jamila. When pregnant with Jamila, Wideman's wife developed placenta previa, a condition that necessitated an immediate caesarean section and threatened the life of both mother and child. Both events haunt Wideman and teach him the importance of "treasuring all the people I loved because nothing could be taken for granted."

Chang-Rae Lee's narrative is similarly about family and memory. Perhaps because he is a first generation Korean American, it is very much about language, speech, and silence as well. The event to which Lee returns is his mother's death from cancer. He narrates his attempt to come to terms with her death as well as with their life together as he grew up in America: her refusal to learn much English, her memories of the Japanese she had to learn when she was young, his own move away from the Korean language into English, and his attempt to write stories "with narrators and chief characters of unidentified race and ethnicity. Of course this meant they were white." For both Wideman and Lee (as it is for all of us), writing is grounded in who they are—their race, gender, social class, age, family, and the significant moments of their lives—and the writing itself becomes a means to make sense of their relation to the world they live in.

"Twas brillig, and the slithy toves/Did gyre and gimble in the wabe": the deliberately nonsensical language of Lewis Carroll's poem "Jabberwocky" is an apt allusion for Barbara Kingsolver's essay on public disinformation and misinformation in the U.S.A. in the late twentieth century. The other literary reference that comes to mind, especially given Kingsolver's shocking list of shocking facts most of us didn't know about the Gulf War, is George Orwell's sinister Newspeak in his dystopian novel *1984*. But Kingsolver's tone here, while quite serious, is ultimately upbeat about the potential for a writer to stay in touch with truth, so her choice of "Jabberwocky" over *1984* as a reference is appropriate. Carroll's poem is not only creatively nonsensical word play; it is also about military combat and deeply ingrained notions of heroism and honor which fathers pass on to their sons. What is the function of the artist in society and what is the responsibility of the artist to her or his society, Kingsolver asks? We live in a society that tries to separate art from politics and conscience, that brands as "political" any artist who does not mirror current conventional beliefs, and that frequently exercises censorship by refusing to publish such people, giving the reason that their work "wouldn't sell." Kingsolver is particularly convincing in this essay about fiction's power of empathy, its ability to put us inside another's point of view. Think about your own experiences of living someone else's life by reading fiction; as an exercise, you might try to write about a day in the life of someone quite different from yourself.

In biographical essays, John Dos Passos and Joan Didion consider two famous American artists, respectively architect Frank Lloyd Wright and landscape painter Georgia O'Keeffe. Both Wright and O'Keeffe are presented as quintessential American artists: they embody American individualism and wide open spaces, on the one hand, and iconoclastic, aggressive, annoying unconventionality, on the other. Dos Passos portrays Frank Lloyd Wright as a preacher and prophet of a new architectural vision that is based on the spaciousness of North American geography and on technological innovations in material. According to Dos Passos, Wright was an artist who "looked toward the American future instead of toward the pain-smeared past of Europe and Asia." Frank Lloyd Wright, as Dos Passos presents him, was a controversial figure, "not without honor except in his own country," rather like the truth-seeking artists Kingsolver mentions in "Jabberwocky."

Joan Didion's brilliant retrospective of Georgia O'Keeffe presents the artist as "hard," spare, uncompromising, and clear in her vision of America through its landscape. Didion chronicles O'Keeffe's move from flowers (however unconventional and sensual) to cow skulls draped in red, white, and blue, a development met by dismay from the art establishment. Like that of Wright, O'Keeffe's artistic vision left behind the crowded, convoluted East for the spacious open landscape and pure horizon line of the American West. Didion's essay is especially interesting in the way it contrasts O'Keeffe's clarity of vision to Didion's own more murky, ambiguous response to that vision, introduced in an anecdote about her daughter's response to one of O'Keeffe's "Sky Above Clouds" paintings.

In "Past Present," poet Jimmy Santiago Baca recounts a disturbing experience in which his past as a prisoner seems to rise up and meld with his present as a free man making a prison film. As do John Edgar Wideman and Chang-Rae Lee, Baca uses his writing to embody, to explore, to sort through, and finally, to come to terms with an experience. Perhaps more than that of either Wideman or Lee, Baca's essay is as much argument as memoir. The merging of the eighteen-year-old convicted prisoner with the thirty-year-old poet causes Baca to argue strongly for reform in the American justice system; he contends that serious criminals "comprise only a small proportion of our prison population." A poignant moment, and perhaps one that marks the reintegration of Baca's two selves, comes when he gives copies of his books of poetry to the prisoners who have worked with him on his film. "As they accepted these books of my poems, I saw respect in their eyes. To me, I was still one of them; for them, I was someone who had made it into a free and successful life. This sojourn in prison had confused me, reawakening the old consuming dragons of hatred and fear. But I had faced them, finally, and perhaps I will be a better poet for it. Time will tell."

We end this section on art and the artist with a sort of spoof, Toni Cade Bambara's "A Sort of Preface." In this brief essay, Bambara raises the question of the relation between fiction and real life from the writer's point of view. How many times when you read a story by someone you know do you ask, "Did that really happen?" It is a question that bubbles up quite readily. Probably, we all use real events, pieces of events, or the insights we gain from those events in our actual writing or in our other modes of self-construction. Even though telling the truth might be inevitable, Bambara warns laughingly of the potential hassles from family and friends if you reveal too much of yourself or of them in published (which means public) work. Bambara concludes by saying she chooses to deal in "straight-up fiction, . . . mostly cause I lie a lot anyway." But what is the difference for a writer between lying and invention, between reality and representation? Of course, the pieces in this section, however autobiographical, are nonfictional prose, not autobiographical fiction, but many of them use techniques of description and narration that we tend to associate with fiction. Whether in fictional or nonfictional prose, if they are good artists, writers select their images, facts, memories, anecdotes, stories, and philosophies to come to some truth about their world.

How does a poet put bread on the table?

Adrienne Rich

Adrienne Rich was born in Baltimore in 1929, studied at Radcliffe College, and won the Yale Younger Poets Award for her first book of poetry, A Change of World *(1951). She was active in the movement against the Vietnam War and in the 1970s became an important spokesperson for the women's movement. Rich has taught at City College in New York, at Douglass College, and elsewhere and has edited the lesbian-feminist journal* Sinister Wisdom. *Among her writings are the poetry collections* Diving into the Wreck *(1973),* The Dream of a Common Language *(1978),* Time's Power *(1989), and* Dark Fields of the Republic *(1995) and the nonfiction works* On Lies, Secrets, and Silence *(1979),* Blood, Bread, and Poetry *(1986), and* What Is Found There: Notebooks on Poetry and Politics *(1993), where the following appeared.*

But how does a poet put bread on the table? Rarely, if ever, by poetry alone. Of the four lesbian poets at the Nuyorican Poets Café[1] about whose lives I know something, one directs an underfunded community arts project, two are untenured college teachers, one an assistant dean of students at a state university. Of other poets I know, most teach, often part time, without security but year round; two are on disability; one does clerical work; one cleans houses; one is a paid organizer; one has a paid editing job. Whatever odd money comes in erratically from readings and workshops, grants, permissions fees, royalties, prizes can be very odd money indeed, never to be counted on and almost always small: checks have to be chased down, grants become fewer and more competitive in a worsening political and economic climate. Most poets who teach at universities are untenured, without pension plans or group health insurance, or are employed at public and community colleges with heavy teaching loads and low salaries. Many give unpaid readings and workshops as part of their political "tithe."

Inherited wealth accounts for the careers of some poets: to inherit wealth is to inherit time. Most of the poets I know, hearing of a sum of

---

[1] Multicultural center in New York City for performance-oriented poetry.

money, translate it not into possessions, but into time—that precious immaterial necessity of our lives. It's true that a poem can be attempted in brief interstitial moments, pulled out of the pocket and worked on while waiting for a bus or riding a train or while children nap or while waiting for a new batch of clerical work or blood samples to come in. But only certain kinds of poems are amenable to these conditions. Sometimes the very knowledge of coming interruption dampens the flicker. And there is a difference between the ordinary "free" moments stolen from exhausting family strains, from alienating labor, from thought chained by material anxiety, and those other moments that sometimes arrive in a life being lived at its height though under extreme tension: perhaps we are waiting to initiate some act we believe will catalyze change but whose outcome is uncertain; perhaps we are facing personal or communal crisis in which everything unimportant seems to fall away and we are left with our naked lives, the brevity of life itself, and words. At such times we may experience a speeding-up of our imaginative powers, images and voices rush together in a kind of inevitability, what was externally fragmented is internally reorganized, and the hand can barely keep pace.

But such moments presuppose other times: when we could simply stare into the wood grain of a door, or the trace of bubbles in a glass of water as long as we wanted to, *almost* secure in the knowledge that there would be no interruption—times of slowness, of purposelessness.

Often such time feels like a luxury, guiltily seized when it can be had, fearfully taken because it does not seem like work, this abeyance, but like "wasting time" in a society where personal importance—even job security— can hinge on acting busy, where the phrase "keeping busy" is a common idiom, where there is, for activists, so much to be done.

Most, if not all, of the names we know in North American poetry are the names of people who have had some access to freedom in time—that privilege of some which is actually a necessity for all. The struggle to limit the working day is a sacred struggle for the worker's freedom in time. To feel herself or himself, for a few hours or a weekend, as a free being with choices— to plant vegetables and later sit on the porch with a cold beer, to write poetry or build a fence or fish or play cards, to walk without a purpose, to make love in the daytime. To sleep late. Ordinary human pleasures, the self's recreation. Yet every working generation has to reclaim that freedom in time, and many are brutally thwarted in the effort. Capitalism is based on the abridgment of that freedom.

Poets in the United States have either had some kind of private means, or help from people with private means, have held full-time, consuming jobs, or have chosen to work in low-paying, part-time sectors of the economy, saving their creative energies for poetry, keeping their material wants simple. Interstitial living, where the art itself is not expected to bring in much money, where the artist may move from a clerical job to part-time, temporary teaching to subsistence living on the land to waitressing or doing construction or translating, typesetting, or ghostwriting. In the 1990s this kind of interstitial living is more difficult, risky, and wearing than it has ever been, and this is a loss to all the arts—as much as the shrinkage of arts funding, the censorship-by-clique, the censorship by the Right, the censorship by distribution.

STUDY AND DISCUSSION QUESTIONS

1. How do poets (and perhaps other writers and artists) tend to support themselves these days?

2. Look up "interstitial." Rich uses the word in two contexts; what does she mean in each case?

3. What amount and quality of time are needed to produce a creative work, according to Rich?

4. How does Adrienne Rich connect the plight of poets to that of other workers?

5. Why does Rich believe life has become harder for poets and other creative artists in the 1990s?

SUGGESTIONS FOR WRITING

1. Do you think poets/writers/artists in the United States should be granted money (and the time that money buys) so that they can produce poems, stories, paintings, sculptures, and other works of art? How might such an arrangement benefit our society, or not? Argue for or against, citing Rich's essay and any other evidence you have available.

FROM *BROTHERS AND KEEPERS*

John Edgar Wideman

*John Edgar Wideman was born in 1941 in Washington, D.C., stud-
ied at the University of Pennsylvania and at Oxford, and has taught at
a number of colleges. Among his books are the novels* A Glance Away
(1967) and Philadelphia Fire *(1990), the story collections* Dambal-
lah *(1981) and* All Stories Are True *(1992), and the nonfiction*
Brothers and Keepers *(1984) and* Fatheralong: A Meditation on
Fathers and Sons, Race and Society *(1994).*

I heard the news first in a phone call from my mother. My youngest brother,
Robby, and two of his friends had killed a man during a holdup. Robby was
a fugitive, wanted for armed robbery and murder. The police were hunting
him, and his crime had given the cops license to kill. The distance I'd put between my brother's world and mine suddenly collapsed. The two thousand
miles between Laramie, Wyoming, and Pittsburgh, Pennsylvania, my years
of willed ignorance, of flight and hiding, had not changed a simple truth: I
could never run fast enough or far enough. Robby was inside me. Wherever
he was, running for his life, he carried part of me with him.

Nearly three months would pass between the day in November 1975
when I learned of my brother's crime and the February afternoon he appeared in Laramie. During that period no one in the family knew Robby's
whereabouts. After the initial reaction of shock and disbelief subsided, people in Pittsburgh had settled into the inevitability of a long, tense wait.
Prayers were said. As word passed along the network of family and friends,
my people, who had long experience of waiting and praying, braced themselves for the next blow. A special watch was set upon those, like my mother,
who would be hardest hit. The best was hoped for, but the worst expected;
and no one could claim to know what the best might be. No news was good
news. No news meant Robby hadn't been apprehended, that whatever else
he'd lost, he still was free. But knowing nothing had its dark side, created a
concern that sometimes caused my mother, in spite of herself, to pray for
Robby's capture. Prison seemed safer than the streets. As long as he was free,
there was a chance Robby could hurt someone or be killed. For my mother

and the others who loved him, the price of my brother's freedom was a constant, gnawing fear that anytime the phone rang or a bulletin flashed across the TV screen, the villain, the victim might be Robert Wideman.

Because I was living in Laramie, Wyoming, I could shake loose from the sense of urgency, of impending disaster dogging my people in Pittsburgh. Never a question of forgetting Robby, more a matter of how I remembered him that distinguished my feelings from theirs. Sudden flashes of fear, rage, and remorse could spoil a class or a party, cause me to retreat into silence, lose whole days to gloominess and distance. But I had the luxury of dealing intermittently with my pain. As winter deepened and snow filled the mountains, I experienced a comforting certainty. The worst wouldn't happen. Robby wouldn't be cut down in a wild cops-and-robbers shootout, because I knew he was on his way to find me. Somehow, in spite of everything, we were going to get together. I was waiting for him to arrive. I knew he would. And this certainty guaranteed his safety.

Perhaps it was wishful thinking, a whistling away of the miles and years of silence between us, but I never doubted a reunion would occur.

On a Sunday early in February, huge, wet flakes of snow were falling continuously past the windows of the house on Harney Street—the kind of snow not driven by wolf winds howling in from the north, but soft, quiet, relentless snow, spring snow almost benign in the unhurried way it buried the town. The scale of the storm, the immense quantities of snow it dumped minute after minute, forced me to remember that Laramie was just one more skimpy circle of wagons huddling against the wilderness. I had closed the curtains to shut out that snow which seemed as if it might never stop.

That Sunday I wrote to my brother. Not a letter exactly. I seldom wrote letters and had no intention of sticking what I was scribbling in an envelope. Mailing it was impossible anyway, since I had no idea where my brother might be. Really it was more a conversation than a letter. I needed to talk to someone, and that Sunday Robby seemed the perfect someone.

So I talked to him about what I'd learned since coming west. Filled him in on the news. Shared everything from the metaphysics of the weather to the frightening circumstances surrounding the premature birth of Jamila, our new daughter. I explained how winter's outrageous harshness is less difficult to endure than its length. How after a tease of warm, springlike weather in late April the sight of a snowflake in May is enough to make a grown man cry. How Laramie old-timers brag about having seen snow fall every month of the year. How I'd almost killed my whole family on Interstate 80 near the summit of the Laramie range, at the beginning of our annual summer migration east to Maine, when I lost control of the Oldsmobile Custom Cruiser and it did a 360 on the icy road in the middle of June.

The letter rambled on and on for pages. Like good talk, it digressed and recycled itself and switched moods precipitously. Inevitably, one subject was home and family. After all, I was speaking to my brother. Whatever the new news happened to be, there was the old news, the deep roots of shared time and place and blood. When I touched on home, the distance between us melted. I could sense Robby's presence, just over my shoulder, a sensation so real I was sure I could have reached out and touched him if I had lifted my eyes from the page and swiveled my chair.

Writing that Sunday, I had no reason to believe my brother was on his way to Laramie. No one had heard from him in months. Yet he was on his way and I knew it. Two men, hundreds of miles apart, communicating through some mysterious process neither understood but both employed for a few minutes one Sunday afternoon as efficiently, effectively as dolphins talking underwater with the beeps and echoes of their sonar. Except that the medium into which we launched our signals was thin air. Thin, high mountain air spangled with wet snowflakes.

I can't explain how or why but it happened. Robby was in the study with me. He felt close because he was close, part of him outrunning the stolen car, outrunning the storm dogging him and his partners as they fled from Salt Lake City toward Laramie.

Reach out and touch. That's what the old songs could do. I'd begun that Sunday by reading a week-old *New York Times*. One of the beauties of living in Laramie. No point in frantically striving to keep abreast of the *Times*. The race was over before the paper arrived in town, Thursday after the Sunday it was published. The *Times* was stale news, all its urgency vitiated by the fact that I could miss it when it was fresh and the essential outline of my world, my retreat into willed ignorance and a private, leisurely pace would continue unchanged.

Five minutes of the paper had been enough; then I repacked the sections into their plastic sheath, let its weight pull it off the couch onto the rug. Reach out and touch. Sam Cooke and the Soul Stirrers, the Harmonizing Four, James Cleveland, the Davis Sisters, the Swan Silvertones. I dug out my favorite albums and lined them up against the stereo cabinet. A cut or two from each one would be my Sunday morning service. Deejaying the songs got me off my backside, forced me out of the chair where I'd been sitting staring at the ceiling. With good gospel tunes rocking the house I could open the curtains and face the snow. The sky was blue. Shafts of sunlight filtered through a deluge of white flakes. Snow, sunshine, blue sky, not a ripple of wind deflecting the heavy snow from its straight, downward path. An unlikely conjunction of elements perfectly harmonized. Like the pain and hope, despair and celebration of the black gospel music. Like the tiny body of the baby girl in her isolette, the minuscule, premature, two-pound-fourteen-ounce bundle of bone and sinew and nerve and will that had fought and continued to fight so desperately to live.

The songs had stirred me, flooded me with memories and sensations to the point of bursting. I had to talk to someone. Not anyone close, not anyone who had been living through what I'd been experiencing the past three years in the West. A stranger's ear would be better than a friend's, a stranger who wouldn't interrupt with questions, with alternate versions of events. I needed to do most of the talking. I wanted a listener, an intimate stranger, and summoned up Robby; and he joined me. I wrote something like a letter to wherever my brother might be, to whomever Robby had become.

Wrote the letter and of course never sent it, but got an answer anyway in just two days, the following Tuesday toward the end of the afternoon. I can pinpoint the hour because I was fixing a drink. Cocktail time is as much a state of mind as a particular hour, but during the week five o'clock is when I usually pour a stiff drink for myself and one for my lady if she's in the mood. At five on Tuesday, February 11, Robby phoned from a bowling alley down the street and around the corner to say he was in town.

Hey, Big Bruh.

Hey. How you doing? Where the hell are you?

We're in town. At some bowling alley. Me and Michael Dukes and Johnny-Boy.

In Laramie?

Yeah. Think that's where we's at, anyway. In a bowling alley. Them nuts is bowling. Got to get them crazy dudes out here before they tear the man's place up.

Well, youall c'mon over here. Which bowling alley is it?

Just a bowling alley. Got some Chinese restaurant beside it.

Laramie Lanes. It's close to here. I can be there in a minute to get you.

Okay. That's cool. We be in the car outside. Old raggedy-ass Oldsmobile got Utah plates. Hey, man. Is this gon be alright?

What do you mean?

You know. Coming by your house and all. I know you heard about the mess.

Mom called and told me. I've been waiting for you to show up. Something told me you were close. You wait. I'll be right there.

In Pittsburgh, Pennsylvania, on November 15, 1975, approximately three months before arriving in Laramie, my youngest brother Robert (whom I had named), together with Michael Dukes and Cecil Rice, had robbed a fence. A rented truck allegedly loaded with brand-new Sony color TVs was the bait in a scam designed to catch the fence with a drawer full of money. The plan had seemed simple and foolproof. Dishonor among thieves. A closed circle, crooks stealing from crooks, with the law necessarily excluded. Except a man was killed. Dukes blew him away when the man reached for a gun Dukes believed he had concealed inside his jacket.

Stop. Stop, you stupid motherfucker.

But the fence broke and ran and kept running deaf and dumb to everything except the pounding of his heart, the burning in his lungs, as he dashed crouching like a halfback the fifty feet from the empty rental truck to an office at one corner of his used-car lot. He'd heard the gun pop and pop again as he stumbled and scrambled to his feet but he kept running, tearing open the fatal shoulder wound he wasn't even aware of yet. Kept running and kept pumping blood and pumping his arms and legs past the plate-glass windows of the office, past a boundary of plastic banners strung above one edge of the lot, out into the street, into traffic, waving his arms to get someone to stop. He made it two blocks up Greys Pond Road, dripping a trail of blood, staggering, stumbling, weaving up the median strip between four lanes of cars. No one wanted anything to do with a guy drunk or crazy enough to be playing in the middle of a busy highway. Only when he pitched face first and lay crumpled on the curb did a motorist pull over and come to his aid.

Meanwhile, at the rear of the rental truck, a handful of money, coins, and wadded bills the dying man had flung down before he ran, lay on the asphalt between two groups of angry, frightened men. Black men. White men. No one in control. That little handful of chump change on the ground, not enough to buy two new Sonys at K Mart, a measure of the fence's deception, proof of the game he intended to run on the black men, just as they'd planned their trick for him. There had to be more money somewhere, and somebody would have to pay for this mess, this bloody double double-cross; and the men stared across the money at each other too choked with rage and fear to speak.

By Tuesday when Robby called, the chinook wind that had melted Sunday's snow no longer warmed and softened the air. "Chinook" means "snow-eater," and in the high plains country—Laramie sits on a plateau seven thousand feet above sea level—wind and sun can gobble up a foot of fresh snow from the ground in a matter of hours. The chinook had brought spring for a day, but just as rapidly as it appeared, the mellow wind had swept away, drawing in its wake arctic breezes and thick low-lying clouds. The clouds which had darkened the sky above the row of tacky, temporary-looking storefronts at the dying end of Third Street where Laramie Lanes hunkered.

Hey, Big Bruh.

Years since we'd spoken on the phone, but I had recognized Robby's voice immediately. He'd been with me when I was writing Sunday, so my brother's voice was both a shock and no surprise at all.

Big Brother was not something Robby usually called me. But he'd chimed the words as if they went way back, as if they were a touchstone, a talisman, a tongue-in-cheek greeting we'd been exchanging for ages. The way Robby said "Big Bruh" didn't sound phony, but it didn't strike me as natural either. What I'd felt was regret, an instant, devastating sadness because the greeting possessed no magic. If there'd ever been a special language we shared, I'd forgotten it. Robby had been pretending. Making up a magic formula on the spot. *Big Bruh.* But that had been okay. I was grateful. Anything was better than dwelling on the sadness, the absence, better than allowing the distance between us to stretch further. . . .

On my way to the bowling alley I began to ask questions I hadn't considered till the phone rang. I tried to anticipate what I'd see outside Laramie Lanes. Would I recognize anyone? Would they look like killers? What had caused them to kill? If they were killers, were they dangerous? Had crime changed my brother into someone I shouldn't bring near my house? I recalled Robby and his friends playing records, loud talking, giggling and signifying in the living room of the house on Marchand Street in Pittsburgh. Rob's buddies had names like Poochie, Dulamite, Hanky, and Bubba. Just kids messing around, but already secretive, suspicious of strangers. And I had been a stranger, a student, foreign to the rhythms of their lives, their talk as I sat, home from college, in the kitchen talking to Robby's mother. I'd have to yell into the living room sometimes. Ask them to keep the noise down so I could hear myself think. If I walked through the room, they'd fall suddenly silent. Squirm and look at each other and avoid my eyes. Stare at their own hands and feet mute as little speak-no-evil monkeys. Any question might get at best a nod or grunt in reply. If five or six kids were hanging out in the little living room they made it seem dark. *Do wop, do wop* forty-fives on the record player, the boys' silence and lowered eyes conjuring up night no matter what time of the day I passed through the room.

My father had called them thugs. Robby and his little thugs. The same word he'd used for me and my cut buddies when we were coming up, loafing around the house on Copeland Street, into playing records and bullshucking about girls, and saying nothing to nobody not part of our gang. Calling Rob's friends thugs was my father's private joke. Thugs not because they were incipient criminals or particularly bad kids, but because in their hip walks and stylized speech and caps pulled down on their foreheads they were declaring themselves on the lam, underground, in flight from the daylight world of nice, respectable adults.

My father liked to read the Sunday funnies. In the "Nancy" comic strip was a character named Sluggo, and I believe that's who my father had in mind when he called them thugs. That self-proclaimed little tough guy, snub-nosed, bristle-haired, knuckleheaded Sluggo. Funny, because like Sluggo they were dead serious about the role they were playing. Dead serious and fooling no-body. So my father had relegated them to the funny papers.

Road grime caked the windows of the battered sedan parked outside the bowling alley. I couldn't tell if anyone was inside. I let my motor run, talked to the ghost of my brother the way I'd talked that Sunday, waiting for a flesh-and-blood version to appear.

Robby was a fugitive. My little brother was wanted for murder. For three months Robby had been running and hiding from the police. Now he was in Laramie, on my doorstep. Robbery. Murder. Flight. I had pushed them out of my mind. I hadn't allowed myself to dwell on my brother's predicament. I had been angry, hurt and afraid, but I'd had plenty of practice cutting myself off from those sorts of feelings. Denying disruptive emotions was a survival mechanism I'd been forced to learn early in life. Robby's troubles could drive me crazy if I let them. It had been better to keep my feelings at a distance. Let the miles and years protect me. Robby was my brother, but that was once upon a time, in another country. My life was relatively comfortable, pleasant, safe. I'd come west to escape the demons Robby personified. I didn't need outlaw brothers reminding me how much had been lost, how much compromised, how terribly the world still raged beyond the charmed circle of my life on the Laramie plains.

In my Volvo, peering across the street, searching for a sign of life in the filthy car on the doorway of Laramie Lanes, pieces of my life rushed at me, as fleeting, as unpredictable as the clusters of cloud scudding across the darkening sky.

Rob. Hey, Rob. Do you remember the time we were living on the third floor of Grandma's house on Copeland Street and we were playing and Daddy came scooting in from behind the curtain where he and Mommy slept, dropping a trail of farts, blip, blip, blip, and flew out the door and down the steps faster than anybody'd ever made it before? I don't know what he was doing or what we were doing before he came farting through the room, but I do remember the stunned silence afterward, the five of us kids looking at one another like we'd seen the Lone Ranger[1] and wondering what the hell was that. Was that really Daddy? Were those sounds actual blipping farts from the actual behind of our actual father? Well, we sat on the floor, staring at each other, a couple seconds; then Tish laughed or I laughed. Somebody had to start it. A choked-back, closed-mouth, almost-swallowed, one-syllable laugh. And then another and another. As irresistible then as the farts blipping in a train from Daddy's pursed behind. The first laugh sneaks out then it's all hell bursting loose, it's one pop after another, and mize well let it all hang out. We crack up

---

[1] Hero of radio, film, and television westerns.

and start to dance. Each one of us takes a turn being Edgar Wideman, big daddy, scooting like he did across the floor, fast but sneakylike till the first blip escapes and blows him into overdrive. Bip. Blap. Bippidy-bip. And every change and permutation of fart we can manufacture with our mouths, or our wet lips on the back of our hands, or a hand cupped in armpit with elbow pumping. A Babel of squeaky farts and bass farts and treble and juicy and atom-bomb and trip-hammer, machine-gun, suede, firecracker, slithery, bubble-gum-cracking, knuckle-popping, gone-with-the-wind menagerie of every kind of fart we can imagine. Till Mommy pokes her head from behind the curtain and says, That's enough youall. But she can't help grinning her ownself cause she had to hear it too. Daddy trailing that wedding-car tin-can tail of farts and skidding down the steps to the bathroom on the second floor where he slammed the door behind himself before the door on the third floor had time to swing shut. Mom's smiling so we sputter one last fusillade and grin and giggle at each other one more time while she says again, That's enough now, that's enough youall.

Robby crossed Third Street alone, leaving his friends behind in the muddy car. I remember how glad I was to see him. How ordinary it seemed to be meeting him in this place he'd never been before. Here was my brother miraculously appearing from God-knows-where, a slim, bedraggled figure, looking very much like a man who's been on the road for days, nothing like an outlaw or killer, my brother striding across the street to greet me. What was alien, unreal was not the man but the town, the circumstances that had brought him to this juncture. By the time Robby had reached my car and leaned down smiling into the open window, Laramie, robbery, murder, flight, my litany of misgivings had all disappeared.

Rob rode with me from the bowling alley to the Harney Street house. Dukes and Johnny-Boy followed in the Olds. Rob told me Cecil Rice had split back to Pittsburgh to face the music. Johnny-Boy was somebody Robby and Mike had picked up in Utah.

Robby and his two companions stayed overnight. There was eating, drinking, a lot of talk. Next day I taught my classes at the university and before I returned home in the afternoon, Robby and his crew had headed for Denver. My brother's last free night was spent in Laramie, Wyoming. February 11, 1976, the day following their visit, Robby, Mike, and Johnny were arrested in Fort Collins, Colorado. The Oldsmobile they'd been driving had stolen plates. Car they'd borrowed in Utah turned out to be stolen too, bringing the FBI into the case because the vehicle and plates had been transported across state lines. The Colorado cops didn't know the size of the fish in their net until they checked the FBI wire and suddenly realized they had some "bad dudes" in their lockup. "Niggers wanted for Murder One back East" was how one detective described the captives to a group of curious bystanders later, when Robby and Michael were being led, manacled, draped with chains, through the gleaming corridor of a Colorado courthouse.

I can recall only a few details about Robby's last night of freedom. Kentucky Fried Chicken for dinner. Nobody as hungry as I thought they should be. Michael narrating a tale about a basketball scholarship he won to NYU,[2] his homesickness, his ambivalence about the Apple,[2] a coach he didn't like whose name he couldn't remember.

Johnny-Boy wasn't from Pittsburgh. Small, dark, greasy, he was an outsider who knew he didn't fit, ill at ease in a middle-class house, the meandering conversations that had nothing to do with anyplace he'd been, anything he understood or cared to learn. Johnny-Boy had trouble talking, trouble staying awake. When he spoke at all, he stuttered riffs of barely comprehensible ghetto slang. While the rest of us were talking, he'd nod off. I didn't like the way his heavy-lidded, bubble eyes blinked open and searched the room when he thought no one was watching him. Perhaps sleeping with one eye open was a habit forced upon him by the violent circumstances of his life, but what I saw when he peered from "sleep," taking the measure of his surroundings, of my wife, my kids, me, were a stranger's eyes, a stranger's eyes with nothing in them I could trust.

I should have understood why the evening was fragmentary, why I have difficulty recalling it now. Why Mike's story was full of inconsistencies, nearly incoherent. Why Robby was shakier than I'd ever seen him. Why he was tense, weary, confused about what his next move should be. I'm tired, man, he kept saying. I'm tired. . . . You don't know what it's like, man. Running . . . running. Never no peace. Certain signs were clear at the time but they passed right by me. I thought I was giving my guests a few hours' rest from danger, but they knew I was turning my house into a dangerous place. I believed I was providing a respite from pursuit. They knew they were leaving a trail, complicating the chase by stopping with me and my family. A few "safe" hours in my house weren't long enough to come down from the booze, dope, and adrenaline high that fueled their flight. At any moment my front door could be smashed down. A gunfire fight begin. I thought they had stopped, but they were still on the road. I hadn't begun to explore the depths of my naïveté, my bewilderment.

Only after two Laramie Police Department detectives arrived at dawn on February 12, a day too late to catch my brother, and treated me like a criminal, did I know I'd been one. Aiding and abetting a fugitive. Accessory after the fact to the crime of first-degree murder. The detectives hauled me down to the station. Demanded that I produce an alibi for the night a convenience store had been robbed in Utah. Four black men had been involved. Three had

---

[2] NYU, New York University; the Apple, New York City.

been tentatively identified, which left one unaccounted for. I was black. My brother was a suspect. So perhaps I was the fourth perpetrator. No matter that I lived four hundred miles from the scene of the crime. No matter that I wrote books and taught literature and creative writing at the university. I was black. Robby was my brother. Those unalterable facts would always incriminate me.

Robby passed through Laramie briefly and continued on his way. That's about it. I wished for more, then and now. Most of what I can recall makes the evening of his visit seem bland, uneventful, though an incident in Jamila's room, beside her crib, is an exception. That and the moment I watched Robby's shoulders disappear down the hallway stairs to the kids' playroom, where a roll-away cot and some extra mattresses had been set out for sleeping. Those moments imprinted. I'll carry the sounds and sights to my grave.

I'd been alone with my brother a few minutes in the kitchen, then in the hall outside Jamila's room. I advised him to stay in Laramie a few days, catch his breath, unwind. Warned him about the shoot-em-up mentality of Western cops, the subtle and not-so-subtle racism of the region. How three black men in a car would arouse suspicion anytime, anywhere they stopped.

Little else to say. I started a thousand conversations inside my head. None was appropriate, none addressed Robby's anguish, his raw nerves. He was running, he was afraid, and nothing anyone said could bring the dead man in Pittsburgh back to life. I needed to hear Robby's version of what had happened. Had there been a robbery, a shooting? Why? Why?

In our first private moment since I'd picked him up at Laramie Lanes, as we stood outside the baby's room, my questions never got asked. Too many whys. Why did I want to know? Why was I asking? Why had this moment been so long in coming? Why was there a murdered man between us, another life to account for, now when we had just a few moments alone together? Perhaps Robby did volunteer a version of the crime. Perhaps I listened and buried what I heard. What I remember is telling him about the new baby. In the hall, then in her room, when we peeked in and discovered her wide awake in her crib, I recounted the events surrounding her birth.

Jamila. Her name means "beautiful" in Arabic. Not so much outer good looks as inner peace, harmony. At least that's what I've been told. Neither Judy nor I knew the significance of the name when we chose it. We just liked the sound. It turns out to fit perfectly.

Your new niece is something else. Beautiful inside and out. Hard to believe how friendly and calm she is after all she's been through. You're the first one from home to see her.

I didn't tell my brother the entire story. We'd need more time. Anyway, Judy should fill in the gory details. In a way it's her story. I'd almost lost them both, wife and daughter. Judy had earned the right to tell the story. Done the bleeding. She was the one who nearly died giving birth.

Besides, on that night eight years ago I wasn't ready to say what I felt. The incidents were too close, too raw. The nightmare ride behind an ambulance, following it seventy miles from Fort Collins to Denver. Not knowing, the whole time, what was happening inside the box of flashing lights that held my wife. Judy's water had broken just after a visit to a specialist in Fort Collins. Emergency procedures were necessary because she had developed placenta previa, a condition that could cause severe hemorrhaging in the mother and fatal prematurity for her baby. I had only half listened to the doctor's technical explanation of the problem. Enough to know it could be life-threatening to mother and infant. Enough to picture the unborn child trapped in its watery cell. Enough to get tight-jawed at the irony of nature working against itself, the shell of flesh and blood my woman's body had wrapped round our child to protect and feed it also blocking the exit from her womb. Placenta previa meant a child's only chance for life was cesarian section, with all the usual attendant risks extremely heightened.

Were the technicians in the back of the ambulance giving blood, taking blood? Were they administering oxygen to my wife? To our child? Needles, tubes, a siren wailing, the crackle of static as the paramedics communicated with doctors in Denver. Had the fetus already been rushed into the world, flopping helpless as a fish because its lungs were still too much like gills to draw breath from the air?

A long, bloody birth in Denver. Judy on the table three and a half hours. Eight pints of blood fed into her body as eight pints seeped out into a calibrated glass contained beside the operating table. I had watched it happening. Tough throughout the cutting, the suturing, the flurries of frantic activity, the appearance of the slick, red fetus, the snipping of the umbilical, the discarding of the wet, liverish-looking, offending bag, tough until near the end when the steady ping, ping, ping of blood dripping into the jar loosened the knot of my detachment and my stomach flip-flopped once uncontrollably, heaving up bile to the brim of my throat. Had to get up off the stool then, step back from the center of the operating room, gulp fresh air.

With Judy recovered and Jamila home, relatively safe after a two-month ordeal in the hospital, I still couldn't talk about how I had felt during my first visit to the preemie ward at Colorado General. I was shocked by the room full of tiny, naked, wrinkled infants, each enclosed in a glass cage. Festooned with tubes and needles, they looked less like babies than like ancient, shrunken little men and women, prisoners gathered for some bizarre reason to die together under the sizzling lights.

Jamila's arms and legs were thinner than my thinnest finger. Her threadlike veins were always breaking down from the pressure of I.V.'s. Since

I.V.'s were keeping her alive, the nurses would have to search for new places to stick the needles. Each time she received an injection or had her veins probed for an I.V., Jamila would holler as if she'd received the final insult, as if after all the willpower she'd expended enduring the pain and discomfort of birth, no one had anything better to do than jab her one more time. What made her cries even harder to bear was their tininess. In my mind her cries rocked the foundations of the universe; they were bellows anything, anywhere with ears and a soul could hear. In fact, the high-pitched squeaks were barely audible a few feet from her glass cage. You could see them better than hear them because the effort of producing each cry wracked her body.

My reactions to the preemie ward had embarrassed me. I couldn't help thinking of the newborns as diseased or unnatural, as creatures from another planet, miniature junkies feeding in transparent kennels. I had to get over the shame of acknowledging my daughter was one of them. Sooner than I expected, the shame, the sense of failure disintegrated and was replaced by fear, a fear I had yet to shake. Would probably never completely get over. The traumas attending her birth, the long trial in the premature ward, her continuous touch-and-go flirtation with death had enforced the reality of Jamila's mortality. My fear had been morbid at first but gradually it turned around. Each breath she drew, each step she negotiated became cause for celebration. I loved all my children, but this girl child was precious in a special way that had brought me closer to all three. Life and death. Pain and joy. Having and losing. You couldn't experience one without the other. Background and foreground. The presence of my daughter would always remind me that things didn't have to be the way they were. We could have lost her. Could lose her today. And that was the way it would always be. Ebb and flow. Touch and go. Her arrival shattered complacency. When I looked in her eyes I was reminded to love her and treasure her and all the people I loved because nothing could be taken for granted.

I had solemnly introduced the new baby to my brother.

This is your Uncle Robby.

Robby's first reaction had been to say, grinning from ear to ear, She looks just like Mommy. . . . My God, she's a little picture of Mom.

As soon as Robby made the connection, its rightness, its uncontestability, its uncanny truth hit me. Of course. My mother's face rose from the crib. I remembered a sepia, tattered-edged, oval portrait of Mom as a baby. And another snapshot of Bette French in Freeda French's lap on the steps of the house on Cassina Way. The fifty-year-old images hovered, opaque, halfway between the crib and my eyes, then faded, dissolving slowly, blending into the baby's face, alive inside the new skin, part of the new life, linked forever by my brother's words.

Robby took the baby in his arms. Coochy-cooed and gently rocked her, still marveling at the resemblance.

Lookit those big, pretty brown eyes. Don't you see Mommy's eyes?

Time continues to loosen my grasp on the events of Robby's last free night. I've attempted to write about my brother's visit numerous times since. One version was called "Running"; I conceived of it as fiction and submitted it to a magazine. The interplay between fiction and fact in the piece was too intense, too impacted, finally too obscure to control. Reading it must have been like sitting down at a bar beside a stranger deeply involved in an intimate conversation with himself. That version I'd thought of as a story was shortened and sent to Robby in prison. Though it didn't quite make it as a story, the letter was filled with stories on which I would subsequently draw for two novels and a book of short fiction.

Even as I manufactured fiction from the events of my brother's life, from the history of the family that had nurtured us both, I knew something of a different order remained to be extricated. The fiction writer was also a man with a real brother behind real bars. I continued to feel caged by my bewilderment, by my inability to see clearly, accurately, not only the last visit with my brother, but the whole long skein of our lives together and apart. So this book. This attempt to break out, to knock down the walls.

At a hearing in Colorado Johnny-Boy testified that Robby had recounted to him a plot to rob a fence, a killing, the flight from Pittsburgh. After his performance as a cooperative witness for the state, a performance he would repeat in Pittsburgh at Robby's trial, Johnny-Boy was carted away to Michigan, where he was wanted for murder. Robby and Michael were extradited to Pittsburgh, charged with armed robbery and murder, and held for trial. In separate trials both were convicted and given the mandatory sentence for felony murder: life imprisonment without possibility of probation or parole. The only way either man will ever be released is through commutation of his sentence. Pennsylvania's governor is empowered to commute prison sentences, and a state board of commutations exists to make recommendations to him; but since the current governor almost never grants commutations, men in Pennsylvania's prisons must face their life sentences with minimal hope of being set free.

Robby remained in custody six months before going on trial. Not until July 1978, after a two-year lockup in a county jail with no facilities for long-term prisoners, was Robby sentenced. Though his constitutional rights to a speedy trial and speedy sentencing had clearly been violated, neither those wrongs nor any others—including a prejudiced charge to the jury by the trial judge—which were brought to the attention of the Pennsylvania Supreme Court, moved that august body to intercede on Robert Wideman's behalf. The last legal action in Robby's case, the denial of his appeal by the Supreme

Court of Pennsylvania, did not occur until September 1981. By that time Robby had already been remanded to Western State Penitentiary to begin serving a life sentence.

STUDY AND DISCUSSION QUESTIONS

1. Where in the introductory paragraphs does Wideman move from introduction into narration? What lets you know he has made this move?

2. Why is John Wideman's experience of his brother's calamity different from that of the rest of their family?

3. What kinds of things does Wideman tell his brother in the letter he doesn't plan to mail? Why does he need to write the letter?

4. What does Wideman say about his brother's adolescence? Was it different from his own? Why do you think he muses about his brother's teenage years?

5. Analyze the paragraph that begins, "Robby was a fugitive. . . ." What emotions is Wideman experiencing here? Is this a turning point in the essay?

6. What happens to the author the day after his brother leaves, and why does it happen?

7. How does Wideman describe and react to the birth experience shared by his wife and child?

8. What does he learn from Jamila?

9. What effect does the fact that Wideman is a black American have on the experiences he writes about in this memoir? To what extent does Wideman address race directly in this piece and to what extent does he let the facts speak for themselves?

SUGGESTIONS FOR WRITING

1. Wideman tells two stories in this memoir: of his fugitive brother's arrival at his house, and of the life-threatening premature birth of his daughter. Why does he associate these two events? What connections do you see between them?

2. Wideman writes in the opening paragraph: "The distance I'd put between my brother's world and mine suddenly collapsed." Later, he writes: "I'd come west to escape the demons Robby personified." What is Wideman referring to and how does he convey to his readers the dangers he's escaped from and the choices he's made?

3. In the paragraph that begins, "Even as I manufactured fiction from the events of my brother's life . . . ," Wideman seems to be giving an explanation for why he is writing. Discuss. Why does this event—having his fugitive brother spend a night with him in Laramie, Wyoming—seem to become a defining moment for Wideman? Have you experienced a significant or defining moment to which your thoughts and emotions keep returning?

The Faintest Echo of Our Language

Chang-Rae Lee

Chang-Rae Lee was born in 1965 in Seoul, Korea, and moved to the United States at age three. He studied at Yale and at the University of Oregon, where he teaches creative writing. His first novel, Native Speaker, *was published in 1995. The following essay originally appeared in* The New England Review *in 1993.*

My mother died on a bare January morning in our family room, the room all of us favored. She died upon the floor-bed I had made up for her, on the old twin mattress from the basement that I slept on during my childhood. She died with her husband kneeling like a penitent boy at her ear, her daughter tightly grasping the soles of her feet, and her son vacantly kissing the narrow, brittle fingers of her hand. She died with her best friend weeping quietly above her, and with her doctor unmoving and silent. She died with no accompaniment of music or poetry or prayer. She died with her eyes and mouth open. She died blind and speechless. She died, as I knew she would, hearing the faintest echo of our language at the last moment of her mind.

That, I think, must be the most ardent of moments.

I keep considering it, her almost-ending time, ruminating the nameless, impossible mood of its ground, toiling over it like some desperate topographer whose final charge is to survey only the very earth beneath his own shifting feet. It is an improbable task. But I am continually traveling through that terrible province, into its dark region where I see again and again the strangely vast scene of her demise.

I see.

Here before me (as I now enter my narrative moment), the dying-room, our family room. It has changed all of a sudden—it is as if there has been a shift in its proportion, the scale horribly off. The room seems to open up too fast, as though the walls were shrinking back and giving way to the wood flooring that seems to unfurl before us like runaway carpet. And there, perched on this crest somehow high above us, her body so flat and quiet in the bed, so resident, so immovable, caught beneath the somber light of these unwinking lamps, deep among the rolls of thick blankets, her furniture pushed to the walls without scheme, crowded in by the medicines, syringes, clear tubing, machines, shot through with the full false hopes of the living and the fearsome calls of the dead, my mother resides at an unfathomable center where the time of my family will commence once again.

No one is speaking. Except for the babble of her machines the will of silence reigns in this house. There is no sound, no word or noise, that we might offer up to fill this place. She sleeps for a period, then reveals her live eyes. For twelve or eighteen hours we have watched her like this, our legs and feet deadened from our squatting, going numb with tired blood. We sometimes move fitfully about, sighing and breathing low, but no one strays too far. The living room seems too far, the upstairs impossible. There is nothing, nothing at all outside of the house. I think perhaps it is snowing but it is already night and there is nothing left but this room and its light and its life.

People are here earlier (when?), a group from the church, the minister and some others. I leave her only then, going through the hallway to the kitchen. They say prayers and sing hymns. I do not know the high Korean words (I do not know many at all), and the music of their songs does not comfort me. Their one broad voice seems to be calling, beckoning something, bared in some kind of sad invitation. It is an acknowledgment. These people, some of them complete strangers, have come in from the outside to sing and pray over my mother, their overcoats still bearing the chill of the world.

I am glad when they are finished. They seem to sing too loud; I think they are hurting her ears—at least, disturbing her fragile state. I keep thinking, as if in her mind: *I'm finally going to get my sleep, my sleep after all this raw and painful waking, but I'm not meant to have it. But sing, sing.*

When the singers finally leave the room and quickly put on their coats I see that the minister's wife has tears in her eyes: so it is that clear. She looks at me; she wants to say something to me but I can see from her stunted expression that the words will not come. Though I wanted them earlier to cease I know already how quiet and empty it will feel when they are gone. But we are all close together now in the foyer, touching hands and hugging each other, our faces flushed, not talking but assenting to what we know, moving our lips in a silent, communal speech. For what we know, at least individually, is still unutterable, dwelling peacefully in the next room as the unnameable, lying there and waiting beside her, and yet the feeling among us is somehow so formidable and full of hope, and I think if I could hear our thoughts going round the room they would speak like the distant report of ten thousand monks droning the song of the long life of the earth.

Long, long life. Sure life. It had always seemed that way with us, with our square family of four, our destiny clear to me and my sister when we would sometimes speak of ourselves, not unlucky like those friends of ours whose families were wracked with ruinous divorce or drinking or disease—we were untouched, maybe untouchable, we'd been safe so far in our isolation in this country, in the country of our own house smelling so thickly of crushed garlic and seaweed and red chili pepper, as if that piquant wreath of scent from our mother's kitchen protected us and our house, kept at bay the persistent ghosts of the land who seemed to visit everyone else.

Of course, we weren't perfectly happy or healthy. Eunei and I were sometimes trouble to my parents, we were a little lazy and spoiled (myself more than my sister), we didn't study hard enough in school (though we always received the highest marks), we chose questionable friends, some from broken families, and my father, who worked fourteen hours a day as a young psychiatrist, already suffered from mild hypertension and high cholesterol.

If something happened to him, my mother would warn me, if he were to die, we'd lose everything and have to move back to Korea, where the living was hard and crowded and where all young men spent long years in the military. Besides, our family in Korea—the whole rest of it still there (for we were the lone émigrés)—so longed for us, missed us terribly, and the one day each year when we phoned, they would plead for our return. What we could do, my mother said, to aid our father and his struggle in this country, was to relieve his worry over us, release him from that awful burden through our own hard work which would give him ease of mind and help him not to die.

My mother's given name was Inja, although I never once called her that, nor ever heard my sister or even my father address her so. I knew from a young age that her name was Japanese in style and origin, from the time of Japan's military occupation of Korea, and I've wondered since why she chose never to change it to an authentic Korean name, why her mother or father didn't change the names of all their daughters after the liberation. My mother often showed open enmity for the Japanese, her face seeming to ash over when she spoke of her memories, that picture of the platoon of lean-faced soldiers burning books and scrolls in the center of her village still aglow in my head (but from her or where else I don't know), and how they tried to erase what was Korean by criminalizing the home language and history by shipping slave labor, draftees, and young Korean women back to Japan and its other Pacific colonies. How they taught her to speak in Japanese. And as she would speak of her childhood, of the pretty, stern-lipped girl (that I only now see in tattered rust-edged photos) who could only whisper to her sisters in the midnight safety of their house the Korean words folding inside her all day like mortal secrets, I felt the same burning, troubling lode of utter pride and utter shame still jabbing at the sweet belly of her life, that awful gem, about who she was and where her mother tongue and her land had gone.

She worried all the time that I was losing my Korean. When I was in my teens, she'd get attacks of despair and urgency and say she was going to send me back to Korea for the next few summers to learn the language again. What she didn't know was that it had been whole years since I had lost the language, had left it somewhere for good, perhaps from the time I won a prize in the first grade for reading the most books in my class. I must have read fifty books. She had helped me then, pushed me to read and then read more to exhaustion until I fell asleep, because she warned me that if I didn't learn English I wouldn't be anybody and couldn't really live here like a true American. *Look at me,* she'd say, offering herself as a sad example, *look how hard it is for me to shop for food or speak to your teachers, look how shameful I am, how embarrassing.*

Her words frightened me. But I was so proud of myself and my prolific reading, particularly since the whole year before in kindergarten I could barely speak a word of English. I simply listened. We played mostly anyway, or drew pictures. When the class sang songs I'd hum along with the melody and silently mouth the strange and difficult words. My best friend was another boy in the class who also knew no English, a boy named Tommy. He was Japanese. Of course, we couldn't speak to each other but it didn't matter; somehow we found a way to communicate through gestures and funny faces and laughter, and we became friends. I think we both sensed we were the smartest kids in the class. We'd sit off by ourselves with this one American girl who liked us best and play house around a wooden toy oven. I've forgotten her name. She'd hug us when we "came home from work," her two mute husbands, and she would sit us down at the little table and work a pan at the stove and bring it over and feed us. We pretended to eat her food until we were full and then she'd pull the two of us sheepish and cackling over to the shaggy remnants of carpet that she'd laid down, and we'd all go to sleep, the girl nestled snuggly between Tommy and me, hotly whispering in our ears the tones of a night music she must have heard echoing through her own house.

Later that year, after a parents' visiting day at school, my mother told me that Tommy and his family were moving away. I didn't know how she'd found that out, but we went to his house one day, and Tommy and his mother greeted us at the door. They had already begun packing, and there were neatly stacked boxes and piles of newspapers pushed to a corner of their living room. Tommy immediately led me outside to his swing set and we horsed about for an hour before coming back in, and I looked at my mother and Tommy's mother sitting upright and formally in the living room, a tea set and plate of rice cookies between them on the coffee table. The two of them weren't really talking, more smiling and waiting for us. And then from Tommy's room full of toys, I began to hear a conversation, half of it in profoundly broken English, the other half in what must have been Japanese, at once breathy and staccato, my mother's version of it in such shreds and remnants that the odd sounds she made seemed to hurt her throat as they were called up. After we said goodbye and drove away in the car, I thought she seemed quiet and sad for me, and so I felt sadder still, though now I think that it was she who was moved and saddened by the visit, perhaps by her own act. For the momentary sake of her only son and his departing friend, she was willing to endure those two tongues of her shame, one present, one past. Language, sacrifice, the story never ends.

Inside our house (wherever it was, for we moved several times when I was young) she was strong and decisive and proud; even my father deferred to her in most matters, and when he didn't it seemed that she'd arranged it that way. Her commandments were stiff, direct. When I didn't listen to her, I understood that the disagreement was my burden, my problem. But outside, in the land of always-talking strangers and other Americans, my mother would lower her steadfast eyes, she'd grow mute, even her supremely solemn and sometimes severe face would dwindle with uncertainty; I would have to speak to a mechanic for her, I had to call the school myself when I was sick, I would write out notes to neighbors, the postman, the paper carrier. Do the work of voice. Negotiate *us,* with this here, now. I remember often fuming because of it, this one of the recurring pangs of my adolescence, feeling frustrated with her inabilities, her misplacement, and when she asked me one morning to call up the bank for her I told her I wouldn't do it and suggested that she needed "to practice" the language anyway.

Gracious God. I wished right then for her to slap me. She didn't. Couldn't. She wanted to scream something, I could tell, but bit down on her lip as she did and hurried upstairs to her bedroom, where I knew she found none of this trouble with her words. There she could not fail, nor could I. In that land, her words sang for her, they did good work, they pleaded for my life, shouted entreaties, ecstasies, they could draw blood if they wanted, and they could offer grace, and they could kiss.

But now—and I think, *right now* (I am discovering several present tenses)— she is barely conscious, silent.

Her eyes are very small and black. They are only half opened. I cannot call up their former kind shade of brown. Not because I am forgetting, but because it is impossible to remember. I think I cannot remember the first thing about her. I am not amnesiac, because despite all this *I know everything about her.* But the memories are like words I cannot call up, the hidden vocabularies of our life together. I cannot remember, as I will in a later narrative time, her bright red woolen dress with the looming black buttons that rub knobbly and rough against my infant face; I cannot remember, as I will soon dream it, the way her dark clean hair falls on me like a cloak when she lifts me from the ground; I cannot remember—if I could ever truly forget—the look of those soft Korean words as they play on her face when she speaks to me of honor and respect and devotion.

This is a maddening state, maybe even horrifying, mostly because I think I must do anything but reside in this very place and time and moment, that to be able to remember her now—something of her, anything—would be to forget the present collection of memories, this inexorable gathering of future remembrances. I want to disband this accumulation, break it apart before its bonds become forever certain.

She wears only a striped pajama top. Her catheter tube snakes out from between the top buttons. We know she is slipping away, going fast now, so someone, not me, disconnects the line to her food and water. The tube is in her way. These last moments will not depend on it. Her line to the morphine, though, is kept open and clear and running.

This comforts me. I have always feared her pain and I will to the end. Before she received the automatic pump that gives her a regular dosage of the drug, I would shoot her with a needle at least five times a day.

For some reason I wish I could do it now:

I will have turned her over gently. She will moan. Every movement except the one mimicking death is painful. I fit the narrow white syringe with a small needle, twisting it on tight. I then pull off the needle's protective plastic sheath. (Once, I will accidentally jab myself deep in the ring finger and while I hold gauze to the bloody wound she begins to cry. I am more careful after that.) Now I fill the syringe to the prescribed line, and then I go several lines past it; I always give her a little more than what the doctors tell us, and she knows of this transgression, my little gift to her, to myself. I say I am ready and then she lifts her hips so I can pull down her underwear to reveal her buttocks.

I know her body. The cancer in her stomach is draining her, hungrily sucking the life out of her, but the liquid food she gets through the tube has so many calories that it bloats her, giving her figure the appearance of a young girl who likes sweets too well. Her rump is full, fleshy, almost healthy-looking except for the hundreds of needle marks. There is almost no space left. I do not think it strange anymore that I see her naked like this. Even the sight of her pubic hair, darkly coursing out from under her, is now, if anything, of a certain more universal reminiscence, a kind of metonymic reminder that not long before she was truly in the world, one of its own, a woman, fully alive, historical, a mother, a bearer of life.

I feel around for unseeable bruises until I find a spot we can both agree on.

"Are you ready?" I say. "I'm going to poke."

"*Gu-rhaeh,*" she answers, which, in this context, means some cross between "That's right" and "Go ahead, damn it."

I jab and she sucks in air between her teeth, wincing.

"*Ay, ah-po.*" *It hurts.*

"A lot?" I ask, pulling the needle out as straight as I can, to avoid bruising her. We have the same exchange each time; but each time there arises a renewed urgency, and then I know I know nothing of her pains.

I never dreamed of them. Imagined them. I remember writing short stories in high school with narrators or chief characters of unidentified race and ethnicity. Of course this meant they were white, everything in my stories was some kind of white, though I always avoided physical descriptions of them or passages on their lineage and they always had cryptic first names like Garlo or Kram.

Mostly, though, they were figures who (I thought) could appear in an *authentic* short story, *belong* to one, that no reader would notice anything amiss in them, as if they'd inhabited forever those visionary landscapes of tales and telling, where a snow still falls faintly and faintly falls over all of Joyce's Ireland, that great muting descent, all over Hemingway's Spain, and Cheever's Suburbia, and Bellow's City of Big Shoulders.[1]

I was to breach that various land, become its finest citizen and furiously speak its dialects. And it was only with one story that I wrote back then, in which the character is still unidentified but his *mother* is Asian (maybe even Korean), that a cleaving happened. That the land broke open at my feet. At the end of the story, the protagonist returns to his parents' home after a long journey; he is ill, feverish, and his mother tends to him, offers him cool drink, compresses, and she doesn't care where he's been in the strange wide country. They do not speak; she simply knows that he is home.

Now I dab the pinpoint of blood. I'm trying to be careful.

"*Gaen-cha-na,*" she says. *It is fine.*

"Do you need anything?"

"*Ggah,*" she says, flitting her hand, "*kul suh.*" *Go, go and write.*

---

[1] James Joyce, Ernest Hemingway, John Cheever, and Saul Bellow are fiction writers; the City of Big Shoulders is Chicago.

"What do you want? Anything, anything."

"*In-jeh na jal-leh.*" *Now I want to sleep.*

"Okay, sleep. Rest. What?"

"*Boep-bo.*" *Kiss.*

"Kiss."

Kiss.

This will be our language always. To me she speaks in a child's Korean, and for her I speak that same child's English. We use only the simplest words. I think it strange that throughout this dire period we necessarily speak like this. Neither of us has ever grown up or out of this language; by virtue of speech I am forever her perfect little boy, she my eternal righteous guide. We are locked in a time. I love her, and I cannot grow up. And if all mothers and sons converse this way I think the communication must remain for the most part unconscious; for us, however, this speaking is everything we possess. And although I wonder if our union is handicapped by it I see also the minute discoveries in the mining of the words. I will say to her as naturally as I can— as I could speak only years before as a child—*I love you, Mother,* and then this thing will happen, the diction will take us back, bridge this moment with the others, remake this time so full and real. And in our life together, our strange language is the bridge and all that surrounds it; language is the brook streaming through it; it is the mossy stones, the bank, the blooming canopy above, the ceaseless sound, the sky. It is the last earthly thing we have.

My mother, no longer connected to her machine, lies on the bed on the floor. Over the last few hours she suffers brief fits and spasms as if she is chilled. She stirs when we try to cover her with the blanket. She kicks her legs to get it off. Something in her desires to be liberated. Finally we take it away. Let her be, we think. And now, too, you can begin to hear the indelicate sound of her breathing; it is audible, strangely demonstrative. Her breath resonates in this house, begins its final cadence. She sounds as though she were inhaling and exhaling for the very first time. Her body shudders with that breath. My sister tries to comfort her by stroking her arms. My mother groans something unintelligible, though strangely I say to myself for her, *Leave me alone, all of you. I am dying. At last I am dying.* But then I stroke her, too. She keeps shuddering, but it is right.

What am I thinking? Yes. It is that clear. The closer she slips away, down into the core of her being, what I think of as an origin, a once-starting point, the more her body begins to protest the happening, to try to hold down, as I am, the burgeoning, blooming truth of the moment.

For we think we know how this moment will be. Each of us in this room has been elaborating upon it from the very moment we gained knowledge of her illness. This is the way it comes to me, but I think we have written, each of us, the somber epic novel of her death. It has taken two and one-half years and we are all nearly done. I do not exactly know of the others' endings. Eunei, my sister (if I may take this liberty), perhaps envisioning her mother gently falling asleep, never really leaving us, simply dreams of us and her life for the rest of ever. I like that one.

My father, a physician, may write that he finally saves her, that he spreads his hands on her belly where the cancer is mighty and lifts it out from her with one ultimate, sovereign effort. Sometimes (and this ought not be attributed to him) I think that his entire life has come down to this struggle against the palpable fear growing inside of his wife. And after she dies, he will cry out in a register I have never heard from his throat as he pounds his hand on the hardwood above her colorless head, *"Eeh-guh-moy-yah? Eeh-guh-moy-yah?"* *What is this? What is this?* It—the cancer, the fear—spites him, mocks him, this doctor who is afraid of blood. It—this cancer, this happening, this time—is the shape of our tragedy, the cruel sculpture of our life and family.

In the ending to my own story, my mother and I are alone. We are always alone. And one thing is certain; she needs to say something only to me. That is why I am there. Then she speaks to me, secretly. What she says exactly is unclear; it is enough, somehow, that she and I are together, alone, apart from everything else, while we share this as yet unborn and momentary speech. The words are neither in Korean nor in English, languages which in the end we cannot understand. I hear her anyway. But now we can smile and weep and laugh. We can say goodbye to each other. We can kiss, unflinching, on our mouths.

Then she asks if I might carry her to the window that she might see the new blossoms of our cherry tree. I lift her. She is amazingly light, barely there, barely physical, and while I hold her up she reaches around my neck and leans her head against my shoulder. I walk with her to the window and then turn so that she faces the tree. I gaze longingly at it myself, marveling at the gaudy flowers, and then I turn back upon her face, where the light is shining, and I can see that her eyes have now shut, and she is gone.

But here in this room we are not alone. I think she is probably glad for this, as am I. Her breathing, the doctor says, is becoming labored. He kneels and listens to her heart. "I think we should be ready," he says. "Your mother is close." He steps back. He is a good doctor, a good friend. I think he can see the whole picture of the time. And I think about what he is saying: *Your mother is close.* Yes. Close to us, close to life, close to death. She is close to everything, I think; she is attaining an irrevocable nearness of being, a proximity to everything that has been spoken or written or thought, in every land and language on earth. How did we get to this place? Why are we here in this room, assembled as we are, as if arrayed in some ancient haunted painting whose grave semblance must be known in every mind and heart of man?

I count a full five between her breaths. The color is leaving her face. The mask is forming. Her hand in mine is cold, already dead. I think it is now that I must speak to her. I understand that I am not here to listen; that must be for another narrative. I am not here to bear her in my arms toward bright windows. I am not here to be strong. I am not here to exchange goodbyes. I am not here to recount old stories. I am not here to acknowledge the dead.

I am here to speak. Say the words. Her nearness has delivered me to this moment, an ever-lengthening moment between her breaths, that I might finally speak the words turning inward, for the first time, in my own beginning and lonely language: Do not be afraid. It is all right, so do not be afraid. You are not really alone. You may die, but you will have been heard. Keep speaking—it is real. You have a voice.

STUDY AND DISCUSSION QUESTIONS

1. Identify and briefly summarize the six sections of this memoir.

2. As you read this essay, list all the words and phrases you notice that refer to language or to speaking.

3. List episodes or anecdotes that are structured around the theme of language.

4. How do the narrator and his mother communicate with each other?

5. How does the narrator's mother feel about Korean, English, and Japanese? For herself? For her children?

6. What is the narrator's relation to English? To his native Korean?

7. What is the difference between the way his mother behaves inside and outside the house?

8. How do the details of caring for a person dying of cancer anchor the narrator's thoughts?

9. Why does the narrator tell us about the short stories he wrote in high school? How do they connect to the situation he is currently in?

10. In Lee's concluding paragraph, who does "you" refer to?

11. What does the title of this essay mean?

SUGGESTIONS FOR WRITING

1. Like John Edgar Wideman in the section from *Brothers and Keepers*, Chang-Rae Lee writes here of a defining moment in his life. Compare/contrast the two autobiographical accounts. How are each of these moments important to Lee and to Wideman *as writers*?

2. Compare the opening and closing scenes of Lee's mother's death. What does Lee focus on or emphasize in the first scene and what in the concluding scene?

3. Choose one of the six sections of "The Faintest Echo of Our Language" and discuss its function in the memoir as a whole. What is Lee's theme in the memoir and how does the particular section help to develop that theme?

JABBERWOCKY

Barbara Kingsolver

Barbara Kingsolver was born in Annapolis, Maryland, in 1955 and studied at DePauw University and the University of Arizona. She has written poetry, Another America *(1991); fiction, including* The Bean Trees *(1988),* Animal Dreams *(1990), and* Pigs in Heaven *(1993); and nonfiction,* Holding the Line: Women in the Great Arizona Mine Strike of 1983 *(1989) and* High Tide in Tucson: Essays From Now or Never *(1996), from which the following is taken.*

Once upon a time, a passing stranger sent me into exile. I was downtown in front of the Federal Building with a small crowd assembled to protest war in the Persian Gulf;[1] he was in a black Ford pickup. As the truck roared by he leaned most of his upper body out the window to give me a better view of his finger, and he screamed, "Hey, bitch, love it or leave it!"

So I left.

He wasn't the first to give me that instruction; I've heard it since I was a nineteen-year-old in a scary barbershop haircut. Now I was thirty-four, mother of a child, with a decent reputation and pretty good hair. Why start listening *now?* I can only say he was finally one too many. I was on the verge of having a special kind of nervous breakdown, in which a person stalks through a Kmart[2] parking lot ripping yellow ribbons off car antennas.

---

[1] 1991 war against Iraq by United States-led coalition following the Iraqi invasion of Kuwait.

[2] Discount department store.

I realize that would have been abridging other people's right to free expression. What was driving me crazy was that very term "right to free expression," and how it was being applied in a nation at war. We were supposed to behave as though we had refrigerators for brains. Open, shove in a slab of baloney, close, stay cool. No questions. Our leaders told us this was a *surgical* war. *Very clean.* The language of the event was a perfect construct of nonmeaning. "Delivering the ordnance," they called it on the nightly news, which sounds nearly friendly . . . "Why, here is your ordnance, friends, just sign on the line." "Deliver the ordnance" means "Drop the bomb."

But we bought the goods, or we kept our mouths shut. If we felt disturbed by the idea of pulverizing civilizations as the best way to settle our differences—or had trouble explaining that to our kids as adult behavior—we weren't talking about it. Typically, if I raised the debate, I was advised that if I liked Saddam so much I could go live in Iraq. As a matter of fact I *didn't* like Saddam, *or* the government of Kuwait. The two countries appeared practically indistinguishable; I doubt if many Americans could have guessed, a few years earlier (as we flooded Iraq with military aid), which one would turn out to be the Evil Empire, and which would require us to rush to its defense in the name of democracy. If *democracy* were really an issue we considered when going into that war, Iraq might have come out a nose ahead, Kuwait being a monarchy in which women held rights approximately equal to those of livestock. (*Since* the war, women's status in Kuwait has actually declined.) But the level of discourse allowed on this subject was "We're gonna kick butt." A shadow of doubt was viewed as treason.

I'm lucky enough to have a job that will follow me anywhere, so I left. I could contemplate from a distance these words on patriotism, written by the wise Garry Wills: "Love of one's country should be like love of one's spouse—a give-and-take criticism and affection. Although it is hoped one prefers one's spouse to other people . . . one does not prove that one loves one's wife by battering other women."

Give-and-take criticism and affection, out the window. And the battery was severe. Upon moving to Spain I read in the papers what was common knowledge, apparently, everywhere but in the U.S.: from the first night onward we bombed Iraqis relentlessly in their homes, killing thousands of civilians every day. Within months, more than 250,000 would be dead—most of them children—because of bombed-out water and sewer systems, hospitals with no antibiotics, hospitals with no roofs. To my horror I read that infections of hands and feet were rampant among Iraqi children, because of bombing debris, and the only available treatment was amputation. It had been an air war on civilians. The Commission of Inquiry for the International War Crimes Tribunal is still compiling the gruesome list of what the United States bombed in Iraq: all the country's major dams and most of its drinking water facilities; enough sewage treatment facilities to contaminate the Tigris River with waterborne killers; virtually all communications systems, leaving civilians unwarned of danger and unable to get help; civilian cars, buses, and taxis; 139 auto and railway bridges; food-processing, storage, and distribution systems; 100 percent of irrigation systems; wheat and grain fields (with incendiary bombs); 28 civilian hospitals and 52 community health centers; clothing factories; a cosmetics factory; an infant formula factory; 56 mosques; more than 600 schools. This was our surgical war.

Soon after the bombing ended, Ramsey Clark wrote a book called *The Fire This Time*, a meticulously researched account of the many ways the U.S. violated the Geneva Convention and perpetrated crimes against civilians in the Persian Gulf War. Clark, as a former U.S. Attorney General, had once been appointed trustee of the nation's conscience. Now he asked us to reckon with some awful responsibilities. But he encountered a truly American form of censorship: free enterprise in the hands of a monkey called See No Evil. His manuscript was rejected by eleven publishers—every major New York house. The editors did not turn it down for lack of merit, they said, but on grounds that it wouldn't be popular. (At length it was released by a small publisher called Thunder's Mouth; hurray for the alternative presses.)

No such hard luck for the memoirs of generals or celebrities, or O. J. Simpson's thoughts from jail while awaiting his verdict. The publisher of the latter (Little, Brown) claimed no moral qualms about providing a forum for Simpson at a time when he already commanded more media attention than has ever been held, probably, by any human being on the planet. The first printing was half a million copies.

This is a spooky proposition: an information industry that narrows down what we'll get to read and know about, mainly on the basis of how eagerly we'll lap it up. Producers and publishers who make these choices seem inclined, if confronted, to throw up their hands and exclaim, "I can't help it if that's what the people want!" A mother could say the same while feeding her baby nothing but jelly beans day after day; so could a physician who administers morphine for head colds. Both would be convicted of criminal neglect. Why is there no Hippocratic Oath for the professionals who service our intellects? Why is it that I knew, without wanting to, every possible thing about a figure skater who got whacked on the leg with a pipe—a melodrama that in the long run, let's face it, is utterly without consequence to anyone but the whackers and the whackee—but I had to go far out of my way to dig up the recent historical events that led to anarchy in Somalia and Haiti.[3] (I

---

[3] In Somalia, the United States backed dictator Muhammad Siad Barre for many years; in Haiti, after supporting the Duvalier dictatorship for decades, Washington covertly undermined Jean-Bertrand Aristide, Haiti's first democratically elected president.

learned, it's worth noting, that the U.S. did embarrassing things in both places.) News stations will move heaven and earth to get their own reporters into the likes of California vs. O. J. Simpson, or backstage with Tonya Harding,[4] but not into hearings on the Clean Air Act. Producers will blame consumers, but blame is hardly the point if we are merrily dying of ignorance, and killing others with our apathy. Few U.S. citizens are aware, for example, that our government has routinely engineered assassinations of democratically elected heads of state in places like Chile and Guatemala, and replaced them with such monstrous confederates as Augusto Pinochet and Castillo Armas.[5] Why do those dictators' names fail even to ring a bell in most red-blooded American heads? Possibly because our heads are too crowded with names like O. J. and Tonya. The guilt for that may not rest entirely with the producers or the consumers, but the crime has nevertheless occurred. To buy or to sell information as nothing more than a consumer product, like soda pop, is surely wrong. Marketed in that way, information's principal attribute must be universal palatability.

This is not to say we only get to tune in to *happy* news—there are wrecks and murders galore. But it's information that corroborates a certain narrow view of the world and our place in it. Exhaustive reports of rare, bizarre behaviors among the wealthy support the myth that violent crime is a random, unpreventable disaster, and obscure the blunt truth that most crime is caused by poverty. There's not much in the news to remind us, either, that poverty is a problem we could decently address, as all other industrialized countries have done. The safest marketing technique is to dispense with historical analysis, accountability, and even—apparently—critical thought.

When the Smithsonian[6] deferred to what it called "public pressure" and canceled an exhibit on the historical use of the atomic bomb in Hiroshima and Nagasaki, Smithsonian Secretary I. Michael Heyman explained, "Veterans and their families were expecting, and rightly so, that the nation would honor and commemorate their valor and sacrifice. They were not looking for analysis, and, frankly, we did not give enough thought to the intense feeling that such analysis would evoke." *Analysis* in that case meant the most elementary connection between cause and effect: what happens when the Ordnance gets Delivered.

---

[4] Olympic figure skating competitor whose husband pleaded guilty to attacking her rival skater.

[5] Augusto Pinochet, head of the military junta that, with United States support, overthrew Chile's democratically elected government in 1973 and executed thousands; Colonel Carlos Castillo Armas, leader of the CIA-supported army of Guatemalan exiles that in 1954 overthrew Guatemala's elected government, which was led by President Jacobo Arbenz.

[6] The Smithsonian Institution, a nonprofit organization that operates museums and other facilities in Washington, D.C.

As a member of that all-important public, I'd like to state for the record that I'm offended. Give me the chance and I'll spend my consumer dollar on the story that relates to what kind of shape the world will be in fifty years from now. I'll choose analysis, every time, over placebo news and empty salve for my patriotic ego. I'm offended by the presumption that my honor as a citizen will crumple unless I'm protected from knowledge of my country's mistakes. I'm made of sturdier stuff than that, and I imagine, if he really thought about it, so is that guy who leaned out of a truck to give me the finger. What kind of love is patriotism, if it evaporates in the face of uncomfortable truths? What kind of honor sits quietly by while a nation's conscience flies south for a long, long winter?

Artists are as guilty as anyone in the conspiracy of self-censorship, if they succumb to the lure of producing only what's sure to sell. The good ones don't, and might still sell anyway, for humans have long accepted subconsciously that good art won't always, so to speak, match the sofa. "Poets are the unacknowledged legislators of the race," Percy Shelley said. They are also its margin of safety, like the canaries that used to be carried into mines because of their sensitivity to toxic gases; their silence can be taken as a sign of imminent danger.

The artist's maverick responsibility is sometimes to sugarcoat the bitter pill and slip it down our gullet, telling us what we didn't think we wanted to know. But in the U.S. we're establishing a modern tradition of tarpapering our messengers. The one who delivers the bitter pill, whether the vehicle is a war-crime documentary or a love story, is apt to be dismissed as a "political artist."

It's a Jabberwockish sort of label, both dreaded and perplexing. Technically the term "political" refers to campaigns, governments, and public institutions. But *Police Academy*[7] was not called political. Barry Lopez is called political, and he writes about dying ecosystems and great blue herons and wolves, for heaven's sake. It took me years to work out what it is that earns this scalding label for an artist or an act.

Now I know, and this is how I know: during the Gulf War some young friend of mine wanted to set up a table in the shopping mall and hand out information about the less cheerful aspects of the war. The administrators of the mall refused permission. My friends contended, "But you let people hand out yellow ribbons and flags and 'We kick butt' bumper stickers!" The mall administrators explained their charter forbids anything political. "Handing out yellow ribbons is public service," they said, "but what *you* want to do is *political.*"

---

[7] 1984 film about bumbling police trainees.

Now you know. This subterfuge use of the word "political," which doesn't show up in my Random House Unabridged, means only that a thing runs counter to prevailing assumptions. If 60 percent of us support the war, then the expressions of the other 40 percent are political—and can be disallowed in some contexts for that reason alone. The really bad news is that the charter of the shopping mall seems to be standing in as a national artistic standard. Cultural workers in the U.S. are prone to be bound and gagged by a dread of being called political, for that word implies the art is not quite pure. Real art, the story goes, does not endorse a point of view. This is utter nonsense, of course (try to imagine a story or a painting with no point of view), and also the most thorough and invisible form of censorship I've ever encountered. When I'm interviewed about writing, I spend a good deal of time defending the possibility that such things as environmental ruin, child abuse, or the hypocrisy of U.S. immigration policy are appropriate subjects for a novel. I keep waiting for the interviewer to bring up *art* things, like voice and metaphor; usually I'm still waiting for that when the cows come home.

In rural Greece some people believe that if you drink very cold water on a very hot day, you will die; here, we have that kind of superstition about mixing art with conscience. It's a quaintly provincial belief that fades out fast at our borders. Most of the rest of the world considers social criticism to be, absolutely, the most legitimate domain of art. If you think I'm overstating this, look who's been winning Nobel Prizes in literature for the last ninety years:

Nadine Gordimer, who has spent her life writing against racism and apartheid in South Africa. Joseph Brodsky, who spent some years in Siberia because of his criticism of Soviet society. Wole Soyinka, who has also logged time in jail because of his criticisms of colonialism in Africa. Gabriel García Márquez, who is possibly the most gifted social critic in a whole continent of social-critic-writers. Czeslaw Milosz, who was active in the anti-Nazi underground and whose poetry is thoroughly ideological. Pablo Neruda, Aleksandr Solzhenitsyn, Miguel Asturias, Thomas Mann, George Bernard Shaw.

U.S. prizewinners do not dominate this list (as they do the Nobel categories of Physics, Chemistry, and Medicine), especially since the 1950s. It's not for lack of great writers, but perhaps because we've learned to limit our own access to serious content. The fear of being perceived as ideologues runs so deep in writers of my generation it undoubtedly steers us away from certain subjects without our knowing it. The fear is that if you fall short of perfect execution, you'll be called "preachy." But falling short of perfection when you've plunged in to say what needs to be said—is that so much worse, really, than falling short when you've plunged in to say what *didn't* need to be said?

And if you should by chance succeed—oh, then. Art has the power not only to soothe a savage breast, but to change a savage mind. A novel can make us weep over the same events that might hardly give us pause if we read them in a newspaper. Even though the tragedy in the newspaper happened to real people, while the one in the novel happened in an author's imagination.

A novel works its magic by putting a reader inside another person's life. The pace is as slow as life. It's as detailed as life. It requires you, the reader, to fill in an outline of words with vivid pictures drawn subconsciously from your own life, so that the story feels more personal than the sets designed by someone else and handed over via TV or movies. Literature duplicates the experience of living in a way that nothing else can, drawing you so fully into another life that you temporarily forget you have one of your own. That is why you read it, and might even sit up in bed till early dawn, throwing your whole tomorrow out of whack, simply to find out what happens to some people who, you know perfectly well, are made up. It's why you might find yourself crying, even if you aren't the crying kind.

The power of fiction is to create empathy. It lifts you away from your chair and stuffs you gently down inside someone else's point of view. It differs drastically from a newspaper, which imparts information while allowing you to remain rooted in your own perspective. A newspaper could tell you that one hundred people, say, in an airplane, or in Israel, or in Iraq, have died today. And you can think to yourself, "How very sad," then turn the page and see how the Wildcats fared. But a novel could take just one of those hundred lives and show you exactly how it felt to be that person rising from bed in the morning, watching the desert light on the tile of her doorway and on the curve of her daughter's cheek. You would taste that person's breakfast, and love her family, and sort through her worries as your own, and know that a death in that household will be the end of the only life that someone will ever have. As important as yours. As important as mine.

At the height of the Gulf War, I found in the *New York Times* this quote from Loren Thompson, director of the national security program at Georgetown University, explaining why the Pentagon wasn't releasing information about deaths in Iraq. When bomb damage is listed only in technical terms, he said, "you avoid talking about lives lost, and that serves both an esthetic and a practical purpose."

The esthetic and practical purpose, of course, is the loss of empathy. We seem to be living in the age of anesthesia, and it's no wonder. Confronted with knowledge of dozens of apparently random disasters each day, what can a human heart do but slam its doors? No mortal can grieve that much. We didn't evolve to cope with tragedy on a global scale. Our defense is to pretend there's no thread of event that connects us, and that those lives are somehow not precious and real like our own. It's a practical strategy, to some ends, but the loss of empathy is also the loss of humanity, and that's no small tradeoff.

Art is the antidote that can call us back from the edge of numbness, restoring the ability to feel for another. By virtue of that power, it is political, regardless of content. If *Jane Eyre*[8] is a great romance, it has also given thousands of men a female experience, and a chance to feel the constraints that weighed upon women of Jane's time. Through art, a woman can give a male reader the unparalleled athletic accomplishment of childbirth, or the annihilation of being raped; if every man knew both those things, I would expect the world to change tomorrow. We have all heard plenty about each other's troubles, but evidently it's not enough to be told, it has to be lived. And art is so very nearly the same as life.

I *know,* for example, that slavery was heinous, but the fate of sixty million slaves is too big a thing for a heart to understand. So it was not until I read Toni Morrison's *Beloved* that I honestly felt that truth. When Sethe killed her children rather than have them grow up in slavery, I was so far from my sheltered self I knew the horror that could make infanticide an act of love. Morrison carved the tragedy of those sixty million, to whom the book is dedicated, into something small and dense and real enough to fit through the door, get in my heart, and explode. This is how a novel can be more true than a newspaper.

One of my favorite writings about writing is this excerpt from Ursula K. Le Guin's introduction to her science-fiction novel *The Left Hand of Darkness,* in which she discusses fiction's role in what we call the truth:

> Open your eyes; listen, listen. That is what the novelists say. But they don't tell you what you will see and hear. All they can tell you is what they have seen and heard, in their time in this world, a third of it spent in sleep and dreaming, another third of it spent in telling lies.
>
> ... Fiction writers, at least in their braver moments, do desire the truth: to know it, speak it, serve it. But they go about it in a peculiar and devious way, which consists in inventing persons, places, and events which never did and never will exist or occur, and telling about these fictions in detail and at length and with a great deal of emotion, and then when they are done writing down this pack of lies, they say, There! That's the truth!
>
> ... In reading a novel, any novel, we have to know perfectly well that the whole thing is nonsense, and then, while reading, believe every word of it. Finally, when we're done with it, we may find that we're a bit different from what we were before we read it, that we have been changed a little ... crossed a street we never crossed before. But it's very hard to *say* just what we learned, how we were changed.
>
> The artist deals with what cannot be said in words.

---

[8] 1847 novel by Charlotte Brontë.

The artist whose medium is fiction does this *in words.* The novelist says in words what cannot be said in words.

This baffling manifesto is a command that rules my writing life. I believe it means there are truths we all know, but can't make ourselves feel: Slavery was horrible. Love thy neighbor as thyself, or we'll all go to hell in a handbasket. These are things that cannot be said in words because they're too familiar to move us, too big and bald and flat to penetrate our souls. The artist must craft missiles to deliver these truths so unerringly to the right place inside of us we are left panting, with no possibility of doubting they are true. The novelist must do this in story, image, and character. And make the reader believe.

To speak of this process as something that must fall either into the camp of "political" or "pure" is frankly absurd. Good art is political, whether it means to be or not, insofar as it provides the chance to understand points of view alien to our own. Its nature is the opposite of spiritual meanness, bigotry, and warfare. If it is disturbing at times, or unpalatable, it may be a good idea to buy it anyway.

In time, I came back from political exile. Not with my tail between my legs, having discovered the U.S.A. was after all the greatest place in the world. On the contrary, I loved the new experience of safety, the freedom to walk anywhere I pleased at any time of day, and the connected moral comfort of a society that cares for all its children, provides universal health care, and allows no one to be destitute. All these foreign things, and more, I loved: the sound of the ocean in my window, and the towering poinsettia trees that blossomed along the roadsides from Christmas till Easter. I missed a few things: Mexican food, certain familiar music on the radio, the blush of a Tucson sunset running hot and sweet up the face of the Santa Catalina Mountains. And I missed the sound of my mother tongue. By accident, it turns out, I've been apprenticed as a writer to my own language and culture. In the midst of a deeply American novel, high and dry in the Canary Isles, I had to beg friends back home for mundanities I couldn't recall—figures of speech, car makes, even commercial jingles.

More than anything, though, I missed people, the beloved relatives and friends I left behind. I had new friends, but it was finally on account of the old ones that I prepared to give up the expatriate's life.

As the time drew near, my feet balked. I dreaded leaving my kind new place to return to the land of the free (*free* to live behind locks at all times; *free* to walk in the evenings from library to parked car with sheer terror in my heart) and the home of the brave (well, yes, *brave*). The land where 7 percent of the world's souls guzzle the lion's share of the world's goods, pitch out a yearly average of sixteen hundred pounds of garbage apiece, and still can drive past homeless neighbors with little awareness of wrongdoing or alternatives. The place I was told to love or leave.

I found I could do neither. Not wholeheartedly. But like the boy who fought the Jabberwock in *Through the Looking Glass,*[9] I took my vorpal sword in hand. For the sake of people who love me and the sight of mountains that move my soul, I would come galumphing back, to face the tyranny of words without meaning and monsters beyond my ken.

I came back because leaving was selfish. A country can be flawed as a marriage or a family or a person is flawed, but "Love it or leave it" is a coward's slogan. There's more honor in "Love it and get it right." Love it, love it. Love it and never shut up.

STUDY AND DISCUSSION QUESTIONS

1. What effect does Kingsolver's opening paragraph have on you? Why does it have this effect?

2. Discuss "empathy" as the concept is used in this essay.

3. What facts and statistics about the Gulf War that Kingsolver tells us did you *not* know?

4. What is the definition of the word "political," as Kingsolver finds it to be currently used in this country? For Kingsolver, what is "real art"?

5. According to Kingsolver, how does a novel work? What is the power of fiction? How are novels different from newspapers, television, and film?

6. What does Kingsolver mean by "the age of anesthesia"? What are its dangers? Discuss Kingsolver's extended medical metaphor.

7. What is truth, according to Ursula K. Le Guin?

8. Go reread the poem "Jabberwocky" in Lewis Carroll's *Through the Looking Glass.* Why do you think Kingsolver borrows Carroll's title for this essay?

SUGGESTIONS FOR WRITING

1. Kingsolver writes: "Good art is political, whether it means to be or not, insofar as it provides the chance to understand points of view alien to our own." Comment. Can you give an example from your own experience?

---

[9] Children's story by Lewis Carroll.

2. Do you find Kingsolver's essay convincing? Discuss what she does as a writer to make an effective argument: how she structures her essay, what choices she makes about her tone, how she begins and ends, what she chooses to tell us, what word choices she makes, and any other factors you want to mention. If you don't find her essay convincing, discuss why.

ARCHITECT

John Dos Passos

John Dos Passos (1896–1970) was a volunteer ambulance driver in World War I, a supporter of leftist causes in the 1920s and 1930s, and a conservative later in life. His most important work is U.S.A., *a trilogy of novels:* The 42nd Parallel *(1930),* Nineteen Nineteen *(1932), and* The Big Money *(1936). Alongside its fictional characters,* U.S.A. *included portraits of actual historical figures; the following portrait of Frank Lloyd Wright is excerpted from* The Big Money. *Among Dos Passos's other novels are* Three Soldiers *(1920),* Manhattan Transfer *(1925), and* Midcentury *(1961).*

A muggy day in late spring in eighteen-eightyseven a tall youngster of eighteen, with fine eyes and a handsome arrogant way of carrying his head, arrived in Chicago with seven dollars left in his pocket from buying his ticket from Madison with some cash he'd got by pawning Plutarch's *Lives,* a Gibbon's *Decline and Fall of the Roman Empire,* and an old furcollared coat.

Before leaving home to make himself a career in an architect's office (there was no architecture course at Wisconsin to clutter his mind with stale Beaux-Arts drawings), the youngster had seen the dome of the new State Capitol in Madison collapse on account of bad rubblework in the piers, some thieving contractors' skimping materials to save the politicians their rakeoff, and perhaps a trifling but deadly error in the architect's plans;

he never forgot the roar of burst masonry, the flying plaster, the soaring dustcloud, the mashed bodies of the dead and dying being carried out, set faces livid with plasterdust.

Walking round downtown Chicago, crossing and recrossing the bridges over the Chicago River in the jingle and clatter of traffic, the rattle of vans and loaded wagons and the stamping of big drayhorses and the hooting of towboats with barges and the rumbling whistle of lakesteamers waiting for the draw,

he thought of the great continent stretching a thousand miles east and south and north, three thousand miles west, and everywhere, at mineheads, on the shores of newlydredged harbors, along watercourses, at the intersection of railroads, sprouting

shacks roundhouses tipples grainelevators stores warehouses tenements, great houses for the wealthy set in broad treeshaded lawns, domed statehouses on hills, hotels churches operahouses auditoriums.

He walked with long eager steps

toward the untrammeled future opening in every direction for a young man who'd keep his hands to his work and his wits sharp to invent.

The same day he landed a job in an architect's office.

Frank Lloyd Wright was the grandson of a Welsh hatter and preacher who'd settled in a rich Wisconsin valley, Spring Valley, and raised a big family of farmers and preachers and schoolteachers there. Wright's father was a preacher too, a restless illadjusted New Englander who studied medicine, preached in a Baptist church in Weymouth, Massachusetts, and then as a Unitarian in the Middle West, taught music, read Sanskrit and finally walked out on his family.

Young Wright was born on his grandfather's farm, went to school in Weymouth and Madison, worked summers on a farm of his uncle's in Wisconsin.

His training in architecture was the reading of Viollet le Duc, the apostle of the thirteenth century and of the pure structural mathematics of Gothic stonemasonry, and the seven years he worked with Louis Sullivan in the office of Adler and Sullivan in Chicago. (It was Louis Sullivan who, after Richardson, invented whatever was invented in nineteenthcentury architecture in America.)

When Frank Lloyd Wright left Sullivan, he had already launched a distinctive style, prairie architecture. In Oak Park he built broad suburban dwellings for rich men that were the first buildings to break the hold on American builders' minds of centuries of pastward routine, of the wornout capital and plinth and pediment dragged through the centuries from the Acropolis, and the jaded traditional stencils of Roman masonry, the halfobliterated Palladian copybooks.

Frank Lloyd Wright was cutting out a new avenue that led toward the swift constructions in glassbricks and steel foreshadowed today.

Delightedly he reached out for the new materials, steel in tension, glass, concrete, the million new metals and alloys.

The son and grandson of preachers, he became a preacher in blueprints,

projecting constructions in the American future instead of the European past.

Inventor of plans,

plotter of tomorrow's girderwork phrases,

he preaches to the young men coming of age in the time of oppression, cooped up by the plasterboard partitions of finance routine, their lives and plans made poor by feudal levies of parasite money standing astride every process to shake down progress for the cutting of coupons:

The properly citified citizen has become a broker, dealing chiefly in human frailities or the ideas and inventions of others, a puller of levers, a presser of buttons of vicarious power, his by way of machine craft . . . and over beside him and beneath him, even in his heart as he sleeps, is the taximeter of rent, in some form to goad this anxious consumer's unceasing struggle for or against more or less merciful or merciless money increment.

To the young men who spend their days and nights drafting the plans for new *rented aggregates of rented cells upended on hard pavements,*

he preaches

the horizons of his boyhood,

a future that is not the rise of a few points in a hundred selected stocks, or an increase in carloadings, or a multiplication of credit in the bank or a rise in the rate on callmoney,

but a new clean construction, from the ground up, based on uses and needs,

toward the American future instead of toward the painsmeared past of Europe and Asia. Usonia he calls the broad teeming band of this new nation across the enormous continent between Atlantic and Pacific. He preaches a project for Usonia:

It is easy to realize how the complexity of crude utilitarian construction in the mechanical infancy of our growth, like the crude scaffolding for some noble building, did violence to the landscape. . . . The crude purpose of pioneering days has been accomplished. The scaffolding may be taken down and the true work, the culture of a civilization, may appear.

Like the life of many a preacher, prophet, exhorter, Frank Lloyd Wright's life has been stormy. He has raised children, had rows with wives, overstepped boundaries, got into difficulties with the law, divorcecourts, bankruptcy, always the yellow press[1] yapping at his heels, his misfortunes yelled out in headlines in the evening papers: affairs with women, the nightmare horror of the burning of his house in Wisconsin.

By a curious irony

the building that is most completely his is the Imperial Hotel in Tokyo that was one of the few structures to come unharmed through the earthquake of 1923 (the day the cable came telling him that the building had stood saving so many hundreds of lives he writes was one of his happiest days)

and it was reading in German that most Americans first learned of his work.

His life has been full of arrogant projects unaccomplished. (How often does the preacher hear his voice echo back hollow from the empty hall, the draftsman watch the dust fuzz over the carefullycontrived plans, the architect see the rolledup blueprints curl yellowing and brittle in the filingcabinet.)

Twice he's rebuilt the house where he works in his grandfather's valley in Wisconsin after fires and disasters that would have smashed most men forever.

He works in Wisconsin,

an erect spare whitehaired man, his sons are architects, apprentices from all over the world come to work with him,

drafting the new city (he calls it Broadacre City).

Near and Far are beaten (to imagine the new city you must blot out every ingrained habit of the past, build a nation from the ground up with the new tools). For the architect there are only uses:

the incredible multiplication of functions, strength and tension in metal,

the dynamo, the electric coil, radio, the photoelectric cell, the internalcombustion motor,

glass

concrete;

and needs. (Tell us, doctors of philosophy, what are the needs of a man. At least a man needs to be notjailed notafriad nothungry notcold not without love, not a worker for a power he has never seen

that cares nothing for the uses and needs of a man or a woman or a child.)

Building a building is building the lives of the workers and dwellers in the building.

The buildings determine civilization as the cells in the honeycomb the functions of bees.

---

[1] Sensationalistic journalism.

Perhaps in spite of himself the arrogant draftsman, the dilettante in concrete, the bohemian artist for wealthy ladies desiring to pay for prominence with the startling elaboration of their homes has been forced by the logic of uses and needs, by the lifelong struggle against the dragging undertow of money in mortmain,

to draft plans that demand for their fulfillment a new life;

only in freedom can we build the Usonian city. His plans are coming to life. His blueprints, as once Walt Whitman's words, stir the young men:—

Frank Lloyd Wright,

patriarch of the new building,

not without honor except in his own country.

STUDY AND DISCUSSION QUESTIONS

1. Why do you think Dos Passos introduces Wright's character for nine paragraphs without explaining who he is or that he is an important historical personage? What kind of person is this young man? Does he seem to be a particular American type?

2. Describe "prairie architecture." How was Wright's style a break from previous American architecture, according to Dos Passos?

3. How is the Imperial Hotel in Tokyo important in Wright's life and career?

4. Look up Frank Lloyd Wright in an encyclopedia. How is the standard historical account like and unlike Dos Passos's?

5. Though Frank Lloyd Wright is today seen as the major figure in modern American architecture, he was still controversial in 1936 when Dos Passos published this piece. Why does Dos Passos characterize Wright as a "preacher" or "prophet"? And why are the lives of "prophets" often stormy?

SUGGESTIONS FOR WRITING

1. Could an architect now, more than one hundred years after Frank Lloyd Wright began his career, land a job with the credentials Wright had? Why or why not? What have we gained and lost from that change?

2. "Building a building is building the lives of the workers and dwellers in the building." Do you agree or disagree? How does the place you live in or work in shape your life? Give examples from your own experience.

GEORGIA O'KEEFFE

Joan Didion

Journalist, novelist, screenwriter, and essayist Joan Didion was born in 1934. She has lived most of her life in California, though she worked for a number of years for Vogue *magazine in New York City. Among her novels are* Play It as It Lays *(1970) and* Democracy *(1984). Her nonfiction has been collected in* Slouching Towards Bethlehem *(1968),* The White Album *(1979), which includes "Georgia O'Keeffe,"* After Henry *(1992), and other volumes.*

"Where I was born and where and how I have lived is unimportant," Georgia O'Keeffe told us in the book of paintings and words published in her ninetieth year on earth. She seemed to be advising us to forget the beautiful face in the Stieglitz photographs. She appeared to be dismissing the rather condescending romance that had attached to her by then, the romance of extreme good looks and advanced age and deliberate isolation. "It is what I have done with where I have been that should be of interest." I recall an August afternoon in Chicago in 1973 when I took my daughter, then seven, to see what Georgia O'Keeffe had done with where she had been. One of the vast O'Keeffe "Sky Above Clouds" canvases floated over the back stairs in the Chicago Art Institute that day, dominating what seemed to be several stories of empty light, and my daughter looked at it once, ran to the landing, and kept on looking. "Who drew it," she whispered after a while. I told her. "I need to talk to her," she said finally.

My daughter was making, that day in Chicago, an entirely unconscious but quite basic assumption about people and the work they do. She was assuming that the glory she saw in the work reflected a glory in its maker, that the painting was the painter as the poem is the poet, that every choice one made alone—every word chosen or rejected, every brush stroke laid or not laid down—betrayed one's character. *Style is character.* It seemed to me that afternoon that I had rarely seen so instinctive an application of this familiar principle, and I recall being pleased not only that my daughter responded to style as character but that it was Georgia O'Keeffe's particular style to which she responded: this was a hard woman who had imposed her 192 square feet of clouds on Chicago.

"Hardness" has not been in our century a quality much admired in women, nor in the past twenty years has it even been in official favor for men.

When hardness surfaces in the very old we tend to transform it into "crustiness" or eccentricity, some tonic pepperiness to be indulged at a distance. On the evidence of her work and what she has said about it, Georgia O'Keeffe is neither "crusty" nor eccentric. She is simply hard, a straight shooter, a woman clean of received wisdom and open to what she sees. This is a woman who could early on dismiss most of her contemporaries as "dreamy," and would later single out one she liked as "a very poor painter." (And then add, apparently by way of softening the judgment: "I guess he wasn't a painter at all. He had no courage and I believe that to create one's own world in any of the arts takes courage.") This is a woman who in 1939 could advise her admirers that they were missing her point, that their appreciation of her famous flowers was merely sentimental. "When I paint a red hill," she observed coolly in the catalogue for an exhibition that year, "you say it is too bad that I don't always paint flowers. A flower touches almost everyone's heart. A red hill doesn't touch everyone's heart." This is a woman who could describe the genesis of one of her most well-known paintings—the "Cow's Skull: Red, White and Blue" owned by the Metropolitan—as an act of quite deliberate and derisive orneriness. "I thought of the city men I had been seeing in the East," she wrote. "They talked so often of writing the Great American Novel—the Great American Play—the Great American Poetry. . . . So as I was painting my cow's head on blue I thought to myself, "I'll make it an American painting. They will not think it great with the red stripes down the sides—Red, White and Blue—but they will notice it.'"

The city men. The men. They. The words crop up again and again as this astonishingly aggressive woman tells us what was on her mind when she was making her astonishingly aggressive paintings. It was those city men who stood accused of sentimentalizing her flowers: "I made you take time to look at what I saw and when you took time to really notice my flower you hung all your associations with flowers on my flower and you write about my flower as if I think and see what you think and see—and i don't." *And I don't.* Imagine those words spoken, and the sound you hear is *don't tread on me.* "The men" believed it impossible to paint New York, so Georgia O'Keeffe painted New York. "The men" didn't think much of her bright color, so she made it brighter. The men yearned toward Europe so she went to Texas, and then New Mexico. The men talked about Cézanne, "long involved remarks about the 'plastic quality' of his form and color," and took one another's long involved remarks, in the view of his angelic rattlesnake in their midst, altogether too seriously. "I can paint one of those dismal-colored paintings like the men," the woman who regarded herself always as an outsider remembers thinking one day in 1922, and she did: a painting of a shed "all low-toned and dreary with the tree beside the door." She called this act of rancor "The Shanty" and hung it in her next show. "The men seemed to approve of it," she reported fifty-four years later, her contempt undimmed. "They seemed to think that maybe I was beginning to paint. That was my only low-toned dismal-colored painting."

Some women fight and others do not. Like so many successful guerrillas in the war between the sexes, Georgia O'Keeffe seems to have been equipped early with an immutable sense of who she was and a fairly clear understanding that she would be required to prove it. On the surface her upbringing was conventional. She was a child on the Wisconsin prairie who played with china dolls and painted watercolors with cloudy skies because sunlight was too hard to paint and with her brother and sisters, listened every night to her mother read stories of the Wild West, of Texas, of Kit Carson and Billy the Kid. She told adults that she wanted to be an artist and was embarrassed when they asked what kind of artist she wanted to be: she had no idea "what kind." She had no idea what artists did. She had never seen a picture that interested her, other than a pen-and-ink Maid of Athens[1] in one of her mother's books, some Mother Goose illustrations printed on cloth, a tablet cover that showed a little girl with pink roses, and the painting of Arabs on horseback that hung in her grandmother's parlor. At thirteen, in a Dominican convent, she was mortified when the sister corrected her drawing. At Chatham Episcopal Institute in Virginia she painted lilacs and sneaked time alone to walk out to where she could see the line of the Blue Ridge Mountains on the horizon. At the Art Institute in Chicago she was shocked by the presence of live models and wanted to abandon anatomy lessons. At the Art Students League in New York one of her fellow students advised her that, since he would be a great painter and she would end up teaching painting in a girls' school, any work of hers was less important than modeling for him. Another painted over her work to show her how the Impressionists did trees. She had not before heard how the Impressionists did trees and she did not much care.

At twenty-four she left all those opinions behind and went for the first time to live in Texas, where there were no trees to paint and no one to tell her how not to paint them. In Texas there was only the horizon she craved. In Texas she had her sister Claudia with her for a while, and in the late afternoons they would walk away from town and toward the horizon and watch the evening star come out. "The evening star fascinated me," she wrote. "It was in some way very exciting to me. My sister had a gun, and as we walked she would throw bottles into the air and shoot as many as she could before they hit the ground. I had nothing but to walk into nowhere and the wide sunset space with the star. Ten watercolors were made from that star." In a way one's interest is compelled as much by the sister Claudia with the gun as by the painter Georgia with the star, but only the painter left us this shining record. Ten watercolors were made from that star.

---

[1] Title of poem by George Gordon, Lord Byron.

STUDY AND DISCUSSION QUESTIONS

1. "I need to talk with her." Discuss Didion's seven-year-old daughter's reaction to seeing a Georgia O'Keeffe painting for the first time.

2. How is Georgia O'Keeffe "hard," according to Didion, and what does Didion mean by "hard"?

3. What did "the city men" want O'Keeffe to do in her painting? And how, specifically, did O'Keeffe overturn those expectations and judgments?

4. "Where I was born and where and how I have lived is unimportant," writes Georgia O'Keeffe. "It is what I have done with where I have been that should be of interest." How does O'Keeffe define how we should look at a work of art? How does this approach contradict the contemporary approach to art and artists, which is relentlessly personal?

5. Still looking at the quote in the fourth question, why do you think "where" is so important for O'Keeffe?

SUGGESTIONS FOR WRITING

1. Both John Dos Passos and Joan Didion are writing biographical essays about major American artistic figures. Compare their approaches to introducing these artists. How does each writer choose to begin, for example? How much of the writer's personality is included in the piece? What do you think the writer's purpose and main point is in each essay?

2. Look at Georgia O'Keeffe's paintings, which are available in reproduction in libraries and bookstores. Choose one painting and write a short essay about it. What is your response to the painting? How is it a thoroughly American painting? Would you describe it as "hard" or "astonishingly aggressive"? If you had to pick one word to describe the painting, what would that word be—and why?

3. Is style character? What do you think Joan Didion finally decides about that question in relation to O'Keeffe and her work?

PAST PRESENT

Jimmy Santiago Baca

Of Chicano and Apache heritage, Jimmy Santiago Baca was born in 1952 in Santa Fe, New Mexico, and spent much of his childhood in an orphanage, until he ran away at age eleven. He lived on the street and, at twenty, was convicted of drug possession and sent to a maximum security prison. He taught himself to read there and soon began writing poetry. His first book, Immigrants in Our Own Land: Poems *(1979), was a critical success and he has since published several other volumes of poetry as well as the essay collection* Working in the Dark: Reflections of a Poet of the Barrio *(1992), from which the following is taken.*

When I finished my last prison term twelve years ago, I never dreamed I would go back. But not long ago I found myself looking up at the famous San Quentin tower as I followed an escort guard through the main gates. I should have been overjoyed since this time I was a free man, the writer of a film which required a month of location-shooting there. But being there had a disquieting effect on me. I was confused. I knew that I would be able to leave every night after filming, but the enclosing walls, the barbed wire, and the guards in the towers shouldering their carbines made old feelings erupt in me. While my mind told me I was free, my spirit snarled as if I were a prisoner again, and I couldn't shake the feeling. Emotionally, I could not convince myself that I was not going to be subjected once more to horrible indignities, that I would not have to live through it all again. Each morning when the guards checked my shoulder bag and clanked shut the iron door behind me, the old convict in me rose up full of hatred and rage for the guards, the walls, the terrible indecency of the place. I was still the same man who had entered there freely, a man full of love for his family and his life. But another self from the past reawakened, an imprisoned self, seething with the desire for vengeance on all things not imprisoned.

As I followed the guard, passing with the crew and the actors from one compound to another, a hollow feeling of disbelief possessed me and I was struck dumb. The grounds were impeccably planted and groomed, serene as a cemetery. Streamlined circles of flowers and swatches of smooth lawn rolled to trimmed green margins of pruned shrubbery, perfectly laid out against the limestone and red brick cellblocks. But I knew that when you penetrated beyond this pretty landscaping, past the offices, also with their bouquets of flowers, past the cellblock's thick walls, there thrived America's worst nightmare. There the green, concealing surface lifted from the bubbling swamp, a monster about to rise from its dark depths. There writhed scaly demons, their claws and fangs primed for secret and unspeakable brutalities.

Even within those walls, the free man that I am eventually found himself able to forgive the sufferings of the past. But the convict in me was inflamed by everything I saw. It was all so familiar, so full of bitter memory: the milk-paned windows and linoleum tiles of the offices, the flyers thumbtacked to cork boards on the walls; the vast lower yard, and the great upper yard with its corrugated shed pocked with light-pierced, jagged bullet holes; the looming limestone cellblocks. The thought of the thousands of human beings whose souls were murdered here in the last hundred years made my blood run cold. The faintly humming body energy of six thousand imprisoned human beings bored a smoking hole in my brain. And through that hole, as if through a prison-door peephole, I saw all the free people going about their lives on the other side, while my place was again with the convicts. Anyone opening that door from the other side must die, or be taken hostage and forced to understand our hatred, made to experience the insane brutality that is the convict's daily lot, and that makes him, in turn, brutal and insane.

Since I was acting in the film, I had to dress out daily in banaroos, prison-issue blue denims. I was made up to look younger than I am, as I might have looked in 1973. After this outer transformation, I seemed more and more to become the person I had left behind twelve years ago, until finally that former self began to consume the poet and husband and father who had taken his place. I didn't know what was happening to me.

Dragged back into dangerous backwaters, I encountered my old demons. The crew seemed to sense this and gave me a wide berth. The familiar despair and rage of the prisoners was like a current sucking me down into the sadness of their wasted lives. The guards who paced the cellblocks now were no different from the guards who had leered and spit at me, beaten and insulted me. Even though I knew that now I wouldn't have to take their shit and that now I could speak up for the cons who had to hold their tongues, part of me was still caught in this time warp of displacement.

When we went to the recreational building, where I was to choose some of the convicts to act as extras, I was surprised by how young they were. I realized I was now the old man among them. In my prison days, the convicts had always seemed to be grizzled older guys, but now, for the most part, they were young kids in their twenties. After I selected the group of extras, I explained to them that the movie was about three kids from East L.A., one of whom goes to prison. As I spoke, my convict stance and manners came back to me, and the old slang rolled off my tongue as if I had never left. Memories of my own imprisonment assailed me, dissolving the barrier between us.

Although technically I was free, that first week I used my freedom in a strange way, venting hatred on anyone who looked at me, the cons included, because they, too, in the prison world, are joined in their own hierarchy of brutality.

One day a documentary crew came to where we were filming in the weight pit and asked to interview me. Prisoners of every race were present. I looked around me and was filled with contempt for every living soul there. After repeatedly refusing to speak, while microphones were shoved in my face, I suddenly decided to answer their questions.

How did I feel about returning to a prison to help film and act in this movie I had written? Was I proud and pleased? I sat on a bench-press seat curling about thirty pounds as I spoke.

I said I hated being back and that no movie could begin to show the injustices practiced here. I said that fame was nothing weighed against the suffering and brutality of prison life. I told them that these cons should tear the fucking walls down and allow no one to dehumanize them in this way. What were my feelings about being here?

I said that I hated everyone and just wanted to be left alone, and fuck them all. Just leave me alone!

I got up and walked away. There was a terrible tearing wound in my heart that I thought no one could see. But Gina, the associate producer, came up to me weeping, pleading for me to come back to myself, to be again the man she knew. She hugged me. One of the actors also approached and talked to me quietly. In spite of their attempts to comfort me, I felt helplessly encaged by powers I couldn't vanquish or control. I was ensnared in a net of memories. When the few convicts who had been hanging with me started to put some distance between us, I felt as if no one could see me or hear me. I was disoriented, as if I had smashed full force into some invisible barrier.

After a couple of days, I came out of it, dazed and bewildered, shocked and weak as if after major surgery. People I previously couldn't bring myself to speak to, I spoke with now. I felt that sense of wonder one feels after a narrow escape from death.

As I continued to live my double life, I became a keen observer of both worlds. On the streets people could cry freely, but in prison tears led to challenges and deep, embittered stares. In prison no one shakes hands, that common gesture of friendship and trust. The talk never varies from the subjects of freedom and imprisonment, the stories and the laughs are about con jobs and scams. Outside everything is always changing, there are surprises, and you talk about that. But in prison the only news is old news. It is a dead land, filled with threat, where there is no appeal from the death sentence meted out for infractions of the convict code. Imagine being hunted through the jungles of Nam day after day for twenty years, and that will tell you a little of what prison is about.

The days went by. When we finished filming, late in the evenings, I would go back to my trailer, change into my street clothes, and walk alone across the lower yard. The dead exercise pit, where many of the men spend a lot of time buffing themselves out, looked forlorn. It was very late as I crossed the lower yard to a waiting van, but the lights around the lower yard, huge, looming, twenty-eyed klieg lights, made it seem like daytime. Everything about prison life distorts reality, starting with the basic assumption that imprisonment can alter criminal behavior, when the truth is that it entrenches it more firmly. Confinement perverts and destroys every skill a man needs to live productively in society.

As I walked on, my mind full of these thoughts, buses from all over California pulled up in the eerie yellow light, disgorging new inmates who were lined up to get their prison clothes before being marched off to the cellblocks. A van was waiting to take me back to my corporate-paid condo, where there was fresh food waiting for me, where I could relax and phone my wife, turn on some soft music and write a little, read a little, in the silence; walk to the window and smell the cool night air and look across the bay to the Golden Gate Bridge and beyond to San Francisco, a city as angelic at night as any heavenly sanctum conjured up in medieval tapestries.

But all of these anticipated pleasures only intensified my anguish for those I was leaving behind, for those imprisoned who have—nothing. The cells in San Quentin's Carson block are so small that a man cannot bend or stretch without bruising himself against some obstacle. And two men share each cell. The cellblocks stink of mildew and drying feces. The noise is a dull, constant, numbing beating against the brain. Had I really inhabited such a cell for seven years? It didn't happen, it couldn't have happened. How did I survive? Who was that kid that lived through this horror? It was me. Since that time I had grown, changed; but I was still afraid to touch that reality with my mind, that unspeakable pain.

On those lonely night walks into freedom, the tremendous grief and iron rage of the convict revived in me. The empty yard, with its watchful glare, mercilessly mirrored the cold, soul-eaten barrenness of those confined within. In the world outside, convicts have mothers and wives and children, but here, in this world, they have nothing but the speed of their fists. They have only this one weapon of protest against the oppression of brain-dead keepers who represent a society whose judicial standards are so disparate for rich and poor.

When a man leaves prison, he cannot look into the mirror for fear of seeing what he has become. In the truest sense, he no longer knows himself. Treated like a child by the guards, forced to relinquish every vestige of dignity, searched at whim, cursed, beaten, stripped, deprived of all privacy, he has lived for years in fear; and this takes a terrible toll. The saddest and most unforgivable thing of all is that most first-time felons could be rehabilitated, if anyone cared or tried. But society opts for the quickest and least expensive alternative—stark confinement, with no attempt at help—that in the future will come to haunt it.

Each day that we filmed at San Quentin, where I was surrounded by men whose sensibilities were being progressively eroded by prison society, the urge grew in me to foment a revolt: tear down the walls, herd the guards into the bay, burn down everything until nothing was left but a smoldering heap of blackened bricks and molten iron. And I was filled with a yearning to escape, to go home and live the new life I had fought so hard to make. The two worlds I inhabited then were so far apart I could find no bridge between them, no balance in myself. My disorientation was radical.

My days were spent in this prison, among men who had been stripped of everything, who had no future; and of an evening I might find myself in the affluence of Mill Valley, attending a ballet with my visiting wife and two sons, my wife's cousin's daughter dancing on stage in a mist of soft lights. . . .

As the weeks passed, I realized I had gone through changes that left me incapable of recognizing my own life. What was most shocking to me was not that I had survived prison, but that the prisons still stood, that the cruelty of that life was still going on; that in San Quentin six thousand men endured it daily, and that the system was growing stronger day by day. I realized that America is two countries: a country of the poor and deprived, and a country of those who had a chance to make something of their lives. Two societies, two ways of living, going on side by side every hour of every day. And in every aspect of life, from opportunities to manners and morals, the two societies stand in absolute opposition. Most Americans remain ignorant of this, of the fact that they live in a country that holds hostage behind bars another populous country of their fellow citizens.

I do not advocate the liberation of murderers, rapists, and sociopaths. But what of the vast majority of convicts, imprisoned for petty crimes that have more to do with wrong judgment than serious criminal intent or character defect? They are not yet confirmed in criminality, but the system makes them criminals. Society must protect itself against those who are truly dangerous. But they comprise only a small proportion of our prison population.

One day, late in the afternoon after we had shot a riot scene, the cellblock was in disarray: burning mattresses, men screaming, hundreds of cons shaking the bars with such force that the whole concrete and iron cellblock groaned and creaked with their rage. The cons were not acting. The scene had triggered an outrage waiting to be expressed. Finally, all that was left were a few wisps of black smoke, the tiers dripped water, and hundreds of pounds of soaked, charred newspapers were heaped on the concrete. Clothing and bed sheets, shredded to rags, dangled from the concertina wire surrounding the catwalks.

Quiet fell, the kind of dead quiet that comes after hundreds of men have been venting their wrath for hours, cursing and flailing and threatening. The smoldering trash on the cellblock floor testified to a fury that now withdrew, expressing itself only in their eyes. One of the convicts walked over to me through the silence. He told me that another convict wanted to speak with me, and led me to a cell that was in total darkness, where he spoke my name. A voice from the top bunk replied. I heard the man jump from the bunk to the floor and come to the bars. He was a tall, young Chicano with a crew cut, whose eyes were white orbs. He lived in the absolute darkness of the blind, in this small cell no bigger than a phone booth. In a soft voice he told me he had a story to tell, and asked my advice. He wanted his story to go out into the world, in print or on film.

Never has a man evoked from me such sympathy and tenderness as this blind warrior. It was plain to me that he had suffered terribly in this man-made hell, and that, somehow, his spirit had survived. I knew that his courage and his heart were mountains compared to the sand grains of my heart and courage. From behind the bars, this tall, lean brown kid with blind eyes told me how, after the guards had fired random warning shots into a group of convicts, he found himself blinded for life. I looked at him and saw the beautiful face of a young Spanish aristocrat who might be standing on a white balcony overlooking a garden of roses and lilies at dawn. I could also see in him the warrior. How softly he spoke and how he listened, so attentive to the currents of sound.

Blind Chicano brother of mine, these words are for you, and my work must henceforth be a frail attempt to translate your heart for the world, your courage and *carnalismo.* While the world blindly grabs at and gorges on cheap titillations, you go on in your darkness, in your dark cell, year after year, groping in your imagination for illumination that will help you make sense of your life and your terrible fate. I couldn't understand you. I could only look at you humbly, young Chicano warrior. You spoke to me, spoke to me with the words and in the spirit in which I have written my poems. Looking at you, I reaffirmed my vow to never give up struggling for my people's right to live with dignity. From you I take the power to go on fighting until my last breath for our right to live in freedom, secure from the brutality in which you are imprisoned. From your blind eyes, I reimagined my vision and my quest to find words that can cut through steel. You asked me to tell your story. I promised I would.

Today, as I was writing these words, a sociologist consulting on the movie led me to a viewing screen to see the eclipse: July 11th, 1991, 11:00 A.M. I looked through the shade glass and saw the sun and moon meet. I thought of you, my blind brother, and how our eyes met, yours and mine, dark moons and white suns that touched for a moment in our own eclipse, exchanging light and lives before we parted: I to tell my people's stories as truly as I can, you to live on in your vision-illuminated darkness. And I thought how the Mayans, at the time of eclipse, would rekindle with their torches the altar flame, bringing the temples to new light; how their great cities and pyramids came out of darkness and they journeyed to the sun in their hearts, prepared to live for another age with new hope and love, forgiveness and courage. The darkness again gave way to the light, and I thought of you in your darkness, and of myself, living in what light I can make or find; and of our meeting each in our own eclipse and lighting the altar flame in each other's hearts, before passing on in our journeys to give light to our people's future.

Copies of my books that I had ordered from New York arrived in San Quentin on the last day of filming. I signed them and handed them out to the convicts who had helped us. As they accepted these books of my poems, I saw respect in their eyes. To me, I was still one of them; for them, I was someone who had made it into a free and successful life. This sojourn in prison had confused me, reawakening the old consuming dragons of hatred and fear. But I had faced them, finally, and perhaps I will be a better poet for it. Time will tell.

The next morning, I woke up early and packed my bags. Then I went back to San Quentin for the last time. The production company vans and trailers, the mountains of gear, the crew and the actors, were gone. I made my way across the sad and vacant yard to make my last farewells. This final visit was a purposeful one: I would probably never set foot in a prison again. I was struck with pity for those who had to stay, and with simple compassion, too, for myself: for the pain I had endured in this month, and for that eighteen-year-old kid I once was, who had been confined behind walls like these and had survived, but who would never entirely be free of the demons he met behind bars. This last pilgrimage was for him, who is the better part of me and the foundation for the man I am today, still working in the dark to create for my people our own unique light.

STUDY AND DISCUSSION QUESTIONS

1. Why does Baca return to prison? Do you think he expected to have the reaction he did?

2. "Dragged back into dangerous backwaters, I encountered my old demons." What conflict is he going through? How does he behave towards his coworkers making the film? Towards reporters? Towards the convicts being filmed?

3. Describe the two worlds Baca contrasts: "on the streets" and "in prison."

4. How does Baca use the physical setting of the prison to embody his emotions? Give a couple of examples.

5. What is Baca's thesis in this essay? What would he like his readers to believe should be changed in this country?

6. How does the blind Chicano prisoner become a symbol for Baca?

7. Discuss Baca's use of the eclipse and of the Mayan ritual of lighting the altar flame.

8. How do the prisoners see Baca?

SUGGESTIONS FOR WRITING

1. Baca writes: "I realized that America is two countries: a country of the poor and deprived, and a country of those who had a chance to make something of their lives." Discuss Baca's arguments, implicit and explicit, for reform of our justice and prison system. Are the two worlds he found himself suspended between limited to those "in prison" and "on the streets"?

2. What does Baca see as the purpose of his own writing?

3. Discuss the function of memory in one, two, or all three of the essays in this section by Baca, Lee, or Wideman.

A SORT OF PREFACE

Toni Cade Bambara

Toni Cade (1939–1995) was born in New York City, attended college there, and worked as a welfare investigator and a community organizer. She took the name "Bambara" from a sketchbook she discovered in her great-grandmother's trunk. She edited The Black Woman: An Anthology *(1970) and published* The Salt Eaters *(1980), a novel; two story collections, including* Gorilla, My Love *(1972), where the following preface appeared; and, with Erroll McDonald and Toni Morrison,* Deep Sightings and Rescue Missions: Fiction, Essays, and Conversations *(1996).*

It does no good to write autobiographical fiction cause the minute the book hits the stand here comes your mama screamin how could you and sighin death where is thy sting and she snatches you up out your bed to grill you about what was going down back there in Brooklyn when she was working three jobs and trying to improve the quality of your life and come to find on page 42 that you were messin around with that nasty boy up the block and breaks into sobs and quite naturally your family strolls in all sleepy-eyed to catch the floor show at 5:00 A.M. but as far as your mama is concerned, it is nineteen-forty-and-something and you ain't too grown to have your ass whipped.

And it's no use using bits and snatches even of real events and real people, even if you do cover, guise, switch-around and change-up cause next thing you know your best friend's laundry cart is squeaking past but your bell ain't ringing so you trot down the block after her and there's this drafty cold pressure front the weatherman surely did not predict and your friend says in this chilly way that it's really something when your own friend stabs you in the back with a pen and for the next two blocks you try to explain that the character is not her at all but just happens to be speaking one of her lines and right about the time you hit the laundromat and you're ready to just give it up and take the weight, she turns to you and says that seeing as how you have plundered her soul and walked off with a piece of her flesh, the least you can do is spin off half the royalties her way.

So I deal in straight-up fiction myself, cause I value my family and friends, and mostly cause I lie a lot anyway.

STUDY AND DISCUSSION QUESTIONS

1. Look up the word "preface." Why do you think Bambara titles this "a sort of" preface?

2. What do you think Bambara means by "autobiographical fiction"?

3. Bambara gives us two examples of what can happen when you use parts of your life in your writing. What are the consequences she details in each case?

4. How serious or tongue-in-cheek do you think this "sort of preface" is? How do you think Bambara might use material from her life in her writing?

SUGGESTIONS FOR WRITING

1. Have you ever used material from your own life in your writing? Do you think writing from experience is harder or easier than pure invention? Where would you draw the line between real events and fiction? Does it matter?

2. Write "a sort of preface" to any group of writings you've done—letters to your parents or friends, papers for this or some other course, a diary or journal you've been keeping, poems or short stories, or even last month's grocery lists.

CREDITS

INDEX OF AUTHORS AND TITLES